Allies at War

Also by Tim Bouverie

Appeasing Hitler: Chamberlain,
Churchill and the Road to War

Allies at War

The Politics of Defeating Hitler

TIM BOUVERIE

THE BODLEY HEAD

LONDON

1 3 5 7 9 10 8 6 4 2

The Bodley Head, an imprint of Vintage,
is part of the Penguin Random House group of companies

Vintage, Penguin Random House UK, One Embassy Gardens,
8 Viaduct Gardens, London SW11 7BW

penguin.co.uk/vintage
global.penguinrandomhouse.com

First published by The Bodley Head in 2025

Typeset in 12/14.75 pt Dante MT Std by Jouve (UK), Milton Keynes
Printed and bound in Great Britain by Clays Ltd, Elcograf S.p.A.

The authorised representative in the EEA is Penguin Random House Ireland,
Morrison Chambers, 32 Nassau Street, Dublin D02 YH68

A CIP catalogue record for this book is available from the British Library

HB ISBN 9781847926227
TPB ISBN 9781847926234

Penguin Random House is committed to a sustainable future
for our business, our readers and our planet. This book is made
from Forest Stewardship Council® certified paper.

MIX
Paper | Supporting
responsible forestry
FSC® C018179
FSC
www.fsc.org

To Clemmie

There is only one thing worse than fighting
with allies and that is fighting without them.

Winston Churchill

Contents

Preface

Stalin was in excellent spirits. As host to thirty-one guests, including three interpreters, he set the tone by telling jokes, clinking glasses and attacking the dinner of whitefish in champagne sauce, caviar, mutton and quail with zeal. Rising from his place at the centre of the table, he proposed a toast to the guest on his left, 'the leader of the British Empire, the most courageous of all Prime Ministers . . . who, when all Europe was ready to fall flat before Hitler, said that Britain would stand and fight alone against Germany, even without any allies'. Later, he paid tribute to the British–Soviet–American alliance that had driven the German Army back from the steppes of Eurasia, the sands of North Africa, the shores of the Mediterranean and the English Channel to the Nazi citadel:

> In the history of diplomacy I know of no such close alliance of three great powers as this . . . Allies should not deceive each other . . . Possibly our alliance is so firm just because we do not deceive each other, or is it because it is not so easy to deceive each other? I propose a toast to the firmness of our Three-Power Alliance, may it be strong and stable, may we be as frank as possible.[1]

The ironies within Stalin's statement, made on the fifth evening of the Yalta conference, 8 February 1945, abound. While Winston Churchill had been vowing to 'fight on' after the fall of France, Stalin had been collaborating with Hitler. Despite his injunction against deception, the Soviets had installed dozens of secret listening devices in the palaces housing the British and American delegations. Every morning before the conference resumed, Stalin was briefed on the private conversations of Churchill and Franklin D. Roosevelt. That afternoon, he had met the American President and received the promise of territory in China and the Pacific in return for the Soviet Union joining the war against Japan. Neither the British nor the Chinese Nationalist leader, Chiang Kai-shek, were consulted. Most serious of all, Stalin had repeatedly stated his wish to see a 'strong', 'independent' and 'democratic' Poland, while remaining steadfast in his determination to preserve the communist puppet regime he had recently installed in Warsaw. Little wonder that Churchill, as he confessed in his toast, felt the burden of responsibility more heavily than at any other moment of the war. The future of Eastern Europe, he had complained to the Soviet diplomat Ivan Maisky two days earlier, 'rests on your bayonets'.[2] And yet, as Stalin himself had said, it would not have been 'possible to win the war without the alliance'.[3]

As Churchill remarked shortly after returning from Yalta, 'There is only one thing worse than fighting with allies and that is fighting without them.'[4] This epigram encapsulates one of the most important themes of the Second World War. In order to defeat the Axis, it was necessary for the British, the French, the Americans, the Soviets and the Chinese to work together. Their collaboration was sophisticated, diverse, mighty and conquering. Yet it was also fractious, suspicious, duplicitous and rivalrous. This book sets out to explore this antagonism: to examine the conflict and co-operation within the anti-Axis alliance, with all its consequences for the twentieth century and beyond.

The only reason why Adolf Hitler, Benito Mussolini and the militarist governments of Emperor Michinomiya Hirohito did not triumph between 1939 and 1945 was that they were confronted by a superior coalition of nations and empires that shared their resources and co-ordinated their plans to thwart them. The combined population of the three main Allied powers – the British Empire, the United States and the Soviet Union – stood at approximately 830 million at the outbreak of war. The total population of the Axis – Germany, Italy and Japan – was less than 260 million. The financial, industrial and material resources of the Allies dwarfed those of their adversaries. In 1943 alone, the Allies produced 2,891 naval vessels, 60,720 tanks and 147,161 aircraft. The Axis, by contrast, built 540 naval vessels, 12,825 tanks and 43,524 aircraft.

Yet the neat statistics are only partially explanatory. In order to bring its economic and demographic weight to bear, the anti-Axis alliance had to be formed and then maintained despite profound differences in ideology, ethics, personality, political systems and post-war aims, as well as disagreements over strategy, diplomacy, finance, imperialism, the allocation of resources and the future peace.

The Second World War is the most chronicled conflict in history. Thousands of books exist on its battles, generals, foot-soldiers and victims. It is not this book's purpose to add to this mountain of military history. Rather, it sets out to explore the politics and diplomacy of the improbable and incongruous alliance that ultimately defeated Hitler. Naturally, some of the events and the most prominent personalities – Winston Churchill, Franklin D. Roosevelt and Joseph Stalin – will be familiar to readers. Yet this book differs from the existing literature. Rather than keeping within the limits of the British–Soviet–American alliance – what Churchill liked to call the 'Grand Alliance' – or the wartime conferences, it examines the salient features of Allied wartime politics and diplomacy in their entirety. Thus, while the first part of the book deals with the Anglo-French alliance and its disintegration, subsequent sections consider the Free French, British colonial policy in light of the Japanese onslaught and Western interaction with that vast, complex and frequently neglected ally, Nationalist China. Other subjects beyond the confines of exclusive 'Big Three' diplomacy include relations with Francoist Spain and neutral Ireland, Allied policy in liberated Italy and war-torn Yugoslavia and British intervention in Greece.

Finally, I have broken my own self-denying ordinance to describe military events involving current or former allies, such as the sinking of the French Fleet at Mers el-Kébir by the Royal Navy, the crushing of the Iraqi revolt of May–June 1941 and the British–Gaullist campaign to oust the Vichy French from the Middle East. These were critical actions with far-reaching consequences and yet they remain little known, with most receiving scarcely more than a paragraph in general histories.

Of course, relations between the three main Allied powers and the politicking of their leaders are at the centre of the text. This was the triumvirate that won the war and shaped the peace. But the lens has been widened to include the foreign ministers, ambassadors, civil servants, emissaries and observers who participated in discussions, tendered advice and commented on events. Writing in 1936, the historian G. M. Young criticised 'much of what passes for diplomatic history' as 'little more than the record of what one clerk said to another clerk'.[5] Yet the opinions of those beneath and around the wielders of power are critical, since they reveal the context in which decisions were made; the nexus of attitudes, prejudices, knowledge, advice and assumptions from which political action derives.

Five years later, the British Director of Military Operations, Major-General Sir John Kennedy, ruminated on the 'frightful task' that awaited the historian of the future. 'I suppose no war has ever been so well documented,' he mused in his against-regulations diary. 'Yet the records do not often reveal individual views. It is essentially a government of committees. Opinions are nearly always collective or anonymous.'[6] Fortunately, thanks to diaries like Kennedy's, we are able to recreate debates and chronicle dissent.

This book has benefited from more than 100 collections of private papers and archives in Britain and the United States. The obvious lacuna is Russia, where archives have been closed to Western scholars for many years. It is possible that there are unpublished documents in Russia that will, when they finally emerge, enhance our understanding of Soviet foreign policy during the 'Great Patriotic War'. Yet we should not set our expectations too high. Unlike in the West, Soviet diplomats rarely expressed their honest opinions and seldom kept diaries or wrote memoirs. Even when they did, as in the case of Ivan Maisky, they were aware that their words were likely to be read by the Soviet secret police (the NKVD) and could be used to incriminate them. Stalin forbade his associates from taking notes during meetings (the exception being translators), while apparatchiks found it safer to repeat party prejudices than speak truth to power. It is therefore unlikely that our understanding of Soviet wartime diplomacy will alter fundamentally from that which we are able to gain from foreign sources, the extensive published documents and digital collections such as the Stalin Archive and the Molotov Secretariat.

The difficulties inherent in maintaining a global alliance between rival great powers with different strategic goals, combat priorities, governmental systems, ideologies and economies were immense. Only Hitler could have brought them together. The Allies were united in their desire to defeat the Nazi dictator and rid the world of German, Japanese and Italian militarism. In this quest they co-operated successfully and to an unprecedented degree. Yet they were at odds over the best way to win the war and about the world they hoped to construct from its ashes.

The Anglo-American alliance was the most formidable, intricate and, in many ways, harmonious military alliance in history. Yet this did not prevent the Roosevelt Administration from trying to dismantle the British Empire and capture British trade. The Free French leader, General Charles de Gaulle, was determined to maintain the unity of the French Empire and see France re-established as a major power but was opposed by the American President and the US State Department. Britain had declared war in accordance with her pledge to preserve Polish independence and yet her wartime partner, the Soviet Union, had participated in the destruction of the Polish state and had every intention of reasserting her control over the region. Far from making the world 'safe for democracy', the tragedy of the Second World War, as prosecuted by the British–Soviet–American alliance, was that it made much of Europe and Asia 'safe' for communism.

Diplomatic history is unfashionable at present. Even more so are the deeds of 'great men'. Yet the history of the Second World War indisputably shows the importance of both. With war raging once more in Europe and with the West struggling to act strategically or in concert, it seems timely to re-examine these events.

PART ONE

The Anglo-French Alliance
1939–1940

I

Allies

Thank God for the French Army.

Winston Churchill, 23 March 1933[1]

As was typical of that fateful spring, the day began in glorious sun-
shine. Walking through central London, the chaff from the plane
trees floating in the breeze, the Senior Assistant Secretary to the
War Cabinet, Colonel Leslie Hollis, marvelled at the serenity of the
city: clerks and civil servants on their way to work, typists in gay
frocks, shoppers and soldiers – all stepped brightly about their business, oblivious to the danger that hung over them. When he reached
Hendon aerodrome, however, Hollis learnt of the storm raging on
the other side of the Channel. The Royal Air Force wanted to postpone the trip but the Prime Minister was adamant: 'To hell with
that . . . I am going, whatever happens! This is too serious a situation to bother about the *weather*!'[2]

The weather was, indeed, the least of Churchill's concerns. Not
only had the Luftwaffe bombed the airfield at which he was due to
arrive the previous evening but the French Prime Minister, Paul
Reynaud, when summoning his ally to this urgent and impromptu
conference, had mentioned both the time and the location of the
rendezvous over an open telephone line. Churchill was furious.
Convinced that the Germans would have been listening in on the
call, he ordered his Assistant Private Secretary, Jock Colville, to ring
up Reynaud's Chef de Cabinet and cancel the meeting, as a deception, before being persuaded that this would cause unacceptable
chaos at the other end.

As it transpired, it is hard to imagine what further mayhem could
have ensued. Landing on the pockmarked airfield near Tours shortly

before 1 p.m. on 13 June 1940, the Prime Minister and his party were disconcerted to find that there was no one to meet them. 'One sensed the increasing degeneration of affairs', recalled Churchill, who walked across the wet, dilapidated airfield towards a group of idling French airmen and requested *'une voiture'*.[3] Eventually, the Station Commander's Citroën was commandeered and the British set off, in considerable discomfort, towards the Préfecture.

Refugees clogged the route – a fragment of the six to ten million French men, women and children fleeing the advancing enemy – and it was with difficulty that the car reached the temporary headquarters of the French Government. There, in keeping with the theme of the day, the British found no one to welcome them, nor any clue as to the whereabouts of the French Prime Minister. Churchill, who had arrived in France looking as if he was 'trying to chew a mouthful of nuts and bolts', took charge.[4] It was already after 2 p.m., he declared, and before anything further was attempted he was going to have some lunch. The British made for the Hôtel Grande Bretagne where, after some forceful negotiations with the proprietor, they were furnished with a private room, some cold chicken and several bottles of Vouvray.

Presently, the Secretary of the French War Cabinet, Paul Baudouin, arrived and ruined the meal by seasoning it 'with an out-pouring of oily defeatism'.[5] Resistance, he maintained, was futile. The Germans were pouring over the Seine bridges and were, at this very moment, on the outskirts of Paris. If the United States agreed to declare war on Germany *immediately* there was, perhaps, the pos-sibility of continuing the struggle but otherwise the situation was beyond retrieve. Responding to this 'Niagara of doom', Churchill was imperturbable.[6] Certainly, he hoped that America would enter the war, he told Baudouin, but Britain would fight on regardless.

At last, Reynaud arrived at the Préfecture. There, the British dele-gation, consisting of the Foreign Secretary, Viscount Halifax, the newly appointed Minister of Aircraft Production, Lord Beaverbrook, the Permanent Under-Secretary of the Foreign Office, Sir Alexander Cadogan, and the Military Secretary to the War Cabinet, Major-General Hastings 'Pug' Ismay, met Churchill's personal liaison with the French Prime Minister, Louis Spears, and the British Ambassador to Paris, Sir Ronald Campbell. On the French side, only Reynaud and Baudouin were present. Although the French Cabinet had invited Churchill to attend their session later that evening – an invitation Reynaud, inexplicably, failed to relay – the absence of the French Commander-in-Chief, General Weygand, or the Deputy Prime Minister, Maréchal Pétain, was an ominous sign.

Reynaud informed his British visitors that, at a Cabinet meeting the previous evening, Weygand had described the military situation as completely hopeless. The French armies were at their 'last gasp'. France had been defeated by the 'God of Battles' and had no choice but to plead for an armistice, to prevent the country from descending into anarchy.[7] Reynaud had insisted that all was not lost. If French forces had suffered great losses, then so had the enemy. If the Army could withstand the German invader for just a few more weeks, he had told the Commander-in-Chief, then they would receive more help from Britain and, eventually, the United States. With rising emotion, Reynaud had spoken of the need to save French honour and, although he did not repeat this to his British guests now, accused Weygand of critically misjudging their adversary: 'You are taking Hitler for Wilhelm I, the old gentleman who took Alsace and Lorraine from us [in 1871] and that was that. But Hitler is a Genghis Khan.'[8]

The French Cabinet had fallen in behind Reynaud. What significance had public order when the honour of France was at stake? What of the agreement signed with Britain not three months ago proscribing a separate peace? And what of the French Empire, from which it would be possible to continue the war?[9] Only Pétain had supported Weygand's proposal. And yet Reynaud now told Churchill that he would not be able to persuade his colleagues to continue the struggle without an immediate declaration of war by the United States. He was compelled, therefore, to ask how the British Government would respond to a French request to repudiate the agreement the two allies had signed on 28 March and seek an armistice with the Germans.

This was the turning point. The moment the British had feared but rarely spoken of for three weeks. An occurrence so shocking that it would have been unthinkable only a couple of months ago:

the defeat, after just six weeks of fighting, of the second largest army in Europe. The end of a political and military partnership that had lasted just ten months.

★

The Anglo-French alliance, which creaked into action upon the outbreak of war, on 3 September 1939, was born not of love or friendship but of necessity. Although the two countries had fought side by side during the First World War, it had not always been a harmonious experience and they had soon found themselves at odds over the peace settlement and the treatment of post-war Germany. Whilst the French, for understandable reasons, wanted to see their still-powerful neighbour hobbled, the British – though happy to administer her colonies – were wary of fuelling the German desire for revenge. They therefore opposed the French demand to detach the Rhineland from Germany and, when Prime Minister Poincaré sent troops into the Ruhr, to seize German coal in lieu of unpaid reparations, publicly denounced the French action. Worst of all, the British Prime Minister, David Lloyd George, had neutered the post-war Anglo-French Treaty of Alliance – the 'ultimate sanction of the Peace Treaty' and 'keystone for European peace', as far as the French were concerned – by inserting the proviso that the agreement would only come into effect once the United States Congress had ratified the concomitant Franco-American Treaty – an event that duly failed to materialise.[10]

With some justification the French responded to these slights and deceptions by invoking the old trope of 'perfidious Albion'. Britain had been one of the architects of the Versailles Treaty but, once the ink was dry, showed little interest in enforcing it or providing the promised guarantees for French security. The British thought the French vindictive and needlessly aggressive. Accused of 'senseless greed' over the issue of German reparations by John Maynard Keynes in his best-selling *The Economic Consequences of the Peace*, the French were considered 'intolerably foolish', 'impossible people' and 'rather insane' for continually poking the German 'tiger'.[11]

Nor did the British attitude change with the advent of Hitler in January 1933. Considering the French largely responsible for this violent strain of German nationalism, the MacDonald–Baldwin Government refused to confront illegal German rearmament and, instead, tried to assuage the militaristic temper of the new regime. On 18 June 1935, it signed a naval treaty with the new Reich, which allowed the Kriegsmarine to expand up to the level of 35 per cent of the Royal Navy. Not only did this agreement abrogate the armaments clauses of Versailles, it was presented to Paris as a *fait accompli*. Understandably, the French Prime Minister, Pierre Laval, was incandescent, while the right-wing journalist Henri Béraud responded to this latest betrayal by castigating *les anglais* for their record of 'violence, perfidy, implacable selfishness and disloyalty'. 'I hate this people for myself and for my ancestors,' Béraud fumed, 'by instinct as much as tradition.'[12]

Yet the French dared not break with the British. Despite the turmoil of French Third Republic politics – which produced fourteen governments between 1933 and 1939 – all French prime ministers were united in the conviction that no French soldier would take up arms against German treaty-breaking unless France enjoyed the unequivocal backing of Britain. This gave the British considerable leverage and allowed first Stanley Baldwin, then Neville Chamberlain, to pursue their policy of appeasement with little regard for French sensibilities. Thus Lord Halifax, then Lord Privy Seal, informed Hitler in November 1937 that Britain had no *a priori* objection to frontier changes in eastern and central Europe and, in September 1938, at the height of the Czech crisis, Chamberlain made the momentous decision to fly to Hitler without informing, let alone consulting, the French Prime Minister, Édouard Daladier. As the French Foreign Minister, Georges Bonnet, noted ruefully after Munich, 'The French Government was only a tail to the British kite.'[13]

Only when appeasement was shown to have failed – when Hitler continued to berate the 'Versailles powers' after Munich and then shredded the Agreement by invading the rump of Czechoslovakia in March 1939 – did the British actively begin to court the French. On 21 March 1939, Albert Lebrun stepped onto the dock at Dover and inaugurated the first state visit to Britain by a French president in more than a decade, or 'Frog week', as the Conservative MP and Wodehouse caricature Henry 'Chips' Channon called it.[14] Over the next four days, the First Gentleman of France and his wife were treated to the full panoply of England's *ancien régime*. The King spoke of an entente destined by 'Providence', while even the pro-appeasement *Times* lauded a renewal of Anglo-French 'solidarity'.[15]

Yet points of tension remained, as the British prevaricated during the summer of 1939 over negotiations with the Soviet Union and when, on 3 September, a combination of French muddle and funk led to the embarrassing spectacle of Britain declaring war on Germany six hours before her ally. This regrettable episode – widely interpreted as a cowardly bout of French chicanery – helped to reinforce the already existing view in Whitehall that however much the British might rely on the French soldier, the same confidence could not be placed in 'French politicians or the Quai d'Orsay [the French Foreign Office]'.[16]

Confidence in the French soldier, however, counted for much. At the outbreak of war, France possessed a regular army of 900,000 men, with five million reservists available for immediate call-up. The British, by contrast, had a professional army of 224,000 men (131,100 of whom were reservists) and 458,000 'Saturday night soldiers', or territorials. The British Expeditionary Force (BEF) that sailed for France in September 1939 was well equipped and, as recent historians have emphasised, uniquely mechanised.[17] But there was precious little materiel with which to furnish the irregulars or the newly conscripted. In April 1939, Viscount Gort, the commander of the BEF, had been appalled to discover a division of territorials without even mugs or cutlery and, one year on, the Conservative MP Quintin Hogg was still training his contingent of the Tower Hamlets Rifles without Bren guns or ammunition. 'Could you please oblige us with a Bren gun?' went Noël Coward's song of the same name. 'The lack of one is wounding to our pride / Last night we found the cutest little German parachutist / He looked at our kit and giggled a bit and laughed until he cried.'[18] Later, when the French Army began to collapse and one of the newly appointed Labour Cabinet ministers, Arthur Greenwood, referred sarcastically to Britain's 'bloody gallant allies', he received a sharp rebuke from the Chief of the Imperial General Staff, General Sir Edmund Iron-side: 'I told him that we had depended upon the French Army. That we had made no army [ourselves] and therefore it was not right to say "these bloody allies". It was for them to say that to us.'[19]

In fairness to Britain's war leaders, it was no part of British, nor for that matter French, strategy to engage in major land offensives for at least two years after the outbreak of war. Aware of their materiel deficiencies, most crucially in the air, and based on the theory that the Allies could lose a short war but, with the mobilisation of their more abundant resources, were bound to win a long one – as they had in 1918 – the initial Anglo-French plan was overwhelmingly defensive. The French, with their large army and chain of fortifications along their eastern frontier – the famous Maginot Line – were to hold the Germans on land, while the British, repeating their actions from the First World War, planned to asphyxiate the German economy by naval blockade. To almost everyone, at least initially, this seemed like prudent strategy. There were several problems with this approach, however, the most immediate of which was that it did nothing to help the country for which the Allies had nominally gone to war: Poland.

On 31 March 1939, having failed to stand by Czechoslovakia and reaped the consequences, Britain and France had pledged themselves to the defence of Poland. Unfortunately for the Poles, it was an empty promise: a political gesture designed to deter Hitler rather than a military plan to aid their country. Although General Maurice Gamelin, the then French Commander-in-Chief, had committed himself to a limited attack three days after the Germans had crossed the Polish frontier, followed by a significant offensive on the seventeenth day of mobilisation, the reality, when war broke out in September, was a timorous incursion of nine divisions, 5 miles into the Saarland, before a full-scale retreat. 'Platoon tried to continue its advance', reads one inglorious entry from a French regimental diary, but 'was halted by the fire of an automatic weapon'.[20]

Understandably, the Poles felt betrayed. 'It is like a shooting party,' exclaimed the distraught Polish Ambassador, Count Edward Raczyński, after one of many fruitless attempts to persuade the British Government to help his country: 'We are the partridges and they [the Germans] are the guns.'[21] The French failed to cause a single German division to be diverted from Poland – despite the paucity of German forces in the west – while the British, sympathetic to French fears of reprisals and reluctant to be the first to cause civilian casualties, insisted on dropping leaflets rather than bombs on the Reich. On 6 October 1939, having suffered more than half a million military casualties and the destruction of much of Warsaw, the Poles were forced to surrender. France's twenty-year strategy of creating a system of eastern alliances capable of containing Germany had ended in brutal failure. The sovereignty of Poland, for which the Allies had finally gone to war, had been extinguished in just four weeks.

*

The swiftness of the Polish collapse was a bitter disappointment to the French, who, despite doing nothing to help, expected the Poles to hold out until the spring. The British were more sanguine. The Chief of Staff to the British Expeditionary Force, Lieutenant-General Henry Pownall, reflected that it would have been impossible to ship the 158,000 men of the BEF safely to France without the 'time and immunity' of the Polish campaign, while the Prime Minister, Neville Chamberlain, retained an improbable faith in a collapse of the German home front. There were, however, problems that derived from a strategy of 'wait and see'.

Unlike in August 1914, the outbreak of war on 3 September 1939 was greeted with neither wild enthusiasm nor foolish jingoism. Most French soldiers, observed the émigré Austro-Hungarian writer Arthur Koestler, 'did not care a bean for Danzig and the [Polish] Corridor . . . They rather disliked Hitler for all the unrest he created but they did not actually hate him. The only thing they really hated was the idea of war.'[22] Captain Daniel Barlone of the 2nd North African Division attributed the lack of zeal among both officers and men to a profound confusion about what they were fighting for. During the Great War, the French Army had been inspired by the need to expel the Germans from their soil and to regain the lost provinces of Alsace and Lorraine. Now the average French soldier felt secure behind the

Maginot Line and dubious of the claim that Hitler would 'hurl himself on us after having swallowed up the little nations, one by one'.[23]

In Britain, the situation was different. Chamberlain's highly publicised attempts to placate Hitler and the no less public failure of his policy had demonstrated the need to resist German aggression beyond all possible doubt. Aside from an embarrassment of dukes and a lunatic fringe from both right and left, opinion polls and Home Intelligence reports showed the nation to be solidly behind the declaration of war. But there was little enthusiasm. Rather, in Britain, as in France, the overwhelming sentiment was 'Let's get it over with.'*

This was easier said than done. Twenty-five years earlier, the Germans had opened the bowling by invading Belgium and driving, with all possible speed, towards Paris. In 1939, politicians feared a similar lightning attack but despite myriad scares and multiple predictions the blow did not come. For Jean-Paul Sartre, serving in a meteorological unit in Alsace, the lull was a boon. Between the outbreak of war and the onset of fighting in the west, he wrote nearly a million words, filling fourteen notebooks with philosophy and completing the first draft of his novel *L'âge de raison*. But most French soldiers were not literary polymaths and morale plummeted. Drunkenness, looting and absenteeism proliferated. 'The army was rotting from inaction', recalled a junior officer at the Ministère de la Guerre, while the 'slovenliness, dirtiness and inefficiency' of the French soldiers he met caused the commander of the BEF's II Corps, Lieutenant-General Alan Brooke, to wonder 'whether the French are still a firm enough nation to again take their part in seeing this war through'.[24]

While the French army stagnated, Parisian social life carried on as normal. Street cafés were full, race meetings continued at Auteuil and Maurice Chevalier sang 'Paris sera toujours Paris' at

---

* 'There was only one consideration which prevented the average French soldier from looking at the war as complete madness,' recalled Koestler, and that was the slogan '*Il faut en finir*' ('This must end'). 'He had been mobilised three times during the past few years and he was sick of having to leave his job and his family every six months and to return after a few weeks, feeling ridiculous and cheated.'

the Casino de Paris. 'Every shop in St Germain and in the outskirts of Paris blazed to high heaven,' noted the young war correspondent Anthony Gibbs. 'The naphtha flares flickered blindingly in the street market stalls. Enormous naked electric light bulbs, of terrifying candle power, shone in batteries from uncurtained windows, lighting up the rain and the puddles and the thronging shoppers with the radiance of the tropic sun.' Soon Gibbs found himself up in front of the British Military Censor.

'You've described here the blackout in Paris. Well, I mean – We don't want the Germans to know *everything*.'

'Can I describe the blackout if I leave out Paris?' enquired Gibbs.

'Well, that's just the trouble. You see you rather give the impression that the French don't pay much attention to the blackout . . . It's a question of annoying our allies.'[25]

Not all British military personnel were so diplomatic. The distinguished medieval historian Marc Bloch, acting as a liaison officer with the BEF, observed that the average English officer, whilst doubtless kindly and good-natured in his own country, had an unfortunate tendency, once across the Channel, to 'confuse his European hosts with "natives" – in other words, with those inhabitants of his colonial possessions who are, by definition, his inferiors.' The British Tommy, wrote Bloch, was arguably worse: 'The soldier immortalised by Kipling knows how to obey and how to fight . . . But he is, by nature, a looter and a lecher: that is to say, he is guilty of two vices which the French peasant finds it hard to forgive when both are satisfied to the detriment of his farmyard and his daughters.'[26]

As the '*drôle de guerre*' or 'Phoney War' dragged on, relations between the Allies became increasingly fractious. French soldiers resented how much better paid their English counterparts were – a grievance the British would later feel towards their American allies – while the fact that Britain had only five divisions in the field (later rising to thirteen), compared to France's ninety-one, helped foster the notion that the British were, as German propaganda alleged, planning to 'fight to the last Frenchman'.[27] Day after day, the giant speakers along the Franco-German frontier, as well as the airwaves of Radio Stuttgart, bombarded French soldiers with lines such as 'It is all the fault of the English!' and 'Britain provides the machines, France provides the bodies.'[28] Louis Spears, the Franco-phile Conservative MP known in Westminster as the 'Member for Paris', reported the view from the French provinces that 'France and France alone appears to be bearing the brunt of the fighting' – this before any fighting had actually taken place – while, in October 1939, Prime Minister Daladier raged to a senior air officer about the 'English, behind the Channel . . . conserving their energies so as to last out'.[29]

In order to counter such sentiments and promote allied unity, fraternisation between British and French soldiers was encouraged at various levels. Although Alan Brooke found the lunches with his French colleagues a strain on both his work and his liver – the lunch-eon on 31 October, hosted by the Préfet du Nord for the Duke of Gloucester, consisted of oysters, lobster, chicken, foie gras, cheese, fruit, wine and liqueurs – his colleague Lieutenant-General Pownall thought they served a useful purpose. British battalions flew the flag by patrolling the French frontier, opposite the Saar, and there was an assortment of inter-Allied sporting events.

In addition to working on an Anglo-French financial agreement (December 1939), cross-Channel trade (February 1940) and industrial co-operation (March 1940), officials in London and Paris spent time pondering increasingly creative schemes to promote Anglo-French unity. 'La Marseillaise', it was suggested, should be played in Brit-ish cinemas after 'God Save the King'; a special stamp featuring the heads of both President Lebrun and King George VI was proposed by the Commissariat Général à l'Information; English, it was urged, should be made compulsory in French schools (and vice versa); and the Minister of Education, Earl De La Warr, wrote to Lord Halifax with a plan for British children to learn something of French gas-tronomy: 'I believe there are a number of unemployed French chefs in London whom we might get to go round the schools and cook French meals!'[30]

But it was action, not cultural exchanges, that British and French public opinion demanded as the 'Bore War' wore on. On 12 September 1939, the first meeting of the Supreme War Council, comprising Chamberlain and the Minister for the Co-ordination of Defence, Admiral Chatfield, for the British, and Daladier and

General Gamelin for the French, took place at Abbeville. The Prime Ministers had no great respect for one another. Having been excluded from Chamberlain's meetings with Hitler and the post-Munich declaration – the infamous 'piece of paper' – the French Prime Minister was naturally suspicious of his British counterpart. When Chamberlain had taken his appeasement caravan to Rome in January 1939, Daladier told the American Ambassador that he 'fully expected to be betrayed', since this was the 'customary fate of allies of the British'. He went on to describe the British Prime Minister as a 'desiccated stick', King George VI as 'a moron' and Queen Elizabeth as an 'excessively ambitious woman who would be ready to sacrifice every other country in the world in order that she might remain Queen Elizabeth of England'.[31] For his part, Chamberlain thought Daladier emotional and vainglorious. He may have been given the soubriquet the 'Bull of Vaucluse' (the southern *département* the Premier represented in the Chamber of Deputies) but he had the horns of a snail.[32]

Nevertheless, at Abbeville, the two leaders put on a good show of Allied unity. Franco-British co-operation had never been stronger, declared Daladier. It was essential that the solidarity of France and Britain 'should be maintained and conveyed to the world', stated Chamberlain. Most satisfactorily from the latter's perspective, Daladier agreed that the Allies should be in no hurry to undertake 'large-scale operations' since time was on their' side.[33]

When the Supreme War Council reconvened in Hove Town Hall on 22 September, however, Daladier urged the establishment of a 'Balkan front' to forestall German penetration of the region. The British considered this pure 'moonshine' – the first of several attempts to shift the focus of the war away from French frontiers.[34] Yet the Balkan project was also symptomatic of the long-standing French interest in creating an eastern front. In April 1938, a French Army Staff study had spoken of the vital need, in the event of war, to establish a 'common front from the Baltic to the Adriatic' and, on 20 September 1939, Daladier spoke of the necessity of sending an expedition to the Balkans, 'to force Germany to disperse its military forces and to make the blockade as effective as possible'.[35]

Either way, Chamberlain threw 'gentle showers of cold water' on the proposal.[36] Haunted by the memory of Gallipoli, the British had no desire to repeat that disaster with another Balkan adventure. This was to set the pattern for Allied strategic discussions during the Phoney War. Whenever the French proposed an expedition to some part of eastern or southern Europe, the British vetoed it and whenever the British suggested anything that might provoke a German response in the west, the French replied with a firm *'non'*. Privately, both partners expressed concerns at this state of strategic stalemate.

For the French, the main cause of restlessness was the growing sense that time was perhaps not on the Allied side after all. French economic malaise, her population deficit, production bottlenecks and a small but influential section of her citizenry in favour of a compromise peace, all contributed to the notion that it was the Germans, not the Allies, who were benefiting from the armed truce. The British shared this fear, while the demoralising effects of prolonged passivity represented an even greater concern. 'There has been a general grouse that here we are suffering gross discomfort, blackouts, rising food prices . . . evacuees in one's spare beds and nothing to show for it,' wrote the Conservative MP Jim Thomas to Viscount Cranborne on 25 September 1939.[37] Cranborne's father, the Marquess of Salisbury, thought the 'dead silence from the front . . . very trying to public nerves', while a 55-year-old woman from Bolton, asked by a Mass-Observation volunteer when she expected the war to end, replied, 'No idea; it hasn't started yet, has it?'[38] Even Chamberlain began to wonder whether the war could ever be won without first giving the Germans 'a real hard punch in the stomach'.[39]

On both sides of the Channel, there was thus a growing desire to do *something* even if there was no clear idea as to what that something should be or, in the words of a French naval officer and later historian, 'to do something even something stupid'.[40] As 1939 turned into 1940 and without any sign of the war starting in earnest, the Allies would come perilously close to doing just that.

II

The Scandinavian Fiasco

Our task in this war is to defeat Hitlerism but it is still
Hitlerism if the aggressor is called Stalin.

Daily Sketch, 22 December 1939[1]

Just before dawn on the morning of 30 November 1939, Soviet forces
crossed the frontier and invaded neutral Finland. Some 450,000 men,
2,514 tanks and 718 armoured cars took part in the initial assault,
which began with an artillery bombardment across the Karelian isth-
mus and the bombing of Helsinki. It was not a war Joseph Stalin had
expected to wage. The Soviet dictator had expected the Finns, when
threatened with the overwhelming might of the Red Army, to relinquish the territories he claimed. When a Finnish delegation arrived in
Moscow on 12 October, however, they had shocked him by rejecting
his demands. Even more astonishing was how this sparsely populated country, with an army of just 150,000 men and thirty-two tanks
(only ten of which were operational at the outbreak of war), then
proceeded to inflict a series of devastating reverses on the Red Army.
Camouflaged Finnish ski-troops flitted through the birch forests
like ghosts, ambushing Soviet columns and severing their communications. The Mannerheim Line – named after the septuagenarian
Finnish Commander-in-Chief – proved a formidable obstacle, while
thousands of underequipped and ill-trained Russian soldiers simply
walked into the Finnish minefields and booby-traps. Inspired by
Finnish resistance – a real instance of David defying Goliath – and
outraged by Soviet aggression, there was soon a clamour in Allied
capitals to aid the Finns, while British and French war leaders saw in
the 'Winter War' an opportunity to shift the focus of their own conflict to Scandinavia and end the strategic stalemate.

Long before the outbreak of hostilities, the British and the French had decided that economic warfare would be integral to their offensive strategy. Germany was deficient in oil, chrome, copper, tungsten, timber, iron ore, bauxite and rubber, as well as foodstuffs. By restricting her imports of these commodities, the Allies, so the theory went, would impair the Nazi war machine and attack the German home front, leading to a precipitous collapse, as had occurred at the end of the First World War. Unfortunately, as so often in political economics, the concept was more beautiful than the reality. Anglo-French estimates of German stocks of raw materials varied wildly – several suggested that they were substantial – while the ability of the Allies to strangle the German economy by means of blockade was undermined by Hitler's conquest of new territories and trade with the Reich's *de facto* ally, Soviet Russia. Yet if Allied leaders engaged in a certain amount of 'mysticism and hope' over the potentials of economic warfare, it is important to remember how few options appeared open to the British and the French in the winter of 1939.[2] With the British opposed to expeditions to the Balkans, the French averse to any action that might invite German reprisals and both countries determined to avoid massacres on the Western Front, the blockade represented a relatively safe arrow in an otherwise bereft quiver. Now, with the growing desire to 'do something' and declining faith in the 'long war' strategy, the Allies began to look northwards.

Germany's dependence on Swedish iron ore, the primary ingredient in the manufacture of steel, had long been recognised in London and Paris. Nine of the eleven million tons of ore imported by Germany each year came from Swedish mines near the northern town of Gällivare, estimated the British Industrial Intelligence Committee in August 1939. Three months later, the senior official at the Ministry of Economic Warfare, Desmond Morton, claimed that the figures were even greater. The conclusion, he argued, was obvious: 'barring unpredictable developments', the halting of Swedish iron ore exports to Germany had the capacity to 'end the war in a few months'.[3] Given such fantastical claims, it is not surprising that some began to refer to Morton's department as the 'Ministry of Wishful Thinking'.[4] But the civil servant had a powerful backer. The report, which Morton submitted on 27 November 1939, had been compiled at the request of the recently reappointed First Lord of the Admiralty, Winston Churchill.

Given the consequences for British domestic politics, most accounts of the Allied intervention in Scandinavia have focussed on the role of Churchill to the exclusion of other factors.[5] Yet the French dimension was just as, if not more, important. By the turn of the year 1940, most French war leaders had lost faith in the notion that 'time was an ally' and were seeking ways to shorten the war. 'We must use our maritime power to precipitate rather than to suffer events,' wrote the French naval Commander-in-Chief, Admiral François Darlan, in January 1940, while as early as November 1939, Daladier described it as 'puerile' to expect a collapse of the German economy from the blockade as currently constituted.[6] In particular, the French Prime Minister was impressed by a report from the German emigré industrialist and former Nazi, Fritz Thyssen, which argued that the side that controlled the Swedish ore fields would win the war.[7]

The Finnish war provided Daladier with the chance to act. French public opinion was outraged by Stalin's wanton aggression; an act, indeed, that united the left with the right for the first time in twenty years. Voices that had remained silent over Poland called for action to save the Finns. The 'civilised world would be abandoning its duty to itself and would ruin all faith in a noble ideal if it allowed heroic Finland to be crushed', opined *Le Temps* in December 1939. 'Finland should be saved at any price,' declared the former leader of the Popular Front, Léon Blum, while, throughout January and February 1940, a growing number of French deputies called for the despatch of military aid and even an expeditionary force to Finland.[8]

Daladier was in no position to resist these calls. Already blamed for French military inertia, he welcomed the prospect of Allied intervention in Finland as an opportunity to shift the focus of the war far away from French frontiers, to disrupt the Swedish ore trade and placate his critics. At a meeting of the Supreme War Council on 5 February 1940, therefore, Daladier placed before the British two operational alternatives: the Allies could mount an expedition to liberate the Finnish peninsula of Petsamo – the hope being that this would provoke the Germans to respond and, thus, allow the Allies to commence operations in Norway and Sweden – or they could land a force at the Norwegian port of Narvik which would occupy the Swedish ore fields *en route* to Finland.

Churchill had been urging his colleagues in the War Cabinet to halt the German iron ore traffic since the third week of the war. His solution was to lay mines in Norwegian territorial waters – thus forcing German transports onto the open sea, where they could be sunk by the Royal Navy – or, as Daladier now suggested, to despatch an expeditionary force to Sweden to occupy the ore fields. The problem was that he had been repeatedly stymied by his colleagues. Although the pugnacious First Lord enjoyed the support of the military planners, the Chief of the Imperial General Staff and the Ministry of Economic Warfare, neither Chamberlain nor the Foreign Secretary, Lord Halifax, was prepared to authorise action that would violate Scandinavian neutrality.

To a certain extent, this was understandable. Britain and France had gone to war, at least nominally, in defence of the rights of small nations and it would undermine the moral plane on which they stood – the salient topographical feature as far as the United States was concerned – to extend the conflict to a new region in defiance of international law. Between December 1939 and February 1940, the Allies tried their best to persuade the Swedish and Norwegian Governments to allow the passage of an Anglo-French force to Finland (which would also occupy the ore fields) and, simultaneously, to reduce the amount of iron ore they shipped to Germany. But the replies from Oslo and Stockholm were consistent and unbending: the Norwegians would do nothing that would risk German retaliation, while the Swedes – for similar reasons – refused to reduce the quantity of ore they sent to Germany.

For the more bellicose Anglo-French war leaders, this obstinacy was infuriating. The Germans were themselves abusing Scandinavian neutrality by sinking British and neutral shipping within Norwegian territorial waters and it was absurd, as Churchill argued in a memorandum for the War Cabinet, for the Allies to be punctilious in their respect for international law when their opponents were gaining advantages 'by tearing up all laws'.[9] On 20 January 1940, during a radio broadcast, he admonished those neutral nations who 'bow humbly and in fear to German threats of violence, comforting themselves meanwhile with the thought that the Allies will win . . . Each one hopes that if he feeds

the crocodile enough, the crocodile will eat him last.'[10] This produced
howls of protest from the Scandinavians, Swiss, Belgians and Dutch,
and Halifax – who, after all, was the one who had to 'be in daily touch
with these tiresome neutrals' – sent his colleague a carefully worded
rebuke.[11] Events, however, were to support Churchill's accusations.

On 14 February 1940, the German tanker *Altmark* was spotted off
the coast of Norway. Believing the vessel to be carrying around 300
captured British merchant seamen, the Admiralty ordered a destroyer flotilla, led by Captain Philip Vian in HMS *Cossack*, to sail
forth and intercept. On the afternoon of 16 February, Vian's force
cornered the *Altmark*, forcing her to take refuge in Jøssingfjord.
There, the *Cossack* followed but was impeded by two Norwegian
torpedo boats whose officers insisted that they had already searched
the tanker and that there were no prisoners abroad. As it transpired,
they had neglected the hold, where the prisoners were kept.* Negotiations with the Norwegians were useless, Vian signalled to the
Admiralty at 4.32 p.m., adding that one of the gunboats 'has a torpedo tube trained on me'.[12] At this fraught moment, Churchill, who
had been following the hunt throughout the day, took charge. He
telephoned Halifax and asked his permission to defy the Norwegians and free the prisoners by force. The Foreign Secretary asked
for some time but Churchill told him that the ships were currently
facing each other and that 'at any moment there might be trouble'.[13]
After ten minutes' reflection, Halifax gave his blessing and Churchill signalled to Vian, ordering him to 'board *Altmark*, liberate the
prisoners and take possession of the ship pending further instructions'.[14] At this, Vian sailed the *Cossack* into the fjord and, after some
further fruitless negotiations with the Norwegians, set course for
the prize. Realising he was about to be overwhelmed, the German
captain tried to ram his assailant but the *Cossack*'s helmsman was
too fast and the *Altmark* ran aground. In scenes reminiscent of the
age of sail, British bluejackets leapt on board the tanker and, after

---

* This bizarre omission takes on a more sinister complexion when one consid-
ers the noise the prisoners made whenever the Norwegian vessels were within
earshot – a distress signal several Norwegian sailors admitted to having heard.

some fierce hand-to-hand fighting, in which six of the *Altmark*'s crew were killed, succeeded in freeing all 299 prisoners.

The *Altmark* incident provided a much-needed fillip to British prestige. Mussolini's son-in-law-cum-Foreign Minister, Count Galeazzo Ciano, complimented the British Ambassador on an action 'reminiscent of the boldest traditions of the Navy at the time of Francis Drake', while the cry 'The Navy's here!' – the phrase by which the prisoners learnt that they were being rescued – went round the world.[15] Yet though Norwegian neutrality had been shown to be woefully ineffectual, fear of Scandinavian opposition continued to exercise a hold on Allied plans.

The British had turned down the French proposal to invade the Finnish peninsula of Petsamo. Offering little prospect of curbing the Swedish ore traffic, it also risked war with the Soviet Union, 'a military gamble without any political prize', according to General Ironside or, to paraphrase Jacques Mordal, an opportunity to do something *extremely stupid*.[16] As compensation, the French demanded that the British enact the Narvik project, by which the Allies would despatch an expeditionary force to the north Norwegian port that would then proceed to Finland, occupying the Swedish ore fields on the way. Temperamentally opposed to any action that might start a 'shooting war', Chamberlain agreed on the condition that the Allies first acquire the assent of the Scandinavians. This, predictably, was not forthcoming. But Daladier refused to let the matter drop. Facing a barrage of criticism over his failure to help the Finns, the French Premier allowed news of the 'impending' operation to spread all over Paris – and, inevitably, further afield – before accepting the Finnish Ambassador's request for 50,000 Allied troops, despite knowing so large a deployment to be impossible. That same day, 1 March 1940, Daladier instructed the French Ambassador in London to impress upon the War Cabinet that his Government would fall unless an Allied expeditionary force was despatched forthwith, adding that his successor would likely feel compelled to pursue 'another policy' – a none too subtle allusion to a compromise peace.[17]

The British were incensed by such obvious blackmail but it had the desired effect. French pressure, alongside the wish 'to divert from ourselves the odium of having allowed Finland to be crushed', combined to give the go-ahead for a military operation that not only risked adding Russia to the list of Allied enemies but could be thwarted by cutting the power to the electric railway that ran between Narvik and Gällivare, the only viable route.[18] Only the capitulation of the Finns, on 13 March, saved the Allies from this 'hare-brained' scheme.[19]

Still, the collapse of Finland was a severe blow to Allied prestige. Neutral opinion, most crucially in the United States, interpreted Stalin's victory as a reverse for the democracies, while the German press crowed about 'an absolutely unique political defeat for London and Paris'.[20] The French Government blamed the British. 'All the influential circles . . . took the view that the fault lay with Great Britain for not having acted at an earlier stage,' explained a French member of the Armaments Commission, while Daladier spoke of a 'loss of faith in his ability ever to induce the British Government to take prompt action or a strong line.'[21]

The British refused to accept these strictures. Britain had despatched, or prepared for despatch, as much aid to Finland as France, noted Sir Alexander Cadogan, while the Under-Secretary of State, 'Rab' Butler, argued that the proposed venture would have ranked alongside the Duke of Buckingham's disastrous attempt to capture the Île de Ré in 1627.[22] They were, however, worried about the effect on French morale and the ramifications for French domestic politics. They were right to be. On 19 March 1940, 300 French deputies abstained in a vote of confidence in Daladier's leadership and the Bull of Vaucluse, as he had predicted, was forced to resign. His successor was the Finance Minister, Paul Reynaud.

No less than Churchill, two months later, Reynaud believed he was the man destined to save his country. Intelligent, dynamic and ambitious, this diminutive politician, whose narrow eyes and natural smirk gave him 'the countenance of a Samurai educated at Cambridge', had distinguished himself during the 1930s as an opponent of Munich and a rare champion of the doctrines of mobile, mechanised warfare, as advocated by Colonel Charles de Gaulle.[23] Churchill rejoiced at his friend's elevation to the premiership but whilst the new head of the French Government may have appeared more resolute than his predecessor, his political position was incomparably weaker, with a majority of just one in the Chamber of Deputies and the smouldering resentment of Daladier, who refused to relinquish his post of Minister of Defence, to contend with.

Reynaud's answer to his political vulnerability was to demonstrate action on the war front. Writing to his British colleagues ahead of the meeting of the Supreme War Council on 28 March, the new Premier exhorted his allies to learn the lessons of their recent defeat and prosecute the war with an energy and determination that had, thus far, been lacking. Understandably, the British did not take well to this scolding. Chamberlain 'went through the ceiling', recorded General Ironside. 'He was horrified when he saw the paper. It gave him the impression of a man who was rattled and who wished to make a splash to justify his position.'[24] When the two men met in London on 28 March, Chamberlain delivered a ninety-minute statement, justifying his handling of the war and demolishing Reynaud's plans with such devastating logic that the French Premier could merely nod along in agreement.[25] The Allies did, however, reach two important decisions: Reynaud consented to Churchill's plan to disrupt German river traffic by dropping over 2,000 fluvial mines into the headwaters of the Rhine (Operation Royal Marine), while Chamberlain agreed to strike at Germany's iron ore supplies by mining Norwegian waters south of Narvik (Operation Wilfred). The meeting ended with the two Prime Ministers signing a joint declaration promising not to conclude a separate peace and pledging to continue to co-operate 'in all spheres' after the war was won.[26]

The mining of the Rhine and the Norwegian coast was due to take place, in tandem, on 4–5 April 1940. On 31 March, however, the French War Committee refused to implement the Rhine project. The obstacle, the British learnt, was Daladier, who feared reprisals against France's aircraft factories and was determined 'to put every possible spoke in Reynaud's wheel'.[27] Daladier 'desires the victory of France but he desires my defeat even more', wailed Reynaud to his liaison with British General Headquarters, André Maurois.[28] The British were dismayed. The operations had been approved concurrently not only to demonstrate the Allies' determination to prosecute the war but also to deflect attention from their violation of Norwegian neutral rights.[29] When Chamberlain saw a clearly embarrassed French Ambassador, he was firm: 'No mines – no Narvik.'[30] But this was, ultimately, a bluff. Having tried and failed to persuade the French to change their minds about Royal Marine, the British decided that it would be a case of cutting their nose to spite their face if they cancelled Wilfred. Notably it was concerns about their French ally, rather than the arguments of Churchill, who had been agitating to mine Norwegian waters for months, that ultimately persuaded the War Cabinet. As Lord Halifax told his colleagues, it was the belief of the British Ambassador that Reynaud would fall if the British refused to proceed with the Norwegian operation. To base such a decision on 'French internal politics' was, he admitted, unorthodox but 'the bad effects which would follow a disturbance in the French political field, coupled with the general psychological position, constituted perhaps the most weighty factors in a very difficult situation.'[31]

During the previous three months, the Swedes and Norwegians had responded to Allied pressure – over ore, over Finland and over German acts of war within their jurisdiction – by restating their intention to maintain their neutrality under all circumstances.* Following the *Altmark* incident and the fall of Finland, however, this line had worn distinctly thin. 'Norway and Sweden are contemptible and lose all claim to be representatives of that higher international morality which they have so long preached at us,' recorded the First Secretary of the British Embassy in Paris, Oliver Harvey, on 14 March.[32] Rab Butler agreed. Although speaking specifically of the Swedes and with unintended irony, given his own previous support for appeasement, his remarks to Chamberlain's Assistant Private Secretary, Jock Colville, on 6 April 1940 are representative of the state of Allied frustration with both Scandinavian countries:

---

* The Swedish diplomat Gunnar Hägglöf was not alone in considering the British attitude towards the Scandinavian dilemma ignorant and callous: 'I have the feeling that England turns its back on Northern Europe, particularly Scandinavia . . . If there really are English hearts beating for Norway, I guess the reason is the salmon fishing.'

The key to their attitude is a determination to avoid fire and the sword at all costs. They would rather sell their souls and their country to the Nazis (provided the sale were effected without bloodshed) than stand up boldly for their beliefs and independence. They would invite Germany to occupy their country peaceably rather than risk an armed invasion.[33]

On the morning of 8 April 1940, four British mine-laying destroyers laid 234 Mark-17 mines in Vestfjord off Narvik. Responding to the news, the Secretary-General of the Swedish Foreign Office (who happened to be in London negotiating an Anglo-Swedish war trade agreement) told Sir Alexander Cadogan that the British had done the 'silliest thing in history'.[34] Yet the mine-laying came too late to have an effect. Well aware of Allied intentions, thanks to French Government leaks, Hitler had ordered his military planners to prepare for the invasion of Norway (Operation Weserübung) as early as 21 January. On the morning of 9 April, a mere twenty-four hours after the British mine-laying operation, German troops landed and captured the Norwegian ports of Kristiansand, Stavanger, Bergen, Trondheim, Narvik and Oslo, while also overrunning neutral Denmark. Belatedly the Allies realised that their months of 'arglebargling', in General Ironside's phrase, had allowed Hitler to steal a march on them.[35] The Germans had been 'very clever', the Chancellor of the Exchequer, Sir John Simon, told Jock Colville, 'and we were ninnies, we were ninnies!'[36]

The ill-fated Anglo-French attempt to expel the Germans from Norway put a further strain on the alliance. Undermanned and grossly underequipped – with a dearth of maps, radios, skis, snow boots and, most crucially, air support – the British, commented one French officer, seemed to have conceived the campaign along 'the lines of a punitive expedition against the Zulus'.[37] Although the Royal Navy succeeded in sinking ten German destroyers in Narvik Fjord (for the loss of two British destroyers), the Allied expeditionary force did not take the town until 28 May. In the meantime, the War Cabinet had decided to shift the focus of operations towards the capture of Trondheim. Between 14 and 21 April, 3,500 British troops and 2,500 French *chasseurs alpins* landed at Namsos, some 130 miles north of the city, while 1,000 British soldiers disembarked at Åndalsnes, 60 miles to the south of the ancient capital. The ensuing attempted pincer movement was a shambles. Bereft of transport, heavy guns and air cover, the uncamouflaged soldiers, floundering through 4 feet of snow, proved easy targets for the Luftwaffe. 'The British troops', wrote Lieutenant-General Adrian Carton de Wiart, 'had been issued with fur coats, special boots and socks . . . but if they wore all these things they were scarcely able to move at all and looked like paralysed bears.'[38] Namsos and Åndalsnes were reduced to splinters. German destroyers sailed up Trondheim Fjord and shelled the expeditionary force from the sea. 'We had rifles, a few Bren guns and some two-inch smoke bombs but none of them were either comforting or effective against a destroyer,' recalled de Wiart.[39] By 27 April, the War Cabinet had decided to cut its losses. Southern Norway would be evacuated but without informing the Norwegians, who were still resisting gallantly. It was a shameful end to a military fiasco.

The British, who had been responsible for the ill-considered and – thanks to the indecisiveness of Churchill and the War Cabinet – perpetually mutating campaign, did not blame the French. Although Reynaud's clumsy attempts to influence strategy caused the British Ambassador to Paris to refer to the French Premier's 'pocket Napoleon proclivities', Norway, it was widely recognised, was a British debacle.[40] Reynaud complained about 'old men who do not know how to take a risk', while Daladier accused the British of pushing France into war and then failing to prosecute it with the necessary vigour.[41] When the War Cabinet decided to evacuate southern Norway without consulting Paris, the French went 'up in smoke'.[42] 'One must think big or stop making war, one must act fast or lose the war,' wrote Reynaud to Chamberlain.[43]

It was, however, in the domestic political sphere that the most important consequences of the Norwegian campaign occurred. Buoyed by ludicrously optimistic press reports, the British public had expected a victory. Instead, they learnt of a humiliating defeat one month after the Prime Minister had assured them that Hitler had 'missed the bus'.[44] Although much of the blame belonged to Churchill, the broad mass of opprobrium fell on Chamberlain.

Eight months of frustration at Allied military inertia was distilled into the two-day parliamentary debate on the Government's handling of the Scandinavian crisis. Norway was a 'shocking story of ineptitude' that 'ought never to have been allowed to happen', declared Sir Roger Keyes, resplendent in the uniform of an admiral of the fleet.[45] The Prime Minister had met Hitler in both peace and war and 'always been worsted', jeered Lloyd George.[46] The former Colonial Secretary, Leo Amery, quoted Oliver Cromwell: 'You have sat too long here for any good you have been doing. Depart, I say, and let us have done with you. In the name of God, go!'[47] On the evening of 8 May, eighty-one Government MPs voted against or abstained on a motion of confidence. Chamberlain was forced to resign and Churchill, in one of the climacterics of the Second World War, became Prime Minister.

In France, Reynaud determined to sack General Gamelin. Appalled by the insouciance with which the French Commander-in-Chief had reacted to the news that the Germans were invading Norway ('You are wrong to get agitated . . . War consists of the unexpected'), the French Prime Minister held this 'nerveless philosopher' culpable for his failure to anticipate or prepare for such an eventuality.[48] At the Cabinet meeting on the morning of 9 May, Reynaud read a long indictment of Gamelin's handling of the Norwegian campaign to his colleagues. When Daladier, still Minister of Defence, refused to dismiss the General, Reynaud announced that he had anticipated this and had already placed his resignation before the President of the Republic. He intended to form a new government that would resolve the question of the high command. Gamelin's fate appeared sealed.

Seven hours later, however, German army groups received the code word 'Danzig'. Soon French and Belgian soldiers stationed along the Western Front heard an ominous murmur as the German vanguard tested its engines and moved towards its jumping-off points. At 4.20 a.m. on 10 May 1940, Hitler's war machine smashed into Holland, Belgium and Luxembourg, while Generaloberst Gerd von Rundstedt's forty-four panzer divisions made their way through the supposedly impenetrable forest of the Ardennes. The Battle of France had begun.

III

The Fall

What hell it is having to fight battles with Allies!

Oliver Harvey, 6 June 1940[1]

The Allies had expected the Germans to repeat their strategy of August 1914, the famous Schlieffen Plan, and attack France through Belgium. This was not unwelcome. Not only did it offer the chance to halt the enemy away from French soil, it would also add twenty-two Belgian divisions to the Allied side – double the size of the British Expeditionary Force – and, potentially, should Hitler extend his front to the north, nine Dutch divisions. The problem was that, in October 1936, the Belgians had reverted to a policy of strict neutrality, while the Dutch continued to cling to that historic neutrality which, so they believed, had saved them from the horrors of the First World War. The British and the French were, therefore, unable to prepare for the German assault as they expected it to unfold.

Considering Hitler's growing record of international brigandage, the Allies expected the Belgians and the Dutch to realise the naïveté of their positions and make the appropriate corrections before it was too late. Put simply, this meant inviting the British and French armies to take up defensive positions within their territory *before* the German invasion began. In February and May 1939, the British and French invited the Belgians for staff talks.* The Belgians refused. After the German attack on Poland in September 1939, the Allies renewed their request and were again rebuffed. The British were

---

* Sharing a frontier with Germany *and* France, as well as being the route through which the Kaiser's armies had marched in 1914, Belgium loomed considerably larger in Allied deliberations than the Netherlands.

disquieted but composed. If the Belgian attitude did not change and the Germans invaded, General Ironside told the War Cabinet, then it would be necessary to 'harden our hearts' and resist the appeal for assistance that would inevitably follow.[2] The French were less calm. Having accused the Belgians of 'playing entirely into German hands', the normally unflappable General Gamelin decried these 'villains . . . [these] unthinking, short-sighted mediocrities'.[3]

The chief villain was the King of the Belgians, Leopold III. A constitutional monarch with considerable power – most notably in his command of the Belgian armed forces – and undemocratic tendencies, this dashing sovereign had fought with bravery during the First World War as the youngest soldier in the Belgian Army. In October 1936, however, it was the 34-year-old monarch who took the lead in renouncing the 1920 'Franco-Belgian defensive military agreement, in the case of unprovoked German aggression' and establishing what he euphemistically called a 'policy of independence'.[4] Over the next four years, the maintenance of Belgian neutrality, although supported by the Foreign Minister, Paul-Henri Spaak, and a majority of parliamentarians, became so identified with the views of the sovereign that it became known as 'the King's policy'. 'I ask each one of you to impose upon himself . . . the rigorous discipline that strict neutrality commands,' Leopold adjured his subjects upon the outbreak of war.[5] In February 1938, as Hitler was preparing to invade Austria, he ordered the fortification of the Franco-Belgian frontier, while, in October 1939, he complained to King George VI that the British Government was asking him to behave dishonourably by requesting staff conversations, since these would entail going 'behind the back of the Germans who had equally guaranteed Belgian neutrality'.[6]

To be sure, Leopold's position was an unenviable one. As the American Ambassador to Brussels put it to Churchill in April 1939, Belgium was balancing on 'the rim of a volcano',[7] terrified of provoking a German invasion by co-operating with the Allies but aware of the need for collaboration if an attack was to be repelled.* Yet the way in which Leopold continued to believe that Hitler would

---

* Churchill expressed irritation with Belgium but confidence in France: 'We are entitled to know where Belgium stands . . . After all we did in the last war and

respect Belgian neutrality, despite the multiple alarms, despite the accruing intelligence to the contrary and despite increasing calls from parliamentarians and the Belgian press for co-ordination with the Allies, savours of a delusional obstinacy.

The first major scare came in mid-November 1939. Following Chamberlain's rejection of his 'peace offer', on 12 October, Hitler had ordered his generals to prepare for an assault in the west, *Fall Gelb* (Case Yellow), to commence exactly one month later. As German troops began to mass along the frontier and the Luftwaffe flew reconnaissance flights over the Low Countries, politicians in Brussels and The Hague began to panic. On 7 November, the Queen of the Netherlands and the King of the Belgians appealed to the belligerents to accept their offer of mediation. The following day, Spaak told the British Ambassador that he expected his Government to allow the Allies to cross their territory if the Germans attacked Holland but not Belgium. When Sir Robert Clive asked about staff talks, the Foreign Minister replied that he thought these would be established imminently, although 'there was still opposition from a certain quarter' (i.e. the King).[8] The British were relieved. 'I should fancy that even the King of the Belgians begins to realise by now that the policy of the ostrich doesn't pay . . . and that he is likely to get the kick in the backside that is due to him,' noted the Chief of Staff of the British Expeditionary Force.[9] But Lieutenant-General Pownall had spoken too soon. After initially delaying the attack, scheduled for 12 November, for three days, due to bad weather, Hitler was subsequently forced to postpone *Fall Gelb* a further twenty-nine times. As the danger receded, the Belgians slipped back into neutrality. The affair was to have important military implications, however, since it was the threat to Holland that persuaded Gamelin to extend his plans for a thrust into the Low Countries, with the left flank of the Franco-British armies now marching beyond the Scheldt estuary to a line running southwards along the River Dyle – 'Plan D'.

The next scare had even more important consequences. On 10

---

the English dead that were left on Flanders fields . . . We do not need Belgium anyway. The French Maginot Line will do the necessary.'

January 1940, a German reconnaissance plane lost its way in fog and crash-landed at Mechelen-sur-Meuse, on the Belgian–Dutch border. The passenger, Major Helmuth Reinberger, was carrying plans relating to *Fall Gelb*, then scheduled for 17 January. Naturally, once he had clambered out of his now wingless Messerschmitt and discovered where he was, Reinberger tried to burn the documents but his lighter failed. Fortunately for him, an obliging farmhand provided him with a match. Less fortunately, some Belgian border guards arrived and, noticing a small bonfire behind a thicket near a crashed German aeroplane, arrested Reinberger and confiscated the papers. When, thanks to some quite staggering incompetence, Reinberger was able to make a second attempt at destroying the documents – grabbing them from the desk of his interrogator and shoving them into the stove, only to have them rescued again – the Belgians were left in no doubt as to their value.

The charred but legible papers revealed the essence of *Fall Gelb*: an attack along a broad front, through Belgium, Holland and northern France, with the decisive thrust coming through Belgium. Still, the Belgians tried to hedge their bets. Rather than inviting the Allies immediately into his country, Leopold III contented himself by having his military adviser hand the French and British Military Attachés a two-page summary of the captured documents. When the French asked to see the originals, the Belgians refused. At 1.20 on the morning of 14 January, however, General Gamelin was woken by the Belgian Military Attaché to be told that the attack was expected that day. Convinced that the Belgians were about to invite the Allies in, Gamelin ordered a general advance. Throughout the night of 14–15 January and during the following day the BEF and a French army, under General Billotte, waited along the Belgian border in freezing conditions. At various points, acting on orders from the Belgian Chief of Staff, General Van den Bergen, Belgian soldiers removed the frontier barriers and, in one place, a French cavalry column crossed into Belgian territory. But the invitation from Brussels never came. Van den Bergen had acted without orders, while the King had temporised until the danger had passed. On 16 January, the Belgian Government formally declined the Allied request to enter their country.

The 'Mechelen incident' increased mistrust and resentment on all sides. The Chief of the Imperial General Staff, General Ironside, complained of trying to help a country that 'is so terrified of infringing its own neutrality that it will make no preparations', while Daladier informed the Belgian Ambassador that henceforth France would reserve 'an entire freedom to form their own appreciations of the situation'.[10] But it was in Germany that the most important ramifications occurred. With the plans having fallen into enemy hands, *Fall Gelb* was substantially revised, with the majority of the German panzers transferred to Generaloberst Gerd von Rundstedt's Army Group A and the focus of the attack shifted from central Belgium to a thrust through the Ardennes Forest in the direction of Sedan. On the morning of 10 May 1940, the guns opened.*

*

The onset of the German *Blitzkrieg* in the west put an intolerable strain on the Anglo-French alliance, as both politicians and military commanders floundered to influence events from which they were increasingly disconnected. It was early on the morning of 15 May 1940 – five days after the battle had begun – that Churchill was woken by a call from Reynaud, who informed him, in near-hysterical tones, that France had been defeated: 'We are beaten; we have lost the battle.'[11] Bewildered, Churchill replied that it surely could not have happened so soon but Reynaud was insistent: while the cream of the French Army and the BEF had charged headlong into Belgium – Gamelin's 'Plan D' – the spearhead of the German invasion had appeared further south. The previous day, the Germans had pierced the French front at Sedan and the various counterattacks had failed. A gaping hole had appeared in the French line and the road to Paris was open.

---

* That the French High Command failed to countenance the idea that the Germans would change their plans following the Mechelen incident, while ignoring the steady stream of intelligence pointing towards the Ardennes, remains the gravest indictment of General Gamelin.

Upon receiving this devastating news, Churchill decided to fly to Paris – the first of five visits the new Prime Minister would make to France during the battle. As he would admit in his memoirs, he was slow to grasp the extremity of the crisis: he had, after all, experienced the First World War, where multiple breakthroughs had occurred before the front had stabilised, while the revolution in mechanised, armoured warfare remained an alien concept to him. Arriving in Paris shortly after 4 p.m. on Thursday 16 May, however, the British party – which included the Vice-Chief of the Imperial General Staff, General Sir John Dill, as well as General Ismay – soon realised that the situation was significantly worse than they had imagined. The Parisians 'seemed listless and resigned', recalled Ismay, while at the Quai d'Orsay officials were pushing wheelbarrows full of secret documents towards a constellation of bonfires, disfiguring the lawn.[12]

At Reynaud's request, Gamelin provided the British with a summary of the battle, his 'ladylike hand' moving over the map, which showed an ominous bulge around Sedan.[13] '*Où est la masse de manœuvre?*' ('Where is the strategic reserve?') enquired Churchill. '*Aucune*' ('There is none'), replied the Commander-in-Chief.[14] It was, Churchill later recalled, among the greatest shocks of his life. According to the French minutes of the meeting, however, the Prime Minister still failed to appreciate the extent of the disaster that was unfolding: 'Mr Churchill hesitated to take the threat presented by the tanks so seriously. So long as they were not supported by strong infantry units, they were only a limited force; so many little flags stuck on the map.'[15] Reynaud disagreed. 'The hard point of the German lance has gone through our troops as through a sand-hill,' the French Prime Minister declared. Then, pointing at the large bulge on the map (which in Churchill's idiomatic French was translated simply as 'boolge'), he stated his profound conviction that upon the outcome of this battle depended 'not only the fate of France but also that of the British Empire'.[16]

Churchill did not agree. Britain's fate, he had already decided, did not depend on France. Yet he did everything he could to rally the French: urging Gamelin to counterattack and disputing the decision to abandon Louvain. Later that night, in Reynaud's flat, 'crowned like a volcano by the smoke of his cigars', he bludgeoned his French counterpart with Britain's determination to continue the war, no matter what: 'We will starve Germany out. We will destroy her towns. We will burn her crops and her forests.' He was convinced that the United States would enter the conflict and even if France was vanquished and Britain razed to the ground, the British Government would continue the struggle from Canada.[17]

The meeting at the Quai d'Orsay brought to the fore the issue that was to cause more controversy during the Battle of France than any other. Responding to Churchill's criticisms of his decision to retreat, Gamelin pointed to the need to check the German advance towards Paris. For this, the British must send more fighter squadrons. Churchill replied that there were only thirty-nine squadrons not engaged in the battle and that these were essential to the defence of the British Isles. Moreover, fighters were no use against tanks, which should be dealt with by the artillery. Nevertheless, the War Cabinet had, that morning, agreed to send an additional four squadrons to France and, following the meeting at the Quai d'Orsay, Churchill obtained their consent for the despatch of a further six.

This was no small act of courage. The previous day, Air Chief Marshal Sir Hugh Dowding, head of Fighter Command, had vigorously opposed the sending of one 'single additional Hurricane' to France, pointing out that if Britain continued to reinforce losses at the current rate then there would not be 'a single Hurricane left in France or in this country'.[18] Yet the decision to throw an additional ten fighter squadrons into the cauldron, though a recognised risk, could be defended on both strategic and political grounds. After a mere six days of fighting, few could believe that the military position was irreparable, while Britain's paltry contribution to the battle – 390,000 soldiers compared to some 600,000 Belgians and over two million French – seemed to justify a further effort.* Before long, however, Churchill's unswerving commitment to the

---

* Contrary to what was believed at the time, the German and Allied forces were, in fact, evenly matched, with the Allies enjoying a superiority in tanks and armoured vehicles.

Anglo-French alliance would lead him into decisions that were militarily unsound and, potentially, disastrous.

★

On 20 May, the German spearheads reached the Channel. By the following day the British Expeditionary Force, along with a considerable body of French troops and the remains of the Belgian army, was encircled. Two British infantry regiments and a tank brigade counterattacked south of Arras but lacked the strength to maintain their momentum or the ground they had gained. On 25 May, the Commander of the British Expeditionary Force, Lord Gort, and Churchill independently decided that the only available course was for the BEF to fight its way to the coast prior to re-embarkation. Three days later, with the evacuation from Dunkirk already underway, Leopold III surrendered. The French, almost relieved to have found a scapegoat, cried betrayal. 'Without warning . . . without a word for the British and French soldiers who, at his agonised appeal, had come to the rescue of his country, King Leopold III of Belgium threw down his arms,' declared a furious Reynaud, in a broadcast to the French people.[19] Belgian refugees were thrown out of French houses while, in Britain, Lloyd George claimed that it would be impossible to find a 'blacker and more squalid example of perfidy and poltroonery than that perpetuated by the King of the Belgians'.[20] Yet it was not Leopold but Reynaud who was responsible for what turned out to be the gravest threat to the independence of France. On 18 May, in an effort to boost morale and replace the lethargic Gamelin, he recalled Maréchal Philippe Pétain, the octogenarian hero of Verdun, and General Maxime Weygand, Chief of Staff to General Foch in the last war, to become Deputy President of the Council and French Commander-in-Chief respectively. It was a decision that was to prove fatal to the Third Republic.

The rout of the British and French armies led to increased suspicions and mutual recrimination. When Gort decided, on his own initiative, to abandon the Arras garrison and withdraw 15 miles to the north-east during the night of 23–24 May, Weygand accused him of compromising his plan for a co-ordinated counterattack, even

though the 'new French Army' designated for the purpose consisted
of a mere five divisions spread over 65 miles. In Paris, the American
writer Clare Boothe Luce watched 'the hatred of the French for the
English growing by giant leaps and bounds', while Reynaud charged
the British with always heading for harbours in an emergency.[21]

The evacuation from Dunkirk brought relations between the
Allies to their nadir. French soldiers, finding that the British had
blocked key sections of the roads so as to facilitate their march to
the sea, talked of 'training their guns on them and shooting'.[22] Priority was given to the BEF – 'every Frenchman embarked is at [the]
cost of one Englishman,' explained Gort to Dill – and when French
soldiers attempted to board the boats, they were (at least initially)
turned away, occasionally at gunpoint.[23] When, at the meeting of
the Supreme War Council held in the Ministère de la Guerre on 31
May, Weygand accused the British of abandoning the French, his
voice, recalled Louis Spears, was 'high, querulous and aggressive'.
For a moment it looked as if Churchill would answer him in kind.
But the Prime Minister's expression then changed and, with tears in
his eyes, he gave the indisputable reply: 'We are companions in mis-
fortune; there is nothing to be gained from recrimination over our
common miseries.'[24]

There were many reasons, Churchill went on to explain, why
only 15,000 French soldiers had so far been evacuated out of a
total of some 165,000. These included the fact that until 29 May,
the French had not received orders to embark. But henceforth
the evacuation would continue on an equal basis, '*bras dessus,
bras dessous* [arm in arm]'.[25] Moreover, Churchill promised that
three British divisions would hold the perimeter, to allow the
remaining French forces to escape. This, as even the Francophile
Spears thought, was excessive. As anyone, except perhaps the
Prime Minister, could see, the Battle of France was lost, the men
around Reynaud actively defeatist. Already on 24 May, seven
days after he had taken over as Commander-in-Chief, Weygand
told Paul Baudouin that he saw no hope of redeeming the situation and wished merely to save 'the honour of the French flag'.
When Reynaud's Chef de Cabinet – a slippery technocrat who
admired Mussolini and had opposed the declaration of war on

Germany – replied that France must be freed from her present ordeal so as 'to rise again' in the future, the General had said that he shared these sentiments.[26]

Fortunately for the British, Churchill's ill-judged magnanimity was not acted upon. Although the Prime Minister's decree was communicated to Admiral Abrial, responsible for the defence of Dunkirk, the commander of the BEF's remaining divisions, Major-General Harold Alexander, received orders from the Secretary of State for War, Anthony Eden, to continue to evacuate his force on a fifty-fifty basis with the French. In the end, it was the French who gallantly held the Dunkirk perimeter between 2 and 4 June, though the rancour this caused was mitigated by the evacuation of 98,000 French troops during this period. Almost all of these would later choose to be repatriated.

The Supreme War Council also considered the perennial problem of Italy. There was little doubt as to where Mussolini's sympathies lay. Since 1938, the Duce had aligned himself with Hitler's determination to redraw the map of Europe and, in May 1939, had entered a formal military alliance with Nazi Germany, the so-called 'Pact of Steel'. The Italian dictator promised to support the Führer over Poland, while Hitler agreed that Mediterranean policy would be in the hands of the Italians. On 25 August, however, Mussolini had been forced to admit to his German ally that Italy was in no fit state to go to war and must remain, at least officially, non-belligerent until 1940. The Allies tried to exploit this reality. Encouraged by the obvious antipathy towards the Nazis of influential sections of Italian society, including Mussolini's son-in-law and Foreign Minister Count Ciano, the strategy the British and French deemed most sensible was to show the Italians that 'neutrality pays' – in other words appeasement.[27]* In January 1940, the British offered to purchase £25 million

---

* This policy horrified those who had opposed previous attempts to appease Mussolini. 'I do not feel that these rather feeble blandishments are the slightest good,' wrote Lord Cranborne, who had resigned as a Foreign Office Minister, in February 1938, upon this very issue. 'On the contrary, they only encourage Italian arrogance.' His correspondent, the Chairman of the Conservative Foreign Affairs Committee, Paul Emrys-Evans, agreed. 'I have a feeling that a completely false

worth of Italian arms and horticultural produce, while the French
did everything they could to assure Mussolini that Italy would benefit from Allied victory. Yet the Duce could not be prised from the
Axis. Although he raged intermittently at German arrogance, he
yearned for the spoils of war and felt certain that Hitler would triumph. He therefore spurned the British and French offers and when
Churchill, upon becoming Prime Minister, sent him a cordial letter,
replied by reaffirming his loyalty to the Führer.

By this stage, the British retained little hope of keeping Italy
out of the war. The success of Hitler's Norwegian venture had
emboldened the Duce and there was a vicious anti-Allied propaganda campaign in the Italian press. Later, when musing on paths
not taken, Lord Halifax wondered whether it might not have been
possible to bribe Mussolini but concluded ultimately that the Allies
could never have 'offered him enough to tempt him' and Sir Percy
Loraine, the British Ambassador to Rome, always disliked the idea
of slipping Ciano '£50,000 on the golf links'.[28]

As the Wehrmacht cut through France, however, the French
became increasingly desperate. On 29 May, in a last-ditch effort to
keep Italy out of the war, Daladier asked the British Government's
permission to make certain specific territorial offers to Mussolini.
This was a sensitive subject. Two days earlier, when Reynaud first
raised the topic in London, he had found a sympathetic listener in
Halifax, who, like him, wanted to use the Duce as an intermediary to explore peace terms. Over the proceeding forty-eight hours,
however, Churchill had succeeded in outmanoeuvring his Foreign
Secretary, thus quashing an initiative that came terrifyingly close to
handing Hitler victory. After the crucial Cabinet meeting on 28 May,
Churchill informed Reynaud of the British Government's rejection
of the Italian approach and, the following day, few were prepared to
take an alternative view. 'Discussion of what to do with ice-cream
vendors,' recorded Sir Alexander Cadogan in his diary, 'drown the
brutes is what I should like to do.'[29]

Nevertheless, the French went ahead with a unilateral approach.

---

impression is being created about the position of Italy,' he noted on 17 March
1940. 'Mussolini is an implacable enemy.' (Emrys-Evans Papers, ADD MSS 58261)

Mussolini did not even deign to reply. 'It is not that he wants to obtain this or that,' noted Ciano. 'What he wants is war and even if he were to obtain by peaceful methods double what he claims, he would refuse.'[30] Indeed, the Duce was in a hurry to enter the conflict before the German victory was complete. By 30 May, the final decision had been made and at 6 p.m. on 10 June Mussolini announced Italy's entry into the war, before an unenthusiastic crowd, from the balcony of the Palazzo Venezia. At his farewell interview with Ciano, the French Ambassador predicted that the Italians would come to regret their alliance with the Germans while Loraine had already expressed his unquenchable faith in Allied victory, since 'the British were not in the habit of being beaten'.[31]

*

By the time of Dunkirk, most British military and political leaders had lost confidence in their French allies. 'There hardly seems to be any mistake the French did not make,' noted Chamberlain, after hearing Gort's damning description of the weeks preceding the evacuation.[32] 'I have an uncomfortable feeling that there is everywhere a lack of direction from the people who ought to be directing and that the subordinates are consequently at sea,' wrote Sir Ronald Campbell to Halifax on 30 May. There was no doubt about Reynaud's integrity but 'he is a bundle of nerves and is hardly up to the herculean task of galvanising his rather flabby team'. Of these, the Ambassador was scathing but accurate. Pétain, unable to follow a discussion for more than a few minutes, gave 'the impression of having lost hope'. Weygand was more alert but, similarly, resigned to defeat. And Daladier had 'gone to pieces' and was being 'worked upon by the wobblers'. 'The fact is', Campbell explained, 'there is practically no single Frenchman among those who know the full gravity of the situation that does not feel – even if he does not admit it – that France is beaten.'[33]

On the evening of 31 May, following the meeting of the Supreme War Council, Churchill gave Spears the impression that he knew the French were played out. He did not say it but, before going to bed, Spears recalled a phrase that the Prime Minister had used during the afternoon's conference: 'The partner that survives will go on.'[34] If this was the case it begs the question why Churchill continued to press for further British military support for France – support which Britain could ill afford to give and which the Chiefs of Staff and a majority of the War Cabinet opposed. As so often with Churchill, the personal combined with the political, the strategic with the sentimental.

Even more than his Francophile colleagues, Churchill loved France, the country he had visited regularly since 1891 and whose cultural achievements appeared to him the apogee of civilisation. ('Winston loves France like a woman,' his physician, Lord Moran, would note at Yalta.[35]) Then there was his sense of chivalry, sharpened by his awareness of history. France was Britain's ally and he would not have it said that Britain had dishonoured herself by abandoning her in her hour of need. 'He nothing common did or mean / Upon that memorable scene.'[36] But there were also strategic reasons. Every day France went on fighting she weakened Hitler's war machine and gave Britain precious hours in which to prepare. The French Empire remained a valuable resource from which, in the last resort, the French might continue the fight, while the French Fleet was a significant asset or major liability depending on who controlled it. Finally, there was the Prime Minister's natural Micawberism: the hope that, so long as the French continued fighting, something might 'turn up'.

Nevertheless, the Prime Minister's sense of chivalry caused him to make at least one decision that was militarily unjustifiable and potentially catastrophic. On 12 June, eight days after the 'miracle of Dunkirk' – in which 338,226 Allied soldiers had been rescued from France – Lieutenant-General Alan Brooke disembarked at Cherbourg. It was only two weeks since he himself had been evacuated but on 2 June he had received the shattering news that he was to return to France and form a new British Expeditionary Force. Looking back, Brooke – who went on to serve as Chief of the Imperial General Staff between December 1941 and June 1946 and experience multiple disasters – described this as one of the 'blackest moments' of his career. As commander of the BEF's II Corps, he had witnessed the collapse of the French Army at close quarters and harboured no illusions as to the ultimate fate of that force. 'The mission I was being sent on from a military point of view had no value and no possibility of accomplishing anything,' the plain-speaking Ulsterman told General Dill.[37] But Churchill was adamant. 'The BEF in France must immediately be reconstituted, otherwise the French will not continue in the war,' he instructed Ismay on 2 June. Even if Paris were lost and organised resistance ended, the French must be persuaded to continue a 'gigantic guerrilla', sustained by an Allied bridgehead in Brittany, the so-called 'Breton redoubt'.[38] When Ismay, who like Brooke was appalled at the idea of sending some of Britain's last trained reserves to reinforce failure in France, suggested that they might quietly delay the departure of these divisions, Churchill was scandalised: 'Certainly not. It would look very bad in history if we were to do any such thing.'[39]

Of course, Brooke and Ismay were right and Churchill was wrong. Meeting General Weygand, who had replaced Gamelin as Commander-in-Chief on 20 May, at Le Mans on 14 June, Brooke was told by the tired-looking General what he already knew: 'the French army had ceased to be able to offer organised resistance and was disintegrating into disconnected groups.'[40] Following this conversation, Brooke immediately telephoned Dill, now Chief of the Imperial General Staff, and told him that the only sensible course was to re-embark the Expeditionary Force as quickly as possible. The Brittany scheme was a 'wild project which was quite impossible'.[41] Four hours later Dill called back and told him that the Prime Minister did not want him to withdraw.

'What the hell does he want?' snapped Brooke.

'He wants to speak to you.'

A difficult conversation ensued but, after half an hour, Brooke succeeded in convincing Churchill that the position was hopeless and that all British forces should be evacuated from France forthwith.[42]

There was also the ever-present question of air support. No sooner had Churchill returned from Paris on 1 June, than the British began to receive near daily French pleas for more fighters. Churchill was torn. 'We must give them more than we can spare', he told a crush of ministers on 3 June, but 'we must not denude this island'.[43] Regarding the former determination, the Prime Minister was in a minority of one. The Air Staff was adamant that to throw further squadrons into the Battle of France was to risk losing the Battle of Britain. The War Cabinet agreed. Echoing the sentiments of Halifax and Chamberlain, Cadogan expressed the blunt view that further assistance to France would not do 'any good' and would not even prevent 'the French reviling us. I'd really sooner cut loose and concentrate on the defence of these islands.'[44] Two days later, however, Churchill returned to the question, arguing that it would be wrong for Britain to have fewer squadrons operating in France than they had at the start of the battle. Lord Beaverbrook was working miracles at the Ministry of Aircraft Production – though Britain's output of fifteen fighters per day was dwarfed by daily losses of twenty-five – and, in any case, 'we could never keep all that we wanted for our own defence while the French were fighting for their lives'.[45] Fortunately for the Air Staff, the Secretary of State for Air, Sir Archibald Sinclair, intervened to emphasise the alarming loss of pilots, in particular squadron leaders, as well as the general disorganisation of Fighter Command. These arguments carried the day and a telegram was despatched to Reynaud, declining to send additional squadrons. Hearing of this refusal, Pétain allegedly told the French Premier, 'Well, there is nothing left but to make peace. If you do not want to do it you can hand over to me.'[46]*

The next few days brought more of the same. The French continued to berate their ally for husbanding their air force, while the British became increasingly convinced that the French were seeking to blame them for the unfolding catastrophe. On 10 June, as the Germans continued their drive towards Paris, Churchill made one of his 'lightning decisions' to fly across the Channel to try and bolster the French. Just as he was about to leave, however, he received news that the French Government was abandoning the capital and, since there appeared 'no perch on which he could alight', he reluctantly gave up the idea.[47]

At 2.30 the following afternoon, however, Churchill, accompanied

---

* There were, nevertheless, 144 British fighters operating in France on 6 June 1940, the equivalent of twelve squadrons.

by Eden, Dill, Ismay and Spears, flew from Hendon to Briare, on the Loire. There they were met by a French colonel 'who might have been welcoming poor relations at a funeral', before being driven to what Spears described as a 'hideous house', a dwelling expanded by 'successful business in groceries or indifferent champagne into a large monstrosity of red lobster-coloured brick, and stone the hue of unripe Camembert'.[48] The name for this incongruous setting of what was to be the penultimate gathering of the Supreme War Council was Château du Muguet – Lily of the Valley Castle.

The Briare conference of 11 June began by Reynaud asking, somewhat embarrassedly, that the joint raid on the Italian heartlands of Genoa, Turin and Milan, planned for that evening, be cancelled. He was aware that he had agreed to this operation only a few days previously – this according with the long-held Allied determination to strike Italy hard the moment she came into the war – but it now transpired that Lyons, as well as the petrol depots around Marseilles, were unprotected by anti-aircraft guns and he feared Italian reprisals. Churchill looked grim but after a brief conference with General Ismay his face softened into a wry smile. The operation could not be cancelled, the Prime Minister's chief military adviser explained, since the bombers had already left England.*

Churchill announced that he and his colleagues had come to France to survey the situation with 'unclouded eyes' and to concert plans for continuing the war.[49] Whatever happened, Britain would continue the struggle and if France could only hold out for a little longer, ideally – though fantastically – until the following spring, then she would receive the assistance of between twenty and twenty-five new British divisions. When Weygand gave an appraisal of the military situation it made for depressing listening. The battle, the Commander-in-Chief explained, was raging along the entire front and consumed the totality of French forces. 'We are fighting on our last line and it has been breached,' he declared, his fox-like

---

* In the end, the operation did not take place as French ground crews, fearful of retaliations, drove cars and lorries onto the aerodrome near Marseilles to prevent the British bombers, which had stopped to refuel, from taking off.

face strained with emotion: 'I am helpless, I cannot intervene for I have no reserves, there are no reserves. *C'est la dislocation.*'[50] Still, the C-in-C asked that Britain deploy her complete air strength, since this was 'the decisive battle that would settle the fate of both nations'.[51] Ismay held his breath. For a moment he worried that his chief's sympathy for France might cause him to repudiate the decision of the War Cabinet and agree to the French request. But his fears proved groundless. 'This is not the decisive point', Churchill intoned; that 'moment will come when Hitler hurls his Luftwaffe against Britain. If we can keep command of the air over our own island – that is all I ask – we will win it all back for you.'[52]

The crossroads was in sight. After Weygand had repeated his stock phrase, that the French were at 'the last quarter of an hour', causing Spears to snap his pencil in frustration, the General declared that if the military situation deteriorated further then he saw no way that France could continue the war.[53] This earned a rebuke from Reynaud, who reminded Weygand that this was a political decision, exclusive to the Government. Churchill continued to urge the French to carry on the fight – to defend Paris, to hold a bridgehead in Brittany, to paralyse Hitler's armies with guerrilla warfare – but his real emphasis was on Britain's determination to fight on '*toujours*, all the time, *partout*, everywhere, *pas de grâce*, no mercy, *puis la victoire!*'[54] When an incredulous Weygand asked him how he proposed to deal with the hundred or so German divisions poised for the invasion of Britain, Churchill replied that he was no military expert but that his technical advisers were of the opinion that the best method was 'to drown as many as possible on the way over and knock the others on the head [*frapper sur la tête*] as they crawled ashore'. Weygand acknowledged that the British had 'a very good anti-tank ditch'.[55]

When the conference resumed the next day, Reynaud told Churchill that Pétain, who was not present, had informed him of his view that it was necessary to seek an armistice. The Maréchal had even written a paper on the subject but, apparently, felt too ashamed to share it.[56] The discussion was no more constructive than the one the day before. Reynaud renewed his request for more fighters and Churchill promised to raise the matter with the War Cabinet. Eden and Dill both spoke of the coming British reinforcements – Brooke and the second BEF were disembarking that very day – while Churchill repeated his entreaties to defend Paris, to counterattack along the lower Seine, to contemplate the possibilities of guerrilla warfare, to hold out until the United States came in. When these suggestions were summarily rebuffed – Weygand had given orders on 10 June that Paris was to be declared an 'open city' – he made an even more solemn request. Speaking slowly and with emphasis so that no one could fail to understand his meaning, he asked that, should there be a 'fundamental change in the situation', the British Government be informed at once so that it might return 'to discuss the new circumstances with you'.[57] The British then flew home.

★

And so we return to 13 June 1940: to the pockmarked airfield at Tours, the cold chicken and Vouvray, the confusion at the Préfecture, the meeting with Reynaud and Baudouin and the French Prime Minister's enquiry about an armistice. Churchill said that he sympathised deeply with France in her suffering. Britain would be attacked next but she was ready. 'The British people have not yet felt the German lash, but they do not underestimate its force . . . far from being cowed, they are looking forward to thrashing Hitler.'[58] When Reynaud pointed out that this did not answer his question, Churchill replied that the British Government would not waste time on reproaches or recriminations but this did not mean that it was prepared to release France from her commitment to continue the war in conjunction with her ally. In any case, the question was premature. Reynaud had proposed making a final appeal for immediate aid to President Roosevelt and until this telegram had been answered it was necessary to wait. Churchill then asked if he might consult his colleagues *dans le jardin*.[59] The British delegation trooped onto the wet grass. For a moment, nobody said a word. Then Beaverbrook spoke for everyone:

There is nothing to do but to repeat what you have already said, Winston. Telegraph to Roosevelt and await the answer. Tell Reynaud

that we have nothing to say or discuss until Roosevelt's answer is
received. Don't commit yourself to anything. We shall gain a little
time and see how those Frenchmen sort themselves out. We are
doing no good here. In fact, listening to these declarations of Reynaud's only does harm. Let's get along home.[60]

Back inside, the British discovered that they had been joined by the
newest member of the French Government, the Under-Secretary
of State for War, Brigadier-General Charles de Gaulle. Churchill
explained that his colleagues had unanimously supported his stance
and the two Prime Ministers then discussed the terms of the appeal
to Roosevelt. Outside the Prefect's office the British found scenes
of disorder and distress. While the British delegation had been
traipsing round the garden, Reynaud had met with the Presidents
of the two French Chambers of Parliament, who protested the
Premier's conduct, arguing that he had no right to contemplate an
armistice. When these patriots saw Churchill, they assured him,
with tears in their eyes, of their desire to continue the fight. It was
then – if Churchill's memoirs are to be believed – that he went up
to de Gaulle and whispered, *'L'homme du destin'*.[61] As he got into his
car, he told General Doumenc: 'You may be sure that, whatever
happens, England will not abandon France.'[62] It was a noble sentiment, sincerely meant and emotionally felt but there was no use
pretending: the Anglo-French alliance was all but over.

IV

Unfriendly Fire

What the consequences . . . will be it is impossible to foretell. But
I imagine the Germans may very possibly force the French into war
against us . . . It was all inevitable, no doubt, but a terrible tragedy.

Leopold Amery to Lord Linlithgow, 4 July 1940[1]

At 9.05 a.m. on 3 July 1940, Captain Cedric Holland descended from
the deck of HMS *Foxhound* and boarded the destroyer's motorboat.
The haze had melted with the North African heat and a perfect day
was developing as the launch chugged towards the harbour sheltering the two modern French battlecruisers *Dunkerque* and *Strasbourg*,
the two elderly (though recently modernised) battleships *Bretagne*
and *Provence*, the seaplane tender *Commandant Teste*, and six destroyers. 'Hooky' Holland, as he was known due to his Roman nose, was
liked and admired in both British and French naval circles. Having
joined the navy at the age of fifteen, he had served in both the North
Sea and the Mediterranean during the First World War, before
being sent to Paris as Naval Attaché in 1938. His two years in the
French capital were a great success. A competent French speaker
with natural charm, he 'enjoyed the confidence and esteem of all
the French officers with whom he was in contact', according to Sir
Ronald Campbell, and 'in particular of Admiral Darlan', who spoke
of the Captain and his work 'in terms of the highest praise'.[2] Now,
however, as the launch cut through the waves towards the harbour
of Mers el-Kébir, Holland was facing the most difficult task of his
career.

His destination was the French flagship *Dunkerque*, where he
wished to speak with the fleet commander, Vice-Admiral Marcel
Gensoul. Just after he had passed the anti-torpedo boom, however,

he was intercepted by the Admiral's barge, commanded by Flag-Lieutenant Bernard Dufay, an old friend of Holland's from his time in Paris. Earlier that morning, when the *Foxhound* had first appeared outside Mers el-Kébir, Dufay had told Holland that Gensoul was too busy to receive him. This was after Holland's decision to signal, at 7.09 a.m., in plain language, the purpose of his presence to the port admiral's signal station:

> The British Admiralty has sent Captain Holland to confer with you. The British Navy hopes that their proposals will enable you and the valiant and glorious French Navy to be by our side. In these circumstances, your ships would remain yours and no one need have anxiety for the future. A British fleet is at sea off Oran waiting to welcome you.

As Holland later explained to his superiors, he had decided to send the signal – which could be read by the entire fleet – 'for the purpose of disseminating the reason of our arrival and giving some indications as to the proposals so that the Lower Deck [i.e. the ordinary sailors] should get to know of them since it was thought that Admiral Gensoul might otherwise keep the matter secret'.[3] Perhaps. But Holland's gambit, which he took on his own initiative, undermined trust with the Admiral, an unfortunate development, compounded by the arrival of a British fleet on the horizon. 'The English may consider this as bringing friendly pressure to bear', commented an irate Gensoul to one of his officers, 'but the presence of a British fleet comprising three battleships and an aircraft carrier is something else. This proposal that I should sail my fleet and join them merits no further examination . . . I will not be threatened in this way. I've told the British destroyer to get out at once.'[4]

This was a considerable blow to Holland, who had been hoping to use his powers of persuasion on Gensoul in person. Instead, he was now forced to negotiate through Dufay, who agreed to relay the British proposals to the Admiral. These were relatively simple. As the War Cabinet had agreed on 1 July, in order to prevent the French Fleet from falling into enemy hands, Admiral Somerville, commander of the hastily assembled British fleet known as Force H, was to offer Gensoul four alternatives: he could join the British and continue the war under his own colours; he could sail his ships to a British port where they would be interned and the crews repatriated; he could remove his fleet to the safety of the French West Indies or the United States; or he could scuttle his ships. If none of these options was accepted then, as Somerville's note concluded, 'I have orders from His Majesty's Government to use whatever force may be necessary to prevent your ships falling into German or Italian hands.'[5]

When Dufay returned with the reply that Gensoul stood by the assurance he had given Admiral Sir Dudley North on 24 June that he would not allow his ships to be captured and would respond to force with force, Holland set about deploying those arguments he had hoped to use upon the Admiral. The British, he said, had complete faith in the French Naval High Command but they were convinced that the Germans intended to seize the French Fleet through some 'dastardly trick' and that, owing to the political situation in France, Admiral Darlan could no longer be regarded as master in his own house.[6] Holland persuaded Dufay to take an *aide-mémoire*, containing these arguments, to Gensoul.

According to the French lieutenant, Holland was noticeably ill at ease: 'hesitant', 'pale-faced' and 'perspiring heavily'. He had confessed that he found Somerville's note 'somewhat *maladroit*' and, despite his years in Paris, seemed to be struggling with his French.[7] If Holland was nervous, he had good reason to be. When briefed on the operation on 30 June he had strongly opposed the use of force. Confident in the reasonableness of the French naval high command, he believed he could talk Gensoul round. But his tactics had rebounded and his negotiations had reached an impasse. Shortly after 9.35 a.m., he had noticed with alarm that the French warships were furling their awnings and getting up steam. A reconnaissance plane from the aircraft carrier *Ark Royal* confirmed the French were preparing to sail and Somerville, in what the French later considered the 'first act of hostility', ordered the mining of the entrance to the harbour.[8]

At 11.09 a.m., Dufay returned to the torpedo boom, accompanied by Gensoul's Chief of Staff. They brought a bellicose response from the Admiral. Gensoul would only confirm the reply he had already sent: he had decided to defend himself by every means possible and would draw Somerville's attention to the fact that the first shot fired would 'put the whole French Navy against the British'.[9] After consulting Holland by signal and delaying the initial deadline of 1.30 p.m. to give the Admiral more time to reconsider, Somerville signalled Gensoul that he had until 3 p.m. to accept the British terms or he would open fire.

★

The question of the French Fleet had first been raised by British political and military leaders as early as 27 May 1940, one day into the evacuation from Dunkirk. On that date, the Chancellor of the Duchy of Lancaster, Lord Hankey, had written to the Foreign Secretary, Lord Halifax, with a draft of demands that the British might consider making in the event that the French asked to be released from the joint agreement prohibiting a separate peace. Unsurprisingly, the French Fleet was top of the list. In 1940, France possessed the second largest navy in Europe, consisting of five battleships, two battlecruisers, two aircraft carriers, eighteen cruisers, fifty-four destroyers and almost seventy submarines. In addition, there were two almost-completed 35,000-ton battleships, the *Richelieu* and the *Jean Bart*, which with their 15-inch guns could rival any warship afloat. If Britain were to thwart a German invasion, let alone maintain her Empire and lines of communication, then it was vital that this powerful weapon should not fall into the hands of the enemy.

As Churchill was leaving the Briare conference on 12 June, he had taken aside the commander of the French Navy, the highly efficient and ambitious Admiral Darlan, and asked for his assurance that he would never surrender the Fleet. That promise was duly given. Yet this was not enough to satisfy the British Admiralty. Three days later, the British Naval Attaché, Captain Edward Pleydell-Bouverie, made a formal request to Darlan's deputy, Contre-Admiral Gabriel Auphan, that, as a precaution, the *Richelieu* and the *Jean Bart* be transferred to British ports and the ships at Mers el-Kébir, the so-called *Force de Raid*, removed to the safety of Gibraltar. Although Auphan rejected this request, he assured Pleydell-Bouverie that the

Richelieu and the *Jean Bart* would sail to England if the danger of air attack became too great or if a 'grave eventuality should arise'.[10]

The fate of the French Fleet and the question of an armistice were inextricably entwined. When, at the Council of Ministers on the evening of 13 June, Pétain had supported Weygand's now hysterical calls for an armistice, several ministers spoke against this proposal on the grounds that the Germans would demand the Fleet. Even if, as Weygand suggested, the ships were sent in advance to North Africa, the Germans could still insist on their return. Reynaud concurred. If the French Government were to break its agreement with the British and sue for peace, only to discover that the Navy was among the German demands, then they would have committed 'a cowardly act for no purpose'.[11]

It is, at this stage, worth considering the options that were open to the French Government. That the Battle of France was lost was now evident to even the most stalwart of French ministers. Since early June, there had been talk of trying to maintain a bridgehead in Brittany – the 'Breton redoubt' – yet this was a wild proposal, bereft of military logic. The alternative was to take the Fleet and as much of the Army as could be saved and continue the war from North Africa. Here too there were practical problems. Although Reynaud had raised the prospect as early as 27 May, neither the military nor the Ministère de la Marine had done anything to prepare for such a contingency. The operation would require 200 ships, Darlan informed the French Prime Minister, while the Army was currently in a state of disintegration. Nevertheless, the Fleet remained intact, while French bases in North Africa had obvious strategic value. Above all, the removal of the Government to some part of the French Empire would have provided a legal rallying point for the forces of resistance, while delegitimising any Quisling regime that attempted to assume power in France.

Reynaud favoured continuing the war from overseas. Yet the French Prime Minister was by now an increasingly isolated and demoralised figure, who lacked the strength to sack the *capitulards* and form a government united in its desire to carry on the struggle. On 15 June 1940, the day after the Germans entered Paris and the French Government moved from the Loire to Bordeaux, he accepted the infamous proposal of the former Prime Minister Camille Chautemps – a notorious defeatist – that the Government, before considering the question of relocating to Algiers, should first ascertain the German armistice demands. The final straw had been the predictable response from Roosevelt, explaining that he was in no position to declare war. That evening, Reynaud formally asked the British Government to release France from her obligations so that she might discover the German terms. If these proved unacceptable – the surrender of the Fleet was cited as an unacceptable demand – then France would continue the war from North Africa. If, however, the British refused this request then Reynaud would have no option but to resign.

Appreciating that there was now almost no chance of keeping France in the war, the War Cabinet responded swiftly and decisively. Early on the afternoon of 16 June, Sir Ronald Campbell informed Reynaud that the British Government agreed to release the French from the agreement of 28 March 'but only provided the French Fleet is sailed forthwith for British harbours pending negotiations'.[12] A few hours later, however, Campbell sent Reynaud a message saying that he should disregard his earlier communication in light of a new proposal: in order to keep France in the war, the British Government was offering to form a complete political union between the two countries.

The extraordinary suggestion for an Anglo-French union is typically portrayed as a desperate snatch at the last tuft of grass before the Franco-British alliance plummeted to its demise.* The idea had, however, been percolating within Whitehall since the beginning of the year. On 28 February 1940, the Deputy Under-Secretary at the Foreign Office, Sir Orme Sargent, produced a minute in which he argued that the Government should consider a 'permanent system of Anglo-French unity' as a counterweight to German power; a 'joint executive machinery', not merely for the direction of military and diplomatic policy but for 'the whole domain of finance, trade

---

* This notion was encouraged by Churchill, who, in August 1944, inaccurately claimed that the offer emanated from 'a wave of Cabinet emotion'.

and economics', so as to make of the two countries 'a single unit in post-war Europe'.[13] This proposal led to the creation of an inter-departmental committee to examine the idea, as well as a full list of proposed articles of association. The Government's chief adviser on foreign publicity, the Earl of Perth, admitted that it was 'going to be very difficult to teach people here to regard the Frenchman as a co-citizen' but with the full support of the Ministry of Information it should be possible to obtain 'popular acquiescence to the [idea of Franco-British] union'.[14]

Similar discussions took place within the Quai d'Orsay, yet French politicians seemed more reticent. As Sargent wrote to the First Secretary at the British Embassy in Paris on 11 April 1940, whilst British ministers made constant references to Anglo-French union, the continuing silence from the other side of the Channel was causing him to wonder 'whether the time has not come when a hint might be dropped to the French that a little bit of reciprocity might not come amiss'.[15] In its final inspiration, however, the forces behind the project were French, not British. Lunching with Churchill at the Carlton Club on 16 June, the head of the Anglo-French Purchasing Commission, Jean Monnet, the French Ambassador, Charles Corbin, and General de Gaulle, in Britain to see about transporting French troops to North Africa, persuaded the Prime Minister that 'some very dramatic move was essential' to keep France in the war. Minutes later, the Prime Minister found himself recommending their proposal for a 'proclamation of the indissoluble union of the French and British peoples' to the War Cabinet.[16]

Fortunately, the 'Declaration of Union' went no further.* Although Reynaud was 'transfigured with joy' when he heard of the proposal, his colleagues did not share his enthusiasm.[17] Minister of State Jean Ybarnégaray accused the British of conspiring to make France an English dominion, while Pétain, reflecting the consensus that Britain too was heading for defeat, asked why France would 'wish to fuse with a corpse'.[18] As Churchill waited on board a special

---

* To give one example of the potential pitfalls of the scheme, the British would have found it extremely difficult to resist French demands upon the RAF once the two countries had become one.

train to begin his journey to Brittany where he intended to meet the French Premier and conclude the union, he received word that a French ministerial crisis was in progress and, a few hours later, that Reynaud had resigned and that Pétain was forming a government. At 1 a.m. on 17 June, Paul Baudouin, now Foreign Minister, informed Campbell that he had asked the Spanish dictator, General Francisco Franco, to obtain the German terms for an armistice.

★

For the next seventeen days, the issue of the French Fleet dominated the agenda of the British War Cabinet. On the morning of 17 June, remembering that they had 'suspended' their previous demand on the subject while offering political union, ministers instructed Campbell to remind Pétain that the 'vital condition' on which the British Government had consented to release France from her obligations was that the Fleet must sail to British ports *before* armistice negotiations began.[19]★ This was followed by a scorching telegram from Churchill, in which the Prime Minister expressed his (obviously doubtful) conviction 'that the illustrious Maréchal Pétain and the famous General Weygand', now Minister of Defence as well as Commander-in-Chief, would not injure their ally by handing the 'fine French Fleet' over to the enemy. 'Such an act', he continued, 'would scarify their names for a thousand years of history.' And yet this situation might well occur, 'by frittering away these few precious hours when the Fleet can be sailed to safety in British or American ports'.[20]

The next day, the First Sea Lord, Admiral Sir Dudley Pound, and the First Lord of the Admiralty, A. V. Alexander, arrived in Bordeaux

---

★ The muddle over the suspended or cancelled telegram of 16 June was to cause much confusion and bitter recrimination. In the eyes of the British Government, the French Government had simply ignored the one condition upon which it had been released from the agreement prohibiting a separate peace. Since the telegram had been cancelled, however, Reynaud had never made his colleagues aware of its contents. What is not in doubt is that the new French Government – which included Weygand, Baudouin and Chautemps – was fully aware of its existing obligations and that by opening armistice talks without even consulting its ally was in clear breach of its obligations.

to confer with Darlan, now Ministre de la Marine as well as Commander-in-Chief of the French Navy. The British were encouraged by the meeting. The Admiral assured his guests that nothing would induce him to surrender the Fleet and that, in the last resort, he would scuttle his ships rather than allow them to fall into the hands of the enemy. Indeed, he had issued orders to this effect that day. In the meantime, the French Navy was continuing to fight – it had just bombarded the Italian coast and sunk two submarines – while plans to sail the *Richelieu* and the *Jean Bart* to West Africa were already in hand. Contrary to the view that 'Darlan was a twister', the British sea lords found the Admiral sincere and 'very friendly'.[21] But the Ministre de la Marine's cordiality was deceptive. Offended by the suggestion that he should remove his Fleet while it was still fighting, the Admiral accused the British emissaries, behind their backs, of acting like 'heirs . . . come to reassure themselves that the dying man has really left them a bequest'.[22]

Tentative British optimism was shattered by the armistice terms. Although Hitler solemnly disavowed any intention of employing the French Fleet – except for 'units necessary for coastal surveillance and minesweeping' – Article 8 stipulated that French ships were to return to ports in metropolitan France where they would be disarmed under German or Italian supervision.[23] 'Our worst fears had been realised,' Pleydell-Bouverie noted in his diary, while Campbell warned the Foreign Office that the 'diabolically clever German terms' had 'destroyed the last remnants of French courage'. 'I do not believe for a moment', he wrote, 'that the French, in their present state of collapse, would hold out against [the] original German condition to recall the Fleet and might even reverse [the] scuttling order.'[24]

Churchill agreed. At 9.30 p.m. on 22 June – three hours after the armistice, which allowed the French Government to retain control of around two-fifths of the country, was signed – the Prime Minister told the War Cabinet that 'in a matter so vital to the safety of the whole British Empire we could not afford to rely on the word of Admiral Darlan', who, however good his intentions, 'might be forced to resign and [have] his place taken by another Minister who would not shrink from betraying us'. Churchill then raised, for the first time, the possibility of resolving the issue by force. The *Richelieu* and the *Jean Bart*, as well as the *Strasbourg* and the *Dunkerque*, had the capacity to 'alter the whole course of the war', he claimed. A British fleet must be sent and the *Richelieu* 'dealt with first'. If the captains refused to parley, 'they must be treated as traitors to the Allied cause. The ships might have to be bombed by aircraft from *Ark Royal* or they must be mined into their harbours . . . In no circumstance must these ships be allowed to escape.'[25]

Over the coming days, attempts were made to ascertain the views of individual French naval commanders and, if possible, persuade them to continue the war. From Alexandria, Admiral Sir Andrew Cunningham, Commander-in-Chief Mediterranean, reported on 23 June that Vice-Admiral Godfroy was considering whether to fight 'under the British crown' but felt that he would be influenced by the orders he received.[26] Similar encouraging noises came from Beirut. But at Mers el-Kébir Vice-Admiral Gensoul made it plain that he would continue to follow orders so long as there existed a legally constituted government in France.

During three long and, at times, rambling discussions on 24 June, the War Cabinet kept returning to the central point that they could not trust Hitler to abide by the terms of the armistice and that French assurances regarding the future of the Fleet were, consequently, worthless. The Pétain Government, declared Churchill, was 'completely under the thumb of Germany'. There was a grave danger that:

> The rot would spread from the top through the Fleet, the Army and the Air Force, and all French Colonies. The Germans would put every form of pressure upon the Government to act to our detriment . . . So long as the position of the French warships was unsecured, they would be used as a blackmailing threat against us. We must at all costs ensure that these ships either came under our control or were put out of the way for good.[27]

By this stage, the Admiralty had already begun to draw up plans to disable the *Force de Raid* at Mers el-Kébir and Oran. On 27 June, Pound presented the War Cabinet with three options: the Royal Navy could mine the entrance to Mers el-Kébir harbour; they could deploy submarines to sink the French battlecruisers if they tried to leave; or they could send a surface fleet to resolve the issue by threat of force. This latter course appealed to Churchill, who claimed that it would chime with public opinion and recalled the sinking of the Dutch fleet in 1801 in similar circumstances. Having obtained the agreement of his colleagues, he ordered Pound to prepare the operation with all possible speed. Five days later, Somerville's Force H sailed from Gibraltar.

★

At 2.50 p.m. on 3 July, ten minutes before Somerville's deadline was due to expire, Holland received a signal from Gensoul stating that he was prepared to receive him 'for honourable discussion'.[28] Once again, the British Captain clambered into the *Foxhound*'s motorboat but this time he sailed beyond the torpedo boom towards the Admiral's flagship, the *Dunkerque*. By this stage, the *Force de Raid* was buzzing with speculation. 'They are mad – absolutely mad,' commented Capitaine Louis Le Pivain of the *Bretagne* to Lieutenant Jean Boutron about '*les anglais*'.[29] As the day wore on, nerves began to fray. When the officers of the *Bretagne* learnt of the British terms and the fast-approaching deadline, Boutron could not keep his views to himself: 'We have not finished paying for this filthy armistice. This is just the beginning.'

Angrily, his neighbour turned on him and demanded to know what he would have done differently: 'Continued the war with those who abandoned us and now are getting ready to fire on us?'

'I tell you, if the English are behaving like bastards now,' Boutron replied, 'well, we behaved like bastards by capitulating to Hitler.' His interlocutor threatened to punch him in the face.[30]

As Holland made his way to the *Dunkerque*, hundreds of pairs of eyes from the upper decks of the French warships followed his progress. 'All ships were in an advanced state of readiness,' wrote Holland in his report. Tugs were waiting next to the sterns of the big battleships, ready to tow them out of the harbour and the guns were trained 'fore and aft', in the direction of the British Fleet.[31]

Gensoul had been disingenuous in his signals to the French Admiralty. At 9.45 a.m., he had reported the arrival of Force H but

only mentioned one of the alternatives offered by the British: 'Ultimatum sent: sink your ships within six hours or we shall force you
to.'[32] Later, in a longer message sent at 1.20 p.m., he falsely claimed
that the choice he was facing was to join the British or scuttle. At
no point did he inform the Admiralty of the third option: to sail
his ships to the French West Indies or the United States, though he
did relay a hint from Holland that the disarmament of his warships
could form the basis of a compromise.

When the first of these messages arrived at Nérac – the French
Admiralty's new temporary headquarters, 80 miles south-east of
Bordeaux – Darlan was with the Government at Clermont-Ferrand.
On his own initiative, however, Vice-Admiral Le Luc ordered the
3rd Squadron at Toulon – consisting of four heavy cruisers and
three divisions of destroyers – as well as the six cruisers stationed
at Algiers, to sail for Oran. When Darlan was eventually reached,
at 1.30 p.m., he fully supported this action. His orders to Gensoul,
relayed half an hour later, were unequivocal: 'You will make it
known to the British intermediary that the Admiral of the Fleet
has ordered all French naval forces in the Mediterranean to join you
ready for action immediately . . . You will reply to force with force.
Summon submarines and aviation if necessary.'[33]

Holland found Gensoul indignant and uncooperative. Enraged
by the British ultimatum but at a nautical disadvantage, his strategy
was to play for time. He had only consented to see the Captain, he
explained, since the first shot fired would be 'tantamount to a declaration of war' between Britain and France. He protested against
the laying of mines at the entrance of the harbour, arguing that this
made compliance with three of the British alternatives impossible.
As for the fourth, he utterly rejected the demand that he sink his
own ships, though he reiterated his pledge to do just this should
there be any danger of their being captured by the Germans.[34]

Time was running out. British Naval Intelligence had intercepted
Darlan's orders and relayed them to Force H. Pound signalled Somerville urging him to 'settle matters quickly or you will have [French]
reinforcements to deal with'.[35] At 5.15 p.m., while he was still arguing with Holland, Gensoul received a fresh message from the British
Admiral: 'If the British proposals are not accepted by 5.30 p.m., I

repeat, 5.30 p.m., I must sink your ships.'[36] Holland's leave taking with Gensoul was more cordial than his greeting. Even at this late stage, the Captain thought that the Admiral did not believe that the British were in earnest – a misapprehension apparently shared by a majority of French sailors, many of whom remained on the upper decks despite the call to 'Action Stations'. At 5.54 p.m., the British opened fire.

Within minutes, the *Bretagne* had received a direct hit, causing a major explosion amidships. Climbing down from the forward gun turret Lieutenant Boutron watched as a tower of black smoke surged into the sky, while the stern had already sunk to the level of the water. The *Dunkerque* was also hit, while the battleship *Provence* and the destroyer *Mogador* were badly mauled. Within two minutes of the start of the bombardment, the French had begun to return fire – the first time since Waterloo the two nations had purposely shot at each other. But it was an unequal contest and none of the French shells found their mark. Nevertheless, the battlecruiser *Strasbourg* and five French destroyers succeeded in slipping their moorings and, aided by the smoke and Gensoul's disingenuous request for a ceasefire, managed to reach the open sea.

The British stopped firing at 6.04 p.m. During the ten-minute bombardment, HMS *Hood*, *Valiant* and *Resolution* had fired twelve salvoes, amounting to 144 fifteen-inch shells. Three days later, twelve torpedo-laden Swordfish aircraft came to finish off the *Dunkerque*. Some 1,290 French sailors were killed in the action – over a thousand from the *Bretagne* alone – and 351 wounded. The survivors could scarcely believe it. 'These English, what can I say!' exclaimed the *Bretagne*'s chaplain when he encountered Boutron on board a hospital ship: 'To think you and I wanted to carry on the fight with them! And they have just murdered us all!'[37]

★

To a man, the British considered 'Oran', as they invariably referred to it, a hateful action. Somerville called it a 'beastly operation' and feared he would, henceforth, be known as the 'unskilled butcher of

Oran' – 'unskilled' because he allowed the *Strasbourg* to escape.[38] Holland wholeheartedly agreed. Having, like Somerville, opposed the threat of force from the outset, he tried (unsuccessfully) to resign from the Navy two days after his parley with Gensoul, citing the 'repugnant' bombardment of Britain's erstwhile allies as the reason.[39] Moreover, both men believed the action to have been unnecessary.

Of course, as with all tragedies, the denouement could have been avoided. Had Gensoul accepted one of the four British alternatives, then he would have preserved the lives of his men and possibly his ships. He could also have proposed a compromise, as Vice-Admiral Godfroy did at Alexandria, where, after painstaking diplomacy with Admiral Cunningham, he agreed to discharge oil, disarm his ships and reduce their crews. Instead, Gensoul failed to report the range of alternatives and wasted precious hours by refusing to meet Holland. He showed neither initiative nor moral courage, only blind subservience to Darlan's orders.

Although an instinctive Anglophobe – a man who liked to remind the British that his grandfather had died fighting their forebears at Trafalgar – Darlan did not initially allow his prejudices to impair his judgement. Disgusted at the idea of capitulating while the navy he had built was still intact, he stated unequivocally on 14 June that he would 'fight to the end' and, if necessary, 'put the whole Fleet under the British flag'.[40] On being reassured that Pétain had no intention of surrendering the French Navy, however, and seduced by the offer of the Ministère de la Marine, he moved swiftly into the armistice camp. 'This Admiral knows how to swim,' commented the former Prime Minister Édouard Herriot.[41] From that moment, like most of the lieutenants of the regime soon to take up residence in the spa-town of Vichy, Darlan was convinced that Britain was heading for defeat and saw no reason to risk Hitler's displeasure by standing in the way of her demise. His order to Gensoul, to meet 'force with force', reflected this view (as well as Gallic outrage at the British ultimatum) but it also led to the destruction of his beloved ships.[42]

With the benefit of hindsight, it is clear that British fears about the French Fleet were exaggerated. Apart from the safeguards that Darlan had put in place (of which the Admiralty was partly aware) the difficulties the Germans would have faced in capturing the French ships, especially those in North and West Africa, were considerable. When German forces began to close in on Toulon in November 1942, following the Allied landings in North Africa, the French naval authorities complied with Darlan's long-standing directive and duly scuttled their ships. To Vichy and its defenders, this was 'proof' that the British should have trusted the regime and its naval commander in 1940. Yet this is to examine events through the wrong end of the historical telescope.

In June 1940, Britain was engaged in a war for national survival. Reeling from the most portentous military defeat in her history, she now faced the threat of invasion. Although morale, bolstered by the Prime Minister's oratory, remained surprisingly high, even Churchill suffered moments of doubt. Waiting to board his aircraft following the meeting of the Supreme War Council at Briare on 12 June, General Ismay expressed his view that, despite the fall of France, 'we'll win the Battle of Britain'. Churchill turned to his military adviser and, in words that could hardly have been at greater odds with his public statements, responded, 'You and I will be dead in three months' time.'[43]

In this welter of danger and uncertainty, there was no room for the benefit of the doubt or the running of even the smallest of risks. Following the Pétain Government's decision to seek an armistice, in contravention of France's agreement with her ally, the Chiefs of Staff concluded that 'we can no longer place any faith in French assurances'. If, as per the terms of the armistice, French warships were to return to metropolitan ports, then 'sooner or later, the Germans will employ them against us'.[44] The Admiralty's greatest concern was the capital ship ratio. In 1940, Britain possessed fourteen capital ships (one on long refit), Italy had six and Germany four, with two on the way. Including the incomplete *Jean Bart*, France had nine. As the First Lord of the Admiralty, A. V. Alexander wrote to Churchill in the immediate aftermath of the bombardment: 'The transfer of this powerful modern capital Fleet to the enemy might have altered the whole balance of naval strength, with incalculable results to our cause.'[45] Instead, thanks to her actions on 3 July, which also included the seizure of all French warships in British ports,* Britain had impounded three capital ships (two in home ports, one in Alexandria), sunk one (the *Bretagne*), immobilised two (the *Dunkerque* and the *Provence*) and damaged another (the *Richelieu*).

This was the metric by which, despite the escape of the *Strasbourg*, Britain's military chiefs considered the operation a success. Yet Churchill had a secondary motive: namely, to demonstrate to the world in general and the United States in particular that Britain was determined to continue the war despite the fall of France. In December 1941, he told the US Secretary of State, Cordell Hull, that 'since many people throughout the world believed that Britain was about to surrender, he had wanted . . . to show that she still meant to fight'.[46] Nor was this a matter of *post facto* justification. Apart from his cryptic references to 'public opinion' in the War Cabinet, Churchill instructed Halifax on 24 June to hold off pressing Roosevelt on the question of giving Britain American destroyers since he thought the President would, ultimately, be influenced 'by what happens to the French Fleet'.[47] Ten days later, the morning after the attack, the British Ambassador in Washington, the Marquess of Lothian, sent the US President this simple, previously overlooked line: 'You will see that Winston Churchill has taken the action in regard to the French Fleet which we discussed and you approved.'[48]

Such considerations may seem callous but there is no denying their importance or the motive that induced them. Mers el-Kébir was a desperate measure born of desperate circumstances. Through their terms, the British offered Darlan and Gensoul a way out. That it was not taken was not their fault. And yet there remains the tragic irony that Britain's first victory of the war was against her former ally.

---

* This was achieved with complete surprise and (with the exception of a fight aboard the French submarine *Surcouf* moored at Plymouth, which resulted in the deaths of two Royal Navy officers and a French warrant officer), without bloodshed. In his memoirs, Churchill would argue that this proved how easy it would have been for the Germans to do the same.

V

Rebels with a Cause

One is always right to bet on France.

Charles de Gaulle, 19 June 1940[1]

The British action at Mers el-Kébir was applauded around the world. 'General reaction to Oran incident very satisfactory in all circles,' reported the Naval Attaché in Rio de Janeiro. 'Chileans consider that action taken [at] Oran only course to pursue' (Santiago); 'Turkish [reaction] – very satisfactory' (Ankara); 'All parties impressed by display of force' (Bucharest). And from Belgrade: 'Impression of all sections of the public was one of relief that Britain [was] not afraid to take extreme measures and looked upon it as indication that she intended . . . to continue the war to [a] victorious conclusion . . . General Staff opinion, as indicated by their liaison officers, is frank jubilation.'[2]

In the United States, the reaction was everything Churchill had hoped for. 'Before the Oran action', reported the British Library of Information in New York, 'there had been pessimism about Great Britain's chances and there had been suspicions about "appeasement" in Britain. The vigorous action of the Royal Navy . . . awakened the realisation here that Great Britain was alive and kicking.'[3] American press commentary was 'almost universally favourable', noted the British Ambassador, Lord Lothian, while in London the American Military Attaché recorded his delight at this 'dashing, old-fashioned, Nelsonian cutting-out expedition . . . which shows that the British are not going to sit quietly and watch Hitler's plans mature.'[4] President Roosevelt would later tell his friend and adviser Harry Hopkins that it was Oran that convinced him that Britain would continue the war – if necessary for years, if necessary alone.

In one Allied quarter, however, the news was decidedly less welcome. For General de Gaulle and his efforts to form a 'Free French' fighting contingent in Britain, Mers el-Kébir was a disaster.

'Rough and unfinished like a Rodin, with carefully done bits here and there', at over 6 feet 4 inches tall, with hooded eyes, a long beak and an indomitable expression, Charles de Gaulle cut an imposing figure.[5] At Saint-Cyr, the French military academy, his height had earned him the nickname 'the Great Asparagus'. Rarely, however, did anyone laugh at him. An exemplary student, he had already developed, by the time he graduated, that 'certain idea of France' – above all, her grandeur – that was to stay with him throughout his life.[6] During the First World War, while serving on the Meuse and at Verdun, he was wounded three times before eventually being taken prisoner. Later he became the foremost advocate of mobile, armoured warfare in France, publishing in 1934 a pioneering book on the subject. In mid-May 1940, he was able to put his ideas into action when he led some of the only successful French counterattacks during the German invasion and on 23 May was rewarded by being promoted to the temporary rank of brigadier-general – the youngest general in the French Army.

By the time de Gaulle joined the French Government, on 5 June, the Battle of France was lost. Yet the General refused to accept defeat and did everything he could to persuade Reynaud to continue the war from Brittany or North Africa. When this plan failed – when Reynaud resigned and Pétain became Prime Minister – he was faced with a stark choice: he could remain in France and accept an armistice, or he could flee to Britain and try to rally the forces of resistance. He did not hesitate. At 9 a.m. on 17 June, accompanied by Churchill's liaison with the French Government, Louis Spears – who was to become first his champion then his implacable enemy – he boarded a British aeroplane and, armed with 100,000 francs from French Government funds and one suitcase, flew across the Channel.

The British knew almost nothing about the man who, for the next five years, was to take up so much of their time and energy. A profile in *The Times* from 7 June described the new French Under-Secretary of War (somewhat inaccurately) as 'aggressively "right wing"', though 'clear-minded, lucid . . . a man of action as well as a man of dreams'.[7] The Permanent Under-Secretary of the Foreign Office was even less well informed. 'I cannot tell you anything about de Gaulle', Sir Alexander Cadogan told colleagues, 'except that he's got a head like a pineapple and hips like a woman.'[8] Churchill, however, had formed a favourable impression of the General during their meetings and when de Gaulle asked him to support a 'Free French' fighting movement under his auspices, on 17 June, he received a sympathetic hearing. At 6 p.m. the following evening, less than thirty-six hours after arriving in Britain, he recorded his celebrated broadcast to France:

> I, General de Gaulle, now in London, call on all French officers and men who are at present on British soil, or may be in the future, with or without their arms; I call on all engineers and skilled workmen from the armaments factories who are at present on British soil, or may be in the future, to get in touch with me. Whatever happens, the flame of French resistance must not and shall not die. Tomorrow, I shall broadcast again from London.[9]*

He would not. At this stage, the War Cabinet was still trying to persuade the Pétain Government to send the French Fleet to Britain and, as a senior Foreign Office official put it, 'it would be disastrous if we should appear at the same time to be coquetting with a possible successor in London'.[10] His boss, the permanently exasperated Cadogan, agreed. 'Told him [Halifax] that this cannot go on. No. 10 . . . is like behind the scenes at the circus and every crank in the world is getting hold of the PM and getting half-baked decisions.' Having got Halifax to square Churchill, Cadogan saw de Gaulle and explained that it was necessary to 'keep quiet until [the] situation clears'.[11]

The signing of the armistice on the evening of 22 June eliminated these scruples. Even before the full details were known, de Gaulle had been let loose on the airwaves again to denounce the capitulation and renew his appeal to 'all French soldiers of the Army,

---

* The speech, broadcast at 10 p.m. and repeated three times the following day, was only celebrated in retrospect. Few Frenchmen heard the original and even fewer acted upon it.

the Navy and the Air Force' to join him in London.[12] The following morning he asked Churchill to recognise a French council of
liberation under his leadership and, at their 10 a.m. meeting, the
War Cabinet agreed to do just that. At first sight, this appears an
astonishingly bold, almost reckless move. In June 1940, Charles de
Gaulle was a virtually unknown brigadier-general who had served
for eleven days in the most disastrous government in French history. When a French lawyer called on de Gaulle two days after his
arrival in England and offered his services, the General had been
frank about the bleakness of his position: 'I have neither money nor
men . . . We are starting from zero. You could begin by holding the
fort. That way de Courcel [his aide] and I can go and have lunch and
at least there will be someone to answer the telephone or open the
door when we are not there.'[13]

Yet Churchill and de Gaulle began with very different ideas about
the role and scope of the proposed committee. In his letter to the
Prime Minister, de Gaulle had spoken of a body that could 'represent the French nation' – in other words a political entity.[14] Writing
to General Ismay, however, Churchill made it clear that he envisaged
de Gaulle's committee as the 'operative authority' of a clandestine
organisation designed to get other Frenchmen out of France – 'a
sort of underground railway' or 'Scarlet Pimpernel organisation'.[15]
It was the failure of more senior French figures to defy the armistice and his own 'certain idea' of himself that allowed de Gaulle to
achieve so much more than this.

For several days in late June, the War Cabinet had harboured
hopes that General Charles Noguès, Commander-in-Chief in
French North Africa, or some other eminent figure would emerge
who could rally the French Empire. On 26 June, they despatched
the Minister of Information, Duff Cooper, to Morocco, to persuade
a group of recently arrived French politicians to establish a government in North Africa. Landing at Rabat, however, Cooper learnt
that these remnants of the Third Republic were being held prisoner
on board their ship. Forbidden from seeing them, he had no more
luck in procuring an interview with Noguès. This left the British
Government with little choice. On the evening of 27 June, Churchill saw de Gaulle in Downing Street: 'You are alone – well, I shall

recognise you alone.'[16] The next morning, a communiqué was published announcing that His Majesty's Government acknowledged General de Gaulle 'as the leader of all free Frenchmen, wherever they may be, who rally to him in support of the Allied cause'.[17]

Although alone, de Gaulle wasted little time in establishing the purpose of his mission. 'Are we rebuilding the French Army as allies of the British and trying to maintain French unity?' enquired his legal adviser, René Cassin. 'We are France!' came the General's succinct and, as his associates would soon learn, characteristic reply.[18] If this was the case, however, few Frenchmen recognised it at the time. Trawling Britain's military camps with Spears – now head of a British mission to de Gaulle – the General succeeded in recruiting a mere two battalions from the Foreign Legion, some 200 *chasseurs alpins* and part of a tank company from the more than 130,000 French soldiers evacuated from Dunkirk and Narvik. The rest chose to be repatriated.

Of course, Mers el-Kébir did not help. Of nearly 500 French naval officers and 18,000 French sailors in England in June 1940, all but 50 officers and 200 men chose to return home. Other hindrances included the War Office which, suffering from a dearth of materiel with which to meet an expected invasion, was understandably reluctant to equip French soldiers who, in their view, had not shown up well during the Battle of France; and pro-armistice French diplomats still in England, who did all they could to discourage recruitment. Nevertheless, by the end of August de Gaulle had a force of 7,000 partially equipped Free French volunteers and by the end of the year this figure would swell to 35,000.

During this time, the British began to learn something of the man they had catapulted from relative obscurity to the symbol of French resistance across the world. On 7 August, the British Government formalised its relationship with de Gaulle by publishing an exchange of letters. The results, from the General's perspective, were highly satisfactory. The British declared that the troops under the General's command would 'as far as possible retain the character of a French force', though under the 'general direction of the British High Command', while Churchill pledged to restore the 'independence and greatness of France'.[19] The negotiations, however, had been gruelling. Over the course of a month and six different drafts, de Gaulle's flounces, hauteur and acerbity succeeded in alienating 'even the best disposed of Foreign Office officials', wrote Spears. 'He was incapable of doing anything personally dishonourable and would always have preferred the truth to a lie but when defending the cause of France . . . he gave the impression of having studied diplomacy at the court of Cesare Borgia.'[20]

The principal sticking point had been the French soldiers, sailors and airmen who, following the fall of France, had joined the British fighting services. Having integrated them into their forces, the British Service Chiefs were loath to let them leave and refuted de Gaulle's claim that, as Frenchmen, they fell under his authority. The dispute was resolved by Churchill, who decreed that, as a matter of principle, new recruits should join their own national forces and that the General would be able to make representations about Frenchmen already serving with the British on an individual basis. Although this infuriated the Service Chiefs, it did not go nearly far enough for de Gaulle, who, according to Spears, tried on at least two occasions to send French aviators serving with the RAF to the Tower of London:

> On the first occasion, the problem . . . was easily resolved without it becoming necessary to remind de Gaulle that we no longer lived in Tudor times . . . The prisoner, escorted in a taxi by a Colonel Brosset, simply opened the door of the taxi at the first red lights in Whitehall and stepped out . . . In the second case I heard of what was afoot in time and the officers of the company on duty in the Tower were kind enough to welcome the bewildered prisoner for long enough to enable us to convey to the head of the Free French that neither the use of the dungeons nor the services of the executioner were among the amenities we were prepared to place at his disposal.[21]

There were similar problems with Vice-Admiral Émile Muselier. The most senior naval officer to rally to de Gaulle, he was given command of the Free French Navy despite a well-deserved reputation for volatility and the appearance of a 'Marseilles pirate'.[22] (He was also an opium addict.) From the start, he infuriated the British by threatening to shoot French sailors who had joined the Royal Navy

and accusing the Admiralty of employing women of dubious reputation to procure their services.[23] Within a few weeks, Spears had
hatched a plot to send Muselier to Alexandria to recruit French sailors. That this was just a ploy to get rid of the turbulent Admiral he
made clear in a letter to Admiral Sir Gerald Dickens: 'He could go
to Gibraltar and nobody need be in any hurry to send him on to
Malta, where he could be kept until the local people could stand
him no longer.'[24] Unfortunately, as Dickens explained, there were
objections to the plan:

> I am afraid as [General] Wavell [Commander-in-Chief, Middle East]
> feels so strongly about Muselier being decanted in Alexandria, we
> shall have to think again. Your scheme was to ooze him through
> Gibraltar and Malta by degrees but the ship going out goes right
> through to Alexandria. Couldn't you make him Colonel-in-Chief of
> the 'Muselier Marins' and land him somewhere in Africa? It would
> be an example of ruthless warfare which even the Germans would
> envy. The physical effect might not be very great but as the man is
> such a crashing bore it would wear down the nerves of even the
> stoutest Touaregs.[25]

Yet if de Gaulle and some of his associates showed an early tendency to exasperate British officials – Cadogan referred to 'that cunt
of a fellow de Gaulle' – the General's persecution by the Pétain Government, located from July in the spa-town of Vichy, only served to
increase his status with the British people.[26] On 25 June, Weygand
had cancelled de Gaulle's temporary rank as brigadier-general. The
following day, he was 'compulsorily retired' from the Army. On 28
June, he received orders, via the French Embassy, to report to Saint-
Michel prison in Toulouse, to answer charges of inciting soldiers to
disobedience. Tried in absentia, he was condemned to four years
in prison and later, after the National Assembly had voted itself
into oblivion and Pétain had granted himself full executive powers
and proclaimed himself Head of State, to death. In his memoirs,
de Gaulle wrote little of these events. All he remembered was the
'unimaginable' kindness of the English people, who set up charities
to support his movement and, on hearing of his sentence, left jewels

and wedding rings at his headquarters, 'in order that the gold might help General de Gaulle in his undertaking'.[27] He would need more than funds, however, if his first enterprise with the British was to prosper.

★

Since 28 June 1940, eleven days after his arrival in England, de Gaulle had been urging the British to help establish him on French territory – somewhere from which his embryonic force could continue the war. His initial preference was North Africa. After Mers el-Kébir, however, this seemed no longer a propitious option and his thoughts turned towards French West Africa and the Senegalese port of Dakar.

Unbeknown to de Gaulle, Churchill's attention had also been drawn to this part of the world. On 4 July – the day after Mers el-Kébir – the Prime Minister had seen a despatch from the British Consul-General at Dakar, Victor Cusden, to the Foreign Office, reporting the suggestion of the city's Mayor that a 'show of force' should be made by British warships off the coast in support of 'semi-official' groups of French patriots who were planning to overthrow the Vichy authorities.[28] Churchill was enthused. The loss of Dakar to the Germans would constitute a grave threat to Britain's already frayed sea communications while, conversely, the seizure of the harbour by Allied forces could prove a decisive advantage in the Battle of the Atlantic. Moreover, Churchill was desperate, like Evelyn Waugh's Brigadier Ritchie-Hook – who in volume one of the *Sword of Honour* trilogy leads an ill-fated commando raid on a thinly disguised Dakar – to get off the defensive and start 'biffing the enemy'.[29] 'The passive resistance war . . . must come to an end,' he had minuted Ismay, a mere day after the completion of the evacuation from Dunkirk. 'I look to the Joint Chiefs of Staff to propose to me measures for a vigorous, enterprising and ceaseless offensive against the whole occupied German coastline.'[30]

To Churchill's annoyance, his military advisers produced a barrage of objections. As Ismay warned the Prime Minister, Dakar was protected by eight 9.4-inch guns, submarine patrols and the *Richelieu*. A naval operation would be foolish 'unless we can be *positive* that the coast defence guns will not fire on us'.[31] There was also the risk that Vichy would respond to an attack on Dakar by declaring war on Britain. After Mers el-Kébir, a furious Darlan and Pierre Laval – a bitter Anglophobe, soon to become Pétain's Prime Minister – had sought retribution in the form of a Franco-Italian assault on Alexandria and an expedition from the Senegalese capital to attack the British in Sierra Leone. In the end, the Vichy Government contented itself with breaking off diplomatic relations and making a desultory raid on Gibraltar. But there was no guarantee that it would act with such restraint in the future. Was it worth risking war with France at the same time as Britain was under threat of invasion?

For a month, nothing happened. Telegrams from the Governors of Nigeria and the Gold Coast suggested that the situation in French West Africa was less favourable to the Allied cause than Cusden had implied and Churchill was persuaded to shelve the idea. At the beginning of August, however, he returned to the operation when de Gaulle presented his own scheme for rallying the French colony. The General had already put plans in train that would, he hoped, bring French Equatorial Africa (Chad, Ubangi-Shari, Gabon and the French Congo), as well as French Cameroon, over to his side. Now, he proposed a Free French expedition, in British ships, to augment these expected gains, by raising the flag of resistance off Dakar. Once again, Churchill was strongly taken with the idea. Telephoning Downing Street from Chequers, he gave orders for plans to be drawn up for the capture of Dakar along the lines adumbrated by de Gaulle, adding that that this was a purely 'political decision and that he didn't want a lot of military objections put up by the Chiefs of Staff'.[32]

As Churchill had anticipated, the Chiefs were less than thrilled by this directive. Indeed, as Rear-Admiral A. D. Nicholl, Assistant Secretary to the War Cabinet, recalled, they were 'extremely disgruntled about the whole thing'. Resentful at having to opine on plans that had not received the scrutiny of the Joint Planners, their main concern was that 'there was far too much optimism about the reception de Gaulle would get at Dakar'. As to the attitude of the British brass towards the Free French, this was encapsulated by the note Nicholl passed Ismay during the discussion: 'Why not let the first flight be our Marines – dressed as Frenchmen if necessary but ready to fight like Royal Marines?' Churchill's chief military adviser grimaced his agreement.[33] It was left to the Joint Planners to point out the essential contradiction between the Government's stated policy of wishing to improve relations with Vichy and the proposal to seize one of its most important colonies.

Still, albeit reluctantly, the Chiefs of Staff approved the operation – known initially as Scipio, later as Menace. They imposed several conditions, however, the most important being that the landing must be unopposed and that the expedition be entirely French – the role of the British would be limited to a naval escort and part of the shipping. When de Gaulle met the First Sea Lord on the afternoon of 5 August, however, the General made it clear that the Royal Navy would be required to counter any opposition from French warships, he having already stipulated that his forces would never fire on their countrymen. This was considerably more than the military planners had bargained for. Yet Churchill took it in his stride and when de Gaulle visited Downing Street the next morning he was treated to the full force of the Prime Minister's verdant imagination:

> Dakar wakes up one morning, sad and uncertain. But behold, by the light of the rising sun, its inhabitants perceive the sea, to a great distance, covered with ships. An immense fleet! A hundred war or transport vessels! These approach slowly, addressing messages of friendship by radio to the town, to the navy, to the garrison. Some of them are flying the Tricolour. The others are sailing under the British, Dutch, Polish or Belgian colours. From the Allied force there breaks away an inoffensive small ship bearing the white flag of parley. It enters the port and disembarks the envoys of General de Gaulle. These are brought to the Governor. Their job is to convince him that if he lets you land, the Allied fleet retires and that nothing remains but to settle, between him and you, the terms of his co-operation. On the other hand, if he wants a fight, he has every chance of being crushed.[34]

In fact, the Dakar expedition was a fiasco from start to finish. As the planners had emphasised, the precondition for success was the accuracy of the reports which claimed that the garrison and French naval forces would welcome de Gaulle and his comrades. Free French intelligence estimated that 70 per cent of the garrison was pro-de Gaulle, 20 per cent was neutral and only 10 per cent supported Vichy. Why there should have been such optimism after Mers el-Kébir is hard to fathom. To be sure, the omens appeared good when de Gaulle's emissaries succeeded in rallying almost all of French Equatorial Africa, as well as French Cameroon, to the Free French in late August. But the assumptions that guided Menace had been laid some weeks before and were never challenged. The British never saw, let alone scrutinised, de Gaulle's sources – chiefly anti-Vichy French West Africans, eager to encourage an expedition – and ignored their own contradictory intelligence.

On 4 July, Vice-Admiral Lyon, Commander-in-Chief South Atlantic, submitted a report to the Admiralty (subsequently circulated within the Foreign Office) based on his visit to the port at the end of June. Apart from stating that he had 'seldom felt less confidence in one of His Majesty's consular representatives than in Mr Cusden' – a man 'of little tact or sense of duty', who, on the day the French Government requested an armistice, had gone fishing with the key to the consular safe in his pocket – he reported that any 'initial resolve to continue the struggle' appeared to have 'evaporated' and that there had even been champagne parties to celebrate the end of the fighting on 29 June. 'All the authorities at Dakar', he concluded, 'find it difficult to break away from the highly centralised system of government to which they are accustomed and as time went on and [the] terms of the armistice became known, the feeling that things were not as bad as they seemed, but would be much worse if they resisted, became stronger.'[35] The Colonial Office was similarly doubtful as to the chances of success, while two former British naval liaison officers at Dakar were adamant that the garrison and ship's companies were loyal to Vichy.* Finally, at no point had there been any indication

---

* They also revealed that the defences at Dakar were considerably stronger than the planners had supposed.

that the Governor-General, Pierre Boisson, a fiercely patriotic right-winger who had lost a leg during the First World War, was likely to co-operate with de Gaulle and his comrades. Indeed, considering the fact that he had just opposed the defection of French Equatorial Africa, the indications were all the other way.

★

From the outset, a sense of black comedy dogged Menace. There were 'Gilbertian breaches of security', complained Air Commodore Slessor.[36] De Gaulle, it was alleged, had mentioned that he was going to West Africa while purchasing tropical equipment from Simpson's on Piccadilly, while, only a street away, inebriated Free French officers toasted '*à Dakar*' and '*à de Gaulle*' at the Écu de France restaurant.[37] On 30 August, the General and his staff left Euston for Liverpool in 'a blaze' of publicity. 'I have never seen so many people from VIPs, civil and military, to wives and girlfriends gathered together to see off the heads of an ultra-secret expedition,' noted Louis Spears' aide, John Watson.[38] Arriving on the platform, another member of the Spears mission, Ronald Wingate, found 'a mass of French officers', as well as 'some hundred or more lovely English girls who were bidding them tearful adieus'. Just as the train was about to leave, a barrow appeared carrying bundles of papers. As these were being loaded onto the train one was dropped and burst open. Tricolour-coloured leaflets bearing the words '*Aux citoyens de Dakar*' flew around the station like rose petals.[39]

Nor did the operetta cease when the scene changed to Liverpool. The French crews of the ships carrying the motorised transport had not been paid for several months and refused to sail until they received their arrears; the motorboat that was to ferry de Gaulle to shore was missing and had to be fetched from Plymouth; and one French *capitaine* declined to put to sea until he had found his mistress. Afterwards, the British would assign much of the blame for the failure of the operation to delays and Free French security breaches. Yet, astonishingly, the Vichy Government remained in ignorance as to the destination of the expedition. Only on the eve of the operation did the authorities in Dakar begin to have suspicions.

As de Gaulle was to say in the aftermath of the expedition, 'fortune cannot always be favourable to us.'[40] Indeed, it is hard to see how she could have been less kind. On the afternoon of 11 September, with his force some 300 miles north-west of Dakar, the naval commander of the operation, Vice-Admiral John Cunningham (not to be confused with his more famous namesake who had secured the demilitarisation of Admiral Godfroy's force at Alexandria), received the devastating news that a Vichy naval squadron had passed through the Strait of Gibraltar and into the Atlantic. A series of communication failures meant that Admiral Sir Dudley North merely flashed the French ships '*Bon voyage!*' (He was later sacked by Churchill.) Led by Rear-Admiral Jean Bourragué, its mission was to recover French Equatorial Africa from the Gaullists. The Admiralty ordered Somerville's Force H to give chase, whereupon Bourragué decided to seek refuge in Dakar. At noon on 14 September, his three heavy cruisers entered the harbour.

Churchill's first thought was to cancel the operation. The arrival of the Vichy cruisers, he told the War Cabinet, had 'altered the whole situation', all but eliminating the chances of a bloodless coup.[41] On board the Dutch ship *Westernland*, de Gaulle and Spears protested violently at this decision – the 'worst example of pusillanimity encountered yet', as the latter complained in his diary – but it was the opinion of the British commanders, Cunningham and Major-General Noel Irwin, that the arrival of the three cruisers did 'not materially alter the . . . situation', that persuaded the War Cabinet.[42] Churchill was impressed by the determination of the men on the spot, while his colleagues feared that de Gaulle would have no future if they abandoned the expedition. From inception to implementation, Menace remained a fundamentally political undertaking.

The operation began at dawn on 23 September 1940. This was when Dakar, 'sad and uncertain', in Churchill's phrase, was supposed to awake to the sight of a vast fleet on the horizon. Instead, the Anglo-French battle force, consisting of two battleships, five cruisers, eleven destroyers and the aircraft carrier *Ark Royal*, was concealed by a thick fog. To some, this appeared 'a wonderful opportunity'. As Lieutenant-Commander Anthony Cobham, a gunnery officer on HMS *Barham*, later wrote, the 4,270 British troops and 2,400 Free French could have got ashore 'almost before our presence was known'.[43]* But despite the 'clammy curtain' rendering his force invisible, thus spoiling the scenario Churchill had envisaged, de Gaulle still hoped for a bloodless coup.[44] Within little over an hour, this was shown to have been a dangerous delusion.

At 5.54 a.m. two Free French aviators landed at Ouakam airfield, tasked with rallying the Vichy pilots. When a bemused-looking airfield commander declared that he had no interest in joining de Gaulle, they tied him up. Then *they* were taken prisoner. While this was going on Swordfish aircraft from the *Ark Royal* were dropping leaflets on the port. At 5.55, Capitaine Georges Thierry d'Argenlieu, a First World War veteran turned monk turned Gaullist, and Captain Henri Bécourt-Foch, grandson of the great Maréchal, accompanied by two dozen men, approached the harbour in motorboats, flying the Tricolour, as well as white flags of truce. Met by the Chief of the Navigation Police, Lieutenant-Commander Lorfèvre, they explained that they bore important letters for the Governor-General and the commanders of the armed forces. While Lorfèvre waited for his deputy to obtain orders from the town, he and 'this dapper little naval monk', as Spears called him, engaged in inauspicious small talk:

> D'Argenlieu: You have a nice little fleet here.
> Lorfèvre: Yes, and it is ready to defend itself.
> D'Argenlieu: We, too, are a group with a lot of *esprit de corps*.
> Lorfèvre: You belong to a religious order and I am myself a believer. We know how to examine our conscience. I have examined mine and I am absolutely convinced that I have done my duty.

---

* After the war, when visiting Dakar as the guest of the French Commander-in-Chief, Irwin was told that if the Anglo-French forces had carried out a surprise landing, at dawn, then they would have been 'welcomed by the troops and the bulk of the population'. The error, his various interlocutors insisted, was to 'broadcast our intentions in advance', allowing the authorities to issue orders and prepare their defences. (Irwin Papers, 1/4, Dakar 23 September 1940)

D'Argenlieu: Our duty was first of all to fulfil our obligations to England.

Lorfèvre: I obey my lawful commanders.

D'Argenlieu: Our superiors have betrayed us.

Lorfèvre: What about Mers el-Kébir?

At this point, d'Argenlieu saw armed soldiers running towards him. Reacting quickly, he kicked the sergeant of the guard in the groin before giving the order: 'Into the boats! Let's go!' As the Free French emissaries sped back towards their ship, they were pursued by machine gun fire.[45]

After this 'dastardly action' (Spears' words), it was obvious that the operation was not developing according to plan.[46] As if to prove this, the shore batteries and the *Richelieu* now opened fire on the Allied fleet just after de Gaulle had completed his fifth broadcast to the inhabitants of the port. At 11.15, shortly after the British ships had begun to return fire, Midshipman Emden, on board the cruiser *Cumberland*, felt a 'dull thud' as a shell tore through the port side, killing the signal crew and starting a fire in the engine room.[47] The destroyers *Foresight* and *Inglefield* were also hit, while the British succeeded in sinking the Vichy submarine *Persée*. In the afternoon, de Gaulle sent three sloops of French marines into Rufisque Bay but sporadic gun fire and the fog, which continued to engulf the operation 'like a slimy jellyfish', caused him to abandon the attack.[48]

The next morning, the mist having become slightly (but only slightly) less impenetrable, Cunningham resumed the bombardment. The previous evening he had received Churchill's blunt instruction: 'Having begun, we must go through to the end. Stop at nothing.'[49] The plan was now to land over 4,000 British troops, once the warships had knocked out the main defences. But Cunningham was unable to silence the shore batteries or the *Richelieu*.* ('Why did you keep on shelling my vegetable garden, couldn't you hit anything else?' the wife of a French battalion commander later complained

---

* 'We might as well have dropped bricks!' commented Lieutenant-Commander Johnstone of the attempt by the British Swordfish to pierce the French battleship's armour with 250-pound bombs.

to Irwin.[50]) At 4.15 p.m. a heavily perspiring de Gaulle in an 'ill-fitting khaki uniform' came on board the *Barham* for a conference with the commanders.[51] He was dejected but dignified. Blaming himself for the withdrawal from Rufisque – where only light opposition had been encountered – he acknowledged that he had underestimated the port's defences, while overestimating his own support. Watching the chain-smoking General in the sweltering heat, Irwin 'felt the greatest admiration for a man with such quiet courage'.[52] De Gaulle would later admit that, in the days that followed, he had contemplated suicide.

The final attempt to subdue the port, on the morning of 25 September – at last, a bright and clear day – was a disaster. At 9.02 a.m., before the British had even opened fire, the last remaining Vichy submarine torpedoed the battleship HMS *Resolution*, causing her to withdraw, listing heavily. At 11.52 a.m., Cunningham signalled to the Admiralty that he was abandoning the operation. It had been an abject failure.

★

In the grand scheme of the Second World War, the Dakar affair was only a minor incident. While Cunningham's force was sailing towards the tropics, RAF Fighter Command was defeating the Luftwaffe in the Battle of Britain. Reading a report of German losses on the deck of the *Westernland*, de Gaulle told Spears: 'They cannot keep this up. You have won.'[53] Yet Dakar had important, or as Churchill put it, 'evil consequences'.[54] Although not, as it transpired, fatal to de Gaulle's future, the failure of Menace was a major setback that lowered the General's already none-too-high reputation in the United States and caused the British to explore *rapprochement* with Vichy. For Churchill, the debacle produced the first serious ripple of criticism about his leadership. Although considerably less deadly, there were disquieting echoes of Norway and even Gallipoli. The aspersion of the press was striking, while the Conservative MP Chips Channon summed up the feeling of his colleagues when he noted: 'We have had enough evacuations and retreats which were unavoidable; why create more?'[55]

It was also revealing. At the same time as 'the few' were defying Hitler's air force in the skies above Britain, a superior British fleet and over 6,000 Allied troops had been unable to capture a port not even held by their official enemies. At the tactical level, it showed that the British could not rival the Germans in combined operations, while at the strategic, it demonstrated the limits of Britain's capabilities. Safe behind her moat, defended by her Navy and the RAF, Britain could withstand the German war machine and deny Hitler victory. But she could not take the offensive. She could not, on her own, roll back the Nazi tide. For that, she would need powerful allies. She would need the United States.

PART TWO

Seeking Allies

1940–1941

VI

The Battle for America

The British may be able to hold the Germans off but they
can't beat the Germans without an ally. It must be either God
Almighty . . . or it must be the United States.

Brigadier-General Raymond Lee, US Military Attaché
in London, 23 September 1940[1]

British reaction to the French surrender was 'practically unanimous', wrote the retired diplomat Sir Horace Rumbold to his
son: 'Thank God that we are now quit of foreigners and doubtful allies and are on our own.'[2] Although this was counterintuitive,
he was not wrong. Boarding HMS *Warspite* three days after the
armistice, Vice-Admiral Tovey greeted Admiral Cunningham with
the words: 'Now I know we shall win the war, sir. We have no
more allies!'[3] King George VI thought that Britain would be better
off now that there were 'no allies to be polite to and to pamper',
while Air Chief Marshal Dowding 'thanked God' when he heard of
the French surrender.[4] Home Intelligence reports revealed a sharp
rise in Francophobia during the Battle of France, while the belief
that it was traditional for Britain to lose every battle except the last
was given cheery expression by one of the doorkeepers at the Foreign Office, who was overheard remarking to his colleague: 'Good
news, Bill, we're in the final!'[5]

Naturally, not everyone felt like this. As Lord Halifax recorded
in his diary, 'the one firm rock' on which British strategy had been
anchored was the impregnability of the French Army.[6] Although
Home Intelligence reports indicated 'a dogged determination to
see the thing through', there was also anxiety and, in some quarters, depression.[7] 'So the French have capitulated,' recorded a

Yorkshire housewife in her diary. 'I couldn't eat my dinner. If we were to continue the fight alone surely we should all be exterminated.'[8] A middle-aged woman from Bolton agreed: 'If France and England can't do it together I don't see what we can do alone.'[9] What indeed? On 18 May, while German tanks were racing across northern France, Randolph Churchill interrupted his father shaving. After a few minutes attacking his stubble, the freshly appointed Prime Minister muttered, 'I think I see my way through.'

His son was astonished. 'Do you mean that we can avoid defeat or beat the bastards?'

'Of course I mean we can beat them,' responded Churchill, dropping his razor.

'Well, I'm all for it but I don't see how you can do it.'

'I shall drag the United States in.'[10]

Strange as it may seem in retrospect, this was not British policy from the outset. Confident in its ability to bring Germany to her knees through the blockade and shielded by the French Army, the Chamberlain Government had felt that US involvement – unlikely in any case – would come at too high a price. 'Heaven knows I don't want the Americans to fight for us,' wrote a cantankerous Chamberlain to his sister Ida on 27 January 1940. 'We should have to pay too dearly for that if they had a right to be in on the peace terms.'[11] Wary of that unique combination of anti-colonial idealism and rapacity – so dangerous to the British Empire – many Britons asked God to save them from 'a German victory and an American peace'.[12] Early in 1940, the Governor-General of Canada, Lord Tweedsmuir (better known as the novelist John Buchan), warned that the entry of the United States into the war would prove a 'dubious blessing', while the Foreign Office's David Scott argued that America was of greater use as a friendly neutral, supplying Britain with arms, than as a full belligerent, husbanding her resources.[13]

Yet if the British did not seek US belligerency during the Phoney War, they desired American mediation even less. On 9 February 1940, President Roosevelt announced that he was sending his cousin, Under-Secretary of State Sumner Welles, to Europe to explore peace options. The British were horrified. Such a mission, Chamberlain told the King, would 'lead to [a] weakening of Allied morale', while

German aggression would receive a veneer of legitimacy.[14] In a long telegram, the Prime Minister begged Roosevelt to reconsider what Sir Alexander Cadogan called this 'awful, half-baked, idea' but the President, despite recognising that the chances of success were 'one in a thousand', ploughed on.[15] As so often with FDR, the President's motives were manifold: he wanted to strengthen his domestic position (it was, after all, an election year) by showing the American people that he had done everything in his power to secure peace; he wanted to dissuade Mussolini from entering the war; he wanted to delay a German onslaught in the west; and he wanted to save the Allies from the 'shooting war' he was far from certain they could win. Although aware of the difficulties, he seems to have genuinely believed he had a chance of brokering a peace deal.

Between 25 February and 19 March, Welles held conversations in Rome, Berlin, Paris and London. None, as the British had predicted, was helpful to the Allied cause. Although suitably revolted by Hitler and Nazi Foreign Minister, Joachim von Ribbentrop, Welles was taken in by Mussolini, who rode the twin American hobbyhorses of free trade and international disarmament.* (Upon his return, Welles told the US Treasury Secretary, Henry Morgenthau Jr, that Mussolini was the 'greatest man he had ever met'.[16]) In Paris, Daladier ridiculed the idea that the Allies could trust Hitler while, in London, ministers from Chamberlain downwards lined up to emphasise Britain's determination to continue the war until she had rid the world of Nazism.†

Chamberlain, despite his instinctive anti-Americanism, liked Welles: 'the best type of American I have met for a long time', he told Ida.[17] Others, however, retained deep suspicions of both the Under-Secretary of State and his master. 'It is now pretty clear . . . that President Roosevelt is ready to play a dirty trick on the world

---

* 'I have rarely seen a man I disliked more,' Welles wrote of his meeting with Ribbentrop. 'The man is saturated with hate of England.' (FDR Papers, PSF, Safe File, Welles Report, 1940)
† The exception was Rab Butler, who, following Welles' visit, told the Soviet Ambassador that any peace proposal would be examined 'without prejudice', sentiments he had earlier expressed to the State Department's Jay Pierrepont Moffat.

and risk the ultimate destruction of the Western democracies in order to secure the re-election of a Democratic candidate in the United States,' wrote the Government's Chief Diplomatic Adviser, Sir Robert Vansittart, on 18 March.[18] A few days earlier, George VI had expressed a rare flash of emotion in his diary after Welles, in an extraordinary act of diplomatic overreach, refused to deliver a letter the King had written to the President on the grounds that it referred to Anglo-American 'collaboration'. 'I am very angry about it,' scrawled the monarch. 'It shows the US and the US Administration are going to do nothing until after the Presidential election [scheduled for 5 November 1940].'[19]

As the British were all too aware, in the spring of 1940 the United States remained firmly isolationist. On 5 September 1939, two days after Britain and France had declared war on Germany, President Roosevelt, in conformance with legislation passed in 1935, 1936, 1937 and 1939, had proclaimed American neutrality. It was, he told his fellow citizens in a radio broadcast – one of his famous 'fireside chats' – his firm intention to keep the United States out of the war. And yet, in the same address, he had cautioned Americans against thinking that events taking place thousands of miles away were of no consequence to the Republic. Indeed, whilst he was proclaiming US neutrality, he was not asking Americans, as Woodrow Wilson had in 1914, to remain 'neutral in thought' as well as deed. 'Even a neutral has a right to take account of facts,' he declared. 'Even a neutral cannot be asked to close his mind or his conscience.'[20]

This was a faithful summary of Roosevelt's position. Sincere in his desire to protect the US from the ravages of war, he nevertheless saw Nazi Germany as a clear threat to the United States and wanted to aid the democracies in their ordeal. In this, he was considerably ahead of US public opinion. As the British Ambassador, Lord Lothian, had to remind London at regular intervals, although 'ninety-five percent' of Americans were 'anti-Hitler', this did not mean they were ninety-five per cent pro-Ally.[21] Indeed, as he wrote to Halifax, on 9 December 1939, 'there are formidable elements [within the US] which are definitely anti-British which take every opportunity to misrepresent our motives and attack our methods'.[22]

This was hardly surprising. With Saratoga and Yorktown as

cornerstones of their national consciousness, many Americans harboured an instinctive distrust of the British Empire – some on moral
grounds, others owing to the closed system of trade ('Imperial Preference') that went with it. Britain's ingrained class system offended
Jeffersonian notions of equality, while Americans were understandably irked by displays of British condescension and superiority. 'To
the British Embassy to dinner – dull,' recorded Assistant Secretary
of State Adolf Berle on 22 September 1939. 'The wife of the Naval
Attaché was presiding . . . and she persisted in talking about "out
here" – the typical county Englishman's method of referring to
the United States as though it were a place much like Egypt . . . I
like Lothian but the conviction rose in me that these English have
learned nothing and forgotten nothing.'[23]* Jay Pierrepont Moffat,
head of the State Department's Western European division,
thought the British continued to regard the US 'as a Dominion gone
wrong', while General 'Vinegar Joe' Stilwell would inveigh against
the 'supercilious Limeys'.[24]

Most acute was the belief, prevalent among isolationists, that
the British were trying to inveigle them into war – a fear supported
by the popular notion that British propaganda had been responsible for 'hoodwinking' the US into joining the First World War.
'BEWARE THE BRITISH SERPENT!' declared posters plastered
across the Midwest during the winter of 1939–40. 'Once more a boa
constrictor – "Perfidious Albion" – is crawling across the American
landscape, spewing forth its unctuous lies.'[25] Later, when the Battle
of France was at its height, Senator Arthur Vandenberg told the
Australian Ambassador, Richard Casey, that the US had no intention of joining the current conflict since she had entered the last
war 'for an ideal and had been let down' by her allies. When the

---

* Although Berle, a renowned Anglophobe, may have been overly sensitive on
this occasion, his general point was valid. In a despatch from March 1937, the
then British Ambassador to Washington, Sir Ronald Lindsay, claimed that the US,
which suffered from a 'famous inferiority complex', resembled 'a young lady just
launched into society and [thus] highly susceptible to a little deference from an
older man'. Three years later the Conservative MP Vyvyan Adams averred that
'like many other uncles, Sam has the mind of an adolescent'.

Australian asked him how he saw the world following a German victory, the senior Senator from Michigan replied that 'it would be unpleasant but not catastrophic'. 'The population of Britain could be transferred to Canada . . . and the United States and democracy could be built up again from North America.'[26]

The 'Phoney War' – an expression coined by another Republican isolationist, Senator William Borah – did not improve British standing in America. Confused by the lack of action on the Western Front, distressed by the fate of Finland and angered by British war measures such as the censoring of US mail and the reduction of agricultural imports to conserve much-needed dollars for war purchases, Gallup opinion polls revealed a slow but steady decline in pro-British feeling among Americans between September 1939 and March 1940.* Of course, public opinion fluctuated. 'On Mondays, Wednesdays and Fridays we are still isolationists,' wrote the British journalist Hessell Tiltman in a sketch of US popular feeling he sent the Foreign Office, 'but on the other days of the week we kinda feel we shall have to give that guy Hitler a kick in the pants.'[27] Nevertheless, the fact was that by December 1939, Britain trailed behind Czechoslovakia, Finland, France and Poland among the nations Americans were said to have most sympathy with, while firm supporters of the British, such as the influential Kansas newspaper editor William Allen White, bemoaned the lack of dynamism on the other side of the Pond: 'The old British lion looks mangy, sore-eyed. He needs worming and should have a lot of dental work. He can't even roar. Unless a new Government takes the helm in Britain, the British Empire is done. These are sad words to say but the truth is the truth.'[28]

The onset of *Blitzkrieg* in the west threw everything into flux. American public opinion swung overwhelmingly behind the Allies but the dominant emotion was one of fear. 'The country has just begun to wake up to the shuddering possibility that

* Lothian thought that among some Americans there was almost a 'resentment that the "drama" of world war is not after all going to be played out'. (Templewood Papers, Part XI, File 5, Lothian to Samuel Hoare, 3 November 1939)

the Germans may win this war, including a seizure of the British Fleet,' recorded Adolf Berle on 26 May 1940.[29] Two days later, he noted the 'steady wave of hysteria' sweeping across the US, as the French Army crumbled and the British Expeditionary Force quit the Continent.[30] Congress, which only months earlier had quailed before additional defence spending requests, rushed to pass a series of appropriations bills, worth $3 billion, to fund the President's plans for a two-million-man army, a two-ocean navy and 50,000 combat aircraft per annum. By May 1941, Congress had appropriated a total of $37.3 billion for the purposes of defence – roughly four times the size of the entire Federal budget for 1939. The votes in the House and the Senate were virtually unanimous. Democrats and Republicans, isolationists and interventionists, almost all agreed that the US was facing the greatest military crisis since the Civil War.

*

With the collapse of France, Britain's war leaders swiftly reached the inescapable conclusion that only the United States could bring about their salvation. 'Our only hope, it seems to me,' wrote Chamberlain on 19 May, 'lies in Roosevelt and the USA.'[31] The Chiefs of Staff agreed. Tasked with assessing Britain's prospects should France be knocked out of the war, their report, delivered to the War Cabinet on 25 May, argued that Britain's ability to continue the war was dependent on 'the full economic and financial support of the United States of America, possibly extending to active participation on our side'.[32] Others went further. Britain's newly appointed Ambassador to Moscow, Sir Stafford Cripps, wanted to establish a permanent Anglo-Saxon grouping between the British Empire and the United States, while, on 15 July, no less an unlikely transatlanticist than Lord Halifax raised the prospect of 'some sort of special association with the USA ... to replace the idea of Anglo-French union'.[33]

Churchill had begun pressing Roosevelt for help within days of entering Downing Street. The two men had established a good epistolary relationship when, at the President's suggestion, the then

First Lord of the Admiralty had begun sending him details of Britain's naval exploits during the Phoney War. Like many Americans, Roosevelt had been critical of Chamberlain's efforts to appease Hitler and admired Churchill's bulldog spirit. 'What the British need today', he wrote to his old Harvard professor in February 1939, 'is a good stiff grog, inducing not only the desire to save civilisation but the continued belief that they can do it.'[34] That Churchill possessed a stiff upper lip no one could doubt. What worried the Roosevelt Administration was that he also possessed the 'grog'. Churchill had 'developed into a fine two-handed drinker', the anti-Churchill American Ambassador to London, Joseph P. Kennedy, informed the President in July 1939.[35] Sumner Welles called Churchill a 'drunken bum' following his visit to London, while on 5 May 1940, Adolf Berle recorded the Washington rumour that 'Churchill is drunk all the time'.[36] Roosevelt noted these stories, yet he also saw the bigger picture. On 12 May he told his Cabinet that 'Churchill was the best man England had, even if he was drunk half the time.'[37]

This, the President and his colleagues would soon learn, was a serious exaggeration. Certainly, Churchill was clear-headed when, on the day the Germans broke through the French line at Sedan, he asked Roosevelt to proclaim a state of 'non-belligerency', meaning that the United States would supply Britain with everything short of armed forces. Specifically, he requested 'the loan of forty or fifty of your older destroyers', to help protect the Atlantic sea lanes – thereby freeing more modern craft to forestall a German invasion – as well as several hundred aeroplanes, anti-aircraft guns and ammunition.[38] When Roosevelt rejected this request, citing the need to obtain Congressional approval as well as America's own defence needs, Churchill was bitterly disappointed. 'Here's a telegram for those bloody Yankees,' he told Jock Colville, handing him a message that painted a doomsday picture for the American President, in which the current British Government went down during the coming battle and 'others' (he would later cite the leader of the British Union of Fascists, Oswald Mosley) 'came in to parley amid the ruins'. 'You must not be blind to the fact', he warned Roosevelt, 'that the sole remaining bargaining counter with Germany would be the fleet and if this country was left by the United States to its fate no one would have the right to blame those then responsible if they made the best terms they could for the surviving inhabitants.'[39]

This was Roosevelt's nightmare scenario. A former Assistant Secretary of the Navy, steeped in the teachings of the American naval strategist Alfred T. Mahan, he appreciated that for over a century the Atlantic had been 'a British lake' and that if the Royal Navy lost control of it, 'the USA could never live', since it was beyond her power to regain it.[40] On 16 May, the American Ambassador to Paris, William C. Bullitt, put to Roosevelt the 'hypothesis that, in order to escape from the ultimate consequences of absolute defeat, the British may install a government of Oswald Mosley . . . which would cooperate fully with Hitler. That would mean that the British Navy would be against us.'[41] A week later, another of the President's long-term associates, the former Ambassador to Moscow and Brussels Joseph E. Davies, sent him two 'violent suggestions'. Convinced that 'short of a miracle, both France and England will be occupied or destroyed this summer', he urged the President to purchase Allied colonial possessions in the western hemisphere and ensure the transfer of their fleets either to the US or to Canada, 'prior to the initiation of any peace negotiations'.[42]

This thought had already occurred to Roosevelt. On 17 May, he put it to Lothian that, 'if the worst came to the worst', the British Fleet should sail to America. Lothian replied that this would depend on whether the United States was in the war, since he doubted whether British public opinion would entrust the Fleet to a neutral America.[43] As the Foreign Office's David Scott commented, this was 'rather like blackmail and not very good blackmail at that but I think we are justified in planting the idea [that the US could not rely upon the protection of the Royal Navy] rather more firmly in Mr Roosevelt's mind'.[44] Churchill agreed. Writing to the Ambassador on 9 June, he explained that his statement in his 'Never surrender' speech of 4 June about continuing the struggle from 'our Empire . . . guarded by the British Fleet', in the event Britain was overrun, was made purely for the benefit of the Axis and ordered Lothian to quash any 'complacent assumption on the United States' part that they will pick up the debris of the British Empire by their present policy'.[45]

Of course, Roosevelt faced considerable difficulties. Although sincere in his desire to aid the Allies, he was hampered by the Neutrality Acts, Congress and US public opinion. The repeal of the arms embargo in November 1939, allowed the US to sell weapons to the Allies on a 'cash and carry' basis but this only revealed a further problem: the dearth of US military equipment. In the spring of 1940, the United States possessed only the eighteenth largest army in the world – 225,000 men – behind Belgium, the Netherlands, Portugal, Spain, Sweden and Switzerland. There was only one tank brigade in the entire US Army, while the US Air Force possessed a mere 160 fighter planes and fifty-two heavy bombers. In these circumstances, many within the Administration and Congress opposed sending precious materiel to the Allies. 'It is a drop in the bucket on the other side and it is a very vital necessity on this side,' explained Army Chief of Staff General George Marshall to Treasury Secretary Henry Morgenthau, as he declined to despatch modern US fighters to France.[46] Later, when Marshall's assistant, Major Walter Bedell Smith, was asked his opinion concerning a British request for 500 pieces of artillery, he replied that if the US was 'required to mobilise after having released [the] guns . . . and was found to be short . . . everyone who was a party to the deal might hope to be hanging from a lamp post.'[47] Secretary of War Henry Woodring, an uncompromising isolationist, and Secretary of the Navy Charles Edison (son of the inventor) both opposed aiding the Allies – a stance that in late June 1940 cost them their jobs – while on 5 June the Senate Foreign Relations Committee overwhelmingly rejected a bill that would have allowed the Administration to sell ships, aeroplanes, rifles and artillery to the British and French. Despite this, Roosevelt, with Marshall and Morgenthau's assistance, succeeded, in early June, in despatching 22,000 machine guns, 25,000 automatic rifles, 500 field guns and half a million rifles to Britain.

Although the Administration would not admit it to the British, a major reason behind American reluctance to send scarce materiel across the Atlantic was the common belief that Britain was heading for defeat. 'There is a wave of pessimism passing over this country to the effect that Great Britain must now inevitably be defeated and that there is no use in the United States doing anything more to help,' cabled Lord Lothian on 27 June 1940.[48] Opinion polls conducted that month suggested that only a third of Americans thought that Britain would win the war, while the commentary of the American press was characterised by only 'the blackest pessimism' regarding Britain's future.[49] Even Roosevelt put Britain's chances of survival at 'about one in three'.[50] Referring to Churchill's request for destroyers in a letter to Interior Secretary Harold Ickes, FDR explained that he always had to think of the possibility that Britain might be overwhelmed and that any ships the United States had lent her 'might fall into the hands of the Germans and be used against us'.[51]

The greatest defeatist of all was the American Ambassador to London, Joseph P. Kennedy. A self-made multimillionaire who had raised and contributed hundreds of thousands of dollars for Roosevelt's election campaigns, this bumptious, ignorant Irish-Bostonian had arrived in Britain in March 1938, where he lost little time in making his opinion known that the democracies were no match for the totalitarians. 'There are signs of decay, if not decadence, here,' he cabled Roosevelt on 30 September 1939. 'I am afraid that I can't conceive [of] the results that this war will bring as running counter to the evolutionary process. England passed her peak as a world power some years ago and has been steadily on the decline.'[52] Later, as first the Battle of France, then the Battle of Britain, raged, he sent a string of increasingly hysterical messages to Washington, insisting that the 'Mother Country' was 'licked' and the time had come for America to cut ties and look to her own interests.[53] The British considered him a menace and a coward: a man who viewed the war purely from the perspective of his own financial and familial interests and was blind to the moral and political dimensions of the conflict.*

Very different was the standing of Britain's Ambassador to Washington. At first sight, Philip Kerr, 11th Marquess of Lothian, was an odd

* Kennedy later told Assistant Secretary of State Breckinridge Long that Hitler had twice invited him to visit him in Germany. 'Hitler must have got the impression Kennedy had views which Hitler might use as an approach to us,' recorded Long on 7 November 1940. 'As a matter of fact, Kennedy thinks we ought to lay the basis for some co-operation. He does not go to the extent of appeasing – but the extent to which he would go is undefined.'

choice to replace the career diplomat Sir Ronald Lindsay as principal resident of Lutyens' vast neo-Georgian mansion on Massachusetts Avenue in August 1939. An intellectual and idealist, who had served as secretary to Lloyd George during the Paris Peace Conference, he was later in the vanguard of those amateur diplomats who tried (and failed) to make a deal with Hitler. For many years, the Foreign Office considered him a dangerous dilettante, while others, disgusted at his ability to sympathise with the Führer's early foreign policy objectives, dubbed him 'Lord Loathsome'.[54] Yet by the time of his premature death on 12 December 1940, he was regarded as one of Britain's greatest ambassadors.

Unlike the majority of his compatriots, Lothian not only knew but *liked* America. As Secretary of the Rhodes Trust during the inter-war years, he had visited forty-four of the forty-eight states and established friendships with an impressive array of politicians, academics, businessmen and journalists. To him, America was a land of excitement and opportunity and it was his firm belief that the two great English-speaking blocs, the British Commonwealth and the United States, should become entwined for their own benefit and that of the wider world. Reflecting on his 'extraordinary flair for public relations', the historian John Wheeler-Bennett (recruited at the start of the war as the Ambassador's personal assistant) analogised Lothian's ability to address the varying currents of American opinion with a 'great musician' playing an intricate composition on the organ: 'Sometimes he would use the *vox humana*, sometimes the *vox angelica*, sometimes a soft and appealing *lieblich gedackt*, sometimes a full and challenging diapason and sometimes he would pull out every stop there was and really "go to town"!'[55]

Every stop but one. Britain must not, the Ambassador insisted, attempt direct propaganda in the United States. Such an effort had been made during the First World War and the memories of that campaign were still a source of suspicion and resentment. 'The fact is', Lord Halifax explained to Lord Beaverbrook in December 1939, 'the Americans . . . have started a regular witch-hunt for propaganda. They see propaganda in the most innocent British statements . . . As I see it, United States sympathy with us will, in existing conditions, only be influenced by what we *do* as opposed to what we may *say*.'[56]

This was to prove true. Informed by reports from American newsmen such as Edward R. Murrow – whose broadcasts began with the increasingly emotive words 'This is London' – Americans watched in wonder during the summer of 1940 as Britain withstood the might of Göring's Luftwaffe. 'The British are an amazing people,' enthused Herschel Johnson, Counsellor at the US Embassy in London. 'With all their faults they are the most generous-minded lot imaginable and what they lack in imagination they make up in courage of which they have an unlimited amount.'[57] His colleague the Military Attaché, Colonel Raymond Lee, concurred. 'What a wonderful thing it will be if these blokes do win the war,' he wrote in his diary three weeks into the Luftwaffe's attempt to destroy Fighter Command, 'they will be bankrupt but entitled to almost unlimited respect.'[58] 'Our British name stands high here,' the Oxford philosopher Isaiah Berlin wrote to his parents from Washington on 26 August 1940. Optimism about Britain's ability to survive was growing, while the heroism of the RAF and the stoicism of the British people were producing a 'terrific swing towards us'.[59]

This was encouraging. Yet, as Lothian remarked in a letter to the Conservative MP Victor Cazalet, 'admiration and sympathy are not much good when one is fighting Hitler in the gate'.[60] On 10 June, Roosevelt had raised British hopes when, at Charlottesville, he pledged to 'extend to the opponents of force the material resources of this nation'.[61] Listening amid the audience at the University of Virginia, John Wheeler-Bennett felt a 'shock of excitement' pass through him: 'This was what we had been praying for – not only sympathy but pledges of support. If Britain could only hold on until these vast resources could be made available to her, we could yet survive and even win the war.'[62] Yet, in the weeks that followed, no tangible assistance emerged, while the President gave little hope regarding the all-important British request for American destroyers.

To Britons engaged in the delicate task of attempting to elicit American aid, this was more than frustrating. 'These people are disgusting,' raged Anthony Rumbold, a young British diplomat working in the Embassy in Washington, in a letter to his mother.

'The plain truth is that the extent of US help to us so far has been limited to allowing us to buy what we could pay for and take away ourselves. The Americans . . . allow themselves to believe that they have been helping us in many often unspecified and important ways but this is *bosh*! I frankly tell Americans that if we go under and they do nothing to help us they will find themselves the best-hated and, at the same time, most friendless nation in the world.'[63]

Although by blood and inclination a proud Atlanticist, Churchill felt similarly. 'Am sure we shall be alright here but your people are not doing much,' he grumbled to his old friend the American financier Bernard Baruch on 28 June.[64] Three weeks later, he warned the Pulitzer Prize-winning journalist Edgar Mowrer that if Britain was beaten, 'while you sat back and watched without lifting a finger to help us', there would be deep resentment.[65] He blocked a move to share Britain's military and scientific secrets with the US unless part of a *quid pro quo* (a ruling he later reversed) and on 31 August, as the Battle of Britain neared its climax, referred sarcastically to the Americans being good at 'applauding the valiant deeds done by others'.[66]

As Roosevelt was increasingly aware, many Americans wanted to do more. In May 1940, the Committee to Defend America by Aiding the Allies had been established under the chairmanship of the widely respected editor of the Kansas *Emporia Gazette*, William Allen White. Convinced that the British Isles constituted America's first line of defence, the 'White Committee', as it was popularly known, set out to garner support for Administration policies aimed at aiding Britain and, by August, possessed more than 700 self-financing local chapters.

Another organisation that lobbied not merely for increased aid but also for American intervention was the so-called 'Century Group'. Holding its meetings in the Century Association, one of New York's oldest and most exclusive clubs, the fifty-odd members – an eclectic mix of writers, publishers, lawyers, businessmen, retired service leaders and religious figures – sought to influence US policy through their network of contacts. On 1 August, the journalist and historian Herbert Agar, along with two other members of the group, called on the President to find out what they could do to help deliver American destroyers to the British. Only recently converted to the necessity of such a transfer, the President asked them to persuade General Pershing, commander of US forces during the First World War and the most respected soldier in the country, to broadcast in favour of the policy. Agar duly visited Pershing and on 4 August the 79-year-old General read out the words that the renowned journalist and Anglophile Walter Lippmann had written for him:

> By sending help to the British we can still hope with confidence to keep the war on the other side of the Atlantic Ocean, where the enemies of liberty, if possible, should be defeated . . . Today may be the last time when measures short of war can still prevent war . . . We have an immense reserve of destroyers left over from the other war . . . If the[se] destroyers help save the British Fleet, they may save us from the danger and hardship of another war.[67]

By this stage, a full-blown public debate – sparked by clandestine briefings by British diplomats – was already showing a preponderance in favour of the British plea. 'All the evidence at our disposal goes to show that there is a rising tide of opinion in America demanding that destroyers be made available to us,' noted the Foreign Office's Jock Balfour.[68] Seven out of ten letters received by Congressmen, according to Reuters, were in favour of the transfer, while isolationist efforts to counter Pershing's intervention were failing.

After a Cabinet meeting on 2 August 1940, Roosevelt recorded that it was agreed, 'without any dissenting voice, that the survival of the British Isles under German attack might very possibly depend on their getting these destroyers'.[69] The newly appointed Republican Secretaries of War and the Navy, Henry L. Stimson and Frank Knox, as well as Interior Secretary Harold Ickes and Treasury Secretary Henry Morgenthau, had long reached this conclusion. But it took further entreaties from Lothian and Churchill, as well as a growing confidence in Britain's ability to survive, to convince the President. Central to this were the reports of Roosevelt's close associate Colonel William 'Wild Bill' Donovan, who informed FDR, after undertaking a whirlwind tour of the beleaguered island in July

1940, that Britain would withstand a German invasion and would never surrender her Fleet. Not that this was the end of the road. As the Cabinet agreed, such a transfer would require legislation and, as Roosevelt explained to Lothian, for this he would have to offer Congress 'molasses'.[70] The Congressional sweeteners he had in mind were a public declaration that the British Fleet would, *in extremis*, sail to North America and, following a suggestion from Knox, the establishment of US air and naval bases on British-held islands in the Caribbean and West Indies, as well as Canada.

The War Cabinet had first discussed the idea of granting the US military rights on certain British possessions as early as 27 May. Enticed by the likely effect on US public opinion and fearful lest the Administration should attempt to occupy the islands unilaterally, Lothian urged the Cabinet to make a spontaneous offer of base rights to the US Government. Although Halifax and the Chiefs of Staff supported the proposal, Churchill demurred. Britain should not make concessions 'except as part of a deal', he argued. The United States 'had given us practically no help in the war and now that they saw how great was the danger their attitude was that they wanted to keep everything which would help us for their own defence'.[71]

On 10 July, Lothian tried again. The American experts in the Foreign Office endorsed his approach. 'The Americans drive a hard bargain,' noted Professor Thomas North Whitehead, a Harvard don seconded to the Foreign Office. 'On the other hand they are generous friends and if we could have seized the opportunity to offer freely and without bargain or quibble the facilities suggested in Lord Lothian's earlier telegram . . .I venture to predict that this might well have constituted a significant step towards the building up of genuinely cordial and collaborative relations.'[72] The Colonial Office opposed the scheme. 'All this is the doing of Philip Lothian,' complained the Colonial Secretary, the die-hard imperialist Lord Lloyd, to Jock Balfour. 'He always wanted to give away the Empire and he now has the perfect opportunity for doing so.'[73] With Churchill in his corner, Lloyd might have carried the day. But the threat of invasion had served to soften the Prime Minister's position and on 29 July the Cabinet gave its consent to an offer to America of facilities in British Guiana, Trinidad and Jamaica.

Two days later, Churchill renewed his plea to Roosevelt for destroy-ers. The enemy was using the entire French coastline to launch attacks upon 'our trade and food', he wrote,' and Britain was losing destroy-ers at a rate of almost four per week. There would be a large number of destroyers – currently under construction – available in 1941 but if American vessels were not sent to plug the gap over the next three to four months then 'the whole fate of the war may be decided by this minor and easily remediable factor'. 'Mr President,' Churchill con-cluded his imploration, 'with great respect, I must tell you that in the long history of the world, this is a thing to do now.'[74]

The War Cabinet's decision to offer the Americans bases coincided with Roosevelt's decision to supply Britain with destroyers. The out-line of a deal was forming. Yet there remained obstacles, the first of which was the President's insistence upon a statement regarding the future of the British Fleet. The issue was similar to that which had obsessed the War Cabinet before Mers el-Kébir. There was, however, a crucial difference: whilst the French had capitulated and were, to a large extent, no longer masters in their own house, the British were still fighting. Summoned to the Cabinet room to hear the Prime Min-ister's comments on the Foreign Office's draft response, Jock Balfour found Churchill 'hunched in an attitude of tense anger like a wild beast about to spring'. 'Pray make it clear at onesh', he lisped, pacing the room, that 'we could *never* agree to the shlightesht compromis-ing of our full liberty of action, nor . . . tolerate any such defeatisht pronounshment . . . The situation is very different to what it was in June . . . very different! We are shewing "that man" [Hitler] that we are resolute. The Americans are asking us to go too far . . . much too far. We can't agree to a proposal of this kind for the sake of a number of old destroyers – very serviceable no doubt, but not vital . . . I told him [Lothian] some weeks ago that if America were our ally there would be no difficulty about giving this kind of assurance. But that is a very different proposition to the one before us. It doesn't do to give way like this to the Americans. One must strike a balance with them.'[75]

Indeed, so strongly did the Prime Minister feel on the subject that his initial reaction had been to spurn Roosevelt's offer of staff talks, on the grounds that they would likely turn on the issue of the future of the British Fleet. It was Halifax who managed to reverse this astonishing decision, pointing out that it was 'sound policy to go as far as we feel we safely can to fall in with any reasonably practical suggestion put forward or known to be favoured by the President'.[76]

Another obstacle concerned the presentation of the deal. Whilst Roosevelt, thinking of Congressional and public opinion, insisted on a straightforward swap, Churchill wanted the transaction to be treated as a free exchange of mutually beneficial gifts. Given his previous preference for hard bargaining, against the Foreign Office's predilection for a more generous approach, this was ironic to say the least. Yet there was method in his madness. As he explained to Roosevelt in a telegram on 22 August, if the transfer was to appear as a *quid pro quo*, then people would, naturally, begin to examine the value of the transaction. Compared to ninety-nine-year leases for air and naval bases on British and Canadian territory stretching from Bermuda to Newfoundland, fifty antique destroyers were nothing. 'If we are going to make a gift, well and good,' explained the Minister for Aircraft Production, Lord Beaverbrook, to Joseph Kennedy, but 'if we are going to make a bargain, I don't want to make a bad one and this is definitely a bad one'.[77]

Yet a 'deal', even a 'tough deal', was considered by Roosevelt and Secretary of State Cordell Hull essential if they were to sell the agreement to Congress. Although a legal opinion, prepared and published by the Century Group, had convinced the President that he possessed the power to transfer the destroyers without recourse to the legislature, there remained the problem of the Walsh amendment (introduced by Senator David Walsh of Massachusetts and passed on 28 June 1940), whereby the Chief of Naval Operations, Admiral Stark, would have to testify that the destroyers were superfluous to American defence – an impossible requirement unless the Admiral could argue that the United States was receiving something more valuable in return. The President had 'no authority whatever to make a gift of public property to any government or individual', explained Hull to Lothian, while the imminence of the Presidential election reinforced the need to win popular approval for the agreement.[78]

In the end a compromise was reached although, reflecting the balance of needs and setting the pattern for the next five years, one that required more from the British than the Americans. The leases on Bermuda and Newfoundland would be accepted as a gift from the British Government, whilst six bases in the British West Indies would serve as 'payment' for the destroyers. The assurance about the Fleet was also given. In an *aide-mémoire*, Hull formally enquired whether the Prime Minister's statement of 4 June, regarding his determination to withdraw the Royal Navy across the Atlantic in the event of it becoming liable to capture, remained the policy of His Majesty's Government. Churchill replied that it certainly did, although such a contingency seemed 'more likely to concern the German Fleet, or what is left of it, than the British Fleet'.[79]

Meanwhile, Roosevelt had received the backing of his Republican challenger, Wendell Willkie, for the swap, as well as an assurance that Senator McNary, the Senate Minority Leader and Willkie's running mate, would raise no objections. On 3 September, the President announced the deal to Congress and the nation. The response from the isolationists was as fierce as it was predictable. Senator Gerald Nye of North Dakota called it a 'dictatorial step', while the *St Louis Post-Dispatch* joined Congressmen Hamilton Fish and George Tinkham in accusing the President of committing 'an act of war'.[80] In the main, however, there was not the storm of protest that Roosevelt had feared. As the British Library of Information in New York noted, the transfer was 'almost universally . . . hailed', with most newspapers, as well as legislators, applauding the palpable enhancement of American security – the greatest addition to the defence of the United States 'since the Louisiana purchase', as Roosevelt put it in his message to Congress.[81]

In London, it was impossible to 'overstate the jubilation in official and unofficial circles caused today by President Roosevelt's announcement that fifty United States destroyers were coming to help Great Britain in her hour of peril', claimed the *New York Times*.[82] By the end of the year, however, only nine of the fifty were in service, while the rest left a lot to be desired. 'I thought they were the worst destroyers I had ever seen,' complained a British Admiral, who, like his colleagues, was appalled to note the vessels' weak armament, cramped accommodation, corroded superstructure, defective engines, faulty steering and innumerable leaks.[83] Lloyd George told the Soviet Ambassador that 'Uncle Sam' had behaved with characteristic cupidity in making Britain pay so dearly for this flotilla of 'old iron', while one Cabinet Minister, reacting to the US demand for bases in Newfoundland, Bermuda, the Bahamas and St Lucia – in addition to those on Jamaica, British Guiana and Trinidad already offered – accused the Administration of unseemly greed.[84]

All of this was true. Yet the realities of the situation afforded the British little choice. In August 1940, Britain's survival as an independent nation hung in the balance. The RAF was Britain's first line of defence but her second was the Royal Navy: the country's historic shield since the days of the Spanish Armada, now stretched across the Atlantic, the Mediterranean, the Pacific and, most importantly, the Channel. The fall of France had brought the Kriegsmarine 500 miles closer to the Atlantic sea lanes and in June alone German U-boats succeeded in sinking thirty-one ships off the British and Irish coasts. Destroyers were needed to protect British shipping against this underwater menace and defend the country against invasion. Of the 176 destroyers with which Britain had entered the war, only sixty-eight were currently fit for service in home waters by July 1940. Taking up the task of guarding Britain's vital supplies were vessels that made American World War I-era destroyers eminently desirable – corvettes with only a single 4-inch gun, no faster than a surfaced U-boat, sloops of war with two 4-inch guns and a slew of converted cargo ships and liners.

Yet the deal's real significance was political not material. As Churchill told the War Cabinet on 14 August, 'If the present proposal went through, the United States would have made a long step towards coming into the war on our side. To sell destroyers to a belligerent was certainly not a neutral action.'[85] This was more than simply putting a brave face on a lopsided deal. It represented the triumph of Halifax and the Foreign Office's view that the most prudent diplomatic strategy was to bind the US to Britain's war effort almost regardless of the terms and that the best tactics were to act with generosity and trust towards the Americans. Two weeks later, six British scientists boarded a Canadian liner bound for America. Their luggage included a small metal deed box containing Britain's most valuable and secret intellectual property: blueprints for rockets, explosives, gyroscopic gunsights, submarine detection devices, the newly created cavity magnetron (the essential component for the next generation of radar devices) and plans for the jet engine and atomic bomb. The British asked for nothing in return.

This then was the importance of the 'Destroyers for Bases' deal. Despite the quality of the ships, a frustrating delay in their despatch and acrimonious negotiations over the scope and location of the bases, the agreement saw the establishment of a *de facto* Anglo-American alliance that would ensure Britain's survival until a full military alliance could come into being.* That the affairs of the two countries should become 'somewhat mixed up together . . . for mutual and general advantage', Churchill told the House of Commons on 20 August (the same speech in which he paid tribute to 'the few' of RAF Fighter Command), was as desirable as it was inevitable: 'I do not view the process with any misgivings. I could not stop it if I wished; no one can stop it. Like the Mississippi, it just keeps rolling along. Let it roll. Let it roll on full flood, inexorable, irresistible, benignant, to broader lands and better days.'[86]

* 'Unfortunately, the negotiations got off on the wrong foot owing to the stupidity of two of our colonial officials,' explained the Secretary of State for the Colonies, Lord Moyne, to the British Ambassador to Madrid, Sir Samuel Hoare, with Sir Hubert Young, the Governor of Trinidad and Tobago, trying 'to plant the Americans in a mosquito haunted swamp'. In the end, however, the British gave way 'on practically everything'. (Templewood Papers, Part XIII, File 18, Lord Moyne to Samuel Hoare, 19 March 1941)

VII

The Reluctant Neutral

> Spain continues to hate the Allies . . . German victories are
> received with joy . . . The instinct for survival, Catholic faith,
> or Latin spirit is drowned by hatred for France and England.
>
> Pedro Teotónio Pereira, Portuguese Ambassador
> to Madrid, 27 May 1940[1]

Sir Samuel Hoare was not popular. In fact, he was distinctly *un*popular. Although hardworking, capable and bright, he was also covetous, conniving and craven – 'the last in a long line of maiden aunts', in Lord Birkenhead's memorable phrase.[2] Whilst he had been an enterprising Air Minister and a successful Secretary of State for India, his brief tenure at the Foreign Office had been a disaster. Seeking to end the Italo-Abyssinian War, he was forced to resign when his scheme to reward Mussolini with around two-thirds of the East African country, concocted with the French Prime Minister, Pierre Laval, became public. Later, while Home Secretary, he had been in the van of attempts to appease Hitler – one of the Cabinet's 'Big Four', responsible for British policy during the Czechoslovak crisis and, ultimately, the Munich Agreement.* When Churchill became Prime Minister, many of his supporters urged him to purge these 'guilty men' from the Cabinet.[3] Yet the new Prime Minister was not politically strong enough – at least initially – to do away with the old guard. Thus, while Halifax retained the Foreign Office, Chamberlain became Lord President of the Council and John Simon was

---

* Sir Samuel, noted three Beaverbrook journalists, 'passed from experience to experience, like Boccaccio's Virgin, without discernible effect upon his condition.'

made Lord Chancellor. Only Hoare was felled. On 17 May 1940, Churchill offered him the Madrid Embassy.

As almost everyone realised, this was little more than a crude attempt to get him out of the country. Although Churchill did not go as far as Sir Alexander Cadogan in viewing Hoare as a potential 'Quisling' – let alone share the diplomat's hope that the former Cabinet Minister might be murdered by Axis agents – he was, nevertheless, determined to rid himself of an arch-appeaser whom he loathed for sponsoring legislation that provided some measure of self-government to viceregal India.[4] And yet, as even Churchill was later forced to admit, there was a serendipitous irony about this otherwise cynical appointment. If there was anywhere in the world where an 'appeaser' was required, any country where 'Slippery Sam' might be an asset, it was Francoist Spain.[5]

The strategic importance of Spain was obvious to all. Situated betwixt the Atlantic and the Mediterranean, she was the geographic hinge upon which the entrance to the 'Great Sea' and the trade routes of the South Atlantic depended. If Spain were to join the Axis and succeed in capturing Gibraltar, the last of Britain's Continental possessions, then the door to the Mediterranean would be closed. German U-boats operating from Spanish ports could wreak havoc on Britain's Atlantic convoys while, from Spain, the Germans would be able to penetrate French North and West Africa. A friendly Spain was desirable but a neutral Spain was 'vital', the military theorist Basil Liddell Hart had advised the British Government in 1938, while, in June 1945, a nostalgic Hermann Göring told the British diplomat Ivone Kirkpatrick that Hitler's greatest mistake had been his failure 'to march through Spain . . . capture Gibraltar and spill into Africa'. It would, the incarcerated Reichsmarschall insisted, 'have altered the whole course of the war'.[6]

To most observers, Hoare's mission appeared doomed from the start. Charged with maintaining Spanish neutrality or, at the least, delaying Spanish belligerency, the sixty-year-old MP for Chelsea was being sent as emissary to a regime overtly sympathetic to the Axis. As the British well knew, the head of the Spanish state, General Francisco Franco, owed his victory in the Spanish Civil War to German and Italian aeroplanes, tanks and guns, as well as some

80,000 troops, pilots and military instructors masquerading as 'volunteers'. By the end of the three-year conflict, the Nationalists had accrued debts of around $500 million to the Axis and, in March 1939, Franco signed the Hispanic-German Treaty of Friendship and joined the Anti-Comintern Pact. That the Spanish dictator disdained the democracies and hoped for a German victory was not in doubt; nor was his desire to unfix Britain's limpet-like hold on the Rock of Gibraltar and sweep the French out of Morocco. There were an estimated 80,000 German nationals in Spain at the start of the war (several hundred of whom were spies), while Ramón Serrano Suñer, the Caudillo's brother-in-law, Minister of the Interior and leader of the Falange – the quasi-fascist party of state, conglomerated by Franco in 1937 – was known to favour intimate co-operation with the Axis.

Into this cauldron of intrigue, resentment and ideological antipathy descended Sam Hoare. His timing could hardly have been worse. Landing in Madrid shortly after 3 p.m. on 1 June 1940, he took command of the British Embassy just as the BEF was being evacuated from Dunkirk. The atmosphere in the Spanish capital, he informed London, was febrile. Falangists, soldiers and spies filled the streets, the Germans and Italians were 'entrenched in every department' and there was a sense of 'impending crisis on all sides'.[7] Escorted by a phalanx of heavily armed police wherever he went, the new Ambassador was a jumble of nerves. Terrified of being kidnapped or shot, he carried an automatic pistol with him, prepared to use it 'either on myself or my assailants'.[8] The fear of a German invasion haunted him. Anxious to preserve the means of escape, he tried (unsuccessfully) to keep the aeroplane that had conveyed him and Lady Maud from England and, according to gossip, placed a ladder against the wall of the Embassy garden each night before going to bed. Justifying his funk to the Ministry of Economic Warfare's Iberian representative, David Eccles, he explained that his capture would naturally be among Hitler's priorities. Eccles replied that the Germans would probably 'attach more value to capturing one or two good British bomber pilots'.[9] Around the same time, Hoare was mid-way through a monologue on his plans for escape when the wife of the British Ambassador to Lisbon, Lady Selby, interrupted: 'You must remember, Sir Samuel, that you are

no longer a politician but have become a diplomat. When a professional diplomat is in a dangerous post, he always acts like the
captain of a sinking ship. He stays to the last.' Hoare turned green.[10]

Yet Hoare was also capable of outward displays of British phlegm.
Although his reception was neither cordial nor encouraging – an
organised mob descended on the British Embassy on the morning
of his arrival chanting *'Gibraltar Español'* – he informed Halifax that
he was going out of his way 'to appear completely unconcerned
as to the way things are going', playing tennis on the weekends and
taking a house next to the one belonging to the German Ambassador.[11] A former intelligence officer, who had served with effect in
pre-revolutionary Russia and then in Italy, his vigilance regarding
German attempts at infiltration and unneutral acts by his hosts was
matched by the speed and robustness of his responses. Learning
of a planned parade of German troops in San Sebastián, following
the arrival of the Wehrmacht at the Franco-Spanish frontier on 27
June 1940, he succeeded in forestalling the event and precipitating
the dismissal of the local commander by informing the Minister of
Foreign Affairs that unless the march was cancelled, he would pack
his bags and return to England.

Frequently, he would invent German acts of penetration, merely
to keep the Spanish on their toes. 'Lomax,' he would say to the
Embassy's Commercial Counsellor, 'make an excuse to see the Minister of Finance and ask about printing the Spanish currency notes.
Bring into the talk something about German soldier-visitors in
northern Spain paying for their purchases in notes overprinted *Ocu-
pación.'* Or: 'Lomax, go and see the Minister of Public Works and
offer to quote him for metalling the highways in northern Spain.
When he asks why, tell him that you've seen German officers meas-
uring up the roads and you supposed Spain must be thinking of a
new road project.'[12]

When, after waiting for three weeks, Hoare finally managed to
gain an audience with Franco, on 22 June 1940, the Caudillo asked
why Britain did not make peace, since it was inconceivable that she
could defeat the Wehrmacht. Six days earlier, the dictator had conveyed to Hitler his offer to join the war against England in return for
territorial expansion and copious supplies. The British were ignorant

of this proposal. Yet the declaration of Spanish 'non-belligerency', as opposed to neutrality, on 12 June, followed by the occupation of Tangier by Spanish troops two days later, were indications of the 'great temptation' being felt within the walls of El Pardo.

Despite these disquieting signs, Hoare felt that Franco and most of his lieutenants (the exception being Serrano Suñer) wished to remain neutral. His reasoning rested on the simple fact that Spain seemed incapable of engaging in another conflagration. Three years of horrendous civil war had left the country economically, materially and emotionally exhausted. Some 344,000 Spaniards had lost their lives during the conflict. A similar number had been condemned to prison or concentration camps. More than 225,000 tons of merchant shipping – a third of the total – had been sunk and almost half the rail network destroyed. Industrial production was down 31 per cent compared to 1935, agricultural production down 21 per cent. Food shortages, exacerbated by the outbreak of the international war and the British blockade, had taken the country to the brink of starvation. The Army was short of tanks, artillery and ammunition and the whole country was short of fuel. In March 1940, the Army High Council told the Caudillo what he already knew: Spain was in no condition to go to war.

To try to ensure that the logic of this situation prevailed, Hoare argued that it was important to keep Franco and his Junta in place, while doing everything possible to strengthen the forces of peace. 'Supposing . . . the present Government were removed by a *coup d'état*,' he wrote to Halifax in mid-June. 'I believe myself that the position would be worse. I believe that it would probably mean the start of another civil war and that it would certainly mean a period of anarchy in which the Germans and Italians could find many pretexts for intervening against us.'[13] Within days of arriving in Madrid, he had lent his support to an audacious scheme, concocted by the buccaneering Naval Attaché, Captain Alan Hillgarth, and the Majorcan businessman Juan March – the richest man in Spain – to bolster the cause of Spanish non-belligerency by bribing senior members of the regime. Churchill, who knew and trusted Hillgarth, approved and within a short period vast sums were being paid to at least thirty prominent individuals, including the Minister of War, the Foreign Minister, Franco's political secretary and even the Caudillo's brother.

How effective this expenditure – which totalled an astonishing £3.5 million by August 1941 – was is hard to gauge. Certainly, the British considered it highly important. When, in the summer of 1941, the US Administration froze several accounts of the Swiss Bank Corporation in New York, including the one that held the Spanish slush fund, British diplomats made frantic efforts to get it unfrozen. 'We must not lose them now, after all we have spent and gained,' Churchill wrote to Anthony Eden, by then Foreign Secretary. 'Vital strategic issues depend on Spain keeping out or resisting.'[14] Similarly, when Franco appointed his Political Secretary, the staunchly anti-Falangist Colonel Valentin Galarza Morante, as Minister of the Interior – the post previously held by Serrano Suñer – in May 1941, Hoare claimed that the change, which precipitated an internal crisis, was a direct result of the 'secret plan'.[15]

In fact, the Cabinet crisis of May 1941 was entirely due to internal Spanish politics, specifically to Franco's determination to keep the Falange in check, a policy that would have received the backing of the military irrespective of British gold. Indeed, while the Spanish generals were never put to the test – in that they never had to face a decision in favour of Spanish belligerency, or a German invasion of the peninsula – the evidence suggests that their response would have been guided by their conception of the national interest rather than personal venality. Mussolini bribed several Greek politicians and generals but this made no difference to the Greek response to the Italian invasion of October 1940, while the profusion of rumours concerning a military coup to remove Franco and restore the monarchy never came to anything.

Of far greater significance was the decision to assist Spain economically. The impetus behind this policy was the Ministry of Economic Warfare's Iberian specialist, David Eccles. Suave and intellectually assured, the former businessman was convinced that by supplying Spain with such necessities as wheat, cotton and oil, Britain could ensure her neutrality. As the Spanish authorities routinely reminded the British, they needed to receive these commodities from somewhere and if they did not come from Britain and her network of global interests, then they would have to turn to the Axis. To such obvious blackmail, Eccles responded with alacrity. 'Who said, "Spain is not for sale?" ' he wrote to the Foreign Office's Roger Makins, cheerfully. 'I want us to buy Spain but entirely from motives of self-interest . . . Could you get the Cabinet to agree a) that we have to bribe Spain; b) that it is infinitely preferable to spend than to lend . . . The orange crop is crucial, a purchase on a satisfactory basis would have an electric effect and be magnificent propaganda.'[16] Lest this appear an argument for undiluted appeasement, the civil servant explained the rationale behind his policy in greater detail on 5 November 1940:

> We are up against it here now. One false step and into the war she [Spain] goes. The balance must be kept if we are to ride it out . . . On the first hand, we are a great people winning a world war, on the second hand we must placate the devils. Pride and prudence must make friends. I see in the Spaniard a kind of awe at the way we control ourselves and when I say, as I often do these days, 'If you want war with us, go ahead, we know what it would mean and have every intention of keeping you from the pit', the Spaniard stiffens, looks you straight in the face and takes off his hat.[17]

His principal opponent was that 'Renegade Etonian', the Labour MP and Minister of Economic Warfare, Hugh Dalton.[18] A long-standing antagonist of dictators and fanatical in his pursuit of the blockade, Dalton saw little reason to comfort a regime so overtly hostile to Britain and which, at any moment, might enter the war against her. 'I would rather that we both kept Spain out of the war and prevented her from being a channel of supply to the enemy,' he wrote to Eccles on 27 August 1940. 'If, however, this cannot be it is not clear to me that we would do better by allowing Spain to be such a channel for some time, and then have her as an enemy all the same, than by letting her come in against us naked and starved, even if a little sooner.'[19]

To Eccles and Hoare, the determination of 'Dr Dynamo' (as the energetic Dalton was known) and some of his subordinates at the MEW to starve Spain was as muddle-headed as it was exasperating. Convinced that Franco, unlike the pre-belligerent Mussolini, had not determined to enter the war, the Whitehall propensity to engage in 'Balkan capers' by withholding 'a case of bananas', as well as more essential items such as tin, copper and sugar, was a perpetual bug-bear.[20] 'Oh Lord, save us from well-fed high-school boys who use statistics as drunkards use lampposts, not to light them on their way but to conceal their own instability!' wrote Eccles to Makins. 'Is it perversity? Is it ignorance? Is it politics? Is it panic? Henry Drogheda [joint Director of the MEW] writes that he has nightmares that the Germans will come into Spain and collar the lot! What lot?'[21]

Fortunately, Halifax and, more importantly, Churchill were sympathetic to the Madrid Embassy's arguments. Although the Prime Minister baulked at Hoare's suggestion that the British should try to appease Franco by offering to discuss the status of Gibraltar ('The Spaniards know that if we lose they will get it anyhow and they would be great fools to believe that if we win we shall mark our admiration for their conduct by giving it to them,' he minuted Halifax), he saw the value of doing everything possible to keep Spain out of the clutches of the Axis.[22] In November 1940, with British supplies proving insufficient and the real prospect of famine in the Iberian Peninsula, he wrote to Roosevelt asking him to send large consignments of food and fuel to Spain, 'so long as they keep out of the war'.[23]

This request received a decidedly mixed response. Although Roosevelt was happy to continue to supply Spain on a limited basis, senior figures within the State Department, including Secretary of State Cordell Hull, were dubious of a policy that smacked of 'appeasement'.[24] Considering the Franco Government 'merely the Spanish glove for a German hand', the Administration had already decided to make a Spanish request for a $100 million loan to buy American wheat, cotton and petrol dependent upon a public pledge in favour of neutrality and saw no reason to drop this condition when the request came from the British.[25] When this assurance was not forthcoming – the Spanish Government could not risk so 'provocative' a statement with the Germans on the Pyrenees, the Minister for Industry and Commerce told the American Ambassador – the onus returned to the British, who, unwilling to wait for Washington to make up its mind, had already authorised shipments of 200,000 tons of wheat and maize from Argentina. In the end, Roosevelt agreed to provide a small amount of humanitarian aid under the auspices of the American Red Cross.

American distrust of the Franco regime was well founded. On 16 October 1940, the increasingly Anglophile Spanish Foreign Minister, Juan Luis Beigbeder y Atienza, was dismissed and the wildly pro-Axis Serrano Suñer was appointed in his place. On 3 November, Franco effectively annexed the Tangiers International Zone and on 21 November – Thanksgiving – a Falangist mob stoned the American Embassy in Madrid. Against this and other provocations, the US Ambassador, Alexander Weddell, a scholarly Virginian, protested with rising emotion. Granted an interview with Serrano Suñer on 19 April 1941, he began by expressing his surprise that Spain appeared to have 'renounced its sovereignty', handing the Minister a pair of letters, addressed to Americans, bearing a German censor's stamp. Later, when objecting to the frequency of attacks not only on Britain but also on the United States in the Spanish press, he remarked that recent editorials gave the impression 'that they had been originally drafted in some foreign language, perhaps German'. Although the head of the Falange confined himself to a grimace, he told the German Ambassador that he had wanted to slap the American in the face.[26]

The truth was, as the Papal Nuncio informed the Vatican, the Spanish Government sought American aid but took no pleasure in receiving it. Standing on the dock at Cádiz as $1.5 million worth of flour, dried and condensed milk and medicines were unloaded from the SS *Cold Harbor*, the *New York Times* correspondent, Thomas J. Hamilton, watched in disgust as Spanish soldiers loaded the awaiting trucks so that the words on the sides of the crates, 'Gift of the American people to the people of Spain', were hidden.[27] The British fared no better. In February 1941, however, Hoare succeeded in outfoxing his hosts. Learning that a fire had destroyed much of the old town of Santander and that the Germans had sent a relief train loaded with wheat, he and John Lomax went straight to the Minister for Industry and Commerce. 'Tell the Minister', Hoare instructed Lomax, acting as interpreter, 'that I've come about the Santander disaster. It needs a prompt and efficient service of relief. I've ordered as a gift the diversion of two shiploads of wheat. Here,

Lomax, show the Minister the telegram.' The Commercial Counsellor was horrified. These cargoes of Argentine wheat were not a
gift but the object of acrimonious and ongoing negotiations with
the Spanish Treasury. 'There is one condition,' Hoare continued
briskly. 'My announcement must be reported in the Spanish press,
in full and promptly, in tomorrow's papers in fact. The ships are still
at sea, you understand. I would not send them to your ports unless
the facts are plainly stated in the press under a Government communiqué. No thanks, just the facts.' When the Minister protested,
Hoare cut him short. 'I see that everything done by the Germans in
Spain is published with headlines, like this trivial German wagon of
wheat, but never a word about supplies and trade arranged by my
Embassy. I must know that there will be full reports before I confirm the offer.' The next day, every Spanish newspaper carried news
of the British 'relief'.[28]

A more consistent and entertaining pursuit was Hoare's campaign to undermine the German Ambassador, the formidable
Eberhard von Stohrer, by inventing clandestine contacts with him.
'Yes, yes, yes,' he would say to Lomax, acting as interpreter with
some Spanish Minister, 'of course the German Ambassador would
be forced to take that line officially but his opposition to my suggestion would be only nominal . . . we understand each other, you
know, the embassy gardens adjoin . . . our wives are keen amateur
gardeners.' Or: 'Yes, yes, yes, of course, there is excellent sport around
Madrid . . . excellent, too, for quiet meetings with colleagues, eh?
Von Stohrer's a keen shot too. We are coaching Señor Lazar [the
German Press Attaché] . . . but, of course, you know them.'[29]

Through such unorthodox means, Hoare won the respect of colleagues and observers alike. 'I am not a professional diplomat, so
I can, perhaps, be allowed to say that at this moment Sir Samuel
Hoare is doing better than any diplomat I know could do,' reported
Hillgarth to Churchill.[30] Although critical of his Cabinet record, the
New York Times' Hamilton could not help admiring the 'magnificent
imperturbability' with which Hoare conducted himself before his
hosts, who, confused by English etiquette, called him 'Sir Hoare'
or 'Don Samuel'.[31] Even the superior Eccles was impressed. Despite
deploring his 'bouts of physical and moral cowardice' (when a bat

found its way into the Ambassador's study, Hoare threw himself behind a sofa while imploring Eccles to kill it with a tennis racket), he was impressed by his 'capacity for skating over thin ice' and for conveying to the Spaniards a sense of imperial *sang-froid* that was 'exquisite and deceives them all'.[32]*

This was most evident in the heady days following Hitler's invasion of the Soviet Union. On 24 June 1941, the British Embassy was attacked by a mob of around 400 Falangists, fresh from listening to an inflammatory speech by Serrano Suñer. That the riot had been carefully organised was barely concealed. The Embassy's police guard was withdrawn, a wagon, filled with stones, was produced and several German cine camera men were on hand to record the event. The protesters tore down the Union Jack, broke the Embassy's windows and tried to force an entry. This was successfully repulsed by the British guards and sixteen escaped British prisoners of war who were sheltering inside. The siege only ended when the police eventually reappeared and dispersed the mob, which, when not throwing rocks or attempting to breach the Embassy's defences, had contented itself by chanting 'Gibraltar for Spain' and 'British assassins'. Hoare was outraged and, accompanied by his diplomatic secretaries and service attachés – the latter in full-dress uniform with swords – descended upon the Spanish Foreign Minister in his private apartment. There, they refused to be seated, while Hoare read a sharply worded protest. When Serrano Suñer tried to offer some form of excuse, the Ambassador cut him off. Having long considered the Falangist 'the nastiest piece of goods' he ever met, he explained that he had not come to argue before turning on his heel and marching the British delegation out of the room.[33]

Naturally, the War Cabinet did not rely solely on the efforts of 'Sam the Conjurer' to guarantee Britain's strategic position.[34] During the second half of 1940 and at various points during 1941, Churchill gave serious consideration to seizing one of the Iberian

---

* 'It is difficult to write nice things about Sir Samuel,' noted the former head of the Iberian division of SIS's Section Five, Kim Philby, in one of the great instances of dialogue between the pot and the kettle. 'But the truth compels me to admit that he rose to the occasion magnificently.'

archipelagos – the Portuguese Azores and Cape Verde Islands or the Spanish Canaries. Britain's Atlantic lifeline depended on denying these islands to the enemy, while their possession would go some way towards mitigating the effects of a successful assault on Gibraltar. 'Must we always wait until a disaster has occurred?' asked the Prime Minister.[35] The Foreign Office, however, urged caution, pointing out that such a course would likely precipitate the very sequence of events they wished to avoid: namely a Spanish declaration of war (Franco was bound to Portugal's defence by the Luso-Spanish Treaty of Friendship and Non-Aggression), the entry of the Wehrmacht into the peninsula and the loss of Gibraltar. Nevertheless, between July 1940 and mid-1942, the Chiefs of Staff would maintain plans to occupy the Atlantic islands the moment the Germans crossed the Spanish frontier or Spain entered the war on the side of the Axis.

This was a wise precaution. On 12 November 1940, Hitler signed Führer Directive no. 18, stating his intention to capture Gibraltar (Operation Felix) and prevent the British from alighting anywhere on the Iberian Peninsula or the Atlantic islands. Moreover, contrary to the post-war claims of Franco and his apologists, the evidence that the Caudillo tried to enter the war in June and again in September 1940 is irrefutable. As Serrano Suñer later attested, Franco's intention was always to join the war at the 'hour of the last cartridges'.[36] With France out of the conflict and the Luftwaffe apparently in the midst of destroying the RAF, the Spanish dictator believed this moment had come. In late September, Serrano Suñer travelled to Berlin to seal the alliance. In contrast to their attitude in June, when Hitler had rebuffed the Caudillo's advances, the Germans were now eager for Spanish belligerency. Appreciating the difficulties of forcing the British to the negotiating table, Hitler was now inclined towards a peripheral strategy, in which the capture of Gibraltar would be key.

They were not, however, prepared to pay the Spanish price. In exchange for entering the war, Franco reiterated his demands for territorial expansion in North and West Africa, as well as a mountain of supplies. These the Germans were unwilling, or unable, to meet. Although Ribbentrop assured Serrano Suñer that there would be an abundance of goods once Spain entered the war, there was simply no way that the Reich could provide the vast quantities of wheat, fuel, railway cars, trucks and ammunition the Spanish demanded. Moreover, Hitler needed to prevent the French Empire from rallying to de Gaulle and the British – an event he was in danger of precipitating if he were to support the annexation of large chunks of French territory by Spain.* When the German dictator met his Spanish counterpart at Hendaye, on 23 October 1940, he found him exasperating. Maundering between effusions of loyalty, personal reminiscences, disquisitions on Spain's economic plight and lectures on Moroccan history, the pot-bellied Caudillo succeeded in outtalking the notoriously garrulous Führer, leading to the latter's remark that he would 'prefer to have three or four teeth taken out' than go through the ordeal again.[37]

Nevertheless, Franco signed the draft German protocol, bringing Spain into the Axis and committing his country to entering the war at an unspecified future date. That this date was never reached was in no small degree due to the pragmatism of British diplomacy. Although Hitler's refusal to meet Franco's territorial and materiel demands may have been the immediate check upon Spanish belligerency in the summer of 1940, the fact was that Spain was never in a position to court British enmity. Woefully unprepared for war, Madrid fully recognised the ability of the Royal Navy to bring the country to its knees through the full imposition of the blockade. This was particularly apparent after the failure of the 1940 harvest. As the American Ambassador reported, it was not uncommon to see people fainting from hunger in the streets. Fights over barely edible scraps of bread broke out. The black market burgeoned and industrial output fell as workers suffered from malnutrition. The country, Weddell informed the State Department, was fast approaching a crisis and:

---

* The Germans also made their own territorial demands. In return for *possible* concessions regarding Morocco, they demanded the Spanish colonies of Guinea and Fernando Po, as well as one of the Canaries as a naval base. An outraged Serrano Suñer rejected the German demands.

Unless some relief, particularly in the way of foodstuffs is forthcoming . . . conditions may be expected to become so chaotic that internal uprisings in Spain will become a distinct possibility with the result that the present regime . . . may either be forced to accept complete Axis domination or be supplanted by other elements who might seize any opportunity to relieve themselves of internal dissatisfaction by a foreign adventure, however hazardous.[38]

This was the thinking behind Britain's gamble to feed Spain and, thus, sustain the Franco regime. It was not that the British were unaware of their clout. As the *Daily Express'* Geoffrey Cox wrote in an editorial – republished in *Arriba*, the official organ of the Falange, on 5 September 1940 – Britain had the ability to make conditions in Spain so intolerable as to reignite the Civil War.[39] What Hoare and his colleagues appreciated, however, was that the consequences of such a policy would be merely to propel Franco into the arms of the Axis or invite a German invasion of the peninsula. As paradoxical as it seemed, Britain's interests were best served by maintaining a regime weak enough to be dependent on British largesse but strong enough to resist German demands. Between November 1940 and February 1941, Hitler subjected Franco to increasing pressure to enter the war, thus enabling the Wehrmacht to initiate Operation Felix, scheduled for 10 November 1941. Yet the Caudillo's answer remained the same: Spain was too vulnerable to become a belligerent. Much as she sympathised with the Axis, she could, as the frustrated Serrano Suñer explained to the head of the Abwehr in February 1941, only enter the war 'when England was about to collapse'.[40]

This was the other determining factor. Since Hitler's failure to take Franco up on his offers of belligerency in June and September 1940, the RAF had won the Battle of Britain. Although the odds still favoured a German victory, the idea that the war would be over within a few months, let alone weeks, had been discredited. In December, further evidence of British vitality was produced when a small band of Imperial forces (36,000 men) succeeded in expelling the 150,000-man Italian 10th Army from Egypt and then advanced 500 miles, deep into Libya. Simultaneously, British and Indian troops crossed into Eritrea, Italian Somaliland and Abyssinia, capturing Keren on 27 March 1941 and liberating Addis Ababa two weeks later. These victories were followed by British reverses in the Balkans and the Sahara but whilst there is some evidence that Franco toyed with entering the war in April 1941, this remained an impossibility owing to Spanish vulnerability to British economic and military coercion.

This is not to imply that British policy succeeded, as its authors hoped, in exercising a positive effect. Despite the best efforts of Hoare and Eccles, economic appeasement and sympathy over Nationalist aspirations in Morocco had a negligible impact upon pro-Allied sentiment, while talk of an 'Anglo-Spanish-Portuguese alliance and a second Peninsular War' was sheer fantasy.[41] Throughout 1940–42, Franco remained firmly in the Axis camp: refuelling German U-boats, furnishing Berlin with intelligence and sending over 18,000 volunteers to participate in Hitler's war against 'Godless communism'. Yet the policy had a restraining effect. The Franco Government realised that only Britain and America could supply Spain with the food necessary to prevent her from starving and that a rigorous blockade might sound the death knell of the regime. By acting pragmatically rather than ideologically, by allowing patience and caution to supersede the desire for pre-emptive action and by constant vigilance, the British managed to keep the reluctant neutral on the sidelines.

VIII

Friend or Foe?

Only the stars are neutral.

Quentin Reynolds, 1942[1]

Owing to its position on the edge of Nazi-occupied Europe, the British Embassy in Madrid became, in Samuel Hoare's words, a 'clearing house' for a miscellany of issues that would not normally have fallen within its province.[2] Writing to Churchill on 27 June 1940, the Ambassador explained that, in addition to trying to shore up Britain's position with the Franco regime, he had been much occupied by 'our friend' the Duke of Windsor – the former Edward VIII – who, along with his wife, two servants, a brace of consuls, a lorry-load of possessions and two Cairn terriers, had crossed from France into Spain on 20 May. The situation was fraught with embarrassment, difficulties and not a little danger. As Hoare relayed to Churchill, wild rumours were flying around the Spanish capital:

> Under the pressure of the German machine, the Spanish press declared that you had ordered his arrest if he set foot in England, that he had come here to make a separate British peace behind your back, that he had always disapproved of the war and considered it even a graver mistake to go on with it etc., etc.[3]

Hoare did his best to ridicule these stories, but they were close to the truth. As the Duke's friend and legal adviser Walter Monckton told the Foreign Office's Charles Peake in January 1940, he had recently witnessed a 'frightful interview' between the Duke and Lord Beaverbrook, during which the pair had agreed that 'the war ought to be ended at once by a peace offer to Germany'. The press baron then urged the Duke to resign his post as a Major-General serving with the British Military Mission in France and return to England, where he would stump the country in favour of peace. At this point, Monckton reminded the Duke that if he were to take this course he would make himself liable to UK income tax, whereupon the 'little man' blanched and declared that 'the whole thing was off'.[4]

Plainly, the sooner the Duke left Spain and returned to Britain the better. This, however, he refused to do until he had received assurances about his employment, his finances and, above all, the status of his wife. When these were not forthcoming and the Duke continued to refuse the Government's summons, Churchill sent him a telegram threatening him with a court martial. This reached him in Lisbon, where the Duke and Duchess had arrived on 2 July. His departure from German-dominated Spain into only slightly less German-infiltrated Portugal came not a moment too soon. As US Ambassador Alexander Weddell reported to Washington, His Royal Highness had told a member of his staff on the evening of 1 July that 'the most important thing now to be done was to end the war before thousands more were killed or maimed to save the faces of a few politicians'.[5] More serious was the German attempt to detain or even kidnap the Duke, so that he could serve as an intermediary in future peace negotiations. 'At a suitable occasion in Spain,' Nazi Foreign Minister, Joachim von Ribbentrop, instructed the German Ambassador in Madrid, 'the Duke must be informed that Germany wants peace with the English people, that the Churchill clique stands in the way of it and that it would be a good thing if the Duke would hold himself in readiness for further developments. Germany is determined to force England to peace by every means of power and upon this happening would be prepared to accommodate any desire expressed by the Duke, especially with a view to the assumption of the English throne.'[6]

The plot, which contained many of the traits of *opera buffa*, foundered on the fact that the Duke showed no inclination to fall into the German trap and that the British Government got wind of it and despatched Monckton to warn him of the danger. Churchill now offered the ex-King the Governorship of the Bahamas – a neat solution to the royal riddle, thought Lord Halifax, though 'I am sorry for the Bahamas'.[7] The task of persuading the Duke to accept banishment to a more comfortable St Helena fell to David Eccles. Unimpressed with the Windsors, whom he described as the 'arch-beachcombers of the world' and 'pretty fifth column', his advice to his former sovereign was blunt: 'I'd take it, Sir. You'll be safe there. You'd get blown up here.'[8] On 1 August, to the relief of British diplomats, the royal couple set sail for the West Indies.

★

Another concern of British diplomacy that found its forum in the Spanish capital was Vichy France. The failure of the Dakar expedition prompted a major reappraisal of British policy. If de Gaulle had reached the limits of his appeal and if Vichy was prepared to defend its territory with equal determination against the Germans, then the case for seeking a rapprochement with the men who commanded the allegiance of the overwhelming majority of French citizens, as well as the French Empire, seemed logical. Setting out his views in a paper for the War Cabinet on 27 September – two days after Admiral Cunningham and de Gaulle had abandoned their attempt to take the Senegalese port – Halifax put the case for a *modus vivendi* with Vichy, in which Britain would relax her blockade in return for assurances that the French Government would resist Axis encroachment on its colonies or remaining Fleet.[9] Following Mers el-Kébir, Vichy had severed diplomatic relations with Britain and even bombed Gibraltar. Unofficial contact, however, had been maintained through the Madrid Embassies and it was to this channel that both Governments now turned.

On 5 October 1940, Hoare informed the French Ambassador, Comte Renom de la Baume, that Britain was prepared to discuss the issue of trade between unoccupied France and her colonies. In return, Vichy would agree not to attempt to recapture those parts of the French Empire that had rallied to de Gaulle, would prevent the re-export of supplies to Germany and deny the extant Fleet and all other French territories to the Axis. So far, so reasonable. Yet Halifax's policy was based upon a false premise. In his paper for the War Cabinet, the Foreign Secretary had spoken of 'encouraging developments in the French Empire and in France itself'. There was, the

Foreign Secretary claimed, a growing sentiment that 'all is not lost and that something may be saved from the wreck'. Although most applicable to the French Empire – free from the German heel – this feeling also appeared to exist in France and 'even in the Vichy Government itself'. At any rate, 'unless the Vichy Government really think it would be to their advantage that Germany should win rather than ourselves, all hope of collaboration need not be abandoned'.[10] Unfortunately, as the British Government was to discover, there were powerful elements within the Vichy Government who felt just this.

For many years, it was held that collaboration arose naturally out of the ashes of the armistice; that the policies of Vichy were dictated by the demands of the conqueror upon the defeated and truncated nation. Certainly, this was among the principal arguments of Vichy's apologists. Yet, as both French and Anglo-Saxon historians have shown, collaboration was a choice: an attempt by the men of Vichy to escape from the purgatory of the armistice; an ingratiation aimed at producing a peace treaty that would restore French sovereignty, territorial integrity and prisoners of war; a quest, among the most fervent, to secure for France the status of 'favoured nation' within the new European order.[11]

On 7 July 1940, amid the outrage over Mers el-Kébir, General Huntziger, Head of the French Armistice Commission at Wiesbaden, proposed a new arrangement with Germany since France found herself 'almost at war with the same enemy as her victorious adversary'.[12] Two days later, Paul Baudouin requested a meeting with Ribbentrop, explaining that France wished to become an 'associated power'.[13] It was, however, the Iago of the Third Republic, the former Prime Minister Pierre Laval, who made the greatest efforts during this period. Appointed Minister of State on 23 June, Laval contrived to have himself named as Pétain's successor on 12 July, having already persuaded the National Assembly to vote itself into oblivion. On 19 July, he made the first of a succession of journeys to Paris where he attempted to cultivate the German envoy, soon Ambassador, Otto Abetz. This he succeeded in doing, at least to a certain extent. Afforded the unique privilege of a semi-permanent pass that allowed him to move freely between occupied and unoccupied zones, he shuttled between Vichy and Paris extolling the virtues of Franco-German co-operation and proffering help for the destruction of Britain, including 200 'volunteer' pilots.

It was to Laval's intense frustration that the Germans showed no interest in these overtures. Hitler was determined to impose a punitive peace on the Reich's 'hereditary enemy' and even the Francophile Abetz wrote of the need to reduce France to 'a satellite state'.[14] The Dakar incident seemed to offer Vichy the opportunity to change this: the defence of the port proved France's loyalty to the armistice. Far from colluding with de Gaulle (as Hitler suspected), Pétain was determined to resist him. He might even wish, the Maréchal told a German industrialist on 22 September – one day *prior* to Cunningham and de Gaulle's arrival off the West African harbour – to join the war against England. But for this Vichy would need consideration. She would need the resources to defend her Empire and expel the Gaullists. She would need to demonstrate the rewards of collaboration to her people: through a relaxation of the demarcation line separating occupied from unoccupied France, by an easing of the financial burden imposed by the conquerors and with the return of French prisoners of war. Most of all, she would need to be assured that the territorial integrity of France and the French Empire would be respected at the peace conference.

Although unwilling to meet almost all of these demands, following the Dakar incident Hitler saw the benefits of trying to 'hook France to the German wagon'.[15] Casting around for a way to win the war, he told Mussolini on 4 October that he intended to draw 'France into the orbit of the anti-British coalition'.[16] Two weeks later, on his way to his conference with Franco, he met Laval at the railway station of Montoire-sur-le-Loir. The Vichy Minister declared that 'he desired the defeat of the British with all his heart' but Hitler refused to provide the prerequisites for French belligerency.[17] France had been 'responsible' for the war, he told Laval, and leniency would depend upon her willingness to cooperate in the final subjugation of England. Two days later, he repeated the same message, at the same railway station, to Pétain.*

---

* The short notice of the meeting and the fury of the Maréchal's foreign policy advisers, Charles Roux and Paul Baudouin (both of whom resigned after

Like Laval, the Maréchal stated that he had always opposed the war and expressed his admiration for Germany and her Führer. In answer to Hitler's question about France's willingness to join his coalition against Britain, he stated that he was in favour of collaboration but warned that he could not declare war without the consent of the National Assembly – the body he had just abolished. In any case, as Laval interjected, France could aid Germany without a formal declaration of war. Nothing officially was agreed and nothing was signed. After the meeting was over, however, a German photographer captured a cordial handshake between the victor of Verdun and the former Austrian corporal. It was to become the iconic image of the policy Pétain announced in a speech six days later:

> Last Thursday, I met the Chancellor of the Reich. It was of my own free will that I accepted the invitation of the Führer . . . it is with honour and to maintain French unity, a unity ten centuries old, within the framework of the new European order that is being constructed that I have, today, entered on the path of collaboration . . . In this way, in the near future, the weight of the sufferings of our country could be lightened, the lot of our prisoners ameliorated, the burden of occupation costs reduced, the demarcation line made more flexible and the administration and supply of the territory facilitated.[18]

The British were alarmed by these developments. They were also perplexed. On 14 October, Renom de la Baume handed Hoare the response to his enquiry in which Vichy, whilst deploring British attacks on its colonies and refusing to recognise the legitimacy of de Gaulle, claimed that it shared Britain's desire for détente, in particular a 'commercial *modus vivendi* as regards trade between France and [her] colonies'.[19] Then, on 22 October, a French-Canadian philosopher arrived in London with what purported to be an offer from Pétain for a truce between the two countries.

Montoire), helped foster the myth that Pétain had been inveigled into attending the meeting against his better judgement. The Maréchal had, however, repeatedly conveyed his desire to meet Hitler and also Göring. The timing was a surprise; the meeting was not.

The activities of Louis Rougier, as well as other unofficial intermediaries such as the Canadian diplomat Pierre Dupuy and Jacques Chevalier – another philosopher and, later, Vichy Minister for Education – were responsible for a considerable amount of confusion and, later, disinformation. A professor at the University of Besançon, specialising in scholasticism, Rougier fancied himself a diplomat. Presented to the Maréchal on 20 October, he obtained permission to travel to London and try his hand at negotiating a relaxation of the blockade.* On 25 October he met Churchill. The day had begun in dramatic fashion when two pre-dawn telegrams arrived from Hoare announcing that the French Cabinet was meeting at noon to decide whether or not to hand over the remains of the Fleet and all French naval bases to the Germans. At Hoare's suggestion, Churchill, who had been woken from his sleep in the safety of an underground station, began drafting a telegram from the King to Pétain, intended to appeal 'to his soldierly honour', while another was sent to Roosevelt asking him to reiterate his warning that the surrender of the French Fleet would 'constitute a flagrant and deliberate breach of faith with the United States Government'.[20]

The French philosopher brought reassurance. Claiming that he spoke in the name of the Maréchal, despite a complete lack of instructions from Pétain, he sketched the same outline of an understanding as had been conveyed by Hoare to Renom de la Baume. That evening, however, news broke of the meeting between Pétain and Hitler at Montoire, accompanied by the rumour that the two men had signed a peace deal transferring control of the Fleet. When Rougier returned to Downing Street the following day, Churchill exploded. 'I will send the Royal Air Force to bomb Vichy,' he yelled at the author of *Philosophy and the New Physics*. 'I will broadcast to

---

* As the authorities at Vichy soon realised, the blockade was not nearly as effective as the British might wish. Overstretched across multiple oceans, the Royal Navy lacked the ships to maintain continuous patrols in the Mediterranean, leading to interceptions of only eight out of 108 French ships that passed through the Strait of Gibraltar during the first three months of 1941. A far greater problem for Vichy was the German tendency to confiscate at least 60 per cent of all goods.

the French people to inform them of my resolve to pursue their government of traitors wherever they go.'[21]

Eventually, Rougier succeeded in assuring the Prime Minister – accurately, as it transpired, though based on nothing more than blind optimism – that no such agreement had been made. Churchill was persuaded to continue along the path of détente and the philosopher departed with an *aide-mémoire* of his conversations with the Prime Minister, the hope being that this might help persuade General Weygand, now Delegate-General for French North Africa, to rally the Empire and re-enter the war. This it failed to achieve. A defeatist in June, the finicky soldier showed no more inclination towards heroics in November. After the war, however, Rougier claimed to have brokered a 'gentleman's agreement' between Pétain and Churchill, allowing the former and his apologists to claim that he had been playing a 'double game': talking with Hitler while negotiating with Churchill.[22] In fact, the assertions of Rougier were not merely bogus but fraudulent. After he had left London, the philosopher added an entire page to the document he falsely described as a 'protocol', while making small but significant changes to the notes of the actual conversation. Pétain and Laval may have been playing a game but it was not the British one.

While hopeful of something from Vichy, the British kept de Gaulle – currently in Brazzaville – at arm's length. As Sir Robert Vansittart commented on Halifax's Vichy paper, which recommended telling the General to rest content with the limited territories that had rallied to him, 'De Gaulle is completely discredited. We had pushed him halfway up the hill but he has now slid back to the bottom.'[23] Evidence that the General had recovered his self-confidence, however, emerged on 2 November when he responded to the news that the British were approaching Weygand by arguing that the former Commander-in-Chief should submit to *him*. 'Ridiculous telegram from Brazzaville, showing that that ass de Gaulle is contemplating "summoning Weygand",' noted Sir Alexander Cadogan on 8 November.[24] That same day Churchill expressed the opinion that de Gaulle, after completing the capture of French Gabon (begun on 27 October), should not proceed to Cairo, where he 'might arouse the antagonism of General Weygand', but return to London:

It is a good thing for him to have captured this South-Western African and Equatorial domain and every effort must be made by us to hold it for him. But he and his movement may now become an obstacle to a very considerable hiving off of the French Empire to our side. There is no doubt that men like Weygand and Noguès [Resident-General in Morocco], when searching their souls about their own misdeeds harden themselves against us by dwelling on the insubordination of de Gaulle.[25]

The Foreign Office's Roger Makins put it more strongly: 'That "creature" de Gaulle is getting much too big for his jack boots,' he wrote to David Eccles (like him, an advocate of rapprochement with Vichy), 'and is quite capable of mixing in rather delicate relations with Weygand. I will not promise to shed a tear for the Maréchal [when he goes] but I understand well enough the place which he shares with Mistinguett [the leading French actress and singer] in the hearts of the French people.'[26]

In the end, de Gaulle prevailed because neither Weygand nor other senior figures of the spa-town regime were prepared to defy the Germans. Following Montoire, Baudouin resigned as Foreign Minister and was succeeded by Laval. A few days later, when Renom de la Baume – now Ambassador to Bern – reported a renewed request from the British for talks, the response from his new chief was unequivocal: 'The collaboration that we have envisaged is exclusive of all ambiguous diplomatic action.'[27] Britain's proposals for economic negotiation went unanswered, while plans for an expedition to expel Anglo-Gaullist forces from Africa were discussed between French and German representatives during November and December.

The British were 'befogged'.[28] Rougier had assured them of the Maréchal's goodwill but power, it seemed, resided with a man bent on collaborating with their enemies.* Optimism revived when Pétain,

---

* After Montoire, Laval ordered the surrender of France's stakes in the Bor copper mines in Yugoslavia to the Germans, followed, a few days later, by some 200 tons of Belgian gold. As with Mussolini, Halifax had thought about bribing the Vichy Vice-Premier but concluded that 'the process would be both unprofitable and unpleasant'. A more important consideration, put forward by Cadogan, was that

disappointed by the poverty of benefits following Montoire and irked by his deputy's lack of deference, dismissed Laval on 13 December. But the essentials remained unchanged. In late December, Churchill sent Pétain a message offering six British divisions to facilitate the rallying of French North Africa but the Maréchal declined even to respond. 'We have not received it,' he told his new Foreign Minister, Pierre-Étienne Flandin, burning the note.[29] Contact between London and Vichy was maintained via the Canadian *Chargé d'Affaires* during January 1941 but it was desultory and, in February, petered out. Reflecting upon these melancholic and ill-conceived diplomatic manoeuvres, Louis Spears analogised the British Government's attempts to propitiate Vichy with 'a well-meaning person bent on feeding a lettuce to a rabbit while it is being chased around its cage by a stoat'.[30] This was apposite. And yet the Vichy Government was also operating under a delusion: the erroneous belief that it could somehow make friends with the stoat.

*

Britain's frustrations with Vichy were mirrored by her dealings with Ireland. When George V declared war on 4 August 1914, he did so on behalf of the entire Empire. Without consultation, let alone consent, millions of Canadians, South Africans, Australians, New Zealanders, Indians, Burmese, Nepalis, Malayans, Kenyans, Rhodesians, Sierra Leoneans, Gambians, Nigerians, Ugandans, Somalians, Jamaicans, Trinidadians, Bermudians, Antiguans, Bahamians, Grenadians, Maltese, Cypriots and sundry others found themselves embroiled in a war with Germany and her allies at one stroke of the imperial pen. This was not the case in September 1939. Although the royal prerogative still applied to the Colonial Empire, the English-speaking Dominions – Canada, South Africa, Australia and New Zealand – were now autonomous nations, imbued with the right to determine their own foreign policy. For a time, it looked as if some would exercise this liberty in favour of neutrality. During the Czech crisis, the South Africans, in particular, had made clear their opposition to war over what was to them a truly 'faraway country' of

---

Laval's attitude was 'dictated by his belief that Germany will win. It would therefore require a very large sum to persuade him to throw over his German friends.'

which they knew little. And, one year on, the vote in favour of South African belligerency was carried with a parliamentary majority of just thirteen. Nevertheless, within a week of Britain's declaration of war, all members of the British Commonwealth had followed suit. All, that is, save one.

The Anglo-Irish Treaty of 1921, which ended two years of guerrilla war between an Irish nationalist paramilitary – the Irish Republican Army (IRA) – and British forces, had created a self-governing Dominion, within the British Commonwealth, under the sovereignty of the Crown. Members of the new Irish Free State Parliament, or Dáil, were required to swear an oath 'to His Majesty King George V, his heirs and successors by law, in virtue of the common citizenship of Ireland with Great Britain and her adherence to and membership of the group of nations forming the British Commonwealth'.[31] This was anathema to many nationalists and the ensuing civil war owed more to disagreement over Ireland's constitutional status than to the effective partition of the island following the creation of a separate parliament at Belfast in 1921, responsible for the six counties of Protestant-majority Ulster.

Although the anti-Treaty forces were defeated, the republican spirit would not be quelled and in 1932 Éamon de Valera's party, Fianna Fáil ('Soldiers of Destiny'), became the dominant force in the Dáil, with its leader assuming presidency of the Executive Council. Over the next six years, de Valera set about eviscerating the Treaty: removing the oath of allegiance, dissolving the post of Governor-General and, in 1937, implementing a new constitution that created a *de facto* republic, known as Éire, though without formally seceding from the Commonwealth or abolishing the monarchy. The following year, the British Government, under Neville Chamberlain, voluntarily surrendered the last, tangible vestiges of British sovereignty by relinquishing the 'Treaty Ports' of Queenstown (Cobh), Berehaven and Lough Swilly, in return for an economic agreement and the vague hope of Irish assistance in the event of war.* In fact, this 'improvident example

---

* 'We hoped that if there was a war and if – or because – we had given up the ports, Éire would come in on our side,' explained the then Dominions Secretary, Malcolm MacDonald, in later life.

of appeasement', as Churchill called it, merely provided the practical conditions for Irish neutrality – the policy de Valera had been proclaiming for over a decade.[32] Thus, while the lamps of the United Kingdom (including Northern Ireland) and the Commonwealth went out both literally and metaphorically during the first week of September 1939, those of Dublin and the twenty-six counties of Éire continued to glow with ostentatious impartiality.

Britain's Vichy policy was vacillating and ambiguous. Not so her diplomacy across the Irish Sea. From the earliest stages of the war, the British, and later the Americans, strove to persuade the Irish to join the war against Germany or, at the very least, to allow the Royal Navy to use the former Treaty Ports that stood guard over the western approaches. The danger of German U-boats operating off the coast of Ireland had been obvious from the earliest hours of the war. At 7.40 p.m. on 3 September 1939, the German submarine *U-30* fired two torpedoes at the passenger liner SS *Athenia*, 200 miles north-west of Donegal, killing 112 of the 1,400 passengers and crew on board.* Five days later, the merchant ship *Regent Tiger* was torpedoed south-west of County Cork. During the first two weeks of the war, 169,000 tons of British shipping – thirty ships – were lost. Considering that this represented more than half the total lost at the height of the U-boat campaign during the previous war, the Admiralty and its aggressive new First Lord were understandably vexed.

At a War Cabinet meeting on 18 September, fifteen hours after the sinking of HMS *Courageous*, one of Britain's few aircraft carriers, off the south-west coast of Ireland, Churchill advanced the case for obtaining use of the Irish ports, though his colleagues deprecated an 'open difference between this country and Éire at the present moment'.[33] A month later, after a further 114,000 tons of Allied shipping had been lost and the battleship *Royal Oak* sunk within the defences of Scapa Flow, he argued that the time had come to tell the Irish Government 'that we must have the use of these harbours and intend in any case to use them'.[34] 'Trouble is looming up about Éire,' noted the consensus-minded Dominions Secretary, Anthony

---

* The captain, Oberleutnant Fritz-Julius Lemp, had mistaken the liner for a merchant vessel.

Eden, in his diary. 'Winston [is] very anxious to use Irish ports . . . The surprising thing is that the Admiralty do not then seem to have attached any great importance to the matter.'[35]

Although not exactly true, the professional advice in the autumn of 1939 was unambiguous.* As the Deputy Chief of the Naval Staff, Rear Admiral Tom Phillips, put it in a memorandum for the Cabinet:

> It has now become imperative that we should escort our convoys both inwards and outwards to and from a position further to the Westward; working as we are from Plymouth and Milford Haven it is impractical to do this. Our destroyers and other escorting vessels have, since the beginning of the war, been running at their extreme capacity. Many of the vessels themselves are beginning to show signs of strain and their crews are worked to the extremity of human endurance from lack of sleep and rest . . . There is one way in which this situation can be drastically and quickly relieved and that is by the Éire Government giving the use of one or more of their ports to the Royal Navy and the Royal Air Force. Berehaven is the most suitable port.[36]

Given that Ireland was dependent on Britain for 50 per cent of her imports and 90 per cent of her exports, such a request, it might be supposed, would be considered with empathy in Dublin. As the Irish Department of Industry and Commerce had noted in April 1939, Éire was almost entirely reliant on foreign countries, in particular the United Kingdom, for her most basic supplies and if these were halted, or substantially reduced, then the economic activities of the entire country could become 'completely paralysed'.[37] This, however, was to reckon without the legacy of a decades-long

---

* The Chiefs of Staff had warned that the loss of the Irish ports – which afforded a 500-mile crescent of protection around Britain's western perimeter – might so increase Britain's difficulties in time of war that 'the life of the nation would be imperilled'. They had, however, concluded that a whole division would be required to hold each port against a potentially hostile Ireland, while the supposition that de Valera would respond with generosity and voluntarily grant Britain facilities in an emergency was a powerful one.

struggle for Irish independence and the granite determination of the Irish Taoiseach.

Born in 1882 in New York, to an Irish mother and a Spanish father, de Valera had been involved in Ireland's fight for emancipation since he joined the Irish Volunteers (the nationalist paramilitary) in 1913. A devout and industrious student, he was working as a professor of mathematics at the time of the Easter Rising in 1916. For his part in the rebellion – during which he commanded a battalion – he was sentenced to death, later commuted to penal servitude. The most senior rebel to escape execution, he spent a year in English prisons before being released in the summer of 1917, winning a parliamentary seat and becoming the recognised leader of Sinn Féin, the primary vehicle for Irish nationalism. Over the next four years, he battled relentlessly for an independent Irish republic, first as President of the Dáil, then as the political head of the anti-Treaty faction during the Civil War.

Although Lloyd George claimed that de Valera was 'not a big man' (he was honest enough to admit that he was 'sincere'), it was hard not to admire the way that 'Dev' succeeded not only in dominating Irish politics throughout the 1930s but in dismantling the last cornices of British rule.[38] By September 1939, despite her nominal position within the Commonwealth, Ireland was a *de facto* independent state and the six-foot-one Taoiseach, with his powerful mind and mellifluous brogue, was determined to keep it that way. Having listened politely to the British Government's request for Berehaven, he replied with what London's recently appointed representative to Dublin, Sir John Maffey, described as a 'categorical "non-possumus"'. 'The creed of Ireland today was neutrality,' de Valera explained to Maffey. 'No Government could exist that departed from that principle. The question of the ports was at the very nerve centre of public interest . . . and the public mood would react with intense violence to any action invalidating their integrity.'[39]

The first half of this statement was little more than the truth. Although Churchill believed that 'three-quarters of the people of Southern Ireland are with us' and that neutrality rested purely on the 'implacable, malignant minority . . . that de Valera dare not do anything to offend', reports from visitors to Ireland showed that this was far from being the case.[40] According to Frank Pakenham, heir to an Irish peerage, 'eight out of ten people strongly support neutrality'. Among these, there was a 'mild' preference for the Allies, 'analogous to the preference felt by most Englishmen for China as against Japan', but this would 'vanish overnight' if Britain violated Irish neutrality.[41] As the de Valera Government repeatedly explained, neutrality was an expression of national independence. By remaining aloof from the war, Ireland was giving practical demonstration to that sovereignty which, so the overwhelming majority of her citizens maintained, rested with the Dáil and the executive in Dublin. To the British, the moral dimension of the conflict appeared obvious and compelling. But in Éire this was tempered by more than seven centuries of British rule and oppression. As Maffey wrote in a remarkably clear-sighted despatch in June 1941, Britons, nostalgic for the 200,000 Irishmen who had fought in the Great War and who liked to claim 'that we are really all one happy family and that this regrettable tiff will blow over', were living in a dream world. Far from being embarrassed by their place on the touchline, most Irish citizens were proud of their stance: admiring of a 'firm Government spurning all cajolery, rejecting all menaces, guiding Ireland on her age-long path to the separate destiny for which her sons have died'.[42]

During interviews with Maffey and other emissaries, de Valera would argue that all might have been different if Britain had coerced the Northern Irish and ended partition. Yet a more important consideration was the fact that Ireland was virtually defenceless. In September 1939, Éire possessed only around 7,000 regular soldiers, augmented by 12,000 poorly trained reservists and volunteers. She had no navy, nothing that could be described as an air force and only one anti-aircraft battery. Fear of German bombs was widespread and increased exponentially following the fall of France, the London Blitz and raids on Belfast in April and May 1941. During this time de Valera made repeated appeals for weapons from Britain. Yet the War Cabinet was little disposed to act with generosity while Britain was experiencing her own critical shortages and while tales of fifth column activities within the twenty-six counties abounded.

'Did you know that the German Gauleiters of Éire are already there, known by name and functioning in a certain way?' wrote the

Prime Minister's intelligence adviser, Desmond Morton, to Lord Swinton, co-ordinator for internal intelligence, on 8 June 1940. Morton's 'informant' was the Anglo-Irish former Commissioner of the Calcutta police, Sir Charles Tegart. Asked by the Secret Intelligence Service's Colonel Valentine Vivian to keep an eye on events in Éire, Tegart had returned to London around the time of Dunkirk convinced that the Germans were planning to invade Britain via Ireland and that there were already 2,000 German agents in Éire preparing the ground.[43] In fact, there were fewer than 500 German and Italian nationals in Ireland according to the Irish authorities, while stories of U-boats being succoured by the inhabitants of west coast villages, though not apocryphal, were similarly exaggerated. German military intelligence, it is true, made various attempts to establish contact with the IRA but the general ineptitude with which the majority of these attempts were carried out meant that most German spies were quickly arrested by the Gardaí.

The fear of a German invasion of Éire was, nevertheless, real. Towards the end of May 1940, while the Wehrmacht was rolling up the French Army, a series of highly secret meetings was held in the Dominions Office between British officials and the Secretary to the Irish Department of External Affairs, Joseph Walshe, and the head of the Irish Army's G2 intelligence section, Colonel Liam Archer. As the Permanent Under-Secretary at the Dominions Office, Sir Eric Machtig, summarised the discussions: Ireland would request British assistance if attacked by Germany but the political situation in the twenty-six counties meant that the arrival of British troops prior to a German assault was out of the question. Profoundly unsatisfactory from a military point of view – the swastikas over Oslo, Copenhagen, Amsterdam and Brussels flying in reproof – Maffey tried, repeatedly, to convince de Valera of the necessity of inviting the British in *before* a German invasion. But the Taoiseach refused to countenance any step that would undermine Irish neutrality. On this rock, the British Government's attempts to gain formal Irish assistance, most importantly on the question of the Treaty Ports, foundered.

Churchill had reacted to de Valera's 'non-possumus' with anger. 'We should challenge the constitutional position of Éire's neutrality,' he told the War Cabinet. 'We should not admit that her neutrality was compatible with her position under the Crown.' Then, having set out 'the juridical position and made clear to the world that we were not committing a violation of neutrality, insist on the use of the harbours'. Meanwhile, 'we should take stock of the weapons of coercion'.[44] This was the closest Britain came to solving the Irish problem by force. Although the question would recur throughout 1940 and 1941 and was even subject to some early-stage planning by General Bernard Montgomery, an invasion of southern Ireland was never seriously considered. Coercion, however, could take other forms, while bribery was also an option.

In June 1940 – the nadir of Britain's military fortunes – the War Cabinet decided to offer de Valera a deal on partition in return for Irish belligerency and the use of the Treaty Ports. Considering the frequency with which the Taoiseach pointed to the division of the north from the south when justifying his country's attitude towards Britain, this approach, it was felt, stood a reasonable chance of success. 'My friends in America say to me "Why don't you take a leaf out of Hitler's book and work the Sudetendeutsche [the German-speaking minority of Czechoslovakia] trick in Northern Ireland?"' de Valera had goaded Maffey, two weeks into Britain's war against Germany.[45] Eight months later, he told the British representative that if there had been a united Ireland at the start of hostilities then both his freedom of action and the spirit of the people would have been transformed. When Maffey enquired whether an end to partition would make Éire Britain's ally as a matter of course, the Taoiseach replied that this would 'probably be the consequence'.[46] When this inducement was proffered, however, de Valera rejected it. The Irish Government refused to subject its defenceless population to German bombs, he told Maffey, while there was understandable scepticism regarding London's ability to deliver the goods. As Northern Ireland's Prime Minister, Lord Craigavon, wrote to Neville Chamberlain upon learning of the proposal, 'To such treachery to loyal Ulster, I will never be a party.'[47]

Confronted with this fresh rebuff, the British reacted with increasing frustration. On 5 November 1940, Churchill publicly condemned the 'grievous burden' imposed on Britain's naval resources by the continued denial of the Treaty ports.[48] When de Valera complained of this, Maffey allowed himself a rare display of emotion: 'The fact is that Mr de Valera is more uneasy today than he has ever been at any stage of his non-stop political career,' he wrote to Machtig. 'Ireland being Ireland, in the mass ignorant and responsive to old hatreds, he is still the chosen tribal leader for their feuds . . . But it is the soul of England which stirs the world today and Éire is a bog with a petty leader raking over old muck heaps.'[49]

In January 1941, in the hope of emphasising Irish dependence on British imports and shipping, the British Government decided to apply the 'cold blast' of trade restrictions to Éire.[50] Shortages of petrol, wheat and other raw materials followed but while much of the ill-feeling of the population was directed towards the Government at Dublin, the Administration remained immovable. There was also increasing American pressure on Éire to change her position. Initially, the Dominions Office had expressed misgivings about the American Minister, David Gray. But this septuagenarian uncle (by marriage) of Eleanor Roosevelt proved himself a doughty, if doltish, champion of Britain's cause. The Irish considered him 'more British than the British'.[51] Walshe complained that he 'brandished the big stick too much', while, in the spring of 1941, de Valera – who had developed a loathing for the tall, patrician, Harvard graduate – considered requesting his recall.[52] Yet in view of the received historiographical view that Gray was a roguish amateur, recklessly exceeding his brief, it is worth recalling the State Department's persistent lobbying of Robert Brennan, Ireland's Minister to Washington, in favour of concessions to Britain, as well as the efforts of Presidential envoys such as Wendell Willkie and Bill Donovan. Willkie told de Valera that he was 'making a great mistake in not giving the bases to the British', that American public opinion would not support him in this stand and that 'even Irish-Americans were getting more and more annoyed with him'.[53]

Understandably, this criticism of Irish neutrality, coming from a country that was itself neutral – and protected from the German threat by a large ocean – was considered annoying and hypocritical. As the Taoiseach remarked to Maffey on 3 January 1941, 'Talk of fighting for the standards and ideals of freedom did not come well from a country which was out of the war zone and did not carry weight in a country which felt itself to be the subject of aggression and invasion.'[54] Yet American opinion, as well as American supplies, remained critical to Ireland. In March 1941, Frank Aiken, the Irish Minister for Defence, travelled to Washington on a mission to obtain ships and weapons from the US. A former Chief of Staff to the IRA, whose anti-British prejudices were stronger than his political acumen (the British considered both him and Walshe potential Quislings), he was not the man likely to appeal to the Roosevelt White House. Even before he had set foot in America, he was reported to have told guests at a lunch party in Lisbon that German victory was not only assured but 'to be hoped for'.[55] Ushered into the Oval Office on the afternoon of 7 April, he succeeded in provoking a rare display of Presidential wrath when he claimed that Ireland was forced to defend herself against *two* potential aggressors, Germany and Britain. 'I never heard anything so preposterous in all my life,' Roosevelt expostulated, grabbing the tablecloth and sending the cutlery flying.[56] Elsewhere, Aiken was pressed repeatedly on the subject of aid for Britain, while the Secretary of the Navy, Frank Knox, informed the Defence Minister that Ireland would receive neither ships nor weapons so long as she insisted on remaining aloof from the conflict. Eventually, the Administration agreed to provide the Irish Government with two freight vessels for transporting food but wished it to be understood that this offer had nothing to do with the mission of the Irish Defence Minister, who appeared to have no appreciation for the fact that 'the future safety and security of Éire depends, inevitably, upon the triumph of the British cause'.[57]

Nor did Allied–Irish relations improve with American entry into the war. On 8 December 1941 – the day following the Japanese attack on Pearl Harbor – Churchill sent de Valera a personal telegram urging him to join the Anglo-American alliance. The Taoiseach – who, upon being alerted to the arrival of the message, assumed that it was a British ultimatum and ordered the Army to its defensive positions – refused. The Irish people, he told Maffey, were 'determined on their attitude of neutrality'.[58] American pressure had no more effect. De Valera continued to deny the Allies the use of Irish ports, while refusing to close the Axis' legations in Dublin in the run up to D-Day. On 2 May 1945, he and Walshe visited the German Legation to pay official condolences following the death of Hitler.*

As was appreciated in Whitehall (if not always in Downing Street), there were in fact numerous instances of *sub rosa* Irish assistance that exceeded the confines of neutrality and aided the Allied war effort. Weather reports, submarine sightings and coast-watching data were readily relayed, while MI5 established a close working relationship with the Gardaí and G2. From early 1941, RAF flying boats were able to traverse a thin strip of Irish airspace, between Lough Erne and the Atlantic – the so-called 'Donegal Corridor' – and, from mid-1942, Allied airmen that crash-landed in Ireland were repatriated to Britain (their German counterparts were interned). British ships and aeroplanes benefited from two wireless detection-finding radio stations at Malin Head (the most northerly point of the Irish mainland), while little was done to impede the 60,000 or so southern Irishmen who volunteered to fight in the British services – roughly the same number that volunteered from Northern Ireland (the only part of the United Kingdom exempt from conscription).†

Against this stands the fact that Irish neutrality was widely recognised within the Nazi foreign policy establishment as a German advantage. 'We should continue to support consolidation of Irish neutrality and independence on a broad national basis,' urged the German Minister in Dublin, Eduard Hempel, on 8 October 1939.[59]

---

* Although the Taoiseach sent a message of condolence to President Truman following the death of Roosevelt eighteen days earlier, there was no corresponding visit to the American Legation.

† The exact figure – complicated by Irishmen already enlisted in British forces at the outbreak of war, desertions, surreptitious border crossings and so on – remains a matter of dispute. As the war approached its end, Irish officials began to make the exaggerated claim that as many as 100,000–250,000 southern Irishmen had fought in the war, prompting attempts by the Dominions Office to ascertain the real number. In June 1945, a British Government memorandum estimated that around 40,000 Irishmen had served in the British armed forces from Éire and Northern Ireland respectively, though they acknowledged that these figures were not certain and historians now consider this figure to be conservative.

Although the Abwehr could not resist dabbling in espionage, including contact with the IRA, Hitler and the German Foreign Ministry heeded this advice and reaped the rewards. More than 3,500 Allied merchant ships, 175 Allied warships and over 72,200 Allied naval and merchant seamen went to the bottom during the Battle of the Atlantic. There were many factors behind these statistics – crucially the fact that the Kriegsmarine had broken the British naval code and was reading Allied signals between March 1941 and June 1942 – but there is little doubt that they would have been lower if Irish air and naval bases had been available to the Allies.

That the Dublin Government disclaimed all responsibility for German U-boat activities was not surprising. What the British found perplexing was how de Valera, his ministers and – thanks to the imposition of draconian censorship – the bulk of the population of Éire seemed blind to the moral aspect of the war. 'England was fighting for everything that Ireland stood for in song and story,' argued Maffey but his interlocutors, embittered by centuries of Anglo-Irish bloodletting, could never accept this.[60] This led to some questionable stances. 'Walshe expressed great admiration for the German achievements,' reported Hempel, three days after the Wehrmacht entered Paris.[61] Six months later, when the Dublin Government became concerned that the British were preparing to seize the Treaty Ports by force, General Hugo MacNeill, commander of Éire's 2nd Division, held discussions with the Counsellor of the German Legation about the possibility of German assistance. De Valera condemned Hitler's invasion of Belgium and Holland but was silent on all other Nazi atrocities, including the mass murder of Europe's Jews, well known by the time he paid his infamous visit to the German Legation.

Irish neutrality was logical, justified and popular. It was never admirable.

IX

Greek Tragedy

The danger of another Norway, Dunkirk and Dakar
rolled into one, looms threateningly before us.

Jock Colville, 5 March 1941[1]

The first two months of 1941 were garlanded with British victories. On
9 December 1940, General Sir Archibald Wavell, the taciturn, cerebral
Commander-in-Chief Middle East, launched Operation Compass
against the Italians in North Africa. By 15 December, the forces of
Marshal Rodolfo Graziani had been driven out of Egypt and soon
British Matilda tanks were racing across Libya. Bardia fell on 5 January 1941, Tobruk just over a fortnight later. By 9 February, the Western
Desert Force, including the 6th Australian Division, had advanced
over 500 miles, capturing 133,298 prisoners, 380 tanks and 845 guns. At
the same time, Imperial forces were waging a successful campaign
in East Africa, driving the Italians from Eritrea and facilitating the liberation of Abyssinia. As the Summer Fields school magazine noted,
'Wavell mi. has done well in Africa.'[2]

Churchill was ecstatic. 'The Army of the Nile has rendered glorious service to the Empire and to our cause,' he telegraphed Wavell
as British forces reached the Libyan frontier. 'Your first objective
now must be to maul the Italian Army and rip them off the African
shore'.[3] No sooner had this injunction been issued, however, than
the Prime Minister began imposing additional responsibilities upon
his already overstretched Middle East Commander.

Resentful of repeated German *faits accomplis* – the latest
being the Wehrmacht's penetration of Romania – Mussolini had
sought to pay Hitler back 'in his own coin' by invading neutral
Greece.[4] On 28 October 1940, 140,000 Italian soldiers had crossed

the border from Albania. 'I shall send in my resignation as an Italian if anyone objects to our fighting the Greeks,' Mussolini had declared.[5] Yet the heirs to Marathon proved more than a match for the impersonators of Rome and, within weeks, the Duce's legions had been driven back across the frontier. When the Greeks broke through the Italian lines at the start of December, capturing the Albanian city of Pogradec, Mussolini lost his nerve. 'There is nothing else to do,' he told his popinjay son-in-law, Count Ciano. 'This is grotesque and absurd but it is a fact. We have to ask for a truce through Hitler.' Ciano explained that this was impossible. Italian Fascism could scarcely survive such a humiliation, while he would 'rather put a bullet' through his head than telephone Ribbentrop.[6]

The British enjoyed the spectacle of the Greeks 'whacking the ice-creamers'.[7] On the question of assistance, however, opinion was divided from the start. From the military perspective, the situation appeared depressingly simple. 'We cannot', telegraphed Anthony Eden on 1 November from Egypt, where, as Secretary of State for War, he was visiting British forces, 'send sufficient air or land reinforcements to have any decisive influence upon [the] course of fighting in Greece', while the diversion of forces from Egypt 'would imperil our whole position in the Middle East'.[8] Others put it more bluntly. The suggestion that Britain should halt a successful campaign against the Italians in North Africa to mount a fresh campaign against the Italians in Greece was, argued the British Ambassador to Cairo, 'completely crazy'.[9]

Yet military considerations were not the only ones that needed to be weighed. In April 1939, following the German invasion of Czechoslovakia, the Chamberlain Government had promised to defend Greece against unprovoked aggression. If Britain now stood by while Greece was overrun, then British prestige, upon which her foreign policy and Empire depended, would suffer. Unlike Germany, who relied on her panzer divisions to wield influence, Britain's war effort, in particular her wartime diplomacy, was bound inextricably to the morality of her cause. For the British in 1940, the question of honour was one not merely of private conscience but also of public necessity. Added to this were diplomatic and strategic considerations. If Greece was defeated, what was to prevent the Axis from dominating the whole of the Balkans, including the Dardanelles? If Greece fell, Turkey would be next. And if Turkey came under the shadow of the swastika then the route would be open not only to Egypt but also to Iraq, the Iranian oil fields and ultimately India.

For all these reasons, Churchill believed that Britain must stand by Greece. 'Greek situation must be held to dominate others now,' he contradicted Eden on 2 November 1940. 'Aid to Greece must be attentively studied lest whole Turkish position is lost through proof that England never tries to keep her guarantees'.[10] When the War Secretary, who, unlike the Prime Minister, had been let into the secret of Operation Compass, continued to demur, he provoked a Churchillian harangue:

> No one will thank us for sitting tight in Egypt with ever-growing forces while Greek situation and all that hangs on it is cast away . . . New emergencies must be met in war as they come and local views must not subjugate main issue . . . Greece resisting vigorously with reasonable aid from Egypt and England might check invaders . . . Trust you will grasp situation firmly, abandoning negative and passive policies and seizing opportunity which has come into our hands. Safety first is the road to ruin in war.[11]

Despite this adjuration, British materiel support for Greece was tokenistic: 100 machine guns, sixty-six anti-tank rifles, twenty-four field guns, twenty anti-aircraft guns, ten light tanks, three squadrons of Blenheim light bombers and two squadrons of Gladiator fighters. Such meagre commons reflected the continuing fear of an invasion of Britain (even if Churchill was inclined to discount the possibility), as well as a paucity of heavy armaments. Then, on 8 November, Eden returned from Cairo and informed the Prime Minister of Compass. Churchill was as excited as a schoolboy. For the next four weeks he bombarded Wavell with telegrams urging him to start his offensive and, once it had begun, exhorting him to capitalise on his success. On 7 January 1941, however, he surprised the Chiefs of Staff by decreeing that 'Greece must have priority after the western flank of Egypt has been made secure'.[12]

Throughout the early winter of 1940–41, British military, diplomatic and secret intelligence had chronicled the steady build-up of German forces in Romania. The inference, Churchill told his colleagues on the Defence Committee, was obvious: Germany was preparing to invade Greece via Bulgaria. In such circumstances, Britain's response appeared no less clear. Although 'it might be that the help which we could bring to the Greeks in the time available would not be enough to save them', the Prime Minister told the meeting, 'there was no other course open to us but to make certain that we had spared no effort . . . From the political point of view, it was imperative to help the Greeks against the Germans.'[13]

Yet the Greeks declined the help the British were offering. On 15 January, General Ioannis Metaxas, the Greek Prime Minister and *de facto* dictator, rejected Wavell's offer of two to three British divisions, deeming this (rightly) too small to do any good but large enough to provoke the Germans. To give the Allies a fighting chance, the Greek Commander-in-Chief, General Alexandros Papagos, had asked for nine British divisions but in their absence thought the British should continue their campaign in Africa, destroying Graziani's forces and securing as much of the Libyan coast as possible.* These were Wavell's sentiments entirely. Appalled at the idea of diverting much-needed resources to Greece just when he had got the Italians on the run, it was with relief that the Commander-in-Chief learnt on 21 January that he was at liberty to push on to Benghazi.

But this was not the end. Following the Greek refusal, Churchill and the Chiefs of Staff turned to Turkey as the country most likely to frustrate a German descent and rally the Balkans. On 31 January, Churchill wrote to the Turkish President, İsmet İnönü, urging him to accept seven squadrons of RAF bombers and three of fighters. Air Chief Marshal Arthur Longmore, Air Officer Commanding Middle East, was aghast. Having already despatched a third of his strength to Greece and coinciding with orders to clear the Luftwaffe from Sicily and Rhodes (as well as supporting the campaigns in Libya

* If a German invasion could not be avoided, the Greek plan was to attempt to delay it for as long as possible, allowing them to defeat the Italians in Albania, before redeploying their depleted divisions to Macedonia.

and east Africa), he wrote to London of his astonishment at being asked to scatter his forces yet further. Fortunately for Longmore, the Turks rejected the British offer, arguing – much like the Greeks and the Yugoslavs, whom the British were also pressing – that such a move would be merely to invite a German response. To the strategists in London, the situation appeared eerily familiar. As with Norway, Belgium and Holland in 1940, so the threatened nations of the Balkans refused to concert their policies or accept British aid, lest their actions precipitate the very scenario they feared.

The Turkish refusal coincided with a deterioration on the Greek front. On 29 January 1941, General Metaxas had died of natural, if still uncertain, causes.* A feared and despised politician in peace, he had proved a unifying and courageous leader in war. His successor, Alexandros Koryzis, was ignorant of military matters and little more than a cipher for the strongly Anglophile King George II. In early February, he informed the head of the British Military Mission in Athens that the situation was desperate. The worst winter in living memory had caused the campaign in Albania to freeze and the Army had only enough ammunition for another two months. When the British Minister, Sir Michael Palairet, asked Koryzis if he maintained the refusal of his predecessor to accept British troops, the Premier handed him a note emphasising his country's determination to resist a German invasion and enquiring as to the size of force Britain was prepared to send.

This softening of the Greek attitude dovetailed with the capture of Benghazi on 6 February. Four days later, at a Defence Committee meeting dominated by Churchill and Eden (now Foreign Secretary), the decision was taken not to pursue the rump of Graziani's army through Tripolitania but to go all out with aid for the Greeks. 'Our first thoughts must be for our ally Greece,' Churchill cabled Wavell. 'If Greece is trampled down or forced to make a separate peace with Italy, yielding also air and naval strategic points against us to Germany, [the] effect on Turkey will be very bad. But if Greece, with British aid, can hold up for some months [the] German advance,

---

* The Germans accused Wavell's aide de camp, Peter Coats, the lover of the Conservative MP 'Chips' Channon, known as 'Petticoats', of assassinating him.

[the] chances of Turkish intervention will be favoured. Therefore, it would seem that we should try to get in a position to offer the Greeks the transfer . . . of the fighting portion of the Army which has hitherto defended Egypt and make every plan for sending and reinforcing it to the limit with men and materiel.'[14]

This decision was, and remains, among the most controversial of the war. As Desmond Morton told Jock Colville on 12 February, there was 'great opposition to the PM's decision not to press on to Tripoli', substituting, as it did, the 'certainty' of complete victory in North Africa for a Balkan gamble that risked turning into 'another Dunkirk'. According to Morton, the Chief of the Imperial General Staff, General Sir John Dill, felt so strongly on the matter 'he was almost thinking of resigning'.[15] Certainly, Dill had raised objections to the venture. At the Defence Committee the previous evening, he had stated baldly that 'all the troops in [the Middle] East were fully employed and none were available for Greece'. At this, Churchill lost his temper. 'I could see the blood coming up his great neck and his eyes began to flash and get more watery,' the CIGS recounted to the Director of Military Operations, Major-General John Kennedy. 'What you need out there is a court martial and a firing squad,' the Prime Minister expostulated, 'Wavell has 300,000 men, etc., etc.'[16]

In fact, Wavell possessed an even greater number of men under his command. Yet the sprawling nature of his responsibilities – encompassing Egypt, Libya, Sudan, Eritrea, Somaliland, Abyssinia, Kenya, Iraq, Transjordan, Palestine, Malta and Cyprus – meant that all he could spare for Greece were two armoured brigades, the recently completed New Zealand Division, two Australian divisions and a Polish brigade. To Major-General Kennedy and his colleagues at the War Office, it seemed as if the Cabinet was determined 'to shove an unsound policy down Wavell's throat':

> What we should do is to keep the water in front of us. Anything we send to Greece will be lost if the Germans come down. It will be another Dunkirk . . . The Greeks and Turks are quite realistic about it. I should like to see Greece make peace now . . . It will be playing the German game if we let them annihilate our forces on the European side of the water and leave the vital places uncovered.

The one hope, Kennedy continued in his diary, was that Eden and Dill were already on their way to Cairo. 'My prediction is that Eden and CIGS will correct the policy . . . Eden is rather chameleon like and will take on the local colour when he sees Wavell.'[17] But what if the Commander-in-Chief was the one to change his hue?

★

In December 1940, Eden had succeeded Halifax as Foreign Secretary. Only forty-three, he was returning to the office he had resigned, in February 1938, owing to Chamberlain's determination to appease Mussolini. During the intervening years his star had dipped if not dimmed. Viewed at one time as the man most likely to succeed Chamberlain, his refusal to assume the leadership of the anti-appeasement forces at Westminster had led to his supersession by Churchill. When war broke out in September 1939, Churchill became First Lord of the Admiralty, with a seat in the War Cabinet, whilst Eden was given the less prestigious post of Secretary of State for the Dominions, outside the War Cabinet. Memorably described as 'half mad baronet, half beautiful woman' by his colleague and sometime rival Rab Butler, the advantages accrued by good looks, charm and intelligence could be vitiated by vanity, timidity and a highly strung temperament.[18] Anthony Quayle, then serving as an aide to the Governor of Gibraltar, thought he seemed 'like an actor playing the part of AE', while Cadogan's diaries provide ample testament to the brittle element in his master's character.[19] Against this stands the Permanent Under-Secretary's retrospective judgement that of all the Foreign Secretaries he served none exceeded Eden 'in finesse . . . as a negotiator, or in knowledge of foreign affairs', while his willingness to stand up to Churchill put him in a small minority among his Cabinet peers.[20] Taking his tenure as a whole, it is hard to imagine any of his contemporaries (including Churchill) fulfilling this difficult wartime role as well as he did.

The Eden–Dill mission was supposed to be top secret. 'For this reason, no doubt,' noted the Deputy Director of Military Operations, Aubertin Mallaby, 'it started by departure in a special train from No. 1 platform at Paddington', with 'every grade of uniformed official in the Great Western Railway ... the Vice Chief of the Imperial General Staff and a number of obvious detectives and MI5 men' in attendance.[21] The party, which included Pierson Dixon from the Foreign Office's Southern Department, was due to fly to Gibraltar that afternoon but gale force winds kept them in Plymouth. The hiatus allowed for a review of policy. As Mallaby recorded:

AE is determined to help the Greeks; in his view it is better to have fought and lost than never to have fought at all. Dill is inclined to say rather little in argument but privately with me he has entirely agreed with my opinion that we can do no real good in Greece and must not throw away our small available forces in a vain attempt to stem the German advance.[22]

Finally, after much delay and an appalling journey, the mission arrived in Cairo on 19 February. There, to Eden's delight and the War Office's astonishment, Wavell and the other Commanders-in-Chief revealed themselves in favour of the Greek venture. Even more astonishing, Dill now stated his support for the scheme. It was certainly 'a gamble', Eden wrote to Churchill, but there was universal agreement that it was better to try and 'run the risk of failure', than to abandon the Greeks to their fate. Indeed, whilst the expedition was without doubt a 'daring venture', both Dill and Wavell were 'not without hope that it might succeed to the extent of halting the Germans before they overrun Greece'.[23]

How are we to account for so startling an about-turn? The most obvious explanation is that the CIGS and the C-in-C Middle East had been converted by the political and strategic arguments. As Dill wrote to his deputy, General Haining, it now appeared clear to him that the 'only chance of preventing the Balkans from being devoured piecemeal was to go to Greece'.[24] Wavell agreed. Over the previous week he had played host to Roosevelt's emissary Colonel 'Wild Bill' Donovan, just back from a tour of Athens, Belgrade and Sofia. According to Donovan's tour guide, Brigadier Vivian Dykes, Donovan:

Put over very well his idea of looking at the Mediterranean not as an east–west corridor but as a no man's land between two opposing fronts. The north–south conception seemed to strike Wavell very forcibly and he was clearly impressed by Donovan's insistence on the need for keeping a foothold in the Balkans.[25]

Struck or not, the wishes of his political masters were unambiguous. When one of Wavell's subordinate generals expressed the view that a Greek expedition could only end in disaster, the C-in-C replied, 'Possibly, but strategy is only the handmaiden of policy and here political considerations must come first. The policy of our Government is to build up a Balkan front.'[26]

Yet the relationship between Churchill and his military advisers and commanders is also of relevance. The autumn and winter of 1940–41 was a difficult time for Britain's strategists. As the threat of invasion declined, the question of where and, more importantly, how to take the fight to the enemy became correspondingly acute. Churchill was for the maximum offensive action. Considering it his duty to battle against 'the dead hand of inaction' and deploring the principle of 'safety first', he proposed a succession of military initiatives, many of them unsound.[27] When the flaws or impracticalities of his schemes were pointed out, he lost his temper. Wavell's refusal to indulge the Prime Minister's fixation on capturing the insignificant Mediterranean island of Pantelleria – a 'wildcat scheme' according to Admiral Cunningham – led to the absurd suggestion that Eden should fly out and replace the General as Commander-in-Chief.[28] Considering him little more than 'a good average Colonel' – a man who might make a 'good Chairman of a Tory association' or worse, 'Chairman of a Golf Club' – Churchill criticised Wavell repeatedly over his failure to take the offensive and the extent of his rearward services.[29]

Nor was Churchill's ire exclusive to the C-in-C Middle East. One night in December 1940, Kennedy was about to leave his desk in the War Office when a visibly agitated Dill, whom Churchill had christened 'Dilly-Dally', came into his room and recounted an appalling argument he had just had in Downing Street. The Prime Minister had said 'things about the Army that he [Dill] could never forgive', including the wish that he had the Greek Commander-in Chief, General Papagos, to run it.[30] One month later and still chuntering that he could get 'nothing done by the Army', Churchill chastised the Chiefs of Staff for proposing the 'minimum of aggressive action', before going on to accuse his military advisers of only wanting to land 'small forces on unimportant islands'.[31] It was sorely tempting for the professionals to reply in kind. 'One wanted to say to him,' wrote Kennedy in his diary: 'Why have you not got [the] USA into the war? Why have you not got Spain on our side? Why have you not got the Balkan states and Turkey aligned with us? And what about the Far East and the attitude of Japan?' But prudence, coupled with the knowledge that diplomacy depends on strength, counselled silence.[32]

Of course, these men were battle-hardened professionals: both Dill and Wavell had been decorated for bravery during the First World War. Yet they would have been less than human had they not allowed an element of chastened pride to influence their decision in favour of a project upon which the Prime Minister had so clearly set his mind. The irony was that at the very moment the Generals were stiffening to the expedition, Churchill was having doubts. 'Do not consider yourselves obligated to a Greek enterprise if in your hearts you feel it will only be another Norwegian fiasco,' he telegraphed Eden on 20 February. 'If no good plan can be made please say so. But of course you know how valuable success would be.'[33]

On 22 February, Eden, accompanied by Dill, Wavell and Longmore, flew to Athens. At Tatoi, the royal palace just outside the city, the Foreign Secretary offered King George, Prime Minister Koryzis and General Papagos 100,000 men, 142 tanks, 240 field guns and 202 anti-tank guns. Eden 'sold the proposition with all the enthusiasm at his command', recalled the secretary to the Commanders-in-Chief Committee, Lieutenant-Colonel Francis de Guingand. After the conference, the Foreign Secretary 'entered the ante-room . . . and preened himself before the chimney-piece on how well he had swayed the meeting. His entourage assisted at this melancholy exhibition of vanity.'[34] When Koryzis asked about the attitude of Turkey and Yugoslavia, Eden had replied that he did not know. He had been trying to meet the Yugoslav Regent, Prince Paul, but the Prince, terrified of antagonising Hitler, had thus far refused. Later, at the purely military conference, it was agreed that the British and the Greeks would attempt to hold a line along the Aliakmon River, between the northern slopes of Mount Olympus and the Yugoslav border. On 24 February, the War Cabinet, augmented by the Australian Prime Minister, Robert Menzies, ratified this decision. As Cadogan recorded in his diary, it was a finely balanced dilemma:

> Read Chiefs of Staff report endorsing proposals for a Balkan expedition to help Greece. On all moral and sentimental (and consequently American) grounds, one is driven to the grim conclusion. But it *must*, in the end, be a failure. However, perhaps better to have failed in a decent project than never to have tried at all. A[nthony] has rather jumped us into this. But it is impressive that *Wavell* and Dill endorse him . . . PM evidently made up his mind.[35]

The next few weeks were dedicated to trying to form a 'Balkan bloc' capable of frustrating a German attack. On 25 February, Eden and Dill landed at Adana, Turkey. There they were met by a guard of honour, representatives of the Turkish Foreign Office and what appeared to be the entire population of the city, cheering and clapping 'furiously'.[36] The British Ambassador, Sir Hughe Knatchbull-Hugessen, was impressed. Turkish crowds were typically 'undemonstrative' but this did not stop the inhabitants of the railway village of Ulukişla from mobbing the British visitors, nor an equally enthusiastic and much larger throng from surrounding the train when it reached Ankara.[37]

Eden had been warned that Turkey, as an active ally, would prove more of a hindrance than a help. The Turks were 'tough fighting soldiers', explained the head of the British Military Mission in Ankara, General James Marshall-Cornwall, but possessed a 'bow-and-arrow army', with scarcely any tanks and even fewer aeroplanes. Under such circumstances, Marshall-Cornwall concluded, there was little that could be done to prevent the Germans from overrunning Thrace, while the largely wooden-built Istanbul could be 'reduced to ashes' by German bombers within a few hours.[38] Far from being an asset, the Turks would merely be a drain on much-needed resources. Wavell and Longmore concurred. In the interests of bolstering Greece and influencing Yugoslavia, however, both Eden and Churchill were determined to try and persuade Turkey to enter the war.

This they failed to do. Although the Turks were obliged under the terms of the Anglo-French-Turkish Treaty of October 1939 to go to war following an act of aggression in the Mediterranean, the *quid pro quo* was extensive economic assistance and vast quantities of equipment. Although the Turks had been provided with the former – a £17 million loan and £25 million worth of credit to spend on British-made arms – the latter was incomplete. Thus, when the British asked their putative allies to join the war, the Turks were able to reply (truthfully) that they were in no fit state to fight the Germans. Indeed, the scarcity of Allied materiel served as a convenient excuse. 'Of course I know that you could not afford to spare those . . . you would be completely lost without them,' a laughing President İnönü told Marshall-Cornwall, following a renewed offer of 100 British fighters and 100 anti-aircraft guns. 'No, no! We are far more useful to you as a friendly neutral country.'³⁹

Despite the Turkish rebuff, Eden was encouraged by the friendliness of Turkish Ministers, in particular the Foreign Minister, Şükrü Saracoğlu, and the obvious sympathy of the population.* The casual optimism of his report on the discussions caused consternation in London. 'Telegram from A[nthony] at Ankara which puzzles me,' recorded Cadogan. 'It is couched in jaunty and self-satisfied terms, talking of the "frankness" and "friendliness" and "realism" of the Turks. The "reality" is that they won't do a damned thing. Has he had his head turned by crowds of hand-clapping Turks?'⁴⁰ Churchill agreed. 'Without in any way blaming [the] Turks, I cannot see that you have got anything out of them,' he telegraphed Eden on 1 March 1941. 'Your main appeal should now be made to Yugoslavia . . . I am absolutely ready to go in on a serious hazard if there is [a] reasonable chance of success . . . But I should like you so to handle matters in Greece that if upon final consideration of all

---

* Certainly, he had a good time, repairing, at Saracoğlu's insistence, on the second night of his visit to the nightclub beneath the Ankara Hotel. The cabaret girls (who had gone to bed) were recalled and Eden, who had taken a First in Oriental languages at Oxford, amused himself by reciting Persian poetry. On the following evening, Saracoğlu coaxed him onto the dance floor leading to what Mallaby described as the 'best sight' of the visit: 'two Foreign Secretaries, doing the Palais Glide at 4 a.m. on a very small floor'. (Mallaby Papers, Diary, 27 February 1941)

the factors . . . you feel that there is not even a reasonable hope, you should still retain power to liberate [the] Greeks from any bargain and at the same time liberate ourselves.'⁴¹

The moment to do this, were it indeed to be done, was when Eden and Dill returned to Athens on 2 March only to discover that the Greeks had not begun to withdraw their troops from Thrace and Macedonia to the Aliakmon line. The British believed that Papagos had agreed to begin this immediately following their meeting on 22 February. Yet the Greek Commander-in-Chief thought that such a manoeuvre was to be implemented only if the British failed to persuade the Yugoslavs to fight, thus rendering a line at Salonika unviable. Papagos had fought hard against the idea of surrendering Greek territory to the Germans and the even more hated Bulgarians, while Eden had sowed the seeds of confusion when, contradicting the Commanders-in-Chief, he had stated that 'preparations' should be made for the withdrawal but that 'execution' should wait until the attitude of Yugoslavia had been ascertained.⁴² Either way, the results were fatal. Bulgaria had joined the Tripartite Pact of Germany, Italy and Japan on 1 March and German forces were already pouring into that country from Romania. In London, the Chiefs of Staff greeted the news of the Greek failure to withdraw with dismay. Promised (or so they thought) thirty-five Greek battalions, dug in along the Aliakmon line, where they would be joined by just over three British and Imperial divisions, they were now being offered a mere twenty-three battalions, currently scattered across Thrace and Macedonia.

Left to its own judgement, there is little doubt that the War Cabinet would have abandoned the operation. Yet the advice from the Middle East – from Eden, Dill and the Commanders-in-Chief – was to proceed. 'Chief of the Imperial General Staff and I, in consultation with [the] three Commanders-in-Chief . . . are unanimously agreed that despite the heavy commitments and grave risks which are undoubtedly involved . . . the right decision was taken in Athens [on 22 February],' Eden telegraphed on 6 March.⁴³ According to his memoirs, Eden felt 'wretchedly anxious' during these days.⁴⁴ Yet the contemporary diaries of the American Minister, Lincoln MacVeagh, suggest that the Foreign Secretary, cheered everywhere by crowds, had not abandoned the jaunty optimism that had so alarmed Cadogan. 'I found Mr Eden very easy and pleasant, a sartorial symphony,' he recorded on 3 March, the day after the British had learnt of the Greek failure to withdraw to the Aliakmon line:

> I liked him at once and felt he was on the ball, though perhaps at the moment the ball is between his pony's legs and he doesn't know how to get at it with his mallet . . . He said he was very pleased with his reception in Turkey and that the Turks are fully loyal . . . Perhaps more interesting was his comment that even if the Germans occupy Greece it will be of no particular effect on the war, since Britain by that time will be 'sitting pretty' in Africa. To fight her way to the domination of the whole Balkans will do Germany no good, since she will be enclosed in the circle of the British blockade and, as he put it, 'playing football in her own cabbage patch' . . . Just about this time, I left, but not before Mr Eden had expressed his belief that sooner or later Greece, Turkey and Yugoslavia would all three be fighting against Germany but that there would be a lot of shifts and hesitations before that happened.

Two days later, Eden exhibited further confidence by gesturing to the American Minister. 'You tell 'em,' he called, taking his leave. 'Thumbs up!' MacVeagh feared that the Foreign Secretary was 'rather at sea'.[45]

Yet if Eden was guilty of wishful thinking, the same was true of Wavell and Dill, both of whom continued to support the expedition despite the material change in circumstances. Indeed, contrary to both contemporary and historiographical claims that Wavell was a reluctant participant in the Greek venture, he repeatedly stated his belief that there was a decent chance of forestalling the Germans, while the dividends accrued from a successful operation would be 'incalculable and might alter the whole aspect of the war'.[46] His junior, the commander of the British Expeditionary Force, Lieutenant-General Henry Maitland Wilson – known as 'Jumbo' on account of his height and girth – took a more realistic view. After listening to Sir Michael Palairet rhapsodising in similar vein, he remarked to a staff officer: 'Well, I don't know about all that but I have already ordered maps of the Peloponnese.'[47]

The odds would have been improved if Yugoslavia could have been persuaded to resist Axis penetration of the region but this Balkan kingdom, comprising Serbs, Croats, Slovenes, Montenegrins, Kosovans, Bosnian Muslims, Macedonians, Slovaks, Hungarians, Germans, Italians, Rusyns and Jews, showed no signs of wishing to become embroiled. The Regent, Prince Paul, was emotionally pro-British. A contemporary of Eden's at Oxford, his closest friends were English aristocrats and dandies like Chips Channon. The majority of the Yugoslav people were similarly pro-Allied. One Sunday, shortly after the fall of France, the British Military Attaché in Belgrade, Colonel J. R. S. Clarke, overheard an old peasant referring to his pig as 'Churchill'. Outraged, Clarke confronted the man. 'Did I hear you correctly? Do you call that pig Churchill?' 'Yes,' came the matter-of-fact reply, 'he's my last hope.'[48] Yet the circumstances of geography, inadequate defences and a well-deserved terror of the Luftwaffe combined to keep the Yugoslav Government from joining the Allied camp.

On 25 March 1941, under intense German pressure and with Britain unable to offer anything beyond brave words, Prince Paul joined the Tripartite Pact. His aim was to spare his country the horrors of war. But he had reckoned without the anti-German sentiments of his people and the unpopularity of his Government. On 27 March, officers of the Royal Guards Corps in Belgrade, along with senior officers in the Royal Yugoslav Air Force, opposition parties and patriotic groups, staged a *coup d'état*, toppling Prince Paul and placing the seventeen-year-old King Peter on the throne. The British, who had encouraged the conspirators, were jubilant. 'The Yugoslav nation [has] found its soul,' declared Churchill, in a speech to the Conservative Central Council.[49] But the expected change in Yugoslav foreign policy failed to materialise. To intense Allied frustration, the new Yugoslav Government – a motley collection of politicians under the leadership of General Dušan Simović – proved no more warlike than its predecessor, refusing to denounce the Tripartite Pact or attack the Italians in Albania. Belatedly, with rumours swirling of an imminent German invasion, the Army was mobilised and talks were held between Greek and Yugoslav staff officers but it was too late. Enraged by Belgrade's defiance, Hitler had ordered the destruction of the Yugoslav state. At dawn on 6 April, over 300 Stukas, Heinkels and Dorniers began to bomb the Yugoslav capital in waves. As the King and Government fled into the mountains and thence to exile, forty-one Axis divisions dissected the country.

The invasion of Greece began at the same time, Hitler having decided in mid-November to eliminate the threat to his southern flank. The Luftwaffe bombed Piraeus (temporarily disabling the port), while the German 12th Army struck south from Bulgaria. Within days, the British Expeditionary Force – consisting principally of Australian and New Zealand troops and only half-deployed – was falling back, alongside its Greek comrades, in disarray. 'Vehicles were jammed nose to tail for miles,' recalled one British officer. 'Buses and private cars, Greeks on horseback and foot, were all jumbled in between our guns . . . We never fired a round on the Venetikos [the river flowing south-west from the Aliakmon], for the enemy found more to interest him in our flanks . . . But the Luftwaffe showed no lack of interest in us, treating us every few hours to a display of machine-gunning and dive-bombing which brought home to us as never before what monopoly of the air meant.'[50]

On 21 April, Wavell gave the order for evacuation. Koryzis had committed suicide three days previously and the Greek Army, exhausted after four months of fighting the Italians, was at its last breath. Between 24 and 29 April, despite relentless attacks by the Luftwaffe, the Royal Navy and the Royal Air Force succeeded in rescuing a little over 50,000 men of the 62,000-strong Expeditionary Force from beaches in Attica and the Peloponnese. Around 14,000 fell into captivity, while some 2,000 had been killed or wounded. Like Dunkirk, it was a deliverance but, as in June 1940, the British lost almost all of their equipment, including over 100 tanks, 192 field guns, 164 anti-tank guns, 40 anti-aircraft guns, nearly 2,000 machine guns and 8,000 vehicles. More than 200 aircraft were lost during the course of the operation, while twenty-six ships were sunk during the evacuation.

At the same time, the British were retreating across the Western Desert. Having decided that he could not allow his Axis partner to be humiliated, Hitler had despatched one of the heroes of the fall of France to North Africa to head a hastily formed *Afrika Korps*.

On 12 February 1941, Generalleutnant Erwin Rommel landed in Tripoli. On 24 March, despite possessing only two German divisions, supported by four underequipped Italian divisions, he attacked. Churchill urged Wavell to counterattack but the Greek expedition left the Commander-in-Chief with few reserves for operations in Cyrenaica. Soon Imperial troops were hurtling back along the coastal road down which they had so recently advanced. Benghazi fell on 4 April and by the 11th the Army of the Nile was almost back at its starting point, though fierce fighting by the Australians prevented Rommel from capturing Tobruk.

Depression among Britain's senior soldiers bordered on defeatism. 'CIGS is miserable and feels he has wrecked the Empire,' recorded Major-General Kennedy, who had come to loathe his title of Director of Military Operations lest 'outsiders think I really "direct" military operations and am partly responsible for this foolish and disastrous strategy that our armies are following'.[51] Elsewhere, the succession of calamities was greeted with incredulity. 'What is the matter with the British?' wondered Lincoln MacVeagh in Athens. 'Can they not create armoured divisions too? They have had a year now since they learned the lessons of modern warfare.'[52] 'I did hope we had done with Dunkirks,' commented Lord Halifax.[53]

The mistakes were many and largely foreseen. For the majority of the soldiers, the cardinal blunder had been not to push on to Tripoli and clear the Italians from North Africa before the *Afrika Korps* arrived in strength. As Kennedy later wrote, faithfully repeating the advice he had given at the time, 'a small force rushed on to Tripoli might well have eliminated the enemy threat from the North African shore for the rest of the war'.[54] That this prize was not seized was, in the words of another soldier, due to the 'chivalrous but quixotic gesture' to go to Greece.[55] Kennedy, General Richard O'Connor (who had led the Western Desert Force during Operation Compass) and Brigadier Eric Dorman-Smith (responsible for much of the operation's planning) all considered it a dereliction of duty that the Chiefs of Staff had not ordered a proper military assessment of the options following the capture of Benghazi, including the Greek venture. In Kennedy's opinion, this failure stemmed from the Chiefs of Staff being 'overawed and influenced unduly by Winston's overpowering personality', a sentiment shared by the Australian Prime Minister, Robert Menzies:

> At War Cabinet [14 April 1941], W.C. speaks at length as the Master-Strategist: 'Tobruk *must* be held as a bridge-head or rally post, from which to hit the enemy.' 'With what?' says I, and so the discussion goes on. Wavell and the Admiralty have failed us. The Cabinet is deplorable – dumb men most of whom disagree with Winston but none of whom dare to say so. This state of affairs is most dangerous. The Chiefs of Staff are without exception Yes Men and a politician runs the services. Winston is a dictator; he cannot be overruled and his colleagues fear him. The people have set him up as something little less than a God and his power is therefore terrific.[56]*

Yet the Greek commitment ultimately arose from political rather than military considerations. Although Wavell gave the venture his blessing, it was Churchill who, in Dill's words, 'led the hunt' towards the decision, propelled by Chamberlain's 1939 guarantee, concern for world opinion and the strategic value of the Balkans.[57] To the Prime Minister's critics, many of whom resided in the War Office, this represented an inversion of priorities. Yet as the military theorist Carl von Clausewitz observed, 'policy is the guiding intelligence and war only the instrument, not *vice versa*'.[58] Over a century after these words were written, with Britain's survival entwined with her prestige, most crucially in the United States, this dictum held good. 'Far from being seen as just another failure, the support of Greece was saluted in the United States as a gallant promise-keeping in a world that had seemed to be corrupted by German promise breaking,' wrote the Century Group's Herbert Agar, a sentiment shared by Under-Secretary of State Sumner Welles.[59] In a radio broadcast on 27 April, Churchill emphasised the chivalry behind the ruined enterprise:

---

* A week later, Menzies told Churchill that he needed Chiefs of Staff who would 'tell him he is talking nonsense'. Churchill exploded but later calmed down and revealed his 'real opinion' of the CoS. 'He knows they are Yes Men', recorded Menzies, 'and does not love them for it.'

They [the Greeks] declared they would fight for their native soil even if neither of their neighbours made common cause with them and even if we left them to their fate. But we could not do that. There are rules against that kind of thing and to break those rules would be fatal to the honour of the British Empire, without which we could neither hope nor deserve to win this hard war. Military defeat or miscalculation can be redeemed . . . But an act of shame would deprive us of the respect which we now enjoy throughout the world and this would sap the vitals of our strength.[60]

Of course, this was of little comfort to the Greeks who, likewise, gained nothing from the disputed claim that the Balkan diversion caused Hitler to delay the launch of Operation Barbarossa, with fatal results. As they retreated from the Aliakmon to the dust-coloured beaches of the Peloponnese, British and Imperial forces felt shame and guilt at the gratitude shown to them by the population, some 300,000 of whom would perish as a result of the Axis occupation. 'We turned . . . to the English,' wrote an Athenian newspaper editor in an open letter to the Greek people. To 'those who were keeping anxious watch and ward on the Channel, those who, they said it themselves, had not sufficient materiel for their own defence. They came and they came immediately.'[61] These were noble sentiments but they could not disguise the fact that, once again, Britain had failed to save an ally from destruction.

X

Desert War

Our radio transmitters are stirring up the Arabs.
We intend to play Colonel Lawrence.

Joseph Goebbels, 17 April 1941[1]

The Royal Air Force base at Habbaniya was a sleepy establishment. Situated on the west bank of the Euphrates, between Ramadi and Fallujah, it was one of two airbases granted to Britain under the terms of the 1930 Anglo-Iraqi Treaty. Although described by one RAF officer as 'the most godforsaken hell-hole in the entire world', the vast camp, covering some 500 acres, contained extensive amenities including schools, shops, cinemas, a hospital, recreation halls, a swimming pool, stables, a pack of hounds, playing fields, a polo pitch, a yacht club, a golf course and twenty-six tennis courts.[2] Water diverted from the river nourished green lawns and herbaceous borders, while the roads bore familiar names such as 'Bond Street', 'Piccadilly' and 'Tottenham Court Road'. The principal business of the base was the flying school. Overseen by Air Vice-Marshal H. G. 'Reggie' Smart, a gallant if staid officer, it consisted of a motley collection of obsolete and obsolescent Gloster Gladiator biplanes, Hawker Audaxes, Fairey Gordons and twin-engine Airspeed Oxfords. Roald Dahl remembered his six months at this 'nonsensical' outpost as insufferably tedious, the humdrum life of the cantonment enlivened only by the menace of the scorpions, or when errant Iraqi tribesmen started sniping from the nearby escarpment.[3] Then, one morning in April 1941, the inhabitants of Habbaniya awoke to find themselves under siege.

For the British in the Middle East, troubles came not in single spies but in battalions. On 1 April 1941, just as Imperial troops were deploying in Greece, the pro-British Regent of Iraq, Emir Abdullah, uncle of the five-year-old King Faisal II, was overthrown in a *coup d'état*. Warned just in time, the Regent managed to pull some women's robes over his pyjamas, sneak out of the palace and seek sanctuary in the American Legation. The conspirators were a pan-Arabist, pro-Axis quartet of colonels in the Iraqi Army, known as the 'Golden Square'. Their figurehead was the former Prime Minister and serial intriguer Rashid Ali al-Gailani.

The British were, understandably, concerned. From a strategic point of view, Iraq was scarcely less important than Egypt. A former British mandate, she had attained her independence in 1932 but only after signing a treaty granting significant military and commercial rights to Britain designed to ensure that country's oil concessions, as well as the land route to India. For much of the remaining decade, the British liked to think of Iraq as a loyal ally, grateful to her former suzerain for founding the modern state after four centuries of Ottoman rule, training and equipping her armed forces and extracting her natural resources (for which the Iraqis received royalties). What this complacency ignored was the rise of anti-British sentiment within the country, fuelled by pan-Arab nationalism, anti-imperialism and anger over Jewish migration to Palestine. Iraqi sympathy for the anti-Zionist Palestinian Revolt, begun in 1936, was practically universal and it was no surprise when, in 1939, following the collapse of the insurgency, many of its leaders, including the Grand Mufti, Haj Amin al-Husseini, sought refuge in Baghdad. As the travel writer and orientalist Freya Stark wrote to a friend on 19 April 1941, 'the Palestine question lies at the root of all our troubles'.[4]

The Germans had been adept at exploiting these feelings: subsidising nationalist newspapers, founding a youth movement (an imitation of the Hitlerjugend) and disseminating anti-British propaganda. The driving force behind these activities was the German Ambassador, Dr Fritz Grobba, who cultivated the leading members of the Iraqi officer corps and whose residence became a centre for intrigue and nationalist ferment. When war broke out, the British prevailed upon the Iraqi Government to sever diplomatic ties with Berlin but not with Rome, whose Legation remained open despite Italian belligerency. In December 1940, Prime Minister Rashid Ali asked the Axis to supply him with captured British military equipment and on 9 April 1941, following the *coup d'état*, the German and Italian Governments promised to support the reinstated Premier in his desire to drive the British from the country.

The Iraq crisis occurred at the worst possible time for Britain's already overstretched Middle East Command. Battling the Germans in Greece, retreating before Rommel in Cyrenaica, mopping up the Italians in east Africa and preparing for an attack on Crete, neither Wavell nor Longmore believed they had the resources for a war against a country that remained, at least nominally, a British ally. Smart's requests for reinforcements were declined while, on 7 April, Wavell informed the War Office that the most he could spare for Iraq was a single battalion, currently in Palestine. Fortunately, Britain's India Command saw matters differently. Long concerned at the vulnerability of the kingdom to either Axis or Soviet penetration, plans had been laid as early as August 1939 to reinforce Iraq with Indian-based troops. On 8 April, Churchill asked Lieutenant-General Claude Auchinleck, Commander-in-Chief India, to implement these plans and on 12 April the vanguard of a division set sail from Karachi.

Informed by the newly arrived Ambassador, Sir Kinahan Cornwallis – an old Middle East hand who had served as an adviser to Faisal I – that Britain intended to avail herself of her treaty rights and land troops in the country, Rashid Ali found himself pre-empted. Unable to oppose the landing without precipitating a war – a scenario for which he was not yet ready – he limited himself to the demand that no further detachments should be sent until those about to arrive had 'passed through' the country, supposedly to Palestine.[5] On 17 April 1941, 364 officers and men of 1st Battalion the King's Own Royal Rifle Regiment landed at Shaibah and, on the following morning, 200 Gurkhas disembarked at Basra. The effect, noted Stark in Baghdad, was 'electrical'. The insurgent Government tried to suppress the news but the BBC undermined its attempts.[6] That day, Rashid Ali sent an urgent message to the Axis Governments via the Italian Minister:

> The Iraq Government was firmly resolved to defend itself and would therefore like to learn as soon as possible . . . first, whether

the Iraqi Army could count on support from the Air Force of the
Axis Powers . . . Second, whether the Iraqi Army could count on
receiving rifles and ammunition by air transports such as Italy
and Germany had used during the Abyssinian and Norwegian
campaigns.[7]

Meanwhile, the residents of RAF Habbaniya were preparing for
trouble. To the horror of the hearties, the polo field and golf course
were bulldozed to create an airfield inside the camp, while bomb
racks were fitted to the antiquated Gordons, Audaxes and Oxfords.
Smart hoped these precautions would prove unnecessary. On 29
April, however – the day after Cornwallis had informed Rashid
Ali that a further 2,000 Imperial troops would be disembarking at
Basra – the British Ambassador became so concerned at the atmosphere in Baghdad that he arranged for the evacuation of 250 British
women and children to Habbaniya. At 3 a.m. the British Embassy
informed Smart of large quantities of men and vehicles moving out
of Rachid Barracks, crossing the bridges over the Tigris and heading
westward. By 4 a.m. he was surrounded.

As a defensive proposition, Habbaniya was hopeless. Never conceived to act as a redoubt, the base was overlooked by a large plateau
atop a 150-foot escarpment. Guarded by six companies of Assyrian,
Kurdish and Arab levies (about 1,200 men in all) – supplemented,
after 29 April, by the 364 men and officers of the King's Own – the
'armour' consisted of eighteen thinly plated Rolls-Royce cars ('like
sardine cans and about as easily opened', as one officer put it) and
two ancient tanks, known as 'Walrus' and 'Seal'.[8] Palestine was 500
miles away, while the bulk of the forces arriving at Basra – 300 miles
away – were unable to reach the base owing to the flooding caused
by the Iraqi decision to cut the 'bunds' on the Euphrates. To all
intents and purposes, Habbaniya was cut off.

Shortly after the sounding of the general alarm, a reconnaissance flight took off from the polo pitch. Clearly visible in the pink
dawn were around 1,000 soldiers of the Iraqi Army, with field guns,
howitzers and armoured vehicles, digging in along the plateau and
beyond them a winding snake of troops and guns stretching back to
Fallujah. No sooner had this information been digested than an Iraqi

officer presented himself at the camp gates and informed Smart that his troops had occupied the heights above the camp for 'training purposes' and that his aircraft were to remain grounded on pain of being shelled. Smart, who had been awarded the Distinguished Flying Cross for bravery in the face of the enemy, replied robustly: 'Any interference with training flights will be considered an "act of war" and will be met by immediate counter-offensive action. We demand the withdrawal of the Iraqi forces from positions which are clearly hostile and must place my camp at their mercy.'[9]

The British Ambassador to Cairo, Sir Miles Lampson, applauded such stoutness. 'It is refreshing to hear something of that kind coming from our people these days,' he noted in his diary.[10] But the path before the Air Vice-Marshal was far from clear. Despite the dramatic decline in Anglo-Iraqi relations, Iraq remained, at least officially, a British ally. Would Smart be thanked for saddling London with another war in the Middle East while Imperial forces were evacuating Greece and retreating in Libya? Could the Arab levies be relied upon? And what of the 9,000 civilians within the cantonment, augmented by the arrival of the women and children from Baghdad? On the other hand, if fighting were to be done then 'twere best it were done quickly, the garrison's only hope lying in a pre-emptive strike against the Iraqi positions. Torn, Smart sent telegrams to Baghdad, Basra, Cairo, Delhi and London asking for instructions. Auchinleck and Cornwallis favoured an immediate display of force but it was the opinion of their political masters that mattered. After a day of agonised suspense – during which the Iraqis consolidated their positions and temperatures soared above 38 degrees Centigrade – a telegram from the Foreign Office arrived providing the Air Vice-Marshal with the unambiguous directive he craved: 'Position must be restored. Iraqi troops must be withdrawn without delay. You have full authority to take any steps you think necessary to ensure this, including air attack.'[11] Later, a more succinct version of the same message arrived from the Prime Minister: 'If you have to strike, strike hard. Use all necessary force.'[12]

Smart resolved to hit the Iraqis at first light. Significantly outnumbered – Iraqi troops on the plateau now amounted to some 6,000, with more on the way – his strategy was to demoralise the enemy with continuous bombing raids, forcing them to withdraw. 'They should be in full flight within about three hours,' he bullishly told his officers.[13] At 2.45 a.m. on 2 May, he issued the Iraqi commanding officer with an ultimatum. Two hours later, no response having been received, the vanishing night was filled with the sound of engines revving. As soon as targets became distinguishable, the thirty-nine available pilots from the training school, supplemented by ten Wellingtons sent from Basra, began to bomb the enemy's gun emplacements and armoured cars. The Iraqis responded by shelling the base and the cantonment, as well as with raids by their own, much larger, air force. By the end of the day, the thirty-nine RAF pilots had flown over 193 sorties, the scene above the plateau resembling 'the front of a wasp's nest on a sunny morning'.[14] But the Iraqis remained in place. During the day their forces had swelled to around 9,000 and, during the night, they maintained a steady hail of shells into the camp.

The failure of the flying school to displace the Iraqis on the first day caused consternation in London and Cairo. 'Are we really going to be beaten by Iraqis?' wondered Sir Alexander Cadogan.[15] Churchill felt the need for reinforcements to resolve the situation as swiftly as possible. British prestige would not survive defeat at the hands of the Iraqi Army. The longer the war continued, the greater the risk of a pan-Arab revolt, while the likely arrival of German reinforcements threatened to encircle Wavell's forces, cut the Empire in two and provide Hitler with the oil fields (Iranian as well as Iraqi) currently nourishing Britain's war effort across the Mediterranean and Middle East. The Commander-in-Chief disagreed. Pressed on all fronts, Wavell argued strenuously for a political solution to the crisis. 'I have consistently warned you that no assistance could be given to Iraq from Palestine,' he responded, tetchily, to a request from the Chiefs of Staff to send a relief force. 'Nothing short of immediate action by at least a Brigade group with strong support of artillery and AFVs [armoured fighting vehicles] could restore [the] situation. There are no guns or AFVs in Palestine and to send forward weak and unsupported forces of cavalry or infantry seems merely asking for further trouble. My forces are stretched to [the] limit everywhere and I simply cannot afford to risk part of [my] forces on what cannot produce any effect . . . I can only advise negotiation with Iraqis on basis of liquidation of regrettable incident by mutual agreement with alternative of war with [the] British Empire, complete blockade and ruthless air action.'[16]

Churchill, the Defence Committee and the Chiefs of Staff were horrified. Fearing that the much-put-upon C-in-C was no longer able to appreciate the wider strategic picture, they responded on 5 May by ordering him to send a relief force to Habbaniya. 'Nice baby you have handed me on my fifty-eighth birthday,' Wavell telegraphed Sir John Dill. 'Have always hated babies and Iraqis but will do my best for the little blighter.' The CIGS responded sympathetically: 'What a birthday present. Sincerely hope you will be able to kill the little brute. Many happy returns for birthday but not of baby.'[17]

The force that assembled at Beit Lid, in Palestine, on 9 May 1941 was distinctly 'scratch'. Commanded by Major-General George Clark and totalling some 6,000 men, it centred around the 4th Cavalry Brigade – comprising the 1st Household Cavalry Regiment, the Royal Wiltshire Yeomanry and the Warwickshire Yeomanry – augmented by a battalion of Essex infantry, a battery of field artillery, eight RAF armoured cars and a squadron of the Transjordan Frontier Force. The cavalry had only recently swapped their horses for vehicles. Known ironically as 'Hitler's secret weapon' owing to their lack of equipment, the comment by one yeomanry officer on plans to resist a German invasion of Palestine with Molotov cocktails was '*C'est magnifique, mais . . . c'est* bloody silly'.[18] There was only one radio set per squadron and one 2-inch mortar per troop, while a dearth of transport led to the requisitioning of dozens of civilian buses and other conveyances. The commander of the once glamorous Household Cavalry was forced to undertake the desert odyssey in a low-slung Haifa taxi.

On 11 May, 'Habforce' crossed from Palestine into Transjordan and began a journey that no army had attempted since the days of Alexander the Great: some 500 miles of open desert, with few distinguishing landmarks, little water and multiple depressions. Their first objective was Rutbah, a fort 85 miles across the frontier, containing the last known well before Habbaniya. Following its seizure by members of the Iraqi Desert Police at the start of the month, Clark had ordered the mechanised squadron of the Transjordan Frontier Force to retake the garrison. The TJFF refused. Composed of Palestinian Arabs, Circassians and a few Jews, they claimed inaccurately that it was contrary to their contract to participate in operations outside Transjordan. After this baleful beginning, Clark decided to despatch a flying column, known as 'Kingcol' after its commander, Brigadier Joe Kingstone, to capture the fort and then strike east towards Habbaniya. On 10 May, after some desultory bombing and a skirmish with the RAF armoured cars, the Iraqis abandoned the stronghold. Arriving at the fort on the night of 13–14 May, Kingstone and his intelligence officer, Captain Somerset de Chair, Member of Parliament for South-West Norfolk, were greeted by a convocation of white-robed soldiers, with pink headdresses and bandoliers of ammunition. These were the Bedouins of the Arab Legion or, more precisely, the 350 men of its Desert Mechanised Force.

Formed in 1920, to provide security for the newly created kingdom of Transjordan, the Arab Legion had developed, during the succeeding two decades, from a tiny police force into an equally small but highly efficient army. When war broke out following the invasion of Poland, Emir Abdullah – second son of Hussein bin Ali, Sharif of Mecca and brother of Faisal I of Syria and then Iraq – demonstrated his loyalty to Britain by placing the resources of his state at her disposal. The crisis in Iraq afforded Abdullah and the Arab Legion the opportunity to prove their fidelity. 'Will the Arab Legion fight?' enquired General Wilson, recently appointed General Officer Commanding Palestine and Transjordan. 'The Arab Legion will fight anybody,' replied its commander, Major Glubb.[19]

John Bagot Glubb – better known as 'Pasha Glubb' – was arguably the most revered and recognised foreigner in Arabia. A former British Army officer, who had served in France and later Iraq, he had brought an end to the raids by Ibn Saud's Wahhabis upon Iraq's southern Bedouin before joining the Arab Legion in 1930. In 1939, he took over its command. Known to the Arabs as Abu Hunaik ('Father of the Little Jaw') on account of a wound sustained during the First World War, his underwhelming appearance belied a gentle charisma. The commander of the TJFF,

Lieutenant-Colonel Peter Wilson, believed that it was owing to Glubb 'more than any other man that the Arabs have not come into the war on the German side'. 'Glubb's influence is unique,' he eulogised to friends in Cairo. 'He knows every tribal chief from the Tigris to the Nile, he is liked and respected in Iraq, Transjordan, Eastern Syria and Northern Arabia. His knowledge of Arab history, poetry and song, which are like the Bible to them, is unprecedented.'[20] De Chair fell immediately under his spell. 'Unassuming as he always appeared, his whole background was glamorous, and I felt that the Glubb legend was more surely rooted in the hearts of the Bedouin than was Lawrence's . . . His men came from tribes all over the Levant (including Iraq) and were proud to serve under him.'[21] Kingstone was not convinced. 'This fellow thinks he is King of Saudi Arabia,' he complained to de Chair, after a brief conference with the keffiyeh-wearing Glubb in the abandoned fort. 'I am going to get him out of the way as soon as we leave here. The trouble is that I don't know whether he is senior to me or not.' De Chair posited that he looked like a lieutenant-general.[22]

The following morning, Kingcol left Rutbah, the Arab Legion leading the way. 'I was unable to decide whether this post was offered to us in order to enable us to guide the column and act as advanced guard, or whether the Brigadier's principal idea was to get us as far away as possible from his column,' Glubb commented.[23] In either scenario, it was a mistake. Despatching Glubb and his men – christened 'Glubb's girls' on account of their long hair and robes – on a wild goose chase to the north, Kingstone turned off the main route at 'Kilo 25' and headed south-east. Soon his trucks were wallowing in the soft sands of a depression.[24] In temperatures exceeding 49 degrees Centigrade, the 500 vehicles of Kingcol began to retrace their tracks. 'We have enough supplies of water to stay here one more day,' the Brigadier announced that evening, 'after that we go on or go back.' Then, turning to Glubb, who had rejoined the column after a day dozing by a salty water-hole, he said: 'I shall want your dusky maidens to help us find an alternative route.'[25]

The lack of water was not Kingcol's only concern. The previous day, as the column wound its way towards Kilo 25, de Chair had been surprised to see 'two black tulips of smoke blossom far down the line'. Seconds later he saw the 'white-hot flash of anti-aircraft fire streaming upwards'.

'It was a Blenheim on reconnaissance,' explained an RAF officer.

'Not one of ours!' de Chair exclaimed.

'No, I expect it is an Iraqi plane. The bastard sprayed the line with machine gun bullets from his rear gun, too.'[26]

In fact it was a Heinkel III. The Luftwaffe had arrived.

Mercifully, no other detachments of the hastily assembled *Fliegerführer Irak* – one squadron of Messerschmitt Bf 110s and one squadron of Heinkel IIIs – located Kingcol, which finally arrived at Habbaniya on 18 May.

The siege had ended twelve days earlier. Despite losing a third of its aircraft and a quarter of its pilots on the first day, the flying school had resumed the attack on the escarpment on 3 May. The rate of attrition had been appalling. Of the twenty-seven Oxfords under Squadron Leader Tony Dudgeon at the start of the battle, only three were considered flyable by the evening of the fourth day, the Gordons, Gladiators and Audaxes having fared no better. Then, suddenly on the morning of 6 May, the Iraqi soldiers on the plateau abandoned their posts. Scrambling down from the escarpment, they began to flee along the road to Fallujah. There they ran into an Iraqi relief column coming the other way. In the ensuing mêlée the few remaining aircraft from the training school inflicted multiple casualties, while British ground forces took over 400 prisoners. After five days of continuous fighting, during which the training school flew over 647 sorties, the Battle of Habbaniya was finally over. The flying school had suffered thirty-four casualties, while estimates of Iraqi losses range between 500 and 1,000.

The succeeding fortnight, though rarely mentioned in general histories, witnessed remarkable feats of British arms. Despite the defeat at Habbaniya, the Iraqi Army remained a formidable opponent. Trained and equipped by the British, it numbered some 60,000 men, 20,000 of whom were concentrated in and around Baghdad. Kingcol, by contrast, comprised 1,450 troops, the Assyrian, Kurdish and Arab levies raising this figure to just over 2,000. The Indian brigades at Basra were impeded by flooding, while the presence of

German aircraft operating from Mosul added piquancy to a situation already fraught with danger. Wavell believed that British forces should content themselves with securing Basra and Habbaniya. The men on the spot, however, were for pushing on. Convinced that they had got the Iraqis on the back foot and anxious to stem the influx of German forces into the country, they attacked Fallujah on 18 May. Four days later the Iraqis counterattacked with tanks (the British had no tanks), employing tactics imparted to them by the British Military Mission. Caught by surprise, the outnumbered defenders came close to disaster but were saved when two companies from the Essex Regiment and a squadron from the Household Cavalry waded through the surrounding flood waters to reinforce the Assyrian levies and hard-pressed men of the King's Own.

The advance on Baghdad began on 27 May, with two squadrons of the Household Cavalry, a troop of 25-pounders and the Arab Legion traversing the desert to attack the city from the north, while Kingstone prepared to lead a column west, along the main Fallujah–Baghdad road. The operation was predicated upon the notion that the Iraqis did not appreciate just how small the British forces were – each column comprising no more than 700 men. This strategy received a fillip when, on 28 May, Somerset de Chair came across a telephone switchboard near the abandoned fort of Khan Nuqta. Deciding to try his luck, he handed the receiver to his interpreter, who was astonished to find himself connected to the headquarters of the Iraqi 3rd Division. 'Tell them that we are surrounded by the British; that the British have got tanks and that the tanks are already across the floods,' instructed de Chair. The interpreter obliged and soon the pair were listening in to panicked reports of 'at least fifty' British tanks closing in upon the capital.[27]

By this stage, Iraqi morale had collapsed. Expecting the beleaguered British to negotiate and confident of considerable German assistance, Rashid Ali and the Golden Square had been disappointed on both counts. Although the Germans had sent aircraft and trainloads of confiscated French military equipment from Syria – as well as Dr Grobba, who arrived in Baghdad on 11 May with £10,000 in gold for Rashid Ali and $15,000 in bank notes for the Grand Mufti – it was not enough to halt the British advance. The Germans are '*shiql ash-Shaitan* [the kin of Satan]', the Iraqi police told Freya Stark, following the fall of Fallujah.[28] A week later, Rashid Ali, the tetrad of colonels, the Grand Mufti and the Italian Minister fled to Iran. Grobba left the country the following day. At 8 p.m. on 30 May, the Mayor of Baghdad and the Chief of Iraqi Military Operations asked for the terms of surrender.

The four-week Anglo-Iraqi War was a relatively old-fashioned affair. Although tough and, in parts, bloody – the British suffered some 200 casualties, while Iraqi losses exceeded 1,000 – it was imbued with a spirit of improvisation and, where possible, chivalry. When the Arab Legion, still under fire from the Iraqi Army, captured the Governor of Baghdad they decided to return him to the city by floating him down the Tigris in a small boat. Later, Glubb told Clark about the important prisoner. 'That's good,' exclaimed the Major-General. 'Got him in the bag, have we?'

'Well, not exactly.'[29]

Yet for all its picturesque romance – the flying school, the relief column and the Arab Legion – the Iraq campaign had greater strategic significance than the contemporaneous loss of Crete. Despite the appalling toll on the Royal Navy – which suffered three battleships and one aircraft carrier damaged and three cruisers and six destroyers sunk, during the evacuation – the fall of Crete did not drive the British from the Mediterranean. The loss of Iraq, on the other hand, had the potential to make Britain's already precarious position in the Middle East untenable, while providing Hitler with enough oil to fuel a long war. 'If the [training] school had been overcome, the Germans would have got a foothold in Iraq,' reflected Air Marshal Arthur Tedder, Air Officer Commanding Middle East, after Longmore had been recalled on 3 May. 'If they had then created a bridgehead behind us, through Vichy-controlled Syria from Greece, our Middle East base could have been nipped out with German forces both to its east and west. Certainly, the whole course of the European war would have been changed drastically, if we had not lost it altogether.'[30] Although it was regrettable – tragic even – that Britain had once again been forced to take up arms against an ally, the decision to counter the pro-Axis intrigues of the insurgent Iraqi Government was both necessary and effective.

XI

Fighting France

We are determined to fight to the end.

Maréchal Pétain, 12 June 1941[1]

Taking a well-earned rest in the 'City of the Kaliphs', Private Harry Chalk, a tiler from Southend-on-Sea, reflected on his good fortune. His company – D Company, 1st Battalion the Essex Regiment – had enjoyed 'days of bliss' in Palestine before crossing 'one of the hottest deserts in the world', relieving the RAF base at Habbaniya, fighting a couple of battles and capturing Baghdad. That they had succeeded in doing so with only four Bren guns and two Vickers machine guns seemed little short of a miracle. 'We had no artillery or tanks' but 'went through Baghdad like a dose of Epsom salts', he recalled. Yet a troubling question remained. Outside Habbaniya, the battalion had been strafed by two Messerschmitts. Taken in isolation, the affair was insignificant. The fighters had failed to hit either the column or the adjacent aircraft. 'But where in the blazes had they come from?'[2] It was not Berlin.

The Iraqi revolt had caught the Germans by surprise. Preparing to invade the Soviet Union, while simultaneously engaged in Libya, Greece and Yugoslavia, there were neither plans nor forces readily available for the *Mittlerer Orient*. Nevertheless, Hitler was determined to do what he could. On 3 May 1941, the Germans requested the use of airfields in French-mandated Syria, from which the soon-to-be formed *Fliegerführer Irak* could refuel on their way to Mosul. Not only did the Vichy Government consent, the new Vice-President of the Council, Admiral Darlan, went further, agreeing to the transfer of confiscated French materiel to Rashid Ali, promising to facilitate delivery of further weapons and supplying the Iraqi Air Force with those 'reconnaissance, pursuit and bomber aircraft' permitted in Syria under the armistice.[3] In return, the Admiral, whose opportunism was matched only by his Anglophobia, hoped to obtain significant concessions, including a reduction of occupation costs, the repatriation of French prisoners of war, a relaxation of the demarcation line separating occupied from unoccupied France and guarantees concerning the French Empire. On 11 May, Darlan discussed the prospect of military collaboration with Hitler and, on 28 May, he appended his signature to an agreement, the so-called 'Paris Protocols', that allowed the Germans to supply Rommel's *Afrika Korps* via the Tunisian port of Bizerte, permitted German U-boats to refuel at Dakar and guaranteed Axis military rights in Syria. Although Pétain and his more cautious colleagues shied away from ratifying this incendiary document, by the time the decision was made the damage was done. On 5 May 1941, the French High Commissioner for the Levant had been instructed to 'welcome' German and Italian aircraft landing within his jurisdiction and on 9 May the first German aeroplanes were spotted above Beirut.[4]

Churchill's reaction to the arrival of the Luftwaffe in the Levant was unhesitating: 'We must go in.'[5] Long concerned about Axis penetration of the region, he had been an early supporter of Free French plans to wrest the mandated territories from Vichy control. The driving force behind these schemes was the former Governor-General of Indo-China, General Georges Catroux. Of medium height, with dark eyes, thick eyebrows and a neatly clipped moustache, this courteous and cultured proconsul with a taste for the high life (his 'luggage' from Hanoi included a suite of Indo-Chinese servants, as well as some extremely heavy furniture), had rallied to de Gaulle in the autumn of 1940. Immediately despatched by Churchill to investigate rumours of an anti-Vichy plot in the Levant, his arrival in Cairo coincided with the betrayal of the conspiracy and the arrest or repatriation of the Gaullists. Undeterred, Catroux's thoughts turned from *coup d'état* to *coup de main*. The difficulty was that any military operation relied upon the co-operation of the British. The Vichy-controlled French Armée du Levant comprised some 25,000 metropolitan and colonial troops, augmented by around 20,000 Syrian and Lebanese levies. The Free French, by contrast, boasted only six battalions (around 3,000 men).

On 1 April 1941, de Gaulle, accompanied by Catroux and Louis Spears, arrived in General Wavell's stiflingly hot office in Cairo, intent on persuading the Commander-in-Chief of the need to oust the Vichy regime from the Levant. The C-in-C was unconvinced. Pressed from north and west, and with some of his forces still engaged in the south, all he sought from the east was tranquillity. When the outbreak of war in Iraq revealed the futility of such hopes, he maintained his position. 'Intervention in Syria meant dispersal of effort and therefore defeat,' he told Catroux and Spears on 4 May. It would be better to lose Syria than 'risk being beaten in detail owing to our intervening with inadequate forces', he repeated the following day.[6] His interlocutors were aghast. Refusing to stand aloof while Syria was subsumed by the Axis, Catroux declared his intention to march his six battalions of Free French troops up to the Palestinian–Syrian frontier and make an emotional appeal to the Vichy forces: 'If you will not fight the enemy of your country, give free passage to other Frenchmen who will. If you will not fight the Germans, will you fight us? Will you shoot Catroux?'[7]

They probably would. The majority of the Armée du Levant despised the Gaullists, deeming them traitors and foreign mercenaries, while the High Commissioner, General Henri Dentz, was unswerving in his loyalty to Vichy, believing that Britain – and by proxy her Free French allies – represented all those elements 'which almost destroyed us: democratic-masonic politics and Judeo-Saxon finance'.[8] On 14 May, Catroux showered the Levant with leaflets, drawing attention to the presence of the Luftwaffe, in contravention of the armistice and exhorting his countrymen to revolt. The failure of this appeal affected him deeply. 'No one seized a rifle to use it against the enemy, no sedition occurred,' he recalled mournfully.[9]

Five days later, Catroux met one of the most renowned French officers in the Levant under a railway bridge on the Syrian–Transjordanian frontier. There, Lieutenant-Colonel Philibert Collet informed him of his desire to bring his ten squadrons of Circassian cavalry over to the Free French. This was welcome but the broader picture was bleak. Far from abandoning Syria, as Catroux had assured Wavell, Dentz was preparing to fight. The Armée du Levant would 'firmly oppose' a Gaullist drive for Damascus. 'They have received their orders and will obey,' explained Collet. 'Not one unit will defect to join our ranks . . . The Air Force, which recently received a visit from General Bergeret, is very hostile . . . and the same is true of the Navy. In short, far from going to Damascus as liberators, we will have to conquer the city with a fierce struggle and if, as is necessary, the Allies want to secure the Levant, it is essential that they come in sufficient force to overcome strong resistance.'[10] On the night of 21–22 May Collet crossed into Palestine. Only three of his ten squadrons of cavalry chose to follow him.

Wavell received Catroux's report with an ironic smile.[11] He had been sceptical about the claim that Dentz was withdrawing from Syria, while the Free French General's belief that he could conquer the Levant with six battalions had always been regarded as fatuous. Events, however, were moving beyond the Commander-in-Chief's control. On 14 May, the RAF attacked German aircraft staging at Vichy-controlled Palmyra. British raids on airfields near Damascus, Rayak and Aleppo followed. On 19 May, the Chiefs of Staff ordered Wavell to improvise the largest possible force and invade Syria at the earliest opportunity. The C-in-C replied that he was preparing a combined British and Free French operation, '*if situation favourable* but you must trust my judgment in this matter or relieve me of command'.[12] Churchill, who had already determined to sack the cautious General, accepted the challenge:

> If the Germans can pick up Syria and Iraq with petty air forces, tourists and local revolts, we must not shrink from running equal small-scale military risks and facing the possible aggravation of political dangers from failure. For this decision we [the Defence Committee], of course, take full responsibility and should you find yourself unwilling to give effect to it, arrangements will be made to meet any wish you may express to be relieved of your Command.[13]

To Major-General Kennedy's surprise, Wavell accepted this reproof without a word. On 25 May – the height of the battle for Crete – he presented London with the outline of Operation Exporter: a three-pronged attack to be undertaken by the 7th Australian Division (less one brigade), the 5th Indian Division and the six battalions of Free French infantry, supported by a smattering of cavalry and armoured cars.

The political strategy was more complicated. To gain the support of the local population, the British were convinced of the need to abolish the mandate and offer the Syrians and Lebanese their independence. From an Arab perspective, this was sound. As even the French were forced to admit, their governance of the region was deeply resented. 'It would be vain to dispute the failure of the French mandate in the Levant in the years before the war,' wrote Catroux (a former Governor of Damascus) to de Gaulle on 31 March 1941. 'It has always encountered subdued hostility, declared or armed . . . We were suffered, we were feared but we were not loved in Damascus or Aleppo and more generally in the Muslim community.'[14]

This was no less than the truth. Ever since the 1915 Sykes–Picot Agreement had carved up the Middle East – the Levant going to France, Palestine and Iraq to Britain – the French had made themselves obnoxious by their peremptory brand of imperialism, venality and penchant for playing off the different tribes and religions (they overwhelmingly favoured the Maronite Christians) against each other. In 1925, their draconian treatment of the Druze provoked the members of this ancient religion to revolt. A decade later, recognising the growing strength of Arab nationalism, the Government in Paris had concluded treaties granting the Levant states the independence they craved but the French Parliament refused to ratify them.

The British were critical of the French Administration. Although they had wrought their own opprobrium – not to mention rebellion – through the Balfour Declaration and subsequent Jewish migration to Palestine, they considered the French brand of colonialism to be heavy-handed and provocative. To Pasha Glubb, the difference was one of attitude:

Wherever the British have penetrated, we meet British officers who believe the Bedouins, the Kurds, the Gurkhas . . . to be the most splendid fellows on earth. The French do not share this passionate interest in other races – they only praise individuals or communities in so far as they have become Gallicised.[15]

A more important disparity by the spring of 1941 was that the British, though bloodied, were unbowed, whilst the French had been humiliated. As Spears noted with characteristic bluntness, the peoples of the Levant did not like 'being occupied by the occupied'.[16]

The original proposal to obtain the support of the native population by offering the Levant states their independence came from Catroux. Delighted, the British despatched Glubb to sound out the Syrian tribes, while Alec Kirkbride, the British Resident in Amman and a former comrade of T. E. Lawrence's, visited the Druze.* The results were encouraging but only because the Syrian leaders were left with the impression that they were being offered genuine autonomy. Yet as Catroux had made clear to London, in both November and December 1940, what he and de Gaulle had in mind was 'independence' on the 'Egyptian model' – that is, formal sovereignty but reserving such military and political rights as to render it practically meaningless.[17] This fundamental and, to some extent, wilful misunderstanding was to bedevil British–Free French relations and the politics of the region for the next four years.

As British, Australian, Indian and Free French troops crossed into Syria and Lebanon on the morning of 8 June 1941, Catroux proclaimed the end of the mandate. 'You are henceforth sovereign and independent,' he informed the Syrian and Lebanese people via a radio address. 'Your status of independence and sovereignty will be guaranteed by a treaty which will also define our reciprocal relations.'[18] At the same time, he appealed to the officers and men of the Armée du Levant not to oppose the Allied forces. Tragically, this entreaty had no effect. Contrary to the expectations of Allied officers, most of whom believed that their little army, bereft of tanks and, for the most part, air cover, would meet only token resistance, the Vichy French fought tenaciously. Advancing in their felt slouch hats to emphasise their friendly

---

* 'The Arabs for twenty-five years past had resented the presence of the French in Syria', recalled Glubb, 'but the alliance between France and Britain had made it impossible to oust them. Now by a fortunate coincidence, as it appeared to the Arabs, the British and French were on opposite sides. The hour for the redemption of Syria had struck.'

intent, the Australians were greeted with bullets. 'All we've got to do tomorrow is walk in, wave our hats to the Frogs and walk on,' one soldier recalled being told.[19] Broadcasting vans, imploring the Armée du Levant to lay down its arms or switch sides, were shelled. When the head of a Gaullist motorcycle unit drew up alongside a Vichy officer and asked him to join the Free French the Vichy man shot him dead. 'Vichy armoured cars contested every yard of our advance,' reported an officer with the Rajputana Rifles, while the invaders were subjected to repeated attacks by the French Air Force.[20]

As with most civil wars, the fratricidal nature of the Syrian campaign made it an ugly affair. Clearly marked British ambulances were shot up by French fighters and there was more than one incident of Vichy forces – which included Tunisian, Chadian and Senegalese troops – using a flag of truce to lure their adversaries into a trap. Laying siege to the fort at T3, a pumping station on the pipeline that ran from Kirkuk to Levantine Tripoli, Lieutenant N. G. P. Boswood of the Warwickshire Yeomanry watched as five Chevrolet trucks approached his troop flying a white flag. Just as Boswood was preparing to take their surrender, French colonial soldiers leapt out of the vehicles and opened up with Tommy guns, while fourteen armoured cars appeared from behind the lorries:

I raced for the nearest trench – the two men with me were killed as they ran, but Sergeant Gillet and I made it. The armoured French vehicles motored backwards and forwards through us but our armour-piercing ammunition did some damage. About a hundred infantry had got into position and opened up on us with a gun of some sort. This went on for about twenty minutes. Then one of my machine guns stopped [working]. The French drew off and, with horror in my heart, I went to discover how much was left of my shattered troop. Of twenty-four men, six were left, eight were dead, five wounded and five prisoners.

When the Vichy French reappeared ten minutes later, Boswood and his few remaining soldiers had no choice but to surrender. After a ferocious argument with the officer in charge, one man was allowed to remain with the wounded but Boswood, Gillet and the others

were bundled into trucks and taken to Deir ez-Zor on the Euphrates. Invited into the Vichy officers' mess, Boswood refused. 'I do
not drink with people who fired under cover of a white flag,' he
explained.[21]

The motives of the defenders were varied but complementary. As
the Vichyites were later at pains to emphasise, they were professional
soldiers carrying out the orders of the 'legitimate' French government. Although the arrival of the Luftwaffe on Syrian airfields caused
some Vichy NCOs to demonstrate their disapproval by refusing to
fraternise with the German pilots (the officers tended to be more hos-
pitable), it was not enough to incite revolt. Then there was the need
to maintain or regain French honour. 'Every drop of French blood
spilled in Syria is a fraction of national honour retrieved,' declared
a prominent Vichy journalist.[22] Failure to put up a 'good show' in
Syria would lead to reprisals against their families in France, Dentz
told his men, while a desire to prove the valour of French arms after
the humiliation of 1940 was common. 'You thought we were yellow,
didn't you?' a Vichy sergeant accused a British war correspondent
outside Sidon. 'You thought we couldn't fight in France. You thought
we were like the Italians. Well, we've shown you.'[23]

Finally, there was the hatred felt towards the British for Mers el-
Kébir and towards the Gaullists for Dakar and French Equatorial
Africa. Fighting between Vichy and Free French forces was so fierce
that most British commanders came to regard the inclusion of the
Gaullists in the invasion force as a grave error. To those who had
accepted the armistice, the Free French represented 'the Devil incar-
nate, the scapegoats for all the anger, resentment and weakness which
had been lurking in the dark places of their consciences for a year',
wrote one Gaullist officer.[24] Yet the bitterness shown towards the British could be almost as great. Occupying the fort of Tel Abid, on the
Turkish frontier, John Masters and the men of the 2nd Battalion, 4th
Prince of Wales' Own Gurkha Rifles, found the wine good but the
inscriptions on the walls sour: 'Wait, dirty English bastards, until the
Germans come. We run away now, so will you, soon.'[25]

But the Germans were not coming. Not wishing to provoke an
Anglo-Gaullist incursion, most of the 120 German aircraft that had
landed in Syria in May and not been destroyed by the RAF had

departed at the start of June. On 12 June, Dentz sent a telegram to Vichy asking for several squadrons of German dive bombers to attack the British Fleet, currently shelling French defensive positions in Lebanon, but his request was rejected. 'We know that we shall lose Syria but we are determined to fight to the end,' Pétain informed the American Ambassador – the irony of his stance compared to his actions of the previous summer apparently eluding him.[26] On 21 June, British, Australian, Indian and Free French troops entered Damascus. Twelve days later, Habforce captured Palmyra. On 11 July 1941 Dentz surrendered. It had been a short but bloody war. Around 4,600 Allied soldiers had been killed or wounded, while Vichy casualties exceeded 6,500. Although some emerged without feelings of enmity, many, including Roald Dahl, who flew Hurricanes during the campaign, were unable to forgive their opponents for what both sides viewed as 'unnecessary slaughter'.[27]

For the Americans it had been a disappointing and embarrassing episode. Following the fall of France, the Roosevelt Administration had taken the controversial decision to recognise the Pétain Government. By maintaining cordial relations with Vichy, the State Department argued, it would be possible to prevent the Maréchal and his ministers from going over to the Axis. In the winter of 1940–41, the Administration had sent food and medical supplies to the unoccupied zone and, in February 1941, the former Counsellor at the American Embassy in Paris, Robert Murphy, had concluded an agreement with General Weygand to supply French North Africa not only with food but also petrol, oil and coal.

The British were incensed. Aware that well over half of all French imports ended up in German hands, they objected to this American-made hole in the blockade, while deploring any act that had the effect of relieving the Reich of its responsibility for feeding the French people. Senior US Administration figures, outside the State Department, agreed. American aid for France was 'a waste of time and money', declared Secretary of the Navy Frank Knox, 'since all Latins, anyway yellow, are now in the complete power of Hitler'.[28] Around the same time, the President's roving emissary, Harry Hopkins, reminded his master that 'anything which promotes economic activity in unoccupied France helps the Germans'.[29]

The justification for ignoring these warnings had been the argument that American support would strengthen the Vichy Government against German demands. When, therefore, the announcement of the Murphy–Weygand Accord was followed by an agreement which saw Vichy supply Germany with 1.5 million heads of livestock, the Darlan–Hitler meeting, the 'Paris Protocols' and collusion in Syria, the Administration was made to look distinctly foolish. '[Cordell] Hull's appeasement policy has failed', crowed Knox, adding that 'all the State Department's pansy balloons were popping and a good thing too'.[30] Yet the Secretary of State was determined to stick to his policy. Although objecting to Darlan's collaboration with Hitler in Iraq and Syria, the US did not break with Vichy. Economic aid was suspended in May but resumed in June, while recognition of the spa-town regime continued until the Germans occupied the whole of France in November 1942. In the intervening period, the Vichy Government provided Rommel with some 1,700 vehicles, a small quantity of arms and 3,600 tons of fuel.[31]

*

Although the Syrian campaign ended in success, it strained relations between the British and the Free French. Exasperated by Wavell's intransigence in April, de Gaulle later chafed at having his forces under British command.* When Eden replied to an early peace feeler from Dentz without consulting the Free French, the General 'went off the deep end'.[32] 'I don't think I will ever get on with *les anglais*,' he raged to Spears. 'You are all the same, exclusively centred upon your own interests and business, quite insensitive to the

---

* At a dinner prior to the invasion, General Marshall-Cornwall raised his glass of Dubonnet and said to de Gaulle, '*Mon général, je bois au succès de nos armées en Syrie.*' The Free French leader replied scornfully, '*Il n'y aura pas de succès.*' When Marshall-Cornwall asked why ever not, de Gaulle replied, 'Because the operation has been planned by the British General Staff.' Outraged, the British General retorted that he had served in France under Weygand's command and that 'every order issued by the French General Staff resulted in a complete disaster'.

requirements of others . . . Do you think I am interested in England winning the war? I am not. I am interested only in France's victory.' When Spears protested that they were synonymous, the General snapped back, 'Not at all in my view.'[33] Around the same time, a British liaison officer serving with the Free French in Syria came across a document instructing Gaullist soldiers on the attitude they should adopt towards their British allies. Divided into three categories, there were '*Les* Gentlemen' – senior officers, who should be treated in a 'frank and respectful manner'; '*Les* Goodfellows' – regimental officers, 'who do not play politics and are therefore worthy of a certain camaraderie'; and, finally, '*Les Officiers de l'*Intelligence Service' – the sly architects of British Imperial policy who should be regarded with the utmost suspicion.[34]

But it was the armistice negotiations outside Acre that caused the real row. Anxious to secure an agreement as quickly as possible, the commander of the Allied expedition, General Wilson, decided to accommodate Dentz's request to exclude the Free French from the negotiations. Worse, he concluded an agreement that completely ignored Free French interests: permitting the Vichy forces to depart the Levant with all their weapons and equipment, excluding any mention of French rights in the region and forbidding contact between Vichy and Gaullist forces, thus denying the Free French the opportunity to recruit. This was completely contrary to de Gaulle's known wishes, yet at this critical moment the General had purposively absented himself. Convinced the British would double-cross him, de Gaulle had flown from Cairo to Brazzaville on 12 July. 'The only way in which I could limit the damage was to give myself space and height, to reach some cloud and from there to swoop upon an agreement that would not bind me and that I should tear up as far as I could,' he recalled loftily in his memoirs.[35] Nine days later, he descended.

'White with suppressed passion', he marched into the office of the newly appointed Minister-Resident for the Middle East, Oliver Lyttelton, and launched into a two-hour tirade against the perfidy of the British.[36] He was 'in the worst mood I have ever known him', recorded Spears. 'He looked frightful . . . as if he had not slept for a week. He was completely intransigent and often extremely rude.'[37] After ranting for an hour, de Gaulle handed Lyttelton a document giving notice that he would be withdrawing his forces from British command and placing the Levant under the authority of General Catroux. Lyttelton refused to accept it. 'It was, in effect, an ultimatum which could only be read as terminating the alliance between Free France and Great Britain,' wrote the British Ambassador to Cairo, Sir Miles Lampson. De Gaulle then stated that he had no confidence in the British High Command, who had conducted the Syrian campaign in 'an unskilful and dilatory way'.[38] Privately, Spears agreed but this was not the time for admitting mistakes and it was with relief that he heard the Minister-Resident declare that they should reflect on the situation 'during the hour of the siesta'.[39]

If de Gaulle slept, the Englishmen did not. Fearing what would happen if the General fulfilled his threat to remove his forces from British command and began to act independently in the Levant, they put in place plans to prevent him from travelling to Syria or communicating with his officers. As a last resort, they were prepared to depose him in favour of Catroux, noting that it might be necessary to 'shut up de Gaulle for a time', either in prison or, preferably, 'a lunatic asylum'.[40]

In the end, such drastic measures proved unnecessary. Returning to Lyttelton's office at six o'clock, de Gaulle appeared transformed. Although not exactly emollient, he was calm, rational and, compared with his earlier performance, relatively polite. Lyttelton wondered if a colleague had exercised a restraining influence but Spears, whilst acknowledging the possibility, noted that de Gaulle had 'cultivated the practice of being . . . intolerably rude' only to change tack suddenly, causing his bruised interlocutor to give way out of sheer relief.[41] 'With the English you need to bang the table [and] they will flatten themselves before you,' the General had advised his subordinates.[42] Over the next three days, Lyttelton and de Gaulle thrashed out an agreement that defined the relationship between the British military and the French civil administration in the Levant and provided the Gaullists with an opportunity to rally the Armée du Levant, though in the event only around 6,000 Vichy soldiers elected to join the Free French.

De Gaulle had triumphed but he was not assuaged. When the

General learnt that a Free French colonel had gone to the airfield to bid farewell to General Wavell – finally sacked by Churchill on 20 June – he placed the officer under arrest. A little later, when Free French forces arrived to take possession of the Druze capital of Suwayda and found the Union Jack fluttering over the fort, de Gaulle sent a blunt message to General Wilson: 'I do not suppose I can vanquish the British Empire but if you do not leave Suweida we shall fire.'[43] Around the same time, he gave an interview to the *Chicago Daily News* in which he claimed that the British were colluding with Hitler for the benefit of Vichy. Incandescent, Churchill gave instructions that no one was to meet de Gaulle upon his return to Britain and 'if he asks to see anybody, he should not be seen'.[44] The General, he wrote to Eden on 27 August, had clearly 'gone off his head'.[45]

For nearly two weeks, Churchill refused to see de Gaulle, preferring to let him 'stew in his own juice'.[46] On 12 September, however, he relented and the General was shown into the Cabinet room. As a mark of his displeasure, Churchill, who typically delighted in exercising his idiosyncratic French, had decided to conduct the interview through an interpreter. 'General de Gaulle, I have asked you to come here this afternoon . . .'

'*Mon Général, je vous ai invité de venir cet après-midi,*' translated Jock Colville.

'I didn't say *mon Général,*' interrupted the Prime Minister, 'and I did not say I had *invited* him.' Realising that this was a game at which two could play, de Gaulle then began to question Colville's rendering of *his* words. '*Non, non, ce n'est pas du tout le sens de ce que je disais,*' interrupted the General. Visibly irritated, Churchill told his unfortunate Assistant Private Secretary that he had better go and find someone who could speak French. After a ten-minute hiatus, during which neither Churchill nor de Gaulle uttered a word, Valentine Lawford, a graduate in modern languages from Corpus Christi, Cambridge, was produced. No sooner had the young diplomat arrived, however, than he too was dismissed. 'They must be mad,' exclaimed Lawford, leaving the Cabinet room: both men had claimed that he too could not speak French.[47]

The pantomime over, Churchill accused de Gaulle (in French) of having left a 'trail of Anglophobia behind him' during his recent travels. He had been 'greatly pained' by the accounts he had received and felt he 'was no longer dealing with a friend'. To these and other charges – including that he was suspected of 'fascist views' – de Gaulle was imperturbable. It was absurd to say that he was the 'enemy of Great Britain', he argued. His position and previous record made it 'inconceivable'. He had, however, been greatly disturbed by recent events in the Middle East and by the attitude of certain British officials towards the Free French.[48] Slowly, the two men moved towards what passed for détente and when Colville re-entered the room he found them sitting side by side, with amiable expressions on their faces, de Gaulle, 'no doubt for tactical purposes . . . smoking one of the Prime Minister's cigars'.[49]

Yet the row left lasting wounds. Spears, previously de Gaulle's staunchest supporter, henceforth became his most bitter opponent. De Gaulle, despite his agreement with Lyttelton, felt sure the British meant to supplant the French in the Levant, while Churchill began to fear that he had created a monster. Over the coming years, these attitudes would come close to causing a complete rupture between de Gaulle and the British Government. Compared to the great events of the summer of 1941, however, these were trivial concerns. Just before dawn on 22 June, the vanguard of 3,600 German tanks, 2,500 aircraft and over three million soldiers invaded the Soviet Union. A few hours later, Churchill announced that Britain would provide the Russian people with all aid in her power. No one knew how long the Red Army would last but, for the moment at least, the British Empire was no longer alone.

XII

The Soviet Enigma

War is bound to intensify the internal, revolutionary crisis both in the
East and West . . . If war breaks out, we shall not be able to sit with
folded arms. We shall have to take action but we shall be the last to do
so . . . in order to throw the decisive weight into the scales.

Joseph Stalin, January 1925[1]

In his first broadcast of the war, on 1 October 1939, Churchill
had described the foreign policy of the Soviet Union as 'a riddle,
wrapped in a mystery, inside an enigma'.[2] Certainly it appeared con-
fusing, if not contradictory. From her foundation in 1922, following
the Bolshevik Revolution and subsequent civil war, the Union of
Soviet Socialist Republics had been the inherent enemy of the 'capitalist democracies'; the propagator of communist intrigue and
proletariat revolution across the world. During the 1930s, however,
following the rise of Hitler, the USSR had reorientated Westwards,
joining the League of Nations in 1934 and placing her faith in the
policy of 'collective security'. Peace was 'indivisible', declared the
Soviet Commissar for Foreign Affairs, Maxim Litvinov, who, in 1935,
concluded defensive alliances with France and Czechoslovakia and
then sought to co-operate with the democracies to contain German
expansion.

The failure of these attempts cost Litvinov his job. Angered by
the Anglo-French appeasement of Hitler – which he believed was
designed to encourage Germany to expand eastwards – Stalin dismissed his Jewish Foreign Minister on 3 May 1939, replacing him
with the known Germanophile Vyacheslav Molotov. As the democracies struggled to convince the despot of the sincerity of their
desire to form an anti-Nazi alliance during the summer of 1939,

so the prospect of a Soviet deal with the German dictator became more enticing.* On 17 August, negotiations between the Russians, the British and the French broke down and on 21 August it was announced that the German Foreign Minister, Joachim von Ribbentrop, was flying to Moscow to conclude a 'Non-Aggression Pact'. Three weeks later, as German forces laid waste to Warsaw, the Red Army crossed into Poland to claim Stalin's share of the spoils.

The news of the Nazi–Soviet Pact 'shook the politicians and young poets of a dozen capital cities', wrote Evelyn Waugh.[3] The left was dumbfounded, while the right considered its anti-communism freshly justified. 'Then I realised that the Russians have double-crossed us, as I always believed they would,' recorded the avowedly anti-Soviet Tory MP Chips Channon. 'They are the foulest people on earth . . . Now it looks like war and a possible partition of Poland.'[4] When this event occurred, following the Soviet invasion on 17 September, Western indignation became even more inflamed. 'The Russians have answered the question "What will Russia do?"' declared the *Evening Standard* on 18 September 1939. 'They have become the accessories in the murder of Poland . . . Today Russia is making an imperialist grab of territory which ranks alongside the crimes of the Nazi gangsters.' In France, Daladier enjoyed widespread support as he moved to suppress the Communist Party while, from his seat in the Scottish borders, Sir Walter Maxwell-Scott (grandson of the novelist) wrote to his friend Lord Halifax to express the by no means uncommon hope that 'we shall [now] have a Holy War against Nazism *and* communism, to save what is left of Christian civilisation'.[5]

Yet for all the sound and fury, there was little appetite to extend the war to the Soviet Union. As Waugh's alias, Guy Crouchback, recalls in *Men at Arms*, disgust at Stalin's actions was countered by

---

* Although the British and French made plenty of errors during the Anglo-Franco-Soviet negotiations held in Moscow, their position was also undermined by SIS officer and Soviet spy, Guy Burgess, who, during August 1939, provided his Soviet handler with a series of reports claiming that the British Government did not want an alliance with the Soviet Union since it was a 'fundamental aim of British policy to work *with* Germany . . . and . . . *against* the USSR.'

simple pragmatism: 'My dear fellow, we've quite enough on our hands as it is. We can't go to war with the whole world.'[6] This was the Government's view. As the Deputy Under-Secretary of State for Foreign Affairs, Rab Butler, put it in a departmental minute, 'A combination of German and Russian men and resources might take time to be effective. But its menace to civilisation and the Empire is so real and great that any future developments in British policy should be judged in the light of a risk of first class magnitude.'[7] Fortunately, the terms of the Anglo-Polish Treaty referred exclusively to aggression by a 'European power' – a euphemism accepted by both sides to stand for Germany – and thus whilst Britain had been obliged to declare war on Germany, there was no corresponding obligation to fight the USSR.[8]

One member of the War Cabinet went further. In a memorandum of 25 September 1939, Churchill, despite his long record of militant anti-Bolshevism, contended that the Soviet incursion may prove a blessing in disguise, since an eastern front was now 'potentially in existence', with the 'left paw of the Bear' blocking German expansion into the Baltic and the Balkans.[9] One week later, in the same broadcast in which he evoked the inscrutability of Soviet action, he went almost as far as welcoming the forward Soviet policy, arguing that Allied and Russian interests in east and south-east Europe were aligned, since neither party wished to see 'Romania, Yugoslavia, Bulgaria and above all Turkey, put under the German heel'.[10] His former (and future) parliamentary colleague, the editor of the *Army Quarterly*, Cuthbert Headlam, appreciated the logic of this argument but not to the extent of overcoming his suspicions. 'So long as Stalin remains in the east and prevents the Nazis from overrunning the Balkans, perhaps there is something to be said for his knavery,' he noted in his diary. 'But my fear is that his main object is to lengthen the war – to exhaust us and the French and Germans and then Bolshevise Europe.'[11]

Such fears were well founded. As Stalin told the Comintern's General Secretary, Georgi Dimitrov, on 7 September:

A war is on between two groups of capitalist countries . . . We see nothing wrong in their having a good hard fight and weakening each other. It would be fine if at the hands of Germany the positions of the richest capitalist countries (especially England) were shaken. Hitler, without understanding it or desiring it, is shaking and undermining the capitalist system . . . We can manoeuvre, pit one side against the other . . . The non-aggression pact is to a certain degree helping Germany. Next time, we'll urge on the other side.[12]

More important were the despot's territorial ambitions. By making a deal with Hitler, rather than the democracies, Stalin was able to regain almost all of the territory Russia had lost at the end of the First World War. In the secret protocol drawn up between Molotov and Ribbentrop on 23 August 1939, Hitler recognised that eastern Poland, Bessarabia (annexed by Romania in March 1918), Finland, Estonia and Latvia all fell within the Soviet 'sphere of influence'. For the loss of 737 men and two weeks' fighting, the Soviet Union was to expand by approximately 78,000 square miles and almost thirteen million people. 'Of course it's all a game to see who can fool whom,' the dictator boasted to the party boss of Ukraine, Nikita Khrushchev. 'I know what Hitler's up to. He thinks he's outsmarted me but actually it's I who have tricked him!'[13] On 27 September – the day Warsaw surrendered – the despot demanded Lithuania, originally earmarked for Germany, in exchange for that portion of 'ethnically Polish Poland' (as opposed to those parts dominated by Ukrainians and Belorussians) currently occupied by the Red Army. Ribbentrop demurred. The Soviet Union was already far larger than Germany, whilst it was the Wehrmacht that had borne the brunt of the fighting. But Stalin insisted. After Hitler reluctantly acceded to this demand, the Red Tsar moved to subsume the Baltic States into his communist empire. In late September and early October, Estonia, Latvia and Lithuania were each blackmailed into signing 'mutual assistance pacts' with their more powerful neighbour, forcing them to accept Soviet air and naval bases on their territory, as well as large detachments of Russian soldiers. When the Estonian Foreign Minister objected, the despot was blunt: Estonia could accept the Soviet demands or suffer the same fate as Poland.

In that partitioned and enslaved former state, Stalin lost little time in imposing the full force of Bolshevism. Private property was abolished, businesses were nationalised and Soviet citizenship was forcibly bestowed. The rounding up of so-called 'enemies of the people' began before the fighting had even ceased. Thousands, soon hundreds of thousands, of politicians, local officials, aristocrats, merchants, intellectuals, lawyers and priests were arrested, often with their families, and sent to the Gulag. Others were simply shot. Between 17 September 1939 and the end of June 1941, when the Red Army retreated before the German invaders, an estimated 500,000 Polish civilians were deported to work as slave labour in the Russian heartlands, alongside 196,000 Polish prisoners of war. Many never returned.

Not that conditions were better in the German-occupied zone. Having murdered at least 12,000 Polish civilians and 3,000 POWs in September, the Wehrmacht and accompanying *Einsatzgruppen* (SS-operated death squads), as well as local German militia, set about the systematic decapitation of the Polish nation. Here too, nobles, professors, clergymen, politicians, journalists, army officers, even musicians and boy scouts were to be eradicated since, as Hitler put it, 'only a nation whose upper levels are destroyed can be pushed into the ranks of slavery'.[15] Around 45,000 Poles were killed in non-combat circumstances between the onset of the German invasion and the end of the year. Of these, around 7,000 were Jews. In the coming weeks and months, hundreds of thousands of Jews would be driven across the border into the Soviet zone or herded into disease-ridden ghettos, the precursors of Belzec, Treblinka and Auschwitz.

Stalin's virtual annexation of the Baltic States was barely noticed in the West. Not so his invasion of Finland in late November 1939. As has already been noted, the USSR's attack on this neutral state provoked more outrage in Western democracies than had the German invasion of Poland three months earlier. 'The Red Tsar is now the executor of the traditional imperialism of Tsarist Russia,' declared Clement Attlee and Arthur Greenwood in a joint state-ment on behalf of the Labour Party, which also took aim at the

USSR's Western apologists. 'Stalin's men in Great Britain use the freedom which they enjoy to defend war and tyranny, a war of conquest by an alien and powerful despot against a small outpost of republican democracy . . . They defend tyranny, either because they do not know, or those who know refuse to tell, that fascism and bolshevism have identical political systems.'[16]

To those who had long argued that fascism and communism were two sides of the same ideological coin, the Soviet invasion of Finland was viewed as a vindication. 'The truth is that we now have two enemies instead of one . . . tied together by a solidarity as profound as it is possible to establish,' claimed the former French Minister of Commerce Paul Bastid in *L'Ère nouvelle*. The editor of the conservative *Journal de débats* agreed. 'There is no difference between Stalin and Hitler. They resemble each other like brothers, brothers who are jealous and hate each other, but who co-operate in the execution of a certain number of crimes.'[17] In the French Senate, Pierre Laval called for a declaration of war against the Soviet Union, while left and right combined to demand aid for Finland.

The British were more circumspect. Although many, like Cuthbert Headlam, considered it 'pitiful' to be 'shutting our eyes to Russian aggression whilst we make such a to do about that of Germany', few saw the sense in declaring war on Russia while Germany remained to be defeated.[18] Certainly, neither Chamberlain nor Halifax had any desire to widen the scope of the war, while Churchill maintained his view that Soviet expansion provided a useful check on German ambitions. Indeed, if the Soviet Ambassador to London, Ivan Maisky, is to be believed, the then First Lord of the Admiralty considered Soviet claims on Finland justified. 'Russia has every reason to be a dominant power in the Baltic and should be one,' he told the Ambassador, two weeks before the Soviet invasion. 'Better Russia than Germany. That is in our, British, interests.'[19]

Yet, within a short period, the War Cabinet was considering plans to strike at the USSR's vital resources. On 31 October 1939, the Minister of Supply, Dr Leslie Burgin, had written to Lord Halifax to draw his attention to the vulnerability of Soviet oil supplies, emanating as they did from three principal oil fields in the Caucasus (the largest being Baku), within range of Allied bombers operating out of Turkey, Iraq, Iran or Syria. Although Burgin declined to speculate on the motives 'of the USSR or her German friends', he thought it of immense importance to have 'some sort of bargaining lever with the USSR' and that 'consideration by our General Staff . . . as to the possibility of annihilating Russian sources of oil might have an immense deterrent effect. If you destroy Russian oil wells, and they are all of the fountain or gusher type and therefore more easily destroyed, you cut off not only Russia from oil but any of Russia's allies [i.e. Germany] looking for her support.'[20]

Responding to this 'somewhat grandiose scheme', the Foreign Office's Soviet expert Fitzroy Maclean, who had served in Moscow during the 1930s, wondered if the Minister had considered the implications of his proposal, which risked war with Russia and in which the Soviet Air Force would be able to deploy over 700 bombers and 1,000 fighters against 'our own supplies of oil', in Iraq and Iran, currently guarded by 'only about thirty-five British military aircraft'.[21] Thus, whilst Halifax sympathised with Burgin's quest 'for a stick with which to threaten, if not to beat, the Russians', he feared that, 'for the present at least, we must look for it elsewhere'.[22]

But the matter would not rest there. The outbreak of the Winter War reawakened fears of Soviet expansion, while the failure of the Red Army to subdue the Finns was felt likely to foment closer collaboration between Russia and Germany. These concerns were particularly acute in France, where the onset of the Soviet invasion produced a wave of anti-Bolshevism. Although the Daladier Government paid lip service to the need to help the Finns, its real aim was to weaken the Soviet Union. To understand this desire, it is important to remember that by the turn of the year 1940 the French Government was having serious doubts about the 'long war' strategy. Comparative analysis of the French and German war economies suggested that the advantage lay with the latter, while the endurance of the *'drôle de guerre'* was having a deleterious effect on morale. In this context, a strike against the Soviet oil fields, as had been suggested in Britain by Burgin, appeared the answer to several problems: it would cripple the Soviet Union's ability to wage war, thus helping the Finns; it would shorten the war by depriving Hitler of a much-needed source of fuel; and it would raise Allied morale.

That the British gave thorough and, in some instances, enthusiastic consideration to this scheme is astonishing but, to a limited extent, explicable. Ever since the announcement of the Nazi–Soviet 'Non-Aggression' Pact, there were those who believed (accurately, as it transpired) that what had in fact been agreed was a plan to redraw the map of Europe for the benefit of the totalitarians. Hitler and Stalin were operating 'hand in glove', argued the Government's Chief Diplomatic Adviser, Sir Robert Vansittart, while, from Moscow, the British Ambassador, Sir William Seeds, contended that the two regimes should be regarded as partners, 'mutually aiding one another's plans'.[23] The Americans agreed. 'The Soviets are as much allied with the Germans as the French are with the British,' wrote the American Ambassador to Moscow, Laurence Steinhardt, to his colleague Loy Henderson. 'It is my personal opinion, which I think both the British and French now share, that Stalin is now definitely committed to a German victory and that the Soviets will do everything within their power to aid and abet Germany.'[24] If a Nazi–Soviet alliance was already in being, what was the sense in allowing it to prosper? British anti-Bolshevism, though less fervent than its French equivalent, was still potent, while the need for action that did not involve hurling troops at the Siegfried Line had already spawned a variety of plans that would threaten or at least impinge Soviet interests in Scandinavia.

Yet the coherence of the 'Baku project' was only superficial. As the Ministry of Economic Warfare was aware, the primary source of German oil was not the Caucasus but the Romanian oil fields at Ploieşti. The British had baulked at the Petsamo operation owing to the risk of war with the Soviet Union but now freely discussed bombing her oil fields. The impetus behind the scheme was the Soviet-Finnish War, yet the climax of Allied planning, including reconnaissance flights, occurred after the Finns had capitulated, while the advice from the Chiefs of Staff was consistent: 'There is no action which we could take against Russia which would bring about the early defeat of Germany.'[25] The sheer absurdity of the proposition – which threatened to add almost 200 million Soviets to the 90 million Germans and Austrians the Allies were already fighting – was captured by the Independent MP and humourist A. P. Herbert:

> It's jolly to look at the map
> And finish the foe in a day.
> It's not easy to get at the chap;
> These neutrals are so in the way.
> But if you say 'What would *you* do
> To fill the aggressor with gloom?'
> Well, we might drop a bomb on Baku,
> Or what about bombs on Batum?[26]

In the end, only the onset of *Blitzkrieg* in the west killed Operation Pike, as the attack on the Soviet oil fields had been designated. Long before this, however, the Soviets had got wind of what the Allies were planning. Well served by his intelligence networks, as well as stories in the Western press (the fact that Herbert's ditty appeared in *Punch* is indicative of the lack of secrecy surrounding the project), Stalin betrayed signs of panic. In early February 1940, the Soviet Government persuaded the standard bearer for Anglo-Soviet rapprochement, Sir Stafford Cripps, currently undertaking a tour of the Far East, to visit Moscow. There, in his magnificently decorated office in the Foreign Commissariat, Molotov spoke of the USSR's willingness to conclude a trade or even a political agreement with Britain, provided she was prepared to act 'in a friendly and not a hostile way to Russia'.[27] A week later, Maisky asked the Under-Secretary of the Foreign Office, Rab Butler, if Britain might act as mediator between Russia and Finland. Stalin was 'hypnotised by the bogey of Allied intervention in the Caucasus', posited the Counsellor at the British Embassy in Moscow, John Le Rougetel, while information gleaned from the Turks suggested that the Russians were so alarmed at the prospect of an attack on Baku that they had sought the advice of American engineers as to the likely effect of such a bombardment.[28] (The Americans replied that, since the whole district was saturated with oil, 'there would be a blaze unequalled in the history of the world'.)[29]

The British viewed these overtures with appropriate cynicism. On 11 February – the same day that General Timoshenko launched a new and decisive offensive against the Finns – Stalin signed a commercial agreement with Hitler that would supply the Reich with 800,000 tons of scrap and pig iron, 500,000 tons of iron ore, 500,000 tons of phosphates, 1 million tons of grains and seeds and 900,000 tons of oil in exchange for a corresponding supply of materiel. As if to underline his cynicism, he also handed over to the Gestapo several hundred German Communist refugees. A little over a year later, the Soviet Government concluded a non-aggression pact with Britain's other potential enemy, Japan. The Russians were simply playing with the Allies, argued Fitzroy Maclean: extending the proverbial olive branch merely to avoid having their oil fields destroyed. Sir Robert Vansittart concurred. 'I hope we shall nibble no more at any Russian bait of any kind but think only of beating her new friend Germany,' he minuted beneath Cripps' report of his interview with Molotov. 'If we can do that, we can then deal with Stalin and his pseudo-communism, which it is just as necessary to destroy.'[30] Yet Cripps remained optimistic about the possibility of detaching the Soviet Bear from the Nazi Wolf and, in May 1940, with Britain's diplomatic and defensive strategy in tatters, Churchill was prepared to clutch at straws however thin. And so it was that Cripps found himself at the end of that month returning to Moscow as Britain's new Ambassador to the Soviet Union.

Sir Stafford Cripps did not fall into that hallowed category of those with whom Churchill considered it 'agreeable to dine'.[31] A vegetarian and teetotaller, he had been expelled from the Labour Party for advocating a 'popular front' with the Communists. His commitment to his own brands of socialism and Christianity was absolute; his enthusiasm for radical, utopian solutions notorious. One day, after the onset of the war in the East, he visited the Kremlin to present Stalin with his own idealistic blueprint for the post-war world. After listening to the Ambassador's starry-eyed exposé for a few minutes, the Soviet leader cut him off. 'Ask the Ambassador if these are his ideas or Mr Churchill's,' the despot instructed the translator. Cripps replied that they were his. 'Ah,' responded Stalin, 'I will study them later. Now pray forgive me, I have urgent business with my Chief of Staff.'[32] A few months later, when it was suggested that the Prime Minister might wish to replace Cripps as Ambassador, Churchill's response was typical: 'A lunatic in a country of lunatics . . . it would be a pity to move him.'[33] Yet he was also brilliant. 'The ablest man in politics', according to one Conservative MP, he had studied chemistry at University College London before going on to earn a fortune at the Bar.[34] The Chinese Nationalist leader, Chiang Kai-shek, was so impressed with him that he offered him the job of industrial adviser to the Chinese Government, while John Russell, who served under Cripps in Moscow, described him as that 'rare combination of moral and intellectual greatness', tempered by 'complete personal simplicity and honesty'.[35]

Cripps arrived at the British Embassy in Moscow, a handsome if somewhat vulgar Italianate mansion on the banks of the Moskva River, on 12 June 1940.* He could not have come at a worse time. Coinciding with the fall of Paris, his mission to persuade the Soviets to strengthen their ties with Britain and loosen those with Germany looked like being stillborn. Although Molotov saw him on 14 June, Stalin kept him waiting until 1 July, by which time the Red Army had annexed the Baltic States, as well as Bessarabia. The imbalance of power was illustrated by an ostensibly light-hearted exchange between Churchill and the (relatively Anglophile) Ivan Maisky. Chaffing the Russian Ambassador over the USSR's 'imperialist aspirations', the Prime Minister explained that it was

---

* The building had been the property of a Ukrainian sugar magnate and was, in the opinion of one member of the Embassy staff, a 'fifth-rate film director's dream'.

alright, since 'we really don't mind, or care, what you do there'. Maisky responded, 'We don't mind if you do; we didn't ask you for permission.'[36]

When Cripps eventually saw Stalin in his office in the Kremlin, known as the Little Corner, he presented him with a letter from Churchill, expressing Britain's desire for improved relations with the Soviet Union and venturing that the USSR no more than Britain wished to see German hegemony in Europe. The despot was unimpressed. 'If the Prime Minister wants to restore the old equilibrium, we cannot agree with him,' he declared, explaining with remarkable frankness that it was Russia and Germany's shared desire to readjust the European balance of power that had led to the 'non-aggression' pact of the previous August.[37] In any case, he did not believe that Germany sought to dominate the entire continent. The Soviet Union and the German Reich had reached an accord and he had no intention of breaking it. Trade with Britain was possible but it could not come at the expense of trade with Germany, which, he freely admitted, was using Soviet raw materials for war purposes. As Cripps was forced to admit in a despatch, the Soviet Union was determined to do 'nothing to help us'.[38]

In fact, the Soviets were alarmed by the size and speed of the German victories. 'Stalin's nerves cracked when he learned about the fall of France,' recalled Khrushchev. 'He cursed the governments of England and France: "Couldn't they put up any resistance at all?" he asked despairingly . . . He let fly with some choice Russian curses and said that now Hitler was sure to beat our brains in.'[39] If the despot was frightened of Germany's increased power, however, the consequence was merely to renew his determination to maintain friendly relations with Hitler. Thus, on 1 August 1940, Molotov went out of his way to emphasise the shared interests of Germany and the USSR in a speech before the Supreme Soviet and on 23 August the Soviet press celebrated the first anniversary of the Nazi–Soviet Pact, contrasting the 'pacific' nature of Soviet and German foreign policy with the 'Anglo-French warmongers'.

Just as Stalin sought to reaffirm relations with Berlin, however, Hitler's mind was moving in the opposite direction. Having been forced to postpone the invasion of Britain in September 1940, he had begun to ponder alternative ways to achieve victory. Even before this date he had told his military commanders that a pre-emptive strike against the Soviet Union might be necessary to deprive Britain of any hope she might have of Russian aid. Stalin's seizure of the Baltic States had angered the Führer, while the USSR's annexation of the Romanian province of north Bukovina (a former Austrian crown land), in addition to Bessarabia, had alarmed Berlin. The Soviet incursion had been 'the first Russian attack on western Europe', Hitler averred, and he warned his paladins of the need to destroy the USSR as a military power if Stalin's lust for territory persisted.[40] Before an irrevocable decision was made, however, he was prepared to contemplate an extension of the 'Devil's bargain' struck in August 1939.

On 12 November 1940, Molotov arrived in Berlin for talks. A guard of honour was drawn up outside the Anhalter railway station and a band played a march of welcome – although out to impress, the Nazis were not going to play *The Internationale*. Compared to the shoal of German officers, resplendent in their grey uniforms, the diminutive Commissar, with his bourgeois fedora, looked like a carpet salesman. If, however, the 'Hammer' was intimidated by his surroundings he did not show it. As Hitler's interpreter, Paul Schmidt, recalled, the Soviet Foreign Minister went in for 'hard, expert boxing' with his German hosts.[41] Unimpressed by Ribbentrop's boast that 'England was beaten', he evinced no more enthusiasm towards the Nazi Foreign Minister's attempts to redirect Soviet expansion towards the Near East and the soon-to-be-former British Empire.[42] When he met Hitler in the Reich Chancellery later that afternoon, he responded to the Führer's typically vague *tour d'horizon* with a hail of specific questions. Did the German–Soviet Agreement still apply to Finland? What did the New Order in Europe and Asia amount to and what part was the USSR to play in it? What was to be the agreed position on Bulgaria, Romania and Turkey? What, precisely, was the nature of the Tripartite Pact, signed between Germany, Italy and Japan on 27 September? If the USSR were to join such a pact she would have to be treated 'as [an] equal partner [. . .] and not [a] mere dumm[y]' and she would require more information on the boundaries of the so-called 'Greater Asian sphere'.[43]

No foreign visitor had ever spoken to Hitler like this, recalled
Schmidt, who, at a second conference the next day, witnessed bad-
tempered and ultimately unresolved haggling over the fate of the
Balkans. That evening, the dinner hosted by Molotov for Ribbentrop
at the Soviet Embassy was interrupted when air-raid sirens announced
the arrival of the Royal Air Force. Sullenly, the Soviet Commissar
followed the Nazi Foreign Minister into his air-raid shelter beneath
Wilhelmstrasse. When the latter continued to harp upon the imminence of England's demise, the Commissar cut him off: 'If England
is defeated, why are we sitting in this shelter? And whose bombs
are dropping so close that we can hear the explosions even here?'[44]
A month later, Hitler confirmed to his generals his determination to
attack the Soviet Union in the spring. It would be a war not merely to
establish 'hegemony in Europe' but to annihilate National Socialism's
ideological enemy, 'Jewish Bolshevism'.[45]

While Stalin negotiated with Hitler, the British were kept in
suspense. Talks over a trade deal were repeatedly postponed and
Cripps was seldom permitted to see Molotov. In his desperation
to improve relations, the Ambassador argued that Britain should
recognise Soviet annexation of the Baltic States and transfer
large sums of Estonian, Latvian and Lithuanian gold, currently
deposited in the Bank of England, to Moscow, as the Russians
demanded. The Permanent Under-Secretary of the Foreign
Office, Sir Alexander Cadogan, condemned this as 'simply silly'.
Recognising that Soviet foreign policy was based on cold-hearted
self-interest, he understood that it would change only 'when and
if they think it will suit them. And if they *do* think that, it won't
matter whether we've kicked Maisky in the stomach. Contrari-
wise, we could give Maisky the Garter and it wouldn't make a
pennyworth of difference.'[46] His Deputy, Sir Orme Sargent, pitied
the hapless Ambassador:

> I am sorry for Sir S. Cripps, who is now entering the humiliating
> phase which all British negotiators in Moscow have to go through
> when they are simply kept waiting on the doormat until such time as
> the Soviet Government consider it desirable, as part of their policy

of playing off one power against the other, to take notice . . . Stalin has meanwhile got Sir S. Cripps exactly where he wants him, that is to say, as a suppliant on his doormat holding his pathetic little peace offerings of tin in one hand and rubber in the other.[47]

Fitzroy Maclean was even more to the point: 'We are solely concerned with the mental processes of a middle-aged Georgian brigand,' he minuted, rejecting the notion that it was possible to tame the Russian Bear through acts of unrequited generosity.[48]

The story of the build-up to Operation Barbarossa is well known. As German forces massed along his frontier, Stalin received a glut of intelligence forecasting the coming invasion. Yet intelligence is open to interpretation and Stalin believed that Hitler was preparing to issue an ultimatum in order to extract concessions, rather than attack without warning. This was the story circulated by the Germans and accepted not only within the Kremlin but, until only a few weeks before the invasion, by British intelligence as well as the Foreign Office. The exception was Cripps. Returning from a visit to Ankara in early March 1941, he told foreign diplomats that he expected Hitler to attack Russia before the end of June. On 24 March, after receiving information from a source in Berlin (via the Swedish Minister in Moscow), he sent the Foreign Office a startlingly accurate précis of German intentions:

> German plan is as follows: the attack on England will be continued with U-boats and from the air but there will be no invasion. At the same time a drive against Russia will take place. This drive will be by three large armies: the first based at Warsaw under von Bock, the second based at Königsberg . . . the third based at Kraków.[49]

On 19 April, Cripps conveyed Churchill's famous 'warning', via Molotov's deputy, Andrei Vyshinsky, to Stalin. Derived from Enigma decrypts, it relayed how, following Yugoslavia's conscription to the Axis, the Germans had begun to move three out of five panzer divisions from Romania to Poland before countermanding this order after the *coup d'état* in Belgrade. In his war memoirs, Churchill made a great deal of Cripps' failure to deliver this 'exceptional' message in person, arguing that if he had been able to have 'direct' contact with Stalin then he might have saved him 'from having so much of his Air Force destroyed on the ground'.[50] Yet Stalin's overriding suspicion was that the British, far from wishing to help, were trying to inveigle him into war. In this context, Cripps' far worse offence – one that did indeed do lasting damage to Anglo-Soviet relations – was his unauthorised warning to Vyshinsky that:

> If the war were protracted for a long period . . . there might be a temptation for Great Britain (and especially for certain circles in Great Britain) to come to some arrangement to end the war on the sort of basis which has again recently been suggested in certain German quarters, that is, that western Europe should be returned to its former status, while Germany should be unhampered in the expansion of her "living space" to the east.[51]

This was Stalin's nightmare: a vision of horror that seemed to gain credence through one of the most bizarre episodes of the war.

On the night of 10 May 1941, Hitler's party deputy, Rudolf Hess, bailed out of his Messerschmitt Bf 110 and parachuted into central Scotland. Discovered by a farmer, he was handed over to the Home Guard and taken to a local police station. There he made repeated requests to see the Duke of Hamilton, whose Lanarkshire seat he had been trying to reach. It was only when the Duke saw him the next day that Hess revealed his identity. A mystic and a fantasist, he had flown to Scotland, he explained, to try and broker a peace deal between Britain and Germany. The mission was entirely his own. The choice of Hamilton was due to the fact that he was a distinguished aviator (the first person to fly over Mount Everest) who had attended the 1936 Berlin Olympics (although he had never met Hess) and was Lord Steward to the King (an influential position in the Nazi's addled mind).

The British were stunned. 'This may be a lunatic', explained Eden's Private Secretary, Valentine Lawford, handing Jock Colville a telephone receiver, but 'he says he is the Duke of Hamilton and that something extraordinary has happened, that he is about to fly down from Scotland to Northolt and that he wants to be met there by Alec Cadogan and the Prime Minister's Secretary . . . It's like an E. Phillips Oppenheim thriller.' Having spoken to the Duke and gathered that 'someone' had arrived, Colville telephoned Churchill at Ditchley, the Oxfordshire home of Conservative MP Ronald Tree, used by the Prime Minister when the brightness of the moon was deemed to render Chequers vulnerable to German bombers.

'*Who* has arrived?' demanded Churchill.

'I don't know,' repeated Colville for the fourth time.

'It can't be Hitler,' mused the PM.

'I imagine not,' replied Colville.

'Well, stop imagining and have the Duke, if it is the Duke, sent straight from Northolt.'[52]

Having established that it was the Deputy Führer they had under lock and key, the British made the risky decision to exploit the mystery surrounding his flight to try and provoke a rift between Moscow and Berlin. A whispering campaign was launched by the intelligence services claiming that there was a split in the Nazi hierarchy, with 'purists', such as Hess, wishing to make peace with Britain so as to launch a fresh war against National Socialism's true enemy, 'Asiatic Bolshevism'. Although Stalin's paranoia required little encouragement, the rumours augmented his existing suspicions. 'Churchill sent us a personal message in which he warns us about Hitler's aggressive intentions . . . and on the other hand, the British meet Hess, who is undoubtedly Hitler's confidant, and conducts negotiations with Germany through him,' the Vozhd (leader) told the Central Committee of the Communist Party.[53] The British, he maintained, were trying to trick him.

Throughout May and June, Stalin would seek to reassure Hitler of his loyalty, unblocking shipments of raw materials to the Reich, severing diplomatic relations with those countries under German occupation and recognising the anti-British Government of Rashid Ali in Iraq. To his paranoic mind, the true intent behind the German military build-up (some 150 divisions by early June) and more than 100 violations of Soviet airspace by the Luftwaffe remained a bluff – the natural crescendo in a 'war of nerves' designed to extract concessions.[54] On 16 June, the Commissar for State Security, Vsevolod Merkulov, sent Stalin a report based on information gleaned from a source in the German Air Ministry, stating that the invasion was imminent. 'Tell your "source" . . . to go fuck his mother!' the despot scrawled across the report. 'This is no source but a *disinformer*.'[55] Six days later, Hitler attacked.

XIII

Allied with Hell

Lord Halifax: A man stuck in the bottom of a well will
accept the hand of a gorilla in the hope of thereby extricating himself.

Republican Congressman: Suppose the gorilla turns
on him when he gets out?

Lord Halifax: We will cross that bridge when we come to it.[1]

At 3.15 a.m. on 22 June 1941, Hitler's juggernaut crashed into the Soviet
defences. Despite the myriad warnings, surprise was achieved along
almost the entire 1,100-mile front. Border guards were killed in their
barracks, communications were sabotaged and 890 Soviet aircraft were
destroyed on the first day alone, the majority lined up in neat rows on
the ground. Within a fortnight, German troops had penetrated deep
into Soviet territory, with Army Group North moving rapidly through
the Baltic States towards Leningrad, Army Group South devouring
large tracts of Ukraine and Army Group Centre cutting into Belorussia, before completing a vast encirclement of Soviet forces near Minsk.
Red Army losses reached into the hundreds of thousands and by 15
July Generaloberst Heinz Guderian's 2nd Panzer Group had reached
Smolensk, less than 250 miles from Moscow. The Russian campaign,
noted the jubilant Chief of the German General Staff, Franz Halder,
appeared to have been won 'in the space of two weeks'.[2]

'The world will hold its breath,' Hitler prophesied of Operation Barbarossa.[3] Eleven hours after learning of the German
invasion, however, Churchill was on the airwaves announcing that
Britain would stand by the Russian people and afford the USSR
all assistance within her power. As King George VI recorded in
his diary, it was a 'very bold' policy decision, one indeed that had

been made without consulting the Cabinet or the Dominions.[4] Churchill's excuse for such unconstitutional behaviour was the importance of providing public opinion with an early lead. In this, he was surely correct. Castigated as the abettor, if not the ally, of Nazism for almost two years – the assassin of Poland, Finland and the Baltic States – there was no denying the fact that the USSR was even more tyrannically governed than Germany. Hitler's pre-war victims stretched into the thousands, Stalin's into the millions. Churchill appreciated these facts. The most militant antagonist of communism during the 1920s – the man who had wanted to use British forces to strangle the Russian Revolution at birth and then inveighed against the 'foul baboonery' of Bolshevism – he recognised that Nazism and communism were non-identical twins.[5] Yet he also understood that Nazi Germany, not Soviet Russia, was Europe's primary foe. Under these circumstances, he was prepared to march with anyone who opposed Hitler or, as he put it to Jock Colville, 'if Hitler invaded Hell he would at least make a favourable reference to the Devil!'[6]

Although Anthony Eden feared that at least 'half the country' would object to close association with the USSR, Churchill's declaration enjoyed broad support.[7] Postal censorship showed that less than a third of correspondents expressed antipathy towards Britain's new ally, the majority taking the view that it was 'a great thing for us to have Russia in' and that if she could only 'hold out for a few months against Jerry' then the war was 'in the bag'.[8] This was at the higher end of professional expectations. As Sir Robert Vansittart told the editor of the *Manchester Guardian*, reflecting the military consensus, the Germans were expected to roll up the Russian armies 'like a carpet'.[9] Despite the USSR's possessing more tanks, more aircraft and more men under arms than any other country in the world, Stalin's purges – which had removed three out of five marshals, eight out of nine admirals, thirteen out of fifteen army commanders and sundry lesser ranks – had, it was believed, all but destroyed the Red Army's fighting potential. When a Republican Congressman asked Lord Halifax, then serving as Ambassador to Washington, whether Britain's share of US war materiel should be reduced to accommodate the Soviets, his Lordship was firm: 'No. Whatever you give

Russia will probably be lost. England, herself, wants all you can give her – and more – without sacrificing for anyone else . . . Russia will not last six weeks.'[10]

This was Roosevelt's concern. Influenced by reports from the Military Attaché in Moscow, the unremittingly pessimistic Colonel Ivan D. Yeaton, US Military Intelligence believed the Germans would be in Moscow by the end of July. The Chiefs of Staff opposed sending much-needed equipment to a distant and by all accounts hopeless theatre, while influential figures within the State Department warned of another 'Brest-Litovsk' (the treaty the Germans had imposed on the Russians in 1918) leading to a full-blown 'Russo-German alliance'.[11] Assistant Secretary of State Adolf Berle was particularly alarmed at the Soviet request to access American technical and military secrets:

> The extreme Anglophile view is that we should turn over everything to the Russians at once. They seem to think that the Russians now love them and will be in all respects a part of their train. Knowing the Russians have almost as great an antagonism to the British as the Germans have to the Jews, I am in no way sanguine. In point of fact, the engineers they wished to let in [to] the plants are the same ones who were doing espionage for Russia and Germany until six weeks ago. I consequently voted 'no' and was glad to see that the Army, Navy and FBI did likewise. We are much better off if we treat the Russian situation for what it is, namely, a temporary confluence of interest.[12]

Roosevelt appreciated these fears. Yet he was also among the first to realise that if the Soviets could hold on then it would mean 'the liberation of Europe from Nazi domination'.[13] On 24 June, he therefore unfroze $39 million of US-held Russian assets and, during July, provided the Soviets with $6.5 million worth of military supplies, though nowhere near the $1.75 billion they had requested. At the end of the month, his friend and emissary, Harry Hopkins, flew to Moscow to assure Stalin that the President was determined to go 'all out' to aid the Russians in their struggle against Nazism.[14] 'The United States was going to provide the Soviet Union with all possible assistance and . . . the details could be worked out later,' the envoy told the dismayed Yeaton.[15] Taking his cue, Stalin asked for 20,000 anti-aircraft guns, as well as machine guns, rifles, aviation fuel and aluminium. His recall of detail and his assurance that the Soviet Union could fight for four years provided she received the necessary equipment impressed the Presidential confidant. Stalin was 'right on the ball', Hopkins told the former US Ambassador to Moscow Joseph E. Davies.[16] Later, in a sycophantic article for *American Magazine*, he described how the Soviet leader spoke 'as he knew his troops were shooting – straight and hard . . . There was no waste of word, gesture, nor mannerism. It was like talking to a perfectly co-ordinated machine . . . Joseph Stalin knew what he wanted, knew what Russia wanted and he assumed that you knew.'[17] His message to Roosevelt was simple:

> I have had two long and satisfactory talks with Stalin and will communicate personally to you the messages he is sending. I would like to tell you now, however, that I feel ever so confident about this front. The morale of the population is exceptionally good. There is unbounded determination to win.[18]*

Despite the bold words, Anglo-American aid to the Soviet Union in the months following the invasion was meagre: 200 Curtiss P-40 fighters and a handful of bombers from the US and 400 fighters and 20,000 tons of rubber from Britain was all that the West was willing to supply at this time. In Washington, the Soviet Ambassador, Konstantin Umansky, complained that he 'was getting the run-around' from the War Department while, in London, Maisky grumbled that the English were withholding 'the weapons we need most badly (small-calibre antiaircraft guns, fighters, etc.)'.[19] On 18 July 1941, in his first telegram to his new ally, Stalin asked Churchill

---

* How Hopkins can have gauged the morale of the Soviet people when he was only in Moscow for three days and had no contact with any Russians outside the Kremlin is hard to tell. A consistent supporter of aid to the USSR, he knew little of the country or her regime. 'The trouble was that Harry only knew two things about the Soviet Union,' an American diplomat later told the journalist John Gunther. 'The first was that they had a bad Tsar named Ivan the Terrible. The second was that Russia was the first country to recognise the United States after 1776.'

to relieve pressure on the Red Army – 350,000 of whose soldiers were currently encircled at Smolensk – by establishing a new front in northern France or Norway. This opening salvo in what was to become the dominating controversy in Anglo-Soviet relations was easily dismissed. The Germans had over twenty divisions in France and the whole Atlantic coast was bristling with 'cannon, wire, pill-boxes and beach mines', explained Churchill to the Soviet leader on 20 July. To attempt a Continental landing at this time would be merely to invite a 'bloody repulse', while minor raids would only lead to 'fiascos'.[20] Although the despot professed to understand Britain's difficulties he applauded Maisky's criticism of British strategy delivered during an emotional interview with Eden on 26 August:

> Your conversation with Eden regarding England's strategy fully reflects the mood of the Soviet people . . . The British Government assists the Hitlerites with its passive wait-and-see policy. The Hitlerites want to beat their opponents one by one – Russians today, English tomorrow . . . The fact that England applauds us and curses the Germans does not change anything. Do the English understand that? I think they do. So what do they want? I think they want us to weaken. If this assumption is correct we have to be careful with the English.[21]

The sheer hypocrisy of these accusations, coming as they did from a man who until recently had been collaborating with Hitler, dividing Europe with the Nazis and literally fuelling the German war machine, did not escape the British. When, on 4 September, Maisky delivered a telegram from Stalin, repeating his demand for a British Expeditionary Force to be sent to France or the Balkans, Churchill reminded the Ambassador that until a few months ago, 'we in this Island did not know whether you were not coming in against us on the German side. Indeed, we thought it quite likely you would . . . Whatever happens and whatever you do, you of all people have no right to make reproaches to us.'[22] One month later, responding to Cripps' plea for a token British force to be sent to fight alongside the Red Army in Russia – Stalin had requested twenty-five to thirty divisions, more than the size of the entire British Army – he addressed the Ambassador in blunt terms:

I fully sympathise with you in your difficult position and also with Russia in her agony. They certainly have no right to reproach us. They brought their own fate upon themselves when, by their pact with Ribbentrop they let Hitler loose on Poland and so started the war . . . That a Government with this record should accuse us of . . . being willing to fight to the last Russian soldier, leaves me quite cool. If they harbour suspicions of us, it is only because of the guilt and self-reproach in their own hearts.[23]

Yet the fear that Stalin, unless encouraged, might seek a separate peace spurred the British and the Americans towards greater commitments. On 28 September 1941, just after the Germans had completed another massive encirclement near Kiev – killing or capturing over 600,000 Soviet soldiers – the British Minister of Supply, Lord Beaverbrook, and Roosevelt's 'expeditor' of aid to Britain, Averell Harriman, arrived in Moscow at the head of a joint mission tasked with providing substantial aid to the USSR.

A larger-than-life character, Beaverbrook had propelled himself from a manse in rural Canada to the heart of British politics and journalism through a combination of opportunism, skulduggery and a surfeit of energy. A millionaire by thirty and a government minister before the age of forty, he had gained control of the *Daily Express* in 1916 and turned it into the best-selling newspaper in the land. Although widely perceived as a bounder, even within his large circle of friends and hangers-on, the vigour with which he promoted his causes, be it Imperial Preference or the appeasement of Germany, made him impossible to ignore. Churchill, despite an abundance of evidence to the contrary, considered him 'a good friend in foul weather'.[24] Clementine Churchill detested him, while Clement Attlee shared General Alan Brooke's judgement that he was 'an evil genius' who exercised an invidious influence on the Prime Minister.[25] Dynamic but mercurial, flawed but indefatigable, his role in almost doubling Britain's aircraft production during the critical summer of 1940, combined with an earthy humour and piratical nature, made him the ideal emissary to appeal to Stalin.

William Averell Harriman shared Beaverbrook's ambition and restlessness but not his irreverence or cynicism. Tall, handsome and aloof, this polo-playing ladies' man had inherited a fortune from his father's railroad empire and then made another, in business and banking. An alumnus of Groton and Yale, he had played a small part in the New Deal before accepting a Presidential commission, in February 1941, to cross the Atlantic and 'recommend everything that we can do, short of war, to keep the British Isles afloat'.[26] After an unsteady beginning – journalists encountering him shortly after his arrival judged him 'rather out of his depth' and 'too legal and dry' – his Anglophilia and obvious determination impressed his hosts.[27] Churchill took to him instantly, while Colville recorded how this earnest, some would say humourless, American succeeded, through a combination of personability, integrity and carefully deployed flattery, in placing himself near the centre of events.

The Anglo-American delegation arrived in Moscow on 28 September 1941, the ninety-ninth day of the war in the East. The journey had been dramatic. Flying from Archangel to the Russian capital, the party had been woken by a barrage of anti-aircraft fire, followed by a sudden dive for the trees. There had been 'a little misunderstanding' involving the city's air defences, they were later informed and, on Stalin's orders, 'there was now a vacancy in the ranks of the Anti-Aircraft colonels'.[28] Their work was tiring and difficult. Although Beaverbrook's instruction to the technical experts was to give and give freely, this simple task was rendered almost impossible by the obfuscation of Soviet officials. When the visitors asked a simple question such as 'How many anti-tank guns are allotted to a division?', they would be told that it depended on 'what sort of division'. When the British and Americans suggested that an infantry division might be taken as an example, their interlocutors replied that it depended on 'where it has to fight'.[29]

Beaverbrook and Harriman's first meeting with Stalin was cordial. The Vozhd described the military situation and requested 4,000 tons of barbed wire and 500 tanks per month, as well as fighters, bombers, anti-aircraft guns and armour plate. When the two men returned to the Kremlin the following evening, however, they found the dictator in querulous mood. Despite being informed that the British and Americans would meet the majority of his demands, Stalin was disgruntled. 'He appeared to question our good faith,' recalled Harriman. 'He seemed to suggest that we wanted to see the Soviet regime destroyed by Hitler; otherwise we would offer more help. He showed his suspicion in a very blunt way.'[30] The two men returned to the National Hotel, where Beaverbrook had been given the 'Lenin Suite', thoroughly depressed. Perplexed by the injustice of Stalin's accusations, the press lord began to fret about the damage to his reputation should the conference end in failure. 'Max was rattled,' recalled Harriman. 'It was for this reason, I suppose, that he asked me to present at the third meeting the combined list of weapons and materials that the British and American Governments were prepared to supply. Then, if things did not go well, the fire would be directed at me.'[31]

He need not have worried. Unaware that they had been played, the emissaries were delighted when, on returning to the Kremlin the following evening, Stalin appeared satisfied with the cornucopia of equipment the British and the Americans were offering. Listening intently, as Harriman ran through the list of more than seventy items the Soviets had requested, the dictator drew a series of wolves on the paper in front of him, filling in the background with red pencil. When Beaverbrook enquired whether Stalin was content, the Vozhd said that he received the list 'with enthusiasm'. At this, Litvinov, who had been dug up at the visitors' request to act as interpreter, jumped to his feet and declared, 'Now we shall win the war!' Relieved, Beaverbrook completely lost his head, describing Stalin in his report to London as 'a kindly man' who 'practically never shows any impatience at all'.[32] The professional diplomats were less impressed. 'Let history record that in those winter negotiations Stalin ran rings round his visitors', wrote the Third Secretary of the British Embassy in Moscow, John Russell, adding that 'for sheer nastiness, Stalin and Beaverbrook were about a match'.[33]

At the banquet on 1 October, an exuberant Beaverbrook asked Stalin – looking like 'a typical jobbing gardener' in his baggy trousers and boots, according to the British Air Minister, Harold Balfour – about the Nazi–Soviet Pact.[34] Unabashed, Hitler's former partner in crime blamed the agreement on Chamberlain's determination to appease the Führer, adding that it had never been repudiated, 'the Germans had simply ignored it'.[35] Stalin then asked after Nancy

Astor and George Bernard Shaw, that unlikely duo who, in 1931, had visited the Soviet Union as part of a credulous 'fact-finding' mission. As Churchill had written in a bitingly funny article at the time, the 'Man of Steel' had 'flung open the closely guarded sanctuaries of the Kremlin and, pushing aside his morning's budget of death warrants . . . received his guests with smiles of overflowing comradeship'.[36] On that occasion, Astor had told Stalin that Churchill's political career was finished. But the despot, as he now relayed to Beaverbrook, demurred: when the Conservatives were confronted by a military crisis, they would assuredly recall the old war horse. 'His curiosity about Churchill was insatiable,' noted Beaverbrook. 'His hatred of Hitler appears to be real. His confidence in the Americans and Great Britain is limited. His power I should have thought is absolute and the bottleneck the most effective in history.'[37]

Izvestiya and *Pravda* hailed the conference as a triumph. 'You can say that the Russians are delighted with Lord Beaverbrook,' the press baron told international correspondents.[38] Well they should have been. Under the terms of the agreement that he and Harriman had brokered, the democracies were committed to supplying the USSR with 500 tanks, 400 aircraft and 200 mini-tanks per month and 1,256 anti-tank guns, 152 anti-aircraft guns and 5,000 scouting cars over the following nine months. Two thousand tons of aluminium, 7,000 tons of lead and 1,000 tons of armour plate were promised on a monthly basis, while Soviet clothes supplies stood at 1.3 million yards of army cloth and 400,000 pairs of army boots per month.[39] Although the burden was evenly spread, the strain was felt most acutely by the British, already under siege in the Middle East and whose proportion of US aid was cut to accommodate the Soviets. 'It was like having all one's eye-teeth drawn out', recalled General Ismay, 'but there was nothing to do but grin and bear it.'[40]

Accompanying the material demands were political ones. As the Anglo-American deputation recorded, Stalin wanted the British to declare war on Finland, which, seizing the opportunity to regain the lands lost in the Winter War, had recommenced operations against the USSR as a 'co-belligerent' of Germany. The situation was embarrassing for the British who but two years previously had sought to aid the Finns against Stalin's unprovoked aggression. Finnish resistance had been 'superb, nay, sublime', Churchill had declared at the time and on 4 November 1941 he wrote to Stalin questioning the wisdom of a formal declaration of war against a country that had so many friends, especially in the United States.[41] The despot's reply was swift and brutal. Describing Britain's reluctance to declare war on Finland as 'intolerable', Stalin claimed that there was a lack of 'clarity' and 'mutual confidence' in Anglo-Soviet relations, while spurning the Prime Minister's offer to send Generals Wavell and Paget to Moscow for strategy discussions.[42] Churchill was apoplectic. On 5 December 1941, however, Britain bowed to Soviet pressure and declared war on Finland, as well as Hitler's southern allies Hungary and Romania.

Even more controversial was the Soviet-British invasion of Iran. The Anglo-Iraqi war had served as a warning as to what could happen if pro-Axis regimes were allowed to flourish in strategically sensitive parts of the world. Situated mid-way between Egypt and India, on the USSR's southern flank, Iran produced around half the oil that fuelled Britain's Middle Eastern and Mediterranean campaigns. The Shah was suspected of being pro-Nazi – a supposition supported by the presence of several thousand German 'technicians', not to mention the Grand Mufti and Rashid Ali, within his kingdom. With the Wehrmacht sweeping all before it to the north, the danger of a German descent, or German–Iranian collaboration on the Iraqi model, appeared real. On 16 August 1941, the British and Soviets demanded the expulsion of the Germans from Iran. When the Iranians refused, they attacked. On 25 August, the RAF and Soviet Air Force dropped bombs on Tehran, Qazvin and Rasht, while three Soviet armies advanced from the Caucasus and two British divisions attacked from Iraq. At Abadan, home to the all-important Anglo-Iranian Oil Company refinery, a Royal Navy sloop sunk the Iranian ship *Palang* and two Iranian gunboats were 'disposed of' at Bandar Shahpur. When the Soviet Military Attaché in London asked Major-General John Kennedy what he meant by 'disposed of', the Director of Military Operations replied, 'liquidated'.[43] Although the Iranians mobilised nine divisions, two with tanks, most units realised the futility of resistance and surrendered without a fight. After four days, it was all over. Reza Shah abdicated in favour of his son and the

British and Soviets divided the country into two zones of occupation. 'When the virtuous once abandon scruples they can go a long way down the rose-strewn path of international immorality – with success and universal approval!' observed Leo Amery cheerfully to Anthony Eden.[44] His colleagues were less sanguine. Aware that the issue of the German nationals was largely a pretext – that Britain's primary objective was to protect the oil fields, the Soviet Union's to secure the only overland route for supplies – Churchill admitted to having qualms about an action 'for which we had justification but no right', while Eden felt 'ashamed' at Britain's 'first act of naked aggression'.[45] In the context of the German onslaught in the east, however, the four-day war was generally felt to be justified, while the desire among the British to assist their allies in a venture that Moscow, even more than London, deemed necessary was also a mitigating factor.

Allies or co-belligerents? It was a moot point. Although Churchill referred to the Russians as 'allies' when announcing the signing of the Anglo-Soviet Agreement on 15 July, others were less happy with the term.[46] 'I avoid the expression "Allies" for the Russians are a dirty lot of murdering thieves themselves and double crossers of the deepest dye', recorded Lieutenant-General Henry Pownall, adding that it was 'good to see the two biggest cut-throats in Europe, Hitler and Stalin, going for each other'.[47] In September 1941, the Minister for Aircraft Production, John Moore-Brabazon, was rash enough to express this sentiment publicly. Although Cuthbert Headlam thought the Minister should confine such opinions to his diary, it was, he admitted in his own journal, 'what a good many of us think'.[48] George Kennan, serving in the American Embassy in Berlin, thought that the Soviet Union should be 'regarded as a "fellow traveller" in the accepted Moscow sense, rather than as a political associate', owing to her system of violence and despotism, while the US Ambassador to Moscow, Laurence Steinhardt, warned the State Department against the naïveté of supposing that it was possible to create 'international goodwill' with people that 'are not affected by ethical or moral considerations, nor guided by the relationships which are customary between individuals of culture and breeding'.[49]

On the other side of the hill, the Soviets demonstrated their suspicion by refusing to provide either the British or the Americans with information regarding their own war effort and through such outrages as the expulsion of three members of the British Naval Mission, on trumped-up charges, even while the Moscow Conference was still in progress. 'Looking back, it seems hard to believe that we spent as much time or more in arranging interviews with the army authorities as at the interviews themselves,' recalled Arthur Birse, interpreter to the British Military Mission in Moscow. 'Some of our specialists spent months waiting to be seen by the Russians and in one or two cases returned to London without having met anyone on the Soviet side. I remember one exceptionally conscientious young officer, a specialist on the technical side, who came out loaded with information of inestimable value to the Russians but whose nerves broke down after months of inactivity.'[50] Nevertheless, the Soviets were provided with British anti-submarine detection technology (later known by the American acronym SONAR); a radio detection set (RADAR); night-flying, radio wave-bending and homing equipment; drawings and specifications for British bombs; and three specimen Mark IX A bomb sights.[51] In addition, the Russians received a steady stream of intelligence from Enigma decrypts (though the British were careful to disguise the source), only for Stalin to accuse his allies of furnishing him with 'incorrect and even misleading' information when events did not evolve exactly as predicted.[52]

To be sure, there were some Soviet attempts to show solidarity with their new ally. On 31 October 1941, to mark the twenty-fourth anniversary of the Bolshevik Revolution, *Pravda* published a list of thirty-four officially approved slogans. Along with such staples as 'Long live . . . the Great October Socialist Revolution, which overthrew the power of imperialists in our country' and 'Death to Hitler's bloody dogs', there were also 'Long live the military alliance between the armies and navies of the Soviet Union, Great Britain and other freedom-loving nations' and 'Long live the United States of America, who support Great Britain and the Soviet Union . . . in their just war against German-fascist aggressors'.[53]

More sincere expressions of comradeship came from outside the official sphere. Called to the switchboard on the morning of 22 June – the first day of Operation Barbarossa – the night watchman at the British Embassy, a Cockney called Harold Elvin, was told that there was a Russian on the line who wished to speak to an Englishman. Perplexed, Elvin picked up the receiver.

'We fight together I think?' enquired the tentative voice at the other end.

'Yes. I think so', replied Elvin.

'I shake your hand.'

'Thank you. Good wishes.'[54]

A few weeks later, when the presence of Cripps and the heads of the British Military Mission was discovered among the attendees at a concert, the audience rose to its feet and began cheering: 'For the brave British people!' 'For the gallant English Army!' 'For the British Ambassador!' 'For the British Military Mission!' 'For Stalin!' 'For the continued friendship and alliance for all time!'[55]

Despite their frustrations, the British recognised that the Russians were engaged in a titanic struggle to which their contribution was necessarily limited.* On 2 October, the Germans launched Operation Typhoon – the drive for Moscow. Eight Soviet armies – 673,000 men – were soon trapped in pockets at Vyazma and Bryansk. When the Soviet Chief of the General Staff, Marshal Zhukov, arrived at the Kremlin on 7 October he overheard, or so he later claimed, Stalin instructing Lavrenti Beria, the sadistic head of the NKVD, to use his agents to contact the Germans and sound out the possibility of a peace deal. A week later, with Hitler's armies still driving forward, the Vozhd ordered the majority of government departments, the theatres and the diplomatic corps to evacuate to Kuibyshev, 675 miles to the south-east. Panic descended upon the capital. Martial law was imposed. A quarter of a million Muscovites, mainly women, were put to work, digging anti-tank ditches. By 26 November, the German 4th Panzer Army had advanced to within 21 miles

---

* Four British convoys had reached Archangel by the middle of November 1941, delivering 466 British Matilda and Valentine tanks. Owing to their narrow tracks, however, these struggled in the Russian snow.

of the city, the men of the SS *Das Reich* Division even able to make out the explosion of Russian anti-aircraft shells above the capital.

But heavy rains – the *rasputitsa* – and Soviet counterattacks had taken their toll on the invaders. While Hitler's armies struggled along roads that turned to quagmires, their strength reduced by more than a third since the start of the offensive, Stalin was transferring troops from the east. By the end of the month, with temperatures having fallen below minus 35 degrees Centigrade, eleven new Soviet armies had been formed behind the lines. On 5 December they attacked. Frost-bitten and exhausted, its vehicles unable to move unless fires were first lit beneath their engines, the Wehrmacht was driven back. Klin was retaken on 15 December, Kalinin the day after. Haunted by Napoleon's fateful retreat in 1812, Hitler ordered his soldiers to fight where they stood. This controversial injunction, liberally interpreted, prevented a retreat from becoming a rout. Yet by 7 January 1942 – the date on which the Soviet counteroffensive began to falter – Army Group Centre had been pushed back between 62 and 155 miles. Moscow, for the moment at least, was saved.

In hindsight, it is possible to identify the failure of the Wehrmacht to defeat the Red Army in a single campaign, symbolised by its reverse before the gates of Moscow, as the turning point of the war: a strategic defeat that, for all the fire and fury of Hitler's 1942 summer offensive, could not be reversed.[56] To contemporaries, however, the future appeared less certain. Although they had underestimated the strength of Russian resistance, most British and American experts continued to expect the Soviet Union to be defeated. Imbued with the myth of the 'invincibility' of the Wehrmacht – already in possession of the majority of Ukraine and more than a third of European Russia – a renewed German offensive, it was commonly assumed, would succeed in capturing Moscow as soon as the snows melted. In this event, the Soviet Union would collapse and Hitler would be free to deploy his full strength against the British Empire. Throughout 1941 and into 1942, therefore, it was to the West and not the East that the British continued to look for salvation.

XIV

'In God's Good Time'

It is impossible for me to understand the ostrich-like attitude of America.
Either we have an interest in the outcome of this war, or we have not. If
not, why are we supplying England with the tools? If we have, why do
we not realise that the situation could not be tougher and every day we
delay direct participation . . . we are taking an extreme risk.

– Averell Harriman to William Bullitt, 21 May 1941[1]

Franklin Roosevelt was not prone to anxiety. On the evening of 5
November 1940, however, he appeared visibly nervous. Sitting in the
dining room at Hyde Park, the family home in which he had been
born on the banks of the Hudson, he recorded the incoming election results on a sheet of paper. As early returns revealed a strong
showing for his Republican rival, Wendell Willkie, the President's
jaw tightened. Perspiring heavily, he summoned the head of his
secret service detail, Mike Reilly. 'Mike, I don't want to see anybody
in here.'

'Including your family?' the bodyguard enquired.

'I said anybody,' the President snapped.

It seemed, the secret service agent recalled, that Roosevelt had
lost his nerve.[2]

Fortunately for his forty-or-so guests, not to mention the wider
world, FDR's jitters proved unfounded. In the most participated
election in US history, Roosevelt received over twenty-seven million
votes to Willkie's twenty-two million, trouncing the Republican in
the electoral college by 449 votes to 82. As the President wheeled
himself onto the balcony and towards an unprecedented third term,
he smiled broadly at the crowd of torch-bearing supporters gathered on his lawn. 'We are facing difficult days in this country,' he

told the throng. 'But I think you will find me in the future just the same Franklin Roosevelt you have known a great many years.'[3] It was an anodyne statement: serviceable and folksy. Yet it concealed an unconscious irony. Far from 'knowing' the President, even Roosevelt's closest associates admitted to having little idea who he really was.

His most obvious characteristics were his bravery and his charm. Struck down by polio when he was thirty-nine, he ended up permanently paralysed below the waist, unable to stand, let alone walk, without heavy leg braces, a stick and someone to lean on. Not only did he refuse to succumb to despair (or retire to Hyde Park as his domineering mother wished), he strove to regain the use of his legs and resumed his political career: nominating Al Smith at the 1924 Democratic National Convention, becoming Governor of New York in 1929 and entering the White House in 1932. His message at his first inauguration – 'The only thing we have to fear is fear itself' – was aimed at a country mired in the Great Depression but was also an expression of his own philosophy.[4] Never heard to complain, his response to being told that Lord Halifax's war-disabled son, Richard, objected to excessive sympathy was, 'Quite right . . . I have no legs but I get around very well.'[5] Later, his physician, Vice-Admiral McIntire, would recall how Churchill, Stalin, Chiang Kai-shek and countless others would watch with a mixture of curiosity and horror as the immobile President was lifted into a chair at the start of meetings, only to be overcome by his 'sheer virility'.[6]

Even more obvious was his charm. The famous grin and easy laugh, the cigarette holder at a jaunty angle, the Presidential cocktails, the well of oft-repeated anecdotes, the colloquialisms – '*dee*lighted', 'grand' and 'bully' – inherited from his fifth cousin and Presidential forebear, the almost offensive overfamiliarity, affected all but the most determined. 'Look out,' his military aide, Major-General Edwin 'Pa' Watson, would warn visitors, 'this is one of the days when he can win the bark off a tree.' When North Dakota Senator Gerald Nye, a vehement opponent of the New Deal and fanatical isolationist, met the President for the first time, he began by boasting that he had 'a hundred per cent' voting record against him, 'on banking, economy and beer'. 'No, Senator,' Roosevelt rejoined. 'You were only twenty-five per cent against me. There were some things in those bills that neither of us liked.' Nye left the meeting 'highly elated'.[7] Later, when a thoroughly disgruntled Joseph Kennedy arrived at the White House on 27 October 1940, nine days before the Presidential election, there was every chance the bruised Ambassador and fervent isolationist would come out for Willkie. After an intimate supper of scrambled eggs and sausages (preceded by the inevitable Presidential cocktail), however, Kennedy agreed to give a radio address endorsing the President.

Charm and bravery were salient features but there were also deep ambiguities. Ostensibly warm and straightforward, FDR could also be cold and manipulative. A consummate politician, capable of all the requisite cynicism, he was, at the same time, one of the great idealists of the twentieth century. Frivolous yet earnest, patient though easily bored, he combined the shibboleths of American egalitarianism with a fetish for European royalty, while his efforts on behalf of the destitute and suffering went hand in hand with an unshakeable sense of himself as a patrician and an attitude towards those around and beneath him that could, on occasion, stray into the cruel. A President of paradoxes, the one feature both allies and opponents agreed on was his addiction to obfuscation and dissemblance. Eleanor Roosevelt noted that her husband's colleagues were often misled by his habit of nodding and saying 'I see' while they were talking, when all he meant to convey was that he was listening – a rarity in itself.[8] But this was only part of it. The worthy recipient of an 8-foot papier-mâché sphinx (a present from bemused White House correspondents), he proudly described himself to his no-less befuddled Hudson valley neighbour and Treasury Secretary, Henry Morgenthau Jr, as 'a juggler . . . I never let my right hand know what my left hand does.'[9] Frances Perkins, who served as Labor Secretary throughout his Presidency, considered Roosevelt 'the most complicated human being I ever knew', while dramatist and speechwriter Robert Sherwood noted the futility of trying to penetrate the President's 'heavily forested interior'.[10] From his perch in the Washington Embassy, Isaiah Berlin provided this penetrating, if largely intuitive, assessment:

The President really is very queer – not at all what you think he is. I
have reached the conclusion that despite the gay and generous nature
and all the manners and sweep of an old-established, landowning
country squire, he is a) absolutely cold, b) completely ruthless, c) has
no friends, d) [is] becoming a megalomaniac . . . His intentions are
humane and decent but the idea that one can trust him or look on
him as a sort of Gladstone is completely false. He does not like the
rich, it is true, but neither does he like the poor or really anyone . . .
His wife is the opposite in every respect, a sentimental, gushing,
heavy liberal, with a great deal of native shrewdness which the very
ugly often develop.[11]

The British were relieved by Roosevelt's re-election. 'President
Roosevelt elected for a third term. *Glory Hallelujah!!* A delicious poke
in the snoot for Hitler,' recorded Churchill's youngest daughter,
Mary, in her diary.[12] Although in selecting Willkie the Republicans
had unwittingly nominated a liberal internationalist, every bit as
convinced as FDR of the need to see Britain through, he was an
untested politician at the head of a still overwhelmingly isolationist party, whilst Roosevelt had eight years of the Presidency behind
him, the last two of which had provided ample demonstration of
the fact that 'he *is* on our side', as George VI put it in his diary.[13] Moreover, there was a general expectation that Roosevelt would start to
lead his country towards active belligerency – might even declare
war – as soon as the tiresome business of appealing to the electorate was over. In this, the British, none more so than Churchill, were
sorely misguided. Standing on the stage of the Boston Arena on
30 October 1940 – six days before polling day – FDR had given his
word to the mothers of America that their sons were not going to
be sent to any 'foreign wars' and he was not going to break it – not
yet at any rate.[14] He therefore made no dramatic policy announce-
ments following his victory but departed on a two-week Caribbean
cruise, leaving a flowery letter of congratulation from Churchill
unanswered.

British depression stemmed not merely from the lack of American GIs on the horizon. As the British Ambassador, Lord Lothian,
announced to reporters at LaGuardia airport on 23 November 1940,

Britain was running out of money.* Forced by the Neutrality Act to pay cash for all goods obtained in the US, Britain had spent more than $1.3 billion on American material since the start of the war. In order to meet such gargantuan expenditure, the British had been liquidating their US securities and gold reserves. By the autumn of 1940, British dollar reserves had fallen to almost $600 million – the minimum deemed necessary to maintain essential trade with other parts of the world – and the Treasury was predicting that by the New Year Britain would no longer be able to finance her purchases in the US. The situation was so desperate that officials contemplated requisitioning gold ornaments and wedding rings, if only to shame the Americans into generosity.

Initially, the Roosevelt Administration was unsympathetic. Blinded by Britain's former economic dominance and sprawling Empire, most Americans believed the British to be far richer than they claimed. As Lothian reported to the Foreign Office, US public opinion is 'saturated with illusions . . . that we have vast resources available that we have not yet disclosed . . . and that we ought to empty this vast hypothetical barrel before we ask for assistance'.[15] Lothian urged Churchill to write to Roosevelt, laying bare the extent of Britain's difficulties and thus, tacitly, placing the future of Britain's war effort in the President's hands. His idea, noted David Scott, 'was that this letter should be continuously in the President's mind and that its existence and the knowledge that some day it might be published would act as a continual spur in meeting our requirements for fear lest it should be said in years to come, "he knew, he was warned and he didn't take the necessary steps."'[16]

On 7 December, the Prime Minister obliged. In a 4,000-word letter that he rightly considered among the most important he ever sent, Churchill spelt out the gravity of Britain's predicament, based on a shortage of ships, munitions and dollars. 'If . . . you are convinced,

---

* The words attributed to Lothian by most historians are, 'Well, boys, Britain is broke, it's your money we want.' None of the reporters, however, recorded these uncharacteristic phrases. Instead, the New York Times told its readers that Lothian had stated that 'available gold and securities had been virtually used up' and, in consequence, Britain was going 'bust'.

Mr President, that the defeat of the Nazi and Fascist tyranny is a matter of high consequence to the people of the United States', he ended his essay, 'you will regard this letter not as an appeal for aid but as a statement of the minimum action necessary to the achievement of our common purpose.'[17]

Roosevelt received the Prime Minister's letter while still on his Caribbean vacation. It provided the catalyst for an idea that had been forming in his mind for some time. Returning to Washington on 16 December, he told reporters that rather than lend Britain money, he proposed to eliminate the 'foolish, old dollar sign' and simply 'lend' Britain the material she needed. 'Suppose my neighbour's house catches fire and I have got a length of garden hose,' the President elucidated. 'What do I do? I don't say to him before that operation, "Neighbour, my garden hose cost me $15, you have to pay me $15 for it" . . . I want my garden hose back after the fire is over.'[18] It was a brilliant homespun metaphor.* No matter that it was imperfect – there was little chance there would be any hose left once the British had finished extinguishing this particular fire – it resonated with millions of Americans and won the Lend-Lease debate before it even began.

In the Commons, Churchill would hail Lend-Lease as 'the most unsordid act in history'.[19] But there was controversy in the detail. While waiting for Congress to pass the requisite legislation, the American Government insisted on the British continuing to pay cash for existing and even future orders.† England's friends expected her 'to fight to the last dollar, to the last man and to the last ship', Secretary of State Cordell Hull had warned Lothian in June.[20] On 10 January 1941, a US cruiser arrived off the western cape of South Africa to carry away £42 million worth of Britain's last remaining gold reserves. A few weeks later, to meet the Administration's insatiable demand for dollars, the Treasury was forced to beg the Belgian Government-in-Exile for a loan of £60 million worth of bullion. The British felt these humiliations keenly. The Americans, fumed Beaverbrook in a letter to Churchill, 'have conceded nothing':

---

* The analogy was first proffered by Interior Secretary, Harold Ickes.
† 'So long as we had dollars to pay,' wrote the Foreign Office's William Strang, 'the policy of the United States was unimaginative and grasping.'

They have exacted payment to the uttermost for all they have done for us. They have taken our bases without valuable compensation. They have taken our gold. They have been given our secrets and offered us a thoroughly inadequate service in return. The American programmes of the Ministry of Supply have lagged to such an extent that it may be said [that] American deliveries are negligible . . . It should be made amply clear that we are not prepared to relinquish any more gold here or in South Africa . . . These are the last resources of the British people and should be held intact to provide us with essential means in the case of a compelling necessity to obtain foodstuffs for our people.[21]

Privately, Churchill agreed. In an unsent telegram to Roosevelt, he described the proposed removal of Britain's South African-held gold as like 'a sheriff collecting the last assets of a helpless debtor'.[22] For the sake of American goodwill, however, he acquiesced.

Equally contentious was Morgenthau's insistence that Britain liquidate some of her direct investments to finance existing obligations and convince a sceptical Congress of British sincerity. The axe fell on the Viscose Corporation, a subsidiary of Courtaulds and Britain's most valuable holding in the US. In a fire sale in March the textile giant was sold to a consortium of American investors for $54 million, less than half its actual worth.* While the British Treasury was obliged to compensate Courtaulds, Wall Street bankers collected $4 million in commission. Morgenthau had wanted the British to go further. Shell, Lever Brothers, Dunlop and Brown and Williamson Tobacco were all considered ripe for the picking and what about Britain's South American holdings and Malaysian rubber plantations? When Sir Frederick Phillips, the Treasury's representative in the US, pointed out that such sacrifices would render Britain bankrupt at the end of the war, Morgenthau conceded the point but argued that Britain could not afford to worry about that now.

---

* Courtaulds' chairman, Samuel Courtauld, behaved with exemplary patriotism. Confronted with the proposed transaction, his one question was whether the sale was essential to the national interest. When Lord Catto, a director of the Bank of England, assured him that it was he made no objection.

To many Britons, American insistence on scraping the bottom of the British barrel smacked of economic imperialism or simple avarice. 'I am afraid they will misuse their strength,' wrote the Foreign Office's Roger Makins to the Ministry of Economic Warfare's David Eccles. 'American imperialism may be very dangerous to Anglo-American relations and more dangerous is the prevalent tendency to strip us to the bone . . . We do all the fighting and are being deprived of our liquid assets while the occupied countries hibernate with their store of riches safely blocked in the USA!'[23] 'Up to date, they've had a damn fine war. On British dollars. Every last one of them,' fulminated Air Marshal Sir Arthur Harris during a tour of American aircraft factories.[24] Churchill feared that Britain was not 'only to be skinned but flayed to the bone', while John Maynard Keynes, sent over to negotiate the 'concession' Britain was required to make for Lend-Lease (in lieu of the 'hose'), accused the Americans of treating their putative ally 'worse than we have ever ourselves thought it proper to treat the humblest and least responsible Balkan country'.[25]

Of course, the frustrations were not all on one side. 'I have never been more outraged,' the highly strung Morgenthau exploded when the British tried to drag their heels over their direct investments. 'Here I stake my reputation . . . and they don't make a god damn move on this thing.'[26] Four days later, the Treasury Secretary told the British Ambassador that Britain must dispose of one major company 'by the end of the week'.[27] (The Viscose sale was swiftly approved.) 'The British, per capita, are the richest in the world and if they care anything about their freedom they ought to be willing to spend all that they have,' boomed outgoing Vice-President John Garner at a Cabinet meeting on 19 January, while Adolf Berle, the Anglophobe Assistant Secretary of State, accused the British of not wanting 'to pay [for] anything, anywhere, at any time'.[28]

The vitriol displayed by the isolationists towards the Administration and, occasionally, the British was far worse. General Robert E. Wood, chairman of the recently created America First Committee, accused the President of requesting 'a blank cheque book' with which to dispose of our 'manpower, our laws and our liberties'.[29] Congressman Hamilton Fish, whose sympathetic view of Nazi foreign policy made him something of an expert on the subject, dubbed HR 1776 (Lend-Lease) 'a fascist bill', while Senator Burton K. Wheeler declared that the President's proposal was tantamount to a declaration of war that would 'plough under every fourth American boy'. If this *was* America's war, the Democrat from Montana and arch-isolationist went on to argue, then 'we ought to have the courage to go over there and fight it. But it is not our war.'[30]

Fortunately, most Americans disagreed. Opinion polls revealed consistent support for the measure (particularly in the South) and on 8 February 1941, the House passed HR 1776 by 260 votes to 165. A month later, it passed the Senate by sixty votes to thirty-one. And on 27 March, Congress approved an appropriations bill for $7 billion worth of Lend-Lease aid. Neither an act of unalloyed altruism – this *was* America's war – nor a plot to strip Britain of her resources, Lend-Lease would make an inestimable contribution to Allied victory, with some $50 billion worth of goods leaving the US for Allied nations between March 1941 and September 1945 and some $8 billion, largely supplied by the British Commonwealth, provided in 'reciprocal aid'. Its effects, however, were not immediate. As Beaverbrook complained in his letter to Churchill, American industry was nowhere near operating on a war footing, with myriad bottlenecks, no central plan for the distribution of raw materials and businesses continuing to prioritise consumer goods over war products. In time, the US would become the great 'arsenal of democracy' (and Soviet communism), as Roosevelt proclaimed in his 'fireside chat' of 29 December 1940.[31] But in 1941, 84 per cent of munitions used by the British Commonwealth were still manufactured in Britain, with only 2.4 per cent deriving from Lend-Lease. Only 100 out of 2,400 aircraft sent from the US to Britain during 1941 were 'lent', while the British continued to pay cash for 60 per cent of US-delivered raw materials during the same year. If the material effect was initially small, however, the psychological impact was massive: a declaration of economic war by the world's foremost industrial power that would, so many believed, lead to a declaration of actual war before long.

Not that the British were always good at expressing their gratitude. Motoring through London one morning in July, the US Military Attaché, Brigadier-General Raymond Lee, was asked by his driver if he had noticed a 'gradual rise of interest in the United States'.

'Well, yes, a trifle,' the Attaché replied. 'But how do you notice it?'

'Well, sir, I can't quite say. It is not that people read more about America, or think about it so much more, sir, but if I might put it so, sir, one might say there is a little more bonhomie about. Don't you think?'

'Well, yes,' Lee agreed. 'Perhaps you might describe it that way but it is only natural, don't you think, that for $7 billion we ought to be entitled to a little bonhomie?!'

'Oh yes, sir, yes, sir, quite. That's just what I mean, sir. I should say there is quite a bit of bonhomie in the air, sir.'[32]

★

While Lend-Lease made its way through Congress, the British played host to a string of influential American visitors. On 9 January 1941, Brendan Bracken, Churchill's man Friday, arrived at Poole to find an emaciated American shivering inside a seaplane. Sent to gauge Britain's chances of survival and, as he put it, act as 'a catalytic agent between two prima donnas – Roosevelt and Churchill – Harry Hopkins was an unlikely emissary to Britain's Conservative Prime Minister.[33] The son of a harness maker from Sioux City, Iowa, he had been a social worker in New York before running a trio of New Deal relief agencies. Irredeemably scruffy, with suits that seemed as if they had been slept in and a hat that appeared to have been sat on, he looked, according to the *New Yorker*, like an 'animated piece of shredded wheat'.[34] His thinness derived from chronic ill-health. In 1937, he had had a large part of his stomach removed and although the surgeons succeeded in eviscerating the cancer, the operation left him prey to a succession of ailments and intestinal trouble. Nevertheless, he was something of a playboy, with a love of women, whiskey and wagers. His devotion to Roosevelt was absolute. Moving into the White House in May 1940, he served the President by combining the roles of troubleshooter, sounding board and drinking companion. To Roosevelt's many critics, he was the sinister influence behind the throne, the target for innumerable press calumnies. But to FDR, he was indispensable. With what one journalist called an almost 'feminine sensitivity' for

Roosevelt's moods, he relieved the President of problems during the day and loneliness during the evenings.[35] When Wendell Willkie, shortly after his election defeat, asked Roosevelt why he kept a man like Hopkins near him, FDR replied by telling Willkie that he might find himself sitting in his chair one day, 'and when you are, you'll be looking at that door over there and knowing that practically everybody who walks through it wants something out of you. You'll learn what a lonely job this is and you'll discover the need for somebody like Harry Hopkins, who asks for nothing except to serve you.'[36] Despite this cold, utilitarian explanation, there was genuine affection between the two men – the closest, arguably, Roosevelt ever came to true friendship.

Hopkins arrived in London sceptical of the British and their famous war leader. Within forty-eight hours, however, he had been transformed into an enthusiastic partisan of both. Alerted to Hopkins' importance by Bracken and Roosevelt's confidant Felix Frankfurter, Churchill gave instructions that he was to be treated 'as one of ourselves – only better'.[37] Taking Hopkins to Ditchley his first weekend in the country, Churchill treated the Presidential envoy to a grandiose discourse on Britain's war aims. 'We seek no treasure, we seek no territorial gains, we seek only the right of man to be free,' he intoned, emphasising the democratic nature of Britain's cause. 'We seek government with the consent of the people, man's freedom to say what he will and, when he thinks himself injured, to find himself equal in the eyes of the law . . . What will the President say to all this?'

Hopkins paused. Then, exaggerating his Midwest accent, replied, 'Well, Mr Prime Minister, I don't think the President will give a damn' for all that . . . You see, we're only interested in seeing that Goddamn son-of-a-bitch, Hitler, gets licked.'[38]

From that moment, Churchill hardly let Hopkins out of his sight, taking him to Scotland to see the Home Fleet and entertaining him at Chequers. His efforts were rewarded. Dining with the Regional Commissioner for Scotland on their return journey from Scapa Flow, Hopkins was asked to say a few words and quoted from the Book of Ruth: 'Whither thou goest, I will go; and where thou lodgest, I will lodge: thy people shall be my people . . . Even to the end.'[39] His report to Roosevelt was more secular but no less emphatic:

> The people here are amazing from Churchill down and if courage alone can win – the result will be inevitable. But they need our help desperately and I am sure you will permit nothing to stand in the way . . . Churchill is the gov't in every sense of the word – he controls the grand strategy and often the details – labour trusts him – the Army, Navy, Air Force are behind him to a man . . . I cannot believe that it is true that Churchill dislikes either you or America – it just doesn't make sense.[40]*

Hot on Hopkins' heels were Wendell Willkie, now acting as a roving Presidential envoy, the new American Ambassador to the Court of St James's, John 'Gil' Winant, and Averell Harriman. For each, the British rolled out the bomb-damaged red carpet and were rewarded in turn. Returning to the US in early February, Willkie gave crucial Congressional testimony in favour of Lend-Lease and then began a campaign to repeal the Neutrality Act. Winant, a progressive Republican who bore a striking resemblance to Abraham Lincoln and was in every way the antithesis of Joseph Kennedy, became a stalwart in the battle to aid Britain, while Harriman threw himself into his role of 'expeditor' of Lend-Lease equipment, making himself so at home within Churchill's ménage that he soon began an affair with the Prime Minister's daughter-in-law.

Less happy, at least initially, and certainly less amorous, was the experience of Britain's principal envoy to the United States. In early December 1940, Lord Lothian had developed a kidney infection. A Christian Scientist, he refused medical treatment and died. As Leo Amery wrote to the Viceroy of India, the Marquess of Linlithgow, the Ambassador's death was regarded as a political as well as a personal tragedy, 'though his most important work was probably

---

* When Hopkins first met the Prime Minister on 10 January, he had told him that there was 'a feeling in some quarters that he, Churchill, did not like America, Americans or Roosevelt'. Churchill blamed Joseph Kennedy for propagating this entirely false impression.

completed'.[41] After mulling a variety of options, including Lloyd George, Churchill alighted on the idea of removing his former rival Lord Halifax from the Foreign Office. The Americans were horrified. Whilst Lothian had a been a clubbable Liberal – one of the few members of the British ruling elite who actually liked Americans – Halifax was a reserved Tory: a former Viceroy and appeaser who looked upon his appointment as a form of transportation.

His tenure began auspiciously – even historically – with Roosevelt sailing out to meet the Halifaxes travelling on board the battleship *King George V*. 'Nothing could have been more charming than he was to us when we went to have tea with him on his yacht,' the freshly minted Ambassador informed the King. 'He told me that he hoped that I should feel free at any time to ask to see him and said that I should do this more easily if I didn't go through the State Department!'[42] From then on, however, it was downhill. Telling reporters that he had discussed the Lend-Lease bill with the Chairman of the Senate Foreign Relations Committee, shortly after his arrival, he was accused of meddling in American politics. Later, attending a baseball game in Chicago, he seemed to disparage the national sport by observing that 'it was a bit like cricket, except that we don't question the umpire's decision so much' and then compounded the error by leaving an uneaten hot dog under his seat.[43] Worst of all, he accepted an invitation for a day's fox hunting in Pennsylvania. Embassy officials begged him not to go. But the Viscount was determined and was duly castigated in the American press for enjoying himself while his countrymen were being bombed.

The truth is that neither Halifax nor his press adviser, Charles Peake, understood America. A man who, by his own admission, knew 'nothing about people', Halifax was bewildered by these 'crude . . . warm-hearted' creatures, who called him by his Christian name (a privilege he denied even his daughters-in-law) and invited him to visit their houses following only the briefest acquaintance.[44]* American politics baffled him. The reverence

* Although she was better at hiding it, his wife, Dorothy, was equally bemused. 'I find this country and the people get queerer and queerer,' she wrote to Walter Monckton on 5 May 1941. 'Press interviewers always ask me what particularly

for public opinion seemed to him disproportionate and cowardly, while the disjointed nature of American Government reminded him of 'a disorderly line of beaters out shooting; they do put the rabbits out of the bracken but they don't come out where you expect'.[45] His dinner with some forty Republican Congressmen, most of whom were staunch isolationists, was a disaster. Looking 'like a church mouse or a poor country cousin', he submitted himself to an interrogation on appeasement, Britain's unpaid First World War debts, her post-war plans, Lend-Lease and Anglo-American co-operation. Although his answers were commendably frank, their effect, if the conclusions of one Midwest Congressman are anything to go by, was merely to reinforce existing prejudices:

General Impressions:
1. England is extremely selfish.
2. She will use anybody to help herself and having gained her ends will dump them overboard.
3. Their statesmen are very smart and have too much experience in power politics for our statesmen to deal with for our own best interests.
4. England looks out for herself first, last and all the time.
5. England has no intention of repayment of any past, present or future war debts.
6. England would like us to help her police the world – she to establish the policies – we to pay the bills.
7. More than ever before I am convinced [that] we should stay out of this war.
8. I had little respect for England before. I have much less now.[46]

___

strikes me as different in the USA and I can never think of anything dramatic or soul-stirring . . . all that occurs to my mind are such things as: 1) Perpetual ice cream; 2) Perpetual handshaking; 3) Keeping their blinds down all day and the electric light on – most strange!; 4) Always hot plates – however cold the food; 5) No one really "grown up", except the children who are terribly sophisticated and hard-baked little wretches.' (Monckton Papers, MS Trustees 5)

Realising that he was floundering – a returning British diplomat informed the Foreign Office that the Ambassador's stock had gone from 'zero to freezing' – Halifax recruited his cousin Angus McDonnell to serve as Honorary Attaché.[47] The second son of an Irish peer, with an irreverent sense of humour, McDonnell had come to know America during his time working for the railroad magnate Chiswell Langhorne (the father of Nancy Astor). As a relation and Eton contemporary, he felt able to tell the Viscount some home truths. When Halifax complained that he found Americans 'odd', McDonnell corrected him. 'On the contrary, it is *you* who are odd. You have led a very sheltered life.' Realising that Halifax was fundamentally shy, he arranged for him to meet small groups of senators and congressmen informally in his Washington apartment. When the Ambassador was having trouble obtaining an interview with the President, McDonnell told him to telephone the President's aide 'Pa' Watson, but insisted that he call him 'Pa'. The Attaché then watched as the Viscount picked up the receiver and, as if overcoming an almost physical pain, managed to stammer, 'Is that you, P . . . Pa?'[48]

Most crucially, McDonnell made the Ambassador leave Washington. Halifax's tours, which eventually encompassed all forty-eight states, were the making of him. Although the Ambassador found it disconcerting to be accompanied by so many policemen, there was little need for protection as friendly crowds welcomed him to such isolationist strongholds as Milwaukee, Chicago and Kansas City. In Detroit, however, he was pelted with eggs and tomatoes by a group of anti-interventionist women, styled 'Mothers of America'. Although the Viscount maintained the silent dignity of 'a French aristo in the tumbril', the British Press Service in New York attributed to him the remark that his only feeling was 'one of envy that people have eggs and tomatoes to throw about. In England, these are very scarce.'[49] This inspired, apocryphal riposte marked the turning point of Halifax's Ambassadorship. Respected for his integrity and pitied for his suffering (his second son, Peter, was killed in action in November 1942, while his youngest son, Richard, lost both his legs in the Western Desert three months later), he came to be regarded as one of Britain's most popular wartime envoys.

Halifax's task was not eased by the slew of Axis victories – in Greece, Yugoslavia, Crete and North Africa – during the spring of 1941, provoking a fresh wave of pessimism in Washington. 'Hull was plain defeatist,' confided David Eccles to Roger Makins, after seeing the Secretary of State in early June, just as the British were trying and failing to relieve the siege of Tobruk. 'Europe and North Africa are gone', he had said, 'and there's nothing to be done but admit we're too late to save England.'[50] His Assistant Secretary of State Breckinridge Long – an extreme nativist who succeeded in curtailing Jewish immigration from Nazi-occupied Europe to the United States – noted that the British were 'damn near licked in the Mediterranean', while the Director of the War Plans Division for the Chief of Naval Operations, Admiral Turner, feared the British would be expelled from the Middle East and that the 'end will then be in sight'.[51]

Such gloom was not confined to America. Dining at Chequers on 27 April, Major-General John Kennedy told Churchill that the time was coming when Britain would, indeed, have to consider evacuating the Middle East. This produced a predictable Prime Ministerial eruption, yet even Churchill had moments of doubt.[52] Five weeks earlier, at another meal, this time in Downing Street, Lady Oliphant (the wife of Britain's interned Ambassador to Brussels) complained about a French governess who had used the expression '*If* we win'. The Prime Minister's response was telling: 'It is not *certain* that we shall win.'[53] Four months later, the British Government signed an agreement with the Soviet Government that prohibited either party from concluding a separate peace with '*Hitlerite* Germany'.[54] The implications of the phrasing, though often overlooked, are unmistakable. Although Churchill utterly rejected any sort of compromise with Hitler or the Nazis, he was not yet in a position to exclude negotiations with an alternative German Government.

Under these circumstances, the need for American belligerency appeared more critical than ever. On 19 May, at a meeting of the Defence Committee, Anthony Eden and Lord Beaverbrook called for urgent action to 'stimulate the United States in the right direction' and for news to 'make the Americans afraid for their own safety'.[55] Although Churchill vetoed the downplaying of any good news (rare enough in any case), the committee concluded by requesting a propaganda campaign to galvanise US opinion towards active participation in the war.

This was hardly a new directive. Under the auspices of William Stephenson – a shadowy Canadian purported to be among the inspirations for Ian Fleming's James Bond – British Security Co-ordination, based in New York, had been working towards this end, by fair means and foul, for over six months. Nor was the trend in American public opinion discouraging. Whilst 93 per cent of Americans had been opposed to US belligerency in May 1940 (according to Gallup), 63 per cent endorsed the statement that the US should go all out to ensure British victory 'even at the risk of getting into the war' in March 1941.[56] By July, opinion polls showed a majority of Americans in favour of US warships acting as escorts for British convoys, while a survey for *Fortune* magazine found that 57 per cent of respondents would support an American declaration of war if Hitler tried to invade the British Isles.[57] The problem, interventionists contended, was not with the American people but at the top. 'The President is waiting for public opinion to lead and public opinion is waiting for a lead from the President,' wrote the former US Ambassador to Paris William C. Bullitt to Harriman, despairingly, in April.[58] The Secretary of War, Henry Stimson, concurred. Long convinced that America must enter the conflict – a conviction shared by Navy Secretary Frank Knox, Interior Secretary Harold Ickes, and the professional heads of both the Army and the Navy – Stimson had visited the White House on 22 April to warn Roosevelt of the perils of inaction. 'I cautioned him on the necessity of his taking the lead and that without a lead on his part it was useless to expect the people would voluntarily take the initiative.'[59]

Roosevelt listened but remained cautious. Although he had ordered the Navy to be ready to commence convoy duties by 1 April, he shied away from the idea after deciding that such an act would require Congressional approval. Instead, he extended US naval patrols in the Atlantic to the twenty-sixth meridian (mid-way between Brazil and West Africa), thus increasing the scope for U-boat and surface raider sightings and ordered the transfer of ten US Coast Guard cutters to the Royal Navy for anti-U-boat work.

The British were grateful. But with Rommel at the gates of Egypt and shipping losses rising to an unsustainable 530,000 tons in March and 668,000 tons in April, it was not enough. On 3 May, raising the spectre of a complete collapse in the Middle East, resulting in Axis domination not only of Europe but also of Asia and Africa, Churchill asked Roosevelt, bluntly, for a declaration of war. The President refused. The most he was prepared to do at this stage was to declare an 'unlimited national emergency'. [60] To intimates, he hinted that he was waiting for an 'incident'. [61] Yet when the US merchant ship the SS *Robin Moor* was sunk by a German U-boat on 21 May he limited his response to freezing German and Italian assets in the US and closing their consulates. Fleet moves, from the Pacific to the Atlantic, had taken place at the start of the month and, on 27 May, Roosevelt made the welcome offer to relieve the British from garrisoning Iceland. Yet there was no escaping the fact that the US remained in 'the Valley of Decision'. [62]

Churchill was thoroughly discouraged. His strategy of 'dragging the United States in' appeared to have failed. Reacting to a particularly unhelpful telegram from Roosevelt, objecting to the suggestion that British forces might have to forestall an Axis coup by occupying the Azores, he minuted Eden: 'It seems to me as if there has been a considerable recession across the Atlantic and that quite unconsciously we are being left very much to our fate.' [63] Then, in July, Harry Hopkins returned to London. His task was simple but momentous: to arrange a meeting between Churchill and Roosevelt.

XV

Atlantic Meeting – Pacific Infamy

Sail on, O Ship of State!
Sail on, O Union, strong and great!
Humanity with all its fears,
With all the hopes of future years,
Is hanging breathless on thy fate.

Verses by Henry Longfellow, sent to Churchill by Roosevelt,
January 1941[1]

Winston Churchill was as 'excited as a schoolboy on the last day of term.'[2] Accompanied by 'a retinue which Cardinal Wolsey might have envied', as Jock Colville put it, including the Chief of the Imperial General Staff, General Sir John Dill, the First Sea Lord, Admiral Sir Dudley Pound, the Vice-Chief of the Air Force, Air Marshal Sir Wilfrid Freeman, his friend and scientific adviser Lord Cherwell and Sir Alexander Cadogan, he travelled north, by special train, on the afternoon of 3 August 1941, to Thurso. There, he boarded a destroyer and thence the battleship HMS *Prince of Wales* – recently in action against the German battleship *Bismarck* – to begin the four-day voyage to Newfoundland and his rendezvous with the President of the United States.

Churchill was determined to enjoy the voyage. Unable to send any but the most important messages since the ship was observing radio silence, he allowed himself to relax, reading C. S. Forester's *Captain Hornblower*, playing backgammon and watching films. 'We do ourselves well on board,' noted Cadogan, who was appreciating the grouse the party had picked up in Inverness and the mountain of caviar brought by Harry Hopkins, fresh from his meeting with

Stalin.* 'As the P.M. said, it was very good to have such caviar, even though it meant fighting with the Russians to get it.'[3]

On 5 August, news leaked of the Prime Minister's voyage, causing panic in Whitehall. 'What a target we were – Winston Churchill and the Chiefs of Staff!' recalled the Daily Herald's H. V. Morton, brought along to record events for propaganda and posterity.[4] But Churchill was unconcerned. Indeed, he rather hoped that the Tirpitz, Bismarck's sister ship, would come out and 'have a dart at him'.[5] Nevertheless, when a U-boat was reported some 40 miles ahead, the battleship, having abandoned its destroyer escort in the interests of speed, altered course and then started zigzagging. Finally, to the intense relief of Captain Leach, on the morning of 9 August 1941 the Prince of Wales slipped into the calm, grey waters of Placentia Bay. As the battleship drew up alongside the USS Augusta, a guard of honour presented arms and the band of the Royal Marines crashed into 'The Star-Spangled Banner'. 'God Save the King' echoed from the other side of the water, where a seated figure in a light-coloured suit was visible beneath an awning on the bridge. At eleven o'clock, the Prime Minister and senior members of his party crossed over to the Augusta to meet the President. To his embarrassment, Churchill had forgotten that the two men had met before. In 1918, when he was Assistant Secretary of the Navy, the 36-year-old Roosevelt had encountered the then Minister of Munitions at a dinner in London. According to Roosevelt, Churchill had 'acted like a stinker . . . lording it all over us'.[6] Fortunately, this disagreeable first impression was expunged as the President, leaning on the arm of his son Elliott, welcomed the Prime Minister aboard the Augusta and then escorted him to a private lunch where the ice broke both ways.

Over the next four days, there was much toing and froing, as the two leaders hosted a series of lunches and dinners, while their staffs discussed the technical aspects of war. Good humour and mutual respect abounded. Churchill 'is a tremendously vital person and in many ways is an English Mayor La Guardia,' Roosevelt reported to his cousin Margaret Suckley, referring to the dynamic, Italian-Jewish Mayor of New York.[7] 'The whole proceedings of the [first]

---

* In 1941, the grouse season opened on 1 August instead of the traditional 12th.

day were marked with much ceremony, everybody being piped on and off ships etc. . . . but behind it all there appeared to be very great friendliness and the Americans had laid themselves out to receive us well,' recorded the Military Assistant to the War Cabinet, Lieutenant-Colonel Ian Jacob.[8] Dill and the US Army Chief of Staff, General Marshall, took an instant liking to one another, while Pound and his opposite number, Admiral Harold 'Betty' Stark, and Freeman and General Henry 'Hap' Arnold were soon on easy terms.

The British were, nevertheless, concerned by what they perceived as a lack of strategic unity among the American Chiefs of Staff. Top secret staff talks held in Washington between January and March 1941, had confirmed existing American plans for a 'Germany First' strategy. Stark was accordingly prepared to see the bulk of the US Fleet transferred from the Pacific to the Atlantic but Marshall wanted to reinforce the Philippines. More disconcertingly, as Jacob noted in his diary, 'not a single American officer has shown the slightest keenness to be in the war on our side. They are a charming lot of individuals but they appear to be living in a different world from ourselves.'[9] The Americans discussed plans for escorting British ships as far as Iceland and Roosevelt promised to supply Britain with a further 130,000 rifles but otherwise the military discussions, to British frustration, focussed on production and the need to equip the US Army.

Meanwhile, Cadogan had been asked to draft a declaration of principles that would serve as a joint statement of war aims. Until now, this was something Churchill had consistently resisted. Although it was easy enough to define what Britain was fighting against, any attempt to define what she was fighting for risked political division both abroad and at home. When a Cabinet Committee attempted to overcome this problem by producing a statement vague enough to satisfy everyone, Churchill complained that it read like a cross between the Sermon on the Mount and an election address. 'Let those who say they do not know what they are fighting for stop fighting and they will see,' he told Colville.[10] For the prize of a joint declaration of war aims with the still non-belligerent United States, however, he was willing to look beyond the immediate exigencies of battle.

As published, the 'Atlantic Charter' was innocuous enough. Building on Roosevelt's post-election State of the Union address, in which the President had looked forward to a world built upon 'four essential human freedoms' – freedom of speech, freedom of worship, freedom from want and freedom from fear – the two leaders disclaimed all territorial ambitions and expressed their opposition to changes in national boundaries that did not accord with the freely expressed wishes of the peoples concerned. 'The fullest collaboration between all nations in the economic field, with the object of securing . . . improved labour standards, economic advancement and social security' was sought and a 'permanent system of general security' was needed, so that the peoples of the world 'may live out their lives in freedom from fear and want'.[11]

Points three and four, however, posed difficulties. In the revised draft, presented by Roosevelt and Under-Secretary of State Sumner Welles, clause four committed the two nations to opening up trade, without 'discrimination and on equal terms'.[12] This, as the British realised, was a none too subtle attempt to abolish Imperial Preference, the system of preferential trade within the British Empire, a long-running obsession of Secretary of State Cordell Hull. Churchill, who was no protectionist but headed a party with a strong protectionist wing, managed to insert the phrase 'with due respect for their existing obligations', but the battle was deferred, not won.[13]

Equally problematic was the commitment, enshrined in clause three, to respect 'sovereign rights and self-government'.[14] In Churchill's mind, this pledge related exclusively to those nations currently 'under the Nazi yoke' and had no bearing on the integrity of the British Empire.[15] The Americans, who sought to dismantle that institution, argued that it applied to all peoples, everywhere. This 'dangerous' ambiguity, as Leo Amery put it to the Viceroy of India, Lord Linlithgow, was to cause trouble in the future.[16] At the time, however, both leaders were pleased to have produced a document that demonstrated unity of purpose and unselfish idealism at a critical stage in the war and the still unofficial Anglo-American alliance.

The Soviet alliance was ignored. Not only was Stalin not consulted but the President and Prime Minister failed even to mention the document in their first joint message to the Soviet leader on 14

August. When the Russians found out they were furious. 'The English and the Americans have dropped all pretences,' raged Molotov's
deputy, Solomon Lozovsky, in a memorandum for his master:

> After indirect hints gathered from the American press about the
> Roosevelt–Churchill declaration, Eden suggested to Comrade
> Maisky that the Soviet Union should take the initiative and offer to
> accept the declaration . . . Lest there be any doubt that the English
> and the Americans want to reduce us to the condition of an English
> dominion and the London-based émigré governments, here is
> Roosevelt's declaration to Congress . . . In order to compel us to
> join the declaration, in the devising of which we took no part, the
> English and the Americans are delaying the transportation of aid
> to us [a falsehood] . . . Naturally, we cannot yield to this coercion,
> for this would only rouse the Anglo-American appetite for political
> demands . . . and lead them further in their quest to equate us to the
> Poles, Czechs, Belgians, Norwegians and 'other Greeks'.[17]

In the end, the Soviet Government endorsed the Atlantic Charter
but would interpret it according to its unique conceptions of 'freedom', 'independence', 'justice' and 'co-operation'.

The most symbolic moment of the Atlantic Conference, codenamed Riviera, was the service held on the quarter-deck of the
Prince of Wales on the morning of Sunday 10 August. Churchill had
taken great trouble over the arrangements, reviewing the prayers
and choosing the hymns ('O God, Our Help in Ages Past', 'Onward,
Christian Soldiers!' and 'Eternal Father, Strong to Save'). Captain
Leach had exhorted his sailors to 'raise steam in an extra boiler so
as to give the hymns full value' and by all accounts they did him
proud.[18] 'You would have to be pretty hard-boiled not to be moved
by it all,' recorded Churchill's Principal Private Secretary, John
Martin, 'one rough British sailor sharing his hymn sheet with one
American ditto. It seemed a sort of marriage service between the
two navies, already in spirit allies, though the bright peacetime paint
and spit and polish of the American ships contrasted with the dull
camouflage of the *Prince of Wales*.'[19] As the national anthems died
away, a hive of cameramen descended upon the Prime Minister and

the President, seated on the deck in wicker chairs. It was, remarked one observer, the sort of shot a 'press photographer would dream of after a good dose of hashish'.[20] As propaganda, it was certainly potent.

At 5 p.m. on 12 August, the *Prince of Wales* set sail for Iceland and thence for home. 'Look after the Prime Minister,' Roosevelt enjoined Churchill's bodyguard, Walter Thompson. 'He is one of the greatest men in the world.'[21] Churchill was equally rapturous. 'I have established warm and deep personal relations with our great friend,' he telegraphed Attlee, describing the signing of the Atlantic Charter as 'an event of [the] first magnitude'.[22] The conference had been characterised by the 'greatest cordiality', he told the War Cabinet on 19 August, the Americans having lost no opportunity 'of identifying themselves with our cause'. As for the President, he was 'obviously determined that they should come in' but could not yet rely on the support of Congress. His plan, therefore, was to become 'more and more provocative'. US destroyers would assume escort duties in the North Atlantic and orders would be given to attack U-boats on sight.[23] The President had said that he would 'not declare war', Churchill told the King that afternoon, but 'he would wage war, with us, against Germany'.[24]

In fact, the Atlantic Conference proved a great disappointment to the British. Writing to the Queen before his departure, Churchill had expressed the view that Roosevelt would not have asked him to travel so great a distance 'unless he had in mind some further forward step'.[25] Yet the President contemplated no such advance. Joining his father on the *Augusta*, Elliott Roosevelt asked about the purpose of the meeting. 'You were there,' his father responded, referring to his son's recent sojourn in Britain. 'You saw the people. You've even told me how they look – grey and thin and strained. A meeting like this one will do a world of good for British morale . . . The Nazis are riding high, these days. Masters of Europe. I don't imagine there are many Americans left by now who don't agree that we've got to lend the British at least *moral* aid.'[26] Although Elliott's recollections should be treated with caution, there is no reason to disbelieve the gist of this vignette. Contrary to Churchill's impression, FDR had *not* committed himself to escorting British ships (this decision was taken later), while the Atlantic Charter, far from foreshadowing US belligerency, was motivated by the American desire to prevent the British from forming 'secret commitments' with other powers and to establish the US's right to influence the future peace. Indeed, there is little evidence, beyond Churchill's claims of what Roosevelt said in their meetings at Placentia Bay, that FDR had decided that America must enter the war. A pacifist in the early 1930s, with a jejune faith in the panacean effects of economic liberalisation and disarmament conferences, his repeated statements during 1939 and 1940 that he was doing everything in his power to keep the US out of war ring true. Although he had told the King, during the latter's visit to the US in June 1939, that if London were bombed America would come in immediately, his failure to honour this pledge suggests that he was merely trying to stiffen the British. Hints of impending US belligerency following the fall of France performed a similar role. The US would sustain Britain but this was to maintain her own first line of defence, not a precursor to an 'inevitable' declaration of war.

By December 1940, most senior Administration figures had concluded that America would have to join the fighting. 'I told Hopkins that . . . if we were going to save England we would have to get into this war and that we needed England, if for no other reason, [than] as a stepping-stone to bomb Germany,' recorded Henry Morgenthau in mid-May 1941.[27] But what of the President? On 17 May, four days after Morgenthau's epiphany, he told the Treasury Secretary that he was 'waiting to be pushed into the situation'.[28] Over the next six months, he made several similar statements. Yet there is also evidence to suggest that he preferred the status of a friendly neutral, furnishing the British and the Soviets with the 'tools' to, if not 'finish the job', then at least hold the line until US public opinion and rearmament were considerably more advanced. Certainly, he proceeded with caution in the Atlantic – anxious, it seemed, to avoid rather than 'provoke' an incident – while American–Japanese diplomacy proceeded on the same basis. It therefore seems reasonable to conclude that the world would have been left waiting for American belligerency for an indefinite period were it not for the events of 7 December 1941.

The British were downcast and increasingly resentful. 'We said last week that from the meeting between Mr Churchill and President Roosevelt had emerged an indication that after the flood America would be interested in the drainage,' complained the *Sunday Times*. 'We also suggested that was not enough. The flood is raging and we are breasting it in an effort to save drowning civilisation . . . It is time these people realised that they are living on earth and not in the clouds. Cloud Cuckootown, as a telegraphic address, confers no immunity.'[29]

Public frustration reflected private bitterness. 'We heartily despise Italians as a race of degenerate, boastful cowards but our feeling toward them pales beside the utter and complete contempt we feel for Americans,' wrote an outraged Anglo-Scot to Harry Hopkins, during the latter's first visit to Britain.[30] 'Roosevelt says the Americans would rather die on their feet than live on their knees,' noted a similarly irate British civil servant in his diary. 'They do not intend to do either – they propose to grovel on their tummies at the shrine of the almighty dollar.'[31] On 28 August, Churchill wrote to Hopkins of the 'wave of depression' that had spread through the Cabinet and the country following Roosevelt's statement that the Atlantic Conference entailed no new commitments and brought the US no closer to war. 'If 1942 opens with Russia knocked out and Britain left alone again, all kinds of danger may arise,' he warned the President by proxy.[32] The following day, he made an impassioned appeal to Ambassador Winant for American belligerency. After the joint declaration, 'America could not honourably stay out. She could not fight with mercenaries. Better she should come in now and give us no supplies for six months than stay out and double her supplies.'[33]

Still, FDR remained cautious. Haunted by the ghost of Woodrow Wilson, whose Presidency imploded when he raced ahead of public and Congressional opinion, he viewed the extension of the Selective Training Act (the draft) by only one vote in the House of Representatives on 12 August with alarm. 'This vote clearly indicates that the Administration could not get a resolution through the Congress for a declaration of war,' Senator Wheeler declared – a fact the British were wont to forget. 'It is also notice that the Congress does not take seriously the cry of the Administration that the

The Devils' Alliance: Vyacheslav Molotov signs the Nazi–Soviet Pact, watched by German Foreign Minister Joachim von Ribbentrop (*centre*) and a clearly pleased Joseph Stalin, 24 August 1939. (Mccool / Alamy Stock Photo.)

'Thank God for the French Army': General Maurice Gamelin inspects a section of the British Expeditionary Force, March 1940. (Hulton-Deutsch Collection / CORBIS / Corbis via Getty Images.)

A house divided against itself will not stand: French Prime Minister Paul Reynaud (*second from right*) with General Maxime Weygand, Paul Baudouin and Maréchal Philippe Pétain, 10 June 1940. (Keystone-France / Gamma-Keystones via Getty Images.)

Catastrophe: German cavalry at the Arc de Triomphe, June 1940.

(Chronicle / Alamy Stock Photo.)

A 'repugnant' action: French warships under bombardment by the Royal Navy, Mers el-Kébir, 3 July 1940. (Süddeutsche Zeitung Photo / Alamy Stock Photo.)

Collaboration: Maréchal Philippe Pétain meets Hitler at Montoire, October 1940.
(Heinrich Hoffmann / ullstein bild via Getty Images.)

'We are France!':
General Charles de
Gaulle inspects members
of the recently created
Forces Françaises Libres,
July 1940. (Everett
Collection Historical /
Alamy Stock Photo.)

Fighting Vichy: British
soldiers descend from
a Bren gun carrier in
the ruins of Palmyra,
Syria, July 1941. (De Luan /
Alamy Stock Photo.)

Enemy at the gates: Soviet troops march straight from Red Square to the front,
November 1941. (Album / Alamy Stock Photo.)

The go-between: Harry Hopkins with Franklin D. Roosevelt.
(Everett Collection Inc / Alamy Stock Photo.)

'Being met together': Roosevelt and Churchill aboard HMS *Prince of Wales*, with US Commander of the Atlantic Patrol Force Admiral Ernest King, US Chief of Naval Operations Admiral 'Betty' Stark, and Lend–Lease 'expediter' Averell Harriman behind, August 1941. (CBW / Alamy Stock Photo.)

Day of infamy: the Japanese attack the US Pacific Fleet at Pearl Harbor, 7 December 1941. (Vintage_Space / Alamy Stock Photo.)

Imperial shame: Lieutenant-General Arthur Percival is led to negotiate the surrender of Singapore to the Japanese Imperial Army, February 1942.

(Ian Dagnall Computing / Alamy Stock Photo.)

Idealists at odds: Sir Stafford Cripps with Mahatma Gandhi, Delhi, March 1942.

(Dinodia Photos / Alamy Stock Photo.)

Second front when? Molotov in Washington, June 1942.
(Hulton-Deutsch Collection / CORBIS / Corbis via Getty Images.)

'The Ogre in his den': Churchill with Stalin and Lend–Lease 'expediter', Averell Harriman, in the Kremlin, August 1942. (GRANGER – Historical Picture Archive / Alamy Stock Photo.)

so-called emergency is greater now than it was a year ago.'[34] Three weeks later, the 'so-called emergency' moved closer to America's shores when a German submarine, *U-625*, fired two torpedoes at the destroyer USS *Greer*. Although the projectiles missed, Roosevelt exploited the incident for all it was worth, announcing in a 'fireside chat' on 11 September that he was ordering the protection of merchant shipping, 'of any flag' within the American defensive zone – now stretching as far as Iceland – and that, henceforth, the Navy would not wait for the Axis to strike first.[35] What he failed to mention was that the *Greer* had been shadowing the submarine for several hours prior to the attack, during which time a British bomber dropped four depth charges.

Even more misleading was the speech he delivered on 27 October – Navy Day – at Washington's Mayflower Hotel. 'I have in my possession', he told the dinner-jacket-wearing audience, as well as millions of American radio listeners, 'a secret map made in Germany by Hitler's Government . . . It is a map of South America and a part of Central America as Hitler proposes to reorganise it . . . This map, my friends, makes clear the Nazi design not only against South America but against the United States as well.'[36] The 'Nazi map', with echoes of the notorious Zimmermann telegram, caused a storm.* While White House correspondents clamoured to see it, the Germans denounced it as a forgery. For once, they were not lying: the map had been made by British Security Coordination.

Meanwhile, relations between the US and Japan were approaching a crisis. For several months, Cordell Hull had been negotiating with the Japanese Ambassador, Admiral Kichisaburō Nomura. The points of contention – the continuing war with China, Japanese membership of the Tripartite Pact and Tokyo's determination to establish a

---

* Intercepted by British intelligence in February 1917, the 'Zimmermann telegram' was a communication from a senior German Foreign Office official, Arthur Zimmermann, to the German Ambassador in Mexico, proposing a German–Mexican alliance in the event of a declaration of war by the United States following the commencement of unrestricted U-boat warfare in the Atlantic. Specifically, Zimmermann stated that the Mexicans would be expected to recover the lost provinces of New Mexico, Texas and Arizona. Published on 1 March 1917, the telegram did much to stimulate American public opinion in favour of war.

new Asiatic order at the expense of the Anglo-Saxon powers – were insurmountable. When Japan occupied the whole of Indo-China, in July 1941, Roosevelt froze her assets and curtailed US oil exports. (In 1940, 60 per cent of Japan's oil came from the US, 30 per cent from the Dutch East Indies and the Caribbean.) A week later, Marshall announced the defence of the Philippines as official United States policy, Roosevelt having already recalled Lieutenant-General Douglas MacArthur for this command. At the Atlantic Conference, the British had asked the Americans to agree to parallel communications, warning Tokyo that 'any further encroachment . . . in the South-Western Pacific' would lead to war with both Britain and the United States.[37] Roosevelt refused. Anxious to avoid a war in the Pacific while one was raging in Europe, he informed Churchill of the Japanese wish to resume negotiations (broken off after the occupation of south Indo-China). Yet the American line remained tough. Encouraged by the power of the B-17 Flying Fortress, now beginning to be stationed in the Philippines, the Japanese, it was believed, could be deterred from southward expansion. The collapse of the Konoye Government and the appointment of the bellicose War Minister, General Hideki Tojo, as Premier on 16 October, belied such complacency. Both Churchill and the Chinese Nationalist leader, Chiang Kai-shek, urged Roosevelt to issue Japan with an explicit warning against a southern thrust or an attempt to cut the Burma Road, China's supply route. But the President, aware that each week of peace added to the defence of the Philippines, preferred to play for time.

The final Japanese proposals, presented in mid-November, offered no prospect of accommodation. When intercepted Japanese diplomatic cables ('Magic') revealed that Tokyo insisted on a resolution by the end of November, the Administration began to speculate on the likelihood of a surprise attack, with targets ranging from Thailand to the Dutch East Indies, Malaya and the Philippines. 'Hull is very certain that the Japs are planning some devilry and we are all wondering where the blow will strike,' noted Henry Stimson after a conference with the Secretary of State.[38] The date was Sunday 7 December 1941.

Some 3,631 miles away, Churchill was dining with Averell Harriman, the envoy's daughter Kathleen, Pamela Churchill and the

American Ambassador, Gil Winant at Chequers. The Prime Minister looked 'very grim and sat in complete silence', recalled the Ambassador. Earlier, Churchill had asked Winant if there was going to be war with Japan.

'Yes', replied the Ambassador, emphatically.

'If they declare war on you, we shall declare war on them within the hour,' Churchill said.

'I understand, Prime Minister. You have stated that publicly.'

'If they declare war on us, will you declare war on them?'

'I can't answer that, Prime Minister. Only the Congress has the right to declare war,' came the unsatisfactory answer.[39] Just after nine o'clock, Churchill turned on his portable wireless to hear the BBC news. As the machine crackled into life, his guests heard about a tank battle in Libya. Then:

> The news has just been given that Japanese aircraft have raided Pearl Harbor, the American naval base in Hawaii.[40]

PART THREE

The Grand Alliance
1942–1943

XVI

Forging the Alliance

Here, where the sword united nations drew

Lord Byron, *Childe Harold's Pilgrimage*[1]

'We looked at one another incredulously', recalled Winant.[2] Harriman remembered a surreal argument with the Prime Minister's aide-de-camp as to whether it was 'Pearl Harbor' or the 'Pearl River' the announcer had just mentioned.[3] Then, after thumping the wireless, Churchill jumped to his feet and, at great speed, began to make for his study. 'We shall declare war on Japan!' he declared. Winant was aghast. 'You can't declare war on a radio announcement!'[4] Churchill conceded the justice of the admonition and asked to be put through to the President. After a few minutes, Roosevelt came on the line.

'Mr President, what's this about Japan?'

'It's quite true,' FDR replied. 'They have attacked us at Pearl Harbor. We are all in the same boat now.'[5] And so Churchill went to bed and, as he later put it, 'slept the sleep of the saved and thankful'.[6]

British relief – elation even – and a retrospective sense of the 'inevitability' of Allied victory have tended to obscure the uncertainty and anxiety of the days following Pearl Harbor.[7] The US was, understandably, in a state of trauma. Having achieved total surprise, the Japanese had succeeded in sinking five battleships and crippling sixteen warships. (Fortunately, the three Pacific Fleet aircraft carriers were at sea and so escaped the attack.) A total of 2,403 Americans were killed, while over 300 aircraft were damaged or destroyed. As news of the disaster began to disperse, panic spread. New York and Washington, it was rumoured, were about to be bombed. Enemy aircraft were 'spotted' off the Virginia coast. When Major-General

Joseph Stilwell arrived at his command post in San Diego on the morning of 11 December he received a call to say that the Japanese Fleet was
164 miles from San Francisco. 'The first reaction to that news was like a
kick in the stomach,' recorded Stilwell, 'the unthinkable realisation that
our defences were down, the enemy at hand, and that we not only had
nothing to defend ourselves with but that time was against us.'[8] Over
the next two weeks there would be many such scares, causing a riot in
Seattle and the near evacuation of Los Angeles.*

Nor was the political scene as serene and straightforward as it
appeared in hindsight. Although Arthur Vandenberg, the influential anti-interventionist Senator from Michigan, claimed that Pearl
Harbor 'ended isolationism for any realist', there were enough non-
realists for Roosevelt to doubt public support for a declaration of
war against Germany – most America-Firsters having been transformed, overnight, into Pacific-Firsters.[9] 'There are some patriotic
citizens', noted Elmer Davis of CBS shortly after Pearl Harbor,
'who sincerely hope that America will win the war but they also hope
that Russia will lose it; and there are some who hope that America
will win the war but that England will lose it; and there are some
who hope that America will win the war but that Roosevelt will lose
it.'[10] When Secretary of War Stimson urged the President to declare
war on Germany 'before the indignation of the people was over',
Roosevelt refused.[11] Nor would he indict the Nazi state during his
address to Congress on 8 December, as Cordell Hull wished. When
Congress gave its almost unanimous approval to his request for a
declaration of war against Japan, his caution appeared justified.[†] Yet
FDR remained wary: reluctant to accede to Churchill's request for
an immediate conference, lest his countrymen interpret the Prime
Minister's arrival as an attempt to divert America away from her
'true' enemy, Japan.[‡]

---

* At Burbank, 500 US troops occupied the Walt Disney Studio to protect Mickey
Mouse and Donald Duck from sabotage.
† There was one dissenting vote in the House of Representatives: Jeannette Rankin,
a lifelong pacifist, who had similarly opposed the declaration of war in 1917.
‡ 'I had a slight feeling that . . . he was not quite sure if your coming here might
not be rather too strong medicine in the immediate future for some of his public

This was, indeed, Churchill's intention. Although Anglo-American Staff conversations had confirmed a 'Germany First' strategy, Churchill feared that outrage over Pearl Harbor might cause the US to throw the bulk of her forces into the Pacific. Already, on the morning following the attack, the US War Office had placed a complete embargo on Lend-Lease equipment, even going so far as to request the return of 250 bombers, previously provided to the RAF, for the defence of Hawaii. 'The whole plan of the Anglo-American defence and attack has to be concerted in the light of reality,' wrote an obviously agitated Churchill to the King, adding that it was also important to ensure that 'our share of munitions and other aid which we are receiving from the United States does not suffer more than is, I fear, inevitable'.[12] To his relief, Roosevelt, having havered, accepted his proposal for an Anglo-American conference, assuring the Prime Minister, on 11 December, that 'production and allocation problems can and will be worked out with complete understanding and accord'.[13]

A few hours later, Hitler stunned the world – if neither Roosevelt nor Churchill – by declaring war on the United States (the only time he bothered with the formality). The decision had been taken within hours of the Japanese assault. Believing that America was already effectively at war and enthused by the deeds of an ally who 'has never been conquered in 3,000 years', the Führer had ordered Admiral Raeder to commence operations against American shipping on the night of 8–9 December.[14] Two days later, standing before the serried ranks of the ornamental Reichstag, he inveighed against Roosevelt and the 'Anglo-Saxon-Jewish-capitalist world'. He portrayed the President as a warmonger, a provocateur determined to deny Germany her natural rights. And yet Germany would fulfil her destiny, 'even if thousands of Churchills and Roosevelts conspire against it'.[15] 'The stars in their courses are fighting for us', was Churchill's comment on the speech.[16]

After a rough voyage – Beaverbrook complained that they might as well have travelled by submarine, so battened down was the *Duke of York* – Churchill and his entourage reached Washington on 22

opinion', wrote Lord Halifax to the Prime Minister on 9 December 1941. (PREM 4/27/9)

December 1941. The President, making up for his earlier hesitation, had invited Churchill to stay in the White House. From the start, it was a familial if huggermugger affair. The Monroe Room was converted into the Prime Minister's map room, while the upstairs hall became, in Robert Sherwood's words, 'the headquarters of the British Empire', with Chiefs of Staff, soldiers and secretaries marching hither and thither.[17] Churchill was given the Rose Suite, opposite Hopkins' room. Every morning, still in his nightshirt and preceded by the inevitable cigar, he would pad across the hall to review the previous day's discussions with the Presidential go-between. 'Certainly [it is] the oddest ménage anybody has ever seen,' noted Halifax, after sitting on a box in the upper hall, waiting for the President to emerge from the Prime Minister's bedroom, while Hopkins wafted by in a dressing gown.[18] On one famous occasion, Roosevelt was wheeled into Churchill's quarters to find his guest in a state of near or total undress. 'The Prime Minister of Great Britain has nothing to conceal from the President of the United States', was Churchill's mock-grandiloquent, if not entirely truthful, response.[19]

During his two-week sojourn at the White House, Churchill and Roosevelt would lunch and dine together almost every day. The lunches were working meals. Attended by Harry Hopkins, it was at these that many of the major issues were agreed. In the evenings there were cocktails, larger, more social dinners and late-night discussions over brandy and cigars. (Vice-Admiral McIntire, FDR's physician, joined Eleanor Roosevelt in considering Churchill 'Public Enemy Number One' for keeping the President up so late.[20]) To onlookers, the contrasts between the two leaders were intriguing. 'Of the two men, the President was the more reserved, suave and diplomatic,' judged White House speechwriter Samuel Rosenman.[21] Eleanor Roosevelt and her confidant Joseph Lash agreed. 'The Prime Minister has the richer temperament', conceded Lash, 'but the President is a more dependable, steadier man in a crisis.'[22] The First Lady thought her husband had a greater grounding in morality. Although she could not help being charmed by the 'very human' Churchill, she was opposed to his Toryism as well as to his imperialism and hoped that he would not have a dominant role in shaping the post-war peace.[23]

The substance of the conference, codenamed Arcadia, proved highly satisfactory. To British relief, the Americans held to the 'Germany First' strategy, the US Chiefs of Staff agreeing, despite the unfolding disaster in the Pacific, that Germany was still the 'prime enemy' and her defeat 'the key to victory'.[24] Lend-Lease was reconfirmed and US troops were promised for Northern Ireland to relieve British forces currently guarding the six counties against invasion. Having decided to create an American Chiefs of Staff Committee, on the British model, General Marshall persuaded first Roosevelt, then Churchill, of the need to *combine* the Chiefs of Staff in one body responsible for the overall direction of the war. Some British officers, not least the newly appointed (and, critically, absent) Chief of the Imperial General Staff, General Sir Alan Brooke, were horrified. For the first time in British history, the supreme military executive would be located outside the British Isles – Marshall having insisted, for political as well as security reasons, on Washington as the home for the new body. Yet while the establishment of the Combined Chiefs of Staff was indicative of a shift in the balance of power – a shift that would only increase as the war continued – it is hard to see how successful strategy, let alone the allocation and co-ordination of resources necessary for global war, could have developed without it. Although its participants would periodically vent their frustration with each other, the Combined Chiefs of Staff provided the structural basis for true partnership – the most integrated and successful military alliance in history.

A scarcely less important innovation was 'unity of command'. After observing British debacles in France, North Africa, Greece and now the Far East, Marshall was convinced of the need for a single commander in each theatre, responsible for all forces of all allies. This was particularly true in South-East Asia, where the scattered nature of British, American, Dutch, Australian and New Zealand territory made inter-Allied and inter-service co-ordination essential. Although the British were initially wary of the proposal, they were persuaded when Marshall recommended Wavell (now C-in-C India) as Supreme Commander of a newly constituted American-British-Dutch-Australian Command for the Far East. The unfortunate General felt like 'a man who wasn't expecting a baby and had been handed quadruplets'.[25]

Churchill's success in persuading Roosevelt of the virtues of an Anglo-American invasion of French North Africa was more contentious. Confined below deck during his voyage across the Atlantic, the Prime Minister had occupied himself by composing four magisterial memoranda on the future of the war. Too weak to attempt an invasion of the European mainland and unable to influence the Russian front beyond the despatch of munitions, the Allied objective for 1942, he argued, should be the occupation of the French colonies of North and West Africa and the control of the whole of the North African shore from Tunisia to Egypt.[26] In certain quarters, this chimed with American thinking. For over a year, Roosevelt had worried about the Axis threat to Dakar, while Stimson, twelve days after Pearl Harbor, considered North and West Africa priorities second only to the security of the British Isles and the Atlantic.[27] Even Marshall was prepared to accept this 'peripheral strategy', provided the Vichy forces could be guaranteed to co-operate. Elsewhere, however – within the War Plans Division and from Generals 'Hap' Arnold, Mark Clark, Brehon Somervell and Joseph Stilwell – there was opposition to an operation that seemed to promise little beyond shoring up Britain's crumbling position in the Mediterranean.* 'The Limeys', complained Stilwell, not for nothing known as 'Vinegar Joe', 'have sold him [Roosevelt] a bill of goods . . . the Limeys have his ear, while we have the hind tit. Events are crowding us into ill-advised and ill-considered projects.'[28] Later, when shown the final Arcadia documents, he ranted in his diary about Britain's senior strategists, who 'shot off their faces as if they were *our* delegates and not theirs':

> So and so simply must be done. The Magnet Plan [the despatch of US troops to Northern Ireland] will relieve several British divisions, which can now go home to jolly old England, thank you. No hint that they might help elsewhere. [In fact, they left the safety of Northern Ireland to fight in North Africa, the Far East and, finally, Europe.] And we must keep up the Lend-Lease torrent to our British cousins, even though our people go without . . . The Limeys

---

* British Imperial forces, now under General Claude Auchinleck, were, currently, advancing in Libya but would soon be pushed back into Egypt.

want us in, committed. They don't care what becomes of us afterwards because they will have shifted the load from their shoulders to ours. So they insist speed is essential and [Roosevelt] has acquired this same itch for us to *do* something and is continually pressing for action against the considered opinion of all his advisers.[29]

Marshall later conceded there was 'too much anti-British feeling on our side . . . Our people were always ready to find Albion perfidious.' The British, by contrast, exhibited less suspicion towards their new ally (at least initially). Musing on the discrepancy, Marshall doubted that it was a compliment: 'They may have just felt we weren't smart enough to cause them trouble,' he told his official biographer.[30] Although the British understood that the Americans had the ability to cause them no end of trouble, he was not far wrong. Like British diplomats, British war planners were appalled at the haphazard nature of the American Government, a *modus operandi* which even Administration insiders recognised as deplorable. 'To our eyes, the American machine of Government seems hopelessly disorganised,' recorded Ian Jacob, Military Assistant to the War Cabinet:

> The President, to start with, has no proper private office. He has no real private secretary and no secretariat for Cabinet or military business. The Cabinet is of little account anyway, as the President is Commander-in-Chief. But he has no proper machinery through which to exercise command. To illustrate this . . . the following day the US Chiefs of Staff met ours in their first formal meeting at the Federal Reserve Building . . . There was no agenda and the first thing Admiral Stark, who was in the Chair, did was to run through the notes he had made of the previous day's meeting. General Marshall had also dictated, on his return to his office, *his* idea of what had happened. We, of course, had our minutes prepared and it was a complete waste of everyone's time to go all over the ground again . . . The Americans are like we were in the days of Jacky Fisher and Kitchener. Personalities, each pushing their own ideas and no real co-operation.[31]*

---

* Jacob was particularly shocked at the state of the President's study: 'A delightful oval room . . . [it] is one of the most untidy rooms I have ever seen. It is full of

The Americans, noted another British staff officer, 'don't understand the drill at all'.[32]

Despite these frustrations, the two staffs got on well. Realising that personalities mattered more than the machine in the American system, the British made efforts to understand and bond with their opposite numbers. By and large, they were impressed. 'General Marshall . . . is alert and young in mind and body . . . seems shrewd and honest and is master in his own house,' noted Jacob. Admiral Ernest King – responsible for naval operations since Pearl Harbor – struck the British as a 'dominating personality, who looks as if he would be the man to inspire the American Fleet with a strong and offensive spirit', while the Air Force commander, General 'Hap' Arnold, was 'a cherubic little man, with white hair and humorous blue eyes', 'quick on the uptake', if slightly impatient.[33]

The most important friendship to emerge from the conference, apart from that between Roosevelt and Churchill, was between Marshall and Sir John Dill. Appointed by Churchill to head the Joint British Staff Mission, the empathetic, courteous Dill developed an affinity with the equally thoughtful, diplomatic US Army Chief. Over the next three years, the two men would work in close partnership, smoothing over many an Anglo-American difference and ensuring that their staffs co-operated in the spirit, as well as the letter, of the alliance. When Dill died of aplastic anaemia in November 1944, the US Chiefs of Staff paid tribute to him as the individual most responsible 'for the achievement of complete co-operation in the work of the Combined Chiefs of Staff', while Marshall overcame precedent and procedure to have his friend interned at the American Valhalla of Arlington National Cemetery.[34]

On Boxing Day, Churchill addressed a joint meeting of Congress. The evening prior to this rare honour he was silent and preoccupied, excusing himself before the end of the White House festivities

---

junk. Half-opened parcels, souvenirs, books, papers, knick-knacks and all kinds of miscellaneous articles lie about everywhere, on tables, on chairs and on the floor. His desk is piled with papers and alongside his chair he has a sort of bookcase also filled with books, papers and junk of all sorts, piled just anyhow. It would drive an orderly-minded man, or a woman, mad.'

to review his speech. His diligence paid dividends. Standing before a podium bristling with microphones in the Senate Chamber he delivered an oration which the *Washington Post* ranked alongside Edmund Burke's defence of the American Colonies. Explaining that the invitation to speak in this historic setting was among the most moving and thrilling experiences of his life – a life 'which is already long and has not been entirely uneventful' – he provoked a ripple of laughter. When he reflected that he 'might have got here on his own', had his *father* been American and his *mother* been British, instead of the other way around, he brought the house down. He warned of a 'time of tribulation before us' but of the final outcome there could be no doubt. 'What kind of people do they think we are?' he asked, referring to the Japanese. 'Is it possible that they do not realise that we shall never cease to persevere against them until they have been taught a lesson which they and the world will never forget?'[35] Four days later, despite having suffered a minor heart attack following his appearance on Capitol Hill, he recalled to the Canadian Parliament the French Generals who, at the time of the fall of France, had predicted that Britain would have her neck wrung like a chicken. 'Some chicken! Some neck!'[36]

The main diplomatic event of the conference was the declaration signed by all members of the anti-Axis alliance, promising to abide by the principles of the Atlantic Charter, pledging to mobilise their resources against the common foe and forbidding a separate peace. Although unremarkable in itself, the agreement presented several difficulties. Whilst the War Cabinet wanted to list the Dominions together – reflecting their shared sovereignty – Roosevelt insisted on enumerating them, along with other belligerents, alphabetically. More contentious was the reference to 'religious freedom'. Freedom of worship may have been a cornerstone of American democracy but was severely curtailed within the 'atheistic' Soviet Union. Maxim Litvinov, the former Soviet Commissar for Foreign Affairs, now Ambassador to Washington, objected to the phrase but the smooth-talking Roosevelt persuaded him that 'religious freedom' included the freedom *not* to have a religion.

The anti-Axis coalition was to be called the 'United Nations', a title conceived by Roosevelt in preference to the less elegant 'Allied

Nations' or 'Associated Nations' and which appealed to Churchill due to its appearance in the third canto of Byron's *Childe Harold's Pilgrimage*. On New Year's Day 1942, Roosevelt, Churchill, Litvinov and T. V. Soong (personal representative of the Chinese Nationalist leader, Chiang Kai-shek) signed the declaration in a small ceremony in the Oval Office, followed by the Ambassadors of twenty-two other nations – including Poland, Norway, Belgium, Greece, Honduras and Nicaragua – the following day, in the State Department.

Not included among the list of signatories were the Free French. On 29 December, the War Cabinet had pressed for their inclusion on the grounds that they were 'in every sense an ally', that they held strategically important territories throughout the world and that, unlike Nicaragua for instance, they were currently collaborating with the British in operations against the Axis.[37] Churchill was sympathetic but Roosevelt refused. The US had never recognised the legitimacy of the Free French and the President considered their inclusion incompatible with Washington's continued recognition of Vichy. Besides, De Gaulle had just infuriated the State Department over the St Pierre et Miquelon affair.

Situated just off the coast of Newfoundland, this tiny archipelago of eight islands was a French colony, housing a valuable weather station and radio transmitter. Assured of the sympathy of the roughly 4,400-strong population, de Gaulle had sought the British Government's blessing to wrest the islands from Vichy and its eleven policemen. Although the Admiralty favoured this *'petit coup de main'*, Churchill, conscious of American reluctance to undermine the Pétain Government, counselled caution.[38] But de Gaulle had gone ahead. On Christmas Eve 1941, 360 Free French sailors in three corvettes under the command of Admiral Muselier descended upon the islands, which duly surrendered without a shot being fired. The Vichy Governor was deposed and on Christmas Day 98 per cent of the population confirmed their support for the Free French in a plebiscite.

Amid the great events of the winter of 1941–42, the peaceful rallying of a cluster of sparsely populated islands off the Canadian coast barely merited a mention in the newspapers. That the event commanded more attention, indeed became a major diplomatic incident, was solely due to the disproportionate reaction of the US Secretary of State, Cordell Hull. Immensely respected, the seventy-year-old Tennessean, with his sad, handsome face and neatly combed white hair was, as the British Embassy informed the Foreign Office, held in higher esteem than 'any other Cabinet officer or member of Congress . . . the most distinguished living embodiment of traditional American virtues'.[39] A veteran of the Spanish–American War, he had served as both a Congressman and a Senator before Roosevelt chose him as his chief diplomat in 1933. For six years, he battled to tear down trade barriers, which he regarded as the 'scourge' of prosperity and the 'cause' of war. But the divergence between his status and his power became increasingly evident as the decade wore on.

Determined, as far as possible, to be his own Secretary of State, FDR preferred to conduct business through his cousin, the suave, ambitious Under-Secretary of State Sumner Welles, or personal emissaries. Understandably, the prickly Hull found such treatment humiliating. 'Hull rankled under what he believed to be Welles' disloyalty and the President's neglect,' recalled Assistant Secretary of State Dean Acheson.[40] Excluded from military discussions, he was left at home when Roosevelt travelled to Allied conferences, forced to glean what had been agreed through interviews with foreign diplomats. Indeed, while Roosevelt appreciated and exploited Hull's standing with Congress, he had little respect for him as a statesman. Although steady and dependable in public (at least normally), he was fretful and querulous in private: a 'hillbilly Polonius' or dissenting nanny goat.[41] Lord Halifax struggled to remember any remarks he made during their frequent interviews that seemed worth relaying to the Foreign Office, while colleagues complained of his slowness, his alternate bouts of obstinacy and indecisiveness and his unfortunate habit of treating political acts as personal affronts. His reaction to the St Pierre et Miquelon affair would justify their disdain.

As soon as Hull heard about the Free French landing, he started agitating to restore the islands to Vichy rule. Enraged at what he saw as a breach of faith – a violation of the Monroe Doctrine, no less – and fearing the collapse of his pro-Vichy policy, he asked

the Canadians to eject the Gaullists. When Prime Minister Mackenzie King declined to act, he asked the British to tame their
creature. On Christmas Day, his anger spilt into the open when
the State Department issued a statement condemning the action
taken by the 'so-called Free French'.[42] The British and Canadians
were flabbergasted. 'I told him [Hull] that it would not do to have
the [Vichy] Governor restored as he was pro-Axis and his wife a
German,' reported a nonplussed King.[43] Far from deploring the
action, Canadians were 'relieved and pleased with the de Gaulle
accomplishment'.[44] More embarrassingly for Hull, so were most
Americans. In the days following his tantrum, Hull found himself
roundly abused by the US press, which accused him of wanting to
'appease Vichy', while hundreds of letters arrived at the Old State
Building, addressed to the 'so-called Secretary of State' at the 'so-
called State department'.[45]

There was no doubt that Hull had made 'a complete ass of
himself', minuted Richard Law, the British Under-Secretary for Foreign Affairs, unaware that the Secretary of State had come close
to resigning over the affair.[46] Yet however great the justice of this
observation, the row over St Pierre et Miquelon was the natural
product of the contradictions of the Administration's French policy.
For more than two years, the US had been the undeclared opponent
of the Axis. Since 11 December 1941, she had been at war with Germany, Italy and Japan. And yet she continued to lend legitimacy to
the collaborationist regime at Vichy, while treating de Gaulle and his
forces as a band of nuisance rebels. It was a discrepancy that would
blight US–Free French relations throughout the war and beyond.

Churchill and Roosevelt were embarrassed by the rumpus over
St Pierre et Miquelon. Yet neither de Gaulle nor Hull could mar the
burgeoning friendship between the two men, nor the spirit of comradeship that prevailed during Arcadia. 'The President punctiliously
made the preliminary cocktails', recalled Churchill, 'and I wheeled
him in his chair from the drawing-room to the lift as a mark of
respect and thinking also of Sir Walter Raleigh spreading his cloak
before Queen Elizabeth. I formed a very strong affection . . . for
this formidable politician.'[47] Roosevelt was also stirred. 'There was
no question but that he grew genuinely to like Churchill,' recorded

Hopkins, after the two men had bid the Prime Minister farewell at Sixth Street station.[48] Two weeks later, in a postscript to a telegram to the 'Former Naval Person', FDR declared, 'It is fun to be in the same decade as you.'[49] The two men would disappoint and annoy each other in the years ahead. But for now, theirs was the alliance that looked on tempests and was not shaken.

XVII

The Rising Sun

To lunch they go at half past one –
Blast me, old chap, the day's half done.
They lunch and talk and fight the Jap,
And now it's time to take a nap.
The staff study starts at three fifteen;
Such progress here you've never seen.
They're working now, as you can see,
But blast me down, it's time for tea.

Verses circulating in Washington, summer 1942[1]

A few hours after Japanese torpedoes struck American warships at Pearl Harbor, Britain's Commander-in-Chief Far East, Air Chief Marshal Sir Robert Brooke-Popham, known as 'Old Pop-Off' due to his habit of falling asleep in meetings, issued an 'order of the day' from his headquarters in Singapore:

We are ready. We have had plenty of warning and our preparations are made and tested . . . We are confident. Our defences are strong and our weapons efficient . . . We see before us a Japan drained for years by the exhausting claims of her wanton onslaught on China. We see a Japan whose trade and industry have been so dislocated by these years of reckless adventure that, in a mood of desperation, her Government has flung her into war under the delusion that, by stabbing a friendly nation in the back, she can gain her end. Let her look at Italy and what has happened since that nation tried a similar base action.[2]

There followed the greatest succession of disasters in British military history.

Even before the first bombs were dropped at Pearl Harbor, the Japanese had attacked the British in Malaya, Japanese Imperial troops having landed shortly after midnight (local time) on 8 December 1941 at Kota Bharu near the Thai frontier. Singapore was also bombed. Within twenty-four hours, British and Australian air strength in northern Malaya had more than halved. In the Philippines, American B-17s and P-40s located at airfields around Manila and Iba were destroyed on the ground. Guam – the largest of the Mariana Islands and a US colony – was bombarded. On 10 December, the battleship *Prince of Wales* (which had conveyed Churchill to Placentia Bay four months earlier) and the battlecruiser *Repulse* were sunk by Japanese bombers. 'I never received a more direct shock,' recalled Churchill. 'Over all this vast expanse of waters [from the Indian Ocean to the Pacific] Japan was supreme and we everywhere were weak and naked.'[3]

Hong Kong fell on Christmas Day. On 31 January 1942, Allied forces, bereft of naval and air support, fell back across the Johore Strait to Singapore. Churchill expected the island, erroneously described as a 'fortress', to hold out for several months. When Japanese forces gained a foothold on the north-west shore, he ordered a last-ditch defence to salvage the honour of the Empire. 'There must at this stage be no thought of saving the troops or sparing the population,' he telegraphed General Wavell, tipped from the frying pan of North Africa into the fire of the Far East. 'The battle must be fought to the bitter end at all costs . . . Commanders and senior officers should die with their troops . . . With the Russians fighting as they are and the Americans so stubborn at Luzon [in the Philippines] the whole reputation of our country and our race is involved.'[4] Five days later, some 85,000 British, Australian and Indian soldiers capitulated to a Japanese force less than half their size. 'We had cause on many previous occasions to be uneasy about the fighting qualities of our men,' recalled Major-General John Kennedy, Director of Military Operations at the War Office, but Singapore represented a new low. 'They had not fought as toughly as the Germans or Russians and now they were being outclassed by the Japanese.'[5]

Nor was this the end of the catalogue of disasters. On 19 February 1942, the Japanese continued their rampage by bombing the Australian port of Darwin, sinking eight ships. A week later, they defeated a combined Dutch, British, American and Australian fleet in the Battle of the Java Sea. On 8 March, the Dutch East Indies surrendered. On the 11th, General Douglas MacArthur, obeying a direct order from Roosevelt, escaped from the Philippines, where his forces were continuing a dogged but doomed defence. Meanwhile, the Japanese were advancing deep into British Burma, severing the 'Burma Road – the supply route for Nationalist China – and threatening to trap the entire British Eastern Army. Flying into a bombed-out Rangoon on 5 March, General Harold Alexander, appointed to save an already hopeless situation, decided to evacuate the city. Driven north, British as well as Chinese Nationalist forces under General Stilwell tried to stem the Japanese tide but without avail. In mid-May, Lieutenant-General William Slim's beleaguered, malaria-ridden 'Burcorps' limped across the border into Assam in north-east India, having conducted a 900-mile fighting retreat. In just five months, the Japanese Empire had expanded as far as New Guinea and the Solomon Islands in the south, the frontiers of India in the west and the Gilbert Islands in the east.

The collapse of British East Asia raised fundamental questions: about empire, about attitudes to race, about strategy and about the coherence of the anti-Axis alliance. Ostensibly, British and American policy towards Japan had been aligned. With major imperial, commercial and strategic interests in the Far East and, in the United States' case, strong sympathy for embattled China, both were opposed to Tokyo's policy of forging a 'New Order in East Asia' under Japanese suzerainty. Beyond this shared objective, however, there were differences and disagreements. Ever since 1931 and Sir John Simon's failure to recommend sanctions following Japan's invasion of Manchuria, the Americans had accused the British of 'appeasing' Tokyo. To this, the British had responded by pointing to the gulf between American words and American deeds. 'We ought to know by this time that [the] USA will give us no undertaking to resist by force any action by Japan short of an attack on Hawaii or Honolulu,' complained Neville Chamberlain, presciently, in July 1934. 'She will give us plenty of assurances of goodwill, especially if we promise to do all the fighting, but the moment she is asked to contribute something she invariably takes refuge behind Congress.'[6] This was, indeed, the form right up until the last days of peace in the Pacific. The US would exhort the British to resist Japanese aggrandisement but when the British enquired about American support the Roosevelt Administration refused to provide the necessary commitment. The antagonism inherent in this discrepancy came to the fore when, in July 1940, the War Cabinet bowed to Japanese pressure and closed the Burma Road. Lord Halifax, contrary to his natural predilection for appeasement, wanted to tell the 'Japs to go to the devil'.[7] But Churchill, faced with the prospect of a German invasion of Britain and a Japanese Government threatening to declare war, felt compelled to temporise. On 16 July 1940, the Government announced that it would suspend the passage of materiel along the road for three months (during the rainy season when few trucks would have been able to make the journey in any case) while negotiations with Tokyo continued. American reaction to this 'teaspoonful of appeasement', as Major-General Kennedy described it, was censorious.[8] Cordell Hull issued a statement deploring the closure of what he euphemistically called one of the major arteries of 'world trade', while Henry Luce's *Life* magazine criticised the British Government for allowing itself to be 'bulldozed' by the Japanese.[9] 'We must try to remember', minuted a member of the Foreign Office, 'that America expects us to take all the knocks and to look as if we liked it.'[10]

As the British explained to Hull and the State Department, the decision to close the Burma Road was a tactical withdrawal, rather than the prelude to a new policy of Far Eastern appeasement. On 27 September 1940, Japan signed the Tripartite Pact with Germany and Italy and on 8 October Britain announced that she was reopening the Burma Road. Thereafter, the positions were somewhat reversed: the British urged a policy of deterrence, while the Americans engaged in secret talks with Tokyo. When the Foreign Office learnt about these conversations – five weeks after they had started – they were alarmed. But the Japanese occupation of southern Indo-China in July 1941 undermined the negotiations, leading to Roosevelt's decision to restrict Japanese oil imports – the policy that, ultimately, convinced Tokyo to go to war with America.*

Churchill was adamant that Britain should support the US in the Far East. Whatever doubts there were in Whitehall about the oil embargo or the Hull–Nomura conversations (which continued until December 1941), these, he insisted, paled before the value of US leadership in the region. If Roosevelt succeeded in keeping the peace in the Pacific, well and good; if he failed, the value of US belligerency would dwarf any injury the Japanese were likely to inflict. 'The advantage of America as an ally to the disadvantage of Japan as an enemy was . . . ten to one,' the Prime Minister told Harry Hopkins in January 1941. 'Why, look at their respective power of steel production and modern war is waged with steel.'[11]

This reasoning was sound. As even the hotheads in Tokyo appreciated, Japan could not hope to defeat the industrial 'giant' that was the United States, once she had woken. In attacking Pearl Harbor, her aim was to cripple the US Pacific Fleet, allowing her to complete her conquest of South-East Asia, trusting that the 'decadent' Americans would quail before the national sacrifices required for victory and seek a compromise peace. Yet there were less rational reasons too. In addition to the Prime Minister's antiquated faith in the power of big battleships was the invidious belief that the Japanese, like all Asians, were 'inferior' beings who could be expected to think twice before confronting the 'might' of the Anglo-Saxons. The Japanese were unlikely to commence hostilities as long as the Germans declined to invade the British Isles, Churchill assured the War Cabinet in April 1941, while to the American journalist John Gunther he predicted that the Japanese would 'fold up like the Italians', being the 'wops of the Far East'.[12]

Such racial arrogance was far from unique. Many Britons and Americans subscribed to the myth that the 'Japs', as they were

* Roosevelt had intended merely to curtail oil exports, sufficient to act as a deterrent but not so extreme as to serve as a *casus belli*. Thanks, however, to the hawkish actions of the Foreign Funds Control Committee – responsible for administering Japan's frozen assets – and Assistant Secretary of State Dean Acheson, no oil was sold to Japan after 26 July 1941.

derisively known, were short-sighted (making them bad pilots), poor jungle fighters and incompetent motorists.* The Japanese 'have peculiarly slow brains', the British Naval Attaché in Tokyo 'informed' the Admiralty in 1935.[13] His superior, Vice-Admiral Sir Charles Little, reflected the views of most Westerners when he spoke of 'these inferior yellow races', while the High Commissioner of the Federated Malay States and Governor of Singapore, Sir Shenton Thomas, responded to the Japanese invasion of his territory with the indelible comment: 'I suppose you'll shove the little men off?'[14]

Not that racial prejudice was confined to Western appreciations of the Japanese. Although many colonialists exhibited a genuine interest, affection even, towards local populations, this did not extend to allowing the 'natives' – often dismissed as 'wogs', 'chinks' and 'pigtails' – into the majority of the clubs, bars and hotels that had become the hallmarks of Britain's latter-day Empire. While Malays, Tamils, overseas Chinese, Burmese and Indians laboured on rubber plantations and down tin mines, pulling rickshaws and tending gardens (Diana Cooper was amazed to see 'natives advancing on all fours', pruning Singapore's lawns with fingers and thumbs), their Western overlords disported themselves at polo matches, gymkhanas, the Hong Kong Jockey Club and the Long Bar at Singapore's Raffles Hotel.[15]† The Australian journalist Ian Morrison blamed the colonial wives for what struck him as the absurdity of British rule: 'The white woman has inevitably tried to recreate England, and usually Surbiton, in the tropics,' he wrote, contemptuously, following the fall of Singapore.[16] Although not entirely fair – the men had much to answer for – the result was the same. Like Disraeli's 'two

---

* So ingrained were these myths that the rumour spread in the US after Pearl Harbor that German pilots had taken part in the attack – their Asiatic allies deemed incapable of such a blow.

† 'Every Asiatic who has travelled much abroad', wrote a Hong Kong journalist, 'must have observed the mental metamorphosis of the Englishman *en route* from London to the East. Before Suez is reached, one could not wish for a more social companion . . . once Suez is crossed, his head begins to turn and, when Colombo is passed, he seems to feel the weight of the whole British Empire upon him and is therefore too proud to rub shoulders with the Asiatics.' (Inverchapel Papers, MS 12101/37)

nations', there were two sets of peoples in East Asia between whom there was little intercourse and limited sympathy. 'British rule and culture and the small British community formed no more than a thin and brittle veneer,' wrote Morrison.[17]*

By the time the British began to comprehend this reality, it was too late. 'We are now faced by vast populations of industrious, intelligent and brave Asiatics who are unwilling to acknowledge the superiority of Europeans or their right to special privileges in Asia,' wrote Duff Cooper, sent by Churchill to assess the situation in the Far East, two months before the Japanese onslaught.[18] While thousands of Malays, Tamils, Chinese, Burmese, Karens, Kachins, Shans and especially Indians fought alongside British Commonwealth forces, others were apathetic, some sympathetic towards the Japanese. This was particularly true of Burma, where the introduction of limited self-government in 1937 had failed to stem demands for full autonomy. Within weeks of Pearl Harbor, the Burmese Prime Minister, U Saw, was caught conspiring with the Japanese. Although the British incarcerated him (it was fortunate from London's perspective that the Premier was returning from a tour of Allied capitals when his 'treachery' was discovered), this did not stop many Burmese, notably the 18,000 members of the Burma Independence Army, from aiding the invaders.

To Americans, antipathetic to empire, the British were reaping what they had sown. 'Today the Japs are at the gates of India', recorded Assistant Secretary of State Breckinridge Long, unable to contain his *Schadenfreude*. 'The province of Bengal is in panic. Fifth columnists are rife, the native Bengali is friendly to the Japs – hostile and resentful of the English . . . India is about to fall. The uncomprehending philosophy of England is meeting its reward. Blind,

---

* Racism was not an exclusively British or Western vice. The Japanese were taught that they belonged to a superior 'Yamato race', destined to supplant the 'decadent' Anglo-Saxons as the new imperial overlords of Asia and the Pacific. American and British Commonwealth prisoners were frequently beheaded, shot, beaten, starved or worked to death. Collectively, non-Japanese Asians fared even worse. During the course of the war, anywhere between six and ten million South-East Asians – the majority Chinese – were massacred by the Emperor's men.

self-centered and tenacious of the phantoms of the past, she refuses
to be convinced of [the] vulnerability of England everywhere but
in England.'[19]

Many Britons dolefully agreed. 'The defect of the British colonial system . . . is that it has been too long and too deeply rooted
in the traditions of a bygone age,' acknowledged *The Times*.[20] An
Englishman whose family had been in Malaya for over a century
reflected that 'it never was right to run a country in the interests
of capitalists at home rather than in the interests of those whose
homes it was'.[21] Foreign correspondents attacked the supercilious
complacency of colonial administrators – the 'gin-swilling pukka
sahibs' and incompetent Colonel Blimps – while Harold Nicolson
expressed the common feeling that Britain's current crop of imperialists failed to show the same levels of determination to hold on to
their Empire that their forebears had shown in gaining it.[22]

These criticisms were justified. Yet the fall of Britain's Far Eastern Empire, like the fall of France, was essentially a military defeat,
attributable to military and strategic factors. Upon the spectrum
of Britain's strategic priorities, the Far East ranked a poor fourth –
behiind the British Isles, the Atlantic and the Middle East. The US
Pacific Fleet, which should have intercepted the Japanese transports
and their escorts, had been crippled at Pearl Harbor. There were
only 165 aircraft allocated for the defence of Malaya (half of which
were Brewster Buffaloes, 'flying beer barrels', rejected for service
in Europe), while the 'fortress' of Singapore was only equipped to
resist a seaward attack. ('The possibility of Singapore having no
landward defences', Churchill later wrote, 'no more entered into my
mind than that of a battleship being launched without a bottom.'[23])
Still, the crisis of Empire was real, leading MPs, the press, Cabinet
Ministers, Chiang Kai-shek and the Americans to urge Churchill
to reach an agreement with Indian nationalists, engaged in a civil
disobedience campaign since October 1940, before the 'jewel' in the
Imperial crown was itself dislodged.

Churchill remained fundamentally hostile to the nationalist aspirations of Britain's Imperial subjects. 'What those people need is
the sjambok [a leather whip],' he told the Governor of Burma, Sir
Reginald Dorman-Smith, when the latter emphasised the Burmese

desire for full Home Rule.[24] His attitude was ideological and had scarcely developed since his days as a cavalry subaltern during the Victorian Raj. Yet it was also pragmatic, deriving, at least in part, from an understandable unwillingness to open a Pandora's box of constitutional issues while Britain was engaged in a global war for national survival.* By the spring of 1942, however, he was no longer in a position to resist calls for a further effort towards an accommodation with India's nationalists. The Far East was in flames. Britain's Imperial prestige was in tatters. In North Africa, Rommel was, once again, pushing British forces back across the Libyan desert. In Canberra, the new Labor Prime Minister, John Curtin, had infuriated Churchill by recalling the 7th Australian Division from the Middle East and then stating, on 26 December 1941, that 'Australia looks to America [for her defence], free of any pangs as to our traditional links or kinship with the United Kingdom'.[25]†

On 27 January 1942, responding to the succession of defeats and mounting criticism of his leadership, Churchill submitted the Government to a confidence vote. Although only one MP dared walk through the 'No' lobby, the Prime Minister was fortunate it was not held any later. On 30 January it was announced that Rommel had taken Benghazi. Two weeks later, the country suffered an even greater humiliation when the German battleships *Scharnhorst* and *Gneisenau* and the heavy cruiser *Prinz Eugen*, accompanied by six destroyers, sailed unimpeded up the English Channel to the safety of the Elbe and Wilhelmshaven. 'Rage', noted Chips Channon, was the national mood. 'This is not the post-Dunkirk feeling but one of anger . . . The Capital seethes with indignation and were Londoners Latins there would be rioting.'[26] Two days later, Churchill broadcast the news of the fall of Singapore.

Churchill's solution to the Indian conundrum was to send Sir

---

* His argument that Britain was also fighting to protect the people of East Asia from 'fascist barbarism' was given retrospective justification by Japanese atrocities.

† He later refused Churchill's and Roosevelt's pleas to divert this force to Rangoon. Although military historians disagreed, Sir Alan Brooke felt that this 'might well have restored the situation and saved Burma'.

Stafford Cripps, recently freed from the frustrations of the British Embassy in Moscow (or Kuibyshev, where the diplomatic corps had been evacuated), on a special mission to Delhi. Although the expelled Labour MP had failed in his attempt to win the trust of the Kremlin, his early advocacy of the Soviet Union, now Britain's gallant ally, and the dogged resistance of the Red Army had caused his popularity to soar. As Churchill's star waned, Cripps rose in the political firmament until, for a brief period in early 1942, he was touted as an alternative Prime Minister. By allowing him to step into the morass of Indian politics, Churchill had the satisfaction of knowing that he was, at least temporarily, removing a dangerous rival from the scene.

The situation in India was worse than even well-informed Westerners realised. As the Japanese advanced across South-East Asia, panic spread across the subcontinent. Hundreds of thousands of Indians along the east coast left their homes and headed inland. Savings accounts from Bihar to Bombay were emptied. As refugees began to pour into Assam and Bengal from Burma, faith in both the competence and compassion of the British collapsed. While Subhas Chandra Bose, the militant nationalist leader, exhorted Indians, via broadcasts from Berlin, to join the Axis and expel the British, colonial administrators ordered the destruction of thousands of boats along the east coast as part of a scorched-earth policy that created one of the causes of the Bengal famine – responsible for some three million Indian deaths the following year.

Not all Indians wanted rid of the British – at least not immediately. As a future leader of the Japanese-sponsored Indian National Army, Shahnawaz Khan, put it, recalling his time in the British-led Indian Army prior to his conversion to the politics of Bose in a Japanese internment camp:

> I was brought up to see India through the eyes of a British officer and all that I was interested in was soldiering and sport . . . At the back of my mind was the traditional urge of loyalty to the King. I owed all my education to him. My family and my tribe were one of the privileged classes in India. They were all prosperous and contented. This too we owed to the British Government and I knew that no change in India would bring them any more prosperity.[27]

Although representative of probably only a fraction of the more than two million Indians who volunteered or were pressured into joining the Indian Army, such views had currency among professional soldiers and the affluent. As General Auchinleck wrote to Leo Amery from his command in the Middle East:

> It really is most striking the way in which all Indian units, combatant or non-combatant, in this theatre have made such a good name for themselves for discipline, courage, willingness and amiability . . . They seem in some mysterious way to have overcome the old and very deep-rooted prejudices against them which persisted in the minds of many 'Britishers', even after the last war.[28]

More significantly, the All-India Muslim League, under Muhammad Ali Jinnah, did not want the British to quit before a separate state had been created that would guarantee the rights of India's 91.5 million Muslims. To Jinnah and his followers, the war which 'nobody welcomed' proved a 'blessing in disguise', as the Muslim League traded support for the war effort in return for safeguards regarding India's constitutional future.[29] When the crisis of the spring of 1942 arose, the future founder of Pakistan rallied his supporters with Nelsonian rhetoric: 'Islam expects every Mussalman to do his duty by his people and by his nation.'[30]

The Indian National Congress, the Hindu-dominated nationalist party, was divided on the question of the war and its relation to the struggle for independence. Some saw the crisis as an opportunity to expel the British. Others, despite their antipathy for the Raj, believed the conflict transcended the fight for statehood. As no less a figure than M. N. Roy – the former Marxist who, during the First World War, had sought an alliance with the Kaiser and later spent five and a half years in a British gaol – put it, 'The present is not England's war. It is a war for the future of the world. If the British Government happens to be a party to this war, why should the fighters for human liberty be ashamed of congratulating it for this meritorious deed?'[31] Chakravarti Rajagopalachari, the former Premier of Madras, wanted to co-operate with the British to defend India against the Japanese but Jawaharlal Nehru, though sympathetic towards the end, refused to endorse the means. Meanwhile, Mohandas Gandhi, who in the summer of 1940 had advised the British to lay down their arms and surrender their 'beautiful island' to Hitler (whom the Mahatma considered 'not as bad as he is depicted'), clung to his doctrine of non-violence, along with the demand that the British leave India immediately, even though 'anarchy may lead to internecine warfare . . . or to unrestrained dacoities [gang robberies]'.[32]

The Cripps mission aroused the keenest attention, later controversy, not only in India but also in Britain, the United States, China and across the colonial world. A common accusation, both at the time and since, was that the British in general and Churchill in particular sabotaged the negotiations. Cripps was tripped up by the unreconstructed imperialist Churchill and the 'Machiavellian' Viceroy, Lord Linlithgow, wrote the foremost historian of the mission, echoing the views of Congress, the Indian press and Roosevelt's personal emissary, Louis Johnson.[33] Yet whilst this description of Churchill is irrefutable, the indictment does not stand up to scrutiny.

Cripps arrived in Delhi on 23 March 1942. After four days staying with the Viceroy, Lord Linlithgow, he left the splendours of Lutyens' Indo-Classical design and moved into more modest quarters at 3 Queen Victoria Road. There he held interviews with leading politicians, including his old friend Nehru, the President of Congress, Maulana Azad, Jinnah and, of course, Gandhi. On Sunday 29 March, Cripps unveiled the War Cabinet's plan for Indian self-governance at a press conference. As soon as hostilities were over, an elected body would draw up a new constitution that would see the 'complete transfer of responsibility from British to Indian hands'.[34] The British Government promised to honour whatever constitution the elected body decided, the only provisos being the right of any province to refuse to accede to the proposed union (thus opening the door to Pakistan) and a treaty between the new nation and Britain, guaranteeing the rights of racial and religious minorities. Until that day, the British Government invited India's political leaders to join the Viceroy's Executive Council during this 'critical period' and assume responsibility for organising the military, material and moral resources of the nation, though command of the armed forces would remain with the British Commander-in-Chief for the duration of the war.[35]

Although the offer was largely the same as that made by Linlithgow a year and a half earlier, the messenger – an independent socialist, known to be a friend of Congress – and the way he elucidated the message, during the ensuing question-and-answer session, underlined its sincerity:

Q. Will the Indian Union be entitled to disown its allegiance to the Crown?

A. Yes . . . The Dominion will be completely free either to remain within or to go without the Commonwealth of Nations.

Q. Will the Indian Union have the right to enter into a treaty with any other nation in the world?

A. Yes.

Q. What will be the power reserved to the British?

A. There will be no power reserved at all.

Q. Will Imperial troops be retained in this country?

A. No Imperial troops will be retained in this country except at the request of or by agreement with the new Indian Union or Unions.

Q. Exactly at what stage does the British Government propose to leave this country?

A. As soon as the constitution-making body has framed a new constitution.

Q. Will India be represented at the Peace Conference?

A. Certainly.[36]

For a while, agreement appeared tantalisingly close. A wrangle over interim defence responsibilities was solved by a formula devised by Louis Johnson. Nehru assured the presidential envoy that he was doing everything he could to reach a settlement. But the talks unravelled over the power of the Viceroy and the nature of the Executive Council. Cripps urged Congress leaders to seize the opportunity before them. An Indianised Executive Council would *be* the Government of India, he explained. The Viceroy would be emasculated; Linlithgow, he hinted, would be replaced. But old suspicions prevailed and on 10 April Congress rejected the proposals.

Cripps believed that Congress had come to the water's edge, stripped but refused 'to make the plunge because the water looks so cold'.[37] In reality, they were never as close to getting wet as their statements, both at the time and subsequently, suggest. Lack of faith in British promises was a major factor. Linlithgow was distrusted, while Churchill's insistence that the Atlantic Charter did not apply to the British Empire had a deplorable effect. Equally pertinent were doubts about Britain's staying power. Gandhi's aphorism that all Cripps was offering was a 'post-dated cheque' was given the journalistic addendum 'on a failing bank'.[38] Most important, however, were divisions within Congress. Whilst Rajagopalachari and his supporters wanted to work with the British, Nehru demanded nothing less than 'complete power'.[39] More critically, while Gandhi had left Delhi after his meeting with Cripps, his influence haunted the negotiations. As all members of the Congress Working Committee knew, the Mahatma's opposition to the proposals, which allowed for the 'vivisection of India', was adamantine.[40] Yet even if the constitutional offer had proved acceptable, his commitment to non-violence was no less absolute. For Gandhi and his legions of followers, the idea of co-operating with the British against the Japanese was never a possibility and Nehru and Rajagopalachari knew it. Faced with the prospect of splitting the nationalist movement in return for a 'dubious' deal with 'an Empire which is crumbling to dust', the Working Committee preferred the status quo.[41] And yet, as several historians have argued, by rejecting the opportunity to work with Jinnah and the Muslim League during the crisis, Congress forwent perhaps the last chance of avoiding partition.

Although Churchill did not wreck the Cripps mission (his telegram expressing doubts over the negotiations was not received until after Congress had rejected the offer), he did not repine over its demise. 'You have done everything in human power and your tenacity, perseverance and resourcefulness have proved how great was the British desire to reach a settlement', he wrote cheerfully to Cripps, adding that the effect throughout Britain and the United States was 'wholly beneficial'.[42] Commentary in the American press bore this out. 'For the first time the American public have woken to the fact that there are difficulties to be met in India besides British obstinacy and have been willing to place the major share of the blame on Indian shoulders,' wrote Halifax to the King.[43]

Not so the American President. Immediately following Congress' rejection of the British offer, Roosevelt's personal representative, Louis Johnson, had fired off an excoriating despatch, blaming London for the collapse of the negotiations. Within twenty-four hours, FDR's own censorious message was on Churchill's desk:

> The feeling is almost universally held that the deadlock has been caused by the unwillingness of the British Government to concede to the Indians the right of self-government . . . American public opinion cannot understand why, if the British Government is willing to permit the component parts of India to secede from the British Empire after the war, it is not willing to permit them to enjoy what is tantamount to self-government during the war.[44]

Churchill was livid. 'The string of cuss words lasted for two hours in the middle of the night,' Harry Hopkins (currently staying with the Prime Minister at Chequers) relayed to Secretary of War Stimson.[45] Warned that Churchill would rather resign than be pressured on India, Roosevelt retreated. However strong his feelings about empire, the war came first. With the Japanese marauding across the Pacific, Rommel advancing in Libya and a new German offensive expected on the Eastern Front, this was no time for disputes with America's closest ally.

Over the next six months, the Indian situation descended into violence as Gandhi launched the 'Quit India' movement in August, adding credence to Cripps' suspicion that the Mahatma 'was actually desirous to bring about a state of chaos while he sits at Wardha eating vegetables'.[46] Vast sit-ins occurred in the major cities. Mobs attacked police stations, post offices and government buildings. A direct challenge to the war effort arose when militants began cutting telegraph wires, destroying bridges and tearing up railway tracks. In the United Provinces, an aerodrome was burnt to the ground. In Bombay and Poona, bombs were detonated. Confronted by the worst crisis since the Indian Mutiny of 1857 and with the Japanese believed to be on the cusp of invasion, the British responded ruthlessly. Demonstrators were met with bullets and metal-tipped bamboo staves. Some 2,500 were shot dead. Houses were burnt, protesters whipped. Sixty-six thousand people were thrown into gaol, including Gandhi and Nehru.* Amazingly, recruitment to the Indian Army kept up and even increased. Muslims, extreme Hindu nationalist organisations such as Hindu Mahasabha and Rashtriya Swayamsevak Sangh as well as the so-called princely states disapproved of the demonstrations. The Army remained loyal. Yet despite British claims to the contrary, 'Quit India' was an overwhelmingly spontaneous mass movement, involving Indians of all classes and from all provinces and requiring the deployment of fifty-two infantry battalions to stop a series of wildfires from blazing into a full-scale inferno.

By the beginning of October, thanks to the severity of the suppression, order had been largely restored. In June, the US Navy had achieved a stunning victory over the Japanese Fleet off Midway Atoll, turning the tide of the war in the Pacific. As the Americans began to roll back the Japanese tsunami and the British made their first, tentative steps towards the reconquest of Burma, politicians and officials in London began to fantasise about an Imperial restoration. But more detached observers knew better. Between February and October 1942, Britain's Asian Empire had suffered a blow from which it would never recover.

---

* However brutal the British reaction, there is little doubt that the subcontinent would have suffered far greater atrocities under either the Germans or Japanese. There was only one solution to the Indian 'problem', Hitler told Lord Halifax in November 1937: 'shoot Gandhi', then 'if that does not suffice to reduce them to submission, shoot 200 and so on until order is established'.

XVIII

Fronts and Frontiers

We'll never forget you if you open the second front now but if anything
happens to Leningrad or Moscow before it comes, some of us will be
inclined to write it against you nearly as much as against the Germans.

Red Army officer to the night porter at the British Embassy in Moscow,
September 1941[1]

Stalin observed the war in the East with detached curiosity. Although
pleased to have gained the United States as an ally, his delight did
not extend to joining the democracies in their war against Japan.
While Hong Kong, Manila, Singapore and Sumatra fell to the
Japanese, the non-aggression pact between Moscow and Tokyo,
signed on 13 April 1941, held. When Anthony Eden visited Moscow
immediately following Pearl Harbor, the Soviet leader ventured that
the Red Army would soon be in a position to march against Hirohito's
expanding Empire. 'We can do nothing now but in the spring we
shall be ready and will then help,' he assured the British Foreign
Secretary.[2] But this was no foretaste of imminent military action.
Rather, as with subsequent promises, Stalin held out the prospect
of Soviet belligerency in the Far East to leverage his own *desiderata*
which, in the winter of 1941–42 and for the next two years, centred
on the twin issues of the second front and the USSR's post-war
frontiers.

The Eden visit arose out of Stalin's complaint that there was 'no
definite understanding' between Britain and the Soviet Union on
war aims, post-war planning or mutual military assistance.[3] Specifically, the dictator wanted the British to recognise the Soviet Union's
borders as they had existed at the time of the German invasion –
to approve the annexation of the Baltic States, Bessarabia and,

although he conceded that this could wait until a later date, a large slice of eastern Poland. When the unfortunate Eden, who had arrived in Moscow on 15 December 1941 with little beyond goodwill to offer, explained that he could not possibly agree to this without consulting his colleagues or the Americans (to whom the British had given a pledge not to enter into any unilateral post-war commitments), the Vozhd became fractious, reminding his guest that it was on this issue that negotiations with the Chamberlain Government had foundered in 1939. Following this threat – a reminder that the Soviets had come to an agreement with the Nazis in the past and could do so again – Stalin proceeded to browbeat Eden about the Baltic States for an hour and a half. Against this barrage of sophistry, intermingled with taunts and threats, the Foreign Secretary stood up reasonably well. After he returned to England, however, he wrote to Churchill urging him to accept Stalin's demands.

Justifying this startling *volte-face* – which contravened both Churchill's pledge to Roosevelt and the Atlantic Charter – Eden contended that the Baltic States had become the 'acid test of our sincerity and unless we can meet him [Stalin] on it his suspicions of ourselves and the United States Government will persist'. This was Cripps' argument. Another, advanced by the Ambassador, repeated by Eden, was that however much the democracies might shrink from endorsing acts of international brigandage, they were powerless to affect the situation on the ground: 'If [the] Russians are victorious they will be able to establish these frontiers and we shall certainly not turn them out', he wrote to Churchill.[4] Finally, there was the contention (again, first made by Cripps) that by recognising the 1941 frontiers, the British and the Americans would in fact be *limiting* Soviet expansion, confining the USSR to Europe's eastern rim, though the Red Army would (if victorious) be likely to occupy territory considerably to the westward. 'Personally', recorded the editor of the *Manchester Guardian*, after meeting Eden upon the latter's return from Moscow, 'he was convinced that Stalin's policy was that of a Peter the Great Russia and that we could, and therefore must, live with her [the USSR] in Europe. Stalin had convinced him that Russia was, and would be, reasonable in her aims.'[5]

Churchill was unimpressed. Having already made it clear that the

Anglo-Soviet alliance should function 'strictly on [the] basis of two people who have come together just to do this job', he wrote to Eden from Florida, where he was enjoying a few days' rest from the Arcadia Conference, to express his displeasure at the Foreign Secretary's conversion to Soviet-inspired *Realpolitik*:

> Your [telegram] surprised me . . . We have never recognised the 1941 frontiers of Russia except *de facto*. They were acquired by acts of aggression in shameful collusion with Hitler. The transfer of the peoples of the Baltic States to Soviet Russia against their will would be contrary to all the principles for which we are fighting this war and would dishonour our cause . . . In any case there can be no question of settling frontiers until the Peace Conference. I know President Roosevelt holds this view as strongly as I do and he has several times expressed his pleasure at the firm line we took at Moscow. I could not be an advocate for a British Cabinet bent on such a course.[6]

Churchill would later alter his position radically. For the time being, however, there was a serious split in the Cabinet, with Eden, supported by Cripps (from February 1942, Lord Privy Seal and Leader of the House of Commons) and the even more fanatical Beaverbrook, arguing in favour of concession and Churchill, supported by Attlee and Ernest Bevin, vehemently opposed. At the heart of the debate stood the difficulty of reconciling Soviet demands with American sensibilities. As Eden put it in a paper of 28 January 1942, 'Soviet policy is amoral, United States policy is exaggeratedly moral', at least, he added, 'where non-American interests are concerned'. Although the US could be relied upon to disapprove of secret agreements in general and secret agreements condoning acts of international piracy in particular, this had to be set against Britain's need to establish a constructive relationship with a European empire whose position at the end of the war might prove 'unassailable'.[7] As quid pro quo, Eden suggested that the British should require the Soviet Government to affirm that it sought no other territorial aggrandisement and should accept Stalin's remarkable proposal that Britain be granted the right to establish post-war air and naval bases in France and the Low Countries and so return to the Continent after a near 400-year absence.

Bitterly divided, the Cabinet agreed on 6 February 1942 to lay the whole problem before the Americans. The reaction was as forecast. Roosevelt thought Stalin's demands impossible to reconcile with the Atlantic Charter, while Sumner Welles argued that if the democracies were to yield on a fundamental matter of principle now there was nothing to prevent 'an indefinite sequence of further Russian blackmail later'.[8] This was the reply Churchill had originally sought. Since 6 February, however, Britain's military fortunes had declined precipitously, with Singapore surrendering on 15 February and the *Prince of Wales* and the *Repulse* at the bottom of the South China Sea. Faced with mounting calamities in the Far East, increasing criticism of his leadership at home and continual pressure from Eden, Cripps and Beaverbrook – the latter of whom had resigned on 19 February, ostensibly due to ill-health but also due to disagreements over Soviet policy – a tired and demoralised Churchill telegraphed Roosevelt on 7 March seeking permission to conclude an Anglo-Soviet treaty acceding to Stalin's demands.

Roosevelt's response was a gauche attempt to assume the lead in Western–Soviet relations. 'I know you will not mind my being brutally frank when I tell you that I think I can personally handle Stalin better than either your Foreign Office or my State Department,' he wrote to Churchill on 18 March. 'Stalin hates the guts of all your top people. He thinks he likes me better and I hope he will continue to do so.'[9] In fact, the Soviets resented the President's efforts to insert himself into the negotiations, Molotov having already informed the Soviet Ambassador to Washington, Maxim Litvinov, that the Politburo preferred 'to deal with one partner, namely the English'.[10] When Roosevelt informed the Ambassador of his opposition to frontier changes while the war was still in progress, the Soviet Government merely acknowledged the communication. According to Litvinov's version of the conversation – held in the White House on 12 March – the President explained frankly that the issue was less the sovereignty of eastern European states, more the sensitivities of US liberal opinion.[11] Six weeks later, he confirmed this departure from Wilsonian idealism, telling Assistant Secretary of State

Adolf Berle that he 'would not particularly mind about the Russians taking quite a large chunk of territory: they might have the Baltic republics and eastern Poland and even perhaps the Bukovina as well as Bessarabia'. When the appalled diplomat suggested that the Atlantic Charter might have some bearing upon the subject and that he hoped the 'President would not be getting generous with Scandinavia', Roosevelt simply laughed.[12] But the issue was serious. Less than a year after promising not to endorse territorial changes that did not accord with the freely expressed will of the people concerned – point two of the Atlantic Charter – the Western powers had demonstrated their willingness to condone Soviet empire building as well as the fissures in their own relationship. Stalin took note and pursued the logical course: ignoring Washington, while increasing the pressure on London, forcing the British to choose between him and the Americans.

Although the British resented the choice, their ire was directed towards the American President rather than the Soviet dictator. Roosevelt's interview with Litvinov (of which the British only heard the American version) was 'a dismal tale of clumsy diplomacy', minuted Eden, complaining that the President had shown 'no consideration for our views and has increased our difficulties'.[13] His left-leaning Private Secretary, Oliver Harvey, reminded his colleagues that the Soviet Union and Britain were allies '*before* [the] USA came in', while Sir Orme Sargent accused Roosevelt of trying to outlaw an independent British foreign policy.[14] Only Sir Alexander Cadogan stood against the tide of pro-Soviet, anti-American feeling within the Foreign Office. 'If we *knew* that compliance with Stalin's demand would make an essential difference to his conduct of the war, would ensure his loyal and intimate consultation and cooperation with us and would not merely lead to further demands, I should say that we could risk trouble in America,' he wrote in a departmental minute. 'But, personally, I feel little assurance on any of these points and I should be very much afraid of getting the worst of both worlds.'[15]

So it transpired. The British attempt to placate Washington by trying to insert a clause into the propsed treaty that would have allowed Estonians, Latvians and Lithuanians to emigrate rather than be incorporated into the Soviet Union was rejected by Moscow, while the decision to press ahead with the negotiations despite American objections provoked fury within the State Department, with Welles, Berle and Hull accusing the British of conniving at a 'Baltic Munich'.[16] Nor was criticism confined to Americans. Learning of the terms of the proposed treaty, a raft of MPs and Ministers rose in protest. 'I feel very hot on the subject', explained Victor Cazalet, Conservative MP for Chippenham and liaison officer with the Polish Government-in-Exile, in a letter to Halifax. 'If, because of the blackmail of Stalin today, we give way on this point, it seems to me we shall divide the nation in two, and what argument is there left against the Germans having taken the Sudetenland and, indeed, Danzig?'[17] His colleague Duff Cooper, recently returned from Singapore, agreed. 'Frankly, I can hardly believe that this is possible,' he remonstrated to Eden. 'Such an act on our part would tear into ribbons the Atlantic Charter and brand us the arch hypocrites of the world.'[18] Other anguished letters came from Harold Nicolson, the Archbishop of Westminster and the Lord Chancellor, John Simon – the man who, as Lloyd George once quipped, had sat so long on the fence that the 'iron had entered into his soul'. On 24 April, Churchill's Parliamentary Private Secretary, George Harvie-Watt, warned the Prime Minister of a growing Parliamentary revolt.[19]

Still, Eden persevered. On 20 May 1942, Molotov arrived in Britain to conclude the negotiations. Fifty-two years old – a decade younger than Stalin – with small, deep-set eyes, a cannonball head and a 'smile of Siberian winter', Vyacheslav Mikhailovich Skryabin was not, as one journalist put it, 'the kind of man you'd want to sit up with late over a bottle'.[20] Wooden, unyielding and unimaginative – despite his proficiency at the violin and incongruous penchant for the tango – he was, wrote Trotsky, 'mediocrity personified'; 'the incarnation of banality', according to the representative of the Polish Government-in-Exile.[21] As Stalin's right-hand man during the 1930s, he had justified his chosen soubriquet of 'Molotov' (meaning 'Hammer') through the alacrity with which he had participated in the purges, his loyalty unimpaired when the despot murdered his aides or, later, imprisoned his wife. A lifelong Anglophobe and Germanophile, it was Molotov who influenced, then implemented, the reorientation of Soviet foreign policy away from collective security and towards an understanding with Nazi Germany, culminating in the Molotov–Ribbentrop Pact of 23 August 1939. The Americans distrusted him, the British detested him. Cadogan considered him 'an ignorant and suspicious peasant'.[22] Yet there was no escaping him. From the moment of his appointment in May 1939, to his dismissal in 1949, he was the indomitable intermediary with whom they had to deal.

As Welles had predicted, Britain's willingness to accept Soviet absorption of the Baltic States merely increased Stalin's demands. As Molotov revealed on the second day of discussions, the despot was now demanding the British recognise the Soviet right to eastern Poland and post-war 'mutual assistance' pacts with Finland and Romania. Neither was acceptable to the British. In accordance with the terms of the 1939 Anglo-Polish Treaty, the British Government had publicly refused to recognise any territorial changes affecting the now occupied country, while agreeing to the latter proposal would be tantamount to endorsing the USSR's right to dominate two other neighbours. Faced with an impasse, Eden produced an alternative treaty that eschewed all mention of frontiers, merely offering a wartime alliance and twenty-year pact of friendship and co-operation. The Soviet reaction was glacial – Molotov exhibiting 'all the grace and conciliation of a totem pole'.[23] Then, on 25 May 1942, the Hammer astonished his hosts by accepting the new treaty.

Why did Stalin give way? Why, having won his point over the Baltic States, did he fail to collect? That the decision was Stalin's and Stalin's alone, there is no doubt. As Molotov commented when transmitting the alternative treaty to Moscow, 'We consider this treaty unacceptable, as it is an empty declaration which the USSR does not need.'[24] But Stalin disagreed:

> We do not consider it an empty declaration [he replied the following evening] but regard it as an important document. It lacks the question of security of frontiers but this is not bad perhaps, for it gives us a free hand. The question of frontiers, or to be more exact, of guarantees for the security of our frontiers . . . will be decided by force.[25]

This, as the British already appreciated, seemed a safe prediction. What the telegram does not explain, however, is why Stalin, having argued so strongly for recognition in December and then maintained the diplomatic pressure throughout the first four months of 1942, suddenly abandoned his core demands. The leading theory within the Foreign Office, repeated by some historians, was that the Soviets had been swayed by the intervention of the American Ambassador, John Winant, who emphasised Washington's hostility to any agreement involving frontier changes. Yet Winant's meeting with Molotov occurred at 10 p.m. on 24 May, three and a half hours after Stalin's telegram ordering the Foreign Commissar to accept the British proposals had been received. Although Soviet diplomats would later try to trade on the fact that they had 'met' American and British sensitivities on post-war issues, the real reason for the about-turn lay in the deteriorating situation on the Eastern Front.

Intoxicated by the success of the Soviet counteroffensive around Moscow, Stalin had ordered an advance along the entire front on 5 January 1942. The result was predictable. Tens of thousands of Soviet soldiers lost their lives and by March the Red Army's counterattack had stalled. At 4.15 a.m. on 8 May, the Germans launched Operation *Trappenjagd* ('Bustard Hunt'), leading to the annihilation of three Soviet armies in Crimea. Four days later, at Stalin's urging, Marshal Timoshenko initiated a pincer movement against German forces around Kharkov. Some 640,000 Soviet troops, 1,200 tanks and over 900 aircraft surged forward. On 17 May, however, the Germans counterattacked, causing the Soviets themselves to be encircled. Faced with disaster on his southern flank (Stalin learnt that the enemy had succeeded in trapping three rifle armies and one tank army on 22 May, two days before he sent his telegram to Molotov) and with a fresh German offensive expected against Moscow, the despot decided to focus his diplomatic efforts upon his more urgent need: the second front.

*

On 29 May, Molotov arrived in Washington. The idea for the visit had been Roosevelt's. Unable to arrange a meeting with Stalin (his request, submitted through Harriman to Maisky on 5 February, had gone unanswered), he had written to the Soviet leader on 11 April asking him to send his deputy to discuss 'a very important military proposal involving the utilisation of our armed forces in a manner to relieve your critical western front'.[26] The President's concern was genuine. As he told Morgenthau on 11 March, 'Nothing would be worse than to have the Russians collapse. I would rather lose New Zealand, Australia or anything else than have the Russians collapse.'[27] The problems were practical. As Roosevelt had explained to Churchill on 8 March, the US currently lacked the shipping to undertake the invasion of French North Africa (Operation Gymnast), let alone a cross-Channel assault. When General Marshall presented plans for an Anglo-American invasion of northern France (Operation Roundup) at the White House on 1 April, the earliest date at which it was admitted the thirty American and eighteen British divisions would be ready to sail was April 1943. Since this was obviously no use to the Russians in 1942, an alternative venture, Operation Sledgehammer, was conceived to land nine divisions on the Cherbourg peninsula in mid-September, should the situation on the Eastern Front appear desperate.

Fearful lest British opposition cause the Americans to repudiate the 'Germany First' strategy and concentrate on the Pacific, Churchill was outwardly welcoming of the proposals. At a meeting of the Defence Committee on 14 April, attended by Marshall and Hopkins (in London to 'sell' their strategy to the British), the Prime Minister declared that 'he had no hesitation in cordially accepting the plan'. The one caveat – so broad as to render this commitment dubious, if not suspect – was the pre-eminent need to defend India and the Middle East.[28] Three days later, Churchill sent Roosevelt an enthusiastic telegram, tinged with the same proviso:

> We wholeheartedly agree with your conception of concentration against the main enemy and we cordially accept your plan with one broad qualification. As you will see from [my telegram] of 15 April, it is essential that we should prevent a junction of the Japanese and the Germans [in the Middle East]. Consequently, a portion of our combined resources must, for the moment, be set aside to halt the

Japanese advance. This point was fully discussed at the meeting and Marshall felt confident that we could together provide what was necessary for the Indian Ocean and other theatres and yet go right ahead with your main project.[29]

In reality, the British had grave doubts about attempting a Continental landing in 1942 and even in 1943. As Major-General John Kennedy noted in his diary:

Any force which we could establish in France would be destroyed by the Germans at this time. They would be unlikely to divest anything from Russia till it suited them – it is not their system to be distracted from [the] main operation. They might well knock us out without moving anything from Russia for they have large forces in France already . . . The only hope for our force would be if the Russians knocked the Germans out . . . and *if* the Russians can knock the Germans out there is no point in our sending the force. We should be the laughing stock of the world if we had another evacuation.[30]

Kennedy's boss, Chief of the Imperial General Staff Sir Alan Brooke, concurred. Regarding Sledgehammer as 'just fantastic', he tried to educate Marshall – whom he considered 'a great gentleman and a great organiser but definitely not a strategist' – as to the immense difficulties of confronting the Germans in France.[31]* At the meeting between Marshall and the Chiefs of Staff on 9 April, he made clear his view that nine divisions were insufficient to maintain a bridgehead, while the Chief of the Air Staff, Sir Charles Portal, warned that the RAF could not provide adequate air cover for a landing at Cherbourg. Later, during dinner in Downing Street, Brooke left Hopkins in no doubt that he had 'a great many misgivings about our proposal'.[32]

Yet the British dared not go too far. Aware that a preponderance of Americans, including the Chief of Naval Operations, Admiral

---

* Marshall's first impression of Brooke – who, it should be pointed out, was scathing about virtually everyone in his diaries – was that he 'may be a good fighting man' but lacked 'Dill's brains'. He certainly lacked Dill's tact.

King, would prefer to focus on the war against Japan, they were loath to douse Administration enthusiasm for action against the main enemy. Moreover, they supported the build-up of American forces in the British Isles (Operation Bolero) – the prerequisite for operations in any European or African theatre. They therefore accepted the American proposals, the 1942 operation contingent upon the situation on the Russian front and the need to prevent the Japanese from invading India.

Later, when the cross-Channel attack was deferred in favour of a series of Mediterranean operations, senior American war planners, including Marshall and Stimson, accused their allies of wilful deceit. 'The British were masters in negotiations,' wrote Albert C. Wede-meyer, a member of the US Joint Planning Staff who attended the London conferences:

> Particularly were they adept in the use of phrases or words which were capable of more than one meaning or interpretation . . . When matters of the state were involved, our British opposite numbers had elastic scruples. To skirt the facts for King and Country was justified in the consciousness of these British gentlemen . . . There was no expressed opposition to Marshall's ideas at this first meeting – just polite sugges-tions that there might be difficulties in undertaking this task or that. What I witnessed was the British power of diplomatic finesse in its finest hour, a power that had been developed over centuries of success-ful international intrigue, cajolery and tacit compulsions.[33]

As this quotation, with its clichéd evocation of scheming, rapacious Limeys, as opposed to the plain-speaking, honest Yankees, implies, Wedemeyer – a Midwesterner of German and Irish descent – was an inveterate Anglophobe, a former supporter of 'America First' who blamed the British for dragging the US into the First World War. Yet the then Lieutenant-Colonel had a point. Although softly worded conditions had been laid, Churchill's reception of the American pro-posals had been enthusiastic, the Prime Minister even having gone so far as to suggest to Roosevelt that the Allies should be prepared to throw 'every available scrap of human and material resources' across the Channel *before* September 1942, should the need arise.[34]

To an extent, this may be interpreted as typical Churchillian exuberance. In his war memoirs, however, Churchill admitted an element of dissemblance: specifically, the failure to mention the invasions of French North Africa or Norway as alternative operations should, as seemed likely, Sledgehammer prove too risky. 'I had to work by influence and diplomacy in order to secure agreed and harmonious action with our cherished ally, without whose aid nothing but ruin faced the world', he wrote.[35]

This disingenuity was to have serious repercussions as American Army chiefs, enraged by what they regarded as rank duplicity, responded by recommending the very policy the British dreaded: the abandonment of Europe in preference for a 'Pacific First' strategy. Although largely a bluff – a petulant attempt to bring their ally to heel – the distrust was long-lasting. It also led to the belief that Churchill and Brooke were fundamentally opposed to a cross-Channel invasion: the conviction that, as Admiral King scornfully put it, the British would 'never go into Europe except behind a Scotch bagpipe band'.[36]

This was not the case. In order to achieve victory, neither Churchill nor the Chiefs of Staff ever doubted the need to confront the Wehrmacht in France. But multiple defeats bred caution, while an axiom of British strategy was to wear down the enemy through a succession of peripheral attacks before engaging his main force on land. Over the coming years, American war leaders would grind their teeth at what they regarded as a British obsession with diversions, 'periphery pecking' and Mediterranean island-hopping.[37] Yet Americans, as well as Britons, had reason to be grateful for Churchill's refusal to sanction an early cross-Channel attack: an effort which, certainly in 1942 and probably in 1943, would have resulted merely in estuaries of Allied blood. Despite legitimate criticism of some of his methods, it was among his greatest acts of the war.

Over dinner at the White House on 29 May, Molotov requested a second front capable of diverting forty German divisions from Russia that year. 'I . . . realised this was a completely impossible operation for them,' the Commissar claimed in retirement. 'But our demand was politically necessary . . . we had to press them for everything . . . for the sake of our people.'[38] Although the Secret

Service had been alarmed to discover a pistol among the Commissar's luggage (as well as a large chunk of black bread and a roll of sausage), his hosts were impressed by what they interpreted as their guest's strained attempts at amiability and Roosevelt described the Foreign Minister's request as 'a legitimate, reasonable demand'.[39] The following day, in a meeting attended by Molotov, Marshall and King, Roosevelt enquired 'whether developments were clear enough so that we could say to Mr Stalin that we are preparing a second front'.[40] Marshall replied that they were but privately cautioned the President against committing the democracies to a date. FDR ignored this advice. On 11 June, following Molotov's departure, the White House issued a communiqué announcing the Commissar's visit and declaring that 'full understanding was reached with regard to the urgent task of creating a second front in Europe in 1942'.[41]

Roosevelt's justification for this cavalier and fateful statement was the need to encourage the Soviets at a critical moment of the war. As the President told Morgenthau on 16 June, 'The whole question of whether we win or lose the war depends upon the Russians. If the Russians can hold out this summer and keep 3.5 million Germans engaged in war, we can definitely win.'[42] In promising more than he could deliver, however, he was committing the very sin he accused the British of. 'I do not want to be in the same position as the English,' he had informed his Treasury Secretary three months earlier. 'The English promised the Russians two divisions. They failed. They promised them help in the Caucasus. They failed. Every promise the English have made to the Russians, they have fallen down on.'[43] By pledging the Americans and the British to a European front in 1942, FDR was inviting a plague on both their houses.

*

Returning to London, where he hoped to extract a similar commitment for an autumn second front from the British, Molotov could take encouragement from the fact that public opinion was demonstrably on his side. The heroic resistance of the Red Army had caused the popularity of the Soviet Union to soar. Thousands of Britons attended rallies in the industrial cities and Trafalgar Square to express their solidarity with the USSR and call for increased military aid. Russian war poems – many by Stalin Prize winners – appeared in both left-wing and conservative periodicals and Tolstoy's *War and Peace* became a best-seller. Maisky, in social Siberia for almost two years, received over a hundred invitations in January and was made an honorary member of the Athenaeum club. (The *Evening Standard* fantasised about the Soviet Ambassador sitting down for a game of bridge with fellow members the Prime Minister, the Archbishop of Canterbury and the Governor of the Bank of England.) When Lord Beaverbrook issued a public call for a second front during a speech in New York – 'Strike out to help Russia! Strike out violently! Strike even recklessly!' – he received plaudits from both sides of the Atlantic.[44] Gallup opinion polls revealed support for this policy 'even if invading the continent this summer might cost more than invading next summer', while Major-General Kennedy noted that Stalin, whose portrait now adorned an alarming number of soldiers' bedsteads, was 'more of a hero than the King or even Winston'.[45] 'I'm afraid the public in our country are politically more unstable and immature than almost anywhere else', bemoaned Eden's Private Secretary, Valentine Lawford, in his diary. 'Their present line on the Soviets is almost sexual':

> I have never claimed to know exactly what to do about our Soviet allies, but it is quite clear what *not* to do. They are fighting for their existence – not for our blue eyes and they are in no position to ask us to do as they wish about the Baltic States, Finland, Poland and Romania and so on. Their victories – for which I thank God – are helping us endlessly but that is no reason why we should kow-tow to them as the press and public opinion seem anxious to do . . . At the end of it all, *we* are the real barrier to the spread over the world of the revolting Soviet doctrine which is to me indistinguishable (except that it is generally less efficient) from National Socialism. And I refuse to forget that for the first year and three quarters of the war, Russia did everything to make us lose it and only fought against our enemy because she [Germany] chose to attack her.[46]

Churchill shared these sentiments. Unmoved by the demonstrations, his views were summed up in doggerel by the Independent MP and humourist A. P. Herbert: 'Let's have less nonsense from the friends of Joe . . . In 1940, when we bore the brunt, / We could have done, boys, with a second front.'[47] When Molotov reported that Roosevelt had said it might be possible to risk 'a second Dunkirk and sacrifice 100,000–120,000 troops', the Prime Minister made it clear that under no circumstances would he agree to such futile butchery.[48] Britain was making preparations for a landing on the Continent but whilst 1943 appeared a fair prospect, there were no guarantees for 1942. In the meantime, Churchill drew attention to Western supplies to the USSR, despite the vulnerability of the Arctic convoys, and to the fact that Britain was already containing a not insignificant portion of the enemy's strength – nine Axis divisions in Libya and thirty-three German divisions in western Europe – though nothing compared to the 217 Axis divisions currently operating in Russia.

The steep decline in Allied military fortunes in June and July 1942, increased the gap between the Soviet demands and the ability of their Western allies to meet them. On 14 June, Rommel broke through the Gazala Line, forcing the British 8th Army to retreat and exposing Tobruk. Wavell's successor, General Claude Auchinleck, assured Churchill that he had no intention of surrendering the stronghold but on 21 June the garrison, which had withstood a 241-day siege the previous year, capitulated. Thirty-three thousand British and South African soldiers went into captivity. The fact that Churchill was at the White House at the time of the disaster compounded his humiliation. He was 'the most miserable Englishman in America since Burgoyne surrendered at Saratoga', he later told a group of senators and congressmen.[49] Roosevelt's response exemplified the attitude that would, ultimately, win the war for the Allies: 'What can we do to help?'[50] Churchill asked for as many Sherman tanks as the Americans could spare. Although they had only just been issued, 300 Sherman tanks and 100 self-propelled guns were stripped from the American 1st Armored Division and sent to the Middle East. Two weeks later, in a rare and less familiar act of generosity, Stalin agreed to the diversion of forty US Douglas Boston bombers, already *en route* to the USSR, to Egypt.

Considering the situation on the Russian front this was a remarkable act of Soviet–Western co-operation. On 28 June, the Wehrmacht had launched its long-awaited summer offensive. Some 1,900 tanks, 1,610 aircraft and 1.3 million men advanced on a line stretching between Kursk and the Sea of Azov, with the objective of seizing the oil fields of the Caucasus. Soviet High Command (the Stavka), expecting a renewal of the attack on Moscow and despite having obtained a copy of the German plan, was caught completely by surprise. Voronezh, an important communications centre 116 miles from the start line, was reached by 5 July. A fortnight later, Generaloberst Ewald von Kleist's 1st Panzer Army was on the lower Don. Rostov fell on 23 July. Hitler then made the catastrophic decision to expand the scope of the campaign, dividing his forces. Henceforth, while Army Group A, under Generalfeldmarschall Wilhelm List, would continue south towards the Caucasus, Army Group B, under Generaloberst Maximilian Freiherr von Weichs, was to proceed east and capture the city of Stalingrad. By 4 August, General Friedrich Paulus' 6th Army had advanced to within 60 miles of the city.

Meanwhile, Churchill had succeeded in persuading Roosevelt to abandon Sledgehammer and revive Gymnast – the invasion of French North Africa, renamed Torch. This decision, combined with the asperity with which Stalin responded to the news that Britain was suspending the Arctic convoys – after twenty-three ships were sunk from Convoy PQ 17 near Bear Island in July – convinced the Prime Minister that the time had come for a face-to-face meeting with his communist partner. The encounter was unlikely to be pleasant. Travelling to Moscow to tell Stalin that there would in fact be no second front in 1942 was like 'carrying a large lump of ice to the North Pole', Churchill reflected.[51] But the Prime Minister hoped that the frankness of his explanation – emphasised by the distance he had travelled to make it – and the revelation of Torch would go some way towards assuaging the dictator. On 2 August, despite War Cabinet concerns about his health, he therefore set off, accompanied by Brooke, Cadogan, Harriman, Ian Jacob, his physician, Sir Charles Wilson, his aide-de-camp, Tommy Thompson, and his Private Secretary, Leslie Rowan.

After a week in Cairo, during which he sacked Auchinleck and appointed General Harold Alexander as C-in-C Middle East and the little-known General Bernard Montgomery in charge of the 8th Army, Churchill flew to Tehran where, early on 12 August, he took off again to begin the nine-hour journey to Moscow. Flying over the Elburz Mountains and the eastern shore of the Caspian (to avoid List's Army group, already surging towards the Caucasus), he awarded Thompson 'ten demerits' for his failure to ensure that there was mustard in the luncheon basket. 'You should know that no gentleman eats ham sandwiches without mustard,' the Prime Minister scolded.[52] Far more serious than the lack of mustard was the fact that the other Liberator, containing Brooke, Cadogan and also Wavell and Air Marshal Tedder (who had joined the party in Cairo), had suffered engine trouble and been forced to return to Tehran. The thought of Churchill meeting 'the Ogre in his Den' without any of his senior advisers scared Cadogan stiff.[53]

Churchill arrived in Moscow shortly after 4 p.m. Although relatively comfortable by wartime standards, the Liberator did not disgorge its passengers with dignity. 'The first glimpse I had of the P.M.', wrote Cripps' successor as British Ambassador, the irreverent Sir Archibald Clark Kerr, 'was a pair of stout legs dangling from the belly of the plane and feeling for *terra firma*.'[54] Greeted by Molotov, a military band and a miscellany of commissars and generals, Churchill delighted his audience by making the 'V' for 'Victory' sign but was distressed when he subsequently learnt that this had been taken as a signal for the second front.[55] He was then driven to State Villa No. 7, eight miles outside the city. Unaware that this was Stalin's own dacha, the British explored their surroundings. Set in a wood of young spruce and Scots pine, the villa – a large, concrete bungalow, painted green – was protected by an inner and an outer wall, 'between which not even a mouse could have hidden', and a spanking new air raid shelter, serviced by electric lifts.[56] Inside, garish lighting revealed a décor of stylish utility, as well as a supper of red and black caviar, suckling pig, *hors d'oeuvres*, vodka and Russian wines. Clark Kerr was impressed by the vigour with which Churchill indulged. Later, however, the epicurean Prime Minister told Stalin that he had not expected such a feast or he would not have spoilt his appetite with mustard-less sandwiches. Ever alert to deception (real or imagined), the despot was unconvinced. 'Church-ill is such a hypocrite!' he exclaimed once the Prime Minister had left the Kremlin. 'He wants me to believe he got that paunch of his eating nothing but sandwiches in London.'[57]

Churchill's first meeting with Stalin took place in the Little Corner at seven o'clock that evening. In addition to Harriman and Clark Kerr, they were joined by Molotov, Marshal Kliment Voroshilov and two interpreters. Photographs of Marx and Lenin stared down from the walls. At Clark Kerr's suggestion, Church-ill began by delivering the bad news: there would be no European second front in 1942 but the Western powers were 'preparing for a very great operation in 1943'.[58] Stalin, who, Harriman noted, was looking older and greyer than when he had seen him almost a year ago, responded with gruff disappointment. What about a demonstration on the Pas-de-Calais? Churchill replied that he had considered such an action but, in a metaphor designed to appeal to a man who had murdered around a million Kulaks for supposedly hoarding grain, regarded it as 'a waste of seed corn.'[59] Stalin then began to heap scorn on the Prime Minister with statements such as 'You can't win wars if you aren't willing to take risks', 'You must not be so afraid of the Germans' and 'Experience showed that troops must be blooded in battle'.[60] Both men were 'very blunt', recorded Clark Kerr, 'as if each one sought by his bluntness to make a dint upon the other'. Stalin, on account of his bad hip but also to express his frustration, kept walking over to a writing table and delving for cigarettes, which he then proceeded to shred and stuff into his pipe, while Churchill, 'once he had "shot his bolt" ', also began to roam, plucking at the seat of his trousers, which, in the heat of the Little Corner, had evidently become stuck.[61]

A discussion about the bombing of German cities took the two men into calmer waters. 'Stalin agreed that this bombing [by the RAF] was of tremendous importance.' He wanted to 'blast the German workmen out of their homes'.[62] Churchill then unveiled Torch, drawing a picture of a crocodile to explain his concept of attacking the 'soft belly' as opposed to the hard snout of the Axis. When the Prime Minister had finished, the despot and former seminarian asked God to bless this enterprise. Stalin showed 'swift and complete mastery of a problem hitherto novel', declared Churchill in a telegram to Roosevelt the following day.[63] It never occurred to him that the dictator might have had foreknowledge of the plan – a far from inconceivable possibility given the number of highly placed Soviet agents in London and Washington. As with subsequent Allied conferences, it is unlikely that Western strategy, both diplomatic and military, was ever entirely 'novel'.

After four hours of discussion, Churchill returned tired but elated to State Villa No. 7. Relieved to have freed himself from the 'millstone' that the American communiqué had hung around his neck, he felt he was on course to establish 'a solid and sincere relationship with this man'.[64] The next day, however, everything was different. After a sticky meeting with Molotov in the morning, the British party – which now included Brooke, Cadogan, Wavell, Tedder and Jacob, though not Clark Kerr – returned to the Kremlin at 11 p.m. There, Stalin presented them with an *aide-mémoire* accusing the British of reneging on their commitments. Torch was now dismissed as irrelevant to the Soviet Union. Stalin complained that the democracies were falling behind with their supplies, claiming that the USSR only received the dregs of materiel. Lounging in his chair, eyes half closed, he then began to taunt his guest, impugning the bravery of the British Army.

To this string of insults, Churchill listened with remarkable forbearance. Resisting the temptation to remind the despot how the Nazi–Soviet Pact had allowed Hitler to divide Europe and initiate their current travails, he merely stated that he pardoned the despot's remarks 'on account of the bravery of the Russian Army'.[65] Eventually, however, his patience snapped. In what Tedder described as the 'most lucid, dramatic and forceful' oration he had ever heard, Churchill explained how he had 'come round Europe in the midst of my troubles. Yes, Mr Stalin, I have my troubles as well as you – hoping, hoping, I said, to meet the hand of comradeship . . . and I am bitterly disappointed. I have not met that hand.'[66]

Back at the villa, Churchill inveighed against the Soviet dictator. When Cadogan pointed out that the room was almost certainly bugged, he responded by declaiming for the benefit of the listening microphones: 'The Russians, I have been told, are not human beings at all. They are lower in the scale of nature than the orang-outang [sic].'[67] Stalin's change of attitude was hotly debated. 'One can hardly suppose', wrote Cadogan, 'that there is a body in the background to which Stalin has to pay deference and which can pull him up.'[68] And yet this is precisely what Churchill did suppose. 'I think the most probable [explanation] is that his Council of Commissars did not take the news I brought as well as he did,' he wrote to the War Cabinet, adding that these shadowy figures had, perhaps, more power than had hitherto been appreciated.[69]

The naïveté of this hypothesis – revealing an almost complete ignorance of Stalin's dictatorship and, ironically, echoing Chamberlain's explanation for Hitler's changes of temper – is astonishing. As Robert Bruce Lockhart – a Soviet expert who had served as Britain's first envoy to Bolshevik Russia – put it in a letter to Sir Orme Sargent in June 1940, evidence that the policy of the Soviet Government 'is the personal policy of Stalin himself and [that] he will brook no opposition, organised or potential' was so abundant as to require no 'further elaboration or emphasis'.[70] And yet the idea of rival powers operating behind the throne persisted in the minds of Churchill, Eden and Clark Kerr to the extent that, in July 1943, Churchill even speculated that he might enjoy greater liberty of action than the man who, as more perceptive observers understood, wielded more power than any Romanov. In reality, the Prime Minister was merely experiencing what had become standard Soviet negotiating technique: cordiality to begin with, hard bargaining in the middle, agreement at the end.

The next morning – Friday 14 August – Clark Kerr arrived at the dacha to find everyone 'scuttling about like startled hens'. Churchill said that he was 'damned' if he was going to keep his engagement and dine with Stalin that evening.[71] Although he eventually agreed to attend, he horrified the Ambassador by insisting on wearing 'a dreadful garment' that 'looked like a mechanic's overall or more still like a child's rompers'.[72] Churchill later claimed to have worn his siren suit to show 'how proletariat I was'.[73] But at the time it was an act of protest to which the 'bourgeois Bolsheviks', attired in neatly pressed uniforms or smart black suits, took great offence.[74]

The dinner was one of those gargantuan Russian affairs that Western visitors learnt to dread. Held in what had been Catherine the Great's bedroom (Clark Kerr enjoyed imagining 'the *ébats*' that had taken place there), over a hundred guests consumed a grotesque amount of food and even more drink, while outside ordinary Muscovites queued for bread.[75] Brooke was as disgusted by the 'orgy' as he was by his neighbour, Marshal Voroshilov. After at least a dozen toasts, the porcine-faced Marshal decided that his white vodka was no good and called for chilli-infused yellow vodka. He then proceeded to knock back two glasses in quick succession at which point 'his forehead broke out in beads of perspiration' and he slumped in his chair, sullen and uncommunicative. Further down the table, Lavrenti Beria – the 'Soviet Himmler' – got so drunk he ended up with his arm round Tedder. Surveying the scene and reflecting on the discussions of the previous evening, Brooke felt that British policy had been wrong from the start. 'We have bowed and scraped to them, done all we could for them and never asked them for a single fact or figure concerning their production, strength dispositions etc. As a result, they despise us and have no use for us except for what they can get out of us.'[76]

Stalin was trying to make himself agreeable. Sitting at the centre of the table, with Churchill on one side and Harriman on the other, he asked the former about British politics and expressed his sympathies over the Gallipoli debacle. In turn, Churchill, though clearly out of sorts, complimented Stalin on the goldfish at State Villa No.7. The despot duly offered to have them killed for the Prime Minister's breakfast. Leslie Rowan was impressed by Stalin. 'Small, sallow, with a dry but human smile, shifty eyes, great strength and a very full realisation of the great power over which he presides. A man to be trusted to beat the Germans, in fact *any enemy*,' he judged after observing him during dinner.[77] Although Brooke agreed, Jacob found it hard to reconcile 'this little peasant, who would not have looked at all out of place in a country lane with a pickaxe over his shoulder', with the Man of Steel: the revolutionary dictator who had condemned millions of Ukrainian, Belorussian and Russian peasants to death, had murdered some of his closest comrades and was now bent on obliterating the Nazi invaders.[78]

At 1 a.m., Churchill decided he had had enough. Still smarting from the insults of the night before, he declined Stalin's suggestion of a film and then made for the exit with such speed that the despot had to trot to keep up with him. His intention was to leave Moscow without seeing Stalin again. Appalled, Cadogan tried to reason with him. When this failed, Clark Kerr was deputed to speak to the Prime Minister. Taking Churchill on a walk around the dacha's garden the next morning, the Ambassador told the PM frankly that if his mission was a failure, 'it was his own fault'. He had not understood the Russians: 'He [Churchill] was an aristocrat . . . They were straight from the plough or the lathe. They were rough and inexperienced. They did not discuss things as we discussed them. They thought aloud and, in thinking aloud, they said many harsh and offensive things.' Churchill, who had got it into his head that Stalin was trying to destroy his Government, stopped stumping through the fir trees. 'The man has insulted me. From now on he will have to fight his battles alone.' Clark Kerr retorted that the situation was too important to allow for hurt feelings. He must 'sweep away all that', he must 'make friends with Stalin'.[79]

At 7 p.m., Churchill was back at the Kremlin. Not expecting the meeting to last long, he had asked the commander of the recently formed Polish Army in the East, General Władysław Anders, to dine with him at 8.30 p.m.. For an hour, the two leaders surveyed the war. Then, just as Churchill was rising to leave, Stalin invited him for drinks in his personal quarters. There they found an old female retainer and the dictator's sixteen-year-old-daughter, Svetlana. Stalin uncorked an alarming number of bottles and started filling glasses. Soon, food began to appear. Just radishes at first, then chicken, beef, mutton, fish and suckling pig. Then the dictator asked, 'Why should we not have Molotov? He is worrying about the communiqué. We could settle it here. There is one thing about Molotov, he can drink.'[80]

Conversation was free and wide-ranging. The two men talked over the Arctic convoys and agreed to conduct a joint operation against northern Norway in November. Stalin listened as Churchill extolled the military prowess of his ancestor, John Churchill, Duke of Marlborough, and then, revealing his humour as well as his sense of history, suggested that England had found an even greater general in the Duke of Wellington. When Cadogan arrived with the

communiqué around 1 a.m., he found the Prime Minister questioning the dictator about the collective farms and the liquidation of the
Kulaks. Revealingly, Stalin confessed that the policy he had overseen
between 1928 and 1933, creating a famine that had killed an estimated
5.7–8.7 million people, was more trying even than the war. But it
'had' to be done. 'We had to do it to mechanise our agriculture.'
Besides, he added in a chilling aside, 'what is one generation?'[81]

Churchill returned to State Villa No. 7 at 3.15 a.m., intoxicated.
Having dismissed the unfortunate Anders, telling him to meet
him in Cairo, he flung himself down on a sofa and began to regale
Wilson and Clark Kerr with tales from the evening. His attitude
to Stalin was transformed. It was now a 'pleasure' to work with
'that great man'.[82] He had been 'taken into the family' and the two
men had parted as friends.[83] The next day, he informed Roosevelt
and the War Cabinet that he was 'definitely encouraged' by his visit
to Moscow. The greatest goodwill had prevailed at his final meeting
with Stalin and the two men had got on easy and friendly terms.
'I feel that I have established a personal relationship which will be
helpful', he wrote, adding that Stalin was now 'entirely convinced
of the great advantages of Torch'.[84]

Jacob was full of admiration for the way Churchill had conducted
himself. He was, however, doubtful about the Prime Minister's
claim to have established a friendship with the Soviet dictator. 'I am
bound to say that I don't believe that it is possible to make friends
with a man like Stalin,' he recorded in his diary. 'The thing that
impressed me most about Stalin was his complete self-possession
and detachment. He was absolute master of the situation at all
times and appeared to be cold and calculating . . . He would have
his closest associate shot without the smallest compunction, if he
calculated that it was necessary . . . I should say that to make friends
with Stalin would be equivalent to making friends with a python.'[85]

Jacob's scepticism had been augmented by the evening he had
just spent with General Anders. A tall, good-looking man, with
high cheekbones and a shaved head, Anders had been awarded
the Silver Cross of the *Virtuti Militari* for his role as a cavalry commander during the Polish–Soviet War of 1919–21. Captured by the
Red Army on 29 September 1939, having fought with equal dis-

tinction against the invading Germans, he was taken to Lubyanka prison in Moscow, where he was interrogated and tortured by the NKVD. Released shortly after Hitler invaded the Soviet Union in June 1941, he was tasked with forming a new Polish army from the hundreds of thousands of Polish soldiers currently languishing in labour camps scattered about the USSR. By the end of October 1941, some 46,000 men had reported to Polish military headquarters in Buzuluk. Although sufficient for two infantry divisions and a reserve regiment (Soviet authorities claimed they were unable to provide rations for more), this represented only a quarter of the 196,000 Polish prisoners of war deported to the Soviet Union between September and October 1939. Of particular concern was the fate of around 15,000 Polish officers and POWs, known to have been captured by the Red Army but who now appeared to have vanished. Enquiries by Anders and the recently appointed Polish Ambassador, Stanisław Kot, were stonewalled. The officers had been released or were in Germany, the Soviet authorities insisted. When General Władysław Sikorski, Prime Minister of the Polish Government-in-Exile, challenged Stalin directly, in December 1941, the despot suggested that the officers had 'escaped' to Manchuria.[86] They had simply 'run away', he later told Anders.[87] It would not be long before the awful truth was revealed.

XIX

The Flickering Torch

Darlan gave me Algiers, long live Darlan! If Laval gives me
Paris, long live Laval!

Franklin D. Roosevelt, 20 November 1942[1]

Just after midnight on 22 October 1942, five American officers and
three British commandos clambered out of a submarine and into four
highly precarious canoes. Silently, they paddled for 2 miles until they
reached a wide beach below a steep bluff. Here, they jumped into
the surf and, lifting their canvas boats out of the water, made for the
darkness of the elevation. The beach was deserted. On reaching the
edge of the bluff, however, they became aware of figures emerging
from the scrub and olive trees. No lights were shown. Then, to the
intense relief of the canoeists, a tall silhouette stepped forward and in
an American accent said, 'Welcome to North Africa.'[2]

So began one of the strangest conferences of the war. The location
was a remote farmhouse near the Algerian town of Cherchell. The
principal cast consisted of Major-General Mark Clark, deputy to the
recently appointed Supreme Commander of the Allied Expeditionary Force, General Dwight D. Eisenhower, and Brigadier-General
Charles Mast, Chief of Staff to the French 19th Army Corps based
at Algiers. Attending the former were four senior American planners, while the latter was accompanied by a coterie of pro-Allied
French officers, as well as representatives of an anti-Vichy conspiracy ring known as 'The Five'. The meeting had been arranged by
President Roosevelt's personal envoy Robert Murphy. Its purpose
was to discuss the possibilities of co-operation between French
North African forces – some 120,000 officers and men nominally
loyal to Vichy – and an American expeditionary force.

Mast was representing General Henri Giraud. One of the most senior generals in the French Army, this swashbuckling patriot had been captured by the Germans while undertaking a reconnaissance mission on 19 May 1940. Imprisoned in the ancient fortress of Königstein, near the old Czechoslovak border, he had escaped by shaving off his moustache, donning a Tyrolean hat and, despite his sixty-three years and gammy leg, abseiling down the wall of the castle. On 29 April 1942, he presented himself at Vichy. Revolted by the defeatism he found there, he was soon in touch with Mast, The Five and the Allies about renewing French military resistance.

Clark confirmed what Mast already knew: the Allies were planning a major intervention in North Africa. Sitting around the kitchen table in the farmhouse, the two sides agreed to put 'their cards on the table; that there would be no holding back of information, no lies'. As Clark recorded in his diary, 'That's when I started lying like hell!'[3] Asked about the size of the operation, the Deputy Supreme Commander stated that the Americans intended to land half a million troops, supported by 2,000 aircraft. If Mast was sceptical, he hid it. Assuring Clark of his willingness to facilitate such an operation, he repeated the claim, already made to Murphy, that Giraud could rally the Army of North Africa without a shot being fired. There were only two conditions: Giraud must be placed in overall command and the conspirators would have nothing to do with Admiral Darlan, no longer Pétain's deputy but still responsible for the French armed forces. When Clark asked about Mast's immediate superior, General Alphonse Juin, Commander-in-Chief in French North Africa, the Frenchman was contemptuous: 'P-f-ft,' he exclaimed, making a breaking motion with his hands, 'I'll handle him just like that.'[4]

The conference then descended into farce. Convinced that there was some sort of smuggling operation taking place, one of the villa's Arab servants had tipped off the police. The news that the authorities were on their way caused pandemonium. 'Officers ran in every direction,' recalled Clark. 'Some of the Frenchmen changed into civilian clothes with a speed I have seen exceeded only by professional quick-change artists. Before I had quite decided what was going on one of General Mast's officers ran past me with a suitcase in one hand out to his car, which immediately took off in the direction of Algiers.

Other Frenchmen went out of the windows and disappeared into the brush along the beach.'⁵ Clark and his officers hid in the wine cellar, while Murphy and the proprietor staged an elaborate performance of drunken revellers at the end of a party. At one point, one of the British commandos was seized by a coughing fit. 'General, I'm afraid I'll choke!' spluttered the unfortunate man. 'I'm afraid you *won't*,' hissed Clark, handing him a well-worn piece of chewing gum.⁶

Eventually, the police departed and the Americans, along with their British pilots, hastened to the beach. Here there was more trouble as the surf was too rough to launch the canoes. After several aborted attempts, during which Clark lost his trousers (a story he would later dine out on), they reached the submarine, which, after one day's sailing, rendezvoused with a flying boat that conveyed them to Gibraltar.

Clark considered the conference a great success. Mast's conception of an Allied landing tallied so closely with the Allies' actual plan that, as one of the American party remarked, it was almost as if he had 'read a copy of Torch'.⁷ The French delegation had handed over a mass of information on troop dispositions, landing sites, fuel depots and airfields. Most importantly, Mast had emphasised his belief that, with Giraud at the forefront of the operation, the Allies would be able to land on the North African shore unopposed. Yet there had also been misinformation and deception within the meeting. Wittingly or not, Mast had exaggerated both his own influence and that of Giraud, while Clark had inflated the size of the Allied expeditionary force fivefold. Most crucially, the American had not revealed the date for the landings. The conspirators, who requested a minimum of ten days' notice, believed that this lay some time off, possibly in the early spring of 1943. In fact, the convoy carrying General George S. Patton's Western Task Force was due to sail from Chesapeake Bay in just thirty-six hours.

★

The decision to postpone a cross-Channel invasion in favour of a North African operation had placed a severe strain on Anglo-American relations. Reacting to the news that the War Cabinet had finally decided against Sledgehammer, Secretary of War Henry Stimson (no Anglophobe) railed against a 'fatigued and defeatist government . . .

blocking the help of a young and vigorous nation'. 'The British leaders have lost their nerve', the War Secretary recorded in his diary, adding that 'this war, if it is to be won, must be won on the morale and the psychology and courage of the American forces and leaders'.[8]

General Marshall agreed. Enraged that a decision he believed had been taken in March had been reopened in June and then rejected in July, he presented Roosevelt with a memorandum, endorsed by Admiral King, recommending a complete reorientation of American strategy towards the Pacific. If, as the US Army Chief later claimed, this was largely a bluff, FDR called it, demanding a comprehensive outline of such a strategy. When Marshall produced a skimpy document on 13 July – the first line of which admitted that there was no 'detailed plan for major offensive operations in the Pacific' – the President said that the Joint Chiefs' attitude amounted to 'taking up your dishes and going away'.[9] He even requested that the record be altered 'so that it would not appear in later years that we had proposed what amounted to the abandonment of the British'.[10] Roosevelt insisted on American forces engaging the principal enemy before the end of the year – preferably before the mid-term elections – and if this could not be done in Europe, then it must be done in Africa. On 25 July, he gave the order for Torch to proceed, 'full steam ahead'.[11]

The operation would be the ultimate test of America's Vichy policy. Up to this point, the benefits of Washington's controversial decision to buttress Pétain's collaborationist regime through aid and diplomatic representation had been negligible. American 'influence', much vaunted by Secretary of State Cordell Hull and later by the State Department's apologetic historian William L. Langer, had not prevented Darlan from seeking to tie France's future to Germany's war effort, nor the Luftwaffe from using Syrian airfields to strafe British troops. For a long time, Roosevelt and the State Department had pinned their hopes on General Weygand but this dyspeptic desk officer was neither as pro-Allied nor as courageous as US diplomats liked to imagine. Although happy to subsist on American supplies, the Délégué Général en Afrique Française showed no interest in re-entering the war and presided over an increasingly authoritarian regime that imprisoned Gaullists and excluded Jews from many aspects of civilian life. When the Germans, despite these credentials, prevailed on Pétain to dismiss him in November 1941, the Americans were disappointed but stoical. US supplies of food and fuel to France's North African colonies continued – albeit sporadically – at the same time as Rommel was receiving trucks, artillery, shells and oil through French Tunisian ports. When German forces repulsed an Anglo-Canadian raid on the port of Dieppe, on 19 August 1942 – resulting in more than 3,000 Allied casualties – Pétain thanked Hitler for 'cleansing French soil of the invader', while Laval, reappointed as Premier in April – the event that finally suspended the US supply programme and precipitated the American Ambassador's recall – used the attack as leverage to strengthen French defences in North and West Africa.[12]

The concierge for America's Vichy policy was Robert Murphy. Tall, with broad shoulders, a sharkish grin and a receding hairline, this genial consular official had been hoicked out of well-deserved obscurity by the fall of France. Counsellor at the American Embassy in Paris when the Germans invaded, he soon found himself representing his country at the insipid spa-town. In December 1940, Roosevelt had appointed him as his personal representative to French North Africa, tasked with rekindling the spirit of resistance. The British disliked and mistrusted him. Considering him a confirmed Vichyite, a snob and social climber, all too at ease in French North Africa's reactionary, Catholic milieu, he had, as his colleague Harold Macmillan later noted, 'neither principles nor judgement'.[13] In February 1941 he had negotiated the North African supply programme. Known as the Murphy–Weygand Accord, the most noteworthy benefit of this deal (as far as the Allies were concerned) was that it allowed the US to despatch twelve 'Vice-Consuls' to the region. Ostensibly responsible for ensuring that American goods did not end up in Axis hands, these 'diplomats', as French and German intelligence well knew, were really spies, who flitted about Morocco, Algeria and Tunisia, making contacts and reporting on military and political dispositions. Although Murphy's so-called 'apostles' were distinctly amateur – their number included a banker, a jeweller, a Parisian playboy and a Coca-Cola salesman – the information they provided was taken seriously, in particular the 'news' that 35,000 Frenchmen in Algeria stood ready for 'offensive action' the moment an American armada appeared.[14] Meanwhile, Murphy cultivated, or rather was cultivated by, The Five, a somewhat disreputable band of right-wingers, all of whom insisted that Giraud was the man to lead a North African revolt. The proof would come on 8 November 1942.

American fears that they may have backed the wrong horse emerged within minutes of Giraud setting foot on Gibraltar. Picked up by submarine off the French coast near Marseilles, the General had no sooner arrived at Eisenhower's headquarters, deep within the bowels of the Rock, on the evening of 7 November, than he demanded to be placed in complete control of the operation. When Eisenhower explained that this was impossible, that the landings were due to take place in under eight hours, the Frenchman refused to broadcast in support of the invasion. For six hours, the Supreme Allied Commander and his Deputy argued with the French General. Eisenhower offered Giraud the command of all French forces in the region, while Clark spelt out the alternative: 'If you don't go along, General Giraud, you're going to be out in the snow on your ass!'[15] Shortly after midnight 'Ike' sent his superiors this bleak assessment of the situation:

> My impression, shared by the *Eagle* [Clark] and [Admiral] Cunningham is that *Kingpin* [Giraud] is playing for time and that he is determined, knowing that there will be some French resistance, not to lay himself open to the charge of being in any way responsible for the shedding of French blood . . . *Eagle* and I are bitterly disappointed, principally because of the help *Kingpin* could have rendered except for his intense personal ambition and ego.[16]

Meanwhile, Murphy and his cohort of conspirators moved to occupy strategic points and detain senior officials in Algiers. The coup was ill co-ordinated and no better equipped. Clark had promised to supply the Resistance with Bren guns but Britain's Special Operations Executive had failed to deliver them. Mast, responsible for the military aspect of the operation, took himself off to one of the landing sites without telling anyone. Nevertheless, over 300 volunteers (many Algerian Jews), armed with antique rifles and a solitary Sten gun, succeeded in seizing the police station, telephone exchange and Préfecture. At around 12.30 a.m. on 8 November, Murphy presented himself at the Villa des Oliviers, where he informed a pyjama-clad

General Juin that an expeditionary force of 'half a million' American troops would shortly be landing along his coastline. Juin, who had lost the use of his right arm during the First World War, was extremely agitated by the news. After pacing the floor for some time, he came to the crux: although he, personally, was prepared to co-operate with the Americans, Darlan was in Algiers (visiting his son, who had been stricken by polio) and could countermand any order he gave. 'Very well,' responded Murphy, 'let us talk with Darlan.'[17]

The adventitious presence of Admiral Darlan offered opportunities as well as complications. On the one hand, Darlan was a duplicitous collaborator: the author of the 'Paris Protocols'; the official who had allowed the Luftwaffe to refuel at French-Syrian airbases; the man who had told the American Chargé d'Affaires, in December 1940, that he preferred a German to a British victory. On the other, he was Commander-in-Chief of all Vichy fighting forces: the figure who could, should he wish, ensure the Allies an unopposed landing and rally the French Fleet at Toulon. Indeed, while there is no truth in the claims that the Admiral's presence in Algiers at the time of Torch was anything other than a freak coincidence, the Americans had given serious consideration to involving him in their scheme.

By early 1942, Darlan had begun to doubt his previously unshakeable faith in German victory and decided to hedge his bets. In April, he authorised his friend Admiral Fenard and son, Alain, to inform Murphy that he wished to open secret talks with the Allies about a resistance plan for southern France. In September, he informed the American Minister, via the head of French North African military intelligence, that he would co-operate with the Americans, provided they arrived in sufficient strength. The Allies weighed this information carefully. Eisenhower wondered whether Darlan would work with Giraud, while Churchill declared that he would crawl on his hands and knees for a mile to meet the Admiral if by so doing he could obtain the remnants of the French Fleet.[18] Ultimately, the Allies decided not to try and incorporate Darlan into their plans but their decision stemmed from Mast and Giraud's refusal to collaborate with him, not from objections about his political record. Indeed, at no point did Washington or London ever state that the Admiral was beyond the political pale, while Roosevelt's instructions to Murphy authorised him to deal with any Frenchman 'whom you consider reliable'.[19] The 'Darlan deal' was thus simultaneously *ad hoc* and premeditated.

Darlan took the news of the approaching Allied force even worse than Juin. 'I have known for a long time that the British are stupid but I always believed Americans were more intelligent,' he raged to Murphy. 'Apparently you have the same genius as the British for making massive blunders!'[20] Unsure whether the American Minister was telling the truth – were half a million Americans landing along the North African coast or was this a raid like Dieppe or a bluff like Dakar? – he refused to act without instructions from Pétain. His mood was not improved by the fact that the Villa des Oliviers (to which he had been invited) had since been occupied by the insurgents. At 3 a.m., the harbour guns started firing.

Between 12.45 a.m. and 8 a.m. on 8 November 1942, 107,000 American and British troops landed at nine beaches in and around Algiers, Oran, Casablanca, Safi and Fedala. That the landings came as a surprise, both to Vichy and to the *Oberkommando der Wehrmacht* (OKW), was miraculous. Six hundred and seventy vessels were involved in Operation Torch, 102 sailing straight across the U-boat-infested waters of the Atlantic to the Moroccan coast. At Gibraltar, the build-up of naval forces was so great that the British Vice-Consul was summoned to appear before General Fernando Barrón. 'I have been trying to emulate your famous Admiral Lord Nelson', the Spaniard explained, 'but if I was blind in *both* eyes I could hardly fail to see those ships lying off our coast.'[21] Barrón urged the British to move them to a less conspicuous anchorage before he was forced to report their presence to Madrid.

Torch, indeed, provided eloquent justification for Sir Samuel Hoare's Spanish policy. When British Intelligence learnt that the Germans were installing a radar and infra-red detection station near the Bay of Gibraltar the Ambassador reminded Franco that he relied on Allied goodwill for the oil on which his regime depended. The station was dismantled. Later, when the Caudillo was informed about the landings, he took the news calmly, accepting Anglo-American assurances that the Allies would respect the neutrality of Spanish Morocco. On the night of 5 November, the convoys carrying the Centre and Eastern Task Forces had passed through the Strait of

Gibraltar. Clearly visible from the North African shore, they were assumed to be heading for Malta, to attack Sicily or to reinforce the British 8th Army, currently driving Rommel from Egypt following the second Battle of El Alamein. Yet whilst the landings achieved complete surprise, hopes that Vichy forces would offer little or no resistance proved baseless. At Algiers, Oran and Casablanca, the Vichy French fought back fiercely. 'At 7.15 a.m., six enemy destroyers came out of Casablanca', recorded General Patton in his diary:

> All ships in range opened on them and they went back. The *Massachusetts* had been shelling the *Jean Bart* for about thirty minutes. I was going ashore at eight and my boat was on the davits [of the USS *Augusta*] with all our things, including my white pistols. I sent an orderly to get them and at that moment a light cruiser and two big destroyers came out of Casablanca, tearing up the coast close to the shore, to try and get our transports. The *Augusta* speeded up to twenty knots and opened fire. The first blast from the turret blew our landing boat to hell and we lost everything except my pistols. At about 8.20 a.m., enemy bombers attacked the transports and the *Augusta* went to protect them. Then we went back into the fight with the French ships and fired hard for about three hours ... It was hazy and the enemy used smoke well. I could just see them and make out our splashes with our ships all firing like hell and going in big zigzags and curves to keep the enemy from our submarines.[22]

At Port Lyautey, near the mouth of the Sebou River, American Stuart light tanks were met by Renault R35s while, at Oran, almost 200 GIs and over 100 Royal Navy sailors were killed trying to storm the harbour. The defenders showed no qualms about firing on US soldiers. This surprised the Americans, who had insisted on concealing British participation – amounting to around a third of ground forces and more than half of naval forces – in the mistaken belief that the defenders would fire on the Limeys but welcome the Yanks. British commandos, pressed into US Army uniforms, were fired upon, while military police attempting to secure the Fedala beachhead were mown down shouting, 'We're Americans!'[23]

Murphy had failed to persuade Darlan to order a general ceasefire.

Liberated from the Villa des Oliviers by a detachment of the *Garde Mobile*, he and Juin had headed to Fort l'Empereur where they proceeded to organise an admittedly half-hearted resistance but which included accepting an offer of Axis air support. Around this time – 7 a.m. in Vichy, 8 a.m. in Algiers – Pétain was woken and approved a telegram, prepared by Laval, to send to Roosevelt: 'We are attacked. We shall defend ourselves. This is the order I am giving.'[24] Within a few hours, Algiers was back in Vichy hands. Giraud's name proved nugatory. Mast's men rallied to General Koeltz and General Roubertie, while, in Morocco, Résident Général Charles Noguès overcame his own internment to arrest the handful of pro-Giraud conspirators and order vigorous resistance against the Americans. When Giraud (who had agreed to Eisenhower's terms late on the morning of 8 November) arrived at Blida airfield, 25 miles south-west of Algiers, on the second day of the operation, he was greeted not by General de Monsabert and the 1st Algerian Tirailleurs as expected but by a young Vichy Colonel who explained that he had agreed to a temporary ceasefire but could regain the airfield from the Allies if so ordered. 'But all this is stupid!' exclaimed Giraud. 'It is not a question of preventing the use of the landing strip . . . On the contrary, it must be made operational again.' Politely, the Colonel explained that he would obey these orders when they reached him through the channel of his direct superiors.[25] 'The actual state of existing sentiment here does not – repeat not – agree even remotely with some of [our] prior calculations,' Eisenhower balefully signalled the Chiefs of Staff.[26]

By this time, Darlan had realised that further resistance was futile. The Vichy forces could inflict multiple casualties upon the invaders but they could not turn back the Allied tide. Returning to the Villa des Oliviers at 3 p.m. on 8 November, he asked Murphy to establish contact with Major-General Charles Ryder, commander of the Eastern Task Force. By early evening a local ceasefire was in place although fighting continued in Oran and Morocco. At 5 p.m. on 9 November, Clark flew into Algiers' Maison Blanche airfield. Realising that Darlan was the man to deal with, he arranged to meet the Admiral, along with Juin and Admiral Fenard, the following morning. The fact that Eisenhower had just promised the command of all French Forces and the Governorship of French North Africa to Giraud was awkward

but, for the moment, irrelevant. The purpose of Torch was to allow
the Allies to attack Rommel's *Afrika Korps* from the rear. For this,
they needed to occupy Tunisia before the Germans. For this, they
needed to stop fighting the Vichy French. And for this, they needed
Darlan.

Clark approached the negotiations with all the subtlety of a
Sherman tank. Desperate to get on with the real battle, he emphasised his demands by swearing and banging his fist on the table.
At one point he threatened to throw the entire cadre of senior
Vichyites – 'yellow-bellied sons-of-bitches' as he referred to them
privately – in gaol and impose an American military government
over the whole of French North Africa.[27] Later, during a break in the
negotiations, Darlan asked Murphy to remind the Major-General
that he, Darlan, was a five-star admiral and should 'stop talking to
me like a lieutenant junior grade'.[28]

Insulted or not, the diminutive sailor, with his 'watery blue eyes
and petulant lips', proved more than a match for the lanky American:

> Clark: It is essential we stop this waste of time and blood.
>
> Darlan: I sent a résumé of the armistice terms to Vichy. Laval was
> absent from Vichy. There will be no reply until the Council of Min-
> isters meets this afternoon . . .
>
> Clark: I am negotiating with you as commander of the troops on
> the ground. I am not prepared nor do I propose to await any further
> word from Vichy.
>
> Darlan: I want to make it clear that I am not here in a[ny] capacity
> of the French Government. I can simply obey the orders of Pétain.
>
> Clark: Then I will have to break off the negotiations and deal with
> someone who can act . . . If the Admiral will not issue orders for the
> cessation of hostilities, I will go to General Giraud . . .
>
> Darlan: I am not certain the troops will obey. This will mean the
> loss of more time and there will be more fighting . . .
>
> Clark: This all boils down to one question. Are you going to play
> with the Vichy Government or go with us?
>
> Darlan: I am simply bound by an oath of fidelity to the Maréchal
> to obey his orders. I can't take the responsibility of giving an order
> to cease hostilities.[29]

While this quasi-Socratic dialogue continued, German troops were pouring into Tunisia. The OKW had demanded the use of French air-bases late on the night of 8 November and Laval had given his consent. The Vichy Vice-Premier had then set off on a torturous, fog-ridden journey to Berchtesgaden, where he hoped to persuade Hitler to preserve some measure of French autonomy. Darlan's filibustering was designed to facilitate these negotiations. Labouring under the delusion that it was still possible to maintain the *zone libre*, even to improve the French lot, he messaged Admiral Auphan on the eve of his meeting with Clark to say that the price for co-operating with Germany in defence of North Africa was the replacement of the armistice with 'another political arrangement which would let us recover our possibilities.'[30] Later, he telegraphed Admiral Esteva in Tunisia and Admiral Derrien in Bizerte: 'The Americans having invaded Africa *first* are our adversaries and we must fight them *alone or with assistance*.'[31]

Fortunately, Juin was able to bring Darlan to his senses. At 11.05 a.m. on 10 November 1942 – fifty-eight hours after the landings had begun and after some 500 Americans, 570 Britons and 1,300 Vichy French had been killed – the trimming Admiral issued orders for French forces to stop resisting the Allies and return to barracks. This directive was swiftly countermanded by Pétain, although a secret, conciliatory message from Auphan would burnish the myth that the Maréchal was playing a 'double game' – collaborating with Hitler while secretly supporting the Allies.

Clark pleaded with Darlan to rally the Toulon Fleet. Still playing for time, the Admiral refused. In the early hours of 11 November, 200,000 German troops, supported by tanks and artillery, crossed into hitherto unoccupied France. Belatedly realising that the prevailing wind was no longer blowing from Vichy, Darlan tried to persuade Contre-Amiral Jean de Laborde to sail the Toulon Fleet to the safety of West Africa. The aristocratic 'Comte Jean' responded by recalling the celebrated response of a French naval commander when asked to join the Free French in 1940: '*Merde!*'[32] Over the next few days, Laborde arrested French officers in favour of joining the Allies and silenced sailors who had begun to chant '*Vive Darlan!*' and '*Vive de Gaulle!*' At dawn on the morning of 27 November, the Germans attempted to seize the ships. But the French sailors were too quick and the Toulon Fleet scuttled itself. This desperate act of self-immolation has been held to vitiate the justification for Mers el-Kébir: if the French Navy could be relied upon to destroy itself then self-evidently there was no need for the British to sink it. What this retrospective argument ignores are the many reasons why the French were considered *unreliable*, as well as the closeness to which the Germans came to succeeding in their enterprise. Far from being a vindication of French 'neutrality', the scuttling of the Toulon Fleet represented the ultimate failure of Vichy to redeem itself by joining the Allies, even after American entry into the war had ensured Allied victory.

Meanwhile, Clark had brokered a deal between the various factions in North Africa. Darlan would head the civil and military administration in French North Africa, while Giraud would command the French armed forces. As soon as this arrangement was announced, it was almost universally condemned. Political opinion, on both sides of the Atlantic, was outraged. Darlan was an infamous collaborator, a 'Nazi stooge', the man who had fired on Allied sailors and handed Indo-China to the Japanese. His state-within-a-state at Vichy was correctly perceived as aspiring fascist, with anti-Semitic laws and a brown-shirted militia who swore to fight 'against democracy, against Gaullist insurrection and against Jewish leprosy'.[33] How could the Allies co-operate with such a man? How could the United States be associated with a politician who, as an aghast Morgenthau reminded colleagues, had sold thousands of people into slavery? There was, he told Stimson:

> A considerable group of rich people in this country who would make peace with Hitler tomorrow and the only people who really want to fight are the working men and women, and if they once get the idea that we are going to sit back and favour these Fascists, these Hitlerites . . . these people are going to have sit-down strikes; they are going to slow up production and they are going to say, 'What's the use of fighting just to put that kind of people back in power?'[34]

In London, the Foreign Office, Parliament and the British press agreed. Far from revelling in Washington's discomfort, as Roosevelt's speechwriter, Robert Sherwood, later suggested, they feared the consequences of Clark's deal for the Allied war effort. 'How can we possibly now represent to the submerged nations of Europe that we are fighting for a new and better system, designed above all to liberate them from the ever-present fear of German aggression?' demanded the Foreign Office's Gladwyn Jebb in a departmental memorandum:

> What guarantee have they now got that we shall not, in the occupation of other countries, make terms with Mussert [the leading Dutch collaborator], Rost van Tonningen [another Dutch Nazi], King Albert [of the Belgians], President Hácha [of Czechoslovakia], General Nedić [of Yugoslavia] and even with Quisling [of Norway] himself, provided only that these reptiles assert that they were really only guided by patriotic motives and were only prompted in their actions by their hatred of 'communism'?[35]

Eden was appalled by the deal, while Cadogan thought the Allies would never do any good 'till we've killed Darlan'.[36]

The Free French, excluded from participating in Torch following the fiasco of Dakar and the bloodletting in Syria, felt justifiably insulted. Roosevelt had even forbidden Churchill from informing de Gaulle of the operation until it was underway. The General, who had already suffered the indignity of a surprise British invasion of French Madagascar in May, was understandably livid. 'I hope the Vichy people throw them back into the sea!' he thundered on hearing of the Allied landings.[37] Later, he calmed down sufficiently to deliver a broadcast in support of the invasion. On 16 November, however, he warned Churchill, during a tense meeting in Downing Street, of the dangers he was courting: 'If France one day discovers that because of the Anglo-Saxons her liberation consists of Darlan, you can perhaps win the war from a military point of view but you will lose it morally and ultimately there will be only one victor: Stalin.'[38]*

Churchill, though less concerned than Eden, appreciated the risk. Writing to Roosevelt on 17 November, he urged that the arrangement with Darlan be treated purely as a 'temporary expedient', lest

---

* Strangely, the Soviet dictator approved the Darlan deal, noting, in a telegram to Churchill, that in war it was necessary to deal not only with Darlans but 'even the devil himself and his grandmother'.

'serious political injury . . . be done to our cause, not only in France but throughout Europe'.[39] Later that afternoon, FDR duly made this point at a press conference. Claiming to sympathise with the indignation expressed at the arrangement with Darlan, he emphasised that this was a 'temporary expedient, justified solely by the stress of battle'.[40] Privately, he was more cynical. 'Darlan gave me Algiers, long live Darlan!' he told de Gaulle's scandalised emissary, André Philip, on 20 November. 'If Laval gives me Paris, long live Laval! I am not like [Woodrow] Wilson, I am a realist.' When Philip replied that he had heard too much talk of 'realism' in France – the term used to salve all the consciences of the men of Vichy – the President repeated his well-known determination not to recognise any prospective French Government until after the liberation.[41] Later, he allowed Darlan to transmit a message to all French diplomatic missions in which the Admiral claimed responsibility for the maintenance and defence of the French Empire, while simultaneously rejecting British suggestions that the time had come to throw the turncoat Admiral overboard. During this time, Vichy's anti-Semitic laws remained in place, while many pro-Allied French officers and conspirators languished in North African gaols.

Roosevelt's argument, first made by Eisenhower, was that the Darlan deal saved American lives. This is debatable. Darlan's ceasefire order was issued only after Algiers and Oran had surrendered and Patton's Western Task Force – despite some 400 casualties – was safely ashore. The Americans were spared a battle for Casablanca but by this stage their armour was in play and the Vichy French situation in Morocco was desperate. Thereafter, there was an argument for maintaining relations with the Admiral in the hope that he could rally the Toulon Fleet and other parts of France's African empire. Although he failed to carry the former – he never, in fact, issued Laborde with a direct order, merely a carefully worded invitation – he was perceived to deliver the latter when Governor-General Pierre Boisson announced on 23 November the rallying of French West Africa to the Allies. Clark believed that Darlan was the only Frenchman capable of facilitating an Allied dash into Tunisia and Eisenhower, no more versed in French politics than his deputy, accepted this assessment.

If the military advantages were debatable, however, the political *dis*advantages were clear. To these, Roosevelt appears to have been curiously blind. In January 1942, de Gaulle had lectured Cordell Hull that modern war was not a 'game of chess' but a 'moral enterprise'.[42] Roosevelt understood this better than anyone. From his 'Four Freedoms' speech to the Atlantic Charter, his hostility towards Iberian and South American dictators and repeated interference in Britain's colonial affairs, he had consistently put morality at the forefront of the Allied war effort. Yet he showed startling indifference to the morality of his French policies. His preferred solution to the North African imbroglio, he told Hull, was to shut Darlan, Giraud and a representative of de Gaulle in a room together and 'give the government of the occupied territory to the man who came out' alive.[43] It is true that de Gaulle was unelected and obstreperous but these were not good reasons to favour men who had slain French democracy and collaborated with America's enemies. Looking back after almost a quarter of a century, Kenneth Pendar, one of Murphy's Vice-Consuls, wondered how it was that the 'most powerful country in the world, girded with military might and holding every card in the pack in the early stages of this diplomatic game, should have fumbled, misplayed and thrown away its political, moral and diplomatic strength as we did'.[44] The answer lay at the heart of America's Vichy policy.

Fortunately for the Allies, Darlan's North African reign proved brief. On Christmas Eve 1942, a young French royalist named Fernand Bonnier de La Chapelle walked into the Admiral's Algiers headquarters and shot him dead. The British and the Gaullists were jubilant. Eden claimed that he had not been 'so relieved by any event for years'.[45] Yet whilst Anglo-Free French involvement remains plausible, nothing beyond circumstantial evidence has yet linked them to the murder.*

The Allies were also fortunate that the Darlan controversy coincided with a shift in the fortunes of the war. On Sunday 15 November, church bells had pealed from steeples throughout Britain in celebration

---

* Stewart Menzies, the head of Britain's Secret Intelligence Service, known as 'C', and Air Commodore Charles Hambro, responsible for the French section of the Special Operations Executive, categorically denied that they were 'mixed up with any "assassination ring" in North Africa'.

of the 8th Army's victory at El Alamein. In two weeks, Montgomery had taken almost 30,000 Axis prisoners, 500 tanks, 250 guns and several thousand trucks. The fact that he enjoyed a 2:1 superiority in men and armour was not publicised. That same month, the US Navy destroyed a heavily protected Japanese troop convoy off Guadalcanal in the Solomon Islands. More significant than both of these events was the great encirclement of German forces at Stalingrad. On 19–20 November, eleven Soviet armies – over a million men – smashed through the Romanian 3rd and 4th Armies to the north and south of the city. Four days later, they met at Kalach, trapping 290,000 Axis troops. General der Panzertruppe Friedrich Paulus sought permission to break out but Hitler refused, sealing the fate of the 6th Army.

The one blemish on this victorious record was the Anglo-American failure to secure Tunisia. A brigade group of General Anderson's 1st Army raced to seize ports east of Algiers but by the end of November 5,000 Axis troops had been airlifted to Tunis, followed by 176 tanks, 131 guns and 1,152 vehicles, right under the nose of Admiral Esteva. 'It is a queer situation in North Africa,' noted Major-General John Kennedy from London. 'The French are allowing the Germans to put forces into Tunisia without firing a shot while they have opposed us in Algeria and Morocco . . . The truth of the matter is that although the French hate the Germans, I am afraid they hate us more.'[46] The battle for Tunisia would drag on for another five months, costing the Allies 76,000 casualties.

Still, the year 1942 ended with improved prospects for the Allies. The Japanese had been decisively defeated at sea and the outcome of the war in North Africa was no longer in doubt. In the Mediterranean, the Italians were forced to look to the defence of their homeland, while 230 of Germany's 260 divisions, thanks to the sacrifices of the Red Army, were now on the defensive. Of course, this was not the end. It was, as Churchill told an audience at Mansion House on 10 November, 'not even the beginning of the end'. But it was, perhaps, 'the end of the beginning'.[47]

XX

Casablanca

The Emperors of the East and West, who in these Eden-like
surroundings had met . . . to determine the future history
of the world.

Pierson Dixon, 22 January 1943[1]

'I shall always feel that the reason the President wanted to meet
Churchill in Africa was because he wanted to make a trip!' mused
Harry Hopkins in his notes of the Casablanca Conference:

> He was tired of having other people – particularly myself – speak for
> him around the world. He wanted no more of Churchill in Wash-
> ington. For political reasons [lest it be claimed that he had been
> beguiled by the British] he could not go to England. He wanted to
> see our troops. He was sick of people telling him that it was danger-
> ous to ride in airplanes. He liked the drama of it. But above all he
> wanted to make a trip![2]

The more serious reason for the conference, held within the safety
of the US compound at Anfa, just outside Casablanca in recently
conquered French Morocco, between 14 and 24 January 1943, was to
determine Anglo-American strategy for 1943.

To US war planners, the conference, codenamed Symbol, constituted nothing less than an American defeat, possibly a swindle. 'We
lost our shirts,' wailed Albert C. Wedemeyer to General Thomas
T. Handy, head of the Operations Division at the War Office. 'We
came, we listened and we were conquered.'[3] Fifteen years later,
the by-then full General was no less bitter, accusing the British of
'politicising' grand strategy, sleight of hand and defaulting on their

commitments. The result, he contended, when coupled with the pronouncements of his own Commander-in-Chief, 'lengthened the war by a full year'.[4]

The US Joint Chiefs had arrived at Casablanca firmly opposed to further operations in the Mediterranean. Such a strategy, they argued, would place a heavy burden on their already stretched shipping while doing little to hasten the final defeat of Germany. The British, by contrast, wished to exploit the opportunities of Torch to strike at what Churchill termed (erroneously as it transpired) the 'soft underbelly' of the Axis. Proposals for operations against Sardinia (Brimstone) and Sicily (Husky) had already been submitted to Washington, along with the recommendation that the Allies should try to prevail on Turkey to enter the war.

The British were aided by unanimity among the services and a Rolls-Royce secretariat. 'It was decided that the best policy would be to take a full bag of clubs,' noted Ian Jacob of the army of planners the British brought with them to Morocco, as well as the 6,000-ton troop ship, equipped with operations rooms, wireless transmitters and a full complement of clerical and cipher staff, that they had commandeered to act as a floating headquarters.[5] The Americans, *per contra*, had travelled light. 'We were overwhelmed by the large British Staff,' recalled General 'Ed' Hull of the US Operations Division:

> The only staff that General Marshall had was small and the other Chiefs of Staff were no better fixed. He had Wedemeyer and one assistant . . . The British had come down there in droves and every one of them had written a paper about something and that was submitted by the British Chiefs of Staff to the American Joint Chiefs of Staff for agreement.[6]

'When the US Chiefs saw how the land lay', recorded Jacob, 'they went out into the highways and byways of North Africa and scraped together some sort of a staff.'[7] Hull was found and one or two others but nothing to blunt the British advantage. 'They swarmed down upon us like locusts,' complained Wedemeyer, 'and if I were a Britisher I would feel very proud. However, as an American, I wish we might be more glib and better organised to cope with these super-negotiators. From a worm's eye viewpoint it was apparent that we were confronted by generations and generations of experience in committee work, in diplomacy, in rationalising points of view. They had us on the defensive practically all the time.'[8]

More serious than their deficiency in staff was the lack of an agreed alternative American strategy. Marshall remained committed to the invasion of France. Although the US Army Chief appreciated that a full-scale invasion of the Continent was scarcely possible in 1943 – Torch, as he had predicted, had diverted too many troops to North Africa – he continued to advocate a cross-Channel assault as the quickest means of defeating Germany. His colleague Admiral King, on the other hand, wanted to send a far greater proportion of US resources into the Pacific. It was a reversion to the debates of the previous summer but the British, with their united front, were able to triumph over their divided allies.

Not that it was all plain sailing. King was a formidable opponent. Characterised by the Secretary of the British Military Mission to Washington, Brigadier Vivian Dykes, as 'a man of great strength of character with a very small brain', he gloried in his reputation as a cantankerous old sea dog, said to trim his toenails with a torpedo net cutter and shave with a blow torch.[9] Admiral Cunningham recognised his abilities as a naval administrator but considered him 'quite ruthless in his methods . . . not an easy person to get on with'.[10] Eisenhower went further. 'One thing that might help win this war is to get someone to shoot King,' he recorded in his diary. 'He's the antithesis of cooperation, a deliberately rude person, which means he's a mental bully.'[11]

King visibly annoyed Brooke, who, in turn, irked the Americans with his clipped, rapid speech and obvious impatience with irrelevances, digressions, verbosity and posturing. At one point it looked as if the talks had reached deadlock. 'It's no use, we shall never get agreement with them,' lamented the CIGS after an antagonistic morning, during which Marshall harped on the importance of reconquering Burma (Operation Anakim) and King remained 'wrapped up in the war of the Pacific at the expense of everything else!'[12] Not for the first time – and certainly not the last – Dill acted as peacemaker. After reminding Brooke of the many areas on which they had already obtained agreement, he took Marshall a moderately revised draft of the British proposals (prepared by Portal) during the lunch break. When the Combined Chiefs reconvened at 3 p.m., the Americans accepted the paper with only minor alterations. The final document, presented to the President and Prime Minister that afternoon, committed the Allies to the invasion of Sicily by July 1943 and the reinvasion of Burma in the autumn. In the Pacific, operations to recapture Rabaul in New Britain and thence the Marshall and Caroline Islands but not, as the Americans wanted, the stronghold of Truk, were approved, while Operation Bolero (the mustering of forces in Britain prior to a cross-Channel assault) would proceed 'as fast as our commitments allow'.[13]

The British could hardly believe their good fortune. 'It has been one of the most difficult tasks I have had to do . . . [but] we have got practically all we hoped to get,' recorded Brooke.[14] 'If I had written down before I came what I hoped that the conclusions would be, I could never have written anything so sweeping, so comprehensive and so favourable to our ideas,' noted Jacob.[15]

The Americans noted it too. 'It taught us a lesson,' recalled Ed Hull. 'Never go to a meeting like that without plenty of help because you need it.'[16] Paul Caraway, a member of Wedemeyer's staff, recalled in uncomradely language how the US never 'lost' another conference. 'Sometimes we didn't win them without a few knocks and bruises, but we won them. Why? Because we stayed ahead of our British friends the whole time.'[17] This was not the case. The British were always meticulously prepared, while the Americans were frequently hampered by Roosevelt's unwillingness to commit himself. What counted was the massive increase in American men and materiel.

That the British triumphed at Casablanca was not simply due to good planning but because the majority of troops and the preponderance of ships available for non-Pacific operations were British. This gave Churchill and the British Chiefs of Staff an effective veto on operations. But the balance of power was about to change. Most British strategists were slow to appreciate the coming shift. Not so Sir John Dill. 'Do you realise that from now on the American war effort and war production is going to increase by leaps and bounds?' the Field Marshal enquired of his aide, shortly after Casablanca.

'They are going to produce two-thirds of everything to our one-third. Therefore, it will become increasingly difficult for us to put forward and sustain our point of view as they will be providing so much more than us.'[18] Symbol was, indeed, the last conference at which an overwhelmingly British conception of strategy would prevail.

Despite the often heated exchanges, the British and American staffs bonded at Anfa. 'The beneficial results of holding such a conference for so long a period and *on a neutral pitch* made themselves clearly manifest', noted Jacob. British and American officers met in the bar at the Anfa Hotel, went for walks along the beach, visited the battered French battleship the *Jean Bart* and dined together in the evenings. 'Mutual respect and understanding ripen in such surroundings,' continued Jacob, 'especially when the weather is lovely, the accommodation is good, and food and drink and smokes are unlimited and free.'[19] Harold Macmillan's Private Secretary, Pierson Dixon, painted an idyllic picture of Anfa Camp:

Within easy walking distance of each other and the hotel but sufficiently screened by palms and flowering shrubs to give an illusion of privacy, numerous pretty villas of modern shape and varying colour – pink, white and Pompeian red – dotted the park-like avenues of the camp . . . Food was provided in the roof-garden restaurant of the hotel and was excellent, consisting of an ideal amalgam of American cooking and local fruit and wine . . . To complete the physical amenities, there was a free bar, amply stocked with gin, whisky, brandy and even port. And strangest of all a free PX (American NAAFI), providing cigarettes, razor blades, soap etc.

It said much for 'the moderation of the Anglo-Saxon temperament', continued Dixon, that this African court did not fall into the way of 'Sardanapalus', the semi-mythical last King of Assyria known for his excess and decadence, 'or Byzantium'.[20] He might have revised this opinion if he had seen more of the conference's principal protagonists. When Roosevelt was wheeled into his sumptuous villa, with its large bed, marble bath and innumerable drapes and frills, he commented: 'Now all we need is the *Madame* of the house.'[21]

Later, when the dignitaries were staying in Kenneth Pendar's villa in Marrakesh, the host entered the salon to discover the President stretched out on one of the couches. 'As I came up to him, he put out his hand to me and said with an engaging smile: "I am the Pasha, you may kiss my hand." '[22] Hopkins, meanwhile, had found Churchill in bed washing down his breakfast with a bottle of white wine. Asked what he meant by this, Churchill replied that he had a 'profound distaste on the one hand for skimmed milk and no deep-rooted prejudice about wine and that he had reconciled the conflict in favour of the latter'. Later that day, Hopkins was cornered by the Chief of Combined Operations, Lord Louis Mountbatten, who told him a 'fantastic story about a non-sinkable ship made of ice which the British were working on' and desired American co-operation.[23] Sometimes the British reputation for eccentricity was well deserved.

In this holiday atmosphere, amid the palm trees, orange groves and cacti, the Churchill–Roosevelt romance continued to blossom. The 'Emperors of the East and West', as Harold Macmillan, Britain's newly appointed Minister for the Mediterranean, dubbed them, ate, drank and played together.[24] At the end of the conference, Churchill persuaded Roosevelt to pay a brief visit to Marrakesh. Insisting that he see the sunset on the Atlas Mountains, he had two of the President's bodyguards carry him up to the roof of the villa, 'his paralysed legs dangling like the limbs of a ventriloquist's dummy', in the unfeeling words of the Prime Minister's doctor.[25] If Roosevelt found this mildly humiliating, he concealed it. At dinner, he proposed the health of the King and the two men made short, affectionate speeches to each other. 'Now, Winston, don't you get up in the morning to see me off. I'll be wheeled into your room to kiss you goodbye', declared Roosevelt.

'Not at all, Mr President, I can get into my rompers in two twos and I'll be on hand to see you off.'

The next morning, Churchill duly accompanied Roosevelt to the airfield in his blue siren suit, Air Marshal's cap, monogrammed slippers and velvet-collared dressing gown. 'If anything happened to that man, I couldn't stand it,' he told Pendar as the President's aeroplane prepared to take off. 'He is the truest friend; he has the

farthest vision; he is the greatest man I have ever known.'[26] His
affection was sincere.

★

Apart from blessing an agreed strategy, the principal task of the
Emperors at Casablanca had been to try to bring some unity to
French affairs. Following the assassination of Admiral Darlan, the
Americans had reverted to their original choice of Giraud as High
Commissioner as well as Commander-in-Chief of French North
Africa but this still left the problem of de Gaulle. Both Roosevelt
and Churchill had been stung by criticism of the Darlan affair.
Accused of favouring collaborators over allies, they sought to repair
the damage by brokering a merger between de Gaulle and Giraud –
the former backed by the British, the latter by the Americans. There
'must be a wedding, even if it [is] a shot-gun wedding', FDR told
Macmillan, parachuted in to keep an eye on French affairs.[27]

On 17 January, the groom, otherwise known as Giraud, arrived at
the chapel. His military bearing and obvious chivalry impressed the
celebrants. 'I said to the German Generals who came to see me [in
prison] that they had lost the war because they had failed to defeat
England,' he told the Combined Chiefs of Staff. 'I could not prophesy
how long the war would last but I told them they could never win
and that sooner or later the USA would come to the help of Great
Britain. Then they asked me to sign a paper to the effect that I would
not attempt to escape . . . I said I would not sign any paper . . . They
were my jailers; I was their prisoner. It was their duty to guard me,
it was mine to escape . . . Well, it took me a year but here I am.'[28]

Unfortunately, his acumen did not match his gallantry. Known to
his fellow officers as the 'eternal lieutenant', his original plan to escape
from Königstein consisted of persuading eighty antiquated French
generals and several admirals to rush the gates.[29] Later, he confirmed
his naïveté by writing to Pétain, pledging his loyalty. To the Americans who had already been exposed to him, the suspicion that Giraud
was not the leader they sought was already current. 'Giraud is not
your man,' Darlan had tried to explain (with admitted self-interest) to

Robert Murphy on the night of the Torch landings. 'Politically he is a child. He is just a good divisional commander, nothing more.'[30] This verity occurred to Roosevelt when the General took up almost the entirety of their first interview with requests for American supplies. Describing Giraud as a 'rather simple-minded soldier', Roosevelt teased Murphy for selecting him as the leader of French North Africa.[31] Not that he proposed to change his plans. Convinced that he was brokering a Victorian marriage, in which the groom, or rather the groom's parents, would exercise control, Roosevelt informed Giraud that he wished him to head the military set-up, 'with General de Gaulle as second in command and some third person as political head of French North Africa'.[32] But where was the bride?

Churchill had written to de Gaulle on 16 January, asking him to fly to Casablanca to reach a settlement with Giraud. To his mortification, de Gaulle refused. He had already made two offers to meet the General, he reminded Eden, but Giraud had been unwilling. Now the time was not 'opportune'. He would meet Giraud at Fort Lamy, or any other part of the French Empire, but declined to meet him under the 'auspices of the other two great Allies', where he would be under pressure to compromise.[33] For over an hour, Eden and Cadogan argued with him but to no avail. 'This, I should think, is the end of the Free French movement,' wrote the latter. 'Roosevelt will say to [the] P.M., "Look at your friend: this is how he behaves." And Winston will have to agree with him – and shed de G.'[34]

In fact, Roosevelt was enjoying his friend's embarrassment. ('He always enjoyed other people's discomfort,' recalled Harriman. 'It never bothered him very much when other people were unhappy.'[35]) 'You've got to get your problem child down here,' FDR teased Churchill.[36] Later he asked, 'Who pays for de Gaulle's food?' Churchill replied that the British did. 'Why don't you stop his food and maybe he will come?'[37] Churchill took this suggestion. On 18 January, he sent Eden a note threatening to disown de Gaulle if he failed to grasp this 'unique opportunity'.[38] Although the War Cabinet softened the message – the General, they appreciated, held a strong position with the press and any suggestion of 'Munich-ing' him would be strongly resented by the public – the seriousness of the situation, as well as the fact that the invitation came from both the Prime Minister *and* the President, was brought home to de Gaulle, who, after a meeting of the Free French National Committee, reluctantly agreed to undertake the journey.[39]

De Gaulle arrived at Anfa on 22 January in vinegary mood. Outraged to find himself surrounded by American soldiers and American flags on what was, technically, French soil, he told Murphy that he never would have consented to stay in his villa had he not learnt that it was the property of a Dane. His first words to Giraud were deliberately provocative: '*Bonjour, mon Général*, I see that the Americans are treating you well!'[40] The pleasantries over, he exploded: 'What is this? I ask you for an interview four times over and we have to meet in this wire enclosure among foreign powers? Don't you realise how odious this is from a national point of view?'[41] His proposal for the future relationship between the two men was simple and uncompromising: Giraud would serve as Commander-in-Chief of Free French forces under *his* authority, the Foch to his Clemenceau.

Later that afternoon, Macmillan persuaded de Gaulle to see Churchill. Upon arriving at the Prime Minister's villa, the Free French leader stated he would not have come had he known he was to be surrounded by 'American bayonets'. Morocco, he complained, was an 'occupied country!'[42] Patiently, Churchill explained the scheme that he and Roosevelt had devised: Giraud and de Gaulle would be joint chairmen of a governing committee for the French Empire, with Giraud in charge of the armed forces, since he was the only man the Americans were prepared to deal with. When de Gaulle replied sarcastically that the arrangement might commend itself to 'American sergeant-majors' but that he could not possibly agree, Churchill threatened to break with him.[43] ('*Si vous m'obstaclerez, je vous liquiderai!*'[44]) But frustration mingled with admiration. 'Look at him,' he invited his physician as the Free French leader stalked off, the issue unresolved. 'He might be Stalin with two hundred divisions behind his words.'[45]

After dinner, de Gaulle met Roosevelt for the first time. 'We vied in good manners,' recalled the General. Beneath the surface, however, the tension was acute. Roosevelt stated that French sovereignty resided with the people; de Gaulle replied that the 'national will had already made its choice'.[46] The atmosphere was not improved by

the sense that the two men were being watched. During the interview, de Gaulle noticed shadows towards the rear of the balcony
and curtains moving at the corners. As he later discovered, a bevy of
bodyguards, as well as the President's naval aide, Captain McCrea,
were behind the 'arras'. The former came as a surprise even to Hopkins. 'In the middle of the conference, I noticed that the whole of the
Secret Service detail was behind the curtains and above the gallery in
the living room and at all doors leading into the room,' he recorded.
'I left the conference and went out to talk to the Secret Service to
find out what it was all about and found them all armed to the teeth
with, perhaps, a dozen Tommy guns among the group . . . They told
me they could not take any chances on anything happening to the
President. None of this hokus pokus had gone on when Giraud saw
the President and it was simply an indication of the atmosphere in
which de Gaulle found himself at Casablanca.'[47]

In his memoirs, de Gaulle depicted Roosevelt as a devious, charming hypocrite, at the helm of a rapacious, imperial power. 'The
United States, delighting in her resources, feeling that she no longer
had within herself sufficient scope for her energies and wishing to
help those who were in misery or bondage anywhere, yielded in
her turn to that taste for intervention which concealed the instinct
for domination.'[48] His suspicion of American designs on the French
Empire was well founded. Addressing the Joint Chiefs just before
their departure for Casablanca, Roosevelt had criticised Murphy's
assurance to Giraud that the Allies would restore the French Empire
in its entirety. 'Mr Murphy had exceeded his authority and . . . he,
as President, was not prepared to make any promises,' Roosevelt
had said. There were some colonial possessions which he was certain 'would not be returned to France and he had grave doubts
whether Indo-China should be'.[49] Later, he discussed with Murphy
and Eisenhower plans to establish Allied military bases at Dakar and
other parts of the French Empire and, on the very evening he met
de Gaulle, extolled the virtues of self-determination to the Sultan
of Morocco.

The next day, de Gaulle categorically refused to accept the American formula. 'What you suggest', he told Giraud, 'boils down to
your having the real power under Roosevelt's protection.'[50] The

British and the Americans then produced a compromise communiqué, stating that the two Generals adhered to the principles of the United Nations and announcing their intention to form a joint committee to administer the French Empire for the duration of the war. De Gaulle's rejection of this face-saving alternative led to a furious row with Churchill, during which the Prime Minister, again, threatened to denounce him. The Free French leader then saw Roosevelt, who, in more measured tones, expressed his sorrow at the impasse. 'In human affairs', he explained, 'the public must be offered a drama. The news of your meeting with General Giraud in the midst of a conference in which both Churchill and I were taking part, if it were to be accompanied by a joint declaration of French leaders – even if it only concerned a theoretical agreement – would produce the dramatic effect required.'[51] Realising that Roosevelt was only interested in the appearance of an agreement, de Gaulle then produced his own communiqué, merely stating that he and Giraud had met and were united in their determination to work towards the liberation of France and the 'triumph of human liberty'.[52] He then, to Roosevelt's delight, agreed to be photographed shaking hands with Giraud – a wedding of sorts but no marriage of minds.

Twenty years later, Murphy marvelled at how this professional soldier, who had never participated in national politics before the war, 'put on such a sparkling performance in international power politics that he took the star role away from the two greatest English-speaking politicians'.[53] Certainly, it had been a remarkable display of will. But was it wise? Four months later, de Gaulle would accept a deal almost identical to the compromise he had spurned at Anfa. His explanation for rejecting the latter was that it had been 'dictated' by the Allies, that it limited his role to the (joint) administration of the French Empire and that it implied agreement with Giraud when no such agreement existed.[54] Was this reason to infuriate his principal benefactor and the President of the United States? Anfa confirmed all of Roosevelt's worst suspicions about the Free French leader: de Gaulle was an egomaniac with dictatorial tendencies. Churchill was more conflicted but left Morocco with his intermittent Gaullophobia operating at a new peak. 'Oh, don't let's speak of him,' he told Kenneth Pendar over dinner in Marrakesh.

'We call him Jeanne d'Arc and we're looking for some bishops to burn him.'[55] Soon, Roosevelt would ask him to fulfil his threats and break with de Gaulle. It would take all the persuasive skills of Eden and the War Cabinet to save *'l'Homme du destin'*.[56]

★

It was at the press conference following the de Gaulle–Giraud handshake that Roosevelt made his famous statement about 'unconditional surrender'. Addressing some thirty reporters crouched on the grass in front of him, Churchill at his side, the President declared that 'peace can come to the world only by the total elimination of German and Japanese war power . . . The elimination of German, Japanese and Italian war power means the unconditional surrender by Germany, Italy and Japan.'[57] Rarely have two sentences led to such confusion and controversy. The confusion stems from the fact that both Roosevelt and Churchill later claimed that this portentous statement was made on a whim. 'We had so much trouble getting those two French Generals together', the President explained, 'that I thought to myself that this was as difficult as arranging the meeting of [Ulysses S.] Grant and [Robert E.] Lee – and then, suddenly, the press conference was on and Winston and I had no time to prepare for it and the thought popped into my mind that they had called Grant "Old Unconditional Surrender" and the next thing I knew I had said it.'[58] This was typical Roosevelt: muddying the historical waters with frivolity. In fact, the President had already mentioned the policy to the Joint Chiefs and discussed it with Churchill, who in turn consulted the War Cabinet. To add to the confusion, Churchill later claimed to have been surprised, annoyed even, by the President's statement.

The theory that Churchill wished to keep open the possibility of negotiating with an alternative German government, either as an end in itself, or in the hope of stimulating opposition to Hitler – an option he had preserved prior to Pearl Harbor – is easily dismissed. On 18 January, Churchill had himself declared, before Roosevelt and the Combined Chiefs, that the conclusion of the conference should be marked with a statement 'to the effect that the United Nations are resolved to pursue the war to the bitter end, neither party relaxing in its efforts until the unconditional surrender of Germany and Japan has been achieved'.[59] The omission of Italy was deliberate. Requesting his colleagues' judgement on such a statement, Churchill explained that he wished to exclude Italy in the hope of encouraging 'a break-up there'.[60] The War Cabinet approved the overall policy but not the exclusion of Italy. Receiving their reply on 21 January, Churchill duly inserted the word 'Italy' into the statement. His grounds for surprise, let alone pique, therefore, remain obscure. Ultimately, it is not important. What is, is that the policy was premeditated and that the Combined Chiefs had ample opportunity to raise any objections.

A more controversial question is whether the declaration stiffened Axis resistance, thus lengthening the war. Most military historians believe not; or at least, not significantly. Ideology, honour, fanaticism, defence of the homeland and rigid military discipline all seem to have been greater motivating factors than anything Roosevelt said at Anfa. Unconditional surrender did not stop the Italians from capitulating in August 1943, nor attempts by the German officer corps to remove Hitler, culminating in the Stauffenberg plot of July 1944. Twenty-three years earlier, the Germans had been forced to accept the '*Diktat*' of Versailles, despite surrendering before a single French, British or American soldier had crossed the German frontier and it is scarcely credible that their successors believed they would receive more lenient treatment.

In any case, the purpose of the Allied statement was not to frighten their enemies but to hearten their friends. Following the Darlan episode, neutral countries and resistance movements across Europe needed reassurance that the Allies would not abandon them for deals with local Quislings. Even more important, Stalin, who had been invited to Casablanca but declined to attend, needed to be convinced that the democracies intended to see the war through to the finish. Both Roosevelt and Churchill had as good as promised to open a second front in France in 1943. Now, they felt unable to honour this commitment. It was only after the Russians had fulfilled their 'allotted role of killing Germans' that the Chiefs of Staff believed they could 'stage a general onslaught on the exhausted animal', noted Oliver Harvey in a bleak but accurate summary of the British consensus.[61] Naturally, neither Churchill nor Roosevelt could say this to Stalin but they could try to placate him: through supplies, through increasingly heavy bombing raids on German cities and by affirming their determination to see the war through to its proper conclusion. The announcement of the policy of 'unconditional surrender' was the ultimate affirmation.

★

Another means of assuaging the Soviet dictator would be to bring Turkey into the war. Replying to a telegram from Churchill on the subject, Stalin had expressed his 'full agreement' as to the need to do 'everything possible to have Turkey enter the war on our side in the spring'.[62] The strategic importance of Turkey was self-evident. Situated on the axis between Europe and Asia, Turkish belligerency would allow the Allies to aid Soviet forces fighting in the Caucasus, to bomb the Romanian oil fields of Ploieşti and to stage offensives against the Germans in the Balkans and the Aegean – the eastern end of the 'soft underbelly'. Churchill had maintained a keen interest in Turkey since before the First World War. Rightly considering her the neutral country with the greatest potential influence once the United States had entered the war, he sought to win her to the Allied side through diplomacy and by supplying her archaic armed forces with British and later American materiel. To his intense frustration, the Foreign Office did not share his enthusiasm. Unsure whether Turkish belligerency would prove an asset or a liability, the department's efforts in this arena were limited to varying and ultimately unsuccessful attempts to dissuade the Turks from supplying the Germans with chromium – a lustrous element essential to the manufacture of armour plating. 'The entire politics of the Foreign Office with Turkey are expressed in the one word, "chrome",' the Prime Minister wrote contemptuously to Eden on 5 November 1942. 'I thought you told me you were going to wind this up but your pertinacious secretariat and your verbose Ambassador continue to wear out the cypher staff and aggravate the paper shortage, to say nothing of wearing out my eyesight, by endless disputation.'[63]

The 'verbose Ambassador' was Sir Hughe Knatchbull-Hugessen. A tall Etonian with kindly eyes and a handsome face, 'Snatch', as he was

known in the Foreign Office, had served with competence as Minister to Persia and then as Ambassador to China, where he had been
severely wounded after a Japanese aircraft strafed his car. Appointed
to the Embassy at Ankara in February 1939, he would later fall into
discredit when it was discovered that his Albanian valet was a German
spy – known as 'Cicero' – who took advantage of his master's hour
of afternoon piano practice to photograph the contents of his safe.*

Knatchbull-Hugessen doubted that it was in the Allied interest for
Turkey to join the war. With little equipment for her undertrained
army, few aircraft and fewer anti-aircraft guns, the country was at
risk of being overwhelmed by the Germans, even after the failure
of Barbarossa. Eden and the Foreign Office sympathised with this
view. Certainly, they did not believe the Turks would declare war
simply because the Allies asked them to.† When, therefore, in a telegram to Eden, the Prime Minister suggested that he go on from
Casablanca to meet members of the Turkish Government, the War
Cabinet demurred. Churchill was furious. Suspecting that this was
a case of Eden guarding his much-trespassed-upon dominion, he
bombarded his colleagues with telegrams until they grudgingly
withdrew their veto. 'We are just off over [the] Atlas Mountains
which are gleaming with their sunlit snows,' he wrote puckishly to
the Foreign Secretary after getting his way. 'You can imagine how
much I wish I were going to be with you tomorrow on the Bench
[in the House of Commons] but duty calls.'⁶⁴

The location for the conference was a loop in the railway line
near the Turkish town of Adana. Multiple precautions were taken
to keep the rendezvous a secret. Knatchbull-Hugessen made out
that he was going on a two-day shooting expedition. Leaving the
Embassy in tweed breeches and appropriate headgear, his guns
placed ostentatiously in the Ambassadorial car, he drove to the small

---

* A school report described Knatchbull-Hugessen aptly as 'decorously inattentive'
but the allegation that Cicero obtained the date for D-Day is pure fiction.
† 'I am anyhow sure that they are entirely on our side and want us to win,' wrote
Knatchbull-Hugessen to the Conservative MP Paul Emrys-Evans on 28 September 1941, 'though they don't see why they should throw themselves uselessly away
and sacrifice all the work of Ataturk merely for our *beaux yeux*.' (Emrys-Evans
Papers, ADD MSS 58261)

station of Kayaş where he met members of his staff and boarded the Presidential train. The military contingent, coming from Cairo, were required to wear mufti. This sparked a frantic search for civilian clothes, the not altogether successful result being to make some of Britain's most senior officers look like a 'band of gangsters'.[65]

The Prime Ministerial party landed at Adana at 12.30 p.m. on 30 January 1943. After inspecting a squadron of Hurricanes, they boarded a train and travelled across flat, flooded country until they reached a siding. There they met the Turkish President's train, to which, with much clanking and shunting, they were attached. Churchill was on the top of his form. After a brief meeting with President İnönü, he read the Turkish delegation – consisting of Prime Minister Saracoğlu, Foreign Minister Menemencioğlu and Marshal Çakmak – a memorandum filled with offers of Allied military assistance. Since none of the Turks spoke English, a secretary from the British Embassy had been deputed to translate. When, however, the young man converted miles into kilometres (for the benefit of the Turks, who preferred this metric), Churchill decided that he was not doing it right and continued his dissertation in his own, idiosyncratic French. 'The result', recorded Ian Jacob, 'was completely intelligible to all the English present, even if they had no knowledge of the language beyond what they learnt at school, but I feel the Turks could only have formed a very hazy idea of what the whole thing was about'.[66]

On the contrary, the Turks knew precisely what the British were about and how they would respond. Understandably averse to having their cities reduced to rubble, the Turks never intended to join the war. They were, however, terrified of Russia, against whose encroachments the Western Allies offered an element of protection. Some members of the British delegation perceived this. 'I never saw men so resolutely disinclined to be drawn into a war,' recalled Cadogan, flown in specially for the conference. 'They were very friendly and pleasant and I am sure their sympathies were genuinely with us but when the conversation began to veer towards anything like practical action on their part it seemed that they found more than the usual difficulty in hearing what was said.'[67] Jacob, who took minutes of all the meetings, noted that the only subject the Turks were interested in was the amount of materiel the Allies could supply:

They asked no question at all about the progress of the war, nor did they try to find out what had been decided at Casablanca. But from little things we picked up here and there it is evident that they are convinced that Germany's days are numbered and that their main preoccupation is the state of Europe following or during the German collapse and what Russia may do. It was this that made them so ready to agree to this meeting. They wanted to be sure of our support if Russia turned nasty. They were a bit apprehensive that the PM would come with proposals for their immediate entry into the war. When they found that he had no intention of trying to push them along, they heaved a sigh of relief and entered whole-heartedly into the fun. Everything was smiles and of course demands for materiel assistance on the largest scale.[68]

Churchill was delighted by his reception. 'This is about the best day's work I have ever done,' he told his doctor before a raucous dinner party. 'The President put both hands on mine. I now understand how he seduces people. I'm sure I have completely won him over. But I don't want the Turks to come in until they are ready. I don't want them massacred. Let them be armed and then, if it is in their interest, they will come in.'[69]

The next morning, Cadogan discovered that the Prime Minister had spent the early hours composing a 'sweeping survey of the future of the world'.[70] Designed to allay Turkish fears of Soviet expansion, these modestly entitled 'Morning Thoughts' included plans for 'a world organisation for the preservation of peace', that would 'embody the spirit but not be subjected to the weakness of the former League of Nations'. Within this would operate not only the great nations of Europe and Asia Minor but confederations of smaller states, such as a 'Scandinavian Bloc', a 'Danubian Bloc' and a 'Balkan Bloc'. Having already assured İnönü that Russia had suffered such heavy losses that she would 'not be anxious for further wars', he explained how the democracies would organise a coalition to counter 'any act of aggression' on her part.[71]

Churchill left Adana believing that 'the Turks have come a long way towards us' and that they would be in the war 'before the year is out'.[72] In fact, as Knatchbull-Hugessen was soon reporting, they had not moved. Although sympathetic towards the British and the Americans, their dearest wish was to preserve their neutrality while preparing for a possible confrontation with the Soviet Union. Over the next two years, the Allies would deploy both threats and blandishments to gain their participation. Churchill, in a bravura evocation of nineteenth-century power politics, suggested offering them Rhodes (since 1912 under Italian occupation) in exchange for helping the Allies capture the island. This drew a sharp response from Eden, who reminded the Prime Minister that the Dodecanese by 'tradition and sentiment' were Greek, that the majority of the population was Greek and that the people would 'almost certainly favour union with Greece'.[73]

In reality, the Allies could have offered the Turks both Crete and Cyprus for all the difference it would have made. In May 1943, Knatchbull-Hugessen reported that the Turkish Cabinet had decided against joining the war, despite receiving more than £14 million worth of Allied equipment. In September, they helped ferry supplies to British forces vainly attempting to hold Leros, Kos and Samos but a request for air facilities in southern Anatolia was denied with catastrophic consequences for the defenders. Churchill's optimism about Turkey had proved as ill-founded as his wild enthusiasm for shoe-string operations in the Aegean. (The British lost six destroyers, two submarines and almost 5,000 men attempting to retain three strategically unimportant islands.*)

In August 1944, after Allied forces had succeeded in reinvading the Continent, the Turks were prevailed upon to sever diplomatic relations with the Reich. Six months later, in the dying days of the Second World War, they would fulfil what the British had always regarded as their treaty 'obligations' and declare war. Neither act affected the outcome in the slightest. As Churchill reflected ruefully at Chequers one evening, all he had ever got out of the Turks were cigarettes.[74]

---

* 'I always felt that Winston placed a wholly disproportionate emphasis in his memoirs on the importance of the islands in the Eastern Mediterranean,' wrote Ismay to Eisenhower in 1951. 'In his original draft the wretched topic appeared so often that it was downright boring and we got him to cut a good deal of it. But on the main issue he was, and still is, as obstinate as a mule.' (Ismay Papers, 4/12, Ismay to Eisenhower, 11 October 1951)

XXI

Special Relationship

If I were to lay down the cardinal principle of our foreign
policy, it would be that we make absolutely sure that now
and forever the United States and Great Britain are going
to see eye to eye on major matters of world policy.

Harry Hopkins, 1945[1]

Wearing the scarlet robes of an Oxford Doctor of Civil Law, a
velvet cap upon his head – the effect being to make him look rather
like a 'genial Henry VIII' – Winston Churchill ascended the stage
of Harvard's Sanders Theatre at 11.30 a.m. on 6 September 1943.[2]
There, before a sea of dignitaries, faculty and students, he extolled
the virtues of the Anglo-American alliance: a partnership cemented
by 'blood and history', by 'law, language [and] literature', common
concepts of right and decency, a marked regard for 'fair play' and
'impartial justice' and the intense 'love of personal freedom'. He
commended the system of the Combined Chiefs of Staff – a body
that disposed of British and American ships, armies and aircraft as
if they were the resources of a single nation – and looked forward
to the day when Britons and Americans might share a common citizenship. As to the apparatus for ensuring the future peace of the
world, there were many schemes being considered but – and here
was the nub of his message:

> I am here to tell you that, whatever form your system of world
> security may take . . . nothing will work soundly or for long with-
> out the united effort of the British and American peoples. If we are
> together nothing is impossible. If we are divided all will fail. I there-
> fore preach continually the doctrine of the fraternal association of

our two peoples, not for any purpose of gaining invidious material advantages . . . but for the sake of service to mankind and for the honour that comes to those who faithfully serve great causes.[3]

The concept of an Anglo-American 'special relationship' – a phrase Churchill did not use at Harvard but was already deploying in private – is easy to ridicule. Undermined by Britain's decline as a global power (a reality already apparent in 1943), transatlantic squabbles and above all the asymmetry of its application, its most frequent appearance is as an empty political cliché. Yet the wartime Anglo-American alliance *was* special. The largest, most integrated, most collegiate politico-military alliance in history, it succeeded – despite a multitude of disagreements and strategic errors – in ridding the Axis from North Africa, the Mediterranean and western Europe, while simultaneously laying the foundations for the post-war order.

Not that its participants always got on. Many Britons who experienced the massive influx of American soldiers, sailors and airmen between 1942 and 1945 (around three million in all) considered their allies a bunch of brash, sex-obsessed parvenus. The Americans, as the popular quip went, were 'overpaid, overfed, oversexed and over here'.* (American soldiers retaliated by pointing out that the British were 'underpaid, undersexed and under Eisenhower'.[4]) American GIs were resented for their superior pay (roughly three times that of the British) and, so the British felt, their too-readily awarded decorations. A typical joke had two GIs going to the cinema to see *Desert Victory*, the film about Montgomery's pursuit of Rommel across Cyrenaica. One fainted but the other made it through and was given a medal.[5] When the US II Corps was routed at Kasserine, in Tunisia, in February 1943, some British soldiers expressed satisfaction but most showed sympathy – an attitude the Americans found even more galling.†

---

* Although probably coined by someone else, the phrase was popularised by the comedian Tommy Trinder.
† 'The outstanding fact to me is that the proud and cocky Americans today stand humiliated by one of the greatest defeats in our history,' noted Eisenhower's aide

For their part, American GIs often found their comrades stiff, cold and supercilious. Fifty per cent of American servicemen questioned in September 1942 disagreed with the statement 'English soldiers are going out of their way to help the American soldiers and show them a good time'.[6] Six months later, a clandestine survey conducted by an American sent on a tour of US Army camps around Cambridgeshire revealed that the average GI, 'knowing nothing . . . of British reserve', was, upon arrival in England, 'rocked back on his heels and flung into a period of bewilderment not unmixed with resentment'. Although these feelings tended to dwindle, dissatisfaction with the small, rainy island on which they had been deposited persisted:

He [the average American soldier] thinks the country is inexcusably old-fashioned. He concedes that there is something to be said for tradition but he will not admit that you can say enough in this direction to counterbalance the agonisingly leisurely shopkeepers, the uncomfortable hotels, the outmoded lavatory equipment, the funny trains, [or] the cut of women's clothes . . . He thinks the monetary system is an example of carrying a national joke a bit too far. He doesn't take pounds and shillings really seriously and, knowing very little or almost nothing about the workings of international rates of exchange, he is convinced they are part of an elaborately contrived device for extracting dollars from the pockets of visiting Americans . . . The Englishman's good manners embarrass him. He realises it is better to have good manners than bad . . . but he prefers to believe that this universal good breeding is 'sissy' and merely another sign of the Englishman's unmanly docility. He thinks English food is abominable, English cooking inexcusable, English coffee atrocious, English restaurants unclean, English waitresses untrained, English dietary habits unhealthy . . . He has very little sincere respect for English girls. By and large he is convinced they are all inferior to American girls . . . He is convinced he can sleep with all of them and will, without much prompting, substantiate

Harry Butcher. 'This is particularly embarrassing to us with the British, who are courteous and understanding.'

his statement with a variety of detailed and colourful examples . . .
He says he can cut out any Englishman, soldier or civilian, with any
girl and admits freely that this is due in large measure to his novelty
as a visitor . . . and the fact that even on the pay of a soldier he has
more money to spend than any Englishman . . . He realises this is
not contributing towards his popularity with Englishmen, particularly with English soldiers . . . but he has no intention of voluntarily
giving up his concrete advantage for so nebulous a thing as better
Anglo-American relations.[7]*

Despite this catalogue of iniquities, relations between the British
and American services improved with familiarity. 'I suppose when
I first went to England I had as many inborn prejudices as anyone
born, reared and educated in the Middle West,' noted Eisenhower's
naval aide, Harry Butcher. But he soon discovered that the British
were not really 'red-coated devils'. 'Beneath the Englishman's exterior, which seems cold to many Americans, are a warmth and a sense
of humour in which I find a particular delight.'[8] Forty per cent of
GIs questioned during the autumn of 1942 had received invitations
to British homes, while 9,000 British and American soldiers and
over 4,000 airmen took part in exchanges between units during the
winter of 1943–4. These exchanges proved overwhelmingly successful, even if the adage about Britain and America being two countries
separated by a common language – not to mention customs – was
regularly proved:

In the Mess at supper [wrote one American home], I mentioned
how beautiful Ingrid Bergman was. 'Be careful, sir,' someone said.
'There is a fine of drinks all round if you mention girls in this Mess,
simply not done!' . . . Other topics which are taboo are religion and

---

* 'British girls need more help on how to deal with American soldiers,' read a
report that made it all the way to the higher echelons of the Foreign Office. They
'need to realise that the more yielding they are, the less Americans will value
them, not in moral terms but in terms of desirability'. (FO 371/34122, The Relationship between American Soldiers and the People of Great Britain, Margaret
Mead, December 1943)

money, which limits the discourse to polo, cricket, dogs and the war. You may tell jokes but they must be from *Punch* and you must always quote *Punch* as your authority. This morning, I dunked my toast and the chappie alongside said, 'I remember so well eight years ago seeing a man who had been to America doing that in the Mess – bit of a shock you know!' . . . In justice to these men I must say that the Colonel was a prisoner in Italy, my chief returned from Africa after his hospital had been blown up, another officer escaped from Germany, many went through Calais and Dunkirk and during air-raids they show no emotion . . . In their way the English are all right.[9]

Crucially, inter-service co-operation was practised at the top. From the moment he was appointed as Supreme Allied Commander of Torch and throughout all his subsequent commands, Eisenhower was determined to lead a truly allied operation. It was a fact, he told his officers at his headquarters in St James's Square, that Americans regarded the British as 'standoffish, conceited snobs', while the British looked on Americans as 'loud-mouthed braggarts'. Yet there would be complete harmony between the nationalities on pain of instant dismissal.[10] Ike was as good as his word. When General Ismay mentioned that a senior American officer was wont to boast that his troops would show the British 'how to fight', Eisenhower vowed to 'make the son-of-a-bitch swim back to America'. (Ismay persuaded him to devise some lesser punishment.) Later, a story circulated about a row between a British officer and an American officer at Allied Force HQ. Eisenhower investigated, decided the American was at fault and sent him packing. Horrified, the British officer appealed for clemency. 'He only called me a son of a bitch, Sir, and all of us have now learnt that this is a colloquial expression which is sometimes used almost as a term of endearment.' The Supreme Commander was unmoved: 'I am informed that he called you a *British* son of a bitch. That is quite different. My ruling stands.'[11]

Outside the purely military sphere, Anglo-American co-operation touched or characterised almost every aspect of the war: from intelligence to production, finance to shipping, neutral diplomacy to propaganda, cryptography to meteorology, pharmacology and,

most significant of all, atomic energy. In March 1940, two émigré
Jewish scientists at Birmingham University, the Austrian-born Otto
Frisch and the German-born Rudolf Peierls, had produced a paper
outlining the theoretical basis of a 'super bomb' based on nuclear
fission.[12] The next year, the British Government's MAUD Committee concluded that Frisch and Peierls were correct: a bomb using
only a small amount of enriched uranium was feasible and would
contain the destructive force of roughly 1,800 tons of TNT.* The
MAUD Committee's report transformed American thinking on
the subject. Previously, 'it appeared that the possibility of a successful outcome [of making an atomic bomb] was very remote,'
Vannevar Bush, Chairman of the National Defense Research Committee, informed Roosevelt.[13] Three months later, in October 1941,
the President wrote to Churchill, suggesting a joint approach to this
vital matter, made urgent by the near certainty that the Germans
were also trying to harness atomic energy. Although Churchill did
not respond until mid-December, collaboration between Britain's
atomic weapons programme – known by the appropriately banal
codename Tube Alloys – and the soon-to-be constituted Manhattan
Project continued under the already established principle of 'full
exchange' of scientific information. In June 1942, while staying at
Hyde Park, Churchill and Roosevelt reaffirmed this principle: agreeing to 'complete cooperation' in atomic research, the results to be
shared fully, as 'equal partners'.[14]

Six months later, however, the Americans abruptly ended 'full
exchange', cutting British and Canadian scientists off from information relating to the electromagnetic method, the production
of heavy water, fast-neutron reactions, fissionable material and
all matters pertaining to the actual manufacture of the bomb.
The argument, made by Bush and his deputy, James B. Conant –
the President of Harvard and, thus, the man who would award
Churchill his honorary degree in September 1943 – was that 'equal
partnership' ran contrary to America's post-war interests. Atomic
energy promised huge commercial advantages. Why share these

---

* Contrary to general belief, MAUD was not an acronym but the name of Danish
physicist Niels Bohr's housekeeper.

with the British? Even more important was the realisation that the bomb might be 'capable of maintaining the peace of the world'.[15] Why accept a duopoly when the US could hold the monopoly? British information had been responsible for galvanising American research but now the Americans, with their vast resources, were well in the lead. Although the Manhattan Project's Military Policy Committee admitted that it would be useful to continue to draw on the expertise of British and Canadian scientists – particularly those working on the heavy-water method of manufacturing the highly fissionable isotope plutonium-239 – it would, they continued, 'not hamper the effort at all fatally if the cessation of interchange resulted in the withdrawal of this group'. In fact, at least one senior American scientist, the Nobel laureate Harold Urey, whose work on isotope separation was crucial to the development of the bomb, believed the sudden decision to end collaboration delayed the programme by six months, possibly by 'a year or more'.[16] Given the unknown state of Germany's atomic weapons programme, it was a criminally parochial decision.

The British were dismayed. 'This development has come as a bombshell and is quite intolerable,' fulminated Sir John Anderson, the Cabinet minister responsible for Tube Alloys.[17] Churchill appealed to Hopkins. Sending the Presidential intimate a complete history of US–UK atomic relations, he asked for the restoration of the status quo ante, both in the interests of the project and on the grounds of 'fair play'.[18] Three months later, he took the matter up with Roosevelt during the Trident Conference, held in Washington between 12 and 25 May 1943. FDR promised that co-operation would be restored but then, on 24 June, agreed with Bush that Britain's interest related to the post-war world and was therefore illegitimate.

The dispute was finally resolved at the First Quebec Conference, codenamed Quadrant. On 19 August 1943, Churchill and Roosevelt agreed to pool their resources in a single, US-based atomic weapons programme. The two leaders promised that the bomb would never be used against each other, that its use against a third power would be decided by mutual consent and that all information would be strictly limited to their two countries. As to any commercial or industrial advantages, these would be left to the discretion of the

President to share or not share with the Prime Minister on the basis of what he considered 'fair and just'.[19] There would be a partnership but not a partnership of equals.

British relief stemmed from the fact that Bush and Conant were in one sense correct: the British *were* worried about the post-war world. Where the Americans erred was in assuming that their ally's interest was chiefly commercial. Although British scientists were fully alive to the civilian potential of atomic energy, Churchill disclaimed all such interest. He could not care less about commercial advantages, he told Bush and Secretary of War Stimson when they visited Downing Street in July 1943. What he was concerned with was Britain's security; her very independence as a country. 'It would never do to have Germany or Russia win the race for something which might be used for international blackmail,' he told his guests, adding that the Soviet Union might well achieve this goal unless Britain and the United States worked together.[20]

Stimson appreciated these arguments. A committed Atlanticist, he was convinced that the dawn of the nuclear age rendered Anglo-American co-operation more, not less, imperative. So, ultimately, did Roosevelt. For all his optimism about the Soviet Union, he never wavered in his determination to exclude the Russians from the secrets of the bomb, even if Soviet penetration of the Manhattan Project – of which he was aware – was already rendering this moot. In June 1944, he and Churchill signed an agreement with the aim of collecting as much fissionable material as possible and, in September, the two leaders initialled an *aide-mémoire* pledging to continue atomic co-operation into the post-war era. Although Roosevelt's thoughts on these agreements are unrecorded – the *aide-mémoire* was signed behind the backs of both the State Department and the President's scientific advisers – they fell within his conception of Great Power co-operation, specifically of the need to maintain the Anglo-American alliance to ensure the peace. As he wrote to Cordell Hull, in a different but related context, eleven days after his meeting with Churchill, 'I just cannot go along with the idea of seeing the British Empire collapse financially and Germany, at the same time, building up a potential re-armament machine to make another war possible in twenty years.'[21] Four days later, the same point was made, with even greater clarity, by Hopkins during a conversation with Churchill's scientific adviser, Lord Cherwell: 'It was vital for the United States to have a strong Britain because we must be realistic enough to understand that in any future war England would be on America's side and America on England's. It was no use having a weak ally.'[22]

As the wrangle over the atomic bomb demonstrated, Anglo-American relations were tainted by old suspicions and ancient prejudices. In the oft-repeated stereotypes of the time, the British were scheming, exploitative and reactionary – the practitioners of secret deals and 'balance of power' diplomacy – whilst the Americans were idealistic, naïve and avaricious – the high priests of international morality but with a convenient myopia when it came to their own practices and history. 'The British just do not know how to play cricket,' complained Assistant Secretary of State Breckinridge Long. Their policy, he posited in January 1942, was:

Suck the United States dry. When the peace comes ally with Russia. Let Russia have Poland, eastern Germany, [the] Baltic States, Finland. Hold the Mediterranean; Turkey hold the Dardanelles. Hold Iraq and Iran and India (if the Japs don't get it) and let the United States alone politically and strangle it commercially . . . If they would take the British businessmen and put them in charge of their Army and Navy, they would win some battles. They are smart boys.[23]

'To the British . . . the true friend might be the man who could be manipulated or enticed to see things as the British themselves saw them,' wrote General Wedemeyer, while five leading US Senators returned from a global tour, in September 1943, filled with tales of how 'smart, hard-headed . . . patriotic British officials and businessmen (in Senator Brewster's words, "a bunch of cunning and scheming brutes") were daily outwitting, ousting and frustrating naïve and inexperienced American officials'.[24] Although Roosevelt and his advisers recognised the hyperbole in parts of these statements – while agreeing with others – they were acutely sensitive to them, leading to the extraordinary decision to refuse to hold a single major wartime conference in the UK. The 'Limeys' may be cunning but it would be harder for Americans to claim they had been 'hornswoggled' if the important decisions were taken on US or neutral soil.

The British considered this absurd and insulting. The Americans, they believed, suffered from an inferiority complex, born of their colonial past and the deficiencies of their own bureaucracy. 'We all know Americans suspect the British "ruling classes" and all their works,' minuted a Foreign Office official in May 1942. 'Their suspicions spring in part from historical causes and therefore cannot be easily removed by changing our policy or even our ruling classes – though the latter course might help!'[25]

Yet if the British were not as Machiavellian as many Americans believed, nor were they as innocent as they themselves claimed. A noteworthy example of British manoeuvring occurred during the Casablanca Conference. With British and American forces engaged in Tunisia and Commonwealth forces advancing through Libya, the question naturally arose of an overall commander. The British recommended Eisenhower for the role, with Sir Harold Alexander as his deputy. Ostensibly a compliment – Alexander was a full general, freshly crowned with the laurels of victory, whilst Eisenhower was a temporary lieutenant-general, struggling to make progress against Generaloberst Hans-Jürgen von Arnim – this was in fact a ploy to leave the important decisions in the hands of the British. 'We were pushing Eisenhower up into the . . . rarified atmosphere of a Supreme Commander, where he would be free to devote his time to the political and inter-allied problems', wrote Sir Alan Brooke, 'whilst we inserted under him one of our own commanders to deal with the military situations and to restore the necessary drive and co-ordination which had been so seriously lacking.'[26]

Indeed, whilst the British laughed at the trope of slippery, sophisticated Limeys manipulating innocent, straight-shooting Yanks, this was a straw to which officials and politicians, alarmed by the inexorable rise of American power, increasingly clung. 'We . . . are Greeks in this American Empire,' explained Harold Macmillan to Richard Crossman, recently arrived as Director of Psychological Warfare in Algiers. 'You will find the Americans much as the Greeks found the Romans – great big, vulgar, bustling people, more vigorous than we are and also more idle, with more unspoiled virtues but also more corrupt. We must run AFHQ [Allied Force Headquarters] as the Greek slaves ran the operations of the Emperor Claudius.'[27] Strength lay 'in the recognition of the sources of power and the ability to use them', the Foreign Office's Alan Dudley reminded his colleagues in the North American Department in November 1943, while an anonymous piece of Whitehall doggerel ran:

> In Washington Lord Halifax
> Once whispered to Lord Keynes,
> 'It's true *they* have the money bags
> But *we* have all the brains.'[28]

More practically, the British possessed an integrated, professional secretariat – the envy of American officials fumbling in the chaos of Roosevelt's Washington. While US diplomats complained that they received more information from their British counterparts than from either the White House or the State Department (Cordell Hull was not even permitted to see the minutes of the Tehran conference*), memoranda flew around Whitehall on every conceivable subject relating to Britain's wartime and post-war standing. 'Between now and next spring, the numbers of US troops here will increase from 130,000 to over a million. This will give us one more big opportunity of doing what may be possible to ensure that an important section of the American electorate will return with a favourable impression of what we are and what we stand for,' read a typical Foreign Office minute of June 1943.[29] Later, responding to recurring concerns about British publicity in the US, the head of the FO's North American Department was able to point to 'our hand-picked consuls', recently increased in number and scattered across the forty-eight states, working 'valiantly and successfully to publicise our country, its virtues and its war effort'.[30] No encounter with an influential American went unrecorded, no debate in Congress went

---

* 'The President runs foreign affairs,' complained Hull to Henry Morgenthau in July 1943. 'I have to find out from Halifax what's going on between the President and Churchill.' (Morgenthau Papers, Diaries, 9 July 1943)

unstudied. Polls and surveys giving clues to emerging trends in US public opinion were pored over, while visits of even lowly US officials were privileged with some mark of attention.

All the diligence and hospitality of the Foreign Office could not, however, eliminate the greatest source of Anglo-American discord: a profound disagreement about colonialism and the continued existence of the British Empire. In poll after poll, imperialism was cited as the leading cause of anti-British sentiment within the United States. This feeling increased significantly during the first half of 1942, when the collapse of Britain's East Asian empire appeared to demonstrate the manifold defects of the system. British colonialism was denounced as 'oppressive, stupid, inefficient and insulting'; the broadcasts of Cecil Brown (CBS) and the articles of Wythe Williams (the *New York Times*) exceeding in vitriol 'anything Dr Goebbels and the Japanese official spokesman have put out', according to British officials.[31] On 30 May 1942, Sumner Welles – widely seen as a Presidential mouthpiece – announced the end of the 'Age of Imperialism'. The war was being fought for the 'liberation of all peoples', the Under-Secretary of State declared. Discrimination between peoples due to 'race, creed or colour must be abolished.'[32] Five months later, Henry Luce published an 'Open Letter . . . to the People of England' in his *Life* magazine. Americans may be divided about what they were fighting for, admitted the press magnate, but one 'thing we are sure we are *not* fighting for is to hold the British Empire together . . . If your strategists are planning a war to hold the British Empire together they will sooner or later find themselves strategising all alone.'[33]

The backlash over the *Life* article was so great that some British officials speculated that it may have done more good than harm. On 24 August, however, Wendell Willkie had embarked on a world tour. A known critic of empire, the former Republican Presidential candidate, who was travelling as Roosevelt's personal representative, had no sooner arrived in the Chinese Nationalist capital, Chungking, than he called for the abolition of the colonial system and the setting of timetables by which dependent territories would be transformed into 'free and independent nations'.[34] 'Men and women all over the world are on the march,' he proclaimed in a broadcast upon his return. 'They are no longer willing to be Eastern slaves for Western profits . . . They are resolved, as we must be, that there is no more place for imperialism within their own society than in the society of nations.'[35] Later, he would publish a best-selling book about his peregrinations, under the title *One World*, in which he characterised the attitude of the British administrators he had met in West Africa and the Middle East as 'Rudyard Kipling, untainted even with the liberalism of Cecil Rhodes'.[36]

Whilst the *Manchester Guardian* and elements of the Labour and Liberal parties praised Welles, Luce and Willkie for their abrasive candour, Churchill, the Colonial Office and most of the Conservative Party raged at American ignorance. 'I am sure at heart that [Willkie] is not anti-British,' wrote Lord Halifax to the King, 'but he is an emotional creature and really knows very little about the subjects that he loosely groups under the title of colonial systems!'[37] As Willkie himself admitted, most Americans had little idea that Canada, South Africa, Australia and New Zealand were independent, self-governing Dominions outside the colonial Empire. Within the latter entity – fifty-five territories, extending from the jungles of Borneo to the deserts of British Somaliland, the islands of the Caribbean to the Gold Coast – there was little consistency except for the profusion of barely suppressed religious, ethnic, tribal or caste antagonisms. To confer immediate independence on many of these 'dependencies', the British argued, was merely to invite anarchy, civil war and genocide. It would be 'like giving a child of ten a latchkey, a bank account and a shotgun', declared the (Labour) Home Secretary, Herbert Morrison.[38] 'Take India if that is what you want!' snapped Churchill during a conversation with Roosevelt's newly appointed envoy to the subcontinent, William Phillips. 'Take it by all means! But I warn you . . . that there will be the greatest blood bath in all history.'[39] Even in Ceylon, where the Colonial Office admitted the demands of the Sinhalese majority for 'responsible self-government', no solution had been found that would protect the interests of the Tamils and other Ceylonese minorities.[40]

Of course, British self-interest went hand in hand with humanitarian concerns. As politicians and officials admitted in private, many imperial possessions, such as Gibraltar, Hong Kong, Malaya and the islands of the Caribbean, were simply too important, either strategically or commercially, to relinquish. Without her Empire, Britain, it was widely appreciated, would soon sink to the rank of a second-rate European power. At the same time, there were those, such as the South African Prime Minister Jan Smuts, who could claim, with complete sincerity, that British imperialism was responsible for the 'widest system of organised human freedom which has ever existed in history'. The British Empire was not like the empires of the past, Smuts argued, but a 'great forward movement of states and territories which have either reached, or are still marching forward to, the goal of full freedom and independent status'.[41] (The fact that this freedom did not extend to South Africa's native black population was conveniently ignored.)

Americans, understandably, had scant sympathy with this perspective. As Willkie told the British Ambassador to Moscow, Sir Archibald Clark Kerr, 'something of the George III tradition' still flourished in the US.[42] What the British found harder to excuse was the American failure to see the mote in their own eye. 'Let me see, Mr President,' replied the Colonial Secretary, Oliver Stanley, when challenged by Roosevelt about Britain's piratical acquisition of Hong Kong, 'that was about the time of the [American-]Mexican War, wasn't it?'[43]* Earlier, while staying at the White House in September 1943, Churchill had been accosted by Helen Reid, the wife of the publisher of the *New York Herald Tribune*, about the plight of the 'wretched' Indians. 'To which Indians do you refer?' enquired Churchill. 'Do you by any chance refer to the second greatest nation on earth which under benign and beneficent British rule has multiplied and prospered exceedingly, or do you mean the unfortunate Indians of the North American continent which under your administration are practically extinct?'[44]

More pertinently, the British found it hard to accept American censure while the US continued to deny basic civil rights to her own black population. Visiting a black technical college in Tuskegee, Alabama, Lord Halifax (a former Viceroy of India) left the campus

---

* Having already annexed Texas, the US expanded by some 500,000 square miles during the two-year conflict (1846–8), incorporating most of the territory of what would become New Mexico, Utah, Nevada, Arizona, California and western Colorado.

feeling depressed. The vocational training appeared meagre and the president of the college, 'a cultured man and a Christian', was obliged to eat his lunch in a separate room. 'One had the impression that the Negroes were demanding some sort of bread and were really being given a stone', the Ambassador wrote to the King. 'One has the impression of a great human problem building up, not being tackled by very wide-seeing people and a good many of the experiments that have been made being pretty hollow or rather like will-o'-the-wisps. Cecil Rhodes' platform of "equal rights for all civilised men" seems better and, indeed, the only solution.'[45] One month later, a mob of several thousand white Alabamians attacked black workers at the Mobile Dry Dock and Shipping Company, inaugurating a summer of violence that saw race riots in Los Angeles, Beaumont (Texas), Detroit and New York.*

Black GIs, by contrast, were popular in Britain, where the Government, despite surreptitious support for American-imposed segregation, refused to impose a colour bar.[46] British publicans resented attempts by white GIs to eject their black brethren, while George Orwell voiced the commonly held view that 'the only American soldiers with decent manners are the Negroes'.[47] A popular story from the spring of 1944 involved a West Country farmer being asked what he thought of all the visiting Americans. The farmer replied that he got on very well with Americans 'but had no time for the white men they had brought with them'.[48] The fact was, wrote Roi Ottley, one of the first black American war correspondents to arrive in the UK, 'the British do draw racial distinctions but not within the doors of the British Isles'.[49]

Finally, there was the suspicion that behind American strictures lurked the ambitions of an imperial rival. As early as February 1941, Henry Luce, the publisher of the much-resented 'Open Letter', had exhorted his countrymen to realise the opportunities, as well as the responsibilities, inherent to their growing power. 'The complete opportunity of leadership is *ours*,' he had declared. Americans must realise that they were the inhabitants of 'the most powerful and vital nation in the world and, in consequence . . . exert upon the

* Eleanor Roosevelt felt that the race riots 'put us on a par with Nazism'.

world the full impact of our influence, for such purposes as we see fit and by such means as we see fit'.[50] The idea of an 'American century' resonated with many influential Americans and would do so increasingly as the war developed and American power grew. The genius of its appeal lay in the amalgam of national and international interests. Trade barriers should be abolished not simply because they caused friction and ultimately wars – at least according to Cordell Hull and other New Dealers – but because American business would be able to dominate free markets. Freedom of the seas and the liberation of air routes would spread commerce and ideas but also allow the United States to rule the waves and the skies. Decolonisation was right in principle and lucrative in practice: opening up new markets and exposing previously husbanded natural resources to the unrivalled power of the dollar.

The British appreciated this duality. 'The book aims at founding an American policy against all Empires and is therefore subtly anti-British,' a Foreign Office official noted of Willkie's travelogue. 'At the same time, it points out equally subtly the great opportunities offered to the USA to exploit the Middle East, Africa, China and Russia, to the commercial advantage of the USA.'[51] 'The Willkie-Welles-Luce group . . . see the world as a vast market for the American producer, industrialist and trader,' warned Isaiah Berlin in a despatch of May 1942. 'They are believers in the American Century, energetic technicians and businessmen, filled with a romantic, equally self-confident, economic imperialism, eager to convert the world to the American pattern.'[52] The London-based High Commissioners of Canada, South Africa, Australia and New Zealand complained regularly of the 'economic imperialism of American business interests . . . quite active under the cloak of a benevolent and avuncular internationalism', while British Cabinet Ministers Amery, Cranborne, Stanley and Beaverbrook became obsessed with what the State Department's leading geographer identified as the quest for American economic '*Lebensraum*'.[53]

There is no doubt that Roosevelt was a sincere anti-colonialist. A Wilsonian liberal (except when he was not), he adhered to the principle of 'self-determination', the fifth of the late President's 'Fourteen Points', even if his own views on race were not as enlightened as is commonly supposed. In sharp contrast to his repeated attempts to interfere in Indian affairs, FDR showed no interest in Burmese independence, telling Churchill in April 1942:

> I have never liked Burma or the Burmese. Thank the Lord you have He-Saw, We-Saw, You-Saw [i.e. U Saw, the Burmese Prime Minister] under lock and key. I wish you could put the whole bunch of them in a frying pan with a wall around it and let them stew in their own juice.'[54]

Later, he evinced an interest in 'racial crossing', positing, in terms that would have appealed to the Nazi racial theorist Alfred Rosenberg, that Chinese–European 'crossings' were 'good' but that Japanese–European 'crossings' were 'bad'. 'As far as I could make it out', reported the British Minister to whom these musings were imparted, 'the President's thought is that an Indo-Asian or Eurasian or (better) Eurindasian race, could be developed which would be good and produce a good civilisation and Far East "order", to the exclusion of the Japanese, languishing in Coventry within their original islands.'[55]

Roosevelt's greatest animus was reserved for the French Empire. Convinced that France was finished as a great power, he saw the seeds of her downfall in the 'corrupt', 'exploitative' nature of her imperialism. '*How* do they [French colonies] belong to France?' he demanded, rhetorically, during the Casablanca Conference. 'Why does Morocco, inhabited by Moroccans, belong to France? Or take Indo-China . . . Why was it a cinch for the Japanese to conquer that land? The native Indo-Chinese have been so flagrantly downtrodden that they thought to themselves: anything must be better than to live under French colonial rule!'[56]* Although he was on record as

---

* The British, keen to defend the principle of colonialism, considered the President's criticisms unjust. Prompted to assess the effects of French rule in Indo-China, the Far Eastern scholar Geoffrey Hudson (attached to the FO's Research Department) noted that the French had a good record 'in the building of road and rail communications, dyke construction and irrigation and agricultural and industrial development'. Exports had risen and the population had increased considerably thanks to 'a service of direct medical assistance . . . begun in 1904'.

pledging to restore the French Colonial Empire at the end of the war – a temporary expedient in FDR's mind, designed to bolster French resistance to the Axis – he repeatedly opposed such a restoration, arguing that Indo-China, New Caledonia and Dakar should, at a minimum, be placed under international trusteeships.

Not that he spared the British. At what seemed like every opportunity, Roosevelt criticised British rule in Gambia, Malaya, Hong Kong, Egypt (where the British ruled *de facto*), India and the Caribbean. He took particular delight in needling Churchill on the subject. 'My friend over there doesn't understand how most of our people feel about Britain and her role in the life of other peoples,' he told the wife of the Slovenian-American journalist Louis Adamic, whose anti-colonial tract, *Two-Way Passage*, he had given Churchill to read before dinner at the White House. 'I've been trying to tell him he ought to consider it. It's in the American tradition, this distrust, this dislike and even hatred of Britain – the Revolution, you know, and 1812 and India and the Boer War and all that.'[57]

Yet he also understood how far he could go. And after Churchill's violent reaction to his interference in the Cripps mission, he drew back, declining appeals both from Chiang Kai-shek and Gandhi to mediate between the British and the Indian National Congress. Over the succeeding years, he would make frequent statements about the need for decolonisation – with international trusteeships the preferred intermediary step – but stopped short of a showdown with his European allies. In part, this was due to his sense that time was on his side. If his analysis was correct – and there was every indication that it was – the European empires were doomed regardless of anything the President said or did. More importantly, however, he and his advisers recognised that the Anglo-American alliance mattered more than their liberal international agenda.

Naturally, this pertained first and foremost to the war. Yet it also stretched beyond the immediate crisis. As J. V. A. MacMurray, a former US Minister to China, noted in March 1943, it was 'more valuable for the peace of the world that we should maintain our relations with the British than that we should jeopardise them . . . by participating in the breaking up of the British Empire'.[58] Few responsible Americans would have dissented from this view. Even before Pearl Harbor, US post-war planners, largely centred around the Council on Foreign Relations in New York, had regarded Anglo-American collaboration as the cornerstone of any future peace. Although US thinking on this issue became increasingly unilateral – as American power grew and British power declined – the need to maintain the Anglo-American partnership, in tandem with a future world organisation, remained axiomatic. According to the Yale Institute of International Relations, what mattered most in the world were 'God, love and Anglo-American relations'.[59] Eighty per cent of Americans questioned in May 1943 thought that US–UK collaboration should continue after the peace, while even the *Washington Times-Herald* (part of the isolationist McCormick-Patterson press) grudgingly accepted the need for a post-war military alliance and combined general staff. Although this same stable would criticise Churchill's Harvard speech – 'the democratic President of the United States and royalist Prime Minister of Great Britain are in close alliance with un-American members of the Republican party to destroy it', declared the *Chicago Tribune* – most US media applauded the Prime Minister's message.[60] 'It was not a plea. It was not a challenge,' declared the *Boston Post*. 'It was the warning of a realist and responsible thinker to the English-speaking people to stand together in a world of great forces.'[61] 'Great Britain and the United States have insoluble bonds of language, creed and goal,' noted the *St Louis Post-Dispatch*. 'In the world of peace as in the world of war, their front must be united.'[62] The *New York Times* celebrated 'the warm friendship and the comrade-like cooperation of two great peoples', while the *Buffalo Courier-Express* shared 'Mr Churchill's confidence that co-operation of the English-speaking countries can be made the foundation stone of a new and better world'.[63]

The 'special relationship' was hedged with mutual misunderstanding and always operated unequally but it was the most versatile, practical and, in some senses, enduring pact to emerge from the Second World War.

XXII

Stress and Strain

Stalin lets no ideological motives influence his actions. He is highly
intelligent. He weighs with suspicious realism all factors involved in
advancing the interests or boundaries of the Soviet Union. He moves
where opposition is weak. He stops where opposition is strong.

William C. Bullitt to Franklin D. Roosevelt, 29 January 1943[1]

While the Western 'Emperors' strategised and enjoyed themselves in Morocco, vast Soviet forces were winning the war in the
East. On 2 February 1943, the remnants of Friedrich Paulus' starved,
frost-bitten army surrendered at Stalingrad. Ninety-one thousand
German soldiers, including the recently created Generalfeldmarschall, went into captivity. The Axis had lost some 850,000 men
during the battle, while Soviet casualties exceeded a million – more
than the combined Anglo-American death toll for the entire war.
On 14 February, Rostov was liberated. In the north, Voronezh was
already in Soviet hands after the destruction of the Hungarian 2nd
Army on the upper Don. Kharkov fell to the Red Army on 16 February but the Germans retook the city on 14 March after an inspired
counterattack by Generalfeldmarschall Manstein's Army Group
South.

Churchill and Roosevelt heaped praise on Stalin. This 'tremendous feat of arms', the Prime Minister told correspondents in
Cyprus, was achieved under the command and direction of a 'great
warrior': a leader whose name must rank among the 'most hon-
oured and most lasting in the history of the Russian people'.[2] But it
was deeds, not words, the Soviet dictator sought. Dismayed at the
delay in clearing the Axis from Tunisia (now projected to be completed by April, rather than February), he was even more disturbed

by the deferment of the cross-Channel assault. 'It seems to me', he wrote to Churchill on 16 February, 'the present situation demands the greatest possible speeding up of the action contemplated – i.e. of the opening of the second front in the West at a considerably earlier date than indicated. In order not to give the enemy any respite, it is extremely important to deliver the blow from the West in the spring or early summer and not to postpone it until the second half of the year.'[3] One month later, he reminded the Prime Minister that he himself had admitted the possibility of opening a 'second front' in 1942 (when Molotov had visited Britain) and as good as promised to open one in the spring of 1943. The invasion of Sicily – Operation Husky – was important but no substitute, while the sluggish progress of American and British forces in Tunisia had supposedly allowed the Germans to transfer thirty-six divisions to the Eastern Front.

Despite these chidings, Western–Soviet relations were on a friendlier footing during the early months of 1943 than hitherto. Although Stalin remained deeply suspicious of his capitalist partners and, as recently as October 1942, had expressed the view that Churchill's opposition to the second front stemmed from his desire to see the Soviet Union defeated, he refrained from those accusations of bad faith and cowardice that had so infuriated the Prime Minister the previous summer. On 6 November 1942, during a speech to mark the twenty-fifth anniversary of the Bolshevik Revolution, he had rejected the claim that the Allies lacked cohesion due to ideological differences, hailing the 'progressive rapprochement' of the 'Anglo-Soviet-American coalition' and forecasting their collective triumph over 'Hitlerite tyranny'.[4] The encirclement of the 6th Army at Stalingrad and the victories at El Alamein and in French North Africa gave substance to these sentiments. British and American audiences applauded the Soviet war film *The City That Stopped Hitler*, while the Soviet leader praised the British documentary *Desert Victory*, informing the British Ambassador, Sir Archibald Clark Kerr, that it would help dispel the sense among the Russian people that 'England is not fighting but watching from the sidelines'.[5]

Clark Kerr had arrived in Moscow in February 1942. A raffish and eccentric Scot – a man who wrote his despatches with a quill and had disguised himself as a Cossack in order to take part in a Russian cavalry raid during the First World War – he was the antithesis of the earnest and austere Cripps. As British Ambassador to Baghdad between 1935 and 1938, he played the role of *éminence grise* to a succession of short-lived administrations, delighting in and despairing of the antics of the 23-year-old King Ghazi, whose fondness for 'pillow fights' was curtailed only after an especially vigorous bout with his Hejazi servants landed him (and subsequently the Queen) with syphilis.[6] He then went to Chungking, where he established a close relationship with Chiang Kai-shek and a reputation as 'the best-liked British Ambassador to China'.[7] In 1929, he had married an eighteen-year-old Chilean beauty, twenty-nine years his junior, named María Salas. But 'Tita', as she was known, fled the squalor of Chungking for the bright lights and marbled floors of America's east coast. This estrangement, which Clark Kerr minded terribly, provides the context for a now famous piece of Foreign Office literature. 'My dear Reggie,' he wrote to his friend and Foreign Office Minister the Earl of Pembroke, on 6 April 1943:

> In these dark days man tends to look for little shafts of light that spill from heaven . . . So I propose to share with you a tiny flash that has illuminated my sombre life and tell you that God has given me a new Turkish colleague whose card tells me that he is called Mustapha Kunt. We all feel like that, Reggie, now and then, especially when spring is upon us, but few of us would care to put it on our cards. It takes a Turk to do that.[8]*

Clark Kerr's rakish side was an advantage in Moscow. Forced to take refuge in a Kremlin air raid shelter during his first meeting with the Soviet dictator, he bonded with his host by telling dirty stories and discussing pipes. It was a case of 'two old rogues, each one seeing the roguery in the other and finding comfort and harmony in it', he reported to Eden.[9] Later, during a banquet in honour of Wendell

---

* Of his later career in the United States, the American journalist Joseph Alsop would criticise Clark Kerr for his love of risqué jokes and inability to suffer fools, noting that there were 'many important fools in Washington'.

Willkie, he demonstrated the correct way to use a Tommy gun by pretending to rake the bellies of Stalin, Molotov and the American guest with the weapon. This caused Stalin to demonstrate his own skill, picking off the members of his own government, with obvious delight, until almost no one in the dining room was left alive.[10] On this occasion, as on others, Soviet hospitality was a bibulous affair. Challenged to a brandy-drinking competition by Andrei Vyshinsky, Deputy Commissar for Foreign Affairs and State Prosecutor during the show-trials, the Ambassador managed to keep pace until rescued by the inevitable after-dinner film, through which he quietly dozed. Later, following a particularly heavy session at the Spiridonovka Palace, he awoke to find himself lying on the floor of his study, fully clothed, with his head in the grate. When he enquired how he had come to be in this indecorous posture, the Embassy butler replied, 'Because, Your Excellency, you insisted.'[11]

On 28 February 1943, Clark Kerr commented on the 'benignity and good temper of Stalin and Molotov' at a recent interview and on 26 March the Foreign Office's Christopher Warner observed that the Soviets had 'not done more than hint at the second front grievance this year in their press'.[12] Then, on 13 April, the Germans announced the discovery of mass graves in the Katyn Forest near Smolensk.

Ten thousand Polish officers, over half of the missing Polish POWs, had been shot in the back of the head, according to Radio Berlin. Their worst fears realised, the Polish Government-in-Exile called on the International Red Cross to investigate. The Kremlin met this request with manufactured fury. Blaming the Germans for the massacre, Stalin – who had indeed sanctioned the murder of what turned out to be 21,892 Polish prisoners, on Beria's recommendation, in March 1940 – accused the Polish Government of colluding with Russia's enemies:

> The Government of General Sikorski has not only not treated the vile fascist calumny against the Union of Soviet Socialist Republics with the contempt it deserves but it did not find it necessary even to put any question in this connection to the Soviet Government or ask for any explanation [he wrote to Churchill on 21 April] . . . The fact

that the campaign hostile to the Union of Soviet Socialist Republics broke out simultaneously in the German and Polish press and is
being conducted in the same direction, cannot leave any doubt that
between the enemy of the Allies – Hitler – and the Government of
General Sikorski there exists contact and understanding with regard
to this hostile campaign.[13]

The British had little doubt the Soviets were responsible. Cadogan
thought Stalin protested too much, while Churchill told guests in
Downing Street that the revelations were 'probably true', the Bolsheviks being 'very cruel' when they wished to be.[14] On 24 May, the
recently appointed British Ambassador to the Polish Government-
in-Exile, Owen O'Malley, produced a masterly analysis of the
available evidence, the cumulative effect of which was 'to throw
serious doubt on Russian disclaimers' and point towards 'a mon-
strous crime . . . committed by a foreign government – albeit a
friendly one'.[15] The Foreign Office was impressed and Churchill
sent a copy to Roosevelt. But its content, no less than its conclusions, were academic. Neither the British nor the Americans had
any intention of upending relations with the Soviet Union over a
historic crime (one of many, as Cadogan noted) even if it did involve
a mutual ally. Stalin understood this and exploited the crisis, severing ties with the Sikorski Government, even though Churchill and
Eden had prevailed upon the unfortunate Premier to withdraw his
request for an independent investigation.

The British were annoyed. Churchill complained to Stalin, while
Eden poured out his disappointment to Maisky. Neither *démarche*
had the slightest effect. The Soviet press continued to castigate the
'London Poles' – or 'Hitler's Polish Allies' as *Pravda* had started
referring to them – while the Vozhd, satisfied with his strategy of
brazening it out, reproved the British for failing to prevent 'one
ally from delivering a blow against another'.[16] This proved the last
word on the matter. Roosevelt refused to be exercised about the
revelations, while Churchill told Maisky that Anglo-Soviet relations
would be unaffected even if the allegations were true. Not for the
first time, the democracies found the principles they were fighting
for at odds with the realities of global war.

In his May Day address, Stalin appeared to reward Anglo-American pusillanimity over Katyn by linking Soviet victories, at Stalingrad and in Ukraine, with Anglo-American success in North Africa. 'For the first time since the beginning of the war, the blow at the enemy from the east, dealt by the Red Army, merged with a blow from the west, dealt by the troops of our allies, into one joint blow.'[17] A few weeks later, he seemed to go further: proving his collaborative credentials by dissolving the Comintern – the body responsible for the co-ordination of communist activities across the world. The British were delighted. A BBC special directive described the announcement as 'by far the most important political event of the war', while Churchill thought the liquidation of the Third International was 'intended by Stalin to be a real contribution' to Western–Soviet understanding.[18] The Americans were even more enthused. Hailed by Hull, Willkie and almost every US radio commentator, the news was greeted with headlines such as 'Reds Dissolve International to End Friction with Allies' and 'Soviets End Comintern to Win War'. The distinguished foreign correspondent John Gunther proclaimed the death of the communist dream of 'world revolution', while the Chairman of the House Committee on Un-American Activities, Congressman Martin Dies Jr, speculated that he might be out of a job.[19]

In fact, Stalin had been thinking of abolishing the Comintern for some time. According to Georgi Dimitrov, the Comintern's General Secretary, the dissolution was first mooted during the era of the Nazi–Soviet Pact but was postponed lest it appear that Moscow was operating under the influence of Berlin. Then, in April 1941, after a performance at the Bolshoi, Stalin made a toast in which he reflected on the recent disaffiliation of the American Communist Party from the Comintern:

Dimitrov has parties leaving the Comintern . . . There is nothing wrong with that. On the contrary, the com[munist] parties ought to be made independent . . . They should turn into national com[munist] parties with various names – the Workers' Party, the Marxist Party etc. The name does not matter. What matters is that they put down roots among their own peoples and concentrate on their own proper tasks . . . Once the com[munist] parties have become stronger in this way, then re-establish their international organisation.[20]

This was one element in Stalin's thinking. As Vyshinsky told Clark Kerr in June 1942, there was a difference between the 'dialectic development [of Marxism] and simple opportunism'. 'I had to remind Kerr that in our opinion revolutions are not made and exported, that we have never done this and have no plans to.'[21] Another was that the Comintern made it easier for capitalists to 'smear' communists by portraying them as the instruments of a foreign power. Stalin empathised with this view. Highly distrustful of foreigners, he looked on his own émigré communists with fear, accusing Dimitrov of harbouring a 'nest of spies' in the heart of the Soviet Union.[22] Yet these were perennial factors and do not explain the decision to dissolve the Comintern in May 1943. The motive for this specific decision appears threefold. First, there was the official justification: the fact that the Soviet Union was engaged in an existential war and that, under these circumstances, it was the duty of the 'widest masses of the people' to aid the 'military efforts of the Governments of those countries [capitalist or not] aimed at the speediest defeat of the Hitlerite bloc'.[23] Second was Stalin's growing respect for traditional nationalism, reflected in his own transformation from revolutionary conspirator to Marshal of the Soviet Union, a title he affected with Romanov pomp from March 1943. And, finally, there was Katyn. Although documentary evidence linking the two events is lacking, the timing of the decision, three weeks after the German revelations, is indicative of cause and effect.* Stalin did not govern by coincidence and while he had succeeded in hurling the German accusations back on the unfortunate Poles, the opportunity to distract his Western allies with a gesture he was going to make anyway seems to have been too good to miss.

The demise of the Comintern revived questions about Stalin and the trajectory of the Soviet Union. For many, the news added to a growing sense that the USSR was shedding her revolutionary

* Dimitrov records being informed of the decision by Molotov on 8 May 1943.

ideology and, under the demands of war and the influence of her Western partners, settling into the mould of a conventional state. The most important subscriber to this thesis was Roosevelt. In the President's mind the USSR was evolving, 'from the original form of Soviet communism . . . toward a modified form of state social-ism'.[24] At the same time, the 'capitalist' powers were becoming increasingly social-democratic, with large bureaucracies and vast government spending. Writing to the banker Thomas Lamont, in a neglected letter of November 1942, FDR recalled a conversation he had had with Maxim Litvinov – then People's Commissar for For-eign Affairs – during the negotiations for American recognition of the USSR in 1933:

> Finally . . . I threw up my hands and said to him, 'What is the use of all this anyway? Your people and my people are as far apart as poles.' Litvinov's answer is worthy of an eventual place in history. He said, 'I hope you will not feel that way, Mr President, because I do not. In 1920 we were as far apart as you say. At that time, you were 100 per cent capitalistic and we were at the other extreme . . . In these thirteen years we have risen in the scale, to let us say, a position of twenty. You Americans, especially since last March, have gone to a position of eighty. It is my real belief that in the next twenty years we will go to forty and you will come down to sixty . . . And while it is difficult for nations to confer with and understand each other with a difference between twenty and eighty, it is wholly possible for them to do if the difference is only between forty and sixty.' Perhaps Litvinov's thoughts of nine years ago are coming true.[25]*

British propaganda promoted this line. Responding to the mass of enthusiasm for the Soviet Union, following the victories at Moscow

---

* 'You Westerners will never understand Bolshevism', the Comintern executive and itinerant revolutionary Karl Radek had warned a US Embassy official in 1934. 'You consider Bolshevism as a hot bath whose temperature can be raised and lowered to suit the taste of the bather. This is not true. You are either 100 per cent in the bath and 100 per cent for it, or you are 100 per cent outside and 100 per cent against it.'

and Stalingrad, Ministry of Information 'Speakers' Notes' emphasised that Soviet communism was no longer a 'malignant Marxist
bogey but . . . a Russian answer to a Russian problem'. Stalin was
a reformer and although his reforms had not gone so far as to turn
Russia into a 'democratic state', the USSR was nevertheless 'moving
towards the democracies'.[26] The re-establishment of the Holy Synod
of the Russian Orthodox Church and the reopening of the Moscow
Theological Academy and Seminary in September 1943, after more
than two decades of religious suppression and persecution, augmented this belief. The Archbishop of York visited Moscow, while
the 'liberalisation' of the USSR was extolled by such sympathetic
commentators as Alexander Werth (for the BBC), Alaric Jacob (for
the *Daily Express*) and E. H. Carr (Deputy Editor of the *Times*).

Naturally, there were sceptics. The *New York Times'* military correspondent, Hanson Baldwin, thought the most compelling argument
for maintaining a large US Army was to 'prevent [the] spread of
Russia and communism over Europe after the war', while Assistant
Secretary of State Adolf Berle saw no evidence that Moscow had
abandoned its dream of world revolution, noting Soviet-sponsored
fifth-column activities in Europe and Latin America.[27] On 29 January
1943, the former US Ambassador to Moscow William Bullitt submitted a 21-page memorandum to Roosevelt in which he dismissed
the notion that Stalin – or 'Uncle Joe', as Churchill and Roosevelt
had incongruously taken to calling him – was a 'changed man' and
warning of the dictator's likely determination to dominate and Bolshevise as many countries as possible:

> The wishful thinkers just now are fond of arguing that 'Stalin has
> become a Russian nationalist, interested only in security for his
> country, therefore, the Soviet Union will become pacific'. They
> forget conveniently that the Russian nationalist state was never
> pacific. Tsarist Russia was, and the Soviet Union today is, an agglom-
> eration of conquered peoples. Since the time of Peter the Great, the
> Russians have extended their rule ruthlessly over one people after
> another. Primary school books in the Soviet Union are issued in 156
> different languages and dialects. The Russians are an immensely
> endowed people, physically strong, intellectually gifted, emotionally

rich. The Ukrainians are even more gifted than the Russians. They were overcome by the Russians by force of numbers. The Russians win their battles in the field and in bed. No race on earth, not even the German, has shown such burgeoning energy as the Russian during the past hundred years. They have conquered one sixth of the earth's surface. They are still bursting with expansive energy . . . Even if Stalin had become a mere Russian nationalist – which he has not – that would be no guarantee of pacific behaviour; indeed, it would be a guarantee of aggressive imperialism.[28]

FDR noted the 'Bullitt thesis' but dismissed it. He had rarely found a problem he could not solve, or at least try to solve, and the rewards of bringing the Soviet Union into the circle of responsible nations were as great as the failure would be catastrophic. In March 1943, he decided to despatch another former Ambassador, Joseph E. Davies, to Moscow with a letter for Stalin, suggesting that the two leaders should meet informally, 'without Churchill'.[29] The Prime Minister had done a 'grand job' in Moscow last August, the President told Davies, but the fact was that Stalin disliked and distrusted him.[30] Churchill's opposition to the second front was well known, as was his fanatical antipathy towards Bolshevism. 'There was no doubt that the Russians had more confidence in our good faith and purposes than they had in the British Empire,' he continued on 11 April, concluding that a Roosevelt–Stalin meeting stood the best chance of establishing a sure basis for future co-operation.[31]

Davies was the perfect choice for such a mission. A publicity-seeking lawyer who had been rewarded for his wife's contributions to Roosevelt's campaigns with the Moscow Embassy in 1937, he was the archetypal 'useful idiot': a man who could sit through the farce of the show-trials and leave convinced that there had, indeed, been a 'conspiracy' against Stalin. In 1941, he had published a best-selling memoir, *Mission to Moscow*: a work of such cloying, pro-Soviet propaganda that its film adaptation, released in 1943, even embarrassed the Kremlin.* Unfortunately, for Roosevelt's purposes,

---

* 'All the Americans present . . . felt that the film was received with rather glum curiosity and doubted if the Hollywood treatment of events described in Davies'

Davies was also a blabbermouth who proceeded to tell everyone he encountered (including the Queen's brother, David Bowes-Lyon) that he was travelling to Moscow with a Presidential letter. When Harriman eventually informed Churchill of the contents of the missive, the latter was dismayed. 'The whole world is expecting and all our side are desiring a meeting of the three great powers,' he wrote to Roosevelt on 25 June. A tripartite conference would be 'one of the milestones of history' but a meeting between the heads of the US and the USSR, with the British Empire excluded, would be a boon to enemy propaganda.[32] FDR's response to this appeal was simply to lie. Responding to the Prime Minister on 28 June, he claimed that the idea for a meeting *à deux* had been Stalin's, when it was in fact him who had ruled out Iceland as a potential rendezvous on the grounds that it would be 'difficult not to invite Prime Minister Churchill'.[33]

As it transpired, Churchill need not have worried, except in so far as Roosevelt's shenanigans revealed the changing power balance within the alliance. Although Stalin accepted Roosevelt's proposal, tentatively agreeing to meet the President in Alaska in July, he then went silent, ignoring the President's subsequent messages, before finally expressing a preference for a tripartite meeting, including Churchill. Although the despot's fear of flying, assassins and intrigues at home made it unlikely that he would ever cross the Pacific, the reason for turning what could have been a polite refusal into a diplomatic snub was the Anglo-American decision to, once again, postpone the invasion of France.

In mid-May, Churchill, Roosevelt and their staffs had convened in Washington where it had been decided, after ferocious argument, that the earliest date upon which a cross-Channel attack could take place was 1 May 1944. Stalin's telegram reacting to this news was, as expected, scalding. Reciting the list of previous Anglo-American promises, he accused his allies of leaving the Soviet Union to absorb the might of the Wehrmacht single-handed. 'It goes without saying', he responded to an emollient message from Churchill,

book met with the general approval of the Russians,' reported the American Ambassador, Admiral William Standley, after a Kremlin showing.

on 24 June, 'that the Soviet Government cannot put up with such disregard of the most vital Soviet interests in the war against the common enemy. You are writing that you fully understand my disappointment. I must say that here is not simply the question of disappointment on the part of the Soviet Government, here is the question of its confidence in the Allies which is severely tried by the above happenings.'[34]

Although Stalin's anger was justified – the Western powers, in their desire to maintain the Russian front, *had* made promises they could not fulfil – Churchill sent an indignant, self-justifying reply. 'I am getting rather tired of these repeated scoldings', he had told Clark Kerr on 16 June, suggesting the Ambassador might warn Stalin of the danger of offending the democracies, 'whose war-making strength is growing with every month that passes and who may play a helpful part in the Russian future'.[35] Although the Vozhd did not deign to reply – nor to any other messages sent during July – he proceeded with plans to withdraw the Anglophile Maisky from London and the internationalist Litvinov from Washington. Both men, remembering the fate of colleagues, feared for their lives and Litvinov considered defecting. They were replaced by the automatons, Andrei Gromyko – a Molotov protégé, whose tenure in Washington, and later at the United Nations would earn him the moniker 'Mr Nyet' – and the equally colourless Fedor Gusev – a dedicated party man who, according to Clark Kerr, looked like a cross between a 'sealion' and a 'pumpkin' and whose English seemed limited to 'I will refer the matter to my superiors'.[36]

In mid-August, Churchill, Roosevelt and the Combined Chiefs of Staff reconvened at Quebec to determine future strategy in light of the successful invasion of Sicily and subsequent fall of Mussolini, following a vote of no confidence in the Fascist Grand Council. Although the second front was foremost on the agenda (at least on the American side) and despite the Red Army's recent spectacular victories at Kursk, Orel and Kharkov, Stalin was not invited. The Soviet dictator made his presence felt, however, by complaining vociferously at the USSR's exclusion from the negotiations for the surrender of Italy. Roosevelt and Churchill were both 'mad' at the despot's accusatory tone, the President announced before dinner at the Citadel on 24 August. Yet FDR's ire took the form of 'making him gayer than usual', recalled Harriman. Churchill, on the other hand, was visibly perturbed, scowling throughout dinner and muttering about 'bloody consequences' afterwards.[37] The next day, the Prime Minister's doctor, Sir Charles Wilson, recently ennobled as Lord Moran, confided to Eden that his patient seemed increasingly depressed, wondering 'whether we shall have to fight Russia after Germany is finished'.[38]

The one encouraging sign in Soviet–Western relations was that Stalin, after much cajoling by Roosevelt and Churchill, had finally agreed to a tripartite conference that autumn. There should be a meeting of the three countries' foreign ministers, in Moscow, to prepare the ground, and the Soviet leader's supposed need to keep in touch with developments on the Russian front would allow him to travel no further than Tehran – necessitating a perilous ten-day voyage for the wheelchair-bound President and a three-day journey for the Prime Minister – but he *was* prepared to meet and even considered the holding of such a meeting 'important'.[39] The Bear might be growling but at least the summer frost was over.

*

In addition to Soviet difficulties, the ten months between the Casablanca Conference and the Tehran Conference were bedevilled by Free French issues: in particular, the recurring problem of what to do with de Gaulle. The handshake between the British-backed de Gaulle and the American-backed Giraud had solved nothing. On the contrary, it was the starting gun for a bitter power struggle: a Gallic cockfight for which the more junior General, with his increasingly attuned political sense and ruthless determination, was immeasurably better suited.

Even before de Gaulle had made his grudging appearance at Anfa, his supporters in North Africa – multiplied by the Darlan deal, with which Giraud was closely associated – had been agitating on his behalf. Giraud, by contrast, had neither political allies nor political judgement. A traditional soldier with little affection for democracy, his early administration was divided between 'honourable, relatively competent, narrow-minded reactionaries', known to Harold Macmillan and his staff as the 'Old Etonians', and 'faintly disreputable adventurers', known as the 'Old Harrovians'.[40] De Gaulle and his disciples exploited this weakness, as well as Giraud's lack of republican credentials. On 23 February 1943, the French National Committee drew up a memorandum (published on 12 March), setting out the terms upon which it was prepared to co-operate with Giraud: there should be a central authority endowed with all the prerogatives of a government; the armistice of 1940 must be recognised as illegal and, thus, null and void; republican law must be re-established in North Africa; and the Empire must be purged of leaders who had collaborated with Vichy.

The day before this document was produced, de Gaulle had requested a British aeroplane to take him to visit Free French troops in North Africa and then on to the Levant. Churchill, still smarting over the General's behaviour at Anfa, refused. *'Alors, je suis prisonnier!'* exclaimed the Free French leader, retiring to his north London home to sulk. Churchill, who fully endorsed this conception of the situation, telephoned Charles Peake, the Foreign Office liaison with the French National Committee, and instructed him to ensure the 'Monster of Hampstead' did not escape.[41] Peake did his best but after a week on the Heath the General renewed his request for air facilities. On 2 April, following painstaking diplomacy by René Massigli, the FNC's recently appointed Commissioner for Foreign Affairs, Churchill agreed to receive de Gaulle in Downing Street.

'Enfin! Je suis prisonnier, bientôt vous m'enverrez à l'Île de Man,' declared the General on entering the Cabinet room.

'Non, mon Général, pour vous, très distingué, toujours la Tower of London,' responded Churchill.[42]

There then followed a fairly well-tempered conversation, during which the Prime Minister urged de Gaulle to postpone his trip until he had reached a deal – currently being negotiated through Georges Catroux – with Giraud. The General appeared receptive. When, however, Churchill forwarded him a similar request from Eisenhower (actually concocted by Macmillan in conjunction with Allied Force Headquarters), he flew into a rage and issued a press release claiming that he was being prevented from concluding a union of

French patriots by the Anglo-Saxons. AFHQ were livid, in particular the Americans who, as Macmillan's adviser Roger Makins noted, nursed a 'dislike and distrust of de Gaulle . . . so violent as to be almost pathological'.[43]

Although he did not know it, the Free French leader was skating on extremely thin ice. On 6 May 1943, Jean Monnet – the former head of the Anglo-French Purchasing Commission, now responsible for mentoring the politically inept Giraud – sent Harry Hopkins a letter denouncing de Gaulle and his agents. Referring to a speech the General had made two days earlier, in which de Gaulle had attacked Giraud for frustrating the unity of the French Empire, Monnet expressed the view that the Free French leader was making 'a straight bid for arbitrary power . . . with all the risks of fascism'. The atmosphere fermented by his supporters was not quite that of a *coup d'état,* but to call it ' "psychological pressure" was to put it very mildly indeed'.[44] Five days later, Churchill arrived in Washington, where he found himself under considerable Presidential pressure to ditch de Gaulle. 'I must now warn you solemnly of a very stern situation developing here about de Gaulle,' he wrote to Attlee and Eden on 21 May. 'Hardly a day passes that the President does not mention it to me. Although this is done in a most friendly and jocular manner, I am sure that he feels very strongly indeed upon it and I see real danger developing if matters are not gripped . . . De Gaulle has hopelessly missed his market in North Africa. He is in my opinion absorbed in his own personal career which depends on a vain endeavour to make himself the arbiter of the conduct of every Frenchman following the military defeat. I ask my colleagues to consider urgently whether we should not now eliminate de Gaulle as a political force and face Parliament and France upon the issues.'[45]

Horrified, the Foreign Office thought the White House atmosphere had gone to the Prime Minister's head. So did the War Cabinet. Meeting on the evening of 23 May, its members, always braver when Churchill was out of the country, came down unanimously against the proposal. 'The name of "de Gaulle" was regarded as a symbol of the Republic and the Gaullist movement stood for the Entente,' commented Attlee, while the service ministers drew attention to the roughly 80,000 Gaullist troops and 6,000 sailors currently serving the Allied cause.[46] Of course, de Gaulle was infuriating. As the head of the British Security Mission in the Levant States, Lieutenant Patrick Coghill, noted, 'Joan of Arc must have been a damned nuisance to her allies and colleagues.'[47] But there was no denying his power. The irony was that the American *démarche* came just when de Gaulle was on the cusp of reaching an agreement with Giraud.

The auguries had been clear for some time. Since the beginning of the year, scores of French soldiers and even more sailors had been defecting to join the Free French. French ships docking in US and British ports were losing up to half their crews, while Anglo-French troops arriving in the newly liberated Tunisian town of Sfax were greeted with cries of '*Vive de Gaulle!*'[48] On 15 May, the General received his trump card. Two months earlier, Jean Moulin, de Gaulle's liaison with the Resistance, had returned to France, tasked with forming a national Resistance council. Now, just as Roosevelt was urging Churchill to break with de Gaulle, this courageous former civil servant delivered the goods. The newly formed Conseil National de la Résistance, comprising not only the Resistance but the old political parties, pledged itself to General de Gaulle and the French National Committee, adding that the 'subordination of General de Gaulle to General Giraud' would never be tolerated by the French people.[49] Two days later, Giraud accepted defeat. De Gaulle was invited to Algiers and on 3 June 1943 the French Committee of National Liberation (Comité Français de Libération Nationale, CFNL) was born with de Gaulle and Giraud as joint Presidents.

Neither the British nor the Americans doubted that de Gaulle had both the capacity and the intention of swallowing Giraud. Yet even they were surprised by the speed with which the Free French leader established his untrammelled authority. Within hours of his arrival in Algiers, de Gaulle had insisted on the dismissal of Charles Noguès (Résident-Général of French Morocco) and Pierre Boisson (Résident-Général of French West Africa) and unilaterally accepted the resignation of Marcel Peyrouton, the former Vichy Ambassador to Buenos Aires, now Résident-Général of Algeria. He then initiated a row over control of the French armed forces, at one stage threatening to resign from the barely week-old Committee. This opening salvo in the 'Battle of the Villas', as one American official

termed it, induced an almost hysterical telegram from Roosevelt to
Churchill, demanding that they rid themselves once and for all of
this turbulent Frenchman.[50]

Churchill sympathised. As early as December 1942, he had
warned MPs against placing all their confidence in a man who was
by no means 'an unfaltering friend of Britain' and, in early June,
made a clumsy attempt to influence the British press away from
its natural Gaullophilia.[51] On 11 June, he adjured Macmillan, who
had relayed de Gaulle's request for Allied recognition of the CFNL,
to recall 'Matthew, chapter seven, verses sixteen and twenty': ' "Ye
shall know them by their fruits. Do men gather grapes of thorns,
or figs of thistles?" ' Macmillan's response was: 'I am doing my
best. But see Revelations, chapter two, verses two to four: "I know
thy works and thy labour and thy patience and how thou canst not
bear them which are evil . . . Nevertheless I have somewhat against
thee because thou hast left thy first love." '[52]

Over the next month, Eden inched Churchill towards recognising
the CFNL – essential, in his view, to Anglo-French relations both now
and in the future. More troublesome were the Americans: not those
at AFHQ – Eisenhower, his deputy, Bedell Smith, and Murphy – all
of whom, under Macmillan's tutelage, had come to appreciate the
wisdom of such a move, but Roosevelt and the State Department.
On 21 July, Churchill sent the President a long telegram explaining
the pressure he was under – from the Foreign Office, Parliament,
his Cabinet colleagues, even the Kremlin – to recognise the CFNL.
Roosevelt's response, received the next day, was that the furthest
he was prepared to go was to 'accept' the Committee's 'local [and]
civil authority', it being simultaneously emphasised that the future
government of France could only be decided by the French people
after the war and that relations with the Committee would continue
to be determined by the military requirements of the British and
American commanders.[53]

The argument continued at Quebec. On 20 August, Eden spent
two hours with Hull but failed to make any headway. 'I told him
we had to live twenty miles from France and I wanted to rebuild
her so far as I could.'[54] Hull, who, according to Eden's Private Secretary, Valentine Lawford, had all the attributes of 'a dried bit of

fruit', responded by accusing the British of financing de Gaulle, the implication being that this money had been used to attack the State Department and its pro-Vichy policy.[55] 'I like the old man but he has an obsession against [the] Free French which nothing can cure,' the Foreign Secretary noted in his diary.[56]*

Eventually, it was decided that the Allies would have to flaunt their disagreement by resorting to separate statements. The British recognised the CFNL as the body responsible for administering those French overseas territories which acknowledged its authority and for directing the French war effort, whilst the American declaration – reflecting Roosevelt's unwillingness 'to give de Gaulle a white horse on which he could ride into France and make himself the master of a government' – was heavily qualified.[57] A little over two months later, de Gaulle succeeded in forcing the hapless Giraud from the Committee but Allied recognition was not withdrawn. As the former Secretary-General of the Quai d'Orsay, Alexis Léger, commented of the General, 'It is not winning he likes, it is conquering.'[58]

The final French drama of the year was an altogether more sordid affair. As we have seen, the Anglo-French invasion of the Levant, in July 1941, was preceded by a declaration by Catroux abolishing the mandate and proclaiming the arrival of Syrian and Lebanese independence. Since then little had been done to turn this pledge into reality. On the contrary, de Gaulle and Catroux were determined to maintain the mandate – at least until treaties guaranteeing France's predominant interests in the region were concluded – and even employed many of the much-despised former Vichy administrators for the purpose. Naturally, the Syrians and Lebanese felt betrayed and appealed to the British, who had guaranteed the Free French pledge and remained responsible for the region's security. They found their champion in Louis Spears.

Spears had been instrumental in 'inventing' de Gaulle. The man who had accompanied the General on his flight to London in June

* Hull was not enjoying the Quebec Conference. A domestic man, who liked to retire early, his attempt to excuse himself from one of Churchill's after-dinner monologues produced the irrefutable adjuration: 'But my dear man, there's a war on!' He stayed until 2 a.m.

1940, he had promoted his nascent movement across Whitehall and taken part in the ill-fated Dakar expedition. By the summer of 1941, however, the two men's relationship had disintegrated. Spears found de Gaulle's impetuosity and mounting Anglophobia impossible to control, while the General had come to regard his former advocate, like most Englishmen, with ill-concealed suspicion. In August, Spears gave up his role as liaison between the British Government and de Gaulle but not his dealings with the Free French, arriving in Beirut a few weeks later as head of a British mission to the newly conquered Levant states.

The British position in the Levant was delicate. 'Time and time again we were told by Syrians and Lebanese that we, the British, could have anything we liked provided we took over the administration, removed the Vichy officials and took care not to replace them with Free French officials,' recalled Charles Mott-Radclyffe, liaison between the Spears mission and General Wilson.[59] This was no exaggeration. Although nationalist feeling would have made itself felt against the subjects of King George – as it already had in Palestine and Iraq – the British were, for the moment, greeted as liberators from French rule. This, as Spears' aide-de-camp, the 25-year-old Earl of Oxford and Asquith, noted in his diary, was 'ticklish' since Churchill had publicly declared that Britain had no intention of supplanting France in the Levant.[60] As far as the Prime Minister and Foreign Office were concerned, this was and remained British policy. Yet there were two British policies operating in the Middle East: the official one, delineated by London, and the unofficial one, pursued by Spears and a coterie of pro-Arab diplomats and intelligence officers. And whilst the former was sincere in its declarations, the latter did indeed seek to oust the French, many wishing to create a 'Greater Syria' under British protection.[61]

Spears was determined to hold the French to their promise on independence. A doughty defender of British interests, he came to see himself as a second Lawrence: defending the Syrians and the Lebanese against the nefarious French. This brought him into conflict with Catroux, the Delegate-General, who paid lip service to independence – nominally conferred on Syria in September and Lebanon in November 1941 – while simultaneously establishing puppet regimes at Damascus and Beirut. Spears' tactic for dealing with the discrepancy was to play the French at their own game: refusing to call on Catroux when he returned as British Minister in March 1942, on the grounds that the states to which he was accredited were now 'independent'. As the head of the British security mission, Patrick Coghill, noted, Spears showed 'sadistic glee in scoring off the French'.[62] In May, he and Richard Casey, the newly appointed Minister-Resident for the Middle East, bullied Catroux into conceding that elections might be held that autumn but Rommel's summer campaign and the threat to Egypt allowed the Free French to renege on this tentative commitment. De Gaulle then entered the scene, making a royal progress through the Middle East and complaining bitterly of British treatment. In Cairo, he and Casey had an 'undignified shouting match' and, in Beirut, he warned the American Consul-General that if the British did not cease their intrigues and recall Spears there would be armed conflict.[63]* Although Churchill had reminded Spears of Talleyrand's *mot* against '*trop de zèle*', he asked the recalcitrant General to return to London, where the two men had one of their blazing rows.[64]

Churchill insisted that elections should take place before the end of the year. De Gaulle and Catroux succeeded in prevaricating for another six months but by the spring of 1943 had run out of excuses. In July, the Syrians went to the polls and returned a nationalist government. The Free French responded by redoubling their efforts to rig the Lebanese vote. Intimidation and bribes were freely dispensed but Spears' own exertions, including the stationing of British military policemen outside the polling booths, had a countervailing effect and nationalist candidates were returned for all constituencies outside Beirut.

---

* It was during this tour that Catroux's wife made an extraordinary proposal to Gardner 'Mike' Cowles, the American magazine publisher and Domestic Director of War Information, currently accompanying Wendell Willkie on his world tour. Simply put, Madame Catroux offered to have de Gaulle assassinated in Beirut, provided she had first received assurances from Roosevelt and Churchill that her husband would take his place. Upon his return Cowles repeated the story to the President, who made him promise not to repeat it until the war was over. In Cowles' opinion, Roosevelt 'seriously considered' taking Mme Catroux up on her offer.

Encouraged by Spears, the new Government set about asserting Lebanese sovereignty. On 7 October, Prime Minister Riad al-Sulh announced plans to amend the constitution to reflect the termination of the mandate and the abolition of French as an official language. Catroux's successor as Delegate-General, Jean Helleu – an ineffectual drunkard whose normal response to difficulty was to disappear into a shed at the bottom of his garden armed with a bottle of whisky – reacted with ill-judged brutality. In the early hours of 11 November, officers of the Sûreté Générale, accompanied by Senegalese soldiers, burst into the homes of the Lebanese President and Prime Minister, dragged them from their beds and arrested them. All but three members of the Cabinet (who could not be found) received similar treatment, while the President's son was thrown in a cellar and beaten with rifle butts to the accompanying cry of 'Son of a dog, son of an Englishman'.[65] At 8 a.m., Helleu announced, in a broadcast, that he had suspended the constitution, dissolved the Chamber and dismissed the Government. Over the coming days, fear mingled with outrage as lorry-loads of Free French troops hurtled around Beirut, plastering the city with Gaullist posters and firing their rifles. Spears was besieged by suppliants: first a delegation of Christian women, then some fifty students from the American University. As the latter waited outside the Legation, a detachment of French marines appeared with fixed bayonets and, at 5 yards' range, opened fire. Eight students and two others were seriously injured, adding to a casualty list spiralling into the dozens.

Eventually, Spears – whom Coghill considered '75 per cent responsible for all the trouble here' – and Casey intervened.[66] On 19 November, the two men presented Catroux (recently arrived to take charge of the crisis) with a note stating that unless the Lebanese Ministers were released and reinstated by 10 a.m. on 22 November General Wilson (Commander-in-Chief Middle East) would impose martial law and liberate the prisoners by force. Although the French General accused the British of perpetrating another Fashoda, he had already decided that retreat was the better part of valour.[67*]

---

* On 18 September 1898, 1,500 British and Egyptian soldiers under Sir Herbert Kitchener faced down a smaller French force under Jean-Baptiste Marchand at

Crucially, a majority of the CFNL were against a showdown with the British over a coup that had so demonstrably backfired. On 22 November, the Lebanese President and his Ministers were released to scenes of immense jubilation and, on the following day, the Government resumed its functions. De Gaulle seethed at the humiliation but was restrained by his colleagues, his representative in London, Pierre Viénot, writing that he would resign rather than 'embark on war against England'.[68]

De Gaulle's role in precipitating the crisis remains a matter of speculation. Although Helleu claimed he was acting on instructions from the top (he had flown to Algiers for consultations with the Free French leader six days before the arrests were made) other evidence suggests the General was surprised by the 'vigour' of the Delegate-General's actions.[69] What is not in doubt is that Helleu – supported if not inspired by de Gaulle – had united the Allies against the Free French on the eve of the much-anticipated conference between the 'Big Three'.

Fashoda on the White Nile. In France, the incident became a totem of Gallic humiliation.

XXIII

The Big Three

Roosevelt was suspicious of Churchill and Stalin was suspicious of
everybody. But outwardly they were all the greatest of buddies.

General Sir Leslie Hollis[1]

At dawn on 3 September 1943, the start of a fine day with calm seas
and blue skies, the Canadian 1st Infantry Division and the British 5th
Infantry Division crossed the Strait of Messina and landed at Reggio
di Calabria on the 'toe' of Italy. Opposition was light, the most serious threat to the Canadians emanating from an escaped puma
which took a shine to Brigadier Penhale. The main Anglo-American
landing at Salerno (Operation Avalanche) proved far bloodier but
by 16 September the bridgehead had been secured and by the 23rd
the Allied armies were pushing north, past Vesuvius, Naples and
the Volturno. Meanwhile, the Red Army, capitalising on its victory
at Kursk, had succeeded in driving a wedge between Army Group
Centre and Army Group South, causing Hitler to sanction a retreat
to the Dnieper. By 22 September the first Soviet soldiers were across
the river, advancing towards Kiev, while, in the north, Smolensk and
Roslavl were liberated after fierce fighting. Amid this atmosphere of
victory, the Foreign Ministers of the United States, Britain and the
Soviet Union convened in Moscow.

The Foreign Ministers' Conference of 19–30 October 1943 has
been obscured by the heads of government conferences that followed in its wake. Yet its achievements were significant: most
notably an increased sense of Allied unity and optimism following
the strongest indications to date that the Soviets were prepared to
extend their collaboration with the West into the post-war period.

The Foreign Ministers arrived at the Spiridonovka Palace, a

neo-gothic mansion filled with marble and gold leaf, with different priorities. Cordell Hull, who had taken his first flight to attend the conference, wanted the Soviets to agree to a declaration pledging the Allies to maintain their co-operation after the war, specifically to the creation of a new international organisation responsible for world peace. Eden wanted a tripartite commission, based in London, to act as a 'clearing house' for all issues relating to the liberation of Europe, while Molotov's agenda was limited to 'measures to be adopted for shortening the duration of the war' – that is, the second front.[2] To everyone's surprise, satisfaction was achieved on all points.

Molotov asked if the British and Americans stood by their commitment to invade France in the spring of 1944. General Ismay, on behalf of the Combined Chiefs, replied that they did. He then enumerated the conditions upon which the cross-Channel operation (codenamed Overlord) was dependent, a disquisition that seems to have satisfied the Soviets more than his own delegation. 'We had better hurry up or we will still be getting ready while they [the Russians] are marching into Berlin,' scrawled Sir Archibald Clark Kerr on a note he passed to the General.

'Lots of time!' responded Ismay, complacently.

'Oh General Pug! Don't you think the trot may any day become a gallop?' entreated the Ambassador. Ismay was unmoved.[3]

The Foreign Ministers agreed to try to bring Turkey into the war before the end of the year and that Austria should be re-established as an independent country. As for Eden's proposal for a trilateral commission to deal with political issues as they arose, this had already been urged by Litvinov in a memorandum arguing the benefits of Western–Soviet co-operation. Molotov studied the paper carefully (his copy is thick with underlinings and annotations) and the European Advisory Council was born without controversy, although the lack of authority conferred on its representatives, in particular the Soviet delegate, Fedor Gusev, ensured that political issues remained the preserve of the Big Three.

The Four Power Declaration was also approved, despite Soviet resistance over the inclusion of China. The Kremlin was reluctant to admit China to Great Power status and objected to Chiang

Kai-shek's elevation to the same level as the three principal Allied warlords. China, however, was an American hobbyhorse – one of four post-war 'policemen' in Roosevelt's conception – and Hull took the opportunity of a break in the conference to impress on Molotov the importance of her inclusion, hinting that a collapse in Chinese confidence would cause the US to redeploy forces from Europe to the Pacific:

> I said to him privately that the American Government is doing every-thing and has done everything possible with respect to the Chinese situation, that it would be impossible in my judgement to omit China . . . that it was the attitude of my Government that China has been in the world picture as one of the Big Four [Allied powers] for the prosecution of the war and for her now to be dumped out on her face by Russia, Great Britain and the United States would create in all probability the most terrific repercussions, both political and military, in the Pacific area and that this might call for all sorts of readjustments by my Government for the purpose of keeping prop-erly stabilised the political and military situation in the Pacific.[4]

Faced with this warning, Stalin yielded, although his insistence on the declaration being signed before the end of the conference represented a final effort to exclude the Chinese since the Chinese Ambassador, Fu Bingchang, lacked plenipotentiary powers. In the end, Chiang's telegram authorising Fu to sign arrived in the nick of time, sparing the Ambassador from perjuring himself by signing the declaration without official status, as he had determined to do. It was one of the 'best days of my life', the Ambassador later told Eden. After years of waiting, China had finally 'become equals with the . . . United States, Britain and the Soviet Union'.[5]

Both the Americans and the British were struck by the spirit of collaboration and the amiable disposition of their hosts. 'Our impression is, and it is confirmed by our press people, that the Sovi-ets are determined that this conference shall be a success,' recorded Eden's Principal Private Secretary, Oliver Harvey. 'Individual Rus-sians all express confidence and pleasure in conversation. For the first time they feel that they are being treated as equals and that we are bringing our troubles to them for unprejudiced discussion.'[6] Molotov, looking awkward in his new black and gold diplomatic uniform – the American interpreter, Charles 'Chip' Bohlen, thought he resembled an SS officer – was 'forthcoming and reasonable', while Stalin appeared in good humour: joking about the time the RAF had forced the Foreign Affairs Commissar to share an air raid shelter with Ribbentrop and teasing the 'Hammer' about his appeasement of Germany.[7]

'Just when we were congratulating ourselves that everything was going splendidly, we got a rude shock,' recalled Ismay.[8] On 27 October, Eden received a telegram from Churchill warning that Overlord might have to be postponed owing to stronger than expected resistance in Italy. The British delegation feared that the news would wreck the conference but Stalin took the blow with unexpected equanimity, merely enquiring whether the delay would be one month or two. Three days later, he gave a banquet for the delegates. Although Harvey found the evening 'interminable' – the Russian habit of constant toasting being a 'barbarous custom, which makes any conversation impossible' – Averell Harriman, recently appointed as US Ambassador to Moscow, thought it the most 'genuine, genial and intimate' dinner he had ever attended in the Kremlin.[9] The conversation was 'free and uninhibited' and Stalin appeared in the best of humour, walking around the table to clink glasses with the Head of the US Military Mission, General Deane, after the latter had proposed a toast to the day when American and British troops would meet Soviet soldiers in Berlin.[10] Most significant from the American perspective, the despot told Hull that he would join the war against Japan after the defeat of Germany.

'There can be no doubt that our Soviet friends have arrived at the decision to attempt to work with us,' wrote Harriman to Churchill.[11] 'Patience and forbearance' would remain the watchwords of Western–Soviet relations but 'long strides forward have been made'.[12] Eden agreed. Writing to the Prime Minister on 29 October, he reported on the many signs indicating that the 'Soviet Government are sincere in their desire to establish relations with ourselves and the United States on a footing of permanent friendship'. The Kremlin had met the democracies on a variety of points in regard 'to which we foresaw difficulties' and the Russian representatives seemed genuinely desirous to open a 'new and happy chapter' in Soviet–Western relations.[13]

This was, indeed, the Soviet intention. The conference was 'a big event in the life of the People's Commissariat', wrote Molotov in an internal minute, instructing Soviet diplomats to study its deliberations and make proposals for the 'realisation of its decisions'.[14] *War and the Working Class*, a recently established fortnightly organ of the Kremlin, spoke of the 'unanimous desire of the peoples of the Soviet Union, Great Britain and the United States to continue the present close co-operation after the end of the war', while Stalin, addressing a meeting of the Moscow Soviet on 6 November, drew attention to Anglo-American victories in the Mediterranean, the bombing of German industrial centres and the supply of munitions to the Soviet Union, all of which 'considerably facilitated the success of our summer campaign'.[15]

The one disappointment, from the British perspective, was their failure to improve relations between the Kremlin and the Polish Government-in-Exile. Eden had solicited Hull's help in this sensitive matter but the Secretary of State had refused, declaring to Harriman in a quite extraordinary outburst: 'I don't want to deal with these piddling little things. We must deal with the main issues.'[16] The British considered this a dereliction of duty but, despite several entreaties, were 'unable to shake Mr Hull'.[17] On 3 November, the delegates departed: Hull for Washington, Eden for Cairo to confer with the Turks.

Churchill, meanwhile, had been pressing for another Anglo-American staff conference before the meeting of the Big Three. Roosevelt had been resisting this for two reasons: he did not want to prejudice the tripartite meeting by giving the Russians the impression that the British and the Americans were attempting to fix the decisions in advance and he wished to avoid a British attempt to obtain a reallocation of resources away from preparations for the cross-Channel invasion in favour of further ventures in the Mediterranean.

As early as 7 October – a mere six weeks after Quebec, where the British had agreed that Overlord should have priority – Churchill had telegraphed Roosevelt asking for his support for operations to capture Rhodes and other islands in the Dodecanese. Sir Alan Brooke thought he was mad. 'I can control him no more,' he wrote in his against-regulations diary. 'He has worked himself into a frenzy of excitement about the Rhodes attack . . . and has set his heart on capturing this one island even at the expense of endangering his relations with the President and with the Americans and also the whole future of the Italian campaign . . . The Americans are already desperately suspicious of him and this will make matters far worse.'[18] Roosevelt, reflecting the views of Eisenhower and the Chiefs of Staff, had replied with a bucket of cold water but on 20 October Churchill was at it again (this time with Brooke's support), asking for a full conference of the Combined Staffs to review the already agreed strategy for 1944. When Roosevelt demurred, citing the sensitivities of the Russians, the Prime Minister sent him a desperate screed:

> The Russians ought not to be vexed if the Americans and British closely concert the very great operations they have in hand for 1944 on fronts where no Russian troops will be present. Nor do I think we ought to meet Stalin, if ever the meeting can be arranged, without being agreed about Anglo-American operations as such . . . Our present plans for 1944 seem open to very grave defects . . . The disposition of our forces between the Italian and the Channel theatres has not been settled by strategic needs but by the march of events, by shipping possibilities and by arbitrary compromises between the British and Americans . . . Early in November a decision must be taken about moving landing craft from the Mediterranean to Overlord. This will cripple Mediterranean operations without the said craft influencing events elsewhere for many months. We stand by what was agreed at Quadrant [Quebec] but we do not feel that such agreements should be interpreted rigidly and without review in the swiftly changing situations of war.[19]

Eventually, Roosevelt agreed to meet Churchill, briefly, at Cairo but insisted on inviting Chiang Kai-shek, thus ensuring that the conference would focus on Far Eastern as opposed to European operations. On 12 November, accompanied by Marshall, Arnold, King, Hopkins and his Chief of Staff, Admiral William Leahy, the President boarded the USS *Iowa* and on 21 November, having narrowly avoided being sunk by one of his own escorts, arrived at the American Ambassador's villa within sight of the Great Pyramid of Giza.*

The Cairo Conference – codenamed Sextant – was very different from that held at Casablanca eight months earlier. Determined not to be hornswoggled by the British – as they felt they had been at Anfa and almost every other Allied conference – the Americans brought a vast staff consisting of some seventy-five officers and thirty warrant officers, supplemented by twenty officers from other theatres.[20] The British fielded a similarly gargantuan team. 'It was astonishing and shocking to see how these conferences grew,' recalled Ismay's deputy, Leslie Hollis. 'It became a question of "getting on the bandwagon", for accommodation was always agreeable, free food and liquor were in abundance and life was in every way more pleasant than in war-time England.'[21] No less than 22,000 pounds of meat, 4,600 pounds of sugar, 78,000 eggs, 5,000 tins of fruit and half a million cigarettes were delivered to the Mena House Hotel where officers could be seen propping up the bar from nine in the morning. When Hollis reprimanded his American counterpart for falling asleep during a crucial plenary session and failing to take the minutes, the officer replied brazenly, 'Now, see here, Jo, don't get mad at me. I'd got one hell of a hangover.'[22]

More important than the size of their staff was the shift in the balance of power. During the voyage to North Africa, Roosevelt and his military advisers discussed their preference for a single commander responsible for all European theatres. When Admiral Leahy predicted that this would likely prove unpalatable to the British, Roosevelt asked for estimates of the total manpower strength of British and American forces, at home and abroad, as of 1 January 1944. The Joint Chiefs replied that whilst the UK would have around

---

* It was on the second day of the voyage, during some anti-aircraft practice, that an officer suddenly shouted, 'It's the real thing! It's the real thing!' A torpedo from the USS *William D. Porter* had got loose and was hurtling towards the flagship. Only some sharp steering on the part of the *Iowa*'s helmsman avoided disaster.

3.7 million men serving overseas by this date, compared to only 3.5 million US, there were an additional 7.5 million uniformed men in America compared to only 800,000 in Britain.[23] The implications were clear: whilst the British had previously been able to play a leading role in determining strategy due to the preponderance of British and British Commonwealth forces, those days were over. FDR may not have been so crude as to have asked, 'Who's senior partner and who's junior?' as claimed by Elliott Roosevelt, who joined his father in Cairo, but he was in no doubt as to the answer.[24]

The British found Sextant a frustrating and acrimonious experience. True to Roosevelt's intentions, Chiang's presence put the conference out of kilter, the first plenary session being dedicated to a meeting with the Generalissimo and his advisers. Although enlivened by the presence of Chiang's wife, Soong May-ling, in a black satin dress with yellow chrysanthemums and a slit that extended all the way to her hip bone – Brooke thought he heard a 'suppressed neigh' from some of the more junior officers – this gathering proved inconclusive and futile.[25] There followed a meeting of the Combined Chiefs of Staff that degenerated into 'a bar-room brawl'.[26] 'Brooke got nasty and King got good and sore', recorded Joseph Stilwell, Chiang's Chief of Staff, after the CIGS suggested that landing craft the Americans wished to deploy against the Andaman Islands (Operation Buccaneer) would be of better use in the Aegean. 'King almost climbed over the table at Brooke. God, he was mad. I wish he had socked him.'[27]

The British wanted to discuss the Mediterranean. As the Director of Military Operations, Major-General John Kennedy noted before the conference, the Chiefs of Staff wished to 'continue the offensive in Italy, to increase the flow of supplies to partisans in the Balkans, to bring about an upheaval in the Balkans by inducing Balkan powers to break away from Germany, to induce Turkey to enter the war and to accept a postponement of Overlord'.[28] The Americans, by contrast, wanted to talk about an offensive in Burma, leaving the European theatre until the tripartite conference when they could count on the support of the Russians. 'We felt almost from the outset . . . that our American associates, so many of whom we looked upon as close friends, had worked themselves into a

state bordering on self-deception,' recalled Air Marshal Sir Sholto
Douglas, Commander-in-Chief Middle East. 'They seemed to be
determined not to listen to our ideas.'[29]

Normally, this was when Churchill would rely on his close relationship with Roosevelt to persuade the President of the British point of
view. But FDR was determined to evade his ally. Tired of the usual
Churchillian eloquence, which the American Chiefs had come to fear
and despise, and looking forward to a new strategic partnership with
the Soviet Union, Roosevelt fell into his old role of 'charming country
gentleman': friendly to all but available to none. This forced Churchill
to play the part of courtier, indulging the President's yarns and seizing opportunities to discuss business 'as and when they arose'.[30] For
the Prime Minister, whose 'whole system' was based on partnership
with Roosevelt, it was a galling experience.[31]

Nor was Churchill able to convince Marshall of the strategic value
of Rhodes. Inviting him to dine with him alone on the evening of 23
November, the Prime Minister had impressed the US Chief of Staff
by reciting whole passages from the Younger Pitt's war speeches
before turning the conversation to the Dodecanese. The next day,
having failed to carry his point – hardly surprising since the British had already been ejected from Kos, Leros and Samos – he tried
again. 'His Majesty's Government can't have its troops standing idle.
Muskets must flame,' he told the Combined Chiefs of Staff, still in
eighteenth-century mode. Marshall replied calmly but firmly: 'God
forbid I should try to dictate but . . . not one American soldier is
going to die on [that] goddamned beach.'[32] Even Hopkins, usually
an important mediator, complained of Churchill's 'bloody Italian
war'. 'Sure, we are preparing for a battle at Tehran,' he warned the
Prime Minister's physician, Lord Moran. 'You will find us lining up
with the Russians.'[33]

In fact, the Americans were not as obdurate as the British claimed.
They agreed that General Alexander could retain sixty-eight landing
craft for the Italian campaign until 15 January and that the date for
Overlord was not immutable. The proposal for a single European
commander was abandoned. All they insisted on was that the British abide by the agreement, made at Quebec, that the cross-Channel
invasion remain the priority for 1944. Not only was this reasonable,

it was also strategically sound. There was no 'soft' underbelly (as Alexander was discovering in Italy) and whilst the Mediterranean campaign may have been prudent in 1942 and 1943, the only route to defeating Germany, short of leaving the task entirely to the Russians, was to strike at her industrial heartlands by way of France.

At 7.07 a.m. on 27 November 1943 the President's specially built Douglas VC-54C Skymaster, nicknamed the *Sacred Cow*, ascended into the indigo sky above Cairo. From there, the Presidential party flew north-east, over Bethlehem and Jerusalem (for the President's benefit), across the Jordan and Baghdad and then on, through the mountain passes, to Tehran, landing at 3 p.m. local time. Stalin, escorted by twenty-seven fighter aircraft, had already arrived, while Churchill, who had lost his voice and called for a medicinal tumbler of whisky at 8.30 a.m., had landed half-an-hour earlier.

Roosevelt was to stay at the American Legation on the outskirts of the city. Late that evening, however, Molotov informed Harriman and Clark Kerr that the Soviets had uncovered a German plot to assassinate the Allied leaders. The Ambassadors were sceptical but Roosevelt, who had been angling for an invitation to stay at the Russian Legation, was happy to play along. The following afternoon, he moved into the central and supposedly more secure Soviet compound. At 3 p.m., Stalin called on his guest. Roosevelt, who had striven for so long to achieve this meeting, was at his most charming. 'I have just a hunch that Stalin . . . doesn't want anything but security for his country', he had supposedly remarked to William C. Bullitt earlier in the year, 'and I think that if I give him everything I possibly can and ask for nothing from him in return, *noblesse oblige*, he won't try to annex anything and will work with me for a world of democracy and peace.' Bullitt had retorted that Stalin was 'a Caucasian bandit whose only thought when he got something for nothing was that the other fellow was an ass'.[34] This conversation may well have been embellished (Bullitt could not remember when it had taken place), yet it contained a fundamental truth. Still confident that he could 'handle' Stalin, Roosevelt sought to forge a working relationship with the Soviet dictator by meeting 'legitimate' Russian security demands. Certainly, there was little in the President's attitude to 'Uncle Joe' that seemed to recognise the ruthless Marxist: the revolutionary from Gori who had rejected his seminarian education to become a bank robber and gun runner for the Bolsheviks, endured exile in the wastes of Siberia, climbed to the top of the party to claim Lenin's state, eliminated his rivals, industrialised the Russian economy, collectivised Soviet agriculture and sent millions of Russians, Belorussians, Georgians, Armenians, Azerbaijanis, Kazakhs, Turkmens, Uzbeks, Kyrgyz, Tartars, Poles, Estonians, Latvians, Lithuanians, Moldovans, Bessarabians and, above all, Ukrainians, to their deaths.

'I am glad to see you. I have tried for a long time to bring this about,' declared Roosevelt, taking the hand of the Soviet dictator, who was dressed in his new, mustard-coloured marshal's uniform, the Order of Lenin pinned to his chest. Over the next fifty minutes, the two men discussed a variety of topics, including the situation on the Russian front and the war in the Far East. Roosevelt said that he wished it was within his power to divert thirty or forty German divisions and, unilaterally, offered Stalin a proportion of the British and American merchant fleets once the war was over. Stalin criticised Chiang Kai-shek and enquired about events in Lebanon. This raised the subject of de Gaulle, a figure the two men proceeded to abuse. Stalin said that he did not know the Free French leader but considered him 'very unreal in his political activities'. De Gaulle claimed to represent the 'soul' of France but 'the real' France was engaged in helping the enemy. Roosevelt – surprisingly for a man who had done so much to legitimise Vichy – agreed. No Frenchman over forty, certainly none who had taken part in the present administration, should be allowed to hold office once the war was over, he argued. Mr Churchill wanted to see France restored as a great power but he did not share this view, feeling that it would take many years of 'honest labour' before France could hope to resume her former place in the world.

After agreeing that Indo-China should not be returned to France, the President steered the conversation to India, confiding that it was easier to discuss this matter without the Prime Minister since he had no answer to this problem and merely proposed to 'defer the entire question to the end of the war'. Stalin agreed that India was a sensitive issue for the British but doubted the practicality of

Roosevelt's proposed solution, namely, 'reform from the bottom, somewhat on the Soviet line'. As the despot pointed out, India was a complicated subject, with different levels of culture and a lack of relations between castes. 'Reform from the bottom would mean revolution.'[35] Harriman, who was waiting outside the meeting room with Molotov, thought Stalin showed 'rather more sophistication than Roosevelt' on this subject.[36]

The first plenary session, held at 4 p.m. around a specially built table in the Russian Legation, was dominated by military affairs. Although Churchill felt he was entitled to be Chairman – on the grounds that he was the eldest (he was about to be sixty-nine, Stalin was sixty-four and Roosevelt was sixty-one), that his name came first alphabetically and because of the 'historic importance of the British Empire' – he waived this right in favour of Roosevelt, who, as head of state as well as government, took charge.[37]* Smiling broadly, like a 'rich uncle paying a visit to his poorer relations', he started by welcoming the Russians to the 'family circle' before embarking on a survey of the war in the Pacific.[38] Stalin regretted that the Soviet Union had been unable to participate in this theatre but repeated the pledge, already given to Hull, to join the war against Japan once Germany had been defeated. As for the European theatre, the Marshal said that the Italian campaign was useful but that Italy was not a suitable jumping-off point for the invasion of Germany. For this, the Allies must look to north and north-west France.

Churchill, who was suffering from a heavy cold, did not dispute this statement. He and the President were agreed that a cross-Channel invasion was essential. The question, he explained, was: what should be done during the next six months? The Allies would take Rome – now expected in January 1944 – but was this to be the extent of their efforts in the Mediterranean? There were the Partisans of Yugoslavia to consider and then there was the Aegean with its links to Turkey and the Black Sea. At this, Roosevelt interjected to reiterate a proposal for a landing at the head of the Adriatic, followed by a drive north-east to join up with the Soviets advancing from Odessa. Considering

---

* Although Stalin enjoyed absolute power, the titular head of state of the USSR was the inconsequential, veteran Bolshevik Mikhail Kalinin.

that this was the very Balkan expedition the US Chiefs sought to avoid – the plan they suspected Churchill of harbouring – this caused some consternation. 'Who's promoting that Adriatic business that the President continually returns to?' demanded Hopkins in a note to Admiral King. 'As far as I know it is his own idea,' the sailor replied.[39] They need not have worried. Stalin had no desire to see his allies entrenched in the Balkans, let alone eastern Europe, and stated his opposition to 'dispersals', arguing instead for an invasion of southern France to coincide with the main cross-Channel assault.[40]

That evening, Roosevelt was the host at a dinner of steak and baked potatoes served by his Filipino mess boys. Reverting to the subject of France, Stalin stated that the French did not deserve considerate treatment from the Allies and should be stripped of their Empire. 'The entire French ruling class was rotten to the core and had delivered France over to the Germans.'[41] Roosevelt said he agreed 'in part' but Churchill declared that he could 'not conceive of a civilised world without a flourishing and lively France'.[42] The conversation then turned to Germany, Stalin explaining that he had no faith in the possibility of reforming the German people. He recalled how, in 1907, he had been in Leipzig when 200 German workers had failed to appear at an important socialist meeting because there had been no railway conductor to punch their tickets. 'The mentality of discipline and obedience could not be changed,' he averred.[43]

After Roosevelt had retired, Churchill broached the question of Poland. The Prime Minister explained that Britain had gone to war for Poland and was committed to her restoration as a strong, independent country. He was not wedded to specific frontiers but her political integrity was paramount. Eden then asked Stalin if he had meant what he had said in an earlier remark about the Poles being able to extend their territory in the west as far as the Oder. The dictator said that he did and offered to help the Poles achieve this object. Churchill said he favoured shifting the Polish frontiers westwards, illustrating his point with three matchsticks. 'The opening moves did not go too badly,' noted Eden in his diary before bed. 'If we could get onto the business soon we might be able to hammer something out.' The difficulty was the Americans, who seemed 'terrified of the subject', Hopkins calling it 'political dynamite' for the 1944 Presidential election. Eden's sympathy for this attitude was limited, not least because it was illogical. 'As I told him, if we cannot get a solution Polish–Russian relations six months from now will be infinitely worse and the elections much nearer.'[44] The time for diplomatic pressure was now, while the Allies still had leverage in the form of Overlord and before the Red Army crossed the Polish border. But neither Churchill nor Roosevelt pressed the point.

The second day saw the British comprehensively outgunned by the Soviets and the Americans. 'Bad from beginning to end', wrote a depressed Brooke, who felt like 'entering a lunatic asylum or a nursing home' after the seven hours of talks.[45] It had begun with a meeting of the Combined Chiefs of Staff at which Marshal Voroshilov – the former Defence Commissar who had been sacked for his incompetence during the Soviet–Finnish War – asked the CIGS if he shared the American view about the importance of Overlord. Brooke replied that he did but that he also appreciated the obstacles. Voroshilov admitted that the Channel posed difficulties but the Red Army had recently had to cross 'several large rivers' and where there was a will there was a way.[46]

Churchill, meanwhile, had tried to see Roosevelt for lunch but had been rebuffed. The President felt that by avoiding Anglo-American tête-à-têtes, he could prevent Stalin from feeling 'ganged-up' upon, Harriman explained. This strategy which had been dominant at Cairo and was to be again at Yalta, was sadly misguided. Stalin expected his capitalist allies to collude and made arrangements accordingly. At eight o'clock every morning he received Sergo Beria, the NKVD chief's nineteen-year-old son, to read through the summaries of the President's and Prime Minister's conversations, furnished by an infestation of listening devices. The candour of Roosevelt and his entourage amazed him. 'They know that we can hear them and yet they speak openly . . . It's bizarre, they say everything in fullest detail.'[47] At 2.45 p.m., Stalin called on his guest, who took the opportunity to elucidate his concept of the future international organisation: a global structure, open to all nations, but dominated by the 'Four Policemen' of the US, the USSR, Britain and China. Although Stalin had doubts about the latter's inclusion, he raised no fundamental objections. The two men then repaired to the outer hall where Churchill, on behalf of the King, presented the despot with the 'Sword of Stalingrad' – a moving ceremony rendered comic when Stalin, having kissed the sword, handed it to Voroshilov, who promptly dropped it.

At the plenary session that followed, Churchill, according to General Deane, 'used every trick in his oratorical bag' to make the case for not denuding the Mediterranean, even if it meant delaying Overlord.[48] Stalin replied by stating that operations in this theatre could only be regarded as 'diversions'; what mattered was Overlord. He asked his allies to set a date for the operation and to name a commander. Roosevelt agreed that it was all a matter of timing and logistics:

> If we launched expeditions in the Eastern Mediterranean, even though initially they might entail only two or three divisions, there was always the possibility that they might develop into a bigger commitment involving the despatch of larger forces. In this event, even the later date of Overlord [June or July 1944] would be prejudiced.

Stalin then asked Churchill a direct question: did the British really believe in Overlord? The Prime Minister's response was forthright but ambivalent: provided the necessary conditions were met, 'it would be our stern duty to hurl across the Channel against the Germans every sinew of our strength'.[49]

Both the British and the Americans were impressed by Stalin's skill as a negotiator. Unlike his loquacious allies, he made no attempt at oratory nor bothered with diplomatic niceties. 'His comments', wrote Deane, 'were terse and to the point.'[50] When Roosevelt suggested that the military issues in question be referred to a committee of the Chiefs of Staff, the Vozhd simply replied: 'The decisions are our business. That is what we have come here for.'[51] 'I thank the Lord that Stalin was there,' wrote Stimson, after reading the minutes. 'In my opinion, he saved the day. He was direct and strong. He brushed away the diversionary attempts of the Prime Minister with a vigour that rejoiced my soul.'[52]

At the dinner that evening, Stalin kept needling Churchill, implying that he nursed a secret affection for the Germans and consequently desired a 'soft peace'. Trailing his coat but also in deadly earnest, he expressed the view that '50,000, perhaps 100,000' German officers should be shot at the end of the war.[53] At this, Churchill intervened to say that the British public would never tolerate mass executions:

> Even if in war passion they allowed them to begin, they would turn violently against those responsible after the first butchery had taken place . . . I would rather be taken out into the garden here and now and be shot myself than sully my own and my country's honour by such infamy.[54]

Roosevelt then suggested a compromise figure of 49,000. Although said in jest – a clumsy attempt to relieve the tension – there were figures within the US Administration who were closer to Stalin's views than Churchill's. As Lord Halifax recorded after a dinner in March, 'Hull surprised me by saying that he would like to shoot and physically kill all the Nazi leaders down to the quite low levels!'[55] The Secretary of State was utterly opposed to 'longwinded trials', noted Hopkins the following day, and 'hoped we could find a way to get the ones that should be shot and do it quietly'.[56] At Moscow, Hull repeated this view, boasting to Henry Morgenthau upon his return that the reason he had 'got along so well with the Russians' was due to his plan to 'hold a secret trial before which I would bring Hitler and his gang and Tojo [the Japanese Prime Minister] and his gang and . . . shoot them all and then . . . let the world know about it a couple of days later'.[57] The Treasury Secretary sympathised, while, back in Tehran, Elliott Roosevelt – the only man who could make Randolph Churchill seem like a paragon of tact – rose to endorse the Marshal's proposal on behalf of the United States Army. Churchill was disgusted. 'Much as I love you, Elliott, I cannot forgive you for making such a dastardly statement,' he told the President's second son.[58]

Churchill returned to the British Legation filled with dark forebodings. 'There might be a more bloody war,' he told Eden, Clark Kerr and Moran in his bedroom.

'You mean a war with Russia?' the doctor enquired.

Churchill, lost in his thoughts, did not respond. Soon, however, he began to expatiate on the need to keep Britain well defended, with a large air force and a militia system like Switzerland. Later, as he was preparing for bed, he said, 'I believe man might destroy man and wipe out civilisation. Europe would be desolate and I may be held responsible . . . Stupendous issues are unfolding before our eyes and we are only specks of dust that have settled in the night on the map of the world.'[59]

Roosevelt, by contrast, had enjoyed his evening. Not only had Stalin's attacks on Churchill amused him – as Marshall recalled, the President always took a certain pleasure in seeing the Prime Minister discomfited – they had also given him an idea. Determined to penetrate the despot's crusty exterior, he sought to establish a rapport at his friend's expense. The next day when the three men reassembled, Roosevelt leant over to Stalin and, in a stage whisper, said, 'Winston is cranky this morning, he got up on the wrong side of the bed.' A vague smile flitted across the Marshal's face and FDR, realising that he was on the right track, began to poke fun at the Prime Minister, 'about John Bull, about his cigars and about his habits'. Stalin enjoyed the teasing. 'Winston got red and scowled', Roosevelt recounted to his Labor Secretary, Frances Perkins, 'and the more he did so, the more Stalin smiled. Finally, Stalin broke out into a deep guffaw and for the first time in three days I saw light. I kept it up until Stalin was laughing with me and it was then that I called him "Uncle Joe" . . . From that time on our relations were personal . . . and we talked like men and brothers.'[60]

Stalin had several reasons to be cheerful. Not only did he relish the cleft in the Anglo-American relationship but the British had given way: agreeing to launch Overlord by 1 June 1944 as well as to a complementary invasion of the south of France, Operation Anvil. That evening, the three leaders were all smiles at a dinner held in the British Legation to mark Churchill's sixty-ninth birthday. The Prime Minister had stipulated that the evening was to be in the 'Russian manner' and there were a great many toasts, with Roosevelt proposing the health of the King and Stalin paying tribute to American industry, without which the war would have been lost.[61] At one point, Churchill remarked that the political complexion of the world was changing and that even Britain was becoming 'a trifle pinker'. Stalin rejoined that this was 'a sign of good health!'[62] The old anti-Bolshevik crusader then drank to the 'Proletarian masses', prompting Stalin to raise his glass 'to the Conservative Party'.[63]

The thirty-four guests were served oyster patties, beef bouillon, poached salmon, roast turkey, cauliflower and cheese soufflé. The *pièce de résistance*, however, was a mountain of ice cream, perched on top of a block of ice, illuminated by a lantern. Various eyes followed this precarious confection as it made its way around the guests, slithering on its plate. For a ghastly moment it looked as if it would fall on Stalin's head but fate intervened and the sugary mass landed on top of his interpreter, Vladimir Pavlov, who continued translating as if nothing had happened. Churchill later recommended Pavlov for a CBE.

In a letter to Roosevelt, thanking him for the twelfth-century Persian bowl he had been given for his birthday, Churchill spoke of their 'sunlit days in Tehran'.[64] Yet the Churchill–Roosevelt friendship had, however subtly, passed its zenith. Despite the warm words of the previous evening – the President had spoken of his 'joy in the friendship which had developed between them in the midst of their common efforts' – the Tehran Conference had seen Roosevelt moving away from Churchill and towards Stalin.[65] Of course, this trajectory was consistent with US strategic thinking. For almost two years, American military planners had been advocating a cross-Channel assault as the quickest route to victory and had no qualms about 'ganging up' with the Russians to achieve this. Yet it also reflected a shift in the alliance; a recognition that the future peace of the world would depend far more upon the United States and the Soviet Union than Britain and her dilapidated Empire.

Roosevelt had come to Tehran determined to establish a genuine US–Soviet alliance. He left with the conviction that he had achieved this. Indeed he believed that the United States would have 'more trouble in the post-war world with the English than with the Russians'.[66] At a press conference on 17 December, he described Stalin as 'like me . . . a realist' and in a 'fireside chat' on Christmas Eve declared his confidence that 'we are going to get along well with him and the Russian people – very well indeed'.[67] A few weeks later the Lend-Lease administrator, Leo Crowley, observed to Morgenthau that the:

> Roosevelt–Stalin axis is gaining strength and the Roosevelt–Churchill axis is losing strength in about equal ratio . . . based on what the President said at the Cabinet meeting right after his return . . . it was perfectly obvious that the President is very much impressed with Stalin and not quite so much impressed as he has been with Churchill.[68]

1943 represented a sea-change in more ways than one.

PART FOUR

Towards Victory

1944–1945

XXIV

The Fourth Policeman

As you probably know, we succeeded in Russia in having China included
in the Four Power Declaration toward saving the world from aggression
during the immediate and post-war periods. I really feel that it is a
triumph to have got the 425 million Chinese in on the Allied side. This
will be very useful twenty-five or fifty years hence.

Franklin D. Roosevelt to Lord Louis Mountbatten, 8 November 1943[1]

The Cairo Conference was, in many ways, an unsatisfactory prelude
to the Tehran Conference. Not only were the Americans determined
to delay the main discussions until they were bolstered by the presence of the Russians but the one strategic commitment made at
Sextant – an amphibious operation to capture the Andaman Islands,
in conjunction with a reinvasion of northern and central Burma –
was reversed after the British failed to persuade their allies to delay
Overlord. Yet the Cairo Conference had great symbolic significance:
the first (and last) time during the Second World War that an Asian
power was admitted to the councils of the Western Allies on terms
of at least nominal equality.

For China the war had begun in 1937 – if not 1931, with the Japanese invasion of Manchuria. A skirmish between Chinese and
Japanese troops near the former Imperial capital of Peking provided the spark and soon the Emperor's armies were swarming over
northern China. Between August and November 1937, the two sides
pitted some of their best forces against each other in Shanghai, turning the once thriving, commercial city into a shambles of masonry
and mortality. From there, the Imperial Armies headed westwards,
spreading the epidemic of violence to the Nationalist capital, Nan-
jing, where anywhere between 50,000 and 200,000 Chinese soldiers

and civilians were massacred and some 20,000 women raped in one of the worst atrocities of the war.* The Chinese Government fled to the city of Wuhan, in Hubei province, where Chiang Kai-shek attempted to rally the remaining forces under his command. In April 1938, the Chinese achieved a rare victory over the Japanese at Taierzhuang. But this only provided a temporary respite and, in October, the Government, along with hundreds of thousands of refugees, was once again on the move, Chiang having taken the desperate decision to blow the dykes on the Yellow River, delaying the Japanese but killing perhaps as many as half a million of his own countrymen. By the end of 1938, the Japanese controlled most of northern China, the eastern seaboard and the Yangtze valley from Shanghai to Wuhan, while the Nationalists had retreated to Chungking, a forlorn dwelling on the mist-covered slopes above the Yangtze, soon to become the most bombed city on earth.

The Western powers sympathised with China in her agony. This was particularly true of the United States, where the idea of Republican China as a fledgling democracy was broadly accepted and tales of Chinese bravery, in the teeth of Japanese barbarism, eagerly devoured. More than 5,000 editorials praising Chinese resistance appeared in the American press during the first three months of the war and, in November 1937, *Time* made Chiang Kai-shek and Soong May-ling its 'Man and Wife of the Year'.[2] Sympathy, however, only went so far: the US showed no desire to abandon her policy of isolationism, while Britain was more concerned with European militarism. Under these circumstances, democratic support for 'democratic' China between 1937 and 1939 was limited to a 'moral embargo' on the sale of American aircraft to the Japanese, a US-facilitated loan of $25 million and a small quantity of munitions. The Soviet Union, by contrast, provided the Nationalists with

* The official figure claimed by the Chinese Government is 300,000 but this is considered by most historians to be an overestimate. The quest for reliable statistics both here and elsewhere is rendered difficult by the fact that the Japanese destroyed so many documents – including 70 per cent of their Army records – between the ceasefire of 15 August 1945 and the arrival of American troops thirteen days later.

348 bombers, 542 fighters, 1,140 pieces of artillery, 9,720 machine guns, 50,000 rifles and 3,665 pilots, advisers and technicians. This was sheer anti-Japanese pragmatism on Stalin's part. Chiang had expelled his Soviet advisers in 1927 and then launched a series of campaigns against the Chinese Communists, resulting in the Long March. But it counted for more than Western idealism.

Nor did Chinese fortunes improve with the outbreak of the European war, as attention turned to the struggle with Germany and the British closed the Burma Road. In May 1941, Roosevelt made China eligible for Lend-Lease but in November the Administration gave serious consideration to a *modus vivendi* with Japan, provoking howls of protest from Chiang. The Nationalists were then forced to watch as the once proud and in many ways despised Western empires crumbled before the Japanese onslaught. Republican China was 'awash with irritation at Britain and America', recalled the US information officer Graham Peck.[3] Having held out against the 'dwarf pirates' (as Chiang called the Japanese) for more than four and a half years, the Chinese could not understand how the democracies, with their superior technology, had lost Hong Kong, Singapore and the Philippines in a matter of months.[4] Peck listened as Nationalist Air Force officers joked that the reason the Americans had abandoned Manila was because the Japanese had bombed their cows and 'American soldiers would not fight when they could not have ice cream every day', while to General Wavell – currently resisting the encroachment of Chinese troops into his Burmese theatre – Chiang delivered a devastating rebuke:

You and your people have no idea how to fight the Japanese. Resisting the Japanese is not like suppressing colonial rebellions, not like colonial wars. The Japanese are a serious great power . . . Fighting against them for many years, we Chinese are the ones who know how to do it. For this kind of job you British are incompetent and you should learn from the Chinese how to fight against the Japanese.[5]

As this lecture suggests, there was no love lost between Chiang and the British. The dominant imperial power in the nineteenth century, it was the British who had sent gunboats to enforce their commercial 'rights' during the Opium Wars, gaining Hong Kong and opening China to a century of foreign exploitation. Like most Nationalists, Chiang seethed with resentment at China's loss of sovereignty, manifested by the so-called Treaty Ports – war-wrought concessions that allowed Europeans, Americans and, finally, Japanese to live, trade and worship, according to their own laws, in specially protected foreign enclaves. On 30 May 1925, British-led police shot dead eleven protesters in the International Settlement in Shanghai, provoking a wave of anti-foreign demonstrations. When British troops, along with French and Portuguese soldiers, participated in a further massacre in Canton, Chiang's anger boiled over. 'The stupid British', he wrote in his diary, 'regard Chinese lives as dirt.' 'How can we', he raged in a subsequent entry, 'emancipate mankind if we cannot annihilate the English?'[6] Later, after the Japanese had invaded Malaya and the *Prince of Wales* and *Repulse* had been sunk, he noted the humility of the British Ambassador, Sir Archibald Clark Kerr, 'but their [the British] greed and their search for a small profit while avoiding the big questions is the same as ever'.[7]* And yet Chiang nursed a grudging respect for his allies, noting, during the Cairo Conference, how Britain had a 'power that extends to the furthest part[s] of the world'. 'Even the untameable Muslim peoples obey their orders. You can't help admiring their magic powers.'[8]†

The United States, by contrast, was viewed by Chiang and the Nationalists as an ideological ally: an anti-imperial power – despite her own concessions, dollar diplomacy and historic involvement in the opium trade – that would help liberate China from both the Japanese and the Europeans. 'The Generalissimo feels that America and China have a common objective which is peculiar to our

---

* It was Clark Kerr's success in China – where he served as ambassador between 1938 and 1942— that led to his appointment to Moscow.
† Not all Chinese despised the British. When the civil servant Sir Arthur Salter was advising the Nanking Government on economic policy in 1931, a Chinese Treasury official asked to be excused so that he could travel to Shanghai to attend the Boat Race dinner. 'What Boat Race dinner?' enquired Salter. The official was shocked. 'There is only one Boat Race! Tomorrow Oxford meets Cambridge at Putney. I always attend the annual dinner at Shanghai on that day.' (Salter Papers, SALT 1/1, Boat Race Dinner in Shanghai)

two peoples because we are both non-aggressive and really love peace,' wrote Soong May-ling to Roosevelt's economist and occasional China envoy, Lauchlin Currie, in May 1942. 'We feel that the President can make the greatest contribution to the world by implementing his ideals through actively espousing the cause of freedom of all races.'[9] Three months earlier, Chiang had enraged Churchill by taking up the cause of Indian independence. Travelling to Delhi to meet Jawaharlal Nehru and Maulana Azad, he then spent five hours in conversation with Gandhi near Calcutta. Although frustrated at his inability to persuade Congress to support the war effort by co-operating with the British, his experience of the Raj left Chiang frightened and disgusted. 'The danger is extreme,' he wrote to Roosevelt on 25 February. 'If the British Government does not fundamentally change their policy toward India, it would be like presenting India to the enemy.'[10] Five months later, he tried again, urging the President to compel the British to come to an accommodation with India's nationalists.

An irony of this attitude – Americanophile but Anglophobe – was that British representatives were often more understanding and supportive of the Nationalist regime than their American counterparts. 'The chiefest of our concerns', wrote Clark Kerr in his valedictory despatch, in February 1942, 'should be to hold the confidence of the Generalissimo, for in him we have a tower of strength and with his confidence, we have that of the vast mass of the Chinese people.'[11] His American colleague, Clarence Gauss, by contrast, was warning as early as January 1942 that the Kuomintang (the Nationalists) had been paying lip service to reform for years but 'little of tangible value has been accomplished'.[12] Like many Americans, Graham Peck was shocked at the discrepancy between the idealised image of Republican China, as existed in the US, and the reality of Chungking. 'I had come back', he recalled, 'with a full set of standard ideas about the Kuomintang's war, acquired from the American press: the gallant losing battles, the brave and clever guerrillas . . . the firmly held fronts beyond which there would be no retreat and behind them a new country a-building.' But instead he found malnourished troops, military inertia, widespread corruption and soaring inflation.[13] 'It is a known fact that the Chinese are great believers in the world of make-believe and that they frequently shut their eyes to hard and unpleasant actualities, preferring rather to indulge their fancy in flattering but fictitious symbols,' reported the head of the US Military Mission, John Magruder, in February 1942. 'As instances of this deceptive symbolism, I may adduce many reports emanating from Chinese diplomatic sources abroad, referring to the marvellous achievements and abilities of the Chinese Army. Such reports are absolutely without foundation . . . The Nipponese [Japanese] forces in China are given no trouble at all, except in places where they [the Chinese] wish to repress guerrillas from roaming around in quest of political or economic gain. It is foolish to label the reoccupation by Chinese forces of territory voluntarily evacuated by the Japs as a smashing victory for China.'[14]

The greatest critic of Chiang and the Kuomintang, however, was the recently arrived Chief of Staff to the Generalissimo, the freshly promoted and notoriously acerbic Lieutenant-General Joseph Warren Stilwell. Rough-hewn and wiry, with close-cropped hair and steel-rimmed spectacles, 'Vinegar Joe' remained spry despite his sixty-one years. A West Point graduate with a flair for languages, he had served in the Philippines and on the Western Front during the First World War (where he had lost most of the sight in his left eye), before going on to spend almost a decade in China, ending up as Military Attaché between the summer of 1935 and the summer of 1939. In a self-assessment written in 1935, he admitted that at times he could be 'unreasonable, impatient, sour-balled, sullen, mad, hard, profane, vulgar'.[15] Yet he was also brave, compassionate, hardworking and determined. The loyalty of those who served under him was considerable, while even his future sparring partner, Lord Louis Mountbatten, was forced to acknowledge his abilities. What he lacked was tact and the capacity to see issues beyond the confines of his own obsessions.

Chiang shared many of Stilwell's characteristics. A seasoned campaigner and veteran political intriguer – a man who, as one contemporary noted, 'never hesitated to forgive his enemies . . . nor to betray his friends' – he had risen to prominence as the commandant of the Soviet-sponsored Whampoa Military Academy and as protégé of Sun Yat-sen, the father of Chinese nationalism.[16] For more than two years, Chiang had concealed his anti-communism (contracted during a visit to Moscow in 1923) but in 1926 he had turned on his Marxist collaborators, gaining the leadership of the National Revolutionary Army and, ultimately, the Kuomintang. He then embarked on the Northern Expedition, defeating or assimilating much larger warlord armies and imposing a unity on China such as had not existed since the collapse of Qing authority at the turn of the century. In April 1927, he conducted a bloody purge of the communists and on 6 June 1928 his forces marched into Peking, his portrait soon replacing Sun's above the Gate of Heavenly Peace.

'One might almost call him supernormal', wrote the American journalist John Gunther of this 'inconspicuous son of a village merchant, who became leader of China's 400,000,000 people'.[17] Five feet nine inches tall, with a bald head, straight back and dark, penetrating eyes, Chiang was an ascetic who rose at five and worked until dusk, save for a short nap in the afternoon, aided by his favourite record, Schubert's *Ave Maria*. A lecherous and violent youth, he later tried to live by the Neo-Confucian principles of sincerity, rectitude, serenity, constancy and determined action. Frequently, he came up short. He had a terrible temper and would often burst into angry tears. Towards his long-term goal – the unity and greatness of China – he was constant and determined. But in more immediate matters of strategy and in dealing with his allies he could be devious and dilatory. In the balanced assessment of the American journalist Joseph Alsop – who served in Chungking on the staff of the aviator Claire Chennault – he had 'the stuff of greatness but he also had more than the average conflicts of greatness'.[18]

Chiang wanted the Allies to concentrate on the war against Japan. This, neither the British nor the Americans – and certainly not the Soviets – were prepared to do. In the grand scheme of global priorities, Japan ranked second to Germany and the China theatre even lower than that. The Chinese were not invited to join the Combined Chiefs of Staff, nor the short-lived American–British–Dutch–Australian Command for South-East Asia, while Chinese Lend-Lease supplies represented a mere 1.5 per cent of the total for 1942 and an even more measly 0.5 per cent for 1943. As compensation, the US agreed to meet Chiang's eye-watering demand for a $500 million loan (Morgenthau called it 'a hold up'), while the Generalissimo was made Supreme Allied Commander for China, Thailand and Indo-China in December 1941, a grand-sounding but meaningless title since almost all troops in this theatre were, and would remain, his.[19] Roosevelt also acceded to Chiang's request for a Chief of Staff: an American who would have 'executive' control of Chinese forces in Burma *subject* to the Supreme Commander.

Stilwell arrived in Chungking at the end of February 1942, just as Burma was going up in flames. Convinced that the success of his mission would depend upon Chiang's willingness to cede control of his armies to him, he was delighted when the Generalissimo proceeded to do just this. The two men disagreed, however, on strategy. Full of fight, Stilwell wanted to launch a counteroffensive to retake Rangoon. 'When I think of how these bowlegged cockroaches have ruined our calm lives it makes me want to wrap Jap guts around every lamppost in Asia,' he wrote to his wife.[20] Chiang was more cautious. Having overcome Wavell's objections, he had committed some of his best troops – the 5th and 6th Armies – to the Burmese theatre and was naturally chary about throwing them away. In his view, the British were fighting poorly and Rangoon was unrecoverable. A more prudent plan was to form a defensive line, east–west, at Mandalay. But Stilwell, who had never held a field command, insisted and the Generalissimo, reluctantly, gave way. The resulting debacle did neither man credit. Although the Chinese fought bravely, Stilwell had underestimated the strength and speed of the Japanese, while Chiang interfered constantly, sending direct orders to divisional commanders. By 25 April, as the American put it, 'the jig was up'.[21] On 5 May, Stilwell took the controversial decision to abandon his forces, some of which had already begun to break up, and escape to India with his staff. After a gruelling two-week trek, much romanticised by the American press, he arrived in Imphal, north-east India. 'I claim we got a hell of a beating,' he told journalists in Delhi. 'We got run out of Burma and it is as humiliating as hell. I think we ought to find out what caused it, go back and retake it.'[22]

Chiang had little doubt what caused it. Although he cursed the British (whose defeat it really was), he also blamed Stilwell for ignoring his orders and squandering some of his best divisions. 'The responsibility for the enormous sacrifice of our forces in Burma lies entirely with Stilwell's command failures,' he raged in his diary. 'When we began to lose, he was all in a fluster and only thought about fleeing to India, having no concern for our forces.'[23] Stilwell, on the other hand, blamed Chiang and his incessant meddling. The Generalissimo, he vented, was a 'stubborn, ignorant, prejudiced, conceited despot', surrounded by yes-men. 'He is not mentally stable, and he will say many things to your face that he doesn't mean fully or exactly.' Soon, he was referring to Chiang as 'the Peanut' and describing Chinese officials as 'Officialdumb'. 'The Chinese Government', he wrote, not inaccurately, 'is a structure based on fear and favor . . . It is interlaced with family and financial ties and influences which could easily tear it to pieces if pulled out.'[24]

The Burmese rout set the tone for the Western–Chinese alliance outside the synthetic world of propaganda. Stilwell had developed a contempt for the man and regime he was meant to serve, while Chiang had suffered a similar loss of confidence in the democracies. When informed, on 26 June, that the US 10th Air Force was being transferred from India to the Middle East, he was furious. Accusing the Americans and the British of treating the Chinese war effort with disdain, he demanded three American divisions to restore the supply route across Burma, 500 aircraft and 5,000 tons of aerial supplies per month, as the 'minimum requirements essential for the maintenance of the China theatre'.[25] Although the US War Department baulked at sending ground troops, Roosevelt agreed to the 500 aircraft and to increase supplies. The chances of China making a separate peace with Japan (as Chiang had hinted) were remote but, as the head of the State Department's Division for Far Eastern Affairs put it, 'the best way to insure against a Chinese collapse lies in the field of sending materials, especially planes, and establishing an effective air transport into and out of China'.[26]

At the start of October 1942, Wendell Willkie arrived in Chungking on the final leg of his world tour. Realising the significance of his visit, the Kuomintang determined to show their regime in the best possible light. Beggars were cleared from the streets, hovels were demolished and hundreds of flag-waving Chinese were driven from their homes to greet him. Willkie, who asked neither Stilwell nor Ambassador Gauss any questions, was whisked from reception, to parade, to arsenal, to factory, to relief organisation, to banquet, and to the front. ('Certainly, Mr Willkie must go,' declared Stilwell, mischievously, of the Republican's projected visit to a well-known section of the line. 'It's where the Japanese and Chinese meet to trade all the goods they need from each other.'[27]) To old Chungking hands, the profusion of 'soft soap, adulation and flattery' was nauseating.[28] But Willkie came up with the goods as far as the Kuomintang were concerned, demanding more aid for China, damning colonialism and praising the Generalissimo as 'a firm and steadfast friend', who exceeded even his 'legendary reputation'.[29]

The acme of his trip was an alleged tryst with Madame Chiang. According to his companion, Gardner Cowles, Willkie and Soong May-ling disappeared one evening, causing Chiang and his bodyguards to mount a search party. When the Republican reappeared, 'cocky as a young college student after a successful night with a girl', he expressed his desire to bring Soong back with them to Washington, for the ostensible purpose of lobbying the President.[30] This latter part of the story is corroborated by Gauss but the liaison is mentioned only by Cowles and must, therefore, remain a matter of speculation. Willkie was certainly a ladies' man but Cowles' account, which has Chiang and a cohort of Tommy gun-wielding guards bursting into his quarters in search of the Republican, appears sensationalist. Either way, Soong accepted Willkie's invitation to visit the US, checking into the Presbyterian Hospital in New York, in November 1942, for various medical treatments.

Soong's American sojourn confirmed the psychological bond between the US and the Chinese war effort. Introduced by the Speaker of the House, Sam Rayburn, and the Senate Chaplain in terms that 'would have been excessive if applied to the Madonna', the Wellesley-educated First Lady of China became the first private citizen, as well as the first woman, to address Congress.[31] Wearing a simple black *qipao*, the jewel-encrusted wings of the Chinese Air Force pinned to her chest, she told America's legislators that China was fighting for the same causes as the United States. 'We in China, like you, want a better world, not for ourselves alone, but for *all* mankind . . . The 160 years of traditional friendship between our two great peoples . . . which has never been marred by misunderstandings, is unsurpassed in the annals of the world.'[32] Later, she would raise millions of dollars for the China Relief Fund, speaking to vast crowds in New York, Boston, Atlanta, Chicago and San Francisco, the climax coming when 30,000 people crammed into the Hollywood Bowl to see what *Life* described as 'a realistic star of the first magnitude'.[33]

Enthusiasm, however, did not translate into strategic or diplomatic equality. Chiang was not invited to attend the Casablanca Conference (Symbol), nor the Washington or Quebec Conferences that followed. The Americans, conscious of the need to sustain Chinese morale, pressed for an offensive to reopen the land route between India and Chungking but the British, whose troops would be in the firing line, repeatedly postponed the reinvasion of Burma. Instead, the Western Allies fell back on gesture strategy: limited operations that fired the imagination but were of dubious military value, such as the jungle raids of Major-General Orde Wingate's Chindits (Special Forces sent to wreak havoc behind enemy lines in Burma) or the efforts of Major-General Claire Chennault to defeat the Japanese with only a few hundred, admittedly well-flown, aeroplanes.

Ultimately, Roosevelt cared less about China's military value – beyond the inestimable service of keeping some 600,000 Japanese pinned down in central China – than about her political potential. As he consistently reminded his Sinosceptic allies, China, despite her manifest weaknesses, was a country of almost half a billion people that was sure to count for something someday. Above all, he wanted to keep China in the Western – specifically the American – camp. The appeal of 'pan-Asianism', it was feared in Washington, as well as London and Canberra, might well survive the defeat of Japan. Nationalist China, unless carefully handled, might easily become a Western antagonist. Explaining his thinking to Stalin during the Tehran Conference, Roosevelt stated that he wanted China to act as one of the 'Four Policemen' of the post-war world, 'not because he did not realise the weakness of China at present but [because] he was thinking farther into the future and that after all China was a nation of 400 million people and it was better to have them as friends rather than as a potential source of trouble'.[34] What he did not mention was his other consideration, namely that 'in any serious conflict of policy with Russia, [China] would undoubtedly line up on our [i.e. the Western] side'.[35]

In this attitude, Roosevelt showed considerably more foresight than Churchill, who struggled to see China as anything more than an eighteenth-century power and a 'faggot vote on the side of the United States in any attempt to liquidate the British Overseas Empire'.[36] Part of this was to do with race. As Lord Moran recalled, Churchill would listen in silence as Roosevelt extolled the virtues of treating China as a great power but later spoke disparagingly of 'little yellow men'.[37] On the other hand, there were plenty of others, less encumbered with imperial prejudice, who struggled to see China as the equal of the British Empire, the United States or the Soviet Union. 'The military weakness of China in contrast to the strength of other powers in the Far East has been the central fact of Far Eastern history for the past one hundred years,' wrote the former Special Assistant to the US Ambassador in Chungking in a paper of September 1943. Such weakness could not be expected to vanish with the outbreak of peace. On the contrary, Chinese 'backwardness' in education, industry, transportation, medicine, agricultural and government practices meant that it 'cannot be conceived that, for a minimum of a generation after the war, she [China] can assume local or world responsibilities for the preservation of peace'.[38]

Yet it was Roosevelt's policy that prevailed and the Chinese who reaped the political benefits: being included in the Four Power Declaration of October 1943 and later, true to this document's intent, as a permanent member of the United Nations Security Council. On 1 October 1942 – China's National Day – Chiang was able to make the momentous announcement that Britain and America had agreed to relinquish their extraterritorial rights and privileges. The Treaty Ports, the concessions, the special tariffs, foreign police, warships and law courts were being abolished. The 'Unequal Treaties' were being reduced to 'a stack of waste-paper'.[39] China was now an 'independent' country on an 'equal footing' with the other Great Powers, crowed the Generalissimo. 'Henceforth, if we are weak, if we lack self-confidence, the fault will be ours.'[40]

The Cairo Conference brought more rewards. Including the symbolism of Chiang sitting alongside Roosevelt and Churchill – the clearest sign to date that China was regarded as one of the Great Powers – Roosevelt agreed that all Japanese territorial acquisitions and conquests since 1914, including Manchuria, Formosa (Taiwan) and the Pescadores (Penghu) should be restored to China at the end of the war. The British hope of 'persuading Chiang and his wife to go and see the Pyramids' while they and the Americans resolved strategy on their own evaporated.[41] In addition to lengthy discussions with Chinese generals – an exercise which even Marshall found a complete waste of time – Roosevelt and Chiang spent hours discussing their vision for a post-imperial world. According to Chiang's diary, the Generalissimo commended the President for his pragmatic approach to the Soviet Union but warned that unless he proved equally successful in eradicating British imperialism the US's contribution to the war would be incomplete. Naturally, FDR agreed and raised the issue of Hong Kong. Although no minutes of the meeting were taken (all we have are Chiang's diary entries, a Chinese memorandum and some tendentious 'recollections' by Elliott Roosevelt), it seems likely that Roosevelt mentioned his periodic efforts to induce Britain to relinquish the island. 'His idea', recalled Halifax, was that if Britain were to surrender the colony voluntarily, the Chinese would be so grateful that they would allow the Union Jack to continue to fly over the island, 'existing British business would be guaranteed its accustomed rights . . . and the port of Hong Kong would be declared and remain for all time a free port for the commerce of all nations'.[42] To this hokum, Halifax responded politely but Eden, when presented with the same argument, enquired whether the President was contemplating a similar gesture affecting US territories such as the Panama Canal Zone. Fortunately for inter-Allied relations, Chiang was more realistic. Although he desired the return of the island, he declined to make it a wartime issue.

Chiang left Cairo in a state of euphoria. China was finally being treated as a full member of the alliance, he felt, while the territorial commitments he had extracted amounted to 'the greatest foreign policy success in Chinese history'.[43] Unfortunately, his elation had caused him to overplay his hand, sending Soong on the final day of the conference to ask Roosevelt for a $1 billion loan to help stabilise China's inflation crisis. According to Soong, the President was sympathetic. But the demand fuelled the sense that Chiang was simply out for as much as he could get: a manipulative sponger who used the threat of a Chinese collapse to obtain 'exorbitant' amounts of US aid while offering little in return.

The sense that the Nationalists were not really fighting but husbanding their strength for a post-war confrontation with the communists had been growing for some time. As the British Military Attaché in Chungking wrote to General Ismay in August 1942, echoing the reports of General Magruder:

> The Chinese are at present showing no signs of taking an active part in the war. All the stuff which is daily put out by the Chungking 'Military Spokesman' is just so much blah and bears practically no relation to the facts at all . . . Since the Pacific war began they have made no attempt to attack the Japs and have allowed a considerable number of divisions to be withdrawn from [central] China for use elsewhere. During the past five years they have received from Russia, Germany, ourselves and others quite a respectable quantity of modern equipment of all kinds. But no one who goes to any of the war zones ever sees any of this, or more than a very small fraction. The general opinion amongst the foreign military community here is that nearly all of this has gone into store, except for some of the aeroplanes which have been flown about in back areas and sooner or later written off. I personally have little doubt that it is the fixed intention of the Chinese to build up now as strong an army as they can with the object of coming to the peace table and confronting the Powers with as formidable a force as they can muster.[44]

This damning assessment, whilst containing some truth, was not entirely fair. Engaged or not, Chiang's forces were holding down more than a half a million Japanese soldiers in central China – troops that could otherwise be redeployed to fight the Americans in the Pacific or the British on the frontiers of India – while defensive operations continued even at the cost of an appalling famine in Henan. (In July 1941, the Chungking Government had begun to collect the land tax in grain to feed the Army, a major cause of the ensuing famine that killed anywhere between 1.5 and 4 million people.) Moreover, Chiang had thrown two of his best armies into the defence of Burma and then placed more troops under Stilwell's command to take part in the reconquest of what was, at least nominally, a British colony.

Stilwell had been planning his revenge for the rout of 1942 even as he traipsed through the Burmese jungle. The remnants of his Chinese forces would form the nucleus of a new army which, supplemented with fresh troops, would be trained with American weapons in India. They would then reinvade Burma with the object of restoring the land link with Chungking. Perhaps surprisingly, given Stilwell's role in the disasters of the first Burma campaign, Chiang agreed to the plan. Although the Generalissimo had lost all confidence in his Chief of Staff, his anxiety to maintain good relations with Washington had caused him to hold off asking for his recall. Instead, he told Stilwell that fifteen Chinese divisions would be ready to take the offensive in northern Burma in the spring of 1943, provided the British played their part by launching an amphibious operation across the Bay of Bengal. The British refusal to do this – made apparent in December 1942 and then again following the Tehran Conference – enraged Chiang, who warned Roosevelt, on 9 December 1943, that the Japanese would be likely to use the respite to launch an all-out offensive 'to liquidate the China affair during the coming year'.[45] Four months later, this prophecy was fulfilled. On 17 April 1944, Japan unleashed Operation Ichigō – her largest operation of the war – designed to capture American air-bases in central China and bring the Nationalist regime to its knees.

Although ultimately unsuccessful, Ichigō was a disaster for the Nationalists. Half a million of the Emperor's best men, supported by 800 tanks, 15,000 vehicles and 100,000 horses, cut through the Chinese First War Zone as if it were made of paper. Within a month they had captured the key city of Loyang, in Henan province, and by the end of May were steaming south into Hunan. Changsha, a beacon of resistance since 1938, fell within three days. Hengyang, 120 miles to the south, endured a 47-day siege but surrendered on 8 August. By October, the Chinese had suffered over 700,000 casualties and the Japanese were in control of Henan, Hunan and Guangxi provinces, threatening Chungking.

The Japanese advance inflamed an already smouldering crisis of confidence in Chang Kai-shek and the Nationalists. As the Second Secretary of the US Embassy in Chungking, John Service, reported in July 1944:

> The situation in China is rapidly becoming critical. The Japanese gamble that slow strangulation would not force the Kuomintang to fight a people's war has been successful. The position of the Kuomintang and the Generalissimo is weakening and there is taking place a progressive internal breakdown. The Kuomintang is not only proving itself incapable of averting this debacle but its policies – internal, economic, foreign and military – are precipitating the crisis. The fundamental cause of this shortsighted bankruptcy of the Kuomintang policies is that, lacking the broad base of popular support, it is allowing the maintenance of its power to overrule all other considerations.[46]

As China's eastern front collapsed and tales of Kuomintang inefficiency, unpopularity and corruption swirled, American diplomats put increasing pressure on Chiang to reach an agreement with his ideological enemies, the communists.

Western understanding of the Chinese communists was poor. The class-warriors whom Chiang had pursued to Yan'an, in northwest China, between 1934 and 1935 – the fabled Long March – were variously described as 'agrarian reformers' (Clark Kerr), 'not communists at all' (Robert Jarvis, US Consul at Hankow), 'social democrats' (Captain Evans F. Carlson, Assistant US Naval Attaché) and the 'most cohesive, disciplined and aggressively anti-Japanese regime in China' (John Paton Davies, political adviser to General Stilwell).[47] In fact, whilst some of this was true – the Chinese Communist Party was overwhelmingly agrarian and certainly disciplined – the CCP was a revolutionary organisation led by a committed communist, Mao Zedong, who used the War of Resistance less to fight the Japanese than to extend his political power.

Mao was a master of propaganda. In a famous interview with

the American journalist Edgar Snow in 1936, he gave the impression of a modest Chinese peasant: a shrewd, empathetic scholar, 'quite free from symptoms of megalomania'.[48] Later, after the outbreak of war with Japan, he and other senior communists issued a statement urging Chiang to collaborate with communist forces to resist the invader. Chiang accepted the united front but after a brief formal collaboration between 1937 and 1938, Mao's view that the communists should engage only in guerrilla warfare prevailed. At the same time, the communists sought to expand their influence by building 'base areas' behind Japanese lines, gaining hundreds of thousands of new recruits. 'The War of Resistance', Mao is alleged to have declared, 'is a great opportunity for us to develop. Our policy is to focus 70 per cent on expansion, 20 per cent on dealing with the Kuomintang and 10 per cent on resisting Japan.'[49] Years later, he would thank Japanese emissaries for enabling the CCP to win the Civil War. 'The "help" of the Japanese invasion', he told Prime Minister Kakuei Tanaka in 1976, had provided the conditions for victory over the Nationalists.[50]

Yet the decline in Kuomintang fortunes caused the Americans to look, with unfaithful eyes, towards the yellow soil of Yan'an. In January 1944, John Paton Davies urged the White House to send an official mission to the communist capital. Convinced that Chiang was determined not to fight the Japanese and was haemorrhaging support, he recommended the mission on the grounds that Yan'an was a major base for military operations, that it offered an abundance of enemy intelligence, that its inhabitants were 'aggressively anti-Japanese', and that it possessed the key to improved relations between China and the Soviet Union.[51] Naturally, Chiang resisted the suggestion. But the combination of American pressure and Ichigō proved too great and on 22 July a US Army observation group arrived in Yan'an.

The impressions of the so-called 'Dixie Mission' were overwhelmingly favourable. In contrast to the squalor and spoils system of Chungking, the Americans, led by John Service, found simplicity, sincerity and social cohesion. Relations between officials and the people were 'open, direct and friendly'. Mao and other communist leaders were mentioned with universal respect. There were no beggars, no signs of desperate poverty nor, so far as they could ascertain, any police. The war seemed 'close and real'. There was no defeatism but rather confidence. Everyone they met appeared imbued with a sense of mission. All in all, the observers felt as if they had 'come into a different country', or, as one correspondent put it, 'the most modern place in China'.[52]

This and similar reports convinced the Americans of the need to press Chiang to strike a deal with Mao. By 1944, the CCP had swelled to more than a million people, with 900,000 regular troops and a similar number of militia. Not only would these forces prove invaluable in the war against Japan – at that stage, prior to the successful test of the atomic bomb, projected to last a further two years – but a coalition between the Kuomintang and the CCP might prevent the country from descending into civil war. To these urgings – made by Ambassador Gauss, Vice-President Henry Wallace and, ultimately, Roosevelt – Chiang reacted badly. 'For twenty years, the communist bandits and the Russians have been plotting against me,' he sobbed into his diary, 'but now the British and Americans are plotting with the communists!'[53] Yet before Sino-US relations could reach a crisis over American desire to work with and possibly arm the communists, the long-running feud between the Generalissimo and his Chief of Staff reached its denouement.

Since December 1943, Stilwell had been battling with his American-trained Chinese divisions – known as X Force – to open a road between Assam in north-east India and Yunnan in south-west China. Critics, including Generals Wedemeyer and Wheeler, doubted the wisdom of cutting through an enemy-infested jungle to build a road that would require constant maintenance, could only facilitate a fraction of the necessary supplies and would, in all probability, be completed too late to make a significant difference to the war. But Stilwell was determined. He wanted to avenge the humiliation of 1942 and he wanted to prove to the cheerleaders of his rival, the aviator General Chennault, the value of ground operations. In March 1944, he was slogging his way down the Hukawng Valley in Burma when the Japanese attempted a massive encirclement of British forces at Imphal and Kohima on the Indian–Burmese border. (It was General Slim's defence of Imphal and Kohima and subsequent counterattack, rather than Stilwell's efforts, that turned the tide in Burma.) Fearing he would be cut off, the American begged Washington to put pressure on Chiang to send the fifteen American-trained Chinese divisions in Yunnan – known as Y Force – into north-east Burma to relieve the pressure. Chiang refused. Having tried to use the divisions as a bargaining chip, to force his allies to honour their operational commitments or to obtain his ridiculously large loan, he was now receiving intelligence about the imminent Ichigō offensive. But a threat from Roosevelt to end Lend-Lease did the trick and on 11 May Y Force crossed the Salween River.

The ensuing military crisis – a battle raging in north-east India and northern Burma, concurrent with an all-out Japanese attempt to crush the Nationalists in central and southern China – showed both Chiang and Stilwell at their worst. While Chiang refused to reinforce generals he suspected of disloyalty, Stilwell, who had deserted his post as Chief of Staff to fight in the Burmese jungle, refused to aid Chiang. 'Let them stew,' he responded when Chennault requested supplies for besieged Hengyang.[54] After a series of meetings with the Generalissimo in June 1944, Vice-President Wallace advised Roosevelt to recall Stilwell. The US War Department's solution was the opposite. On 6 July, Roosevelt wrote to Chiang asking him to place Stilwell in command of all Chinese forces, including the communists.

Chiang prevaricated. The request was deeply offensive but he feared a rift with the Americans. Accepting the President's request in principle, he asked for time as well as a specially appointed representative to 'adjust the relations between me and General Stilwell'.[55] Roosevelt sent the former Secretary of War Patrick J. Hurley. On 7 September, Hurley met with Chiang, who agreed to hand over command to Stilwell. Considering this was a man he distrusted and despised and who more than reciprocated these feelings, this was no small concession. His condition was control of Lend-Lease. Hitherto, Stilwell had kept this precious resource in his own hands – denying the Nationalists supplies during the Battle of Hengyang to increase the pressure on Chiang to relinquish his command. 'If the G-mo controls distribution, I am sunk,' he recorded in his diary. 'The Reds will get nothing. Only the G-mo's henchmen will be supplied and my troops will suck the hind tit.'[56]

On 15 September the two men quarrelled over how to respond to the Japanese counteroffensive against Y Force in northern Burma. Chiang wanted X Force to draw off the attackers. Stilwell said they needed to rest. In response, Chiang said that unless X Force came to the rescue he would have to withdraw Y Force. Stilwell was enraged. Wiring Marshall, who along with Roosevelt and Churchill was attending the Second Quebec Conference, he stated that the 'crazy little bastard' (as he called Chiang in his diary) was threatening to throw away 'the results of all our labours'.[57] The response he got from Quebec was as hot as a 'firecracker'.[58] Accusing Chiang of bringing the war in the Far East to the brink of disaster, Roosevelt warned the Generalissimo that unless he continued to support the operations in Burma, 'you must yourself be prepared to accept the consequences and assume the personal responsibility'.[59]

Hurley begged Stilwell not to deliver the message. 'Joe, you have won the ball game. The Gimo has agreed to everything.'[60] But Stilwell would not listen. Having driven to Chiang's residence on Yellow Mountain, he was determined to hand the 'bundle of paprika to the Peanut' in person. 'The harpoon hit the little bugger right in the solar plexus,' he recorded gleefully. 'It was a clean hit but beyond turning green and losing the power of speech, he did not bat an eye. He just said to me, "I understand."'[61] Two days later, Stilwell sent a victory ditty to his wife:

> I've waited long for vengeance –
> At last I've had my chance.
> I've looked the Peanut in the eye
> And kicked him in the pants.[62]

As soon as Stilwell had left, Chiang burst into tears. He could not accept the insult. He would break with Stilwell come what may. The Presidential message, he instructed T. V. Soong to inform Hurley, represented 'the lowest point in the history of the US leadership of the alliance'.[63] On 24 September, he asked Roosevelt to recall his Chief of Staff. He would cede control of China's armies to another general but he could not trust General Stilwell. Although Marshall wanted to argue, Roosevelt acceded to Chiang's request. Later,

'Temporary expedient': Admiral François Darlan flanked by Supreme Allied Commander General Dwight D. Eisenhower and General Mark W. Clark. (Associated Press / Alamy Stock Photo.)

Gallic cock fight: General de Gaulle and General Henri Giraud shake hands at Anfa camp, near Casablanca, 24 January 1943. (Piemags / WW2Archive / Alamy Stock Photo.)

Blame game: mass graves of Polish officers, murdered by the NKVD, are discovered in the Katyn Forest, April 1943. (World History Archive / Alamy Stock Photo.)

Master and commanders: Churchill with Foreign Secretary Anthony Eden, Chief of the Imperial General Staff General Sir Alan Brooke, Air Chief Marshal Sir Arthur Tedder, Admiral of the Fleet Sir Andrew Cunningham, General Sir Harold Alexander, US Army Chief of Staff General George Marshall, Supreme Allied Commander General Dwight D. Eisenhower and General Sir Bernard Montgomery, Algiers, June 1943.

(Piemags / WW2Archive / Alamy Stock Photo.)

Both alike in dignity: Anthony Eden and Cordell Hull at the Foreign Ministers Conference in Moscow, October 1943. (Photo 12 / Alamy Stock Photo.)

'I can handle Stalin': Roosevelt and the self-created Marshal Stalin at Tehran, November 1943. (Everett Collection Inc / Alamy Stock Photo.)

The Big Three: Churchill hosts a dinner to celebrate his sixty-ninth birthday, Tehran, November 1943. (Fremantle / Alamy Stock Photo.)

Sino-American fellowship: Generalissimo Chiang Kai-shek, his wife, Soong May-ling, and General 'Vinegar Joe' Stilwell, April 1942. (Alpha Stock / Alamy Stock Photo.)

The Yugoslav imbroglio: Tito (*right*) with partisan commanders, May 1944. (Niday Picture Library / Alamy Stock Photo.)

Money talks: US Treasury Secretary Henry Morgenthau Jr and British Treasury envoy Lord Keynes at Bretton Woods, July 1944. (World History Archive / Alamy Stock Photo.)

Warsaw in flames: members of the Polish Home Army fight the Germans, August 1944.
(World History Archive / Alamy Stock Photo.)

Liberation and civil war: British soldiers on the streets of Athens, December 1944.
(AFP via Getty Images.)

Feeling the strain: Churchill, Stalin and a visibly ailing Roosevelt at Yalta, February 1945.
(Science History Images / Alamy Stock Photo.)

'Uncle Joe': Stalin with Churchill at Yalta.
(Fremantle / Alamy Stock Photo.)

Shadows of victory: a Red Army soldier plants the hammer-and-sickle flag above the ruins of the Reichstag, May 1945. (Shawshots / Alamy Stock Photo.)

he authorised the publication of a story in the *New York Times* – fed by Stilwell to the journalist Brooks Atkinson, during his last days in Chungking – which lambasted Chiang for dismissing 'the ablest field commander in China since "Chinese Gordon" '.[64] The Sino-US relationship would never be the same. Although American military supplies continued, the sense that China was an ungrateful ally – a 'moribund, anti-democratic regime that is more concerned with maintaining its political supremacy than driving the Japanese out of China', according to Stilwell and his sympathisers – took root.[65] Between December 1944 and May 1945, the Japanese were evicted from Burma but this was overwhelmingly the accomplishment of Lieutenant-General Sir William Slim and his 'Forgotten Army' of Indian, British and West African soldiers. When the Allies gathered to discuss the post-war world at Yalta, in February 1945, Chiang was not invited to attend. Nor were the Chinese included at Potsdam, where the war against Japan and the post-war order of Asia were due to be discussed. Rather, China ended the war in much the same diplomatic position as she had been at the time she joined the alliance: a phantom member of the illusory 'Big Four'.

XXV

Turncoats and Partisans

My task was simply to find out who was killing the most
Germans and suggest means by which we could help them to
kill more. Politics must be a secondary consideration.

Fitzroy Maclean[1]

The town of Cassibile, on the east coast of Sicily, possessed a historic symbolism. It was here, in 413 BC, that the Athenians had
capitulated to the Syracusans and it was here, on 2 September 1943,
that representatives of the Italian Government arrived to sign the
Allied terms of surrender. Or so the Allies thought.

For over a month, since the fall of Mussolini in a palace coup, emissaries of the new Italian Prime Minister, Marshal Pietro Badoglio,
had been attempting to extricate their country from the Axis. At 10
p.m. on 1 September, the Allies received word that the Italians had
agreed to their terms. The following morning, however, General
Giuseppe Castellano told his British and American interlocutors
that he lacked the authority to sign the necessary document. With
the invasion of Calabria less than eighteen hours away, the British
Minister-Resident in the Mediterranean, Harold Macmillan, decided
that the time had come for a display of firmness. Apprising General Sir
Harold Alexander of the situation, he requested an intervention. The
General entered into the spirit of the enterprise with gusto. Donning his
best parade uniform, complete with gleaming boots and golden spurs,
he climbed over the wall at the back of the Allied camp (so as to avoid
the less imposing entrance of traipsing across a stubble field), mounted
his vehicle and, along with his staff, roared round to the tent where
the Italians were holding out. With icy politeness, Alexander demanded
to know who the officers were. If they were plenipotentiaries, they

would sign; if they were spies, he would have them arrested. He then threatened to bomb Rome unless the armistice was agreed within twenty-four hours. The Italians signed the following day.

Alas, not all Italian difficulties could be so easily resolved. In July 1943, Churchill and Roosevelt had agreed to deal with any non-Fascist Italian government capable of 'delivering the goods'.[2] The Badoglio Government offered half of this. The landings at Salerno were unopposed by the Italians, the Italian Fleet was transferred to the Allies and civil order was maintained. Although the administration preferred to flee rather than defend Rome – leaving the Germans to occupy the capital for the next nine months – a handful of Italian units, most notably at Bari and on Cephalonia, turned their guns on their former allies. On 13 October 1943, King Victor Emmanuel declared war on Germany. Yet neither the King nor Badoglio could be said to be untainted by fascism. Although military defeat had finally caused the feeble and fatalistic monarch to dismiss Mussolini, he had sustained both him and his accomplices for over twenty years. Even now, after his country's surrender, the little sovereign was prone to referring to the Duce as 'a kind of factor who ran the estate very well for about ten years and then let it go to ruin'.[3] The record of his fellow septuagenarian Pietro Badoglio was even worse. As Governor of Tripolitania and Cyrenaica between 1929 and 1933, he had waged a near-genocidal campaign against the indigenous population and, in 1935 and 1936, deployed mustard gas against the Abyssinians. In 1940, he had resigned as Chief of Staff – following the Army's disastrous showing in Greece – but had waited until the Allies had landed on Italian soil before moving against Mussolini.

Churchill had no problem with 'seeming to recognise the House of Savoy or Badoglio'.[4] His commitment to monarchy was both romantic and practical. The last believer in the divine right of kings (according to his wife), he also saw the institution as a unifying and stabilising influence. In *The Gathering Storm*, he would lament the 'prejudice of the Americans' which prevented the Allies from fortifying post-1918 Germany with a constitutional sovereign around which all elements, both liberal and feudal, could rally.[5] Now he saw the preservation of the Piedmontese dynasty and its choice of First Minister as a bulwark against 'chaos, bolshevisation or civil war'. It might be some time before the Allies could drive the Germans out of Italy (as indeed it was) and 'we have no right to lay undue burdens on our troops'.[6]

The Americans had other ideas. Apart from their 'prejudice' against monarchy, they were committed (as, theoretically, were the British) to the principles of self-determination, liberal democracy and anti-fascism. Above all, they wanted to avoid the opprobrium of a second 'Darlan deal'. On 2 September 1943, therefore, Cordell Hull and Adolf Berle agreed to help facilitate the journey of Count Carlo Sforza, the former Italian Foreign Minister and fierce opponent of fascism, from political exile in the US to Italy. The British, not wishing to undermine Badoglio, queried the decision. Berle explained that there were some six million Italian-Americans in the US and that they held an important electoral position. (The Presidential election was just over a year away.) The anti-fascists, naturally, wanted a liberal regime, while the former admirers of Mussolini wanted to redeem themselves in the eyes of their American compatriots. Neither would understand an interdiction of Sforza – the leader of 'Free Italy' – returning to his homeland. On 23 September, Berle received a letter from Sforza promising to support Badoglio in his efforts to 'drive every German soldier from Italian soil'.[7] This pacified the British but only for a moment. Two weeks later, the Count told the *New York Times* that Churchill was 'badly informed' of the Italian situation, likening the Prime Minister's appeal to the Italian people to rally round the Crown to 'a preacher for the Stuarts [going] among the enraged soldiers of Cromwell'.[8]

Churchill was furious. Sharing the Foreign Office view that Sforza was an 'elderly peacock', a bore and a snob, whose 'astonishing vanity entirely warped his judgement', he asked the Count to call on him in Downing Street as he passed through London.[9] There he gave him a 'good schooling' and was rewarded with a ten-minute lecture on the seniority of the House of Sforza in relation to the House of Savoy.[10]* 'It is quite evident to me that the old fool wants to be king himself, hence his republicanism,' scrawled the Premier.[11] (The 'old fool' was only a couple of years older than Churchill.) Yet

---

* In fact, Francesco Sforza only became Duke of Milan (through marriage) in 1450, whereas the House of Savoy was established in 1003.

the Count promised to support the King and Badoglio provided that the Italian people would, in due course, be free to choose their own regime. Within a few weeks he was back in Italy and within as short a space of time was, as Macmillan recorded, 'running an intrigue to force the abdication of the King, to get Badoglio to act as Regent . . . and to become Prime Minister himself'.[12]

The Americans supported Sforza. Early indications were that Badoglio was unacceptable to Italian liberal and democratic opinion, while the King was widely reviled. The Russians, on the other hand, favoured the status quo. This was no compliment to the ageing duopoly. Although Stalin told the Italian Communist leader, Palmiro Togliatti, that the war came first, it did not escape Moscow's notice that the unpopularity of the King–Badoglio regime was acting as a recruiting sergeant for the Italian Communists. In March 1944, the Soviet Union unilaterally recognised the Badoglio Government and in April Togliatti joined the Ministry, along with Sforza and Benedetto Croce, Victor Emmanuel having been persuaded to retire in preference to his son. Two months later, Togliatti reported to the supposedly dissolved Comintern that the Italian Communist Party was growing rapidly.[13]

On 18 May 1944, the British 8th Army and the American 5th Army finally broke through the Gustav Line, precipitating the capture of Rome. (A Pyrrhic victory, as it turned out, since General Mark Clark's determination to take the city, in disobedience of his orders, allowed the German 10th Army to escape.) Churchill had been adamant that Badoglio should remain until the capital was secured; ideally until the whole peninsula was liberated. On 8 June, however, General Sir Noel Mason-MacFarlane, Chief Commissioner of the Allied Control Commission for Italy, brought the Government to Rome to make contact with the leaders of the political parties. The result was the fall of Badoglio and the appointment of the moderate socialist and former War Minister, Ivanoe Bonomi, as Prime Minister. Although this represented no threat to Allied interests – the composition of the Government was little changed and Bonomi, unlike Badoglio, was unsullied by fascism – Churchill was incandescent. 'I am surprised and shocked about Badoglio being replaced by this wretched old Bonomi,' he minuted Eden. (Bonomi was even

closer in age to Churchill than Sforza.) 'We have lost the only competent Italian with whom we could deal.'[14] In telegrams to Roosevelt
and Stalin, Churchill implied that the Allies should refuse to recognise this 'cluster of aged and hungry politicians'.[15] But by 16 June he
was forced, reluctantly, to agree with Macmillan that it was impossible 'to put Humpty Dumpty [Badoglio] in place again'.[16]

The coda to the saga came four months later when Churchill
ordered the British High Commissioner in Italy, Sir Noel Charles, to
oppose the appointment of Sforza as Foreign Minister. The Americans, who liked Sforza and his influence on Italian-Americans (many
of whom had just helped re-elect Roosevelt to a fourth term), were
indignant. On 5 December 1944, the new Secretary of State, Edward
Stettinius, issued a statement rebuking the British for their interference. Eden was furious and Churchill sent Roosevelt a protest that
was tantamount to an accusation of disloyalty:

> I was much astonished at the acerbity of the State Department's
> communiqué to the public and I shall do my best . . . to avoid imi-
> tating it. I feel however entitled to remind you that on every single
> occasion in the course of this war I have loyally tried to support any
> statements to which you were personally committed, for instance
> in the Darlan affair . . . I do not remember anything that the State
> Department has ever said about Russia or about any other allied
> state comparable to this document with which Mr Stettinius has
> inaugurated his assumption of office.[17]

To Roger Makins, watching from his vantage point in the Washington Embassy, it was yet another manifestation of 'the shifting of
relative power within the Anglo-American alliance'.[18]

★

The Italian squabble had a Rossinian quality but the situation in
Yugoslavia, with its mythologies, sub-plots and innumerable betray-
als, was positively Wagnerian. In April 1941, the Royal Yugoslav
Government and the seventeen-year-old King Peter had fled before
the advancing Germans. Travelling first to Athens, the King declared

his intention to maintain the struggle, before continuing his journey, along with his ministers, to London by way of Cairo. Since their arrival coincided with the onset of Operation Barbarossa, their hosts paid little attention to Balkan affairs for some months. As the summer wore on, however, reports of anti-Axis resistance in the hills of Croatia, Serbia and Montenegro began to penetrate Whitehall. The man behind these activities, the British learnt, was Draža Mihailović: a Serbian Colonel in the Royal Yugoslav Army who had retreated to the mountains around Ravna Gora, in western Serbia, to organise a resistance movement on the Četnik model.*

With encouragement from the Political Warfare Executive, the British press built up Mihailović into a hero: a man deserving the 'admiration and gratitude' of all free people; a General who was carrying on a 'regular war' against three fully equipped Axis divisions.[19] Unfortunately, such encomia were not matched by practical support. Although Churchill instructed both Ismay and Hugh Dalton (responsible for the Special Operations Executive) to do everything 'in human power' to aid the guerrillas, four Liberator bombers were all that were available to drop an inadequate quantity of munitions – often on the wrong locations – between November 1941 and November 1942.[20] During the following four months only two drops – comprising a mere 23 tons – were made, while the delivery of 500 left-footed boots sparked claims of sabotage.

British attempts to unify the resistance were even less successful. During the early autumn of 1941, an uneasy alliance had existed between the royalist Četniks under Mihailović and the communist Partisans under Josip Broz, better known as 'Tito'. This short-lived collaboration ended in November when the rival factions fell out and began to fight each other. Not wishing to contribute towards the incipient civil war, the British halted the meagre supplies being sent from Cairo. On 22 November, however, Mihailović informed the Yugoslav Government-in-Exile that he had succeeded in stopping the

---

* The Četnik organisation had its origins in the nineteenth century and the Serbian fight against Ottoman rule. Led by Serbian officers, operating through both central and local structures, these bands of hardy guerrillas played an important role in both the Balkan Wars and the First World War.

fratricide, causing the British to resume parachute drops. In fact, the civil war was still raging even as the Germans drove both movements from Serbia: the Četniks to Montenegro, the Partisans to eastern Bosnia. In mid-November, both the Yugoslav Government-in-Exile and the British made the first of a series of requests to the Soviet Government to force the Partisans to submit to Mihailović's command and end their internecine activities. The Soviets, concealing their radio link with Tito, replied that they had neither contact with nor influence over the Yugoslav Communists. Within a few days, however, Moscow radio began to praise Mihailović, while Tito was rebuked for his overtly political agenda: 'Do not call your proletarian brigades proletarian,' the Comintern General Secretary, Georgi Dimitrov, wrote in August 1942. 'Instead call them shock brigades . . . Understand that this has enormous political significance . . . within the country and for foreign countries. You are waging a people's liberation war . . . you are not waging a proletarian struggle . . . Quit playing right into the hands of the enemies of the people.'[21]

Such messages, combined with the complete lack of Soviet materiel support, were obviously discouraging. In the summer of 1942, however, the Soviets began to broadcast anti-Mihailović stories, claiming that the Partisans were the only group doing any fighting and accusing the Četniks of collaborating with the enemy. These reports alarmed the Yugoslav Government-in-Exile, which produced a lengthy document refuting the allegations. The Foreign Office was impressed but not entirely convinced. Minuting colleagues in the Southern Department on 19 August, the diplomat Victor Coverley-Price drew attention to the 'dangerous difference of opinion between ourselves and the Russians', while admitting that 'we ourselves are not altogether clear as to M's singleness of purpose'. His conclusion, reflecting London's growing scepticism, was stark: 'Either we or the Russians must be wrong about M.'[22]

The British had established loose contact with Mihailović in the autumn of 1941. Deposited off the coast of Montenegro by submarine, Captain D. T. 'Bill' Hudson of SOE had reached the Colonel's headquarters at Ravna Gora just as the short-lived alliance between the Četniks and the Partisans was disintegrating. In late October, the Germans had responded to the nascent insurgency by massacring

1,700 Serbs at Kraljevo, followed by a further 2,778 at Kragujevac. For every German killed, Hitler ordered that a hundred Serbs were to be executed. Mihailović, whose purpose was to protect the Serbian people and preserve the Serbian-dominated state, was horrified. Deciding that such reprisals were too high a price to pay for rebellion – particularly when viewed in conjunction with the genocide of Orthodox Serbs in Croatia and Bosnia-Herzegovina by the Croatian Catholic-fascist Ustaše – he decided to end formal resistance, ordering his forces to disperse until such time as assistance would enable them to drive the Axis from their land. Not only was this the policy of the Yugoslav Government, it was also to a large extent the policy advocated by SOE. As Dalton wrote in August 1941, the guerrillas:

> Should show sufficient active resistance to cause constant embarrassment to the occupying forces ... But they should keep their main organisation underground and avoid any attempt at large scale risings or ambitious military operations, which could only result at present in severe repression and the loss of our key men. They should now do all they can to prepare a widespread underground organisation ready to strike hard later on, when we give the signal.[23]

The problem was that Mihailović was not prepared to maintain 'active resistance', at least not to the level desired by SOE or Middle East Command. Although the Četnik leader responded to Allied requests to disrupt Axis supplies by conducting a campaign of railway sabotage during the summer and early autumn of 1942, the severity of the German response caused him, once again, to suspend his activities. The Partisans, by contrast, viewed reprisals as recruiting opportunities. In November 1942, Bill Hudson, whose mission had been blighted by poor radio communication, complained that Mihailović was not merely passive but capable of collaborating 'with either [the] Italians or [the] Germans' if this 'serve[d] his purposes without compromising him'.[24] At the same time, Enigma decrypts revealed that the Axis was being forced to deploy significant resources in areas beyond the reach of the Četniks. In March 1943, the decision was made to contact the Partisans.

Captain William Deakin was an Oxford historian. A graduate of

Christ Church and Fellow of Wadham, he had served as Churchill's research assistant for the later volumes of the future Prime Minister's life of Marlborough and later on his *History of the English-Speaking Peoples*. A man of intelligence and charm, he had joined the Queen's Own Oxfordshire Hussars before the outbreak of war but was soon recruited into SOE. December 1942 saw him working on Balkan matters in Cairo and in the early hours of 28 May 1943 he found himself descending through the night air to join the Partisans on Mount Durmitor, in north-west Montenegro.

Deakin's mission and that of his successor, Fitzroy Maclean, were highly influential. Landing in the midst of a battle, the Oxford don was exhilarated as he and his new comrades scrambled up mountains, down gorges and across rivers, in a desperate attempt to escape the advancing Germans. 'In a small space of days we had been buffeted, protected by an evaporating innocence, into an epic now being fought out within a cauldron,' he wrote in his vivid, Churchillian memoir. 'There was no front and no quarter. We had been pulled into a closed and simple world. We had no past and the future would be counted out by minutes.'[25]

Deakin reported that 20,000 Partisans were battling 100,000 Germans (only a slight overestimation on both sides) and that whilst the Partisans were sustaining heavy losses the Germans were also suffering. (What he was unaware of was that the Germans were also trying to liquidate the Četniks.) He called for all possible aid to be sent to the Partisans and, on 25 June 1943, the first parachute drop was made. More significantly, he endorsed the Partisan claim that the Četniks were collaborating not only with Milan Nedić, the Serbian Quisling, but also the Germans and Italians. Years later, Vlatko Velebit, the smooth-talking Partisan liaison to the British mission, described his bucolic method of propaganda:

> My system . . . was to take him [Deakin] to a stream nearby, very nice and cool and fresh water where we used to bathe the whole afternoon. I always took a bunch of captured documents with me . . . I think the course of indoctrination, if I may call it that, worked very well because Deakin got more and more convinced that the Mihailović movement was really no good at all and was

really a kind of fifth column supporting the enemy rather than a resistance force.[26]

Although the bathing was optional, Maclean received similar treatment.

Fitzroy Maclean was an unlikely Partisan sympathiser. An adventurous diplomat turned amateur soldier, he had served in Moscow at the time of the purges, when 'fear hung over the city like a mist' and the 'highest and the lowest alike were dragged from their beds at three in the morning to vanish forever'.[27] One night, at the theatre, a Belgian colleague watched as a Russian turned to Maclean and asked, innocently, 'Comrade, may I borrow your programme?' The Scotsman gave him a cold Caledonian look and replied, 'I am no comrade of yours.'[28] Summoned to Chequers for a Prime Ministerial briefing, Maclean asked Churchill, after the latter had prised himself away from a Donald Duck cartoon, how the British Government felt about supporting a communist movement with almost certain links to Moscow. As Maclean recalled, the Prime Minister's response was unequivocal:

> So long . . . as the whole of Western civilisation was threatened by the Nazi menace, we could not afford to let our attention be diverted from the immediate issue by considerations of long-term policy . . . My task was simply to find out who was killing the most Germans and suggest means by which we could help them to kill more.[29]

Maclean parachuted into Partisan headquarters in central Bosnia during the early hours of 18 September 1943. The situation, owing to the Italian surrender, was in flux. The Partisans had seized the Dalmatian coast – allowing the Allies to unload 600 tons of supplies – but the Germans were bearing down on them and would soon force a retreat to the mountains. Like Deakin, the romantic Maclean was enthralled:

> While we sat there [at a local Partisan command], messengers kept bringing in situation reports from nearby areas where operations were in progress. As they delivered their messages, they . . . gave the clenched-fist salute. Somehow it all seemed strangely familiar: the peasant's hut, the alert young Commander, the benign figure of the Political Commissar with his walrus moustache and the

hammer and sickle badge on his cap, the girl with her pistol and hand-
grenades, the general atmosphere of activity and expectation . . . In
Russia I had only seen the Revolution twenty years after the event,
when it was as rigid and pompous and firmly established as any regime
in Europe. Now I was seeing the struggle in its initial stages, with the
revolutionaries fighting for life and liberty against tremendous odds.[30]

Both officers were captivated by Tito. Born in 1892 in the northern
Croatian region of Zagorje, then part of the Habsburg Empire, Josip
Broz had fought with courage against both Serbia and Russia as a
conscript of the Croatian Home Guard during the First World War.
Captured in 1915, he spent two years in a Russian military hospital
and prisoner of war camp until the February Revolution offered
him the chance of escape. Over the next three years he participated
in the Russian Civil War, before returning to his homeland where he
joined the Communist Party of Yugoslavia. In 1937, after a decade of
illegal activity and six years in prison, he became its leader. Unlike
Mihailović – described by an SOE officer as 'narrow-minded and
stubborn, very pan-Serb, wily and a master of evasion and procras-
tination' – Tito exuded sincerity, dynamism and a roguish charm.[31]
Both Deakin and Maclean were struck by his 'surprisingly broad
outlook; his never-failing sense of humour; his unashamed delight
in the minor pleasures of life; a natural diffidence in human relationships, giving way to a natural friendliness; a violent temper, flaring
up into sudden rages; a considerateness and a generosity constantly
manifesting themselves in a dozen small ways'.[32] Far from being a
'rigid doctrinaire', a 'fanatic . . . narrow in out-look and impervi-
ous to open debate', Tito appeared surprisingly human: a natural
leader, 'broadened by the experience of exile and prison, flexible in
discussion, with a sharp and humorous wit and a wide curiosity'.[33]

On 5 October 1943 – a mere seventeen days after he had arrived
in Yugoslavia – Maclean began his return journey to Cairo. He had
not travelled outside a small area of Bosnia and Croatia, he had not
moved without Partisan supervision, he had not encountered the
Četniks or their British Liaison Officers and he had not – unlike
Deakin – witnessed any fighting. His sole source of information,
as with Deakin, were the Partisans. His report was, consequently,

wildly exaggerated. Instead of the roughly 60,000 men operating under Tito's command, Maclean attributed to the Partisan leader a force of 220,000 soldiers – more than double the number of Germans in the entire country. Well disciplined, highly motivated and centrally controlled, these guerrillas were held to dominate the greater part of Yugoslavia. In fact, the Četniks controlled most of rural Serbia, along with large parts of Montenegro and sections of Bosnia-Herzegovina. The Partisans, by contrast, held sway in Croatia (although they would shortly be evicted from the coast), Slovenia and the other parts of Bosnia-Herzegovina. Not only were they apparently more 'numerous, infinitely better organised, better equipped and better disciplined' than the Četniks, they were also, according to Maclean, amazingly effective: with five Germans killed for every Partisan. Repeating the familiar claim that Mihailović was a collaborator and thus 'thoroughly discredited in the eyes of most of the population', the 32-year-old Maclean, who had visions of becoming a Balkan Lawrence, concluded his report by recommending that the Allies withdraw their support from Mihailović and transfer it all to Tito.[34]

The twin claims that the Partisans were fighting whilst the Četniks were not, and that the Četniks were collaborating whilst the Partisans were not, were central to the British decision to abandon Mihailović. Both had a basis in fact. In November 1941, following the breakdown in co-operation between the Četniks and the Partisans, Mihailović had allowed himself to be persuaded by German intelligence officers to meet with representatives of the occupying power. The meeting came to nothing. The Germans demanded the unconditional surrender of the Četniks, while Mihailović, though prepared to leave Serbia's main arteries under German control, insisted on maintaining his force as guardians and future liberators of the state. Elsewhere it was different. Local Četnik commanders in Montenegro and Slovenia collaborated with the Italians against the Partisans. The extent to which Mihailović authorised this collaboration is unclear (he was frequently incommunicado) but the evidence suggests that he approved of local arrangements that allowed his forces to gain arms and territory but disapproved of agreements that could prove politically damaging. It was in this spirit that he allowed his supporters, at certain intervals, to join the forces of the Serbian puppet, Milan Nedić.

Short of food, clothing and equipment, Mihailović encouraged his
followers to enlist in the collaborationist Serbian State Guard in order
to obtain arms that could later be used against their enemies.

Naturally, the Partisans denounced the Četniks as traitors. Yet
the Partisans' own hands were by no means clean, participating in
prisoner exchanges and, in March 1943, sending three high-ranking
representatives to confer with a senior German officer about the possibility of a truce. While these talks were ongoing, Tito ordered his
forces to cease operations against the Axis, granting the Germans
safe passage to attack the Četniks. The reality was that the civil war
was more important to both sides than fighting the Axis. One day
the Germans and the Italians would be gone – the Allies would see
to that – but the battle for the future of Yugoslavia would still have
to be fought. Mihailović, therefore, tried to preserve his dwindling
band of followers, while Tito frequently ordered his soldiers to avoid
fighting the Germans and concentrate on annihilating the Četniks,
'the greatest danger to the development of the National Liberation
Struggle'.[35] Both movements committed atrocities – the Četnik massacre of Croats and Muslims in Croatia and Bosnia-Herzegovina
amounting to genocide – and battles were multidimensional. A
good illustration of this Russian-doll war is provided by an American Liaison Officer attached to the Četniks. On 2 October 1943,
Mihailović's forces attacked one German and two Ustaše companies
at Višegrad on the River Drina. They then drove on towards Sarajevo
and started fighting the Partisans. The Partisans counterattacked and
captured Višegrad. Allied radio then announced that the Partisans
had destroyed two bridges on the Užice-Višegrad-Sarajevo railway
when in fact this had been the work of the Četniks.

The situation was thus complicated and yet Britain's liaison officers
with the Partisans – both of whom enjoyed direct links to the Prime
Minister – presented an unambiguous picture. After reading the
Maclean report and questioning the two officers in Cairo, Churchill
decided that he had heard enough. On 10 December 1943, the Prime
Minister announced that he wanted to be rid of Mihailović by the end
of the year. The Yugoslav Government-in-Exile was appalled and the
Foreign Office was sceptical but Churchill insisted. Against cries of
protest from British Liaison Officers operating with Mihailović, who

had witnessed the General's popularity in Serbia, all Allied supplies to the Četniks were stopped. In March 1944, the British Liaison Officers to Mihailović were withdrawn. In May, King Peter bowed to British pressure and dismissed the Government of Božidar Purić, including Mihailović from his post as Minister of War. Three months later, the monarch removed the General from his role as Chief of Staff to the Yugoslav Army and on 12 September he urged all Yugoslavs to 'join the National Liberation Army under the leadership of Marshal Tito'.[36]

It was not long before the British began to realise their mistake. In November 1943, while the Big Three were meeting at Tehran, Tito, in a speech filled with praise for the Soviet Union, had proclaimed the end of royal authority and the creation of a new National Committee of Liberation. Appointing himself Prime Minister and Defence Minister, as well as Marshal, he then announced that the King was forbidden from returning to Yugoslav territory until the end of the war, when the future of the monarchy would be decided. All subsequent attempts by Churchill to save the young King's throne failed. The only sure means would have been to back the Četniks against the Partisans, the very reverse of the Prime Minister's policy. In August 1944, Churchill met Tito at Naples. Earlier, when Maclean had warned Churchill that the newly created Marshal planned to establish a communist regime in Yugoslavia, the Prime Minister had seemed relaxed. 'Do you intend to make Yugoslavia your home after the war?' he enquired.

'No, Sir', replied Maclean.

'Neither do I. And that being so, the less you and I worry about the form of Government they set up, the better.'[37]*

Now, however, he decided that it did matter. He asked Tito if he was planning to impose communism on the liberated Yugoslavia and received an assurance that he was not. He then warned the Marshal, who was sweating under the Neapolitan sun and his 'absurd' new uniform of thick, blue cloth and gold lace, that Britain could not recognise his movement as a future government unless he came to an agreement with the King. He also warned against using '*our* war materiel against rival Yugoslavs'.[38] That evening, according

---

* Despite this statement, Maclean later obtained Tito's permission to purchase a villa on the island of Korčula where he spent time in later life.

to the Foreign Office's Pierson Dixon, Churchill was 'very realistic' about Tito, who he thought was 'getting away with too much'. Drafting a memorandum he intended to hand the Partisan leader, he emphasised the importance of the Serbs (the majority of whom were staunchly anti-communist) and the need for unity if Allied supplies were to continue. 'It is a pity the PM did not use this sort of language with Tito in the early days,' reflected Dixon in his diary. 'Now it is too late. Tito is essential now to our war plans and knows it and the Russian armies are nearer to Yugoslavia than we are. So Tito snaps his fingers at us and is conciliatory only to the extent necessary to make a show of helpfulness.'[39] Eden was even more explicit. When Churchill sent him a note on 31 August, reminding him of the great responsibility they would incur if Tito were able to 'subjugate the rest of the country by weapons supplied by us', the Foreign Secretary noted that it was the Prime Minister who had 'persistently pushed Tito despite our warnings'.[40]

On 18 September, Tito 'levanted' from the island of Vis, where he had been living under British protection, and flew in secret to Moscow.[41] There he obtained promises of hitherto absent Soviet supplies and guarantees concerning the territorial integrity of Yugoslavia. The Partisans showed no gratitude for 'capitalist' supplies. On the contrary, they believed, or chose to believe, that the British were merely transporting munitions made in the Soviet Union. One story, probably apocryphal but nevertheless illustrative, involved a British officer attempting to persuade a Partisan Commissar that the cargo he had just brought at great risk across the Adriatic was indeed British. When the Commissar continued to insist that it was Russian, the Captain lost patience: 'Well, I've come to the wrong bloody port – cast off for'ard!'[42]

During the autumn of 1944, relations between Tito and the Western Allies deteriorated as the Partisans moved into Serbia and the Marshal complained about British troops operating alongside his forces in Montenegro. In the spring of 1945, the two sides engaged in an unseemly dash to occupy Venezia Giulia and Carinthia. The Partisans won the race for Trieste but lost the race for southern Austria. By this stage, the British were in no doubt that the bulk of their munitions had been used to attack the Četniks rather than the Germans. 'Keep in mind that the basic aim of this operation is to liquidate the Četnik forces of Mihailović and the Nedić forces as well,' Tito had instructed his commanders prior to the conquest of Serbia.[43] On 1 September 1944, despite being abandoned by the British, Mihailović had issued orders for a general uprising to drive the Germans out of Serbia and forestall a communist takeover. Around 30,000 Četniks answered his call but without weapons they were powerless. Attacked by the Partisans, even as they were attacking the Germans at Kruševac, many deserted after they heard the King disown their leader a few weeks later. Forced to retreat to the hills of the Sandžak, Mihailović sent his agents in Italy a desperate message:

> The Partisans have instituted a ruthless terror in which the best among the leaders of the community and the heads of the old established families are being indiscriminately killed. Concentration camps are being set up and filled with the flower of the Serbian people. In the hopes of bare survival, people are fleeing to the mountains like animals . . . We entreat you to send a delegation to the country to inform the Allies of our tragic situation.[44]

The Allies ignored Mihailović's appeal. Worse, they forcibly repatriated thousands of anti-communist refugees, as well as Croatian, Slovenian and Serbian collaborators from Austria, whom the Partisans then shot. Estimates of the number of victims range between 18,000 and 25,000. In March 1945, King Peter was forced to appoint three Regents – two of whom were Partisans – to govern in his stead. The ensuing Provisional Government was dominated by the Communists, who, following demonstrably unfree elections, succeeded in abolishing the monarchy in November. Appointed Prime Minister in the spring, Tito ruled Yugoslavia with authoritarian ruthlessness until his death in 1980. In 1948, he broke with Stalin and the Soviet Union, providing retrospective justification (for some) for the West's decision to back him. Meanwhile, Mihailović had been captured near Višegrad. Brought to Belgrade, he was subjected to a five-day show-trial and executed on 17 July 1946. Later that year, Eden was asked at a political dinner what troubled his conscience most after five years as Britain's wartime Foreign Secretary. Eden's answer was simple: 'Our betrayal of Mihailović.'[45]

XXVI

Brave New World

Something big will come out of this war: a new heaven and a new earth.

Eleanor Roosevelt, echoing her husband's views, November 1943[1]

As dawn broke on 6 June 1944, 5,300 Allied ships came into view off the Normandy coast. The Germans who beheld the scene could hardly believe their eyes. The 'full might of the English and the Americans' was drawn up, wrote one, 'limitless ships small and great assembled as if for a parade'.[2] One hundred and thirty thousand British, American and Canadian troops came ashore in the first wave. By dusk, despite heavy American casualties on Omaha Beach, they had secured a perimeter between half a mile and 3 miles deep. Over the coming days, they would link up and push inland. Bayeux was captured on D-Day +1, Cherbourg on 26 June. Over the next two months, little progress was made and much blood spilt as the Germans took advantage of the dense Normandy countryside – the *bocage* – and Allied caution to mount a stubborn defence. In late July, however, the American 1st Army broke through the German defences south of Saint-Lô and were soon racing across open country. Paris was liberated on 25 August, Brussels on 3 September. By the middle of the month, Eisenhower's forces were on the doorstep of Germany, having advanced 400 miles and destroyed eight German divisions in just three weeks.

The outcome of the war had not been in doubt since the winter of 1942–3 – arguably since Pearl Harbor – yet the breakthrough in the west, which coincided with major advances in Belorussia and in Italy, allowed the Allies to pay increasing amounts of attention to the world that would emerge once victory had been achieved. The issues were multifarious and intertwined but broadly fell into three categories: international security and the structures for its maintenance; empire and the future of colonies; and economics and trade.

At the centre of the security question loomed the problem of Germany. All three main Allied powers agreed that this great, industrious nation should never be able to wreck the peace of the world again. All three agreed that she should be disarmed and broken up. The differences were ones of emphasis and detail. As he had made clear at the Tehran Conference, Stalin favoured only the harshest treatment for his erstwhile collaborators. The Germans, he argued, were an ingenious people. In the space of just twenty-one years, they had recovered from their defeat in 1918 to renew their pursuit of European hegemony. Disarmament was not enough: German industry must be gutted; the country occupied; the state dismembered. Of the democratic nations, the Americans were closest to this perspective. Believing that the word 'Reich' should be 'stricken from the language', Roosevelt favoured the division of Germany into at least five separate states.[3] Harking back to the Europe of the eighteenth century, he recalled how Germany had been less dangerous 'when divided into 107 small principalities'.[4] The British were more circumspect. Whilst the Labour Cabinet Ministers – Attlee, Bevin and Dalton – were enthusiasts for partition, the Foreign Office considered the proposal impractical and counterproductive. Churchill was somewhere in between. Although he supported the excision of Prussia, his natural magnanimity, combined with the desire to maintain a barrier against the Soviet Union, caused him to shrink from wholesale vivisection. In his opinion, the war had largely been the fault of Hitler and his henchmen and whilst 'during wartime no distinction could be made between the leaders and the people . . . nevertheless, with a generation of self-sacrificing, toil and education, something might be done with the German people'.[5] Less than a year later, however, he initialled a paper calling for the complete destruction of German industry: a plan to reduce Bismarck's creation of blood and iron to a pastoral state.

The author of this radical proposal was Henry Morgenthau. Appalled by War and State Department plans to revive the German economy so that she could pay reparations, the Treasury Secretary devised a scheme to 'divide Germany up into a number of small provinces, stop all industrial production and convert them [the

Germans] into small agricultural landholders'.[6] 'Just strip it,' he instructed his chief economic adviser, Harry Dexter White, referring to the Ruhr and the Saar. 'I don't care what happens to the civilian population . . . I would take every mine, every mill and factory and wreck it . . . Steel, coal, everything . . . This is the cauldron which gives forth war and I don't know any other way to stop them from making war other than to shut down this area completely.'[7] Although he did not say so officially, knowledge of the Holocaust contributed to this diluvial proposal. 'It seems inhuman,' admitted Morgenthau to Treasury colleagues. '[But] we didn't ask for this war. We didn't put millions of people through gas chambers. We didn't do any of these things. They have asked for it.'[8]

Morgenthau's reference to the genocide of Europe's Jews was exceptional. In general, this vast crime – of which the British and Americans were aware by the summer of 1942 – was seldom cited in Allied policy discussions and never raised at Heads of Government or Foreign Ministers' conferences, save for brief mention during the Trident meetings of May 1943. One month earlier, responding to increasing pressure from Jewish and Christian groups (though not the Vatican, whose silence on this issue would become infamous), women's clubs and the press, British and American delegates convened in the Caribbean to discuss the 'refugee problem'. Hopes among the Jewish community were raised. But the Bermuda Conference proved little more than a cynical propaganda exercise: 'a conflict of self-justification, a façade for inaction', in the words of British Foreign Office Minister Richard Law.[9] Rescue would come 'through victory', insisted the State Department – which, thanks to the obstructionist efforts of Assistant Secretary of State Breckinridge Long, had issued a mere 228,964 visas (out of a potential 460,000) to refugees between 1938 and 1942 – while the British refused to risk a revival of the Arab Revolt by permitting mass migration to Palestine.

In desperation, some Jewish leaders asked the Allies to bomb the railway lines leading to the extermination camps and even Auschwitz itself. The response from the civilian-controlled military was negative. The aircraft were needed for existing operations, argued US Assistant Secretary of War John McCloy, while the attempt would 'in any case be of such doubtful efficacy that it would not warrant the use of our resources'.[10] In fact, Allied aircraft were already flying over Auschwitz, bombing nearby industrial targets and dropping supplies to the Polish resistance in Warsaw. Practical questions were valid but the moral imperative, as with other rescue schemes, was consistently ignored. In the end, it is hard to escape the conclusion that the Allied failure to do more to save Jewish lives derived not merely from a lack of initiative but also a lack of sympathy.

Roosevelt supported the Morgenthau Plan. 'We have got to be tough with Germany and I mean the German people, not just the Nazis,' he reassured his Treasury Secretary on 19 August 1944. 'You either have to castrate the German people or you have got to treat them in such a manner so they can't just go on reproducing people who want to continue the way they have in the past.'[11] His Secretary of War passionately disagreed. An old-fashioned Republican, who as Herbert Hoover's Secretary of State had grappled with the effects of the Versailles Treaty, Stimson saw 'enormous general evils' emanating from the proposal to transform one of the world's leading industrial centres into a non-productive 'ghost territory' and reduce the German people to a level of bare subsistence.[12]

Churchill concurred. Apprised of the policy during the second Quebec Conference (codenamed Octagon), held between 12 and 16 September 1944, he gave Morgenthau a 'verbal lashing' such as the Treasury Secretary had never received in his life.[13] He was all for disarming Germany, he said, 'but we ought not to prevent her living decently. There are bonds between the working classes of all countries and the English people will not stand for the policy you are advocating.'[14] The following day, however, he and Roosevelt initialled a document promising to eliminate 'the war-making industries in the Ruhr and in the Saar' and turn Germany into a country 'primarily agricultural and pastoral in its character'.[15] The reason for this startling about-turn was simple if ignoble. Britain desperately needed American economic assistance – both for the war against Japan and to stave off post-war bankruptcy – and the two issues were linked. On 14 September – the day after the Prime Minister's laceration of Morgenthau – Roosevelt toyed with Churchill, refusing to commit to Lend-Lease Stage II ($7 billion to support the war in the Pacific) until the Prime Minister agreed to the Treasury plan for the post-war treatment of Germany. At one point, Churchill grew so frustrated he exclaimed, 'What do you want me to do, stand up and beg like Fala [the President's Scottish terrier]?'[16] Roosevelt relented but only after his friend had given a verbal commitment to the Morgenthau Plan. Over the succeeding twenty-four hours, Lord Cherwell (Churchill's anti-Teutonic scientific adviser) and, through him, Morgenthau, per-suaded the Prime Minister that Britain would be the beneficiary of German economic sterilisation. 'I explained to Winston', the 'Prof' told Moran, 'that the plan would save Britain from bankruptcy by eliminating a dangerous competitor. Somebody must suffer for the war and it was surely right that Germany and not Britain should foot the bill. Winston had not thought of it in that way and he said no more about a cruel threat to the German people.'[17]

Ultimately, these calculations and machinations came to nought. On 23 and 24 September – one week after Octagon – details of the Mor-genthau Plan appeared in the American press and the ensuing uproar was sufficient for Roosevelt to forget that he had ever supported the scheme. 'Henry Morgenthau pulled a boner [a tactical mistake in base-ball]', FDR, hypocritically, told Stimson, while Goebbels exploited the revelation of this 'Jewish murder plan' to incite an already defeated people to fight for every building, street and field.[18] When Marshall saw Morgenthau for lunch five days after the story broke, his response was admirably restrained: 'Well, we have got loudspeakers on the German lines telling them to surrender and this doesn't help one bit.'[19]

Other aspects of post-war planning were less incendiary. At the Foreign Ministers' Conference in Moscow, the Allies had agreed to create an international organisation for the maintenance of peace and global security. At Dumbarton Oaks, in Washington, in the late summer of 1944, flesh was put on these idealistic bones. There was to be a General Assembly, open to 'all peace-loving states', an inter-national court and a secretariat.[20] Power was to reside in the Security Council. The smaller states would be allowed to 'blow off steam' in the General Assembly, Roosevelt told Eden, but the important deci-sions would be made by the Great Powers.[21]

Who qualified as a Great Power proved more contentious. Both the British and the Soviets had grave doubts about including China in this venerated category but the Americans insisted. Conversely,

it was the British who fought against American and Soviet resistance for the restoration of France as a Great Power. At the Tehran
Conference, Roosevelt and Stalin had vied with each other in den-
igrating the French, placing Churchill in the unlikely position of
defending de Gaulle. Since then, the Free French leader had infuriated the Prime Minister by arresting former Vichy satraps (including
Churchill's old friend Pierre-Étienne Flandin), refusing to visit him
at Marrakesh (before finally relenting) and throwing a tantrum on
the eve of D-Day. And yet Churchill never wavered in his belief that
a strong France was essential to a 'peaceful and happy Europe'.[22]

A 'peaceful and happy Europe' was foremost among Churchill's
post-war concerns. Although generally bored by anything other than
the war, he looked forward to the 'revival of the glory of Europe, the
parent continent of the modern nations and civilisation'.[23] 'Hard as it
is to say now,' he had continued in a minute to Eden of October 1942:

I look forward to a United States of Europe in which the barriers between the nations will be greatly minimised and unrestricted
travel will be possible. I hope to see the economy of Europe studied
as a whole. I hope to see a Council consisting of perhaps ten units,
including the former Great Powers, with several confederations –
Scandinavian, Danubian, Balkan, etc. – which would possess an
international police and be charged with keeping Prussia disarmed.
Of course, we shall have to work with the Americans, in many ways,
and in the greatest ways but Europe is our prime care and we certainly
do not wish to be shut up with the Russians and the Chinese when
Swedes, Norwegians, Danes, Dutch, Belgians, Frenchmen, Spaniards,
Poles, Czechs and Turks will have their burning questions, their desire
for our aid and their very great power of making their voices heard.[24]*

---

* In a pre-war article, Churchill wrote of Britain being 'with Europe but not of it'.
This, however, was written at a time when the British Empire covered a quarter
of the globe, encompassing approximately 500 million people in its own preferential trade system. Ultimately, attempts to divine what he would have thought of
Britain's entry into the European Union (eight years after his death) or exit from
it (fifty-five years after his death) fall into that category of speculation which, as
Gwendolen says in the *Importance of Being Earnest*, bears 'very little reference at
all to the actual facts of real life as we know them'.

Stalin's attitude was considerably less co-operative. Although he favoured an independent Italy, in preference to what he assumed would be a British client state, and instructed French communists to work with de Gaulle for similar reasons, he opposed confederations in central and eastern Europe that could be turned against him. Not only was Germany to be eviscerated in the Soviet plan; France was to be kept in her emaciated state: her colonies stripped, her strategic bases purloined. 'The result', noted Chip Bohlen of the US Embassy in Moscow, 'would be that the Soviet Union would be the only important military and political force on the continent of Europe.'[25]

Roosevelt shared Stalin's low opinion of the French. Although publicly committed to the restoration of France and the French Empire, in private he set his face against the return of French colonies, while doubting the feasibility, sometimes even the desirability, of a French renaissance. In part, this stemmed from his animosity towards de Gaulle. 'The only thing I am interested in', he told Under-Secretary of State Edward Stettinius in May 1944, 'is not having de Gaulle and the National Committee named as the government of France.'[26] Two months later, however, he received the Free French leader at the White House and agreed to recognise the French National Committee as the *de facto* authority for the civil administration of France. More significantly, he agreed that France, though unrepresented at Dumbarton Oaks, might be considered for a seat on the United Nations' Security Council. He even began to soften on the issue of French colonies in South-East Asia.

In January 1944, Roosevelt had reiterated his long-standing belief that Indo-China ought not to be returned to France. The territories – which the Vichy regime had surrendered to the Japanese in 1940–41 – were too important strategically and economically, while the French record of administration, he argued, had been appalling. France had held the colony for nearly a hundred years, the President told Halifax, and 'the people are worse off than they were at the beginning'.[27] The Foreign Office and the State Department disagreed with the President's view, noting the increase in the Indo-Chinese population, as well as advances in education, transportation, agriculture and public health. By November, however, FDR was saying that 'no final decisions' had been made and, in January, looked the other way while the British infiltrated French saboteurs into the region.[28] Two months later, US aircraft were providing assistance to the French in Indo-China, Roosevelt having reversed his position to the extent of telling his adviser on Caribbean and colonial affairs, Charles Taussig, that France might retain her colonies under trusteeship, providing independence was the final goal.

The British were relieved by the President's change of attitude. Not only were they committed to the restoration of France as a global power – 'a strategic necessity' to protect against both a resurgent Germany and the Red Army, according to the Post-Hostilities Sub-Committee – but the French Empire was seen as the obvious first line of defence against American interference in Britain's own overseas possessions.[29] 'We do not know where the United States would stop if they were once allowed or encouraged to imagine that the conception of "parent states" in the Pacific might be discarded', minuted one Foreign Office official in February 1944, while Halifax feared the day when the President might 'have the bright idea that the Netherlands East Indies or Malaya' should be placed under 'international trusteeships'.[30]

The British position was well known. During his Mansion House speech of 10 November 1942, in which he had celebrated the victory at El Alamein, Churchill had made the famous – or as it was seen on the other side of the Atlantic, notorious – statement that he had 'not become the King's First Minister in order to preside over the liquidation of the British Empire'.[31] One month later, speaking to Taussig, he was even more frank:

> Nations live on their traditions or die. Your country has its traditions which you cherish . . . We also have our traditions and as long as I am here, we will hold to them and the Empire. We will not let the Hottentots by popular vote throw the white people into the sea; nor let the Syrians by popular vote throw out the Jews.[32]

The US position was equally well known. In most American minds, the Age of Empire was over and the winds of change were starting to blow. 'Winston, you have four hundred years of acquisitive instinct in your blood and you just don't understand how a country might not want to acquire land somewhere if they can get it,' the President had lectured the Prime Minister at Cairo. 'A new period has opened in the world's history and you will have to adjust yourself to it.'[33] In the American view, colonies should be placed under international trusteeship, in preparation for independence. The Philippines was their proud example. Acquired by the United States following the Spanish–American War of 1898 – which also saw the US gain Puerto Rico and Guam – the archipelago had been granted self-government in 1935 and the promise of independence after ten years. The Japanese invasion disrupted this timetable but the loyalty of the population and the effectiveness of Filipino resistance – which at its height controlled 60 per cent of the islands – seemed to prove the virtues of decolonisation.*

Between August 1942 and the spring of 1944, Washington and London engaged in a protracted wrangle over a joint declaration on colonial policy. The Americans wanted the British to commit to the principle of colonial independence. The British wished to emphasise the responsibilities of 'parent states' towards 'dependent peoples'. The Americans wanted the British to commit to a system of international trusteeships. The most the British were prepared to accept were 'regional councils' that would have a consultative but not supervisory capacity. For the British, self-government within the British Commonwealth was the goal; for the Americans, nothing but full sovereign independence would suffice.[34]

This fundamental difference, naturally, led to an impasse. At times, the British toyed with a unilateral declaration; at others, Cordell Hull tried to resurrect his draft from the shallow grave the Foreign Office had dug for it. In Moscow, the Secretary of State tried to outmanoeuvre the British by slipping a copy to Molotov behind Eden's back. The British considered this pretty shabby (a none too subtle attempt 'to put us in a minority of one', as Richard Law commented) but the

---

* 'Incidentally, does there exist any American statement showing exactly what benefits US administration purports to have conferred on the islands during the forty-odd years of occupation before their partial restoration of the Philippine constitution which they had suppressed?' enquired the Foreign Office's Neville Butler, tartly. (FO 371/35310, Butler Minute, 19 January 1943)

Soviet Commissar missed or eschewed the opportunity to cause mischief, merely commenting that the matter should 'receive further study'.[35]

Still, Roosevelt persisted. Asked by Under-Secretary of State, Edward Stettinius, and Isaiah Bowman – the eminent geographer and President of Johns Hopkins University – whether he wanted them to raise the subject of trusteeships during their visit to London in April 1944, the President replied, 'Yes, by all means. It is something I think we should discuss with them at every opportunity.'[36] During the second week of April, therefore, Bowman took up the topic with Law and, on 19 April, had a long, unsatisfactory interview with the Colonial Secretary, Oliver Stanley. He even raised it with Churchill and received a rehash of the Prime Minister's Mansion House speech in return: 'We entered this war for honour and to redeem our pledge to Poland and we shall say to the world at the close of the war that we do not want one foot of ground in addition to what we had at the beginning of the war. But we shall not give up one foot of ground.'[37]

Meanwhile, Imperial forces were battling to regain Britain's Eastern Empire. In August 1943, Churchill had persuaded the Combined Chiefs of Staff to create South East Asia Command under the auspices of the glamorous, if grossly overpromoted, Lord Louis Mountbatten. Designed to inject some much-needed vigour into the region, SEAC's unspoken purpose was to ensure that British forces were the ones to 'liberate' Burma and Malaya. The Americans understood this and resented it. Stilwell accused Mountbatten of 'playing the "Empah" game', while SEAC was held to stand for 'Save England's Asian Colonies'.[38] The contradictions between Great Power co-operation and the desire to reform the world according to American shibboleths was highlighted by Stilwell's political adviser, John Paton Davies:

> Our policy is apparently based on the conviction that we need Britain as a first-class power; Britain cannot be a first-class power without its Empire; we are accordingly committed to the support of the British Empire . . . [Yet] in the minds of most Americans a better world is identified with the abolition of imperialism and there is a very real danger that the United States may again become isolationist after

the war as a result of a feeling by the American people that they have been made dupes of British imperialism.[39]*

Others expressed less high-minded concerns. 'Let the recovery of the Netherlands East Indies, the Philippines . . . as well as the removal of the Japanese from Singapore and all of South East Asia, follow as the manifest results of American naval and aerial operations,' wrote William Howard Gardiner, a former President of the Navy League, to the State Department's Joseph Grew. 'Such a procedure would improve immeasurably the peace settlements we would be able to make in the regions of the Pacific *and* our future . . . commercial opportunities.'[40] A former Republican Congressman serving with the Marines, Philip C. Ferguson, wanted the American public to know 'what over a million potential customers out here [South East Asia and the Pacific] can do toward keeping our tremendous shop open for business', while the former Consul-General in Batavia looked forward to the day, not far off, when the US would be able to insist on 'the "open door" in the matter of imports, exports, industries, the development of resources and the improvement of the condition of the native'.[41]

Although some Cabinet Ministers – Amery, Beaverbrook, Cranborne, Grigg, Lyttelton and Stanley – worried about American economic imperialism, Churchill was more concerned with his country's dwindling status as a world power. He insisted, therefore, on Britain playing her full part in the war against Japan and, at Octagon, obtained Roosevelt's consent for a British fleet to operate in the Pacific under US command. (Admiral King was so enraged by this decision, he later denied all knowledge of the President's commitment and had to be read the minutes of the meeting.)

By this stage, the American threat to Britain's colonial empire had passed its peak. British intransigence had had the desired effect, while

---

* A corrective to this thesis came, surprisingly, from the pen of Adolf Berle: 'I think Mr Davies is probably getting into pretty deep water,' the Assistant Secretary of State commented. 'For one thing, I doubt if the British Empire is going to exist solely because of our "commitment to recreate" it. It would equally be argued that Great Britain, by defending us against the Germans, had chosen to maintain the United States as a first-class power.'

the loss of confidence in Republican China undermined Roosevelt's concept of an Asiatic 'policeman'. Other factors included the US Navy and War Department's desire to retain the Japanese mandated islands for strategic purposes and growing unease about the Soviet Union. From mid-1944, therefore, the word 'independence' began to be replaced by 'self-government' in State Department memoranda and at the Yalta Conference the Administration's proposals would be limited to trustee-ships for former League of Nations mandates, ex-enemy territories and *voluntarily* surrendered colonies. Yet it was Roosevelt who would have the last (albeit posthumous) laugh as India and Burma gained inde-pendence in 1948, Indonesia in 1949 and Indo-China five years later. All the King's horses and all the King's men could not, as the President had predicted, put Europe's Asian empires back together again.

★

The mellowing of the Roosevelt Administration in its attitude towards colonialism was not reflected in its approach to economic matters. Since the autumn of 1943, the US Treasury had been trying to cap Britain's gold and dollar balances at $1 billion. These reserves – which had stood at around $4 billion before the war, had been virtually exhausted by 1941 and then, thanks to Lend-Lease and dollar spending within the sterling area, rebuilt to just over a quarter of their pre-war level – were vital to Britain's financial health.* As the Chancellor of the Exchequer, Sir John Anderson, explained to Stettinius during his April 1944 visit, British losses in overseas assets and increases in overseas liabilities amounted to a staggering $15 billion. In this context, a small rise in the country's gold and dollar balances was irrelevant. It was, as Churchill put it, as if 'a man two years ago had ten thousand dollars in the bank and five dollars in his pocket, whereas now he has one hundred dollars in his pocket but he owes the bank several thousand dollars'.[42]

The State Department was sympathetic. 'Certainly, it is unrea-sonable to set a hard and fast limit on assets without regard to liabilities,' argued Dean Acheson, who pointed out that the Soviet

* By the war's end, the United States had accumulated $21 billion in gold bullion.

Union was thought to possess almost twice as much gold as the United Kingdom but was not being asked to make financial sacrifices.[43] Later, at a meeting attended by Morgenthau, Stettinius, White and Leo Crowley (responsible for Lend-Lease), he voiced the rarely heard verity that:

> The British are devoting to the war as large a share of their national income as we are, if not a larger one. Their tax burden and war costs, in relation to population and national income, are as great or greater than our own. For us to request the British, therefore, to pay in dollars for a part of American production used in the war is in effect to shift to the British part of the financial costs which are properly ours.[44]

Roosevelt, however, sided with the Treasury. Dubious, like many Americans, of British protestations of penury, he joked to Morgenthau that if the situation was really that bad, he would 'go over there and make a couple of talks and take over the British Empire'.[45] The Treasury rationale was political: accusations that the British were profiting from American largesse – a calumny of the 'Five Senators Tour' – were damaging and the Senate Committee to Investigate the National Defense Program, chaired by one Harry S Truman, was on the war path. Yet restricting British gold and dollar reserves also increased British dependence on the US and, thus, American leverage when it came to such long-standing economic campaigns as the elimination of Imperial Preference. In the end, the Administration abandoned the idea of a formal cap but achieved the same end by reducing the list of items eligible for Lend-Lease.

The negotiations over Lend-Lease Stage II and Article VII – the clause in the Mutual Aid Agreement by which the British had agreed to work towards the 'elimination of all forms of discriminatory treatment in international commerce' (i.e. Imperial Preference) – proved similarly fraught.[46] The Hull thesis was both high-minded and self-serving. Barriers to trade caused friction between countries, lower living standards and, ultimately, wars, the Secretary of State argued. At the same time, the chief beneficiary of free markets would be the country most able to exploit them – in this case the United States. The British were not wholly opposed to multilateralism. Although protectionists were wont to refer to 'the lunatic proposals of Mr Hull', Churchill and Keynes were prepared to move in the direction of tariff reductions.[47] Their conditions were a corresponding reduction in US tariffs and the means to rebuild Britain's devastated export trade.

In mid-1944, the British sought to secure an extension to Lend-Lease that would allow them to start the process of turning their economy back to its peacetime function. The quantity desired was $7 billion in supplies. Roosevelt, having kept Churchill dangling, agreed to $3.5 billion in munitions and $3 billion in non-military equipment. Churchill, with tears in his eyes, thanked his friend and then asked to take a second look at the Morgenthau Plan. But the President's promise was never formalised. Over the coming months, with his advisers predicting a storm in Congress, FDR backed away from ratifying the agreement. When Morgenthau pointed out that he would be reneging on the commitment he had made at Quebec, Roosevelt replied that the British would have to rely on American 'goodwill'.[48] Five months later, Roosevelt was dead and this unpredictable resource was in short supply. The Stage II provisions, negotiated by Keynes, were whittled away and on 17 August 1945 – two days after the surrender of Japan – President Truman abruptly terminated Lend-Lease, leaving Britain to face her 'financial Dunkirk'.[49]*

At the same time, the British were forced to make concessions to their more powerful ally in the fields of civil aviation, the supply of Middle Eastern oil and the import of Argentinian meat. Each reduced the country's post-war standing and each was correspondingly resented. Yet all were made due to the paramount need to maintain, or attain, American economic assistance. 'Our lack of bargaining power', Churchill's sometime adviser Desmond Morton stated frankly, 'was . . . because we were broke.'[50] The Americans

---

* Keynes later negotiated a $3.75 billion loan from the United States and a $1.19 billion loan from Canada. Although the Americans behaved generously over Lend-Lease – cancelling Britain's debts – the loans, at 2 per cent interest, contained damaging conditions, including the convertibility of sterling. The UK made her last repayment in December 2006.

understood this and exploited it. British economic dependence meant that the US could obtain agreement for 'any reasonable course of action upon which we may choose to insist', boasted the State Department's Stanley Hornbeck, while Roosevelt threatened to hold up Stage II (a particularly devious bit of politicking since this was what he was already doing) unless the British accepted an agreement on civil aviation highly advantageous to the United States.[51] 'Pure blackmail', commented Jock Colville.[52]

This dynamic was equally apparent at the United Nations Monetary and Financial Conference at Bretton Woods. In February 1943, Morgenthau's prinicipal economic adviser, Harry Dexter White, had published his plan for a new international economic order. This prompted Keynes to advance his own plan. The schemes were superficially similar but fundamentally different. Both men wanted to stabilise exchange rates, prevent balance of payments crises, unblock capital and liberalise trade. Yet whilst White proposed a lending fund, made up of individual member currencies, securities and gold, Keynes wanted to create a new, non-convertible, international currency, accrued through trade, that would facilitate international transactions via an international clearing bank. Crucially, Keynes wished to place punitive restrictions not only on excessive borrowing but on excessive accumulation – thus making surplus countries, not just deficit countries, bear some of the burden for correcting payments imbalances. Since the United States was then the world's leading surplus economy, this was, obviously, anathema to White and the US Treasury. White's purpose was to open the world to American commerce (members of his fund would be banned from erecting new trade barriers and competitive devaluations), not weaken US economic dominance in the interests of poorer countries. Above all, he sought to make the dollar *the* international currency: the sole surrogate for gold, the lodestar for all other currencies. Henceforth, the US would not only have complete discretion over her own financial affairs but also be able to dictate monetary policy to the entire world.

Keynes hoped to effect a compromise but White was obdurate. The Americans had no interest in weakening the power of the dollar – especially not with some 'phoney international unit' that could not be converted into gold – nor in allowing poorer countries to accumulate vast overdrafts at American risk.[53] The negotiations, which took place in Washington in the autumn of 1943, were long, complex and frequently acrimonious. 'Absolute Bedlam,' recorded one British official. 'Without any agenda or any prepared idea of what is going to be discussed they [Keynes and White] go for each other in a strident duet of discord, which after a crescendo of abuse on either side leads up to a chaotic adjournment.'[54] Typically, the tall, brilliant, condescending, effervescent, temperamental product of Eton and King's College, Cambridge, would outdebate the short, scrappy, Harvard-educated, Treasury assistant. 'White was full of vigour and manful thrust,' wrote Keynes' friend and fellow economist Roy Harrod. 'His earnestness carried him forward in a torrent of words, which sometimes outstripped his grammatical powers. Keynes . . . detected any inconsistency in the opposition, even in the most abstruse matter, with lightning celerity and pointed it out with seeming gentleness in barbed and sometimes offensive sentences.'[55]

Keynes persuaded White to increase the fund's size (though not to the extent of the $26 billion he had proposed) and secured concessions relating to 'scarce currency'. But the American held the trump cards and the scheme that emerged was undeniably his. At Bretton Woods, the bucolic resort in the White Mountains of New Hampshire, Keynes was fobbed off with the Chairmanship of the Commission on the International Investment Bank (the future World Bank), while White took charge of the fund (the future International Monetary Fund). Outmanoeuvred and outbargained, the British delegation was reduced to arguing over the location of the institutions. Since the Americans had refused to hold a single wartime conference in the United Kingdom, the chances of their allowing either of these temples to international finance to be based in the British Isles were always slim and White duly insisted that both the Fund and the Bank be housed in Washington.

In contrast to their treatment of the British, the Americans went to great lengths to accommodate the Soviets: granting them a larger quota than they deserved of the Fund; allowing them to pay a smaller contribution than they ought to the Bank; providing them with clauses which would allow them to keep their already reduced gold subscription in Moscow; and offering them an escape from exchange fixes. In part, this may be attributed to the pro-Soviet proclivities of Harry White. A long-time admirer of the economic planning of the USSR, White was denounced as a member of a Soviet spy ring by defecting members Whittaker Chambers and Elizabeth Bentley in September 1939 and August 1945 respectively. Their claims subsequently corroborated by Soviet intelligence decrypts (though never to the extent of incontrovertible proof), White was hauled before the House Committee on Un-American Activities in August 1948 (where he denied the charges) and died of a heart attack three days after giving evidence.

Yet White was not the only member of the Roosevelt Administration to show greater solicitude towards the USSR than the UK. From the President down, the conviction that the future peace depended upon the closest possible co-operation between the United States and the Soviet Union was axiomatic. Admiration for the Russian people and their fighting prowess far outweighed that accorded to Britain, while the sense that the Soviet and American systems were in the process of 'converging' – the former becoming freer, the latter more state-driven – was shared by Cabinet members and officials alike.* Finally, the USSR, with her closed economy, was not considered an economic rival to the US whereas Britain, with her Empire and discriminatory trade, was.† The conclusion drawn by many New Dealers, some of whom were communist sympathisers, was stark: the Soviet Union was a more important and, in some ways, more desirable partner than the British Empire. There would be space for only two truly Great Powers in the Pax Americana, not three.

---

* In April 1944, a leading American newspaper claimed that the Soviet Union was pursuing 'state capitalism', while the *New York Times* declared that 'Marxian thinking in Soviet Russia is out'.

† 'On the face of it we had no serious conflict over vital interests with Russia,' the journalist Edgar Snow told Maxim Litvinov in October 1944. 'Economically speaking, we were not rivals on the world market, our needs seemed to be complementary. On the other hand, everywhere in the world we were coming into conflict with British economic interests and the war had profoundly deepened this rivalry.' (Roosevelt Papers, PSF, Diplomatic Correspondence, Box 49, Russia 1945, Record of a Conversation between Snow and Litvinov, 6 October 1944)

XXVII

The Polish Agony

Are we not allies? Who wants a weak ally? We shall share
everything with the Poles in a fraternal manner.

Joseph Stalin to Stanisław Kot, 14 November 1941[1]

At 10.20 a.m. on 18 May 1944, a 25-year-old second lieutenant named
Kazimierz Gurbiel attached the blue and red pennant of the 12th
Podolski Lancers to a branch and planted it in the ruins of the once
great Benedictine abbey of Monte Cassino. The Poles had suffered
3,784 casualties capturing the German stronghold – the capstone of
the Gustav Line, which had withstood three previous assaults – but
had accepted the task in order to draw attention to their country's
cause. Later, the Polish II Corps lost more than 7,500 officers and
men battling up the spine of Italy, while the Polish Parachute Brigade, under Major-General Stanisław Sosabowski, was reduced by
23 per cent in Operation Market Garden – Montgomery's hubristic
attempt to leapfrog into Germany by seizing key bridges over the
Rhine.*

Polish losses, like all military casualties, were tragic. Yet Poland's
political story represents a unique tragedy within the vast architecture of the Second World War: a tale of woe and injustice surpassed
only by the suffering of her citizens – the more than two million
Polish Christians who perished and the roughly three million Polish

---

* British Generals Frederick 'Boy' Browning, Brian Horrocks and, ultimately,
Montgomery were, later, highly critical of Sosabowski but neither he nor his
men – who fought with great bravery – deserved an ounce of blame for this British military disaster.

Jews who were robbed, starved, beaten, ghettoised and gassed between 1939 and 1945.

In April 1943, Stalin had used the revelation of the Katyn massacre as an excuse to break off diplomatic relations with the Polish Government-in-Exile. Three months later, the Poles suffered an even greater blow when the aeroplane carrying the Polish Commander-in-Chief and Premier, General Władysław Sikorski, crashed just after take-off from Gibraltar.* A man of great courage and distinction, a war hero and a democrat who had served as Prime Minister in the early 1920s and opposed the dictatorship of Marshal Piłsudski, the General was, by common consent, the only figure capable of maintaining a semblance of unity among the rival Polish political factions and preventing his compatriots' natural suspicion of the USSR from descending into outright hostility. His successor, Stanisław Mikołajczyk, had neither his prestige nor his sense of destiny. A farmer turned politician from Poznań, the leader of the Polish Peasant Party, he was described by Churchill as 'a fat, slightly bald, old fox' and, more pertinently, by his fellow exile, the Czechoslovak President Edvard Beneš, as 'a good party politician' but 'not a first-class political figure'.[2] Less chauvinist than his colleagues, he sought to improve Soviet–Polish relations while relying, ultimately, on the democracies to save his country from communism.

The central issue was Poland's eastern frontier. Stalin had made it clear that he wanted the Soviet Union to extend to the Curzon Line – the border recommended by Lord Curzon in 1920 that ran from the Polish–Lithuanian frontier to Eastern Galicia and only slightly more generous to the Poles than the Molotov–Ribbentrop Line of September 1939. Since the proposal emanated from a British Foreign Secretary and since the Poles were a minority (albeit a large one) in these eastern provinces – the majority consisting of Belorussians and Ukrainians – the British found this difficult to dispute. Russia sought 'only the return of that territory with which she entered the war in 1914', Churchill told Sikorski – an inaccuracy since the oil-rich region of Eastern Galicia had never been part of

---

* Conspiracy theories claiming that Churchill or the Soviets were responsible for the crash are baseless.

the Tsarist Empire – while Oliver Harvey, now an Assistant Under-Secretary, thought the Poles should accept the demarcation on the grounds of 'justice and ethnography.'[3] At Tehran, Churchill conceded the Soviet demands and sought compensation for the Poles in East Prussia. Stalin accused the Polish Government-in-Exile of collaborating with Hitler and murdering Soviet partisans (an outrageous slander which none of the Western statesmen challenged) but said that the Poles might expand in the west as far as the Oder.

Convinced that they had the basis of a deal, the British set out to cajole and bully the Poles. Eden told Mikołajczyk he thought the Polish Government would be making a 'great mistake should they reject the Soviet proposal', which offered 'new rich provinces' in East Prussia, Lower Silesia and Pomerania, while Churchill told the Premier frankly that 'the Curzon Line was the best that the Poles could expect and all that he would ask the British people to demand on their behalf'.[4] The Russians were entitled to Wilno (Vilnius), Lwów (Lviv) and Eastern Galicia. When Mikołajczyk protested – when he reminded Churchill of his pledge not to recognise territorial changes obtained by force; of the Atlantic Charter, which foreswore geographical adjustments 'that do not accord with the freely expressed wishes of the people concerned'; of the 200,000 Poles fighting under Allied command, many of whom came from these provinces; and of the fact that Stalin was seeking not ethnographic 'justice' but 'domination' – Churchill got angry.[5] Poland owed her 'liberation' to the Red Army, which, even now, was marching across her pre-war frontier, he lectured. If the Poles did not make an agreement now, it would be too late: the Russians would be in possession of the entire country and would lose no time in establishing a puppet government. Britain might sympathise with the Poles but neither she nor the United States would 'go to war to defend the eastern frontiers of Poland'.[6] If the Polish Government would not see sense and seize this, he must 'look at the matter from the British point of view and make his own agreement with Stalin'.[7]

Some Foreign Office denizens considered Churchill's bludgeoning of the Poles unwise as well as unedifying. 'Let me here say', recorded Valentine Lawford, Eden's Private Secretary, in his unpublished diary, 'that Winston's attitude towards Stalin is still more sycophantic and nauseating than his attitude towards Roosevelt:

> Never was a great man so unwise in his judgements of other people. In this Polish frontier trouble, he has been giving Stalin every point Stalin didn't happen to have on his side by the nature of things. I suppose one day the world will be enlightened. Today all that happens is that Uncle Joe wisely cashes in on all Winston's gratuities. It is fantastic, or very depressing.[8]

Pierson Dixon thought Churchill 'astonishingly childish' in his handling of the Russians, while Owen O'Malley, Britain's Ambassador to the Polish Government-in-Exile, annoyed the Prime Minister by commenting that 'what is . . . morally indefensible generally turns out, in the long run, to have been politically inept'.[9] 'The real choice', O'Malley wrote to Eden, 'seems to me . . . to lie between . . . selling the corpse of Poland to Russia and finding an alibi to be used in evidence when we are indicted for abetting a murder; and . . . putting the points of principle to Stalin in the clearest possible way and warning him that our position might have to be explained publicly with equal clearness. In the second alternative we might indeed fail to deflect him from violent and illegal courses but it would be on record that we had done our utmost to do so.'[10]

On the other hand, there were many influential Britons whose pro-Soviet enthusiasm caused them to look askance at the Poles. The 'Red Professor of Printing House Square', E. H. Carr – who had transferred his services as a dictator's apologist from Hitler to Stalin without so much as a twinge of embarrassment – produced a string of editorials for *The Times* welcoming Soviet hegemony in eastern Europe and criticising those, especially the Poles, who sought to thwart it. He was supported, pictorially, by the *Evening Standard*'s David Low, who lashed out at 'irresponsible' Poles for waging a 'private war on Russia'.[11] Brendan Bracken believed that much of the British public considered the Poles a 'feckless race', while Lord Beaverbrook argued that the Poles had 'always been unsatisfactory', their war effort 'consistently over-valued', their politics tainted by 'antisemitism in a virulent form'.[12] The trouble was, noted Dixon:

The English do not feel warmly about [the] Poles, as they do about a few other foreign states . . . Realism tells them that Poland is too far off for any help of ours to be effective and Poland, as a continental power, does not excite the same sympathies in English breasts as does an island power like Greece . . . It is obvious that no Englishman is going [to go] to war with Russia, or even to risk imperilling relations with Russia, for Poland.[13]

Be this as it may, Stalin's refusal to meet the Poles half-way caused alarm in Downing Street and Whitehall. On 28 January 1944, Churchill had written to Stalin, relaying his attempts to get the Poles to agree to the Curzon Line and seeking assurances regarding Poland's future independence, the underground movement with its army and officials and the return of the Polish Government-in-Exile. The Vozhd replied on 4 February, demanding that the Poles not only publicly accept the Curzon Line but also reconstitute their Government so as to rid themselves of those 'pro-Fascist' elements hostile to the Soviet Union.[14] Although this appears like an obvious pretext – the precursor to the establishment of a Soviet puppet regime – the evidence suggests that Stalin had not shut his mind to working with *some* non-communist Polish representatives. During discussions with Edvard Beneš, shortly after Tehran, the despot had kept quizzing his guest about the London Poles, especially Mikołajczyk. 'Who among the Poles is a really prominent personality?' he asked. Later he exclaimed, rhetorically, 'Where can one find any Poles one could talk to?' The thrust of his questions suggests that Stalin, at this stage, was seeking a pro-Soviet Polish government with at least a veil of legitimacy.[15]*

Encouraged not so much by Stalin's missive as by his assurances to Clark Kerr about his desire to see a strong and independent Poland after the war, Churchill arranged a lunch at Chequers to 'soften up' the Poles.[16] Although Mikołajczyk and the Polish Foreign Minister, Tadeusz Romer, protested vigorously, Churchill was able to inform Stalin on 20 February that the Polish Government was ready to

---

* In a short-sighted and disgraceful attempt to curry favour with the Soviet leader, Beneš recommended that the Russians occupy the whole of Poland and install their own regime.

declare that the pre-war frontier 'no longer corresponds to realities' and to discuss a new frontier between Poland and the Soviet Union as part of a 'general settlement'.[17] For the briefest of periods, optimism appeared in the corridors of the Foreign Office. On 28 February, however, Stalin gave his response to Clark Kerr. 'It was not', relayed the Ambassador, 'a pleasant talk.' With a snigger, the Vozhd had dismissed the Polish overture. 'The Polish Government did not want a settlement,' Stalin claimed. 'Its purpose was to embroil us [the British] with the Soviet Government . . . If the Poles meant business they should clearly and openly accept the Curzon Line.' More accusations were levelled against the Poles, followed by the suggestion that the Allies should seek more amenable Poles in the United States and the Soviet Union to work with.[18] When Churchill sent further appeals, explaining that he would soon have to explain the situation to Parliament, the dictator responded with a violent cable warning the Prime Minister against issuing threats which may 'lead to contrary results'.[19]

The Soviets could not understand the British obsession. 'What is Poland?' demanded Alexander Bogomolov, Soviet Ambassador to the French National Committee, of Roger Makins. 'Why, the industrial production of Magnitogorsk is greater than the whole industrial production of Poland.'[20] Stalin complained that he was spending all his time on 'unimportant' Polish affairs, while even the relatively pro-Western Maxim Litvinov told the American journalist Edgar Snow that the Politburo was:

> Absolutely right about Poland. In fact, we have been too lenient, if anything . . . Poland has got to be friendly towards this country and must abandon the idea that she can be a springboard against Russia and in that way get back her sixteenth century empire. Before the war, the Becks and Sosnkowskis [former Polish Foreign Minister and current Polish Commander-in-Chief] offered their services in that respect to Germany. Now, they offer themselves to Britain and America. We won't have it.[21]

The British were extremely depressed. Although the Soviet-sympathising Geoffrey Wilson (a former First Secretary at the British Embassy in Moscow, now in the Foreign Office's Northern

Department) denied that Stalin had imperial ambitions, Eden con- fessed to 'growing apprehension that Russia has vast aims and that these may include the domination of eastern Europe and even the Mediter- ranean and the "communising" of much that remains'.[22] Although he fond it harder to shake off the 'spirit of Tehran', Churchill was inclined to agree. He was full of 'gloomy forebodings', recorded Jock Colville on 30 April, and, on 8 May, he sent Eden an apocalyptic minute: 'I fear that very great evil may come upon the world. The Russians are drunk with victory and there is no length they may not go.'[23]

Meanwhile, the Polish underground was experiencing the 'fra- ternal manner' of its Soviet allies first-hand. Ordered to co-operate with the advancing Red Army, the Armia Krajowa (Home Army) began a series of local uprisings in January 1944, just as the Sovi- ets were crossing the pre-war frontier. Armed mainly with machine guns and rifles, the AK engaged the Germans in a series of bloody confrontations and gained control of small areas of eastern Poland. In March, the 27th Division of the AK encountered the vanguard of the Red Army and took part in joint operations to capture Turzysk (Turiisk) and Kowel (Kovel). Soviet orders, however, were to disarm the AK and kill anyone who resisted. As the Red Army swept for- ward in Operation Bagration – capturing Minsk, Wilno, Lublin, Brześć (Brest) and Lwów between 3 and 27 July – AK units were told they must disband and join the Polish 1st Army, the Soviet-formed communist force. When they refused – sometimes even when they accepted – the officers and many of the men were arrested and deported to the Soviet Union.* Some were shot, others hanged. In despair, the Poles appealed to the Western Allies to intervene: to despatch a military mission that 'could serve as a witness to Soviet moves and oppose them'; to make diplomatic representations in Moscow; and to send weapons with which to fight the Germans. But the British and the Americans did nothing.[24]

The Poles considered the British attitude towards their pre- dicament callous and dishonourable. Yet it contained an element of honesty: the frank admission that the democracies could not

---

* By the end of September 1944, an estimated 21,000 Polish AK soldiers had been arrested by the Soviets.

prevent Stalin from redrawing the Polish–Soviet frontier by force. (It also contained a deception, in that the British never revealed that they had approved the Curzon Line at Tehran.) The behaviour of the Roosevelt Administration, on the other hand, was broadly dishonest and even cynical. In March 1942, while on the one hand opposing the British attempt to recognise Soviet sovereignty over the Baltic States, Roosevelt, on the other, told Litvinov that he did not anticipate any difficulty regarding the Soviet Union's post-war territorial claims. He had always considered it a mistake to remove those provinces (eastern Poland and the Baltic States) from Russia, he told the Ambassador, and bade him inform Stalin that the United States was sympathetic to his desire to redraw the Soviet border but that he could not say so for 'political reasons'.[25] Not only were such statements a flagrant breach of the Atlantic Charter, they were also at odds with what he was saying to the Poles.

In December 1942, Sikorski visited the White House and obtained, or so he thought, Presidential approval for Polish expansion into East Prussia *as well as* for the retention of Lwów and Wilno. 'Stalin would accept very reasonable terms for his west frontier,' FDR assured the General. He would take Estonia and Latvia, as well as the Finnish port of Petsamo, but would leave Lithuania and most of eastern Poland.[26] One year later, Roosevelt informed his advisers of his intention to appeal to Stalin 'on grounds of high morality' to respect the eastern Europeans' right to self-determination.[27] Yet at Tehran, the President told Stalin that he would like to see the entire Polish state moved westwards but that, due to the existence of some six million Polish-American voters, he could not say so in an election year. He then proceeded to reassure the despot that he understood the Soviet desire to incorporate the Baltic States but hoped that there would be plebiscites to satisfy world opinion. In any event, 'he did not intend to go to war with the Soviet Union on this point'.[28]

Such double-dealing may be seen to support several historiographical theses: that FDR was naïve about the Soviet Union; that he believed he could 'charm' Stalin, as George Kennan later claimed, or could 'outwit' him, as Walter Lippmann would come to argue.[29] Yet a conversation he had with Archbishop Francis Spellman, the

Catholic prelate of New York, shortly before Tehran, suggests that Roosevelt had fewer illusions than is sometimes imagined. According to the Archbishop's notes, FDR told him:

The world will be divided into spheres of influence. China gets the Far East; the US the Pacific; Britain and Russia, Europe and Africa. But as Britain has predominantly colonial interests it might be assumed that Russia will predominate in Europe . . . He hoped, 'although it might be wishful thinking', that the Russian intervention in Europe would not be too harsh . . . He believes that he will be better fitted to come to an understanding with Stalin than Churchill. Churchill is too idealistic; he is a realist. So is Stalin. Therefore, an understanding between them on a realistic basis is probable. The wish is, although it seems improbable, to get from Stalin a pledge not to extend Russian territory beyond a certain line. He would certainly receive Finland, the Baltic States, the eastern half of Poland [and] Bessarabia. There is no point to oppose these desires of Stalin because he has the power to get them anyhow. So better give them gracefully. Furthermore, the population of eastern Poland wants to become Russian. Still, it is absolutely not sure whether Stalin will be satisfied with these boundaries . . . On the direct question of whether Austria, Hungary and Croatia would fall under some sort of Russian protectorate, the answer was clearly yes . . . It is natural that the European countries will have to undergo tremendous changes in order to adapt to Russia but he hopes that in ten or twenty years the European influences would bring the Russians to become less barbarian . . . Finally he hopes the Russians will get [i.e. adopt] forty per cent of the capitalist regime [and] the capitalists will retain only sixty per cent of their system and so an understanding will be possible.[30]

Such stark realism – albeit sprinkled with astonishing simplicity – is rare among Roosevelt's utterances and was certainly absent from the meeting he had with Mikołajczyk in June 1944. 'Poland must be free and independent,' the President declared. 'What about Stalin?' Mikołajczyk enquired. 'Stalin is a realist,' Roosevelt replied, lighting a cigarette. 'And we mustn't forget, when we judge Russian actions, that the Soviet regime has had only two years of experience in international relations. But of one thing I am certain, Stalin is not an imperialist.'[31] According to the memorandum of the conversation compiled by Edward Stettinius, Roosevelt said he was 'convinced the Russians were sincere in their desire for a strong independent Poland and indicated that he thought they could trust the Russians to give them fair treatment'. When Mikołajczyk demurred, the President said that he was 'not worried about territorial matters, that they [the Poles] would get East Prussia and Silesia and if they had to give up a little something somewhere else, he thought it was a pretty good exchange'.[32] He felt confident he could secure both Königsberg (Kaliningrad) and Lwów – despite the fact that Stalin had laid claim to both cities at Tehran – as well as Tarnopol (Ternopil) and Drohobycz (Drohobych).* He stressed the importance of the Poles reaching an agreement with Russia, since neither he nor Churchill had any intention of fighting the Red Army, but averred that 'Stalin doesn't intend to take freedom from Poland. He wouldn't dare to do that because he knows that the United States Government stands solidly behind you.'[33]

Roosevelt gave Mikołajczyk two specific pieces of advice: to dismiss the members of his Cabinet the Soviets objected to and to fly to Moscow to negotiate directly with Stalin. Before the Polish Premier could be 'bundled off', however, as the unsympathetic Harvey put it, Stalin announced that he was recognising the Soviet-sponsored Polish Committee of National Liberation – shortly to be ensconced at Lublin – as the sole authority responsible for the administration of Poland.[34] The move had been a long time coming. On 27 August 1941 – a mere two months after the onset of Operation Barbarossa – Stalin had ordered Georgi Dimitrov to create a new Polish Workers' Party and, in February 1943 – two months prior to the Katyn revelations – he founded the Union of Polish Patriots, a thinly disguised communist alternative to the Polish Government-in-Exile. Mikołajczyk, nevertheless, persevered with his trip, arriving

---

* When Churchill heard this, he was horrified. Although he would be 'the first to rejoice if it were really so', he told Mikołajczyk, the Polish Prime Minister should not 'harbour illusions'.

in Moscow on 30 July. The talks were a grim charade: Molotov asked Mikołajczyk why he had come (something the Polish Prime Minister must have occasionally wondered himself), while Stalin insisted that he recognise the legitimacy of his Polish stooges. The real tragedy, however, was not in Moscow but Warsaw.

Convinced that the Russians were about to take the city and determined that the Poles should be the ones to liberate the capital, the commander of the Polish Home Army, General Tadeusz Bór-Komorowski, gave the orders for a mass uprising to begin on 5 p.m. on 1 August 1944. The venture was based on a series of fateful misconceptions. The Germans were not, as the Poles believed, preparing to evacuate the city but rushing troops forward to check the Soviets. Western aid, due to the great distances involved, would necessarily be minimal, while the country's regular forces were many hundreds of miles away fighting in Italy. Most critically, the Red Army was not about to enter the city but remained several miles off, on the far side of the Vistula.

For sixty-three days, armed with only 1,000 rifles, 1,200 revolvers, 300 pistols, 60 light machine guns, 7 heavy machine guns and 25,000 hand grenades, the AK battled the Germans. Early successes were limited and fleeting. By the end of the first day the Poles were in control of five municipal districts on the west bank of the river but had failed to secure any of the bridges or the capital's two airports. Thereafter, it became increasingly a matter of survival as Hitler ordered the city to be 'wiped from the face of the earth' and Himmler encouraged the SS to commit murder with impunity.[35] On 5 August – the fifth day of the rising – an estimated 40,000 Poles were massacred in the suburb of Wola. The suffering was beyond belief. Hospitals were torched; nurses raped; women and children tied together and forced to walk in front of German infantry as human shields. 'On every conceivable little piece of ground are graves of civilians and soldiers,' wrote an escaped British POW, John Ward, in one of sixty-five reports he sent to London that were read by the Government but suppressed by the Ministry of Information for fear of antagonising the Soviets. 'Worst of all, however, is the smell of rotting bodies, which pervades over the whole centre of the city. Thousands of people are buried under the ruins . . . Soldiers defending their battered barricades are an awful sight. Mostly they are dirty, hungry and ragged. There are very few who have not received some sort of wound. And on and on, through a city of ruins, suffering and dead.'[36]

On 2 October the rising, which was supposed to have only lasted a few days, ended. Around 22,200 members of the AK and a similar number of Germans had been killed or seriously wounded. The civilian losses were far higher. Anywhere between 150,000 and 200,000 Polish citizens perished in the inferno, while 100,000 evacuees were deported to the Reich as slave labour.

The Poles believed, and the British suspected, that the Red Army had been held back to allow the Germans to crush a powerful, patriotic force, loyal to the legitimate Government in London. In fact, the majority of the Soviet 1st Belorussian Front was still some way off at the start of the revolt, which coincided with a German counterattack. Yet Stalin's attitude was made plain not merely by the lack of support he gave the Poles but through his successful efforts to frustrate Western assistance.

Events in Warsaw had caught the Kremlin by surprise. When Mikołajczyk first begged Stalin to aid the insurrection on 3 August, the despot's response had been to belittle the Home Army: 'What is an army without artillery, tanks and an air force?' he asked. 'In modern warfare such an army is of little use. They are small partisan units, not a regular army . . . As a matter of fact, these people do not fight against the Germans but only hide in woods.'[37] Mikołajczyk disputed this slander hotly but Stalin persisted, claiming in a telegram to Churchill on 5 August that the revolt was 'greatly exaggerated and does not inspire confidence'.[38] Three days later, he promised Mikołajczyk that the Red Air Force would drop guns and ammunition by parachute but nothing was done and on 15 August Vyshinsky rejected an American request for US aircraft to be allowed to land on Russian bases, having flown in supplies from Britain. Averell Harriman, who until this time had been a pronounced optimist on Western–Soviet co-operation, was disturbed. 'For the first time since coming to Moscow, I am gravely concerned by the attitude of the Soviet Government,' the Ambassador wrote to Roosevelt and Hull. 'If Vyshinski correctly reflects the position of the Soviet Government, its refusal is based not on operational difficulties or denial that the resistance exists but on ruthless political considerations.'[39]

Churchill did all that he could. On 18 August, he wrote to Roosevelt requesting a joint appeal to Stalin. The President agreed but the telegram he sent (drafted by Admiral Leahy) was wetter than the Vistula and the Vozhd responded by merely repeating his calumnies against the 'group of criminals, who have embarked on the Warsaw adventure'.[40] Meanwhile, Marshal Rokossovsky, commander of the 1st Soviet Belorussian Front, had informed Stalin that he would be able to resume his advance on 25 August but the despot did not reply. Instead, the main Russian effort was directed southwards, while the Soviet press gave rare publicity to the setback suffered by Rokossovsky's forces in the north.

In desperation, Churchill urged Roosevelt to send Stalin a further message stating that unless 'you directly forbid it', American aeroplanes would land on Soviet airfields in Ukraine after dropping supplies on Warsaw.[41] Wary of risking Soviet–Western relations on a cause he already regarded as lost, Roosevelt refused. 'I do not consider it advantageous to the long-range general war prospect for me to join with you in the proposed message to U[ncle] J[oe],' he replied.[42] Undeterred, Churchill telephoned Eden on Sunday 3 September to suggest a joint Anglo-American *démarche* informing Stalin that the next convoy of Lend-Lease material would not sail due to his refusal to help Warsaw.[43] Eden persuaded him against this course but the following day Churchill sent Roosevelt a cable urging him to 'consider the big stakes involved' and authorise his air force to land on Russian airfields with or without Soviet permission.[44] Meanwhile, British aircraft, manned by Polish, British and South African pilots, were attempting to deliver supplies from bases in southern Italy. The journey was extremely dangerous – taking the bombers to the limits of their range and requiring them to drop to below 500 feet to try and avoid German and sometimes Russian anti-aircraft fire – but almost 200 sorties were flown between 4 August and 21 September. Fifty per cent of the canisters ended up in enemy hands and forty-one aircraft never returned, leading to Air Marshal Sir John Slessor's calculation that one Allied air crew was lost for every ton of supplies delivered.

On 4 September, the War Cabinet sent a collective message to the Soviet Government, warning that British public opinion was 'deeply moved' by events in Warsaw and the 'terrible suffering of the Poles there'.[45] This was only recently true. The excitement of events in France – the Allies had broken out of Normandy in early August – combined with a lack of detailed reporting on the situation in Warsaw meant that few Britons paid much attention to the rising during its first two weeks. On 11 August, however, the *Daily Mirror* questioned Soviet inaction:

> No doubt there are good reasons why the Russians paused; why no arms were sent until now [by the Western Allies] at the last minute. But they will have to be the best reasons for the crumbling walls of Warsaw and the broken bodies of her children demand an explanation of why the help was delayed.[46]

Two weeks later, the *Scotsman*, which had led the reporting on the Katyn affair, and *The Economist* drew attention to the scandalous lack of Russian assistance for Warsaw, while George Orwell took aim at those left-wing intellectuals – or, in Beaverbrook's case, right-wing press barons – who sought to excuse Soviet barbarism: 'Do remember that dishonesty and cowardice always have to be paid for. Don't imagine that for years on end you can make yourself the boot-licking propagandist of the Soviet regime, or any other regime, and then suddenly return to mental decency. Once a whore, always a whore.'[47]

Eventually, a combination of Western pressure and the advance of the Soviet-sponsored Polish 1st Army caused the Kremlin to change tack. On the night of 13–14 September, the Red Air Force began delivering supplies to Warsaw and on the night of 18–19 September, 110 American B-17 bombers were permitted to land at Soviet airbases, having jettisoned 1,300 canisters of food and munitions over the beleaguered city. These efforts fell into the fatal category of 'too little, too late'. Only 388 of the American canisters were retrieved by the AK, while most of the ammunition the Soviets dropped was Russian-made and did not fit the Polish guns. Pondering the tragedy, US Assistant Secretary of State Adolf Berle articulated the West's military-political dilemma:

Somewhere a voice must be found for the voiceless: the little people who fought in our fight and are being condemned to death by our common victory. I am rapidly getting to the point where I have had all of this I can take. But until the Germans are beaten, we have to follow the rule either to be quiet or to be helpful.[48]

★

The rising over, Poland's political tragedy hurtled towards its wartime coda. On 9 October, Churchill flew to Moscow to negotiate a 'spheres of influence' agreement with Stalin, and on the same day the two leaders summoned Mikołajczyk, along with representatives of the Lublin Committee, to try to settle the 'Polish question'. Churchill's conduct during the negotiations was intemperate and, at times, unfeeling. Yet it stemmed from two understandable precepts: a refusal by him, no less than Roosevelt, to allow the Polish issue to undermine Soviet–Western co-operation; and the knowledge that the longer the Polish Government-in-Exile prevaricated, the slimmer the chances of a free, democratic Poland emerging at the end of the war.

The talks, which took place in the Spiridonovka Palace, covered familiar ground. Stalin demanded that the Polish Government publicly accept the Curzon Line and come to an arrangement with the Committee of National Liberation, already entrenching itself in Soviet-occupied Poland. Churchill, speaking of the 'sacrifices made by the Soviet Union in the course of the war . . . and its effort towards liberating Poland', gave the Marshal his full support.[49] Mikołajczyk replied that he was not empowered to cede 40 per cent of his country. This provoked a predictable argument, ending only when Molotov revealed the secret of Tehran: 'We all agreed at Tehran that the Curzon Line must divide Poland,' the Commissar declared, looking to Churchill for corroboration. 'You will recall that President Roosevelt agreed to this solution and strongly endorsed the Line. And then we agreed that it would be best not to issue any public declaration about our agreement.'[50] Mikołajczyk could not believe what he was hearing. Roosevelt had told him in June that he would fight for Poland's eastern territories, while the

British had disclaimed making any deal behind Poland's back. Harriman, who was attending merely as an observer, looked at the rug. Churchill, however, met the Prime Minister's disbelieving eyes and said, 'I can confirm this.'[51]

That evening, Churchill and Eden returned to the Spiridonovka Palace to meet the Lublin Poles. They were not impressed. Eden described Bolesław Bierut and Edward Osóbka-Morawski as 'the rat and the weasel', while Churchill would mock these Polish apparatchiks as a pair of ventriloquist's dummies:

> They had learned and rehearsed their part so carefully that even their masters evidently felt they were overdoing it. For instance, M. Bierut, the leader, spoke in these terms: 'We are here to demand on behalf of Poland that Lwów shall belong to Russia. This is the will of the Polish people.' When this had been translated from Polish into English and Russian I looked at Stalin and saw an understanding twinkle in his expressive eyes, as much as to say, 'What about that for our Soviet teaching!'[52]

Not that it caused him to spare Mikołajczyk. When the Polish Premier continued to resist the Russian demands in a private meeting with the British on 14 October, Churchill exploded:

> I wash my hands . . . as far as I am concerned we shall give the business up. Because of quarrels between Poles we are not going to wreck the peace of Europe. In your obstinacy you do not see what is at stake. It is not in friendship that we shall part. We shall tell the world how unreasonable you are. You will start another war in which 25 million lives will be lost. But you don't care.[53]

Wearily, the British tried to extract some sort of compromise from the Soviets. The Poles were prepared to accept the Curzon Line as the *temporary* demarcation between Poland and the USSR (the final frontier to be drawn at the peace conference) or to accept a slightly modified Curzon Line with Lwów remaining in the reconstituted Poland. Eden took this latter proposal to Stalin but the despot, who seemed to savour the irony, replied that he was committed to the claims of the Ukrainians – those unwilling inhabitants of the Soviet Union whom he had robbed, persecuted and starved by the million. Churchill's mood, meanwhile, was not improved by Eden's fondness for weak puns: 'Anthony, *don't* tell me *again* that we are Poles apart!' he berated the Foreign Secretary on returning to the British Embassy.[54]

Faced with little choice and under immense pressure, Mikołajczyk returned to London to try to persuade his colleagues to accept the Allied terms: a public commitment to the Curzon Line and a willingness to work with Stalin's communist stooges. His one remaining hope was that Roosevelt stood by his words of June 1944, not his deeds of December 1943. The omens were, ostensibly, encouraging. Determined to retain the Polish vote at the forthcoming Presidential election, Roosevelt had invited representatives of the Polish American Congress to visit him at the White House on 11 October. When the delegates entered the President's study, they noticed a large map of Poland behind the President's desk, marked with the country's pre-war frontiers. Two weeks later, FDR assured the President of the Polish American Congress, Charles Rozmarek, that the 'territorial integrity of Poland was his goal' and received his endorsement.[55] Yet the Poles were as much pawns in the American election campaign as they were in the wider game of Allied diplomacy. Mikołajczyk's appeal to the President of 26 October was ignored until two weeks *after* Roosevelt's historic fourth-term victory – aided by the votes of 90 per cent of American-Poles – and when FDR did respond he disclaimed all responsibility for the Polish–Soviet dispute: 'In regard to the future frontiers of Poland, if a mutual agreement on this subject . . . is reached between the Polish, Soviet and British Governments, this Government would offer no objection.'[56]

In fairness to Roosevelt, American enthusiasm for the deeds of the Red Army and its Commander-in-Chief made a serious row with the Kremlin politically difficult as well as militarily inexpedient. As the new Secretary of the Navy, James Forrestal, complained to a friend:

I find that whenever any American suggests that we act in accordance with the needs of our own security he is apt to be called a

god-damned fascist or imperialist, while if Uncle Joe suggests that
he needs the Baltic Provinces, half of Poland, all of Bessarabia and
access to the Mediterranean, all hands agree that he is a fine, frank,
candid and generally delightful fellow who is very easy to deal with
because he is so explicit in what he wants.[57]

In late October 1944, Roosevelt finally saw the newly appointed
American Ambassador to the Polish Government-in-Exile, Arthur
Bliss Lane. Lane expressed the view that the US should be firm
and insist upon a free and independent Poland. If the US was not
going to be strong now, when she had 'the largest Army, Navy and
Air Forces in the world and at a time when the President had just
received another mandate from the American people', then he did
not see when she would ever be strong. Roosevelt's reply was sharp
and sarcastic: 'Do you want me to go to war with Russia?' Later
in the conversation, he stated that 'Stalin's idea of having a *cordon
sanitaire*, in the shape of Poland under Russian influence, as a bulwark to protect the Soviet Union against further aggression was
understandable'.[58] The world had come full circle. In 1919, the Allies
had looked to the newly constructed Poland and the Baltic States as
a barrier against Bolshevik Russia. Now it was these states that were
to be sacrificed in the interests of the vastly more powerful USSR.
Lane later entitled his memoirs *I Saw Poland Betrayed*.

On 24 November, Mikołajczyk resigned. Abandoned by the
Americans and the British, he had tried and failed to persuade
his colleagues to accept Stalin's terms. His successor, Tomasz
Arciszewski – an old socialist and veteran of Poland's struggle for
independence – was rejected by the Allies. Eden told the Commons that the Polish Government was no longer representative,
while Churchill looked forward to Mikołajczyk's speedy return.
'I trust', he wrote to Stalin on 3 December, 'that you will agree
that our respective influence should be used with the Poles here
and with those at Lublin to prevent any steps on either side which
might increase the tension between them and so render more difficult M. Mikołajczyk's task when, as I hope, he takes it up again
in the not far distant future.'[59] He trusted in vain. In his reply, five
days later, Stalin disclaimed all interest in both the 'Polish émigré

Government' and Mikołajczyk, whom he accused of being a front for 'criminal' and 'terroristic' elements, murdering Soviet soldiers on Polish soil. The Committee of National Liberation, by contrast, had achieved 'notable successes in strengthening its national democratic organisations', in carrying out land reform and 'in broadening the organisation of its Polish forces'.[60]

Seeing which way the wind was blowing, Churchill and Roosevelt tried to prevent their ally from recognising the Lublin Committee as the official government of Poland. On 16 December 1944, Roosevelt asked Stalin to defer any such step until the Big Three could meet again, most probably in late January. It seemed a small favour to ask but the Vozhd had no intention of surrendering even a fraction of his advantage. Having kept the President waiting a week for an answer (Roosevelt's message was delivered by Harriman on 20 December), Stalin replied with fresh invective against the 'émigré Polish Government' and praise of the Lublin Committee. He called on the democracies to cut ties with the London Poles and recognise the Committee of National Liberation.[61] Roosevelt protested but the despot was unmoved. On 28 December, the Lublin Committee declared itself the provisional government of Poland and on 1 January 1945, Stalin informed Roosevelt that he had no choice but to recognise this body.

The iron curtain had begun its slow descent.

XXVIII

Spheres of Influence

My observation is that in the present state of affairs in Europe your writ
runs just as far as your army of occupation goes and no farther.

Adolf Berle, 26 August 1944[1]

Despite Soviet intransigence over Poland, the road from World War
to Cold War was not pre-laid, even if the Soviet siege mentality and
Russian espionage made a breakdown in East–West relations highly
likely. Although Stalin had no intention of compromising over his
western frontiers, he still hoped to continue the Grand Alliance into
the post-war period. When Roosevelt had outlined his scheme for
Great Power co-operation, including an international police force,
in May 1942, the despot had reacted with enthusiasm. 'Roosevelt's
considerations about peace protection after the war are absolutely
sound,' he cabled Molotov in Washington. 'There is no doubt that
it would be impossible to maintain peace in future without creating
a united military force by Britain, the USA and the USSR, capable
of preventing aggression . . . Tell Roosevelt . . . [he] is absolutely
right and that his position will be fully supported by the Soviet Government.'[2] Two years later, after British, American and Canadian
troops had stormed the Normandy beaches and the Red Army had
driven the Germans from Soviet soil, he hailed the 'solidity' of the
Allies before the Moscow Soviet:

> One should not be surprised that there are disagreements [between
> the Allies] but that there are so few and that, as a rule, they are
> resolved almost every time in a spirit of unity and coordination
> among the three great powers . . . The alliance between the USSR,
> Great Britain and the United States of America is founded not on

casual, transitory considerations but on vital and lasting interests . . .
Can we expect the actions of this world organisation to be sufficiently effective? It will be effective if the great powers which have
borne the brunt of the war against Hitlerite Germany continue to
act in a spirit of unanimity and accord.[3]

This did not mean that the Soviet leader had shed his habitual and
ideological suspicions. 'Perhaps you think that just because we are
the allies of the English, we have forgotten who they are and who
Churchill is', he challenged the Yugoslav communist Milovan Ðilas
in March 1944. 'There is nothing they like better [than] to trick their
allies. During the First World War they constantly tricked the Russians and the French. And Churchill? Churchill is the kind of man
who will pick your pocket of a kopeck [the smallest unit of Russian
currency] if you don't watch him . . . Roosevelt is not like that. He
dips in his hand only for bigger coins. But Churchill? Churchill will
do it for a kopeck.'[4] Later, when passing a map of the Soviet Union,
the Vozhd declared that the Anglo-Americans would 'never accept the
idea that so great a space should be red', while a reprimand he sent his
commanders for allowing 'hostile elements', otherwise known as British and American air crews, to land on Soviet-controlled bases in August
1944 sheds additional light on his refusal to aid the Warsaw airlift.[5]
　　The fact is that whilst Stalin's attitude towards his allies fluctuated,
as theirs did towards him, he looked to the Grand Alliance and the
new international organisation (which would be its forum) to check
a resurgent Germany. That Germany would revive and become a
renewed threat to European peace, he had no doubt. 'You can't change
the Germans,' he told the Czechoslovak President, Edvard Beneš,
'they'll begin again to prepare themselves for war and after some time
another war will come.'[6] The difficulty was that he also demanded an
exclusive sphere of influence in eastern Europe. This too was born of
security concerns. From the time of Lenin, Soviet leaders and propagandists had been obsessed with the sinister intentions of the ring of
capitalist countries that surrounded them. Like the Romanovs, they
fretted constantly about the insecurity of their vast borders. The victims of three European invasions in 130 years, the Russians saw their
immediate neighbours – many of which had been part of the old

Tsarist Empire – as an essential buffer zone. Were it not for the Soviet incorporation of eastern Poland, the Baltic States and Bessarabia – the fruits of the Molotov–Ribbentrop Pact – Stalin told Churchill during the Prime Minister's first visit to Moscow, the Germans would have got considerably further than they had in 1941. Yet these strategic demands were irreconcilable with Western democratic ideals. Spheres of influence were all very well – the British had long defended their predominance in a range of geographies, while the United States had famously declared a sphere of influence over the entire western hemisphere (the Monroe Doctrine) – yet the spheres had to remain open and broadly free. Roosevelt called his Latin American doctrine the 'Good Neighbor Policy', while the British pointed with pride to the development of democratic institutions in Egypt, Iraq and India. To condone the creation of closed, oppressive puppet governments in eastern and central Europe would be to repudiate the principles the democracies were fighting for. Moreover, there was the growing concern that Poland, Finland and the Baltic States represented the despot's *minimum* demands; the fear that the Soviet Union would continue to expand her territory and influence until the West forced her to stop.

The military were generally more apprehensive than the civilians, the British, for reasons of geography, more than the Americans. As Alan Brooke noted on 27 July 1944:

> Germany is no longer the dominating power of Europe, Russia is. Unfortunately, Russia is not entirely European. She has, however, vast resources and cannot fail to become the main threat in fifteen years from now. Therefore, foster Germany, gradually build her up and bring her into a federation of Western Europe.[7]

This argument, repeated in notes the Chiefs of Staff sent the Post-Hostilities Planning Staff, alarmed the Foreign Office. More optimistic than the COS about the maintenance of Great Power co-operation after the war and placing greater faith in the Soviet need to focus on internal reconstruction, the FO feared that talk of Russia as 'enemy number one', already current among the military, would become a self-fulfilling prophecy.[8] 'If we suspect them, ergo they will suspect us,' the Russia expert Robert Bruce Lockhart had argued as early as 1942. 'Treat them like civilised beings and decent people and they will try to behave like civilised beings. Treat them like gangsters and they will out-gangster gangsterdom.'[9]

Nevertheless, the Foreign Office was interested in the idea of a 'Western bloc' as a counter to a revived Germany and – though this was never stated publicly – a potentially hostile USSR. Writing to his colleagues in King Charles Street on 30 May 1944, Duff Cooper, now serving as Britain's representative to the French Committee of National Liberation, set out the case for such an alliance. Starting from the premise that Britain had, throughout her history, striven to prevent any one nation from dominating the Continent (the crux of his argument against the appeasement of Germany during the 1930s), it was only logical, the former Cabinet Minister averred, for Britain to fear Russia:

Russia has a population more than twice as numerous as that of Germany. She possesses resources both of food and raw materials, largely undeveloped, which might render her almost independent of foreign imports. In courage and endurance her people are second to none. She has but lately embarked on a programme of development which is likely to transform a mainly agricultural into a mainly industrial population. She has adopted a system of government which combines the efficiency of totalitarianism with an ideology which appeals to the hearts of the people and which they have accepted with the enthusiasm with which men embrace a religious faith . . . It would be difficult to overestimate the potential menace which all these advantages create.

Whether the USSR intended to exploit these 'advantages' in pursuit of European hegemony was a moot point. 'There is nothing in the short history of the USSR to suggest that they harbour aggressive designs on their neighbours,' wrote Cooper, strangely forgetting the Polish–Soviet War, the Molotov–Ribbentrop Pact and the Soviet–Finnish War. Yet prudence, he continued, prescribed caution. Alliances were infinitely preferable to isolation and the obvious combination for Britain to work towards, he argued, was a concert of the western European states 'bound together by the most explicit terms of alliance'.[10]

The Foreign Office were united in considering this a 'remarkable despatch'.[11] Yet whilst there was broad agreement as to the attractions of a 'Western bloc', few, at this stage, shared the Ambassador's fears about the Soviet Union. The Post-Hostilities Planning Staff had acknowledged 'the *possibility* that she [Russia] might at some stage attempt the domination of Europe', wrote Gladwyn Jebb, 'but that does not mean that she will . . . and at the present time we think it extremely unlikely'.[12] Sir Orme Sargent thought an alliance directed against Germany 'welcome' but a bloc aimed at balancing Russia 'a most dangerous experiment', while Eden minuted that Cooper had reached the right conclusion even though his reasoning was 'faulty'.[13]

Similar divisions existed within American opinion. Whilst General Groves – responsible for the Manhattan Project – spoke for many in the military when he claimed that he had never been under 'any illusion . . . but that Russia was our enemy', the diplomats tended towards greater optimism.[14] In particular, Harriman hoped to use American financial aid as a lever with which to extract concessions over eastern Europe. As 1944 wore on, however, the Ambassador's despatches became increasingly gloomy. 'I believe that it is their intention to have a positive sphere of influence over their western neighbours,' he wrote to Cordell Hull on 20 September. 'It can be argued that American interests need not be concerned over the affairs of this area. What frightens me, however, is that when a country begins to extend its influence by strong-arm methods beyond its borders under the guise of security it is difficult to see how a line can be drawn. If the policy is accepted that the Soviet Union has a right to penetrate her immediate neighbours for security, penetration of the next immediate neighbours becomes at a certain time equally logical.'[15]

His recently arrived deputy, the forty-year-old George Kennan, who had served in the Moscow Embassy during the purges, agreed. In September 1944, Kennan sent the State Department a masterly 5,000-word despatch that exhibited greater prescience than his more famous 'Long Telegram' of February 1946:

People at home would find Soviet words and actions easier to understand if they would bear in mind the character of Russian aims in

Eastern and Central Europe. Russian efforts in this area are directed to only one goal: power . . . It is a matter of indifference to Moscow whether a given area is 'communistic' or not. All things being equal, Moscow might prefer to see it communised, although even that is debatable. But the main thing is that it should be amenable to Moscow influence and, if possible, to Moscow authority.[16]

Churchill oscillated between extreme pessimism and rarely justified optimism. An emotional creature, his judgement was frequently determined by the tone of Stalin's latest telegram. As the Red Army swept westwards, however, he became increasingly preoccupied with trying to 'save' as much of eastern and central Europe as possible from the Soviets, while simultaneously preserving British interests. His strategy was both diplomatic and military. On the military side, he wanted the Americans to provide General Alexander with enough forces to break into the Po valley and then drive north-east through the 'Ljubljana Gap' towards Vienna. Such an action, he told Roosevelt and the Combined Chiefs during the Second Quebec Conference, would forestall the 'dangerous spread of Russian influence in this area'.[17] A secondary motive was that it would be a British operation, yielding prestige and justifying the Prime Minister's Mediterranean strategy, but this went unmentioned.

Understandably, the Americans refused. The war was being won in eastern and north-west Europe and the appetite for Balkan adventures, particularly ones that involved crossing the Alps in winter, was no greater in the autumn of 1944 than it had been in the autumn of 1943. A decade later, Churchill told the historian John Wheeler-Bennett that the two greatest foreign policy mistakes of his lifetime had been Woodrow Wilson's insistence on abolishing the German monarchy and Roosevelt's 'decision' to allow the Russians to reach Prague and Vienna before the British and the Americans.[18] Seen from a Cold War perspective, such a contention had obvious currency. Nor was it entirely a matter of hindsight. Responding to the American's rejection of his preferred strategy – a cause to which he kept returning between June 1944 and February 1945 – Churchill accused Roosevelt of committing 'the first major strategic and *political* error for which we two have been responsible.'[19] Yet his argument rested on a false military premise. The 'Ljubljana Gap' was a 2,000-foot pass leading to the Sava Valley. Between the Sava and Vienna rise the Karavank mountains, 6,000-foot peaks from which only two roads descend to the Klagenfurt valley. The ideal terrain for defence, it was here and in the surrounding mountains that the Austrians had held the Italians for four years during the First World War. Eisenhower rightly dismissed the scheme as an unwarrantable conjecture, while Brooke complained of Churchill's 'strategic ravings': 'It was hard to make him realise that if we took the season of the year and the topography of the country . . . we should have three enemies instead of one,' he wrote in his diary.[20] The only sure way to have beaten the Russians to central Europe would have been to cross the Channel in 1943 – a venture the Prime Minister, for sound military reasons, had successfully opposed.

Churchill's diplomatic strategy was more successful. With the Soviets advancing in the Balkans, his plan was to sacrifice what was already lost in the hope of saving what remained. 'Are we going to acquiesce in the communisation of the Balkans?' he minuted Eden on 4 May, by which time the Soviets had driven the Germans from almost all of Ukraine and were approaching Romania. 'If our conclusion is that we resist the communist infusion and invasion we should put it to them pretty plainly.'[21] The following day, Eden asked the Soviet Ambassador, Fedor Gusev, to call on him. The British understood, the Foreign Secretary stated, that the Russians would take the lead in Romanian affairs but wished to have the decisive voice in Greek matters. In particular, the British wanted the Soviets to cease their support for the Greek communist partisans. Two weeks later, Gusev – or 'Frog-face', as Cadogan called him – told Eden that the Soviet Government agreed to his proposals but wondered whether the Americans approved.[22] Hastily, Eden instructed Halifax to sound out Hull. This the Ambassador did but, owing to the Secretary of State's well-known aversion to 'spheres of influence', pretended that the proposal was a Soviet initiative. Unfortunately, Churchill sent Roosevelt a separate telegram on 31 May and gave the game away. Justifiably annoyed, the State Department prepared a cable for the President to send the Prime Minister repudiating the agreement. Now it was Churchill's turn to be affronted. 'I think you might trust me in this,' he retorted in an impassioned message on 11 June. 'The Russians are ready to let us take the lead in the Greek business, which means that EAM [the communist National Liberation Front] and all its malice can be controlled by the national forces of Greece.'[23]

Reluctantly, Roosevelt agreed to give the policy a three-month trial but now the Russians, exhilarated by the scale of their recent victories and scenting Anglo-American discord, began to prevaricate. Both Churchill and Eden were irritated at losing what they considered to have been an opportunity for limiting Soviet interference in the Balkans. 'Does this mean that all we had settled with the Russians goes down through the pedantic interference of the US?' the Prime Minister minuted Eden.[24] The Foreign Secretary told the War Cabinet that it probably did. Yet neither man was prepared to let the matter drop. Travelling on board the *Queen Mary* to the Second Quebec Conference in early September, Churchill emphasised his wish to 'forestall the Russians in certain areas of Central Europe' by military means, while Eden's response to the Soviet invasion of Bulgaria – begun on 8 September – was to argue for the immediate despatch of British troops to Greece to prevent the Soviets from penetrating further south.[25] On 12 October 1944, British paratroops duly landed in Athens as part of Operation Manna, their comrades in 'Fox Force' and 'Bucket Force' having already gained control of the Peloponnese. Since the Germans were already in the process of withdrawal, progress was swift and on 14 October Fox Force was driven into the Greek capital by buses provided by the Mayor of Athens. Meanwhile, Churchill and Eden had arrived in Moscow to try to secure a more diplomatic and wide-ranging division of the Balkans.

The Tolstoy Conference was a British initiative to which the Americans had given only grudging approval. On 29 September, Churchill had informed Roosevelt of his desire for another meeting with Stalin to 'clinch' Soviet participation in the war against Japan, to effect a settlement over Poland and to discuss 'other points' relating to Greece and Yugoslavia.[26] Although Roosevelt seemed relaxed about the proposed Anglo-Soviet get-together, the State Department's Russia expert, Chip Bohlen, and Hopkins were not and persuaded Roosevelt to send Churchill a message asking that Harriman be present during the discussions. They also prepared a message for the President to send Stalin, stating that 'there is literally no question, political or military, in which the United States is not interested', as well as Roosevelt's conviction that 'the three of us and only the three of us' were capable of resolving the fundamental questions of war and peace.[27] This amused Stalin, who on the one hand criticised the President's cable to Churchill – complaining that 'it seemed to demand too many rights for the United States [while] leaving too little for the Soviet Union and Great Britain' – while on the other agreeing with Harriman that all major questions should be dealt with on a tripartite basis. Once again, Anglo-American disagreement equalled Soviet opportunity.[28]

The first meeting, which took place in Molotov's study at 10 p.m. on the evening of 9 October, consisted of Churchill, Eden, Stalin, Molotov and their interpreters. Although Churchill had told Roosevelt that he would be 'very glad' to have Harriman sit in on the discussions, he was sure the President did not 'wish this to preclude private *tête-à-têtes* between me and UJ . . . as it is often under such conditions that the best progress is made'.[29] After discussing Poland, Churchill turned to the issue of the Balkans. He was 'not worrying much about Romania. That was very much a Russian affair . . . But in Greece it was different. Britain must be the leading Mediterranean power and he hoped Marshal Stalin would let him have the first say about Greece in the same way as Marshal Stalin [would have] about Romania.'

Stalin replied that he understood that Britain had suffered greatly owing to her communications having been cut in the Mediterranean and that Greece was very important to her. 'He agreed with the Prime Minister that Britain should have the first say in Greece.' Churchill then produced what he called a 'naughty document': a list, written in his own hand, of Balkan countries and the proportions of post-war influence he proposed that Britain and the Soviet Union should have in them. Russia would have 90 per cent influence in Romania, while Britain would have 90 per cent influence in Greece. Bulgaria would be 75 per cent under Russian influence but the two countries would share Yugoslavia and Hungary on a fifty-fifty basis.

After a slight pause, Stalin took out his blue pencil and made a large tick upon the paper. This was the sort of politics he liked: an old-fashioned carve-up. Suddenly embarrassed, Churchill suggested that they burn the document. But Stalin told him to keep it.[30]

Of course, as Churchill wrote in a letter he drafted the following day but did not send Stalin, the percentages were no more than a 'guide for the conduct of our affairs'.[31] Chip Bohlen later quipped that to try to divide a country on a percentage basis 'is almost like saying that someone should be eighty per cent or twenty per cent pregnant'.[32] Yet Stalin was prepared to play the game in order to increase his influence in eastern Europe. The following day, Molotov accordingly insisted that the Soviet Union must have 75 per cent predominance in Hungary and 90 per cent in Bulgaria. Although Eden persuaded the Foreign Commissar to accept 80 per cent in the latter, the difference was immaterial. The Soviet Union had already been acknowledged as the dominant power in Bulgaria but for a worthless 10 per cent had gained the right to dominate Hungary. The deal was thus distinctly one-sided but then this merely reflected the realities of power and the tyranny of geography.

Meanwhile, the Americans were beginning to discover what had been decided. On 10 October, Harriman informed Washington that the British were trying 'to work out some sort of spheres of influence with the Russians, the British to have a free hand in Greece and the Russians in Romania' and on 13 October the Ambassador reported that percentages representing proportionate influence had been allotted to Bulgaria, Hungary and Yugoslavia.[33] These were supplemented by more general messages from Churchill to Roosevelt, emphasising the necessity of preventing civil war from breaking out in the Balkans and alluding to the steps he had taken to 'save' Greece and Yugoslavia from Soviet domination.[34]

'We have found an extraordinary atmosphere of goodwill,' the Prime Minister informed the President.[35] Stalin appeared in genial mood – except when it came to the Poles – and even agreed to dine at the British Embassy. The next evening, there was a command performance at the Bolshoi Theatre during which both leaders received a thunderous ovation from the audience. 'I have had very nice talks with the Old Bear,' Churchill wrote to his wife. 'I like him the more

I see him. *Now* they respect us here and I am sure they wish to work with us.'[36] The first test would come in little over a month.

★

Since their departure from Greece in April 1941, the British had given sanctuary to the Greek Government-in-Exile, as well as to His Majesty King George II of the Hellenes. Described by Roosevelt as a 'charming fellow, considering what an empty head' and by Jock Colville as among the two worst 'advertisements for hereditary monarchy' (the other being King Peter of Yugoslavia), the King was unfailingly pro-Allied but unpopular in his own country owing to his support for the dictatorship of General Metaxas.[37] The resistance which formed in his absence was dominated by the left. The National Liberation Front (Ethniko Apeleutherotiko Metopo, EAM) – which, at its height, had around 700,000 members – had been founded by the Communists (the KKE, Kommounistiko Komma Elladas) and an assortment of socialist and agrarian parties. Its nearest rival and sometime collaborator was the National Republican Greek League or EDES (Ethnikos Dimokratikos Ellinikos Syndesmos). A broadly republican body under the command of the charismatic yet disorganised Colonel Napoleon Zervas, EDES stood for a democratic constitution and a popular plebiscite to resolve the question of the monarchy. The British supplied both movements but it was the guerrilla arm of the EAM, the Greek People's Liberation Army (Ellinikos Laïkos Apeleutherotikos Stratos, ELAS), that proved the more powerful, forcibly amalgamating smaller resistance groups and murdering rivals. As the British Ambassador to the Greek Government-in-Exile, Rex Leeper, pointed out, there was a fundamental contradiction in Britain's Greek policy: 'His Majesty's Government . . . were speaking with two voices. The political voice, i.e. the Foreign Office, was giving full support to King George and his Government, [while] the military voice, i.e. GHQ Middle East [and SOE], was giving support with arms and gold sovereigns to the King's worst enemies in the Greek mountains.'[38]

Attempts to bridge the multiple divides – between the resistance movements and the Government, between the Government (largely consisting of republicans) and the King and between the resistance movements themselves – proved futile. In the autumn of 1943, civil war broke out between ELAS and the more liberal partisans and, in April 1944, the Greek Brigade and the Greek Navy mutinied in support of the EAM. The British suppressed the rising and a new government was formed under the leader of the Social Democrats, George Papandreou. In May, Papandreou presided over a conference attended by representatives of all the major political parties as well as the resistance groups. Hopes rose. Under the terms of the Lebanon Charter (the conference was held in the Grand Hôtel du Bois de Boulogne, near Beirut), the civil war was ended, the resistance was unified and the armed forces were reorganised under a newly created Government of National Unity. But the peace was fragile and ELAS paid scant attention to its terms. On 3 June, Eden circulated to the War Cabinet a report from a British liaison officer, recently returned from eight months with the communist partisans:

> Our Mission has kept this movement alive and unless British troops control matters in the towns after the German evacuation I foresee the tragedy going really deep into all Greece . . . ELAS . . . are now a well-organised gang of terrorists. Ares, their leader, has many brutal murders to his credit and he is quite ruthless . . . These bands have only been allowed to grow and thrive through our policy and we have saddled Greece with these troubles. It is up to us to rid her of them . . . bag and baggage.[39]

Originally, the British had hoped to return to Greece in strength and restore the King. After the Tehran decision in favour of Overlord, however, this was no longer possible and the King was forced to concede that he would not return to his country without a mandate inviting him to do so. This vexed Churchill, whose judgement was wont to desert him on the subject of royalty and who was already chiding the Foreign Office over its alleged failure to protect Europe's monarchs, despite his backing of the anti-monarchist Tito. Nevertheless, on 12 October Operation Manna began and on Wednesday 18 October the Greek Government arrived in Athens.

At first, all went well. The Athenians were overjoyed by the arrival of British troops and Harold Macmillan persuaded their commanding officer, Lieutenant-General Ronald Scobie – 'a charming man but *not* gifted with brains' – to enter into the spirit of the occasion, bowing, waving and blowing kisses from an open car.[40] A *Te Deum* was sung in the cathedral and Papandreou made a rousing speech in Constitution Square. Beneath the bouquets, however, there were deep problems. The Axis occupation – which included a particularly murderous Bulgarian regime in eastern Macedonia and Thrace – had devastated the country. Half a million people had died and 1,700 villages had been destroyed between April 1941 and October 1944. Industry had been gutted, infrastructure shattered. Famine, which had killed an estimated 5 per cent of the population during the winter of 1941–2, continued to haunt the archipelago, while mass unemployment and runaway inflation threatened a complete breakdown of law and order. At the same time, there were around 60,000 heavily armed guerrillas – some 50,000 ELAS and 10,000 EDES – who would need to be disarmed or incorporated into a new national army.

The British were in no doubt as to the dangers. As Macmillan, who had recently added Greece to his Mediterranean Proconsulship, told a meeting of officers and diplomats in the British Embassy on the day of his arrival, 'Unless Papandreou deals *at once* with the currency situation there will be a most serious crisis [and] unless some way can be found to disarm ELAS . . . there will be a most dangerous situation leading, inevitably, to civil war.'[41] Over the next week, he and Leeper despatched a stream of cables calling for 'cruisers, coffee, gold sovereigns, oil seeds, aeroplanes and various other commodities . . . believed to be useful in a monetary crisis'.[42] Most were slow to arrive. On 29 October, however, assistance appeared in the diminutive form of the Under-Secretary of His Majesty's Treasury, Sir David Waley. As Macmillan recorded, his coming was like that of Trollope's ubiquitous physician, Sir Omicron Pie:

At last the great London specialist had come – a guinea a mile and a big fee as well. He is a splendid little man, obviously a strong character, with a charming, even boyish, smile and sense of fun. He listened patiently (at a consultation which took place after dinner), approved the remedies so far applied, thought an operation urgent, thought the patient would probably die but nevertheless there would be no trouble about the death certificate – and sent us all to bed a little deflated but much impressed.[43]

The Greek Government accepted Waley's medicine – which included the introduction of a new currency backed by the British Military Authority – but the situation remained desperate, with workers rushing to spend their wages before they lost all value and the price of a newspaper reaching 10 billion drachmas before stabilising. Meanwhile, the political atmosphere became increasingly febrile as the EAM kept up a steady stream of propaganda and bands of ELAS guerrillas established roadblocks along the approaches to the capital. Papandreou planned to dissolve the partisans and replace them with a newly formed National Guard. He was authorised to do this by the Caserta Agreement, signed by the leaders of ELAS and EDES on 26 September, as well as the Greek Government, with its six EAM members. Since then, however, the situation had deteriorated owing to the arrival from Italy of the Mountain Brigade, a British-trained Greek unit known for its loyalty to the monarchy. If the partisans were to be disbanded then the Mountain Brigade should also be dissolved, argued the EAM ministers, strongly supported by the Communists. Papandreou refused. Acts of terrorism by ELAS were increasing and the forces at the disposal of the Government were still dwarfed by those of the guerrillas. On 2 December, with rumours of a coup abounding and battalions of ELAS fighters converging on the capital, the six EAM ministers resigned from the Government. The next morning, violence broke out in Constitution Square. The 'second round' of the Greek Civil War had begun.

Churchill reacted to events in Athens by raining brimstone. 'You must force Papandreou to stand to his duty and assure him he will be supported by all our forces if he does so,' he wrote to Leeper. 'Should he resign [as the Greek Premier was threatening to do] he should be locked up till he comes to his senses.'[44] To Scobie, who was having to cope with an ELAS takeover of Athens' police stations and attacks on Greek sailors, he wrote:

> You are responsible for maintaining order in Athens and for neutral-
> ising or destroying all EAM-ELAS bands approaching the city . . .
> Naturally, ELAS will try to put women and children in the van
> where shooting may occur. You must be clever about this and avoid
> mistakes. But do not hesitate to fire at any armed male in Athens
> who assails the British authority or Greek authority with which we
> are working . . . We have to hold and dominate Athens. It would be
> a great thing for you to succeed in this without bloodshed if possible
> but also with bloodshed if necessary.[45]*

Unfortunately, this message, which was dictated late at night after a
good dinner, was seen by the American representative to the Advisory Council for Italy, who forwarded it to the State Department,
who then proceeded to leak it to Drew Pearson of the *Washington
Post*. American public opinion was outraged. Britain was accused of
trying to force an unpopular, right-wing government and an even
more unpopular monarch upon the Greek people with bayonets.
The fact that neither Papandreou nor his Ministers were right-wing,
or monarchists, was unknown or ignored. Newly appointed Secretary of State Edward Stettinius issued a statement disassociating the
US from British action, while Admiral King ordered American ships
to cease ferrying supplies to British forces in Greece – an order that
was rescinded only after Churchill complained to Hopkins.

   Nor was criticism confined to the US. Throughout the crisis,
most of the British press and much of the Labour Party were out-
spoken in their denunciation of the Government. On 8 December,
Churchill answered his critics in the House of Commons. It 'was
a superb Parliamentary performance', recorded Macmillan (in
London to discuss Italian affairs), but not 'a very *profound* speech –
that is, I think it simplified the problem'.[46] This was fair. Not all EAM
members were communists; not all ELAS fighters were terrorists.

---

* The Prime Minister sat there, 'grunting in his armchair and dictating . . . to
Miss Layton who did not bat an eyelid at the many blasphemies with which the
old man interspersed his official phrases', recorded Pierson Dixon. 'He was in
bloodthirsty mood and did not take kindly to suggestions that we should avoid
bloodshed if possible.' (Dixon Papers, Diary, 4 December 1944)

Fear of a right-wing coup co-existed alongside the fear of a left-wing revolution – an understandable apprehension given the Metaxas dictatorship, British support for the monarchy and the continued employment of known collaborators within the Greek gendarmerie – while the outbreak of violence on 3 December was as much the fault of the Athenian police as of *agents provocateurs* within the pro-EAM crowd.

On the other hand, ELAS was not the noble, democratic resistance movement many in the West believed it to be. Led by a renowned sadist, Aris Velouchiotis – 'the most ruthless man I have ever met, the most cold-blooded, the cruellest', according to one SOE officer – it had prioritised the liquidation of its ideological enemies over opposition to the Germans.[47] ELAS/EAM had brought schools and improved communications to the territories it administered but also terror and firing squads. In October 1943, it had launched an assault upon its liberal, social-democratic rivals, EDES and EKKA (Ethniki kai Koinoniki Apeleutherosis, National and Social Liberation), while its behaviour during the events of December 1944 revealed a determination to dominate the country by force. As Churchill told the Commons, 'Democracy is no harlot to be picked up in the street by a man with a Tommy gun.'[48]

Meanwhile, the British Embassy in Athens was under siege. A large pink building on Kefisia Boulevard, easily identified by the Union Jack flying from the roof, it was an obvious target for snipers, whose bullets, the Ambassador reflected, made the same noise as a 'ball hitting a fives court'.[49] One day, Macmillan's Private Secretary, John Wyndham, decided to go skipping in the Embassy garden:

> I hadn't been skipping very long when ping, a bullet landed at my feet. I looked up and there was a man on a neighbouring rooftop aiming a rifle at me. He kept on taking pot-shots at me while I darted about trying to avoid them. Osbert Lancaster [the Embassy Press Secretary and cartoonist] appeared at the French windows and called out: 'What *are* you doing?' I explained that a man up there was trying to kill me. Osbert said: 'Hang on!' and disappeared. Presently, he reappeared at the French windows shouting: 'Keep him in play; we've summoned the military to come and pick him off.' By

this time I was getting rather fed up. The Ambassador, the Ambassadress, Mr Macmillan and various members of the Embassy staff now appeared at the window, shouting, 'Keep it up, keep it up.' This I did. At one stage I dived into the border, only to hear the Ambassadress cry from behind the French window: 'Oh, John, not the dahlias!' . . . [Finally], an armoured car lumbered up and the man was picked off . . . We then got on with our work.[50]*

Macmillan had returned to Athens on 11 December, accompanied by Field Marshal Alexander, freshly appointed Supreme Allied Commander for the Mediterranean. With ELAS in possession of four-fifths of the city and Piraeus, the latter's assessment of the military situation was bleak: 'Your seaport is cut off, your airport can only be reached by tank or armoured car, you are outnumbered, your dumps are surrounded and you have three days' ammunition. I can put that right in time but it may take a fortnight.'[51]

Convinced that a political solution had to be found – even as reinforcements were rushed from Italy – Macmillan and Alexander recommended that the King be prevailed upon to appoint the Archbishop of Athens, Damaskinos Papendreou, regent. This solution – which would provide a new figure of authority in Athens and dispel the accusation that the British were planning to restore the King by force – had been knocking about since the autumn of 1943. It had foundered because it proved unacceptable to King George and because Churchill *and* Roosevelt refused to give up the King. Since then, Churchill had developed the erroneous belief that the Archbishop was 'a quisling placed there by the Germans . . . longing to be Head of State'.[52]† Nevertheless, he and Eden saw the King on

* Although probably exaggerated, this anecdote captures the Gilbert and Sullivan side of the Embassy siege, during which some fifty British men and women camped in rooms and corridors at the back of the house. Macmillan increased the jollity of an otherwise tense situation by breaking into the previous Ambassador's wine cellar. 'I have decided that in sieges it is permissible to drink the former Ambassador's champagne,' he wrote in his diary.
† In fact, Damaskinos had done his best to protect his flock against German reprisals and, in March 1943, publicly condemned the deportation of Greek Jews. When the local SS commander, Jürgen Stroop, threatened to have him executed

12 and 14 December and, at the urging of the War Cabinet, asked him to relinquish his authority. When the monarch refused, Churchill returned his attention to the military situation and to pleading with Roosevelt for a statement of support. Although the former would slowly improve, the President maintained a disapproving silence throughout December.

On Christmas Eve, Churchill decided to fly to Athens to try and resolve the crisis himself. Hitler had recently launched his surprise counteroffensive through the Ardennes and British forces could not remain in Greece indefinitely. At 3 p.m. on Christmas Day the Prime Minister landed at Kalamaki airfield and within two hours a plan had been devised to hold a conference of all the parties, under the chairmanship of Damaskinos. This 'pestilent priest', as Churchill was still referring to him, was currently in bed – the only place in the powerless city where one could keep warm – but was roused by Leeper and presented himself at HMS *Ajax* (where Churchill was staying) at 7 p.m. in full regalia.[53] Unfortunately, his arrival coincided with a Yuletide fancy dress party and some of the ship's company mistook the immensely tall Archbishop – complete with black beard, robes, staff and mitre – for a fellow reveller. Luckily, the captain intervened before any serious injury could be done and the cleric was hastily shown into the boardroom. Churchill, despite his prejudices, took to Damaskinos, who had that day issued an encyclical condemning ELAS for taking thousands of civilian hostages (several of whom were shot each day) and who promptly accepted the Prime Minister's invitation to chair the proposed conference. This took place in the Ministry of Foreign Affairs, illuminated (due to the lack of power) by six hurricane lamps. Earlier in the day, the *Ajax* had been straddled by enemy shells and, as Churchill left the British Embassy, there was a burst of machine gun fire down Kefisia Boulevard. It was probably the closest he came to death during the Second World War.

The conference was due to begin at 4 p.m. Just before the

---

by firing squad, the Archbishop replied, 'According to the traditions of the Greek Orthodox Church, our prelates are hanged, not shot. Please respect our traditions.'

appointed time, however, a message was received stating that the ELAS delegates were delayed. Some wondered if they would come at all and Churchill was well into his introductory remarks when, as Colville recorded, 'there were noises off and three shabby desperados, who had been searched and almost stripped before being allowed to enter, came into the dimly lit conference room'.[54] The British delegation rose but the members of the Greek Government and of the other political parties remained firmly seated. Churchill would have shaken the ELAS delegates by the hand had it not been for Alexander's bodily intervention. They were Dimitris Partsalidis (the General Secretary of the EAM), Georgios Siantos (Secretary of the Communist Party) and General Manolis Mandakas (commander of ELAS forces in Attica). 'The contrast between these three red-faced, hale representatives from the barricades and the aged Greek elder statesmen, one of whom had to be carried to his seat,' relayed Alexander's political adviser, Harold Caccia, to his wife, 'was not encouraging.' The saving grace was the Archbishop: a 'vigorous medieval prelate of some six foot four or more. Apart from him the only other man to catch the eye was the ex-dictator [Nikolaos] Plastiras, who sat rigidly throughout the proceedings and whose only recorded remark later in the meeting was to silence Partsalidis with the words, "Sit down, butcher." '[55]

Churchill assured the delegates that Britain had no intention of interfering in Greece's internal affairs. 'Whether Greece is a monarchy or a republic is a matter for Greeks and Greeks alone to decide.' But Britain could not stand by and allow Greece to descend into anarchy; not when her troops had been invited into the country by the legitimate Government (of which EAM was a part) to expel the Germans and ensure order. After brief remarks by Eden and Alexander and a rather more prolix speech by Papandreou, Partsalidis rose and paid tribute to 'our great ally, England'.[56] Considering that his words were accompanied by the sound of British Beaufighters strafing ELAS strongholds and near constant rifle fire, the irony was palpable. Churchill then got up and, announcing that they would now leave the Greeks to their deliberations, began shaking hands with the Greek Government delegates. When he reached the ELAS representatives he paused. 'Can no one introduce me to these

gentlemen?' he asked. The Prime Ministerial hand was extended
and the Communists took it, making low, deferential, bows as they
did so. 'We have begun the work,' Churchill enjoined the remaining
company. 'See that you finish it.'[57]

This they did not do. Although all parties (including the monarchists) agreed to the appointment of Damaskinos as Regent, the
Communists made unacceptable demands, including 40–50 per cent
representation in the new government. Crucially, they refused to
disband ELAS before elections were held or to return the hostages.
Thus, while King George proclaimed a regency on 30 December
(following heavy British pressure), fighting in Attica continued until
15 January. Over the coming weeks, the true nature of ELAS was
revealed as mass graves were discovered in previously held communist areas: the hands of the victims tied behind their backs,
the burn marks of a revolver discharged at close range still clearly
visible. Over 200 British soldiers had died in the Battle of Athens,
alongside 3,480 Greek Government troops and gendarmes and 2,
000–3,000 ELAS combatants. Some would continue to criticise
Churchill's actions. Yet there seems little doubt that his decision to
commit British troops saved Greece from protracted civil war or
a communist takeover, at least temporarily.* Certainly, the enthusiasm with which he was received by a crowd of 40,000–50,000
Athenians when he returned to the Greek capital a month later
belied the EAM claim to represent the majority of the Greek
people. On 18 January 1945, he rebuked his detractors in what Colville considered his best oratorical effort 'since 1941 or even 1940'.[58]
There had been no instance in his experience, Churchill told the
House of Commons:

> Where a British government has been so maligned and its motives
> so traduced . . . by important organs of the press . . . We went to
> Greece . . . on the invitation of a Greek Government in which all

---

* Fighting between the Communists and Government forces resumed in March
1946 and continued until the autumn of 1949. Although precise figures are impossible to obtain, well over 100,000 Greeks were killed in the Civil War, which saw
atrocities committed by both sides.

parties, even the Communists, were represented ... We came with good gifts in our hands, stability and assistance ... We brought food, clothing and supplies ... We were received with flowers and cheers and other expressions of rapture and we British, the wicked British ... busied ourselves in the distribution of supplies throughout those parts of the country to which we had access ... For three or four days, or more, it was a struggle to prevent a hideous massacre in the centre of Athens, in which all forms of government would have been swept away and naked, triumphant Trotskyism installed ... However, by the skin of our teeth and thanks to the resolution of the handful of British soldiers on the spot, the assailants were hurled back and Athens, and, as I firmly believe, Greek freedom were saved.

He had chosen his words carefully. 'Trotskyites', he told MPs, seemed the correct definition and 'has the advantage of being equally hated in Russia'. Earlier in his speech, he had drawn attention to the fact that British military intervention in Greece had been approved by 'both our great Allies'.[59] Yet whilst Roosevelt had refused to lift a finger to stem American criticism, Stalin had adhered to the terms of the percentages agreement.* Neither ELAS nor the KKE (the Greek Communist Party) received even a modicum of Soviet support during the crisis. On the contrary, the Kremlin made its disapproval plain when Soviet authorities arrested Petros Rousos, a senior Greek Communist attempting to reach Moscow to solicit aid, and deposited him back on the Greek frontier. No word of censure regarding British action appeared in the Soviet press, while the head of the Soviet Military Mission to Greece, Lieutenant-Colonel Grigory Popov, made his allegiance clear by requesting a British armed guard to accompany his movements.[60]

Churchill, therefore, had reason to be grateful to Stalin. When the Foreign Office drew attention to the Soviet policy of deporting tens of thousands of Romanians of German descent to work in Russian labour camps in mid-January, he defended the Kremlin

---

* 'How the British can dare such a thing!' FDR allegedly exclaimed during the battle for Athens. 'The lengths which they will go to hang on to the past!'

on the grounds of Soviet suffering (not least at the hands of the Romanians) but more importantly because of 'what we promised about leaving Romania's fate to a large extent in Russian hands'.[61] Greece may have been 'saved' but the price was the subjugation of Romania, Bulgaria, Hungary and, probably, Yugoslavia. The fact that there was little the West could do to prevent this remains the foremost argument in favour of the percentages agreement. Better to save one Balkan country, Churchill reasoned, than to allow them all to fall under Moscow's sway. Yet it was a far cry from the Atlantic Charter and boded ill for the post-war world. Spheres of influence may have worked in the past but they had required the balance of power to keep them from expanding. Now, as 1944 turned into 1945, the power dynamic was looking distinctly imbalanced, with the Soviet Union increasingly dominant in Europe, the British Empire in visible decline and the United States looking forward to withdrawing her troops to the far side of the Atlantic at the earliest possible date.* The scene was thus set for the final meeting of the Big Three at the Black Sea resort of Yalta, in Crimea.

---

* 'Don't ask me to keep any American forces in France. I just cannot do it!' Roosevelt had warned Churchill in February 1944. 'I would have to bring them all back home. As I suggested before, I denounce and protest the paternity of Belgium, France and Italy. You really ought to bring up and discipline your own children. In view of the fact that they may be your bulwark in future days, you should at least pay for their schooling now!'

XXIX

Yalta

We seemed to be friends.

Winston S. Churchill, 1951[1]

The *Sacred Cow* landed on the makeshift airfield at Saki shortly after noon on 3 February 1945. A few minutes later, the Prime Minister arrived in another Skymaster. Greeted by Molotov, a military band and a guard of honour, the British party – which included Eden, Cadogan and the Prime Minister's second daughter, Sarah Oliver – then watched as the President was lowered in his wheelchair from his aircraft by means of a specially installed lift. Everyone was shocked by Roosevelt's appearance. 'His face was . . . a sort of yellow, waxen and very drawn, very thin,' recalled the British translator, Hugh Lunghi.[2] Churchill thought him 'very frail', almost 'transparent', while the Prime Minister's doctor, Lord Moran, correctly diagnosed 'hardening of the arteries of the brain in an advanced stage'.[3]

After inspecting the Soviet troops, the dignitaries and their entourages set off on the near-80-mile drive to Yalta, on the southern tip of the Crimean peninsula. The entire route was lined with Red Army soldiers at 300-yard intervals, who snapped to attention as the cavalcade of black Lend-Lease Packard and ZIS limousines passed. Anna Boettiger (née Roosevelt), who was accompanying her father, was impressed by these 'smart' figures in their long, thick overcoats.[4] Less impressive was the state of the roads, which were so strewn with potholes that the British and Americans had to bump along at 20 miles per hour. Admiral Leahy complained that the journey was 'breaking every bone in his body', while Churchill, on being told that they had only travelled an hour, exclaimed, 'Christ! Five more of this.'[5] The snow-covered steppes were flat and dreary and all around were the vestiges of conflict. The landscape was littered with 'burned-out tanks, gutted buildings and destroyed German freight trains', recalled the head of Roosevelt's Secret Service detail, Mike Reilly.[6] Sarah Oliver thought the vista 'as bleak as the soul in despair', while Roosevelt was so shocked by the scenes of destruction that he told Stalin during their first meeting that he 'was more bloodthirsty in regard to the Germans than he had been a year ago' and hoped the Marshal would again propose a toast to the 'execution of 50,000 officers of the German Army'.[7]

The Americans were housed in the Livadia Palace, where the talks were to be held. Built in 1911 as a summer retreat for the Tsar and his family, this Italianate mansion, 4 miles outside the city, enjoyed panoramic views of the Black Sea and the surrounding mountains. 'Pug' Ismay thought the Livadia 'quite lovely' but Pierson Dixon found the setting 'melancholy . . . steeped in memories of the Romanovs'. 'Even the road along which we drove every day was built by them and the whole landscape, with its trees and boulders, seemed still to belong to an imperial and luxurious aristocracy,' he wrote to his wife.[8] His colleague Valentine Lawford agreed. 'There is an air of sorrow brooding over the place, particularly the gardens that go down to the sea,' he noted.[9]

The British were billeted in the Vorontsov Palace, half an hour's drive from the Livadia. An incongruous blend of baronial castle and Moorish palace, this Gothic-Arabian pile had been built by Prince Mikhail Vorontsov, a hero of the Napoleonic Wars and later Governor of Crimea, in the mid-nineteenth century. Described by Cadogan as a 'house of indescribable ugliness', with furnishings of 'almost terrifying hideosity', it had served as Generalfeldmarschall Erich von Manstein's headquarters during the German occupation.[10] This meant that it had remained relatively intact. Although every single window had had to be replaced, many of the portraits and some of the furniture were still in their original setting. The Livadia, on the other hand, had been completely gutted by the retreating Germans. For three weeks, an army of carpenters, plumbers, painters and Romanian POWs had worked twelve-hour shifts to make the Palace and surrounding sanatoria habitable. Overseen by the head of the NKVD, Lavrenti Beria, the result was a triumph of totalitarian planning and terror. More than 1,500 railway carriages carrying wood, glass, food and furniture stripped from the capital's hotels, made the three-day journey from Moscow to Yalta. The rugs in the President's suite were changed four times; the walls of his bathroom repainted seven times.

Yet not even the feared head of the secret police could expand the size of the buildings. The result was severe overcrowding, with eight American generals in one room, sixteen colonels in another and forty lesser ranks in another. The dearth of bathrooms was an even greater problem. Each morning, the Chiefs of Staff would send their batmen to represent them in the queue for the ablutions. Chief of the Air Staff Sir Charles Portal thought it unacceptable for inhabitants to lock the bathroom door when the lavatory lay beyond. One morning, Leslie Hollis watched as the frustrated Air Marshal stood on a chair to see who was taking so long in the bath through the fanlight. 'It's Jumbo,' he said, clambering down, dejectedly. A few minutes later, the elephantine figure of Field-Marshal Sir Henry Maitland Wilson emerged in a vast towel and hurried away.[11] There was a shortage of desks and almost everyone, from Churchill down, was bitten by bedbugs. 'If we had spent ten years on research, we could not have found a worse place in the world,' the Prime Minister grumbled.[12]

★

The Yalta Conference is considered the most important and certainly the most controversial of all the wartime summits. To many – particularly the populations of eastern Europe, Chinese Nationalists and American Republicans – Yalta soon became a synonym for gullibility, duplicity and betrayal. The arch-isolationist Senator Robert Taft charged the American delegation, in a radio address of 1951, with having taken the position:

> That Soviet Russia was a peace-loving democracy, as much interested in liberty and justice as the American people themselves . . . They accepted the promises of Stalin that he would establish freedom in Poland and other countries, although he had never kept a promise

and was as much of an aggressor in Poland as Hitler was. They set him up in control of Berlin, Prague and Vienna and American troops were turned back from Berlin and Prague because of the agreements made at Yalta. The Administration established Stalin in Manchuria, contrary to every principle of American foreign policy since the days of John Hay [US Secretary of State, 1898–1905] and contrary to our obligation to our ally who had so long fought the Japanese.[13]

William Bullitt, Roosevelt's first Ambassador to Moscow, accused the President of 'wishful appeasement', while the Australian historian Chester Wilmot dubbed Yalta 'Stalin's greatest victory'.[14]

In fact, the decisions made at Yalta had far less significance than those taken at previous meetings between 1941 and 1945, while accusations of 'betrayal' rest on the unfounded supposition that there were genuine alternatives. By February 1945, the Red Army was only 43 miles from Berlin. Having begun a general offensive on 12 January, the Soviet 1st Belorussian Front and the 1st Ukrainian Front had advanced rapidly, capturing Warsaw on 17 January and Łódź two days later. On 23 January, Soviet forces entered Elbing in East Prussia and on 30 January they crossed the Oder. Estonia, Latvia, Lithuania, Poland, Romania, Bulgaria, Yugoslavia and Hungary were already under the Soviet sway. The Western Allies could try to temper Stalin's influence, as Roosevelt attempted to do, or cut deals, as Churchill had at Moscow, but they could not reverse the Russian advance. In this context, the crucial decisions were not those taken at Yalta but those of 1942 and the Casablanca Conference of January 1943, when Churchill had persuaded Roosevelt to delay the cross-Channel assault in favour of the invasion of French North Africa and then of Italy. The fact that this went against the wishes of the Soviets, who had been begging the democracies to reinvade the Continent since the autumn of 1941, is among the ironies of the politico-military dilemma. The Western powers had let the Soviet Union pay the blood-price for defeating the Wehrmacht and were now reaping the consequences.

Furthermore, Yalta was not a 'peace conference' like Versailles, nor a peacetime settlement of a territorial dispute like Munich. In February 1945, the Anglo-American armies were still 370 miles from

Berlin, on the far side of the Rhine. Eisenhower's forces had only recently regained the initiative following Generalfeldmarschall von Rundstedt's Ardennes offensive, while the British 8th Army and the American 5th Army were yet to reach Bologna. More significant still was the need to defeat Japan. Although MacArthur's forces were making slow progress in the Philippines, the surrender of Hirohito's armies was still estimated to be anywhere between eighteen months and two years away. (The successful test of the atomic bomb in Alamogordo, New Mexico, on 16 July would radically alter this forecast.) To hasten their capitulation and save American lives, the US Chiefs of Staff insisted upon the need for Soviet assistance. The USSR, according to a JCS memorandum dated 23 January, would be required to tie down the million-strong Japanese army in Manchuria and provide bases for US air forces in Siberia.[15] Roosevelt needed no convincing. From Pearl Harbor to his death on 12 April 1945, his priority was to defeat the Axis in the shortest possible time and if political concessions had to be made to achieve this, then so be it. Unlike Churchill and Stalin, FDR continued to put the war before the coming peace, while the President's overriding political aim also behoved a consensual approach at Yalta: the maintenance of Great Power co-operation in the post-war period.

In many ways, the Yalta Conference – codenamed Argonaut – mimicked the dynamics and choreography of the Tehran Conference. As in 1943, Churchill tried to meet Roosevelt beforehand to concert strategy and, as in 1943, FDR refused. Equally distressing was the President's suggestion that the tripartite conference should only last five or six days. Churchill was appalled. Regarding the meeting as of cardinal importance to the post-war world, with major issues such as the occupation of Germany, the role of France, the liberty of eastern Europe and the new international organisation to settle, he pressed Roosevelt to allow Secretary of State Stettinius and the American Chiefs of Staff to join their British counterparts on Malta, prior to their departure for the Black Sea. 'I do not see any other way of realising our hopes about world organisation in five or six days,' he cabled the President on 10 January 1945, 'even the Almighty took seven.'[16]

On 30 January, Churchill and Eden had arrived on Malta. The Foreign Secretary was just as anxious as the Prime Minister to confer with the Americans before the formal sessions. 'I am much worried that the whole business will be chaotic,' he confided to his diary, 'Stalin being the only one of the three who has a clear view of what he wants and is a tough negotiator. PM is all emotion in these matters, FDR vague and jealous of others.'[17] The following evening, Stettinius and Hopkins arrived. To British relief, they appeared 'disarmingly frank and . . . pliable to our point of view'.[18] 'We found ourselves in complete agreement on all major points,' noted Eden. 'They seemed to me to give rather too much weight to [the] World Council and too little to Poland, in the sense that unless the Russians can be persuaded or compelled to treat Poland with some decency there will not be a World Council that is worth much. But this is more a matter of emphasis than anything else since they seem fully alive to [the] seriousness of [the] Polish issue.'[19]

Within a few hours, however, British optimism evaporated as Roosevelt arrived but refused to discuss the impending conference. Instead, he spent most of his time on Malta sightseeing. The State Department's Soviet expert, Chip Bohlen, had assured the President that prior consultation with the British would not perturb the Russians (who expected it) but Roosevelt was adamant: 'he did not want to arouse Stalin's suspicions'.[20] After both lunch and dinner on board the USS *Quincy*, during which Churchill and Eden found it impossible to get near business, the Foreign Secretary rounded on Hopkins, pointing out that they were about to enter a 'decisive conference and had so far neither agreed what we would discuss nor how to handle matters with a Bear who would certainly know his mind'.[21] Hopkins, who had lost his old intimacy with Roosevelt and was desperately ill at Yalta, tried to persuade the President, through Anna Boettiger, to meet the Prime Minister prior to the opening session of the conference but FDR refused. He would not see Churchill before the start of formal proceedings. But he would see Stalin.

Stalin had arrived at Yalta ahead of his guests, having travelled by armoured train from Moscow. Ensconced in the Yusupov Palace in Koreiz – once the property of Prince Felix Yusupov, one of the assassins of Rasputin – he was protected by a bevy of bodyguards, as well as a bunker that could withstand a direct hit by more than

1,000 pounds of explosive. As Eden had predicted, the despot had come to the Black Sea with a clear set of demands. He wanted Germany to be occupied and dismembered. He wanted reparations to compensate the Soviet Union and rebuild her economy. He wanted territorial concessions in the Far East. And he wanted to ensure that the Soviet Union could not be outmanoeuvred in the new international organisation. Although Soviet diplomatic preparations for Yalta were less extensive than they had been for the Foreign Ministers' Conference of October 1943 and for Tehran, this simply reflected the fact that the most important of Stalin's war aims – the domination of eastern Europe – had already been achieved thanks to the victories of the Red Army.

Still, the paranoid Marshal was leaving nothing to chance, receiving reports from Soviet doctors stationed at Saki airfield on Roosevelt's appearance and benefiting from dozens of listening devices installed across the palaces by Sergo Beria. Although the American and British delegations were warned to expect Soviet eavesdropping they continued their conversations with reckless candour. Roosevelt frequently 'spoke against the English', recalled the NKVD boss's son, who wondered if this was deliberate misdirection designed to appeal to Stalin.[22] Even more valuable were the briefings the Soviet dictator received on 23 and 28 January on British and American aims for the conference, gleaned from confidential documents stolen from the Foreign Office in London and the British Embassy in Washington by Guy Burgess and Donald Maclean. As the effective secretary of the US–UK commission on the political and economic future of liberated Europe in Washington, Maclean had access to almost all papers pertaining to the post-war world, while also being able to supply his Soviet handlers with a summary of Roosevelt's and Churchill's discussions at the Second Quebec Conference.*

---

* The American delegation even included a Soviet agent, the State Department's Director of Political Affairs, Alger Hiss. Yet, as recently uncovered Soviet documents have shown, Hiss was working for the military branch of Soviet intelligence and only became known to the political branch after Yalta. His presence at the conference does not seem to have helped the Soviets.

'Franklin had high hopes that at this conference he could make real progress in strengthening the personal relationship between himself and Marshal Stalin,' wrote Eleanor Roosevelt of her husband's preparations for Yalta.[23] As at Tehran, FDR had asked Stalin to call on him for a private meeting before the first plenary session and, as at Tehran, the Vozhd was happy to oblige. 'The two leaders greeted each other as old friends,' recalled Bohlen. 'Smiling broadly, the President grasped Stalin by the hand and shook it warmly. Stalin, his face cracked in one of his rare, if slight, smiles, expressed pleasure at seeing the President again.'[24] The conversation mirrored their *tête-à-tête* at Tehran. Roosevelt flattered Stalin by predicting that the Russians would reach Berlin before the Americans took Manila and flaunted his differences with Churchill by saying that he hoped the Marshal would again propose the summary execution of German officers – the 'jest' that had so appalled the Prime Minister at Tehran.[25]

The conference, which opened in the ballroom at the Livadia Palace at 5 p.m. on 4 February, had no fixed agenda. The effect was to render the discussions somewhat haphazard, with most issues being referred to the Foreign Ministers for closer examination. The topics included the progress of the war, the future of Germany, the role of France, the proposed international organisation, the Dardanelles, prisoners of war, Iran and Poland. Contrary to Cold War critiques, the democracies scored some important successes. The British were anxious for France to be one of the occupying powers of post-war Germany. The Soviets were opposed. In December 1944, de Gaulle had visited Moscow to negotiate a defensive treaty. Seeking to raise his country's diplomatic status, he also sought to win Stalin's approval for his desire to annex the Rhineland and the Saar. The Free French diplomat Jean Laloy, who acted as interpreter, was appalled. Such an act would 'permanently poison' Franco-German relations, leading inevitably to another war, he argued.[26] Fortunately for Laloy, Stalin refused to commit himself. Less fortunately, he tried to insist on the recognition of the Lublin Committee as the Provisional Government of Poland as the precondition for any Franco-Soviet pact.

In his memoirs, de Gaulle made great play of his rejection of this

demand, contrasting his unbreachable principles, which nevertheless resulted in a Franco-Soviet Treaty of Mutual Assistance, with
Anglo-American pusillanimity at Yalta. In fact, he went some way
towards accommodating Stalin's wishes. Although he refused to
recognise the Polish communists – infuriating Stalin and amazing
Molotov – he agreed to meet them and to an exchange of representatives. Indeed, had the Vozhd been prepared to support de Gaulle's
territorial requests it is possible that he would have gone further.
'My intention in going to Moscow was not simply to exchange
signatures with Stalin on a piece of paper,' the General told his
aide-de-camp two years later, 'I wanted to see what he was really
thinking about the Rhine. And I was ready, deep down, to engage
myself to support him in Poland, Romania etc. in exchange for
categorical support from him in our combat for the Rhine.'[27] The
ruthless pursuit of self-interest was not only a Soviet vice.

Stalin found de Gaulle an 'awkward and stubborn man'.[28] It was
'unrealistic', he told Roosevelt, of the General to expect France to
be treated as an equal of the three main allies when her contribution
to the war had been 'very small' and in 1940 she had 'not fought at
all'.[29] When the question of a French zone of occupation came up
on the second day of the conference, he made plain his opposition
to France having a say in the control of Germany. Churchill put the
French case strongly. This owed nothing to de Gaulle. When Eden
had suggested that the General – now recognised as head of the
Provisional Government of France – be invited to attend the conference, the Prime Minister had vetoed the proposal. 'I cannot think
of anything more unpleasant and impossible than having this men-
acing and hostile man in our midst, always trying to make himself
a reputation in France by claiming a position far above what France
occupies and making faces at the Allies who are doing the work,' he
wrote.[30] Yet he never wavered in his belief that France was a great
nation that ought to be restored. More importantly, with Roosevelt
threatening to withdraw American troops two years after the termination of hostilities, the British would need the French to share
the burdens of occupation and mitigate the imbalance of power.

Positioning himself as mediator between Churchill and Stalin,
Roosevelt supported the Prime Minister's plea for a French zone (to

be carved out of the British and the American zones) but sided with Stalin in opposing French participation in the Allied Control Commission. This stance, as the President's advisers subsequently persuaded him, was ludicrous. The French could not be expected to contribute troops to the occupation of Germany without having some say on policy, nor would they agree to. At the seventh plenary session on 10 February, Roosevelt announced that he had changed his mind, whereupon Stalin raised his arms above his head and said, '*Sdayus*' ('I surrender').[31]

The British were also successful in postponing the decision on the dismemberment of Germany. At the second plenary session, Stalin recalled that the President and Prime Minister had supported the division of Germany at Tehran and enquired whether they adhered to this position. Although the Soviets were yet to decide on the number of German states they wished to create, dismemberment represented one of their most important and long-standing war aims. As early as November 1941, with the Wehrmacht closing in on Moscow and the diplomatic corps being evacuated to Kuibyshev, Molotov had informed Maisky that the Politburo believed that 'Austria should be separated from Germany . . . and that Germany itself, including Prussia, should be divided into a series of more or less independent states so as to provide a guarantee for the peace of European states'.[32]

Roosevelt supported the Soviet proposal. Recalling his childhood visits to the only recently unified Germany, he made a 'rambling and inconclusive statement' about the virtues of Bavaria and Hesse-Darmstadt (a landgraviate that had been abolished in 1806) to which the Soviets listened with 'polite indifference' and the British with 'slight signs of boredom'.[33] Although Churchill had indeed supported the dismemberment of Germany at Tehran – in particular the excision of Prussia – he had since encountered opposition from the Foreign Office as well as from members of his Government. With a general election looming, he was averse to committing himself on this contentious issue.

'In principle all were agreed on the dismemberment of Germany,' the Prime Minister declared. 'But the actual method was much too complicated to settle here in five or six days. It would require a very searching examination of the historical, ethnographic and economic facts and would need prolonged consideration by a special committee.'[34] This view carried. Although Stalin kept returning to the issue, Roosevelt suggested that the conference ask the Foreign Ministers to consider the problem and submit a recommendation as to the best method for studying plans for the division of Germany. The following day, Molotov tried to tie the British 'hand and foot' to dismemberment but Eden, who was against creating multiple German states that would strive for reunification, held his ground. When Maisky (now one of several Deputy Commissars and Stalin's interpreter for the conference) complained that he did not understand the Foreign Secretary's attitude, Eden snapped at him, reminding the former Ambassador that Britain was still an independent power. 'My obstinacy did good, I think,' noted Eden in his diary. 'Anyway, after luncheon Stalin greeted me most warmly . . . and said: "You have won again." '[35]

Ultimately, although it was decided to include the word 'dismemberment' in the surrender documents, the precise meaning of this term was left to be decided by a tripartite commission in London. On 7 March, Eden, the Soviet Ambassador, Fedor Gusev, and the American Ambassador, John Winant, met to consider the issue. But now Stalin was having doubts. Gusev lacked instructions from Moscow and, on 24 March, Molotov asked the Ambassador to inform the commission that the Soviet Government viewed dismemberment 'not as an obligatory plan . . . but as a possible option to put pressure on Germany'.[36] Six weeks later, in his address to the Russian people following the German surrender, Stalin declared that the USSR was not going to 'dismember or destroy Germany'.[37] What prompted this startling about-turn remains a matter of speculation. Yet it seems likely that Stalin did not wish to assume the responsibility, and therefore the opprobrium, for a policy with which his allies disagreed, while a united Germany was more attractive from the point of view of extracting reparations.

The Soviet demand for reparations was understandable. The Germans had wreaked unimaginable damage during four years of war and occupation against the USSR. Equally understandable was Western opposition to vast indemnities. Haunted by memories of the 1920s, when the victors had had to furnish Germany with loans in order to receive only a fraction of the 50 billion marks they demanded, while simultaneously sowing the seeds of lasting resentment, both Roosevelt and Churchill approached the issue with trepidation. Responding to the Soviet demand for $10 billion in reparations – half taken in industrial equipment, half in payments, spread over ten years – Churchill recalled how the Allies had indulged themselves with similarly fantastic figures at the end of the last war but that these had 'turned out to be a myth'.[38] If he could think of a way that the British people could benefit from reparations, he would gladly concede the point but he had grave doubts on the matter: 'once bit, twice shy'.[39]

Roosevelt agreed that the financial settlement that emerged from the First World War had been a fiasco. He was, however, in favour of reparations 'in kind' to the Soviet Union, whose people, he argued, should not have a lower standard of living than the Germans. On 20 January, Maisky had made it clear to Harriman that these included plans to transfer millions of Germans to the USSR to work as forced labour. At the second plenary session on 5 February, Roosevelt asked Stalin about this but the despot, not wishing to get into a debate on slave labour before the democracies had conceded the wider issue, claimed that the Soviet Government was not yet ready to discuss the matter.

Churchill succeeded in limiting Western acquiescence to Stalin's reparations demands to the creation of another tripartite commission to consider the question. On 9 February – the sixth day of the conference – however, Roosevelt informed Stettinius that he had decided to meet the Soviets on this point. The US Government, Stettinius informed Molotov and Eden at noon, was willing to accept the principle of reparations in kind as well as the Soviet figure of $20 billion ($10 billion for the USSR, $10 billion for the other Allies) to serve as the basis for discussions. The British were horrified. 'We consider $20 billion . . . as far too great', the War Cabinet telegraphed Churchill the following day. It was 'roughly the equivalent of Germany's pre-war gross exports (i.e. not allowing for any imports) in an average year' and it was not to be believed that this could be paid by a Germany that had been 'bombed, defeated [and] perhaps dismembered'.[40]

Throughout the plenary session on 10 February, Churchill held the line against an increasingly irritated Stalin. At the dinner at the Vorontsov Palace that evening, however – with the atmosphere improved and 'Winston . . . always a bit inclined to weep tears of brandy in gratitude for anything he interprets as a friendly gesture from his great compeer', according to Valentine Lawford – the Prime Minister gave way.[41] Stalin said that he feared having to return to Moscow and 'tell the Soviet people they were not going to get any reparations because the British were opposed to it'. 'On the contrary', Churchill responded; he 'very much hoped that Russia would receive reparations in large quantities but he remembered the last war when they [the Allies] had placed the figure at more than the capacity of Germany to pay'.[42] The principle of reparations in kind and the figure of $20 billion appeared in the final protocol.

Roosevelt was happy to side with the Soviets on the issue of reparations because he had achieved his two primary objectives. The first and most important was Soviet support for the world peace organisation. This had been agreed in principle at the Foreign Ministers' Conference in October 1943 but the discussions at Dumbarton Oaks had exposed differences over the use of the veto in the Security Council and the composition of the General Assembly. Neither the Soviets nor the British (nor for that matter the US military) were willing to allow the Security Council to impose sanctions by a simple majority vote. The American solution was to grant each member a veto over actual decisions but not with respect to procedure or discussions – thus allowing the voices of small nations to be heard. 'Unless this freedom of discussion in the Council is permitted,' Stettinius warned the conference on 6 February, 'the establishment of the World Organisation, which we all so earnestly desire . . . would be seriously jeopardised.'[43]

The Soviets, aware that they would be in an ideological minority within the new body and contemptuous of the rights of small nations, were sceptical. During the dinner hosted by Roosevelt on the first night of the conference, Stalin had insisted that the responsibilities of peace must rest solely with the principal Allies. 'It was ridiculous to believe', he declared, 'that Albania would have an equal voice with the three great powers who had won the war.'[44] Yet Roosevelt and Churchill succeeded in persuading Stalin that

Russia had nothing to fear and on 7 February, the dictator accepted the American formula. His price was the inclusion of at least two of the 'Soviet Republics' in the General Assembly. American hearts sank. Unlike the British Dominions, which enjoyed full sovereignty (including the right to secede from the Commonwealth), the Soviet Republics were constituents of a highly centralised, authoritarian state. If Stalin insisted on their inclusion, Roosevelt had told senators before his departure, then *he* would insist on the admission of all forty-eight American states. But Churchill, who wished to include India, supported Stalin and the President reluctantly gave way. Later, he would be criticised for bending to Soviet pressure. Yet whilst the inclusion of Ukraine and Belorussia as 'independent' members of the United Nations was patently absurd, it was a chiefly cosmetic concession. In Roosevelt's conception, the General Assembly was purely a forum for the smaller nations to 'blow off steam' and the inclusion of two Soviet constituents would not affect the deliberations or the decisions of the Security Council.[45] As a means to ensure Soviet support for the new international organisation, it was cheap at the price.

The inducements to get Stalin to join the war against Japan were far greater. The Soviet leader had made clear his willingness to participate in the Far Eastern war as early as December 1941. At Tehran, he promised to be at war with the Japanese three months after the end of the European conflict. Since then, however, the Soviets had resisted American attempts to engage in military planning. 'Antonov [Deputy Chief of Staff of the Red Army] . . . literally turned white when I mentioned the word "Japan",' recalled the head of the US Military Mission to Moscow, General John Deane.[46] In October 1944, Stalin told Harriman and Deane that the USSR would enter the war against Japan, provided the US supply the weapons and provided agreement was reached on certain 'political aspects'.[47] Two months later, the dictator was explicit. Handing Harriman a map, he stated that the Kurile Islands and lower Sakhalin should be 'returned' to Russia. He wanted to 'lease' the ports of Dairen and Port Arthur and he wanted to 'lease' the Chinese-Eastern Railway in Manchuria. Finally, he wanted the Soviet-client state of Outer Mongolia recognised as an independent entity.[48]

None of this came as a surprise to Roosevelt. Stalin had intimated his demands at Tehran and both the President and Churchill had expressed their sympathy for Russia's long-standing desire to obtain 'warm water ports'.[49] Indeed, contrary to the oft-repeated claim that Roosevelt was 'pressured' into making territorial concessions to Stalin by the US military, FDR had already decided to satisfy the despot's Far Eastern *desiderata* in the interests of future Great Power co-operation. On 12 January 1944, fresh from his sojourn at Tehran, the President had told the Pacific War Council that Stalin had agreed that Manchuria, Formosa and the Pescadores should be returned to China:

> That the Koreans are not capable of exercising and maintaining independent government and that they should be placed under a forty-year tutelage; that Russia, having no ice-free port in Siberia, is desirous of getting one and that Marshal Stalin looks with favour on making Dairen a free port for all the world . . . He wishes all of Sakhalin to be returned to Russia and to have the Kurile Islands turned over to Russia in order that they may exercise control of the straits leading to Siberia . . . It was extremely gratifying to him [Roosevelt] to find that . . . Marshal Stalin saw 'eye to eye' with him on all major problems in the Pacific and that he felt that there would be no difficulty in reaching agreements about the control of the Pacific once Japan had been completely conquered.[50]

Between Tehran and Yalta, nothing occurred to cause Roosevelt to alter his view. Although the State Department pointed out that the Kuriles had never belonged to Russia in their entirety and that southern Sakhalin contained an ethnic Japanese population of 400,000, these papers – completed in December 1944 and January 1945 – were not included in the President's Yalta briefing book. Even if they had been, it is unlikely they would have changed Roosevelt's opinion. A peaceful, satisfied Soviet Union that would co-operate with the US in Asia represented the President's long-term political goal, while US military planners believed that Soviet participation in the war in the Far East would save tens of thousands of American lives.

Nor is it true, as Churchill implied in his memoirs, that this was an entirely American project of which the British disapproved.

Eden, it is true, opposed tempting Stalin with Asian territorial concessions. Although it would be hard to reject Soviet claims to southern
Sakhalin, he wrote in a pre-Yalta memorandum, since this had been
'lost' following the Russo-Japanese War of 1904–5, Soviet penetration
of Manchuria and Korea threatened to create a 'cauldron of international dispute'.[51] Churchill disagreed. Stalin's promise to 'march
against Japan' constituted the most important statement of the Tolstoy conference, he minuted Eden on 23 October 1944, adding that it
would be 'absolutely necessary to offer Russia substantial war objectives in the Far East'.[52] Three months later, responding to the Foreign
Secretary's reiterated concerns, he was even more blunt:

> A speedy termination of the Japanese war, such as may be procured
> by the mere fact of a Russian declaration of war against Japan,
> would undoubtedly save us thousands of millions of pounds. The
> Staffs see no particular harm in the presence of Russia as a Pacific
> power. I should not be able to oppose the kind of Russian wishes
> which you mention, especially as the quid pro quo far outvalues any-
> thing we are likely to get out of China.[53]

As events transpired, it was the Foreign Secretary, not the Prime
Minister (and certainly not the President), who proved wiser on this
issue.

The Soviet military delegation refused to discuss the war in the
Far East until the issue had been addressed by the heads of government. Roosevelt accordingly asked Stalin to call on him before
the fifth plenary session on 8 February. At 3.30 p.m., the dictator
arrived at the Livadia Palace and, after various diversions, restated
his demands. Roosevelt said that he felt there would be 'no difficulty whatsoever in regard to the southern half of Sakhalin and the
Kurile Islands going to Russia at the end of the war'.[54] Concerning
Chinese territory, he was more cautious: he had not had an opportunity to discuss the Marshal's demands for a warm water port at
the end of the south Manchurian railroad, nor his desire to 'lease'
the Chinese-owned Manchurian railways, with Chiang Kai-shek.
Increasing the pressure, the despot said that if these conditions
were not met it would be difficult for him to explain to the Russian

people why the Soviet Union was declaring war on Japan. But then he offered a solution: the two leaders would simply agree the issue between themselves. Roosevelt accepted this proposal and then began to discuss Korea. Not considering the peninsula ready for independent government, he proposed a trusteeship under American, Soviet and Chinese but not British auspices. Assuming the unlikely role of defender of British interests and upholder of Great Power unity, Stalin replied that the British would certainly be offended – indeed, he feared the Prime Minister might 'kill us' – and advised the President to include them. Finally, the two leaders touched on their shared desire to create an international trusteeship for Indo-China and the importance of a power-sharing agreement between the Kuomintang and the Chinese communists. The meeting lasted half an hour.[55]

Roosevelt's speechwriter and Hopkins' biographer, Robert Sherwood, considered the Roosevelt–Stalin Asian deal the 'most assailable point in the entire Yalta record'.[56] Later, when the agreement became public, it was attacked by Republicans and other Cold War warriors as a base example of appeasement, committed behind the back of America's ally, Nationalist China. The fact that the atomic bomb – successfully tested on 16 July and dropped on Hiroshima and Nagasaki on 6 and 9 August respectively – rendered Soviet assistance in the war against Japan moot was central to these critiques. This, however, was wisdom in retrospect. Roosevelt did not know when the atomic bomb would be ready, while leading members of his entourage, most notably Admiral Leahy, doubted that it would ever work. What is not a matter of hindsight is that Roosevelt had engaged in just the sort of secret deal and territorial carve-up that both he and Cordell Hull had railed against in public and private. As to the substance of the deal, Roosevelt was uneasy about what he was doing but had decided that it was worth it to ensure Soviet–American co-operation in Asia, including on the all-important issue of preventing civil war in China. Had he succeeded, few would have questioned his tactics. But he did not. As with Munich, appeasement may be justified but only if it works.

Even more controversial – though principally in retrospect – was the agreement on prisoners of war. As the Red Army swept west-wards, tens of thousands of British and American servicemen fell into Soviet hands as the German internment camps – the majority of which were in central and eastern Europe – were overrun. Con-versely, the British and the Americans found themselves responsible for hundreds of thousands of Soviet POWs who had been forced to fight alongside the Wehrmacht or had chosen to do so, if only as a means of survival. (Of the roughly 5.7 million Soviet prisoners cap-tured by the Germans between 1941 and 1945, an estimated 3.5 million died in captivity.) The British wanted their servicemen repatriated as swiftly as possible and realised that the Soviets would demand their combatants, whom they regarded as traitors, in return. This presented an obvious dilemma. As the Secretary of State for War, Sir James Grigg, wrote to Eden on 24 August 1944:

> If we do as the Russians want and hand over all these prisoners to them whether or not the prisoners are willing to go back to Russia, we are . . . sending some of them to their death and though in war we cannot, as you point out . . . afford to be sentimental, I confess that I find the prospect somewhat revolting and I should expect public opinion to reflect the same feeling . . . On the other hand, if we don't do what the Russians wish there may be the danger that they will not be ready to co-operate in getting back speedily to us the British and other Allied prisoners who fall into their hands as they advance into Germany. Obviously, our public opinion would bitterly and rightly resent any delay in getting our men home or any infliction of unnecessary hardship on them and if the choice is between hardship to our men and death to the Russians the choice is plain.[57]

This was Eden's view. At the Tolstoy Conference in October 1944, he conceded to Molotov the right of the Soviet Government to receive not only all Soviet prisoners of war (despite the USSR not being a signatory to the Geneva Convention, protecting POWs against maltreatment) but all 'Soviet citizens', including Polish, Estonian, Latvian, Lithuanian, Ukrainian and White Russian refugees. During the next three months, shipping shortages ensured that few POWs could be repatriated to the USSR, while Soviet authorities refused to allow Western officers even to visit the camps in which American and British Commonwealth prisoners were held. This unsatisfactory situation determined Eden to make a fresh effort at Yalta. 'We greatly hope that an agreement can be concluded before the Conference breaks up,' he wrote to Churchill in an *aide-mémoire* on 9 February. 'We shall be grateful if the Soviet authorities will communicate all information available to them about repatriated prisoners of war and civilians in their hands. The delay in doing so is causing great embarrassment. A list of camps overrun is attached. The men may number as many as 50,000 . . . We are making sacrifices to provide shipping . . . to transport the Soviet citizens from the United Kingdom and the Mediterranean. We consider that ships used for repatriating Soviet citizens should be fully used on the return journey for bringing back British Commonwealth prisoners and civilians.'[58]

Up to this point, the Americans had shown none of the enthusiasm of their British allies for a quid pro quo on prisoners of war. But Eden won Stettinius round to the British perspective at Malta and the negotiations proceeded without regard for the Geneva Convention. On 11 February, the last day of the conference, the British and the Americans signed separate agreements with the Soviets that stipulated:

> All Soviet citizens liberated by the forces operating under [British/] American command and all [British/] American subjects liberated by the forces operating under Soviet command will, without delay after their liberation, be separated from enemy prisoners of war and will be maintained separately from them in camps or points of concentration until they have been handed over to the Soviet or [British/] American authorities, as the case may be, at places agreed upon between those authorities.[59]

As several historians have pointed out, the agreement made no mention of *forcible* repatriation: that is, the repatriation of prisoners of war or 'Soviet citizens' against their will. Yet this became the tragic reality, as British and American soldiers, ordered to 'fulfil' the Yalta agreement, tricked and bludgeoned hundreds of thousands of men, women and children onto trucks and ships. This led to horrific scenes, with many repatriates, aware of the fate that lay in store for them, preferring suicide to being handed over to the NKVD. Allied servicemen, some of whom came close to mutiny, found the repatriations a loathsome task. 'With few exceptions, the men, whether claiming Polish or Soviet nationality, protest violently at being sent back to the Soviet Union or even to their homes in Poland,' wrote Brigadier Roy Firebrace, charged with assessing cases of disputed nationality, to the Foreign Office's Christopher Warner in April 1945. 'A large number insisted on giving reasons for their not wishing to go back and related with a wealth of detail their experiences in the Soviet Union or Poland after the entry of the Red Army. It was one long story of shootings, arrest, ill treatment and deportation of families . . . There were cases of kulaks' sons who had been chased from pillar to post and one young man stated that he had been in prison from the age of twelve until released to join the Red Army. Most of them said they preferred death to returning to the Soviet Union and some even invited the British to shoot them in preference to handing them over. I have never in my life seen such human misery or such despair.'[60]

One month later, a Canadian liaison officer recorded the scene following the arrival of a cargo of repatriated Russian POWs at Odessa:

> The Soviet authorities refused to accept any of the stretcher cases as such and even the patients who were dying were made to walk off the ship carrying their own baggage . . . The prisoner who had attempted suicide was very roughly handled and had his wound opened up and allowed to bleed. He was taken off the ship and marched behind a packing case on the docks; a shot was then heard but nothing more was seen. The other thirty-two prisoners were marched or dragged into a warehouse fifty yards from the ship and, after a lapse of fifteen minutes, automatic fire was heard coming from the warehouse; twenty minutes later a covered lorry drove out of the warehouse and headed towards the town.[61]

In all, the Allies repatriated some 2 million POWs and 'Soviet citizens' between 1945 and 1947. Many of these, such as the Russian

Liberation Army under General Andrei Vlasov or the more gen-
eric *Hilfswillige* ('willing helpers'), had fought against the Allies in
both the East and the West. Yet many others were forced labourers
or refugees. Still others were not 'Soviet citizens' at all but Russian
émigrés who had fled to central Europe in the aftermath of the
Bolshevik Revolution. As early as July 1944, Harold Macmillan, who
would later be severely criticised for his role in repatriating some
60,000 Cossacks from Austria, asked the Foreign Office to define a
'Soviet citizen'. The final response, which arrived on 6 March 1945,
was clear: a Soviet citizen was someone who had lived within the
boundaries of the USSR as they had existed before the outbreak
of war. Those who had left the Soviet Union prior to that date or
had been incorporated into Stalin's empire following the Molotov–
Ribbentrop Pact did not fall into this fatal category. But Allied
soldiers lacked the time, the expertise, the orders and, in some
instances, the inclination to differentiate. The result was that some
of those that were 'repatriated' had not seen Russia since the Tsar's
days, while others were innocent Poles, Estonians, Latvians, Lithuanians, Bessarabians and Cossacks.

★

As expected, the greatest point of contention at Yalta was Poland.
On 3 February, the Polish Prime Minister, Tomasz Arciszewski, had
sent Roosevelt a letter, begging him not to betray the Polish people.
'The whole world expects that these important discussions . . . will
result in the creation of foundations for a future peace, a peace which
should bring to nations the freedom of conscience and speech and
secure for them freedom from fear and want,' he wrote, reminding
the President of his celebrated 1941 State of the Union address. 'I
trust that these essential freedoms will also be granted to our nation
which has been fighting unflinchingly for their realisation at the side
of the great American and British democracies. In particular, I trust
you will not permit any decisions to be taken which might jeopardise the legitimate rights of Poland or her independence and that you
will not recognise any *faits accomplis* with regard to Poland.'[62]

The British and the Americans were united in their desire to ensure a free and independent Poland. Yet by the time of Yalta they lacked leverage and that which they did possess – the continued supply of Lend-Lease and the promise of post-war economic aid (the Soviets had recently requested a $6 billion loan from the US Treasury) – they declined to employ. Instead, both Churchill and Roosevelt appealed to Stalin on emotional grounds, the two leaders invoking the spirit of magnanimity and compromise without which the Grand Alliance could not survive. Raising the topic at the third plenary session on 6 February, Roosevelt announced that he was still in favour of the Curzon Line but felt that if the Soviet Government would allow the Poles to retain Lwów then this would have a salutary effect. In November 1944, while talking to Harriman, FDR had mused that Stalin might allow the disputed city – a Polish island surrounded by a sea of Ukrainians – to be governed by an international committee. 'I tried to tell him', recalled Harriman, 'that it was impossible to have a Polish, capitalistic city in a Ukrainian, socialist countryside. The President saw no problem with that. He said the peasants could come into Lwów and sell their produce to Poles for rubles.'[63] Not for the first time, the realities of Bolshevism eluded the American President.

Churchill said that he was more interested in the question of Poland's independence than frontiers:

> Our sole interest was one of honour because we had drawn the sword to help Poland against Hitler's brutal onslaught. We could never be content with any settlement which did not leave Poland a free and independent sovereign State . . . Poland should be mistress in her own house and captain of her own soul.[64]

After a brief recess, Stalin responded, rising from the table and, according to Maisky, speaking with 'unusual fervour'.[65] The Prime Minister had said that Poland was a matter of honour but for the Soviet Union it was 'not only a question of honour but also of security'. Throughout history, Poland had been a corridor through which Russia's enemies had passed to attack her. During the last thirty years alone, the Germans had used this route twice. This was why the Soviet Government no longer maintained the policy of the old

Tsarist Government. 'That government had wanted to suppress and assimilate Poland' but the Soviet Union had embarked upon a policy of friendship, 'and friendship, moreover, with an independent Poland'. As to the Curzon Line – which granted Lwów to the USSR – this was not an invention of the Soviets but of Western statesmen. How could he return to Moscow and say that he had been less Russian than Curzon and Clemenceau? What would the Ukrainians say? No, it was better for the war to continue a little longer so that Poland could be compensated at the expense of Germany. Turning to Churchill, he ridiculed the Prime Minister's suggestion that they should try to form a new Polish government, representative of all the political parties, during the conference. How was this possible without the Poles? 'They all say that I am a dictator but I have enough democratic feeling not to set up a Polish government without Poles.'[66] As an exercise in shameless cynicism, it was virtuosic.

Roosevelt suggested adjourning the discussion until the next day. Before he could do so, however, Churchill declared that he wanted it put on record that the British Government had different information on the situation in Poland to the Soviets. According to their sources, the Lublin Government could not be regarded as representing more than a third of the Polish people. He feared that unless they resolved this issue, the Polish underground would come into conflict with the Lublin Government, leading to 'arrests', 'deportations' and 'bloodshed'.[67] After the session had been adjourned, he complained to Maisky:

> Stalin is too unyielding. In my last speech I tried to be as delicate and careful as I could . . . but, to speak frankly, every day we receive many reports that cast the internal situation in Poland in an extremely murky light: the Lublin Government is unpopular; many detest it; all dissidents are being arrested and exiled to Siberia *en masse*, everything rests on your bayonets.[68]

That evening, Roosevelt decided to appeal to Stalin personally. 'I am greatly disturbed that the three great powers do not have a meeting of minds about the political setup in Poland,' he wrote in a letter, drafted by Bohlen, stiffened by Eden. 'It seems to me that it puts all of us in a bad light throughout the world to have you recognising one government while we and the British are recognising another in London. I am sure this state of affairs should not continue and that if it does it can only lead our people to think there is a breach between us, which is not the case. I am determined that there shall be no breach between ourselves and the Soviet Union. Surely there is a way to reconcile our differences.'

Having warned the dictator that the United States could not 'recognise the Lublin Government as now composed', Roosevelt suggested that they invite representatives of both governments, as well as other prominent Poles, to join them at Yalta.[69] The following day, Stalin said that he had attempted to contact Bierut and Morawski but had been unsuccessful and that he lacked the addresses for the other proposed attendees. Then, with impeccable timing, he accepted the American voting formula for the United Nations Security Council. When the discussion returned to the subject of Poland, he asked Molotov to present a set of Soviet 'compromise' proposals. These stated that the Russians recognised the desirability of augmenting the Lublin Government (now based in Warsaw) with 'some democratic leaders from Polish émigré circles' and that once this had been achieved the Polish population would be able to express its opinion in an election.[70]

Over the next two days, the British and the Americans tried to improve on these proposals. The Curzon Line was accepted but the democracies urged the creation of a new Polish Provisional Government that would hold 'free elections in Poland as soon as conditions permit'.[71] This was unacceptable to the Soviets. It was impossible to ignore the existence of the current Polish Provisional Government, which enjoyed 'great authority and prestige', claimed Molotov.[72] When Churchill made an impassioned speech on behalf of the lawful Polish Government in London and its importance to the British people, Stalin rejoined that these men might be clever but they were not liked in Poland because they had been absent during the occupation. Elections were desirable but until then they must deal with the Provisional Government just as the Allies were dealing with the unelected Provisional Government in France under General de Gaulle. It was a clever debating point that the Marshal exploited deftly. Later, once Roosevelt had moved the discussion onto the subject of the Balkans, the despot asked, pointedly, 'what was going on in Greece'. He said he had 'no intention of criticising British policy there but he would merely like to know what was going on'. This was Stalin's way of reminding Churchill that he had not interfered as the British suppressed the attempted communist takeover of Greece, as per the percentages agreement, and expected a free hand in eastern Europe in return. Churchill was forced to acknowledge that he had been grateful to Stalin for 'not having taken too great an interest in Greek affairs'.[73]

On the morning of 9 February, Roosevelt – having achieved his principal aims of Soviet participation in the United Nations and the war against Japan – instructed Stettinius to soften the American stance on Poland. The Americans would no longer insist on a Presidential Council or a new Polish Provisional Government but would be content to see the existing Provisional Government enlarged so as to become 'fully representative', pending free elections.[74] The British objected but the Soviets, aware that they were on the cusp of winning this crucial point, hastened to close the issue. Accepting the American compromise proposal as the basis for an agreement, Molotov announced that he would like to make only a couple of small amendments. He wanted to substitute the phrase 'fully representative' with 'reorganised', and he objected to the Anglo-American proposal for the Ambassadors of the three Great Powers to act as observers of the Polish elections to ensure they were 'free and unfettered'. After a short interval, Roosevelt said that he thought the remaining differences were 'largely a matter of the use of words' and could be resolved by a further meeting of the Foreign Ministers.[75] He and Churchill then made speeches urging that the elections, when they came, should be honest and free. The vote, the President insisted, must be 'beyond question . . . like Caesar's wife'. 'They said that about her,' responded Stalin, 'but in fact she had her sins.'[76]

The next day, Roosevelt, anxious to depart, abandoned the stipulation that the elections should be overseen by the Allied Ambassadors. The British were appalled. '[The] Americans gave us

no warning and I don't propose to agree to their action,' scrawled
Eden in a note to Churchill during the Foreign Ministers' meeting
at the Vorontsov Palace. 'Certainly do not agree,' replied the Prime
Minister.[77] But agree they did. With no American support, Russian
troops on the ground and time running out, there was little the
British could do. The final declaration, approved on the afternoon
of 10 February, spoke of 'free and unfettered elections' but not of
supervision. The existing Polish Provisional Government was to
be 'reorganised on a broader democratic basis' but whom this would
involve and what the proportion of democrats to communists
would be was left unstated.[78] As Roosevelt's Chief of Staff, Admiral
Leahy, warned the President, the agreement was 'so elastic that the
Russians can stretch it all the way from Yalta to Washington without technically breaking it'. 'I know, Bill. I know it. But it's the best
I can do for Poland at this time,' the President replied.[79]

On the other hand, the democracies succeeded in persuading
Stalin to endorse a Declaration on Liberated Europe. An American initiative, this document pledged the three powers to consult
together to provide assistance to those countries liberated from
Nazism so that they might rebuild their economies and 'create democratic institutions of their own choice'. Reaffirming their adherence
to the principles of the Atlantic Charter, the Allies promised to foster
the conditions in which the liberated peoples of Europe might live in
peace and prosperity and provide the stability necessary for the creation of interim authorities 'broadly representative of all democratic
elements in the population', followed by 'free elections'.[80]

Although intended to placate FDR's domestic critics and to galvanise American support for the new international organisation more
than to constrain Russian actions, the Declaration on the Liberation
of Europe would stand as lasting reproof against Stalin's determination to dominate his neighbours by force. Bohlen was surprised the
dictator signed it. So was Molotov. But the dictator, unlike Neville
Chamberlain, knew the value of paper agreements – particularly
ones containing such nebulous terms as 'broadly representative'
and the 'will of the people'. 'Don't worry,' the Vozhd assured the
Foreign Commissar. 'We can deal with it in our own way later. The
point is the correlation of forces.'[81]

Confronted with Soviet intransigence over Poland, there were moments of acute pessimism during the conference. Churchill, who had already christened 1945 'this new, disgusting year', told Moran on 6 February that 'the next war' would be 'an ideological one'.[82] Later, when observing the sun reflected on the sea as he and Sarah drove to the Livadia Palace, he remarked: 'The Riviera of Hades.'[83] Much of this gloom derived from his fear of Soviet imperialism and the spread of communism across Europe. As he was heard to comment shortly after his return from Crimea, 'What will lie between the white snows of Russia and the white cliffs of Dover?'[84] Yet it also stemmed from Britain's obvious decline in significance within the alliance and Roosevelt's indifference to what the Prime Minster considered to be vital issues.

For many years and still to this day, it was alleged that Roosevelt's physical deterioration had allowed Stalin to outmanoeuvre the democracies at Yalta. Certainly, Roosevelt was in poor health at Argonaut. Diagnosed with hypertension, atherosclerosis, angina pectoris and congestive heart failure in March 1944, he had less than ten weeks to live by the time he arrived on the shores of the Black Sea. Yet whilst Roosevelt was below par at Yalta, he was able to perform to the satisfaction of the American delegation, persuading Stalin to join the United Nations and the war against Japan. 'For those who attributed Roosevelt's decisions to illness,' wrote Eden in his memoirs, 'it must be remembered that though the work of the Conference was strenuous enough to keep a man even of Churchill's energy occupied, Roosevelt found time to negotiate in secret and without informing his British colleague or his Chinese ally, an agreement with Stalin to cover the Far East.'[85]

Crucially, FDR's actions at Yalta were consistent with his policies since 1942. Convinced of the need for Great Power co-operation in the post-war world, he sought to build a US–Soviet alliance that would survive the demise of Nazi Germany. The fate of eastern Europe – beyond his grasp in any case – the sensibilities of the Chinese and even, or especially, the feelings of the British were subordinate to this aim. Britain had been crucial to US foreign and defence policy in 1940 and 1941 but the balance of power had altered dramatically since then. Whilst Britain was demonstrably weaker, having sacrificed a quarter of her national wealth to ensure her survival, the US economy was booming, while the Soviet Union had already replaced Germany as the dominant power in Europe. As Hopkins told George VI, prior to his departure for Yalta, he feared that 'Great Britain and America' were going to 'drift apart again after the war'. 'He is still with the President', the monarch recorded in his diary, 'and notices that he [Roosevelt] has changed a great deal in the way of making up his mind about foreign policy.'[86] Around the same time, Roosevelt revealed his frustrations with Churchill to Joseph Davies. The Prime Minister, the President complained, was 'becoming more and more mid-Victorian and slipping farther and farther back into last century thinking'. Referring to the punishment of war criminals – a subject on which FDR was very much a 'hanging judge' – he thought it likely that Churchill would 'not go along' with the US proposals but if that were the case 'they could go ahead their own way and we and the Soviets could go ahead in our own way'.[87] This summarised FDR's attitude at Yalta.

All of this said and despite the tendency of the Cold War to loom over Yalta in subsequent accounts, the atmosphere of the Crimea discussions was remarkably cordial. 'I have never known the Russians so easy and accommodating,' wrote the normally acerbic Cadogan to his wife. 'In particular, Joe has been extremely good. He *is* a great man and shows up very impressively against the background of the other two ageing statesmen.'[88] 'I suppose it is one of the most remarkable meetings that have ever been held,' wrote Pierson Dixon to his wife. 'Between them the three protagonists can decide the future of the world. Never before have the three agreed so closely on great matters. The problem will be to keep them together, though the auguries are good.'[89]

At the dinner he hosted at the Yusupov Palace on 8 February, Stalin went out of his way to praise his fellow warlords. 'The "Bear" as host was in terrific form and it was very friendly and gay,' wrote Sarah Oliver to her mother.[90] Rising from the table covered with caviar, whitefish in champagne sauce, Caucasian mutton and pilaf with quails, the dictator proposed a toast to the 'leader of the British Empire . . . who, when all of Europe was ready to fall flat before Hitler, said that Britain would stand and fight alone against

Germany, even without any Allies . . . He [Stalin] knew of few examples in history where the courage of one man had been so important to the future history of the world'.[91] Later in the evening, the Soviet leader raised his glass to the alliance. In his thick Georgian accent, he declared:

> In the history of diplomacy, I know of no such close alliance of three great powers as this . . . A change has taken place in European history, a radical change, during these days. It is good to have an alliance of the principal powers during a war . . . But an alliance against the common enemy is something clear and understandable. Far more complicated is an alliance after the war for securing lasting peace and the fruits of victory. That we fought together was a good thing but it was not so difficult; on the other hand, that these days the work of Dumbarton Oaks [on the future United Nations] has been consummated and the legal foundations laid for organising security and strengthening peace is a great achievement. It is a turning point.[92]

With speeches such as this, it is little wonder that both the American and British delegations departed Yalta in a state of exaltation. 'We really believed in our hearts that this was the dawn of the new day we had all been praying for and talking about for so many years,' commented Hopkins. 'We were absolutely certain that we had won the first great victory of the peace . . . The Russians had proved that they could be reasonable and far-seeing and there wasn't any doubt in the minds of the President or any of us that we could live with them and get along with them peacefully for as far into the future as any of us could imagine.'[93] Ismay thought the manner of the Russians transformed since the early days of the alliance, while Bohlen recalled the feeling of 'hope, as we left Yalta, of genuine cooperation with the Soviet Union on political questions after the war'.[94]

Even Churchill was affected. Although he feared a new 'ideological war', he told Moran that he did not expect such an event 'while Stalin is alive'.[95] Two days later, he repudiated a paper by Clark Kerr that argued that 'the only bond of [the] victors is their common hate'.[96] At the Yusupov Palace, he proposed a toast to the Soviet leader, whose life was 'most precious to the hopes and hearts of all of us', and to Coalition Ministers in London he predicted that as long as Stalin survived in power Western–Soviet relations would remain friendly and secure.[97] 'Poor Neville Chamberlain believed he could trust Hitler,' Churchill told the 'crush' in his room in the House of Commons, 'but I don't think I'm wrong about Stalin.'[98]

XXX

Triumph and Tragedy

Never before have the major Allies been more closely united – not
only in their war aims but also in their peace aims. And they are
determined to continue to be united . . . so that the ideal of
lasting peace will become a reality.

Franklin D. Roosevelt, Address to Congress following the
Yalta Conference, 1 March 1945[1]

The Yalta agreements were hailed in Washington, London and
Moscow. 'All doubts about the Big Three's ability to co-operate in
peace as well as in war seem now to have been swept away,' proclaimed *Time* magazine.[2] 'Unbounded satisfaction was expressed . . .
with the results of the Crimea Conference,' reported *The Times*.[3]
Pravda and *Izvestiya* were effusive in their praise, while Molotov
informed Soviet Ambassadors that the atmosphere had been cordial, the *modus operandi* one of 'striving for agreement on disputed
questions'.[4] His deputy, Ivan Maisky, was more candid. Writing to
his friend Alexandra Kollontai – the first female member of the
Politburo, now Soviet Ambassador in Stockholm – he boasted that
'seventy-five percent of the conference decisions are ours'. The
influence of the Soviet Union in general and of Stalin in particular
had been 'extraordinarily great'.[5]

Churchill felt Soviet obstinacy over Poland acutely. Yet even he
was swept up in the adulation, telling the War Cabinet on 19 February 1945 that he felt 'quite sure' that Stalin 'meant well to the world
and to Poland'.[6] Of course, the real test of Soviet sincerity would
be their willingness to allow Mikołajczyk to return to Warsaw and
join a properly reorganised Polish Government but 'his own feeling
was that the Russians would honour the declaration that had been

made'.[7] As Jock Colville noted, the PM was 'trying to persuade himself that all was well'.[8] On 27 February, Churchill defended the Yalta agreements in the Commons, his aim being to make Stalin responsible for implementing the Western interpretation of the accords:

> Most solemn declarations have been made by Marshal Stalin and the Soviet Union that the sovereign independence of Poland is to be maintained . . . The impression I brought back from Crimea and from all my other contacts, is that Marshal Stalin and the Soviet leaders wish to live in honourable friendship and equality with the Western democracies. I feel also that their word is their bond. I know of no government which stands to its obligations . . . more solidly than the Russian Soviet Government.[9]

In Washington, Roosevelt's address to a joint session of Congress – which he delivered sitting down, rather than use his leg braces as he had in the past – was less rhetorical but no less emphatic: 'Never before have the major Allies been more closely united, not only in their war aims but *also* in their peace aims,' he told legislators. Decisions affecting the countries of liberated Europe would be taken 'jointly' by the three Great Powers. Naturally, this would involve an element of 'give and take' but the Allies were united in their commitment to free elections and to 'making Poland a strong, independent and prosperous nation'.[10]

This was not mere bombast. Recalling his work on the address, White House speechwriter Samuel Rosenman remembered how the President 'made it clear . . . that he was certain the Yalta conference had paved the way for the kind of world that he had been dreaming, planning and talking about' for so long:

> He felt that he understood Stalin and that Stalin understood him. He believed that Stalin had a sincere desire to build constructively on the foundations that had been laid at Yalta; that Stalin was interested in maintaining peace in the world so that the Soviets could make the industrial and social changes he thought necessary. The only reservation Roosevelt had was whether or not the others back in the Kremlin would sincerely go along with what Stalin had signed

at Yalta . . . He was also worried about what would happen if Stalin
should die or be stripped of his power. But there was no doubt in his
mind that if the Soviet leaders would back Stalin, a new era in world
peace was at hand.[11]

It was not long before events exposed the naïveté of this view.

On 3 March, two days after his address to Congress, Roosevelt
sent Stalin a telegram requesting permission for American aircraft
to evacuate liberated US prisoners from Polish soil. Stalin refused.
Unwilling to allow his allies access to the country while he was
tightening his hold, he claimed that all US prisoners of war had
been evacuated to Odessa. This was followed by the revocation of
General Deane's only recently granted permission to visit Poland
and the barring of American 'contact officers', agreed at Yalta.
Enraged, Roosevelt sent Stalin a second telegram – drafted by Stettinius and Stimson – expressing his indignation: 'This Government
has done everything to meet each of your requests. I now request
you to meet mine in this particular matter.'[12] Five days later, Stalin
replied, claiming that the presence of US officers in Poland would
put an intolerable strain on the Red Army and accusing the Americans of mistreating Soviet POWs in the West.

At the same time, the Soviets were asserting their influence in
those parts of eastern Europe accorded to them by the percentages
agreement. Since December 1944, the Romanian communists had
been agitating to bring down the Government of General Nicolae
Rădescu. On 24 February 1945, violence broke out following mass
demonstrations in Bucharest. Three days later, the Soviet Deputy
Commissar for Foreign Affairs, Andrei Vyshinsky, descended on the
Romanian capital. Marching into the royal palace, he ordered the 23-
year-old King Michael to dismiss Rădescu and appoint a communist
ministry. He then slammed the door so hard the ceiling cracked. For
a while the monarch resisted but with Soviet armour on the streets
there was little he could do and on 6 March he agreed to appoint a
government entirely subservient to Moscow.

Churchill was alarmed by Soviet actions in Romania. Since this
country fell within the Soviet sphere of influence and since Stalin
had refrained from supporting ELAS in Greece, however, he felt

unable to protest directly. Instead, he appealed to Roosevelt to take the lead, arguing that the 'principles of Yalta' were being 'trampled' on the streets of Bucharest.[13] FDR sympathised. But with the Red Army in control of the country since November and with the British already having 'sold' this portion of eastern Europe to Stalin, the President did not consider Romania 'a good place for a test case'.[14] That, as both Prime Minister and President knew, was Poland.

The task of implementing the vague and in many respects contradictory compromise on Poland, devised at Yalta, had been handed to a commission consisting of Molotov, Harriman and Clark Kerr. As Eden reported to Churchill, the proceedings of this body were a grim 'farce', with Molotov – pre-briefed on the Anglo-American negotiating position thanks to the treachery of Donald Maclean – refusing to invite leading Polish democrats to augment the Soviet-puppet Government.[15] Once again, Churchill appealed to Roosevelt, pointing out, in a telegram of 8 March, that unless the Western leaders sought justice on behalf of the Poles, they were liable to be accused of having underwritten a 'fraudulent prospectus' at Yalta.[16] Roosevelt sympathised but shied away from a direct confrontation with Stalin on tactical grounds. Two days later, the Prime Minister sent the President a further cable, lamenting the collapse of the Crimean accords as well as the cleavage in Anglo-American diplomatic strategy:

> We can, of course, make no progress at Moscow without your aid and if we get out of step the doom of Poland is sealed . . . I do not wish to reveal a divergence between the British and the United States Governments but it would certainly be necessary for me to make it clear [to Parliament] that we are in the presence of a great failure and utter breakdown of what was settled at Yalta . . . The moment that Molotov sees that he has beaten us away from the whole process of consultations among Poles to form a new government, he will know that we will put up with anything.[17]

Meanwhile, the NKVD was busy rounding up former members of the Polish Home Army and deporting them to labour camps in Siberia. According to a British intelligence report, 'more Poles have been arrested [in the town of Sandomierz] during the few months of Soviet occupation than during the whole five years of German occupation'.[18] Between February and May 1945, some 90,000 Polish men were sent to the Gulag. On 27 March, the Russians lured fifteen leading members of the Polish Underground Government to a meeting to discuss 'co-operation' with the Soviet authorities. Arrested shortly after they arrived, they were flown to Moscow and thrown in prison, pending trial for sabotage. As Kathleen Harriman wrote to her sister, Mary: 'The war is going wonderfully . . . but the mood is slightly dampened . . . by our gallant allies who at the moment are being most bastard-like.'[19]

On 3 April, Stalin sent Roosevelt a blistering message, accusing the British and the Americans of colluding with the Germans. The context for this extraordinary diatribe – the nadir of the Big Three's correspondence – was putative negotiations for the surrender of German forces in Italy. On 8 March, the regional head of the SS, Obergruppenführer Karl Wolff, had made contact with American intelligence officers in Bern about a potential deal. Honouring agreements made at the Foreign Ministers' Conference in October 1943, the British informed the Russians and received a request for a Soviet representative to be included in the talks. The British were happy to oblige but the Americans objected. Infuriated by Soviet obstinacy over American POWs and alarmed by the deadlock over Poland, Harriman and the head of the US Military Mission, John Deane, had persuaded Washington to reject the Soviet request, arguing that the Russians would never allow the democracies to participate in the surrender of German forces in their sector and that the Kremlin would, moreover, regard acquiescence as a 'sign of weakness', leading to 'even more untenable demands . . . in the future'.[20]

The Soviet response was explosive but also practical. Paranoid that the Western powers might, even at this late stage, be planning to cheat him of his great victory, Stalin ordered Marshals Zhukov and Konev to take Berlin before the British or the Americans. In fact, Eisenhower had already decided against a drive for the Nazi capital, informing the Soviet leader on 31 March of his intention of linking up with the Red Army near Leipzig and in Bavaria. The British had disputed this decision vigorously. Aware of the post-war significance of beating the Russians to Berlin, they railed against the Supreme Commander's cautious, politically obtuse, 'broad front' strategy. 'The Russian armies will no doubt overrun all Austria and enter Vienna,' Churchill telegraphed Roosevelt on 1 April. 'If they also take Berlin will not their impression that they have been the overwhelming contributor to our common victory be unduly imprinted in their minds and may this not lead them into a mood which will raise grave and formidable difficulties in the future?'[21]

Although the Americans refused to change course, Roosevelt – or rather his advisers, who by now were responsible for almost the entirety of the President's correspondence – had sent Stalin a telegram expressing his concern at the deterioration of East–West relations since Yalta. On 3 April, he provided an uncharacteristically irate rebuttal to the dictator's imputations of collusion regarding the surrender of German forces in Italy:

> It would be one of the great tragedies of history if at the very moment of victory, now within our grasp, such distrust, such lack of faith should prejudice the entire undertaking . . . Frankly I cannot avoid a feeling of bitter resentment toward your informers, whoever they are, for such vile misrepresentations of my actions or those of my trusted subordinates.[22]

Churchill rejoiced at Roosevelt's message. But the President's telegram, written by Marshall and Leahy, did not betoken a change of policy. Although Roosevelt agreed that the democracies 'must not permit anybody to entertain a false impression that we are afraid' and spoke of taking a 'tougher' line with the Russians as the British and American armies advanced, he had not given up hope of Soviet–Western co-operation and gave no indication that he viewed Stalin and the USSR as a threat to the coming peace.[23] Indeed, in the last message he sent Churchill – a four-line telegram he drafted personally from the Little White House at Warm Springs, Georgia – he suggested that the two leaders should 'minimise the general Soviet problem as much as possible because these problems, in one form or another, seem to arise every day and most of them straighten out as in the case of the Bern meeting. We must be firm, however, and thus far our course is correct.'[24]

The following day, Roosevelt suffered a massive intracerebral haemorrhage and died. The world, including Stalin, was stunned. Whilst wary of Churchill, whom he always suspected of trying to trick him, the Soviet leader had developed a genuine respect, bordering on admiration, for the American President. 'I do not believe Roosevelt will violate the Yalta Agreement', he told Zhukov, following his return from the Black Sea, 'but as for Churchill, he can do anything.'[25] When Harriman saw Stalin on 13 April, he found him 'deeply distressed'. 'He greeted me in silence and stood holding my hand for about thirty seconds before asking me to sit down.'[26] After assuring the Vozhd that the new President, Harry Truman, would continue the late President's policies, the Ambassador urged the Soviet leader to send Molotov to the imminent conference in San Francisco on the founding of the new international organisation. Following the row over the surrender of German forces in Italy, the Foreign Commissariat had announced that only a low-level delegation, headed by the Soviet Ambassador to Washington, Andrei Gromyko, would be travelling to California. Now, however, Stalin agreed that Molotov would participate in this historic meeting.

If Stalin was nervous about the new President, he was right to be. Inexperienced and insecure, Truman was determined to 'stand up to the Russians'.[27] On 23 April he rebuked Molotov, during the latter's visit to the White House, over Soviet failure to 'honour' the Yalta accords. 'I have never been talked to like that in my life,' expostulated the Foreign Commissar. 'Carry out your agreements and you won't get talked to like that,' retorted the President, according to his memoirs.[28] Although Harriman was the architect of this new 'tough' stance – Stalin, he told Truman on 20 April, had 'misinterpreted our generosity and our desire to cooperate as an indication of softness' – it was, he later admitted, 'an unfortunate conversation'.[29] 'His [the President's] behaviour gave Molotov an excuse to tell Stalin that the Roosevelt policy was being abandoned. I regretted that Truman gave him the opportunity. I think it was a mistake, though not a decisive mistake.'[30]

A week later Hitler shot himself in the bunker of the Reich Chancellery. Since 16 April, Berlin had been under relentless attack on three fronts by some two-and-a-half million Soviet troops, 6,250 tanks and 7,500 aircraft. Soviet artillery reduced much of the city to rubble, while Red Army soldiers, scavenging from house to house, committed rape on an industrial scale.* Soviet casualties were high – over 350,000 – but Stalin was indifferent. He wanted the Nazi capital both as a prize and because it had been the centre of German atomic research. (The dictator was unaware that most of the German uranium, as well as the scientists, had been evacuated to Haigerloch in the Black Forest.)

On 2 May, the Red Flag was implanted on the roof of the Reich-stag. Five days later, Generaloberst Alfred Jodl signed the act of unconditional surrender at Supreme Headquarters, Allied Exped-itionary Force in Rheims. Enraged that this moment of theatre should have occurred in the West, Stalin insisted that the Germans sign a separate surrender in Berlin.

The war in Europe ended on 8 May 1945. The struggle to defeat Hitler – the *raison d'être* of the short-lived Anglo-French alliance and then of the Anglo-American-Soviet alliance – had taken five years, nine months and eight days. It had been the deadliest conflict in history. Famine, disease, homelessness, bombing, reprisals, mas-sacres and genocide – most notably the murder of more than six million Jews – had accompanied battlefield casualties that stretched into the millions. Some 270,000 British and 292,000 American sol-diers, sailors and airmen had died fighting the Germans and their continental allies in Europe, the Middle East, North Africa and the Atlantic. A staggering eight to ten million Soviet servicemen and women had perished on the Eastern Front. The Reich lost more than five million men in battle, while Italian, Romanian, Hungar-ian and Finnish military deaths equalled a further million. Through toil, tears, sweat and oceans of blood, the Allies had rolled back the Wehrmacht from the shores of the Mediterranean, the Volga and the Atlantic, all the way to the Nazi capital. The Allies were victori-ous but the alliance was fraying.

Already, on 4 May, Churchill had written to Eden of his fear of US troops withdrawing to their agreed lines of occupation, thus

---

* More than two million German women and girls are believed to have been raped by members of the Red Army in 1945.

allowing 'a tide of Russian domination [to sweep] forward 120 miles on a front of 200 or 400 miles'. Such an event, he continued, would be 'among the most melancholy in history':

> The Russian frontier would run from the north cape of Norway, along the Finnish–Swedish frontier, across the Baltic, to a point just east of Lübeck . . . and half-way across [Austria] . . . to the Isonzo river. Thus the territories under Russian control would include the Baltic Provinces [*sic*], all of Germany to the occupational line, all Czechoslovakia, a large part of Austria, the whole of Yugoslavia, Hungary, Romania, Bulgaria, until Greece in her present tottering condition is reached'[31]

Having stated his refusal to be cheated out of a fair deal for Poland even if it meant going to the 'verge of war with Russia', the Prime Minister ordered the Chiefs of Staff to consider the possibility of driving the Red Army back by force.[32] On 8 June, the planners presented him with Operation Unthinkable. The object was to 'impose the will of the United States and the British Empire' upon the Soviet Union regarding Poland and the liberty of eastern Europe. The means were forty-seven British and American divisions, the Polish armed forces and, controversially, what remained of the Wehrmacht. The proposition was an offensive along a curved line from Stettin (Szczecin) to Bydgoszcz in the north and from Leipzig to Breslau (Wrocław) in the south. The combined British and American air forces and Anglo-American generalship were considered superior to their Soviet equivalents but these were minor advantages. As the military planners pointed out, the Soviets could field 170 divisions against any Western offensive – a preponderance of almost four to one. Even if the democracies were able to achieve a 'quick success' there was nothing to suggest that the Soviets would submit. They could withdraw, as they had in 1941, and there was 'virtually no limit to the distance to which it would be necessary for the Allies to penetrate into Russia in order to render further resistance impossible'. All in all, the Chiefs of Staff concluded: 'It would be beyond our power to win a quick but limited success and we should be committed to a protracted war against heavy odds. These odds, moreover, would become fanciful if the Americans grew weary and indifferent.'[33]

Confronted with this reality – which he surely must have known all along – Churchill retreated, asking the planners to consider, instead, the measures necessary to ensure the security of the British Isles, should the Americans withdraw their forces from Europe and the Russians advance as far as the Channel. Five weeks later, following the successful test of the atomic bomb in the Jornada del Muerto desert, Truman told Stalin at Potsdam – where the Allies had gathered to discuss the administration of Germany, reparations and the war against Japan – that the democracies had developed 'a new weapon of special destructive force'.[34] According to the former's memoirs, the Soviet leader was nonchalant – thanks to the treachery of Klaus Fuchs, Nunn May, Morris Cohen and others, Stalin was well aware of the Manhattan Project – but this did not change the fact that, for the moment, the Americans had the bomb and the Russians did not.* That evening, according to Zhukov, Stalin sent Soviet atomic scientists a telegram instructing them to hasten their work on a Russian weapon. The arms race that would define the relationship between the superpowers for the next forty-five years had begun.

At Potsdam, the Allies issued a declaration calling on the Japanese to surrender unconditionally or face 'prompt and utter destruction'.[35] Truman, Stimson and newly appointed Secretary of State James Byrnes were determined to use the atomic bomb to save American lives – the US had just lost 49,000 men on Okinawa – and end the war in the Far East before the Soviets could overrun Manchuria, northern China and perhaps Korea.† Churchill, who gave his ready consent, was especially taken with this latter consideration. 'It was no longer necessary for the Russians to come into the Japanese war,' he enthused to Brooke, 'the new explosive alone was sufficient to settle the matter.'

---

* Henceforth, as Senator Edwin C. Johnson of Colorado later put it, the United States could 'compel mankind' to follow the American vision of a 'lasting peace . . . or be burned to a crisp'.

† The fact that Roosevelt had expended considerable political capital in 'persuading' Stalin to join the war against Japan was an irony ignored by the new Administration.

Furthermore, we now had something in our hands which would redress the balance with the Russians. The secret of this explosive and the power to use it would completely alter the diplomatic equilibrium which was adrift since the defeat of Germany. Now we had a new value which redressed our position . . . now we could say, 'If you insist on doing this or that, well we can just blot out Moscow, then Stalingrad, then Kiev, then Kuibyshev, Kharkov, Sebastopol etc, etc.'[36]

Although the Americans were never as explicit, there is no doubt that the behaviour of the Soviet Union and the increasingly tense state of East–West relations played a part in the decision to employ what Truman called the 'most deadly' weapon in the 'history of the world'.

At 8.15 a.m. (local time) on 6 August 1945, the B-29 Superfortress *Enola Gay* opened its doors and dropped a uranium bomb on the southern Japanese city of Hiroshima. At least 70,000 people were killed instantly, with a further 60,000–80,000 dying of burns, radiation poisoning, shock and other injuries by the end of the year. Three days later, with nothing having been heard from Tokyo, a second bomb – this one containing plutonium – was dropped on the capital of Kyūshū, Nagasaki. A further 70,000 civilians perished. In the meantime, the Red Army had invaded Manchuria, Molotov having informed the Japanese Ambassador to Moscow on the afternoon of 8 August that the USSR was abrogating the Soviet–Japanese Non-Aggression Pact of 13 April 1941. This did it. Without the Soviets to act as mediators – an avenue the Japanese had been exploring since July – the situation was finally realised as hopeless. On 10 August the Japanese Foreign Minister, Shigenori Tōgō, informed the Allies that the Japanese Government would accept the Potsdam proclamation provided that the role and status of the Emperor were protected.

The Second World War ended on 14 August 1945. Scenes of jubilation erupted across the world. The war that had killed some seventy-five million people, and displaced and maimed millions more, was finally over. But the Allies, whose joint endeavours had brought it to an end, were at odds over Poland and the fate of eastern and central Europe; over the Turkish straits, the occupation of

Iran and the future of East Asia; and over post-war financing and the termination of Lend-Lease. The possibilities of co-operation had not disappeared but the drift was unmistakably towards increased suspicion, imperial rivalry and ideological antipathy. Politicians and journalists in the United States and Britain openly discussed the 'inevitability' of war with Russia – even if most went into print to dismiss such talk – while the Moscow *New Times* warned its readers that the advent of the atomic bomb was 'a signal for reactionaries all over the world to agitate for a new crusade against the Soviet Union'.[37] On 11 July, Harriman had warned that 'the principles of ethics with which humanity had occupied itself for centuries were now subordinated in Moscow to the single question of whether men, individually, or collectively, were willing to accept all the policies of the Kremlin' and on 16 August – seven months before his more celebrated pronouncement at Fulton, Missouri – Churchill spoke in the House of Commons of an 'iron curtain' dividing the continent.[38]

The Cold War may not have begun but the division of the continent, if not of the world, into two opposing ideological blocs had become a fearful possibility.

Epilogue

None of its constituents desired the break-up of the Grand Alliance. That this should have occurred despite their unity of intent, and so quickly, appears at first sight to require some special kind of historical explanation. As Churchill recalled, wistfully, of Yalta: 'We had the world at our feet. Twenty-five million men marching at our orders by land and sea. We seemed to be friends.'[1] Seen in the broader context of East–West relations, however, the disintegration of the wartime alliance appears unsurprising.

The Soviet Union was a revolutionary enterprise, founded upon an ideology that both forecast and preached the overthrow of capitalism through violence. Between 1918 and 1919 the Allies had sought to destroy this basilisk by aiding the Whites against the Reds in the Russian Civil War. The Bolsheviks never forgot this incursion. Terrified of encirclement without and enemies within, their actions were governed by the twin principles of wholesale distrust and constant vigilance. In 1924, the British recognised the fledgling Soviet state but severed diplomatic relations (temporarily) three years later, after a raid on the headquarters of the Soviet 'trade delegation' in London revealed evidence of Soviet espionage within the British Isles. The United States, meanwhile, delayed recognition until 1933, the hearings of the Senate Overman Committee having fostered the impression that the USSR was 'a kind of bedlam inhabited by abject slaves completely at the mercy of homicidal maniacs whose purpose was to destroy all traces of civilisation'.[2]

During the 1930s, the British and French ignored the pleas of the internationalist Soviet Foreign Minister, Maxim Litvinov, for a policy of collective security and instead tried to appease Hitler. Stalin's deal with the Nazi leader was cynical and avaricious yet it also reflected his fear that the democracies were conniving to direct the Wehrmacht eastwards. Thereafter, for the first twenty-two months of the Second World War, the 'Allies' were on opposite sides: the

Soviets aiding the German war economy and dividing eastern
Europe with their fascist partners; the British and French drawing
up plans to oppose the Red Army in Finland and destroy the Soviet
oil fields in the Caucasus.

In this context, the break-up of the Grand Alliance following
its victory over Nazi Germany is not startling. Ideological antago-
nists and imperial rivals, the British, Americans and Soviets came
together to defeat a common enemy and then reverted to the *status
quo ante*. As these pages have shown, the alliance itself was perme-
ated by lies, suspicions, secrets and spats. For the Soviets, the most
important issue, between June 1941 and June 1944, was the opening
of the second front. The Anglo-American failure to honour a commitment to this effect in 1942 and 1943 caused consternation within
the Kremlin and led Stalin to question his partners' fidelity to the
alliance. Although the democracies considered this rich coming
from the man who, until lately, had been collaborating with Hitler,
there was substance to this grievance. Between 1942 and 1944, the
British and the Americans led the Soviets a merry dance over the
timing of the cross-Channel assault. The Russians were excluded
from Western military planning, while the democracies' most
important secret, the Manhattan Project, was not officially revealed
until 1945.

The political differences between the Allies were always wide
and, arguably, unbridgeable. Having invaded eastern Poland in
1939 and annexed the Baltic States the following year, Stalin was
determined to regain these territories once the Germans had been
expelled. His first request for Western recognition of the USSR's
pre-Barbarossa frontiers came in December 1941, mere days after the
Red Army had stopped the Wehrmacht before the gates of Moscow.
As we have seen, Eden took a pragmatic approach. 'If [the] Russians
are victorious they will be able to establish these frontiers [regard-
less] and we shall certainly not turn them out,' he cabled Churchill.[3]
The Prime Minister disagreed. 'You are making a very large assumption about the conditions which will then prevail [at the end of the
war],' he wrote from the United States. 'No one can foresee how the
balance of power will lie, or where the winning armies will stand. It
seems probable that the US and the British Empire, far from being

exhausted, will be the most powerful armed and economic bloc the world has ever seen and that the Soviet Union will need our aid for reconstruction far more than we shall need theirs.'[4]

If this was optimistic in 1941, it bore little relation to reality in 1944–5. The decision to delay the cross-Channel invasion until the summer of 1944, though militarily sound, ensured that it was the Red Army, rather than the British and the Americans, that ended up liberating and then occupying all of eastern and much of central Europe. From late 1943, the democracies anticipated this state of affairs and tried to persuade Stalin to grant genuine autonomy to those states that fell within his grip. At times, they flattered themselves that they were on the brink of success. But the auguries were never good. The imposition of Stalinism on eastern Poland and the Baltic States, following the annexations of September 1939 and August 1940, had been instantaneous and savage. In April 1943, Stalin had used the discovery of his own massacre of Polish officers to cut ties with the legitimate Polish Government in London and promote a puppet regime. Neither the pleadings of Churchill nor, occasionally, those of Roosevelt had the slightest effect. At Yalta, the Western powers prevailed on the Soviet leader to allow some democratic Poles to augment the Lublin Government, pending free elections, but the reality remained unchanged. As the Vozhd told Zhukov following his return from Crimea: 'Churchill wants the Soviet Union to [share a] border with a bourgeois Poland, hostile to us, we cannot allow this to happen.'[5]

The crux of the matter was that there was a fundamental contradiction at the heart of the alliance. The British and the Americans were fighting an aggressive, totalitarian, ideological, murderous, hegemonic power in the name of liberty, democracy and the rights of small nations. The Soviet Union *was* an aggressive, totalitarian, ideological, murderous power, with hegemonic potential, that did not give a kopeck for the rights of small nations. Neither side understood the other properly. The British and the Americans thought the Soviets were becoming more open and would become yet more so as they continued their collaboration with the West, shedding the vestiges of their old inferiority complex in the process. The Soviets thought the British and American emphasis on parliament and public opinion merely cover for their own imperial purposes.

'Roosevelt refers to Congress. He thinks that I will believe that he is really afraid of it,' declared Stalin. 'Nonsense! He is the military leader, the Supreme Commander-in-Chief. Who dares object to him? It is convenient for him to hide behind parliament. But he won't fool me.'[6] As Litvinov lamented to the American journalist Edgar Snow, the Foreign Commissariat was 'run by three men' – Molotov, Vyshinsky and Vladimir Dekanozov – 'and none of them know or understand America or Britain'.[7]

Considering these facts, it may seem that the break-up of the Grand Alliance was all but inevitable. In the opinion of the distinguished American Cold War historian Vojtech Mastny, the fault of the Western leaders was less their inability to prevent the disintegration of the wartime alliance than their failure to 'prepare themselves and their peoples for the disheartening likelihood of a breakdown'.[8] Yet there were alternative courses. In June 1941, just after the onset of Operation Barbarossa, George Kennan wrote to the State Department's Loy Henderson, arguing that the West should view the inchoate Russian alliance in strictly pragmatic terms:

> It seems to me that to welcome Russia as an associate in the defence of democracy would invite misunderstanding . . . In following such a course I do not see how we could help but identify ourselves with the Russian destruction of the Baltic states, with the attack against Finnish independence, with the partition of Finland and Romania, with the crushing of religion throughout Eastern Europe and with the domestic policy of a regime which is widely feared and detested . . . [Russia] has no claim on Western sympathies and there is no reason apparent to me why its present plight should not be viewed realistically at home as that of one who has played a lone hand in a dangerous game and must now take the moral consequences. Such a view would not preclude the extension of material aid wherever called for by our own self-interest. It would, however, preclude anything which might identify us politically or ideologically with the Russian war effort.[9]

This view was shared by Assistant Secretary of State Adolf Berle, who feared the consequences of Churchill's early embrace of the

USSR and her leader. The British and the Americans, he wrote in his diary, should view the Russian situation for what it is: 'namely a temporary confluence of interest'.[10] What this argument ignored was the power of public opinion – which responded to the deeds of the Red Army with considerable enthusiasm – and the desire of politicians and public alike to create a new world, based on international dialogue and Great Power co-operation.

An extension of this argument, also made by Kennan, foundered on the same reef. In late January 1945, the then Counsellor at the American Embassy in Moscow wrote to his friend and fellow Soviet expert Chip Bohlen just before the opening of the Yalta Conference. Aware that there was little the West could do to prevent the Soviets from subjugating eastern Europe, Kennan advocated a frank 'spheres of influence' deal that would see the democracies excluded from the Soviet sphere and the Soviets excluded from the democratic sphere. Eastern and south-eastern Europe should be 'written off', he argued. Plans for the United Nations should be abandoned. The US should accept the partition of Germany and should begin 'consultations with the British and French about the formation of a Western European federation, which would include West German states'.[11]

Although this plan bore a remarkable resemblance to what later occurred, it was, as Bohlen pointed out, impossible to contemplate as official policy in early 1945. The British and the Americans had at least to attempt to work with the Soviets: public opinion demanded it. To embark upon a new period of ideological antagonism and Great Power rivalry while the smoke from the current conflict was still in the air was unconscionable. If the attempt failed, the democracies could not be blamed for not trying. Roosevelt was determined to prevent the United States from returning to a policy of isolationism and a majority of the American people seemed to support him. The democracies had been fighting to create a new era of international engagement – 'One World' in Wendell Wilkie's pithy phrase – not to substitute one foe for another.

The only feasible alternative that might, conceivably, have had an effect would have been to take a firm line with the Soviets from the outset. 'Why did you Americans wait till right now to begin opposing us in the Balkans and Eastern Europe?' asked a bewildered Litvinov of Edgar Snow in June 1945. 'You should have done this three years ago. Now it's too late and your complaints only arouse suspicion here.'[12] The democracies could have drawn a direct link between the liberty of eastern Europe and the future of the alliance during the critical years 1941–3. They might have made the vast quantities of material they were sending the USSR conditional upon a satisfactory agreement on Poland and the Baltic States. The Americans, after all, had shown themselves more than happy to use Lend-Lease as a lever to obtain political and economic concessions from the British: on Imperial Preference, on civil aviation, on Middle Eastern oil, on Argentinian meat, on the World Bank and on the International Monetary Fund. The Soviets 'cannot understand giving without taking', wrote the US Military Attaché in Moscow, John Deane, to General Marshall in December 1944. 'Gratitude cannot be banked in the Soviet Union. Each transaction is complete in itself without regard to past favors. The party of the second part is either a shrewd trader to be admired or a sucker to be despised.'[13]

Whether such a strategy would have produced the desired results is, of course, a matter of speculation. What is certain is that it would have entailed an element of risk. Stalin had come to terms with Hitler before and could, in theory, do so again. Rumours of a separate German–Soviet peace – which appeared periodically between 1941 and 1943 – sent shivers down the spines of even the most inured Soviet sceptics. 'The gloomiest morning I have had since Pearl Harbor', recorded Senator Vandenberg – one of only two US Senators to vote against the recognition of the USSR in 1933 – after hearing of one such rumour in April 1943. Just over a week later, the Senator found himself haunted by an almost intolerable dilemma. What if Stalin were to demand American recognition of the Soviet 'right' to subsume eastern Poland, Bessarabia and the Baltic States? If the US agreed, it would be a repudiation of the very principles the democracies were fighting for but if she refused she risked alienating Stalin. No, *'we must win the war first'*, concluded Vandenberg: 'Russia's withdrawal would cost a million needless casualties.'[14]

Of course, it would have been extremely difficult for Stalin to extricate himself from the war. The humiliation of Hitler's perfidy and the sacrifices of the 1941 and 1942 campaigns demanded nothing less than total victory. Equally, it is almost impossible to imagine Hitler accepting any sort of peace offer prior to the dramatic reversal of military fortunes in 1943, by which time Stalin had no incentive for such a deal. Yet in the context of global war – one the Germans had come perilously close to winning – it is understandable that Churchill and Roosevelt shrank from confronting the man whose armies were responsible for over 75 per cent of German combat casualties between 1939 and 1945 and who had the capacity to save hundreds of thousands of British and American lives by joining the war against Japan.

The British, Americans and Soviets were able to defeat the Axis because the alliance endured. Hitler's only hope – one to which he and his courtiers clung, even as the 'thousand-year' Reich crumbled around them – was that the Allies would realise the contradictions inherent in their collaboration and go their separate ways. That they did not do so may be defended on both political and ethical grounds. Communism may have been 'indistinguishable' from many of the worst features of Nazism, as Churchill said in his first broadcast after the onset of Operation Barbarossa, and was responsible for millions more deaths than Nazism before 1939, but it was not attempting to subjugate an entire continent or exterminate an entire people.[15] Not then, at any rate. Of course, this was no comfort to Stalin's victims: to the millions of Poles, Estonians, Latvians, Lithuanians, Finns, Ukrainians, Belorussians, Romanians, Bulgarians, Moldovans, Georgians, Armenians, Azerbaijanis, Kazakhs, Turkmens, Uzbeks, Kyrgyz, Tartars and Russians who suffered and died under communism. Yet on both a strategic and a utilitarian basis, the decision to fight Nazism in collaboration with Soviet communism was unquestionably the right one. Even within the dark context of the twentieth century, Nazism represented a singular evil and a unique threat to the world that had to be conquered by whatever means available.

This meant sacrifices. Between 1939 and 1945, the Allies made vast sacrifices in men, money and material to defeat Hitler. The democracies also made moral and political sacrifices. In order to maintain the coalition against Nazism, it was necessary to forget the Molotov–Ribbentrop Pact and the Soviet invasions of Finland, eastern Poland, Bessarabia and the Baltic States. It was necessary to ignore the characteristics of the Soviet regime and the murder of more than 21,000 Polish prisoners. Most distasteful of all, it was necessary to acquiesce to the resumption of the USSR's pre-1941 frontiers and a Soviet sphere of influence in eastern Europe. That they managed to do so while maintaining their claim to be fighting a 'just war' says most about international hatred of Hitler but also something for Allied statecraft. Indeed, contrary to the historiographical assertion that Allied diplomacy during the Second World War was 'undistinguished', it was responsible for a whole range of policies and decisions of vast significance.[16]

In June 1940, Britain faced the very real prospect of defeat. Her principal ally, France, had been conquered in just six weeks. 'The one firm rock' on which British strategy had relied, the impregnability of the French Army, was gone.[17] Faced with the prospect of invasion, the need to augment the Royal Navy was paramount. The destroyers-for-bases deal, announced on 3 September 1940, was not merely the achievement of Churchill but of a whole team of British diplomats and propagandists, most notably the British Ambassador to Washington, Lord Lothian. Once the British had proved their determination to survive – first by the ruthless decision to sink the French Fleet at Mers el-Kébir, later by the heroic actions of RAF Fighter Command in the skies over southern England – they received a steady stream of American aid, negotiated by Churchill, the British Embassy in Washington and the British Purchasing Commission under Arthur Purvis. When Britain's dollar supplies began to run out, a fresh diplomatic initiative – masterminded by Lothian, led by Churchill, negotiated by the Treasury's Sir Frederick Phillips and John Maynard Keynes – led to the creation of Lend-Lease. True, Churchill failed to persuade Roosevelt to declare war – an event that, but for Pearl Harbor and Hitler's suicidal declaration of war on the United States, remains doubtful – but by December 1941 the British had managed to obtain the means of survival, even if they lacked the resources for victory, while US public opinion had swung from outright isolationism to broad support for the British war effort. Meanwhile, British and American war planners had agreed the general strategy they would pursue in the event of the US becoming involved in a war against Germany and Japan.

At the same time, the British avoided making unnecessary enemies and made the most of allies, however militarily insignificant. British diplomacy in Francoist Spain was pragmatic and deft; the decision to back de Gaulle courageous and far-sighted. On the other hand, the British failed in their efforts to enlist Irish or Turkish assistance. In both cases, there was little that could have been done to alter this fact. Neutrality was the ultimate expression of Irish independence, while the Turks were resolved not to suffer the fate of France, Yugoslavia or Greece. The difference is that whilst the British realised the futility of their remonstrances and occasional bribes in Dublin, they continued to nurse hopes of the Turks, to whom they sent a steady trickle of materiel.

British policy with respect to Greece suffered from similar wishful thinking. Thanks to a combination of misplaced optimism and Prime Ministerial bullying, Eden, Wavell and Dill allowed themselves, in 1941, to become the champions of an intervention that stood little chance of military success. And yet Churchill and his admittedly temperamental Foreign Secretary were surely right to help the Greeks. In 1941, Britain possessed few advantages over the Axis. Among the few she did enjoy was her moral authority and the prestige that came from defying German hegemony, without allies, for a year following the fall of France. Had she abandoned Greece to her fate – in contravention of the guarantee bestowed by the Chamberlain Government in April 1939 – these assets would have been tarnished. Equally, though moral considerations were absent from the British decision to crush the pro-Axis revolt in Iraq, to overthrow the collaborationist Vichy regime in Syria and, along with the Soviet Union, to occupy Iran in August 1941, these acts showed that the old Empire was not prepared to risk, let alone suffer, an injury during its years of peril.

The German invasion of the Soviet Union and the Japanese attack on the US Pacific Fleet at Pearl Harbor transformed the war. Henceforth the British Empire was no longer a lonely actor in a European and Mediterranean struggle but one part of a triple alliance engaged in a truly global conflict. Neither the Soviet Union nor the United States placed as much emphasis on diplomacy as the British. Habitually isolationist, these emerging superpowers could rely on their growing strength, in men and material, to win almost any argument they chose. Naturally, the British resented this. At regular intervals between 1941 and 1945, they complained of having to accept Soviet or American decisions that ran contrary to their own sense of sound military or political strategy. And yet the British were able to influence the war in several critical ways: most notably in the decision to postpone the cross-Channel invasion in favour of a landing in French North Africa and then the invasion of Italy.

Much of the credit for this belongs to Churchill and the relationship he had cultivated with Roosevelt since the beginning of the war – a political and emotional friendship that peaked in the winter of 1942–3. Yet it also shows the leadership of Roosevelt, who, in this vital matter, went repeatedly against the wishes of his own Chiefs of Staff to side with the British, thus avoiding a bloodbath on the beaches of northern France. The 'Germany First' strategy survived and the Anglo-American alliance flourished as American and British Imperial forces cleared the Axis from North Africa and then Sicily.

Thereafter, however, the balance of power within the coalition shifted dramatically as Russian victories accrued and American confidence grew. At Tehran, the US President joined with the Soviet dictator in forcing the British Prime Minister to set a spring date for the invasion of France, effectively hobbling the PM's quixotic desire for further operations in the Mediterranean. Churchill felt his diminution of power acutely – Britain, he lamented after Tehran, was but a 'poor little donkey' beside the 'big Russian bear' and the great 'American elephant' – and yet he managed, on certain notable occasions, to pursue an independent line within the alliance: negotiating a spheres-of-influence agreement with Stalin in October 1944 and ordering British troops onto the streets of Athens two months later. Both decisions were and remain controversial. Accused of consigning much of eastern Europe to a 'spiritual and cultural gas chamber', on the one hand, Churchill is charged with bloody interference in the affairs of an ally, on the other.[18] And yet, as we have seen, there was little the West could do by the autumn of 1944 to prevent Stalin from communising most of eastern Europe and the Balkans. All that was left was to try and prevent Greece from falling into the Soviet sphere and to attempt to preserve some sort of influence in Yugoslavia. Churchill failed in the latter (at least initially) but succeeded in the former.

The American record, though by no means flawless, was similarly impressive. Having kept Britain afloat and prepared the American people for the task that lay ahead – through the destroyers-for-bases deal, Lend-Lease and increasing involvement in the Atlantic – Roosevelt imbued the alliance with a sense of morality and idealism that inspired millions. Under his leadership, the democracies defined their war aims through the Atlantic Charter and the Declaration of the United Nations. Although he did not live to see them inaugurated, the International Monetary Fund and the World Bank were lasting achievements, while the creation of the United Nations may be considered among his most significant and personal legacies. Similarly, although he failed to establish a system of colonial trusteeships during his lifetime, the break-up of the European empires so soon after the end of the war vindicated his anti-imperial stance, while also owing something to it. Perhaps most importantly for the US herself, the Roosevelt Administration ensured that the post-war international financial system would be of her own making, with the United States assuming the role of international creditor *par excellence*. The American Century was born and then sustained through the inexorable power of the dollar.

Of course, there were blemishes. American sympathy for Nationalist China prevented a cool assessment of the aims and aptitude of Chiang Kai-shek's regime, leading to bitter disappointment on both sides. The State Department's pro-Vichy policy was equally unsuccessful. Yielding little of substance – except Robert Murphy's network of American 'consuls' in French North Africa – it came dangerously close to undermining the moral basis of American action. Roosevelt's dislike of de Gaulle was irrational and extreme and did lasting damage to Franco-American relations. The President's greatest wartime foreign policy failing, however, was his lack of frankness in dealing with Stalin.

In May 1942, Roosevelt had given Stalin a commitment that the democracies would open a second front, in Europe, that year. The Red Army was preparing to face a renewed German offensive and the President wanted to dissuade the Soviet leader from any thoughts of a separate peace. Yet it was a hasty promise and one that, when broken, would cause lasting suspicion in the Kremlin. Similarly, while Churchill and Eden tried to impress on Stalin the importance of a fair deal for Poland and at least a modicum of liberty for eastern Europe, Roosevelt and Hull failed to convey the depth of American interest in these matters. In their calculation, it was better to leave such contentious issues until the peace conference: when Germany and perhaps Japan would have been defeated and the Soviets would need American credit to rebuild their economy. Yet such a strategy had its perils, particularly with a President in such poor physical health. These dangers became apparent when Roosevelt died and Truman challenged Molotov over the Yalta accords – agreements that, again thanks to Roosevelt's unwillingness to confront Stalin, were deliberately vague. The Soviets assumed there had been a fundamental change in US policy, when in fact there had only been a change of personality and tactics. Roosevelt's postponement of difficult discussions eased the course of US–Soviet wartime relations but it stored up serious trouble for the future.

Stalin had every reason to be satisfied with his conduct of foreign affairs during the war. Within weeks of Hitler's betrayal and the calamity of the German invasion, he had repositioned himself as the courageous ally of his traditional ideological foes, the capitalist democracies. Between June 1941 and May 1945, the USSR received 17.5 million tons – worth more than $13 billion – of Western aid.* The trucks that transported the Red Army from Stalingrad to Berlin were American made; the Spam that kept Soviet soldiers from starving was produced in Minnesota. Unlike the British – who were expected to return or 'replace' the material they had been 'lent' – Lend-Lease to the Soviet Union came with neither conditions nor expectations of repayment. Although the Soviets would later belittle the contribution made by Lend-Lease, the fact was, as Zhukov admitted in 1963, without Western aid the Soviet Union 'could not have continued the war'.[19]

In June 1942, Stalin agreed a twenty-year mutual assistance treaty with Britain, proscribing either party from concluding a separate peace. Although the dictator failed in his bid to gain Western

---

* The Soviets received some $11 billion in US Lend-Lease aid and £428 million worth of British aid.

recognition of his absorption of the Baltic States, he carried the point *de facto*, with neither the British nor the Americans challenging the legitimacy of the annexations. A year later, he succeeded in turning the discovery of his murder of the Polish officer corps to his advantage by severing relations with the lawful Polish Government in London. At Tehran, the British and the Americans accepted his demand for the Curzon Line and at Yalta they agreed that the Lublin Government should merely be 'reorganised', with the addition of some democratic politicians, rather than 'replaced'.

In the meantime, the Soviet Union had been accepted as one of the 'Big Three' Allied powers – the equal of the United States and the British Empire – after years of ostracism. Courted by both Roosevelt and Churchill, Stalin exploited the divisions between these democratic 'prima donnas' with skill, while giving physical proof of his new-found power by compelling the wheelchair-bound President and the 69-year-old Prime Minister to travel thousands of miles, across U-boat-infested waters and precarious air routes, to treat with him. The Soviet Union would be a permanent member of the UN Security Council – where, thanks to Stalin's insistence, the Great Powers would be able to avail themselves of a veto on proposed action – and would be the principal beneficiary of German reparations. The only major Soviet foreign policy failure in this period was Stalin's inability to persuade the democracies to open a second front in France before the summer of 1944. This, paradoxically, proved a Soviet advantage, however, since it ensured that it was the Red Army and not the British and the Americans that ended up 'liberating' eastern and central Europe.

In May 1945, Stalin was triumphant. The costs of war had been horrendous. Some twenty-seven million Soviet citizens had lost their lives between the onset of Operation Barbarossa and the signing of the German surrender, four years later. More people died during the siege of Leningrad than the total number of British and American casualties for the entire war. But the USSR had prevailed. The Red Army had held the Wehrmacht at Stalingrad and then driven it back, all the way to the Reich Chancellery. In the process, the Soviet Union had emerged as a new superpower, with Stalin the master of more territory than any of his Romanov predecessors. And yet, even in his hour of triumph, there were doubts and fears.

Like his Western counterparts, Stalin wished to maintain the wartime alliance. Convinced that Germany would rise again, he, no less than Roosevelt and Churchill, saw it as the responsibility of the Great Powers to keep the peace. The war had undermined the certainties of traditional Bolshevik diplomacy. 'Lenin in his time did not dream of the correlation of forces which we have attained in this war,' Stalin boasted to a delegation of Yugoslav Communists in January 1945. 'Lenin reckoned with the fact that everyone was going to attack us and it would be good if any distant country, for example America, might remain neutral. But it has now turned out that one group of the bourgeoisie went to war against us and another was on our side. Lenin previously did not think that it was possible to remain in alliance with one wing of the bourgeoisie and fight with another. This is what we have achieved.'[20]

On the other hand, the Soviet dictator was distrustful of his Western comrades, who had failed to inform him of their efforts to build an atomic bomb and now possessed the monopoly of this uniquely destructive weapon. In April 1945, he accused the democracies of colluding with the enemy. This was a fantasy, bordering on wilful misinterpretation. Yet the knowledge that his allies were considering rolling back the Red Army with British and American tanks and German manpower (Operation Unthinkable) – information he obtained almost contemporaneously, thanks to Soviet espionage – can only have increased his suspicions. Above all, Stalin was determined to prevent the West from interfering in his plans to dominate eastern Europe. The security of the USSR, it was his sincere and longstanding belief, required a chain of proxy states along her frontier. Yet this was anathema to the Western powers with whom he hoped to maintain friendly relations.

The irony at the heart of the breakdown of the Grand Alliance was that it was an event that none of its participants desired and yet each seemed powerless to prevent. After six years of unrelenting struggle and untold suffering, victory was achieved in the summer of 1945 but not before the seeds of a new conflict had already been sown.

Acknowledgements

To my slight horror, I realise that I have been working on this book for longer than the events it describes – that is, for longer than the Second World War. During this time, I have incurred a great many debts. The first I must acknowledge are to those persons and institutions that kindly gave me access to and permission to quote from private papers. In this context, I am extremely grateful to Balliol College (Oxford), the Beinecke Library (Yale), the Bodleian Library (Oxford), the British Library, the Cadbury Research Library (University of Birmingham), Cambridge University Library, the Churchill Archive Centre (Churchill College, Cambridge), the Citadel Archives (Clemson University), the Library of Congress, Lord Egremont, Eton College, Georgetown University, the Earl of Halifax, the Imperial War Museum, Lady Hamilton of Dalzell, the Hoover Institution (Stanford), the Houghton Library (Harvard), Johns Hopkins University, King's College (University of London), the Middle East Centre (St Antony's College, Oxford), the Liddell Hart Centre for Military Archives (King's College, University of London), Antony Mallaby, the Royal Maritime Museum, the Royal Navy Strategic Studies Centre, David Mortimer, Rosaleen Mulji, the National Records of Scotland, the University of North Carolina, Nuffield College (Oxford), the Earl of Oxford and Asquith, the Parliamentary Archives, Sue Peake, Nicholas Pleydell-Bouverie, Lord Roberts of Belgravia, the Franklin D. Roosevelt Presidential Library, Sir Henry Rumbold, Alexander Russell, the Royal Archives (Windsor), the Marquess of Salisbury, St Antony's College (Oxford) and the Wren Library (Trinity College, Cambridge). Attempts have been made to contact all copyright holders. If, however, I have unintentionally infringed anyone's copyright then both I and the publishers offer our sincere apologies.

I would like to express my gratitude to St Antony's College, Oxford – specifically to the Warden, Professor Roger Goodman,

Professor Timothy Garton Ash and Camilla Swift – for appointing me as the Alistair Horne Fellow for 2020 – 21. Although my tenure coincided with the pandemic, depriving me of the benefits of college life and academic fraternity, the support the fellowship gave me was invaluable for my research. In a similar vein, I would like to thank Stephen and Jane Poss for their generosity in aiding my work in US archives. Since I delivered the Poss Distinguished Churchill Lecture at the International Churchill Society Conference in Kansas City, Missouri, in 2022, Stephen and Jane have become dear friends as well as champions of historical truth.

For answering various questions or pointing me towards material, I would like to thank James Barr, Catherine Katz, Robert Lyman, Professor Vladimir Pechatnov, Andrew Riley, Sir Barney White-Spunner and Professor Brian Young. Iris Harmsworth, James Smith and Nicholas Wingfield-Digby helped by photographing documents in various archives, while Dmitri Kravets and Francis Parham provided translations of assorted Russian books and documents. Domenica Dunne's assistance with the letters of General Charles de Gaulle and General Georges Catroux, as well as the papers of Louis Spears, was stalwart, selfless and significant. To her and all of the above I express my utmost thanks.

I am deeply grateful to Eleanora Kennedy, Hank and Sarah Slack and Margaret Thornton for hosting me in the US while I was working in the archives, and to Lonti Ebers for allowing me to write part of the book as a resident of Amant Siena. The rest of the text was written chiefly in the London Library, where I have benefitted from the superb collection and peerless staff. Other books were kindly lent by Sir Max Hastings.

I would like to thank my agent, Bill Hamilton, for his encouragement and unfailing wisdom. This book would not exist without my editors, Stuart Williams at Bodley Head and Kevin Doughton at Crown. To them and to Jörg Hensgen, for his meticulous edit of the text and unfailing good humour, I am deeply grateful.

For reading all or parts of the typescript, offering their criticisms and fielding my dyslexia, I would like to express my sincere thanks to Andrew Gilmour, Jamie Pleydell-Bouverie, Jane Pleydell-Bouverie, Peter Pleydell-Bouverie, Stephen Poss and Nicholas

Wingfield-Digby. My gratitude to Richard Davenport-Hines for his many helpful suggestions for improvements is unbounded. Naturally, the judgements, as well as any errors that remain, are mine and mine alone.

Finally, I would like to thank my wife, Clemmie, not only for examining each sentence with lawyerly precision but also for enduring the book's creation over the last three years. It is dedicated to her with love and gratitude.

Sources and Bibliography

Archives

Joseph Alsop Papers, Library of Congress

Leopold Amery Papers, Churchill College Cambridge

Earl of Avon Papers, Birmingham University Library

Sir John Balfour Papers, King's College London

Lord Beaverbrook Papers, Parliamentary Archives

Adolf A. Berle Papers, Franklin D. Roosevelt Presidential Library

Isaiah Berlin Papers, Bodleian Library, Oxford

2nd Earl of Birkenhead Papers, private collection

John Boettiger Papers, Franklin D. Roosevelt Presidential Library

Lord Boothby Papers, National Records of Scotland

Lieutenant N. G. P. Boswood Papers, Imperial War Museum

Lieutenant-Commander Bowers Papers, Imperial War Museum

Isaiah Bowman Papers, Johns Hopkins University

A. E. Buddell Papers, Imperial War Museum

Sir Reader Bullard Papers, St Antony's College, Oxford

R. A. Butler Papers, Trinity College, Cambridge

James F. Byrnes Papers, Clemson University

Sir Harold Caccia Papers, Eton College

Sir Alexander Cadogan Papers, Churchill College, Cambridge

Victor Cazalet Papers, Eton College

H. W. Chalk Papers, Imperial War Museum

Neville Chamberlain Papers, Birmingham University Library

Lord Chandos Papers, Churchill College, Cambridge

Chartwell Papers, Churchill College, Cambridge

Lord Cherwell Papers, Nuffield College, Oxford

General Mark Clark Papers, Citadel Archives

Cobham Papers, Imperial War Museum

Lieutenant-Colonel Patrick Coghill Papers, St Antony's College, Oxford
    and Imperial War Museum

Alfred Duff Cooper Papers, Churchill College, Cambridge
Coupland Papers, Bodleian Library, Oxford
Oscar Cox Papers, Franklin D. Roosevelt Presidential Library
Joseph E. Davies Papers, Library of Congress
Sir Pierson Dixon Papers, private collection
Sir Reginald Dorman-Smith Papers, British Library
Emden Papers, Imperial War Museum
Paul Emrys-Evans Papers, British Library
L. F. Flanakin Papers, Imperial War Museum
Edward J. Flynn Papers, Franklin D. Roosevelt Presidential Library
Felix Frankfurter Papers, Library of Congress
HM King George VI Papers, Royal Archives, Windsor
Major-General G. F. Grimsdale Papers, Imperial War Museum
Halsted Papers, Franklin D. Roosevelt Presidential Library
Lord Hankey Papers, Churchill College, Cambridge
Kathleen Harriman Papers, private collection
W. Averell Harriman Papers, Library of Congress
Oliver Harvey Papers, British Library
Loy Henderson Papers, Library of Congress
Hickleton Papers, Borthwick Institute, University of York
1st Earl of Hillsborough Papers, Churchill College, Cambridge
Vice-Admiral Sir Cedric Holland Papers, National Maritime Museum, Greenwich
Marion Holmes Papers, Churchill College, Cambridge
Harry Hopkins Papers, Franklin D. Roosevelt Presidential Library and Georgetown University
Cordell Hull Papers, Library of Congress
Harold L. Ickes Papers, Library of Congress
Inverchapel Papers, Bodleian Library, Oxford
Lieutenant-General N. M. S. Irwin Papers, Imperial War Museum
Lord Ismay Papers, Liddell Hart Centre for Military Archives, King's College London
Sir Ian Jacob Papers, Churchill College, Cambridge
Lord Jebb Papers, Churchill College, Cambridge
Hershel Johnson Papers, University of North Carolina
Major-General Sir John Kennedy Papers, Liddell Hart Centre for Military Archives, King's College London

Sir Hughe Knatchbull-Hugessen Papers, Churchill College, Cambridge

Valentine Lawford Papers, Churchill College, Cambridge

Admiral Willliam D. Leahy Papers, Library of Congress

Marquess of Linlithgow Papers, British Library

Lord Lloyd Papers, Churchill College, Cambridge

Breckinridge Long Papers, Library of Congress

Marquess of Lothian Papers, National Records of Scotland

Hugh Lunghi Papers, Churchill College, Cambridge

Harold Macmillan Papers, Bodleian Library, Oxford

Brigadier Aubertin Mallaby Papers, private collection

Sir John Martin Papers, Churchill College, Cambridge

Jay Pierrepont Moffat Papers, Houghton Library, Harvard

V. M. Molotov Papers, Molotov Secretariat

Sir Walter Monckton Papers, Balliol College, Oxford

Henry Morgenthau Jr Papers, Franklin D. Roosevelt Presidential Library

Lord Moyne Papers, private collection

Robert Murphy Papers, Hoover Institution, Stanford

2nd Earl of Oxford and Asquith Papers, private collection

Charles Peake Papers, private collection

Edward Pleydell-Bouverie Papers, Royal Navy Strategic Studies Centre

Lieutenant-General Sir Henry Pownall Papers, Liddell Hart Centre for Military Archives, King's College London

Lord Roberts of Belgravia Papers, private collection

William Rigdon Papers, Franklin D. Roosevelt Presidential Library

Franklin D. Roosevelt Papers, Franklin D. Roosevelt Presidential Library

Anna Roosevelt Halstead Papers, Franklin D. Roosevelt Presidential Library, Columbia University (Oral)

Rowan Papers, private collection

Sir Anthony Rumbold Papers, Bodleian Library, Oxford

John Russell Papers, private collection

5th Marquess of Salisbury Papers, private collection

Sir Arthur Salter Papers, Churchill College, Cambridge

General Sir Ronald Scobie Papers, Imperial War Museum

Sir Walford Selby Papers, Bodleian Library, Oxford

Lord Sherfield Papers, Bodleian Library, Oxford

Mary Soames Papers, Churchill College Cambridge

Sir Edward Spears Papers, St Antony's College, Oxford and Churchill College, Cambridge

Josef Stalin Papers, Stalin Digital Archive

Laurence A. Steinhardt Papers, Library of Congress

Henry L. Stimson Papers, Yale University

Lord Strang Papers, Churchill College, Cambridge

Charles W. Taussig Papers, Franklin D. Roosevelt Presidential Library

Lord Templewood Papers, Cambridge University Library

United Kingdom Government Papers, National Archives, Kew

Sumner Welles Papers, Franklin D. Roosevelt Presidential Library

Sir John Wheeler-Bennett Papers, St Antony's College, Oxford

John G. Winant Papers, Franklin D. Roosevelt Presidential Library

Ivan D. Yeaton Papers, Hoover Institution, Stanford

Document collections

Arbatov, G. A., Komplektov, V. G. and Kornienko, G. M. (eds), *Sovetsko-amerikanskie otnosheniia vo vremia Velikoi Otechestvennoi voiny, 1941–1945*, 2 vols (Moscow, 1984)

Chandler, Alfred D. et al. (eds), *The Papers of Dwight D. Eisenhower: The War Years*, 5 vols (Baltimore, MD, 1970)

Churchill, Randolph S., Gilbert, Martin and Arnn, Larry P. (eds), *The Churchill Documents*, 19 vols (Hillsdale, MI, 2009–2018)

Documents diplomatiques français, Series 1936–39 (Paris, 1986)

Documents on German Foreign Policy, 1918–1945, Series D (London, 1949–1964)

Dokumenty vneshnei politiki SSSR (Moscow, 1992–2000)

Domarus, Max (ed.), *Hitler, Reden und Proklamationen, 1932–1945*, 4 vols (Munich, 1965)

Eade, Charles (ed.), *Secret Session Speeches* (London, 1946)

Foreign Relations of the United States: Diplomatic Papers, 1939–1945 (Washington, DC, 1949–66)

General Sikorski Historical Institute (ed.), *Documents on Polish–Soviet Relations, 1939–1945*, 2 vols (London, 1961)

Gilbert, Martin (ed.), *The Churchill War Papers*, 3 vols (London, 1993–2000)

Kynin, G. P., Sevostianov, P. P. and Suslov, V. P., (eds), *Sovetsko-angliiskie otnosheniia vo vremia Velikoi Otechestvennoi voiny, 1941–1945* (Moscow, 1983)

McNeal, Robert H. (ed.), *Sochineniia I. V. Stalina*, 3 vols (Stanford, CA, 1967)

Mansergh, Nicholas (ed.), *The Transfer of Power, 1942–1947*, 12 vols (London, 1970–1983)

Moggridge, Donald (ed.), *The Collected Writings of John Maynard Keynes*, 30 vols (Cambridge, 1978)

Muggeridge, Malcolm (ed.), *Ciano's Diplomatic Papers* (London, 1948)

Nicholas, H. G. (ed.), *Washington Despatches, 1941–45: Weekly Political Reports from the British Embassy* (London, 1981)

Parliamentary Debates, House of Commons, Official Report, Fifth Series

Pétain, Philippe, *Discours aux Français, 17 juin 1940–20 août 1944* (Paris, 1989)

Rhodes James, Robert (ed.), *Winston S. Churchill: His Complete Speeches*, 8 vols (London, 1974)

Rzheshevsky, Oleg A. (ed.), *War and Diplomacy: The Making of the Grand Alliance – Documents from Stalin's Archives* (Amsterdam, 1996)

Simpson, Michael (ed.), *The Cunningham Papers: Selections from the Private and Official Correspondence of Admiral of the Fleet Viscount Cunningham of Hyndhope, KT, GCB, OM, DSO*, 2 vols (London, 1999)

Simpson, Michael (ed.), *The Somerville Papers: Selections from the Private and Official Correspondence of Admiral of the Fleet Sir James Somerville, GCB, GBE, DSO* (Aldershot, 1995)

Sontag, Raymond James and Beddie, James Stuart (eds), *Nazi–Soviet Relations, 1939–1941: Documents from the Archives of the German Foreign Office* (Washington, DC, 1948)

Van der Poel, J. (ed.), *Selections from the Smuts Papers*, 7 vols (Cambridge, 1966–73)

Various (eds), *Towards Freedom: Documents on the Movement for Independence in India, 1938–1947* (New Delhi, 1997–2016)

Primary published sources

Acheson, Dean, *Present at the Creation: My Years in the State Department* (London, 1969)

Adamic, Louis, *Dinner at the White House* (New York, 1946)

Addison, Paul and Crang, Jeremy A. (eds), *Listening to Britain: Home Intelligence Reports on Britain's Finest Hour, May to September 1940* (London, 2010)

Agar, Herbert, *Britain Alone: June 1940–June 1941* (London, 1972)

Alsop, Joseph, *I've Seen the Best of It: Memoirs* (New York, 1992)

Amery, L. S., *My Political Life*, 3 vols (London, 1953–5)

Anders, W., *An Army in Exile: The Story of the Second Polish Corps* (London, 1949)

Arnold, Henry H., *Global Mission* (New York, 1949)

Astley, Joan Bright, *The Inner Circle: A View of War at the Top* (London, 1971)

Attlee, C. R., *As It Happened* (London, 1954)

Attlee, C. R., Greenwood, A. et al., *Labour's Aims in War and Peace* (London, 1940)

Auden, W. H. and Isherwood, Christopher, *Journey to a War* (London, 1939)

Auphan, Gabriel, *La Marine française dans la seconde guerre mondiale* (Paris, 1967)

Avon, Earl of, *The Eden Memoirs*, 3 vols (London, 1960–5)

Balfour, Harold, *Wings over Westminster* (London, 1973)

Ball, Stuart (ed.), *Parliament and Politics in the Age of Churchill and Attlee: The Headlam Diaries, 1935–1951* (Cambridge, 1999)

Banac, Ivo (ed.), *The Diary of Georgi Dimitrov, 1933–1949* (New Haven, CT, 2003)

Barclay, Sir Roderick, *Ernest Bevin and the Foreign Office, 1932–1969* (London, 1975)

Barlone, D., *A French Officer's Diary: 23 August 1939–1 October 1940* (Cambridge, 1942)

Barman, T., *Diplomatic Correspondent* (London, 1968)

Barnes, John and Nicholson, David (eds), *The Leo Amery Diaries*, 2 vols (London, 1980–8)

Baudouin, Paul, *The Private Diaries of Paul Baudouin* (London, 1948)

Beaufre, André, *Le Drame de 1940* (Paris, 1965)

Beaufre, André, *La Revanche de 1945* (Paris, 1966)

Beneš, Eduard, *Memoirs of Dr Eduard Beneš* (London, 1954)

Berezhkov, V. M., *Kak ia stal perevodchikom Stalina* (Moscow, 1993)

Beria, Sergo, *Beria, My Father: Inside Stalin's Kremlin* (London, 2001)

Berle, Beatrice Bishop and Jacobs, Travis Beal (eds), *Navigating the Rapids, 1918–1971: From the Papers of Adolf A. Berle* (San Diego, 1973)

Berlin, Isaiah, *Personal Impressions* (London, 1980)

Bew, Paul (ed.), *A Yankee in de Valera's Ireland: The Memoir of David Gray* (Dublin, 2012)

Biddle, Francis, *In Brief Authority* (Garden City, NY, 1962)

Bilainkin, George, *Diary of a Diplomatic Correspondent* (London, 1942)

Bilainkin, George, *Maisky: Ten Years Ambassador* (London, 1944)

Bilainkin, George, *Second Diary of a Diplomatic Correspondent* (London, 1946)

Billotte, Pierre, *Le Temps des armes* (Paris, 1972)

Birse, A. H., *Memoirs of an Interpreter* (New York, 1967)

Bloch, Marc, *Strange Defeat* (London, 1949)

Blum, John Morton (ed.), *From the Morgenthau Diaries*, 3 vols (Boston, 1959–1967)

Blum, John Morton (ed.), *The Price of Vision: The Diary of Henry A. Wallace, 1942–1946* (Boston, 1973)

Bohlen, Charles E., *Witness to History, 1929–1969* (London, 1973)

Bois, Elie J., *Truth on the Tragedy of France* (London, 1941)

Bond, Brian (ed.), *Chief of Staff: The Diaries of Lieutenant-General Sir Henry Pownall*, 2 vols (London, 1972–4)

Boothe Luce, Clare, *European Spring* (London, 1941)

Borden, Mary, *Journey down a Blind Alley* (London, 1946)

Boutron, Jean, *De Mers el-Kébir à Londres* (Paris, 1980)

Bradshaw, Tancred (ed.), *The Glubb Reports: Glubb Pasha and Britain's Empire Project in the Middle East, 1920–1956* (Basingstoke, 2016)

Brennan, Robert, *Ireland Standing Firm: My Wartime Mission in Washington* and *Éamon de Valera: A Memoir* (Dublin, 2022)

Bullard, Sir Reader, *The Camels Must Go* (London, 1961)

Bullitt, Orville H. (ed.), *For the President, Personal and Secret: Correspondence between Franklin D. Roosevelt and William C. Bullitt* (London, 1973)

Burdick, Charles and Jacobsen, Hans-Adolf (eds), *The Halder War Diary, 1939–1942* (London, 1988)

Butcher, Harry, *My Three Years with Eisenhower* (New York, 1946)

Butler, Lord, *The Art of the Possible: The Memoirs of Lord Butler, KG, CH* (London, 1971)

Byrnes, James F., *All in One Lifetime* (New York, 1958)

Byrnes, James F., *Speaking Frankly* (London, 1947)

Campbell, Sir Gerald, *Of True Experience* (London, 1948)

Campbell, Shelagh, *Resident Alien: An Englishwoman in New York and Washington, 1939–43* (London, 1990)

Campbell, Thomas M. and Herring, George C. (eds), *The Diaries of Edward R. Stettinius Jr., 1943–1946* (New York, 1975)

Carton de Wiart, Adrian, *Happy Odyssey* (London, 1950)

Casey, Lord, *Personal Experience, 1939–1946* (London, 1962)

Cassin, René, *Les Hommes partis de rien: le réveil de la France abattue, 1940–41* (Paris, 1975)

Casson, Stanley, *Greece against the Axis* (London, 1941)

Cato, *Guilty Men* (London, 1940)

Catroux, Georges, *Dans la bataille de Méditerranée, Égypte, Levant, Afrique du Nord, 1940–1944* (Paris, 1949)

Chair, Somerset de, *The Golden Carpet* (London, 1944)

Chandos, Lord, *The Memoirs of Lord Chandos* (London, 1962)

Churchill, Sarah, *A Thread in the Tapestry* (London, 1967)

Churchill, Sarah, *Keep on Dancing* (London, 1981)

Churchill, Winston S., *The Second World War*, 6 vols (London, 1948–53)

Clark, Mark, *Calculated Risk: His Personal Story of the War in North Africa and Italy* (London, 1951)

Colville, John, *The Churchillians* (London, 1981)

Colville, John, *Footprints in Time* (London, 1976)

Colville, John, *The Fringes of Power: Downing Street Diaries, 1939–1955* (London, 1985)

Cooper, Artemis (ed.), *Durable Fire: The Letters of Duff and Diana Cooper, 1913–1950* (London, 1983)

Cooper, Diana, *Trumpets from the Steep* (London, 1960)

Cooper, Duff, *Old Men Forget* (London, 1953)

Coupland, R., *The Cripps Mission* (London, 1942)

Cowles, Gardner, *Mike Looks Back: The Memoirs of Gardner Cowles, Founder of* Look *Magazine* (New York, 1985)

Cowles, Virginia, *Looking for Trouble* (London, 1941)

Crozier, W. P., *Off the Record: Political Interviews, 1933–1943* (London, 1973)

Cunningham of Hyndhope, Admiral of the Fleet Viscount, KT, GCB, OM, DSO, *A Sailor's Odyssey: The Autobiography* (London, 1952)

Dahl, Roald, *Going Solo* (London, 1986)

Dallin, Alexander and Firsov, F. I. (eds), *Dimitrov and Stalin, 1934–1943: Letters from the Soviet Archives* (New Haven, CT, 2000)

Dalton, Hugh, *The Fateful Years: Memoirs, 1931–1945* (London, 1957)

Danchev, Alex (ed.), *Establishing the Anglo-American Alliance: The Second World War Diaries of Brigadier Vivian Dykes* (London, 1990)

Danchev, Alex and Todman, Daniel (eds), *War Diaries, 1939–1945: Field Marshal Lord Alanbrooke* (London, 2001)

Davie, Michael (ed.), *The Diaries of Evelyn Waugh* (London, 1976)

Davies, John Patton, Jr, *China Hand: An Autobiography* (Philadelphia, 2012)

Davies, John Patton, Jr, *Dragon by the Tail* (London, 1974)

Davies, Joseph E., *Mission to Moscow* (New York, 1941)

Deakin, F. W. D., *The Embattled Mountain* (London, 1971)

Deane, John R., *The Strange Alliance: The Story of American Efforts at War-time Co-operation with Russia* (London, 1947)

Dilks, David (ed.), *The Diaries of Sir Alexander Cadogan, OM, 1938–1945* (London, 1971)

Dixon, Pierson, *Double Diploma: The Life of Sir Pierson Dixon, Don and Diplomat* (London, 1968)

Djilas, Milovan, *Conversations with Stalin* (London, 1962)

Djilas, Milovan, *Memoir of a Revolutionary* (New York, 1973)

Douglas, Sholto, *Years of Command* (London, 1966)

Dunford Wood, James (ed.), *Big Little Wars: The War Diaries of Colin Dunford Wood, 1938–41* (London, 2020)

Eade, Charles (ed.), *Churchill, by His Contemporaries* (London, 1953)

Eccles, Sybil and Eccles, David, *By Safe Hand: Letters, 1939–42* (London, 1983)

Eeman, Harold, *Clouds over the Sun: Memories of a Diplomat, 1942–1958* (London, 1981)

Eeman, Harold, *Inside Stalin's Russia: Memoirs of a Diplomat, 1936–1941* (London, 1977)

Egremont, J. E. R. W., *Wyndham and Children First* (London, 1968)

Eisenhower, Dwight D., *Crusade in Europe* (London, 1948)

Elvin, Harold, *A Cockney in Moscow* (London, 1958)

Evans, Trefor E. (ed.), *The Killearn Diaries, 1934–1946* (London, 1972)

Farley, James A., *Jim Farley's Story: The Roosevelt Years* (New York, 1948)

Farrer, David, *G for God Almighty: A Personal Memoir of Lord Beaverbrook* (New York, 1969)

Feinberg, Barry and Kasrils, Ronald (eds), *Bertrand Russell's America: His Transatlantic Travels and Writings*, 2 vols (London, 1973)

Foo, Yee Wah (ed.), *Chiang Kaishek's Last Ambassador to Moscow: The Wartime Diaries of Fu Bingchang* (Basingstoke, 2011)

Freedman, Max (ed.), *Roosevelt and Frankfurter: Their Correspondence, 1928–1945* (London, 1968)

Fröhlich, Elke (ed.), *Die Tagebücher von Joseph Goebbels*, 15 vols (Munich, 1993–6)

Gamelin, Maurice Gustave, *Servir*, 3 vols (Paris, 1946–7)

Gandhi, Mahatma, *The Collected Works of Mahatma Gandhi*, 100 vols (New Delhi, 1958–94)

Garfield, Simon (ed.), *A Notable Woman: The Romantic Journals of Jean Lucey Pratt* (Edinburgh, 2015)

Gaulle, Charles de, *Lettres, notes et carnets* (Paris, 1980–97)

Gaulle, Charles de, *Mémoires de guerre*, 3 vols (Paris, 1954–9)

Gibbs, Anthony, *Gibbs and a Phoney War* (London, 1967)

Gillois, André, *Histoire secrète des Français à Londres de 1940 à 1944* (Paris, 1973)

Glubb, John, *A Soldier with the Arabs* (London, 1957)

Glubb, John, *The Story of the Arab Legion* (London, 1948)

Gorodetsky, Gabriel (ed.), *The Complete Maisky Diaries*, 3 vols (New Haven, CT, 2017)

Gorodetsky, Gabriel (ed.), *Stafford Cripps in Moscow, 1940–1942: Diaries and Papers* (London, 2007)

Gromyko, Andrei, *Memories* (London, 1989)

Guingand, Major General Sir Francis de, *Generals at War* (London, 1964)

Guingand, Major General Sir Francis de, *Operation Victory* (London, 1947)

Gunther, John, *Inside Asia* (London, 1939)

Gunther, John, *Inside Europe* (London, 1938)

Gunther, John, *Procession: Dominant Personalities of Four Decades as Seen by the Author of the 'Inside' Books* (New York, 1965)

Hadley, Peter, *Third Class to Dunkirk: A Worm's-Eye View of the BEF, 1940* (London, 1944)

Hägglöf, Gunnar, *Diplomat: Memoirs of a Swedish Envoy in London, Paris, Berlin, Moscow & Washington* (London, 1972)

Halifax, Lord, *Fullness of Days* (London, 1957)

Hamilton, Thomas J., *Appeasement's Child: The Franco Regime in Spain* (London, 1943)

Hammond, Nicholas, *Venture into Greece: With the Guerrillas, 1943–44* (London, 1983)

Hardy, Henry (ed.), *Flourishing: Isaiah Berlin Letters, 1928–1946* (Cambridge, 2004)

Harriman, W. Averell, *America and Russia in a Changing World: A Half Century of Personal Observation* (Garden City, NY, 1971)

Harriman, W. Averell and Abel, Elie, *Special Envoy to Churchill and Stalin, 1941–1946* (New York, 1975)

Hart-Davis, Duff (ed.), *King's Counsellor: Abdication and War – The Diaries of Sir Alan Lascelles* (London, 2006)

Harvey, John (ed.), *The Diplomatic Diaries of Oliver Harvey, 1937–1940* (London, 1970)

Harvey, John (ed.), *The War Diaries of Oliver Harvey, 1941–45* (London, 1978)

Harvie-Watt, G. S., *Most of My Life* (London, 1980)

Hassett, William D., *Off the Record with FDR, 1942–1945* (New Brunswick, NJ, 1958)

Hayter, Sir William, *A Double Life* (London, 1974)

Heffer, Simon (ed.), *Henry 'Chips' Channon: The Diaries*, 3 vols (London, 2021–2)

Herbert, A. P., *Less Nonsense!* (London, 1944)

Herriot, Édouard, *Épisodes, 1940–1944* (Paris, 1950)

Hoare, Sir Samuel, Viscount Templewood, *Ambassador on Special Mission* (London, 1946)

Hodgkin, E. C. (ed.), *Letters from Tehran: A British Ambassador in World War II Persia* (London, 1991)

Holborn, Louise (ed.), *War and Peace Aims of the United Nations, September 1939–December 1942* (Boston, 1943)

Hooker, Nancy Harvison (ed.), *The Moffat Papers: Selections from the Diplomatic Journals of Jay Pierrepont Moffat, 1941–1943* (Cambridge, MA, 1956)

Hornbeck, Stanley K., *The United States and the Far East: Certain Fundamentals of Policy* (Boston, 1942)

Hull, Cordell, *The Memoirs of Cordell Hull*, 2 vols (London, 1948)

Iatrides, John O., *Ambassador MacVeagh Reports: Greece, 1933–1937* (Princeton, NJ, 1980)

Ickes, Harold L. (ed.), *The Secret Diary of Harold L. Ickes*, 3 vols (London, 1955)

Ismay, Lord, *The Memoirs of General the Lord Ismay* (London, 1960)

Israel, Fred L. (ed.), *The War Diary of Breckinridge Long: Selections from the Years 1939–1944* (Lincoln, NE, 1966)

Jackson, Robert H., *That Man: An Insider's Portrait of Franklin D. Roosevelt* (New York, 2003)

Jacob, Alaric, *A Window in Moscow, 1944–1945* (London, 1946)

Jebb, Gladwyn, *The Memoirs of Lord Gladwyn* (London, 1972)

Jovanovich, William (ed.), *The Wartime Journals of Charles A. Lindbergh* (New York, 1970)

Kelly, Sir David, *The Ruling Few: Or, the Human Background to Diplomacy* (London, 1952)

Kennan, George, *Memoirs, 1925–1950* (London, 1968)

Kennedy, John, *The Business of War: The War Narrative of Major-General Sir John Kennedy* (London, 1957)

Keynes, J. M., *The Economic Consequences of the Peace* (London, 1920)

Kimball, Warren F., (ed.), *Churchill & Roosevelt: The Complete Correspondence*, 3 vols (Princeton, NJ, 1984)

King, Cecil H., *With Malice toward None: A War Diary* (London, 1970)

Kirkpatrick, Ivone, *The Inner Circle: Memoirs* (London, 1959)

Knatchbull-Hugessen, Sir Hughe, *Diplomat in Peace and War* (London, 1949)

Kot, Stanisław, *Conversations with the Kremlin and Dispatches from Russia* (London, 1963)

Kumanev, G. A., *Riadom so Stalinym* (Moscow, 1999)

Kuśnierz, Bronisław, *Stalin and the Poles: An Indictment of the Soviet Leaders* (London, 1949)

Kuznetsov, Nikolai, *Kursom k pobede* (Moscow, 2003)

Lane, Arthur Bliss, *I Saw Poland Betrayed: An American Ambassador Reports to the American People* (Indianapolis, 1948)

Latimore, Owen, *China Memoirs* (Tokyo, 1990)

Lawford, Valentine, *Bound for Diplomacy* (London, 1963)

Leahy, Fleet Admiral William D., *I Was There* (London, 1950)

Leasor, James, *War at the Top: Based on the Experiences of General Sir Leslie Hollis* (London, 1959)

Leeper, Sir Reginald, *When Greek Meets Greek* (London, 1950)

Leutze, James R. (ed.), *The London Observer: The Journal of General Raymond E. Lee, 1940–1941* (London, 1972)

Liddell Hart, B. H., *The Defence of Britain* (London, 1939)

Lockhart, Sir Robert Bruce, *Comes the Reckoning* (London, 1947)

Lockhart, Sir Robert Bruce, *Friends, Foes and Foreigners* (London, 1957)

Lockhart, Sir Robert Bruce, *Giants Cast Long Shadows* (London, 1960)

Lomax, John, *The Diplomatic Smuggler* (London, 1965)

Lukacs, John (ed.), *George F. Kennan and the Origins of Containment, 1944–1946: The Kennan–Lukacs Correspondence* (Columbia, MO, 1967)

McCrea, John L., *Captain McCrea's War: The World War II Memoir of Franklin D. Roosevelt's Naval Aide and USS Iowa's First Commanding Officer* (New York, 2016)

McIntire, Ross T., *Twelve Years with Roosevelt* (London, 1948)

McIntire, Ross T., *White House Physician* (New York, 1946)

MacKenzie, Norman (ed.), *The Letters of Sidney and Beatrice Webb* (Cambridge, 1978)

Maclean, Fitzroy, *Eastern Approaches* (London, 1949)

Macleod, Roderick and Kelly, Denis (eds), *The Ironside Diaries, 1937–40* (London, 1962)

Macmillan, Harold, *The Blast of War, 1939–1945* (London, 1967)

Macmillan, Harold, *War Diaries: Politics and War in the Mediterranean, January 1943–May 1945* (London, 1984)

MacVane, John, *War and Diplomacy in North Africa* (London, 1944)

Maiskii, Ivan Mikhailovich, *Izbrannaia perepiska s rossiiskimi korrespondentami*, 2 vols (Moscow, 2005)

Maisky, Ivan, *Memoirs of a Soviet Ambassador: The War, 1939–1943* (London, 1967)

Marshall-Cornwall, James, *Wars and Rumours of Wars: A Memoir* (London, 1984)

Martin, A. W. and Hardy, Patsy (eds), *Dark and Hurrying Days: Menzies' 1941 Diary* (Canberra, 1993)

Martin, Sir John, *Downing Street: The War Years* (London, 1991)

Masters, John, *The Road Past Mandalay: A Personal Narrative* (London, 1961)

Mauriac, Claude, *Un autre de Gaulle: journal, 1944–1954* (Paris, 1970)

Maurois, André, *Tragédie en France* (Paris, 1940)

Maurois, André, *Why France Fell* (London, 1941)

Mikołajczyk, Stanisław, *The Pattern of Soviet Domination* (London, 1948)

Miller, Robert L. and Pugliese, Stanislao G. (eds), *Diary 1937–1943: The Complete, Unabridged Diaries of Count Galeazzo Ciano* (London, 2002)

Millis, Walter (ed.), *The Forrestal Diaries* (London, 1952)

Montague Browne, Anthony, *Long Sunset: Memoirs of Winston Churchill's Last Private Secretary* (London, 1996)

Moran, Lord, *Winston Churchill: The Struggle for Survival, 1940–1965* (London, 1966)

Morrison, Ian, *Malayan Postscript* (London, 1942)

Morton, H. V., *Atlantic Meeting* (London, 1943)

Mott-Radclyffe, Charles, *Foreign Body in the Eye: A Memoir of the Foreign Service Old and New* (London, 1975)

Muggeridge, Malcolm (ed.), *Ciano's Diary, 1939–1943* (London, 1947)

Murphy, Robert, *Diplomat among Warriors* (London, 1964)

Nicolson, Harold, *Why Britain Is at War* (Harmondsworth, 1939)

Nicolson, Nigel (ed.), *Harold Nicolson Diaries and Letters*, 3 vols (London, 1966–8)

Norwich, John Julius (ed.), *The Duff Cooper Diaries, 1915–1951* (London, 2005)

O'Malley, Sir Owen, *The Phantom Caravan* (London, 1954)

Papagos, Alexander, *The Battle of Greece, 1940–1941* (Athens, 1949)

Passy, Colonel, *Souvenirs*, 2 vols (Monaco, 1947–8)

Patton, George S., *War as I Knew It* (Boston, 1947)

Pawle, Gerald, *The War and Colonel Warden: Based on the Recollections of C. R. Thompson, Personal Assistant to the Prime Minister, 1940–1945* (London, 1963)

Pearse, Richard, *Three Years in the Levant* (London, 1949)

Peck, Graham, *Two Kinds of Time* (Boston, 1950)

Pendar, Kenneth, *Adventure in Diplomacy: The Emergence of General de Gaulle in North Africa* (London, 1966)

Perkins, Frances, *The Roosevelt I Knew* (London, 1947)

Pertinax, *The Gravediggers of France: Gamelin, Daladier, Reynaud, Pétain, and Laval* (Garden City, NY, 1944)

Peterson, Sir Maurice, *Both Sides of the Curtain: An Autobiography* (London, 1950)

Philby, Kim, *My Silent War* (London, 1968)

Phillips, William, *Ventures in Diplomacy* (London, 1955)

Pimlott, Ben (ed.), *The Second World War Diary of Hugh Dalton, 1940–1945* (London, 1986)

Ponsonby, Col. Sir Charles, *Ponsonby Remembers* (Oxford, 1965)

Pottle, Mark (ed.), *Champion Redoubtable: The Diaries and Letters of Violet Bonham Carter, 1914–1945* (London, 1998)

Pringle, J. D. M., *China Struggles for Unity* (London, 1939)

Raczynski, Edward, *In Allied London* (London, 1962)

Ranfurly, Hermione, *To War with Whittaker: The Wartime Diaries of the Countess of Ranfurly, 1939–1945* (London, 1994)

Reilly, Michael E., *Reilly of the White House* (New York, 1947)

Resis, Albert (ed.), *Molotov Remembers: Inside Kremlin Politics* (Chicago, 1993)

Retinger, Joseph, *Memoirs of an Eminence Grise* (Brighton, 1972)

Reynaud, Paul, *In the Thick of the Fight* (London, 1955)

Reynaud, Paul, *La France a sauvé L'Europe* (Paris, 1947)

Reynolds, David and Pechatnov, Vladimir (eds), *The Kremlin Letters: Stalin's Correspondence with Churchill and Roosevelt* (London, 2018)

Reynolds, Q. J., *Only the Stars Are Neutral* (New York, 1942)

Ribbentrop, Joachim von, *The Ribbentrop Memoirs* (London, 1954)

Roosevelt, Eleanor, *This I Remember* (New York, 1950)

Roosevelt, Elliott, *As He Saw It* (New York, 1946)

Roosevelt, Elliott (ed.), *The Roosevelt Letters: Being the Personal Correspondence of Franklin Delano Roosevelt*, 3 vols (London, 1949–52)

Rosenman, Samuel I., *Working with Roosevelt* (New York, 1952)

Rougier, Louis, *Mission secrète à Londres: les accords Pétain–Churchill* (Paris, 1947)

Salter, Arthur, *A Slave of the Lamp: A Public Servant's Notebook* (London, 1967)

Sartre, Jean-Paul, War Diaries: *Notebooks from a Phoney War, November 1939–March 1940* (London, 1984)

Schmidt, Paul, *Hitler's Interpreter* (London, 1951)

Self, Robert (ed.), *The Neville Chamberlain Diary Letters*, 4 vols (Aldershot, 2000–2005)

Sherwood, Robert E., *The White House Papers of Harry L. Hopkins*, 2 vols (London, 1948–9)

Smith, Amanda (ed.), *Hostage to Fortune: The Letters of Joseph P. Kennedy* (New York, 2001)

Snow, Edgar, *Journey to the Beginning* (London, 1959)

Snow, Edgar, *Red Star over China* (New York, 1937)

Soames, Emma (ed.), *Mary Churchill's War: The Wartime Diaries of Churchill's Youngest Daughter* (London, 2021)

Soames, Mary (ed.), *Speaking for Themselves: The Personal Letters of Winston and Clementine Churchill* (London, 1998)

Sosabowski, Stanisław, *Freely I Served* (London, 1960)

Spears, Sir Edward, *Assignment to Catastrophe*, 2 vols (London 1954)

Spears, Sir Edward, *Fulfilment of a Mission: The Spears Mission to Syria and Lebanon, 1941–1944* (London, 1977)

Spears, Sir Edward, *Two Men Who Saved France: Pétain and De Gaulle* (London, 1966)

Stark, Freya, *Dust in the Lion's Paw: Autobiography, 1939–1946* (London, 1961)

Stark, Freya, *East Is West* (London, 1945)

Stettinius, Edward R., Jr, *Roosevelt and the Russians: The Yalta Conference* (Garden City, NY, 1949)

Stimson, Henry L. and Bundy, McGeorge, *On Active Service in Peace and War* (New York, 1948)

Stirling, Lt-Col. W. F., *Safety Last* (London, 1953)

Strong, Sir Kenneth, *Men of Intelligence: A Study of the Roles and Decisions of Chiefs of Intelligence from World War I to the Present Day* (London, 1970)

Sudoplatov, Pavel and Sudoplatov, Anatoli, *Special Tasks: The Memoirs of an Unwanted Witness, a Soviet Spymaster* (Boston, 1994)

Sulzberger, C. L., *A Long Row of Candles: Memoirs and Diaries, 1934–1954* (London, 1969)

Talbott, Strobe (ed.), *Khrushchev Remembers*, 2 vols (London, 1971–4)

Tedder, Lord, *With Prejudice: The War Memoirs of Marshal of the Royal Air Force Lord Tedder* (London, 1966)

Thayer, Charles, *Bears in the Caviar* (London, 1952)

Thayer, Charles, *Hands across the Caviar* (London, 1953)

Thierry d'Argenlieu, Georges, *Souvenirs de guerre: juin 1940–janvier 1941* (Paris, 1973)

Thompson, W. H., *I Was Churchill's Shadow* (London, 1951)

Tree, Ronald, *When the Moon Was High: Memoirs of Peace and War, 1897–1942* (London, 1975)

Truman, Harry S, *Memoirs*, 2 vols (London, 1955–6)

Tully, Grace, *FDR, My Boss* (New York, 1949)

Vandenberg, Arthur H., Jr (ed.), *The Private Papers of Senator Vandenberg* (London, 1953)

Verney, John, *Going to the Wars: A Journey in Various Directions* (London, 1955)

Vian, Sir Philip, *Action This Day: A War Memoir* (London, 1960)

Villelume, Paul de, *Journal d'une défaite: août 1939–juin 1940* (Paris, 1976)

Watchman, *What of the Night?* (London, 1940)

Watson, John A., *Échec à Dakar: septembre 1940* (Paris, 1968)

Wedemeyer, Albert C., *Wedemeyer Reports!* (New York, 1958)

Weil-Curiel, A., *Le Temps de la honte*, 3 vols (Paris, 1945–7)

Welles, Sumner, *Seven Major Decisions* (London, 1951)

Welles, Sumner, *The Time for Decision* (London, 1944)

Werth, Alexander, *Moscow '41* (London, 1942)

Weygand, Maxime, *Recalled to Service: The Memoirs of Maxime Weygand* (London, 1952)

Wheeler-Bennett, John, *Special Relationships: America in Peace and War* (London, 1975)

Wheeler-Bennett, John (ed.), *Action This Day* (London, 1968)

White, Theodore H. (ed.), *The Stilwell Papers* (London, 1949)

White, Theodore H. and Jacoby, Annalee, *Thunder out of China* (London, 1947)

Willkie, Wendell, *One World* (London, 1943)

Wilson, Field-Marshal Lord, *Eight Years Overseas, 1939–1947* (London, 1948)

Winant, John G., *A Letter from Grosvenor Square: An Account of Stewardship* (London, 1948)

Wingate, Sir Ronald, *Not in the Limelight* (London, 1959)

Young, Kenneth (ed.), *The Diaries of Sir Robert Bruce Lockhart*, 2 vols (London, 1973–80)

Zhukov, G., *The Memoirs of Marshal Zhukov* (London, 1971)

Zhukov, G., *Reminiscences and Reflections*, 2 vols (Moscow, 1985)

Secondary sources

Aglion, Raoul, *De Gaulle et Roosevelt: la France Libre aux États-Unis* (Paris, 1984)

Alexander, Martin S., *The Republic in Danger: General Maurice Gamelin and the Politics of French Defence, 1933–1940* (New York, 1992)

Allen, Louis, *Singapore, 1941–1942*, 2nd ed. (London, 1993)

Allport, Roger, *Britain at Bay: The Epic Story of the Second World War, 1938–1941* (London, 2020)

Alperovitz, Gar, *The Decision to Use the Atomic Bomb and the Architecture of an American Myth* (London, 1995)

Ambrose, Stephen E., *Eisenhower*, 2 vols (London, 1984–5)

Andrew, Christopher, *The Secret World: A History of Intelligence* (London, 2018)

Applebaum, Anne, *Iron Curtain: The Crushing of Eastern Europe, 1944–56* (London, 2012)

Auty, Phyllis and Clogg, Richard, *British Policy towards Wartime Resistance in Yugoslavia and Greece* (London, 1975)

Baram, Philip J., *The Department of State in the Middle East, 1919–45* (Philadelphia, 1978)

Barker, Elisabeth, *British Policy in South-East Europe in the Second World War* (London, 1976)

Barker, Elisabeth, *Churchill and Eden at War* (London, 1978)

Barr, James, *A Line in the Sand: Britain, France and the Struggle That Shaped the Middle East* (London, 2011)

Barr, Niall, *Yanks and Limeys: Alliance Warfare in the Second World War* (London, 2015)

Barré, Jean-Luc, *Devenir de Gaulle, 1939–1943* (Paris, 2003)

Bayly, Christopher and Harper, Tim, *Forgotten Armies: The Fall of British Asia, 1941–1945* (London, 2004)

Beaumont, Joan, *Comrades in Arms: British Aid to Russia, 1941–45* (London, 1980)

Beesly, Patrick, *Very Special Admiral: The Life of Admiral J. H. Godfrey, CB* (London, 1980)

Beevor, Antony, *The Battle for Spain: The Spanish Civil War, 1936–1939* (London, 2006)

Beevor, Antony, *Berlin: The Downfall, 1945* (London, 2002)

Beevor, Antony, *The Second World War* (London, 2012)

Beevor, Antony, *Stalingrad* (London, 1998)

Bell, P. M. H., *A Certain Eventuality: Britain and the Fall of France* (Farnborough, Hants, 1974)

Bell, P. M. H., *France and Britain, 1900–1940: Entente and Estrangement* (London, 1996)

Bell, P. M. H., *John Bull and the Bear: British Public Opinion, Foreign Policy, and the Soviet Union, 1941–1945* (London, 1990)

Bellush, Bernard, *He Walked Alone: A Biography of John Gilbert Winant* (The Hague, 1968)

Bennett, M. Todd, *One World, Big Screen: Hollywood, the Allies, and World War II* (Chapel Hill, NC, 2012)

Beschloss, Michael, *The Conquerors: Roosevelt, Truman and the Destruction of Hitler's Germany, 1941–1945* (New York, 2002)

Bethell, Nicholas, *The Last Secret: Forcible Repatriation to Russia, 1944–7* (London, 1974)

Birkenhead, Earl of, *Halifax: The Life of Lord Halifax* (London, 1965)

Bloch, Michael, *Operation Willi: The Plot to Kidnap the Duke of Windsor, July 1940* (London, 1984)

Bloch, Michael, *Ribbentrop* (London, 1992)

Bohlen, Charles E., *The Transformation of American Foreign Policy* (New York, 1969)

Bond, Brian, *France and Belgium, 1939–1940* (London, 1975)

Bouverie, Tim, *Appeasing Hitler: Chamberlain, Churchill and the Road to War* (London, 2019)

Brendon, Piers, *Dark Valley: A Panorama of the 1930s* (London, 2000)

Browder, Robert Paul, *The Origins of Soviet–American Diplomacy* (Princeton, NJ, 1953)

Brown, David, *The Road to Oran: Anglo-French Relations, September 1939–July 1940* (London, 2004)

Brown, Judith M. and Louis, Wm Roger (eds), *The Oxford History of the British Empire, Vol. IV: The Twentieth Century* (Oxford, 1999)

Burns, James MacGregor, *Roosevelt: The Soldier of Freedom, 1940–1945* (London, 1971)

Butler, Ewan, *Mason-Mac: The Life of Lieutenant-General Sir Noel Mason-Macfarlane* (London, 1972)

Butler, J. R. M. (ed.), *A History of the Second World War: Grand Strategy*, 6 vols (London, 1956–76)

Calder, Robert, *Beware the British Serpent: The Role of Writers in British Propaganda in the United States, 1939–1945* (Montreal, 2004)

Carlton, David, *Churchill and the Soviet Union* (Manchester, 2000)

Carter, Zachary D., *The Price of Peace: Money, Democracy, and the Life of John Maynard Keynes* (New York, 2020)

Chadwin, Mark, *The Hawks of World War II* (Chapel Hill, NC, 1968)

Chamberlain, W. H., *America's Second Crusade* (Chicago, 1950)

Chang, Jung, *Big Sister, Little Sister, Red Sister: Three Women at the Heart of Twentieth-Century China* (London, 2019)

Chang, Jung and Halliday, John, *Mao: The Unknown Story* (London, 2005)

Charmley, John, *Churchill's Grand Alliance: The Anglo-American Special Relationship, 1940–1957* (London, 1995)

Charmley, John, *Duff Cooper: The Authorized Biography* (London, 1986)

Chisholm, Anne and Davie, Michael, *Beaverbrook: A Life* (London, 1992)

Chubarian, Alexander O. and Shukman, Harold (eds), *Stalin and the Soviet–Finnish War, 1939–1940* (London, 2002)

Cienciala, Anna M., Lebedeva, Natalia S. and Materski, Wojciech (eds), *Katyn: A Crime without Punishment* (New Haven, CT, 2008)

Clarke, Peter, *The Cripps Version: The Life of Sir Stafford Cripps, 1889–1952* (London, 2002)

Close, David H., *The Origins of the Greek Civil War* (London, 1995)

Close, David H. (ed.), *The Greek Civil War, 1943–50: Studies of Polarization* (London, 1993)

Cointet, Jean-Paul, *Nouvelle histoire de Vichy, 1940–1945* (Paris, 2011)

Cole, Wayne S., *Roosevelt and the Isolationists* (Lincoln, NE, 1983)

Connell, John, *Wavell: Scholar and Soldier, to June 1941* (London, 1964)

Cosgrave, Patrick J., *R. A. Butler: An English Life* (London, 1981)

Coutau-Bégarie, Hervé and Huan, Claude, *Darlan* (Paris, 1989)

Cray, Ed, *General of the Army: George C. Marshall, Soldier and Statesman* (New York, 1990)

Crémieux-Brilhac, Jean-Louis, *La France libre: de l'appel du 18 juin à la Libération* (Paris, 1996)

Crémieux-Brilhac, Jean-Louis, *Les Français de l'an 40*, 2 vols (Paris, 1990)

Cross, J. A., *Sir Samuel Hoare: A Political Biography* (London, 1977)

Cull, Nicholas, *Selling War: The British Propaganda Campaign against American 'Neutrality' in World War II* (New York, 1995)

Dallek, Robert, *Franklin D. Roosevelt* (London, 2017)

Dallek, Robert, *Franklin D. Roosevelt and American Foreign Policy, 1932–1945* (New York, 1979)

Danchev, Alex, *Very Special Relationship: Field Marshal Sir John Dill and the Anglo-American Alliance, 1941–44* (London, 1986)

Dannreuther, Raymond, *Somerville's Force H: The Royal Navy's Gibraltar-Based Fleet, June 1940–March 1942* (London, 2006)

Davies, Norman, *Rising '44: The Battle for Warsaw* (London, 2003)

Davis, Kenneth S., *FDR: The War President, 1940–1943* (New York, 2000)

Dawson, Raymond H., *The Decision to Aid Russia, 1941: Foreign Policy and Domestic Politics* (Chapel Hill, NC, 1959)

Deakin, William, Barker, Elisabeth and Chadwick, Jonathan (eds), *British Political and Military Strategy in Central, Eastern and Southern Europe in 1944* (Basingstoke, 1988)

Dilks, David, *Churchill and Company: Allies and Rivals in War and Peace* (London, 2012)

Dilks, David (ed.) *Retreat from Power: Studies in Britain's Foreign Policy of the Twentieth Century*, 2 vols (London, 1981)

Douglas-Hamilton, James, *Motive for a Mission: The Story behind Hess's Flight to Britain* (London, 1971)

Dudgeon, A. G., *Hidden Victory: The Battle of Habbaniya, May 1941* (Stroud, 2000)

Duroselle, Jean-Baptiste, *L'Abîme, 1939–1945* (Paris, 1982)

Eastman, Lloyd et al., *The Nationalist Era in China, 1927–1949* (Cambridge, 1991)

Edgerton, David, *Britain's War Machine: Weapons, Resources and Experts in the Second World War* (London, 2011)

Edwards, Robert, *White Death: Russia's War on Finland, 1939–40* (London, 2006)

Egremont, Max, *Under Two Flags: The Life of Major-General Sir Edward Spears* (London, 1997)

Erickson, Ljubica and Erickson, Mark (eds), *Russia: War, Peace and Diplomacy* (London, 2004)

Feingold, Henry L., *The Politics of Rescue: The Roosevelt Administration and the Holocaust, 1938–1945* (New Brunswick, NJ, 1980)

Feis, Herbert, *The China Tangle: The American Effort in China from Pearl Harbor to the Marshall Mission* (Princeton, NJ, 1953)

Feis, Herbert, *Churchill, Roosevelt, Stalin: The War They Waged, the Peace They Sought* (Princeton, NJ, 1957)

Fenby, Jonathan, *The General: Charles de Gaulle and the France He Saved* (London, 2010)

Filene, Peter G., *Americans and the Soviet Experiment, 1917–1933* (Cambridge, MA, 1967)

Fishman, Sarah et al. (eds), *France at War: Vichy and the Historians* (Oxford, 2000)

Fisk, Robert, *In Time of War: Ireland, Ulster and the Price of Neutrality, 1939–1945* (Dublin, 1983)

Fleming, D. F., *The Cold War and Its Origins, 1917–1960*, 2 vols (Garden City, NY, 1961)

Flower, Desmond and Reeves, James (eds), *The War, 1939–1945* (London, 1960)

Folly, Martin H., *Churchill, Whitehall and the Soviet Union, 1940–45* (Basingstoke, 2000)

Fort, Adrian, *Wavell: The Life and Times of an Imperial Servant* (London, 2009)

Franco Salgado-Araujo, Francisco, *Mis conversaciones privadas con Franco* (Barcelona, 1976)

Freidel, Frank, *Franklin D. Roosevelt: A Rendezvous with Destiny* (Boston, 1990)

Funk, A. L, *The Politics of TORCH: The Allied Landings and the Algiers Putsch, 1942* (Lawrence, KS, 1974)

Gaddis, John Lewis, *The United States and the Origins of the Cold War, 1941–1947* (New York, 1972)

Gannon, Robert I., *The Cardinal Spellman Story* (London, 1963)

Gard, Maurice Martin du, *La Carte impériale: histoire de la France outre-mer, 1940–1945* (Paris, 1949)

Gardner, Richard N., *Sterling–Dollar Diplomacy: Anglo-American Collaboration in the Reconstruction of Multilateral Trade* (Oxford, 1956)

Garver, John W., *Chinese–Soviet Relations, 1937–1945: The Diplomacy of Chinese Nationalism* (New York, 1988)

Gaunson, A. B., *The Anglo-French Clash in Lebanon and Syria, 1940–45* (Basingstoke, 1987)

Gilbert, Martin, *Auschwitz and the Allies* (London, 1981)

Gilbert, Martin, *Sir Horace Rumbold: Portrait of a Diplomat, 1869–1941* (London, 1973)

Gilbert, Martin, *Winston S. Churchill, Vol. VI: Finest Hour, 1939–1941* (London, 1983)

Gilbert, Martin, *Winston S. Churchill, Vol. VII: Road to Victory, 1941–1945* (London, 1986)

Gillies, Donald, *Radical Diplomat: The Life of Archibald Clark Kerr, Lord Inverchapel, 1882–1951* (London, 1999)

Gladwyn, Cynthia, *The Paris Embassy* (London, 1976)

Glantz, Mary E., *FDR and the Soviet Union: The President's Battles over Foreign Policy* (Lawrence, KS, 2005)

Gori, Francesca and Pons, Silvio (eds), *The Soviet Union and Europe in the Cold War, 1943–1953* (Basingstoke, 1996)

Gorodetsky, Gabriel, *The Grand Delusion: Stalin and the German Invasion of Russia* (New Haven, CT, 1999)

Gorodetsky, Gabriel, *Stafford Cripps' Mission to Moscow, 1940–42* (Cambridge, 1984)

Gunther, John, *Roosevelt in Retrospect* (London, 1950)

Hall, H. Duncan, *North American Supply* (London, 1955)

Harrison, Mark (ed.), *The Economics of World War II: Six Great Powers in International Comparison* (Cambridge, 1998)

Harrod, Roy, *The Life of John Maynard Keynes* (London, 1951)

Hart-Davis, Duff, *Man of War: The Secret Life of Captain Alan Hillgarth* (London, 2012)

Hastings, Max, *All Hell Let Loose: The World at War, 1939–1945* (London, 2011)

Hastings, Max, *Bomber Command* (London, 1979)

Hastings, Max, *Finest Years: Churchill as Warlord, 1940–1945* (London, 2009)

Hemming, Henry, *Our Man in New York: The British Plot to Bring America into the Second World War* (London, 2019)

Herring, George C., Jr, *Aid to Russia, 1941–1946: Strategy, Diplomacy, and the Origins of the Cold War* (New York, 1973)

Hewlett, Richard G. and Anderson, Oscar E., Jr, *A History of the United States Atomic Energy Commission, Vol. I: The New World, 1939–1946* (Philadelphia, 1962)

Hinsley, F. H. et al, *British Intelligence in the Second World War*, 4 vols (London, 1977–90)

Holland, James, *Italy's Sorrow: A Year of War, 1944–1945* (London, 2008)

Horne, Alistair, *Macmillan: The Official Biography*, 2 vols (London, 1988–9)

Horne, Alistair, *To Lose a Battle: France, 1940* (London, 1969)

Iatrides, John O., *Revolt in Athens: The Greek Communist 'Second Round', 1944–1945* (Princeton, NJ, 1972)

Iatrides, John O. (ed.), *Greece in the 1940s: A Nation in Crisis* (Hanover, NH, 1981)

Imlay, Talbot C., *Facing the Second World War: Strategy, Politics and Economics in Britain and France, 1938–1940* (Oxford, 2003)

Isaacson, Walter and Thomas, Evan, *The Wise Men: Six Friends and the World They Made – Acheson, Bohlen, Harriman, Kennan, Lovett, McCloy* (New York, 1986)

Isono, Fujiko (ed.), *Owen Lattimore: China Memoirs – Chiang Kai-shek and the War against Japan* (Tokyo, 1990)

Jäckel, Eberhard, *La France dans l'Europe de Hitler* (Paris, 1968)

Jackson, Ashley, *The British Empire and the Second World War* (London, 2006)

Jackson, Julian, *A Certain Idea of France: The Life of Charles de Gaulle* (London, 2018)

Jackson, Julian, *The Fall of France: The Nazi Invasion of 1940* (Oxford, 2003)

Jackson, Julian, *France on Trial: The Case of Marshal Pétain* (London, 2023)

Jackson, Julian, *France: The Dark Years, 1940–1944* (Oxford, 2001)

Jeffery, Keith, *MI6: The History of the Secret Intelligence Service, 1909–1949* (London, 2010)

Jordan, Anthony J., *Churchill: A Founder of Modern Ireland* (Westport, Ireland, 1995)

Jordan, Nicole, *The Popular Front and Central Europe: The Dilemmas of French Impotence, 1918–1940* (Cambridge, 1992)

Kammerer, Albert, *La Tragédie de Mers el-Kébir: l'Angleterre et la flotte française* (Paris, 1945)

Karski, Jan, *The Great Powers & Poland, 1919–1945: From Versailles to Yalta* (Lanham, MD, 1985)

Kearns Goodwin, Doris, *No Ordinary Time: Franklin and Eleanor Roosevelt – the Home Front in World War II* (New York, 1994)

Keegan, John (ed.), *Churchill's Generals* (London, 1991)

Kennan, George F., *American Diplomacy, 1900–1950* (New York, 1951)

Kennan, George F., *Russia and the West under Lenin and Stalin* (London, 1961)

Kennedy, David M., *Freedom from Fear: The American People in Depression and War, 1929–45* (Oxford, 1999)

Kersaudy, François, *Churchill and De Gaulle* (London, 1981)

Kersaudy, François, *Norway 1940* (London, 1990)

Kershaw, Ian, *Hitler*, 2 vols (London, 1998–2000)

Kersten, Krystyna, *The Establishment of Communist Rule in Poland, 1943–1948* (Berkeley, CA, 1992)

Khan, Yasmin, *The Raj at War: A People's History of India's Second World War* (London, 2015)

Khlevniuk, Oleg V., *Stalin: New Biography of a Dictator* (New Haven, CT, 2015)

Kimball, Warren F., *Forged in War: Roosevelt, Churchill, and the Second World War* (New York, 1997)

Kimball, Warren F., *The Juggler: Franklin Roosevelt as Wartime Statesman* (Princeton, NJ, 1991)

Kimball, Warren F., *The Most Unsordid Act: Lend-Lease, 1939–1941* (Baltimore, MD, 1969)

Kirby, S. Woodburn, *The War against Japan*, 4 vols (London, 1957–69)

Kitchen, Martin, *British Policy toward the Soviet Union during the Second World War* (New York, 1986)

Kochanski, Halik, *The Eagle Unbowed: Poland and the Poles in the Second World War* (London, 2012)

Kochanski, Halik, *Resistance: The Underground War in Europe, 1939–45* (London, 2022)

Kolko, G., *The Politics of War: The World and United States Foreign Policy, 1943–1945* (New York, 1968)

Kotkin, Stephen, *Stalin*, 2 vols (London, 2014–17)

Lacouture, Jean, *De Gaulle: The Rebel, 1890–1944* (London, 1990)

Langer, William L., *Our Vichy Gamble* (Hamden, CT, [1947] 1965)

Lash, Joseph P., *Roosevelt and Churchill, 1939–1941: The Partnership That Saved the West* (London, 1977)

Laufer, I. and Kynin, G. P. (eds), *SSSR i germanskii vopros* (Moscow, 1996)

Lees, Michael, *The Rape of Serbia: The British Role in Tito's Grab for Power, 1943–1944* (New York, 1990)

Lehrman, Lewis, *Churchill, Roosevelt & Company: Studies in Character and Statecraft* (Guilford, CT, 2017)

Li, Zhisui, *The Private Life of Chairman Mao* (London, 1994)

Long, Gavin (ed.), *Australia in the War of 1939–1945, Series 1: Army*, 7 vols (Canberra, 1952–63)

Longford, Earl of and O'Neill, Thomas P., *Éamon de Valera* (Boston, 1971)

Louis, William Roger, *Imperialism at Bay, 1941–1945: The United States and the Decolonization of the British Empire* (Oxford, 1977)

Lownie, Andrew, *Traitor King: The Scandalous Exile of the Duke and Duchess of Windsor* (London, 2021)

Lyman, Robert, *First Victory: Britain's Forgotten Struggle in the Middle East, 1941* (London, 2006)

Lyman, Robert, *Iraq, 1941: The Battles for Basra, Habbaniya, Fallujah and Baghdad* (Botley, Oxford, 2006)

MacIntyre, Captain Donald, *Fighting Admiral: The Life of Admiral of the Fleet Sir James Somerville, GCB, GBE, DSO* (London, 1961)

Mackenzie, Compton, *Eastern Epic, Vol. I: Defence, September 1939–March 1943* (London, 1951)

McLynn, Frank, *Fitzroy Maclean* (London, 1992)

McMeekin, Sean, *Stalin's War: A New History of the Second World War* (London, 2021)

Marder, A. J., *From the Dardanelles to Oran: Studies of the Royal Navy in War and Peace, 1915–1940* (London, 1974)

Marder, A. J., *Operation 'Menace': The Dakar Expedition and the Dudley North Affair* (Oxford, 1976)

Masson, Philippe, *La Marine française et la guerre, 1939–1945* (Paris, 2000)

Mastny, Vojtech, *Russia's Road to the Cold War: Diplomacy, Warfare, and the Politics of Communism, 1941–1945* (New York, 1979)

Mazower, Mark, *Inside Hitler's Greece: The Experience of Occupation, 1941–1944* (London, 1993)

Mazower, Mark (ed.), *After the War Was Over: Reconstructing the Family, Nation, and State in Greece, 1943–1960* (Princeton, NJ, 2000)

Medlicott, W. N., *The Economic Blockade*, 2 vols (London, 1952)

Melton, George E., *Darlan: Admiral and Statesman of France, 1881–1942* (Westport, CT, 1998)

Militärgeschichtliches Forschungsamt (ed.), *Germany and the Second World War*, 13 vols (Oxford, 1990–2017)

Miner, Stephen Merritt, *Between Churchill and Stalin: The Soviet Union, Great Britain, and the Origins of the Grand Alliance* (Chapel Hill, NC, 1988)

Minnen, Cornelis A. van and Sears, John F., *FDR and His Contemporaries: Foreign Perceptions of an American President* (Basingstoke, 1992)

Mitter, Rana, *China's War with Japan, 1937–1945: The Struggle for Survival* (London, 2013)

Mockler, Anthony, *Our Enemies the French: Being an Account of the War Fought between the French and the British, Syria, 1941* (London, 1976)

Moore, R. J., *Churchill, Cripps, and India, 1939–1945* (Oxford, 1979)

Moorehead, Alan, *African Trilogy: The North African Campaign, 1940–43* (London, [1944] 1998)

Moorhouse, Roger, *The Devils' Alliance: Hitler's Pact with Stalin, 1939–1941* (London, 2014)

Moorhouse, Roger, *First to Fight: the Polish War, 1939* (London, 2019)

Mordal, Jacques, *La Campagne de Norvège* (Paris, 1949)

Murphy, David E., *What Stalin Knew: The Enigma of Barbarossa* (New Haven, CT, 2005)

Neal, Steve, *Dark Horse: A Biography of Wendell Willkie* (Garden City, NY, 1984)

Neiberg, Michael S., *When France Fell: The Vichy Crisis and the Fate of the Anglo-American Alliance* (Cambridge, MA, 2021)

Nester, William, *Franklin D. Roosevelt and the Art of Leadership: Battling the Great Depression and the Axis Powers* (Barnsley, 2004)

Nolan, Aengus, *Joseph Walshe: Irish Foreign Policy, 1922–1946* (Cork, 2008)

O'Brien, Philips Payson, *The Second Most Powerful Man in the World: The Life of Admiral William D. Leahy, Roosevelt's Chief of Staff* (New York, 2019)

O'Halpin, Eunan, *Spying on Ireland: British Intelligence and Irish Neutrality during the Second World War* (Oxford, 2008)

Olson, Lynn, *Citizens of London: The Americans Who Stood with Britain in Its Darkest, Finest Hour* (New York, 2010)

Olson, Lynn, *Those Angry Days: Roosevelt, Lindbergh, and America's Fight over World War II, 1939–1941* (New York, 2013)

Osborn, Patrick, *Operation Pike: Britain versus the Soviet Union, 1939–1941* (Westport, CT, 2000)

Ousby, Ian, *Occupation: The Ordeal of France, 1940–1944* (London, 1997)

Overy, Richard, *Blood and Ruins: The Great Imperial War, 1931–1945* (London, 2021)

Overy, Richard, *Russia's War* (London, 1998)

Overy, Richard, *Why the Allies Won* (London, 1995)

Owen, Nicholas, 'The Cripps Mission of 1942: A Reinterpretation', *The Journal of Imperial and Commonwealth History*, vol. 30. no. 1, January 2002

Papastratis, Procopis, *British Policy towards Greece during the Second World War, 1941–1944* (Cambridge, 1984)

Pavlowitch, Stevan K., *Hitler's New Disorder: The Second World War in Yugoslavia*, rev. ed. (London, 2020)

Paxton, Robert O., *Vichy France: Old Guard and New Order, 1940–1944* (New York, 1972)

Payne, Stanley G., *Franco and Hitler: Spain, Germany, and World War II* (New Haven, CT, 2008)

Payne, Stanley G. and Palacios, Jesús, *Franco: A Personal and Political Biography* (Madison, WI, 2014)

Phillips, Hugh D., *Between the Revolution and the West: A Political Biography of Maxim M. Litvinov* (Boulder, CO, 1992)

Pike, David Wingeate, *Franco and the Axis Stigma* (Basingstoke, 2008)

Playfair, I. S. O. et al., *The Mediterranean and the Middle East*, 6 vols (London, 1954–88)

Plokhy, S. M., *Yalta: The Price of Peace* (New York, 2010)

Pogue, Forrest C., *George C. Marshall*, 4 vols (New York, 1963–87)

Porch, Douglas, *Defeat and Division: France at War, 1939–1942* (Cambridge, MA, 2022)

Porch, Douglas, *Hitler's Mediterranean Gamble: The North African and Mediterranean Campaigns in World War II* (London, 2004)

Preston, Diana, *Eight Days at Yalta: How Churchill, Roosevelt and Stalin Shaped the Post-war World* (London, 2019)

Rankin, Nicholas, *Defending the Rock: How Gibraltar Defeated Hitler* (London, 2017)

Raugh, Harold E., Jr, *Wavell in the Middle East, 1939–1941: A Study in Generalship* (London, 1993)

Rees, David, *Harry Dexter White: A Study in Paradox* (London, 1974)

Reynolds, David, *The Creation of the Anglo-American Alliance, 1937–41: A Study in Competitive Co-operation* (London, 1981)

Reynolds, David, *From World War to Cold War: Churchill, Roosevelt, and the International History of the 1940s* (Oxford, 2006)

Reynolds, David, *In Command of History: Churchill Fighting and Writing the Second World War* (London, 2004)

Reynolds, David, *Rich Relations: The American Occupation of Britain, 1942–1945* (London, 1995)

Reynolds, David, Kimball, Warren F. and Chubarian, A. O. (eds), *Allies at War: The Soviet, American, and British Experience, 1939–1945* (New York, 1994)

Rhodes James, Robert, *Anthony Eden* (London, 1986)

Rhodes James, Robert, *Victor Cazalet: A Portrait* (London, 1976)

Roberts, Andrew, *Churchill: Walking with Destiny* (London, 2018)

Roberts, Andrew, *The Holy Fox: A Biography of Lord Halifax* (London, 1991)

Roberts, Andrew, *Masters and Commanders: How Roosevelt, Churchill, Marshall and Alanbrooke Won the War in the West* (London, 2008)

Roberts, Geoffrey, *Stalin's Library: A Dictator and His Books* (London, 2022)

Roberts, Geoffrey, *Stalin's Wars: From World War to Cold War, 1939–1953* (New Haven, CT, 2006)

Roberts, Walter E., *Tito, Mihailović and the Allies, 1941–1945* (Durham, NC, [1973] 1987)

Romanus, Charles F. and Sunderland, Riley, *Stilwell's Command Problems* (Washington, DC, 1956)

Romanus, Charles F. and Sunderland, Riley, *Stilwell's Mission to China* (Washington, DC, 1953)

Roskill, Captain S. W., *The War at Sea, 1939–1945*, 3 vols (London, 1954–1961)

Royle, Trevor, *Glubb Pasha: The Life and Times of Sir John Bagot Glubb, Commander of the Arab Legion* (London, 1992)

Schofield, Victoria, *Wavell: Soldier and Statesman* (London, 2006)

Schuker, Stephen A., *The End of French Predominance in Europe: The Financial Crisis of 1924 and the Adoption of the Dawes Plan* (Chapel Hill, NC, 1976)

Sebag-Montefiore, Simon, *Stalin: The Court of the Red Tsar* (London, 2003)

Service, Robert, *Stalin: A Biography* (London, 2004)

Shaw, Louise Grace, *The British Political Elite and the Soviet Union, 1937–1939* (London, 2003)

Sherwin, M. J., *A World Destroyed: The Atomic Bomb and the Grand Alliance* (New York, 1975)

Short, Philip, *Mao: A Life* (London, 1999)

Sima, William, *China and ANU: Diplomats, Adventurers, Scholars* (Acton, ACT, 2015)

Simms, Brendan and Laderman, Charlie, *Hitler's American Gamble: Pearl Harbor and the German March to Global War* (London, 2021)

Smith, Colin, *England's Last War against France: Fighting Vichy, 1940–1942* (London, 2009)

Smith, Neil, *American Empire: Roosevelt's Geographer and the Prelude to Globalization* (Berkeley, CA, 2003)

Smyth, Denis, *Diplomacy and Strategy of Survival: British Policy and Franco's Spain, 1940–41* (Cambridge, 1986)

Snyder, Timothy, *Bloodlands: Europe between Hitler and Stalin* (New York, 2010)

Snyder, Timothy and Brandon, Ray (eds), *Stalin and Europe: Imitation and Domination, 1928–1953* (New York, 2014)

Stafford, David (ed.), *Flight from Reality: Rudolf Hess and His Mission to Scotland, 1941* (London, 2002)

Stahel, David, *The Battle for Moscow* (Cambridge, 2015)

Stahel, David, *Operation Typhoon: Hitler's March on Moscow, October 1941* (Cambridge, 2013)

Stahel, David, *Retreat from Moscow: A New History of Germany's Winter Campaign, 1941–1942* (New York, 2019)

Stavrakis, Peter J., *Moscow and Greek Communism, 1944–1949* (Ithaca, NY, 1989)

Steil, Benn, *The Battle of Bretton Woods: John Maynard Keynes, Harry Dexter White, and the Making of a New World Order* (Princeton, NJ, 2013)

Steiner, Zara, *The Triumph of the Dark: European International History, 1933–1939* (Oxford, 2011)

Stoler, Mark A., *Allies and Adversaries: The Joint Chiefs of Staff, the Grand Alliance, and US Strategy in World War II* (Chapel Hill, NC, 2000)

Stoler, Mark A., *The Politics of the Second Front: American Military Planning and Diplomacy in Coalition Warfare, 1941–1943* (Westport, CT, 1977)

Strang, Lord, *Home and Abroad* (London, 1956)

Suárez, Luis, *Franco* (Barcelona, 2005)

Sulzberger, C. L., *The Last of the Giants* (New York, 1970)

Tamkin, Nicholas, *Britain, Turkey and the Soviet Union, 1940–45: Strategy, Diplomacy and Intelligence in the Eastern Mediterranean* (Basingstoke, 2009)

Taylor, A. J. P., *Beaverbrook* (London, 1972)

Taylor, A. J. P., *The Origins of the Second World War* (London, 1961)

Taylor, Jay, *The Generalissimo: Chiang Kai-shek and the Struggle for Modern China* (Cambridge, MA, 2009)

Taylor, Philip M., *The Projection of Britain: British Overseas Publicity and Propaganda, 1919–1939* (Cambridge, 1981)

Terraine, John, *The Right of the Line: the Royal Air Force in the European War, 1939–1945* (London, 1985)

Thomas, R. T., *Britain and Vichy: The Dilemma of Anglo-French Relations, 1940–42* (London, 1979)

Thorne, Christopher, *Allies of a Kind: The United States, Britain and the War against Japan, 1941–1945* (London, 1978)

Thorpe, D. R., *Eden: The Life and Times of Anthony Eden, First Earl of Avon, 1897–1977* (London, 2003)

Tolstoy, Nikolai, *Stalin's Secret War* (London, 1981)

Tolstoy, Nikolai, *Victims of Yalta* (London, 1977)

Tombs, Robert and Chabal, Emile (eds), *Britain and France in Two World Wars: Truth, Myth and Memory* (London, 2013)

Tombs, Robert and Tombs, Isabelle, *That Sweet Enemy: The French and the British from the Sun King to the Present* (London, 2006)

Tompkins, Peter, *The Murder of Admiral Darlan: A Study in Conspiracy* (London, 1965)

Tooze, Adam, *The Wages of Destruction: The Making and Breaking of the Nazi Economy* (London, 2006)

Trotter, William R., *A Frozen Hell: The Russo-Finnish Winter War of 1939–1940* (Chapel Hill, NC, 2000)

Tuchman, Barbara W., *Stilwell and the American Experience of China, 1911–1945* (New York, 1970)

Tusell, Javier and Queipo de Llano, Genoveva G., *Franco y Mussolini: la política española durante la segunda guerra mundial* (Barcelona, 2006)

Tute, Warren, *The Deadly Stroke* (London, 1973)

Van de Ven, Hans, *China at War: Triumph and Tragedy in the Emergence of the New China* (London, 2017)

Verrier, Anthony, *Assassination in Algiers: Churchill, Roosevelt, de Gaulle, and the Murder of Admiral Darlan* (New York, 1990)

Volkogonov, Dmitri, *Stalin: Triumph and Tragedy* (London, 1991)

Wang, Dong, *China's Unequal Treaties: Narrating National History* (Lanham, MD, 2005)

Wapshott, Nicholas, *The Sphinx: Franklin Roosevelt, the Isolationists, and the Road to World War II* (New York, 2015)

Ward, Geoffrey C. (ed.), *Closest Companion: The Unknown Story of the Intimate Friendship between Franklin Roosevelt and Margaret Suckley* (Boston, 1995)

Warner, Geoffrey, *Iraq and Syria, 1941* (London, 1974)

Warner, Geoffrey, *Pierre Laval and the Eclipse of France* (London, 1968)

Werth, Alexander, *Russia at War, 1941–1945* (London, 1964)

Wiggan, Richard, *Hunt the Altmark* (London, 1982)

Williams, Charles, *Pétain* (London, 2005)

Williams, Heather, *Parachutes, Patriots and Partisans: The Special Operations Executive and Yugoslavia, 1941–1945* (London, 2003)

Wilmot, Chester, *The Struggle for Europe* (London, 1952)

Woodward, Llewellyn, *British Foreign Policy in the Second World War*, 5 vols (London, 1970–76)

Wylie, Neville (ed.), *European Neutrals and Non-belligerents during the Second World War* (Cambridge, 2002)

Zamir, Meir, *The Secret Anglo-French War in the Middle East: Intelligence and Decolonization, 1940–1948* (Abingdon, 2015)

Articles

Alexander, Martin S., 'The Fall of France', *Journal of Strategic Studies*, vol. 13, no. 1 (1990), pp. 10–44

Bell, P. M. H., 'War, Foreign Policy and Public Opinion: Britain and the Darlan Affair, November–December 1942', *Journal of Strategic Studies*, vol. 5, no. 3 (1982), pp. 393–415

Binion, Rudolph, 'Repeat Performance: A Psychohistorical Study of Leopold III and Belgian Neutrality', *History and Theory*, vol. 8, no. 2 (1969), pp. 213–259

Cairns, J. C., 'Great Britain and the Fall of France: A Study in Allied Disunity', *Jounal of Modern History*, vol. 27, no. 4 (1955), pp. 365–409

Cairns, J. C., 'A Nation of Shopkeepers in Search of a Suitable France, 1919–1940', *American Historical Review*, vol. 79, no. 3 (1974), p. 710–43

Chan Kit-cheng, 'The United States and the Question of Hong Kong, 1941–45', *Journal of the Hong Kong Branch of the Royal Asiatic Society*, vol. 19 (1979), pp. 1–20

Chase, J. L., 'The Development of the Morgenthau Plan through the Quebec Conference', *Journal of Politics*, vol. 16, no. 2 (1954), pp. 324–59

Costigliola, Frank, '"I Had Come as a Friend": Emotion, Culture and Ambiguity in the Formation of the Cold War, 1943–54', *Cold War History*, vol. 1, no. 1 (2000), pp. 103–28

Dieterich, Renate, 'Germany's Relations with Iraq and Transjordan from the Weimar Republic to the End of the Second World War', *Middle Eastern Studies*, vol. 41, no. 4 (2005), pp. 463–79

Dvoinykh, L. and Tarkhova, N., 'What Military Intelligence Reported: Historians Have a Chance to Analyse Soviet Dispatches on the Eve of War', *Russian Studies in History: A Journal of Translations*, vol. 36, no. 3 (1997), pp. 76–98.

Gaunson, A. B, 'Churchill, de Gaulle, Spears and the Levant Affair, 1941', *Historical Journal*, vol. 27, no. 3 (1984), pp. 697–713

Halstead, Charles R., 'Diligent Diplomat: Alexander W. Weddell as American Ambassador to Spain, 1939–1942', *Virginia Magazine of History and Biography*, vol. 82, no. 1 (1974), pp. 3–38

Herring, George C., 'The United States and British Bankruptcy, 1944–1945: Responsibilities Deferred', *Political Science Quarterly*, vol. 86, no. 2 (1971), pp. 260–80

Hill, Alexander, 'British Lend-Lease Aid and the Soviet War Effort, June 1941–June 1942', *Journal of Military History*, vol. 71, no. 3 (2007), pp. 773–808

Huan, Claude, 'Les négociations franco-britanniques de l'automne 1940', *Guerres mondiales et conflits contemporains*, no. 176 (1994), pp. 139–54

Kern, Gary, 'How "Uncle Joe" Bugged FDR', *Studies in Intelligence*, vol. 47, no. 1 (2003), pp. 19–31

Kimball, Warren F., 'Lend-Lease and the Open Door: The Temptation of British Opulence, 1937–1942', *Political Science Quarterly*, vol. 86, no. 2 (1971), pp. 232–59

Kitchen, Martin, 'Winston Churchill and the Soviet Union during the Second World War', *Historical Journal*, vol. 30, no. 2 (1987), pp. 415–36

Kozhanov, Nikolay A., 'The Pretexts and Reasons for the Allied Invasion of Iran in 1941', *Iranian Studies*, vol. 45, no. 4 (2012), pp. 479–97

La Feber, Walter, 'Roosevelt, Churchill and Indochina, 1942–1945', *American Historical Review*, vol. 80, no. 5 (1975), pp. 1277–95.

Macrakis, Michael S., 'Russian Mission on the Mountains of Greece, Summer 1944 (A View from the Ranks)', *Journal of Contemporary History*, vol. 23, no. 3 (1988), pp. 387–408

Mark, Eduard, 'October or Thermidor? Interpretations of Stalinism and the Perception of Soviet Foreign Policy in the United States, 1927–1947', *American Historical Review*, vol. 94, no. 4 (1989), pp. 937–62

Mastny, Vojtech, 'The Beneš–Stalin–Molotov Conversations in December 1943: New Documents', *Jahrbücher für Geschichte Osteuropas*, vol. 20, no. 3 (1972), pp. 367–402

Mayers, David, 'Soviet War Aims and the Grant Alliance: George Kennan's Views, 1944–1946', *Journal of Contemporary History*, vol. 21, no. 1 (1986), pp. 57–79

Millman, Brock, 'Toward War with Russia: British Naval and Air Planning for Conflict in the Near East, 1939–1940', *Journal of Contemporary History*, vol. 29, no. 2 (1994), pp. 261–83

Morley, Joel, 'The Memory of the Great War and Morale during Britain's Phoney War', *Historical Journal*, vol. 63, no, 2 (2020), pp. 437–67

Morriss, Agnieszka, 'The BBC Polish Service during World War II', unpublished PhD thesis, City, University of London (2016)

O'Halpin, Eunan, 'Irish–Allied Security Relations and the "American Note" Crisis: New Evidence from British Records', *Irish Studies in International Affairs*, vol. 11 (2000), pp. 71–83

Owen, Nicholas, 'The Cripps Mission of 1942: A Reinterpretation', *Journal of Imperial and Commonwealth History*, vol. 30, no. 1 (2022), pp. 60–89

Pechatnov, Vladimir, 'How Soviet Cold Warriors Viewed World War II: The Inside Story of the 1957 Edition of the Big Three Correspondence', *Cold War History*, vol. 14, no. 1 (2014), pp. 109–25

Reynolds, David, 'The Churchill Government and the Black American Troops in Britain during World War II', *Transactions of the Royal Historical Society*, vol. 35 (1985), pp. 113–33

Reynolds, David, 'Lord Lothian and Anglo-American Relations, 1939–1940', *Transactions of the American Philosophical Society*, vol. 73, no. 2 (1983), pp. 1–65

Rieber, Alfred J., 'The Crack in the Plaster: Crisis in Romania and the Origins of the Cold War', *Journal of Modern History*, vol. 76, no. 1 (2004), pp. 62–106

Roberts, Geoffrey, 'Stalin at the Tehran, Yalta, and Potsdam Conferences', *Journal of Cold War Studies*, vol. 9, no. 4 (2007), pp. 6–40

Roof, Abraham M.,'A Separate Peace? The Soviet Union and the Making of British Strategy in the Wake of "Barbarossa", June–September 1941', *Journal of Slavic Military Studies*, vol. 22, no. 2 (2009), pp. 236–52

Rosenberg, Joseph L., 'The 1941 Mission of Frank Aiken to the United States: An American Perspective', *Irish Historical Studies*, vol. 22, no. 86 (1980), pp. 162–177

Sbrega, John H., 'Anglo-American Relations and the Selection of Mountbatten as Supreme Allied Commander, South East Asia', *Military Affairs*, vol. 46, no. 3 (1982), pp. 139–45.

Small, Melvin, 'How We Learned to Love the Russians: American Media and the Soviet Union during World War II', *Historian*, vol. 36, no. 3 (1974), pp. 455–78

Smyth, Denis, ' "Les Chevaliers de Saint-George": la Grande-Bretagne et la corruption des généraux espagnols (1940–1942)', *Guerres mondiales et conflits contemporains*, no. 162 (1991), pp. 29–54

Sokolov, V. V., 'Molotov, Viacheslav Mikhalilovich', *Diplomaticheskii vestnik*, July 2002

Steil, Benn, 'Keynes: The Dunkirk Diplomat', *History Today*, vol. 63., no. 6, June 2013

Stewart, Andrew, 'The British Government and the South African Neutrality Crisis, 1938–39', *English Historical Review*, vol. 123, no. 503 (2008), pp. 947–72

Thomas, Martin, 'The Discarded Leader: General Henri Giraud and the Foundation of the French Committee of National Liberation', *French History*, vol. 10, no. 1 (1996), pp. 86–111

Van Creveld, Martin, 'Prelude to Disaster: The British Decision to Aid Greece, 1940–41', *Journal of Contemporary History*, vol. 9, no. 3 (1974), pp. 65–92

Venkataramani, M. S. and Shrivastava, B. K., 'The United States and the "Quit India" Demand', *India Quarterly*, vol. 20, no. 2 (1964), pp. 101–39

Woods, Randall Bennett, 'FDR and the Triumph of American Nationalism', *Presidential Studies Quarterly*, vol. 19, no. 3 (1989), pp. 567–81

Zamir, Meir, 'An Intimate Alliance: The Joint Struggle of General Edward Spears and Riad al-Sulh to Oust France from Lebanon, 1942–1944', *Middle Eastern Studies*, vol. 41, no. 6 (2005), pp. 811–32

Zamir, Meir, 'De Gaulle and the Question of Syria and Lebanon during the Second World War: Part I', *Middle Eastern Studies*, vol. 43, no. 5 (2007), pp. 675–708

Zamir, Meir, 'The "Missing Dimension": Britain's Secret War against France in Syria and Lebanon, 1942–45 – Part II', *Middle Eastern Studies*, vol. 46, no. 6 (2010), p. 791–899

Notes

Preface

1 Martin Gilbert and Larry P. Arnn (eds), *The Churchill Documents, Vol. XXI: The Shadows of Victory, January–July 1945* (Hillsdale, MI, 2018), 'Argonaut' Conference, Birse Notes, Dinner Toasts, 8 February 1945, pp. 405–6. • 2 Quoted in S. M. Plokhy, *Yalta: The Price of Peace* (New York, 2010), p. 176. • 3 Gilbert and Arnn (eds), *Churchill Documents, Vol. XXI*, 'Argonaut' Conference, Birse Notes, Dinner Toasts, 8 February 1945, p. 406.• 4 Alex Danchev and Daniel Todman (eds), *War Diaries, 1939–1945: Field Marshal Lord Alanbrooke* (London, 2001), 1 April 1945, p. 680. • 5 G. M. Young, *Victorian England: Portrait of an Age* (London, 1936), p. 103.• 6 Kennedy Papers, 4/2/3, 26 January 1941

I: Allies

1 Hansard, HC Deb, 23 March 1933, vol. 276, col. 542. • 2 James Leasor, *War at the Top: Based on the Experiences of General Sir Leslie Hollis* (London, 1959), p. 85. • 3 Winston S. Churchill, *The Second World War, Vol. II: Their Finest Hour* (London, 1949), p. 158; *The Memoirs of General the Lord Ismay* (London, 1960), p. 144. • 4 Martin Gilbert (ed.), *The Churchill War Papers, Vol. II: Never Surrender, May 1940–December 1940* (London, 1994), Antony Goldsmith 'recollection', p. 309. • 5 Edward Spears, *Assignment to Catastrophe, Vol. II: The Fall of France, June 1940* (London, 1954), p. 199. • 6 Leasor, *War at the Top*, p. 87. • 7 CAB 99/3/2, Supreme War Council Minutes, 13 June 1940; Paul Reynaud, *In the Thick of the Fight* (London, 1955), p. 490. • 8 CAB 99/3/2, Supreme War Council Minutes, 13 June 1940; Paul Reynaud, *La France a sauvé l'Europe* (Paris, 1947), vol. 2, p. 315. • 9 Reynaud, *In the Thick of the Fight*, p. 491; *The Private Diaries of Paul Baudouin* (London, 1948), 12 June 1940, pp. 97–100. • 10 Quoted in Antony Lentin, 'Une aberration inexplicable'? Clemenceau and the Abortive Anglo-French Guarantee Treaty of 1919, *Diplomacy and Statecraft*, vol. 8, no. 2 (1997), p. 31. • 11 J. M. Keynes, *The Economic Consequences of the Peace* (London, 1920), p. 95; Arthur Balfour quoted in Stephen A. Schuker, *The End of French Predominance in Europe: The Financial Crisis of 1924 and the Adoption of the Dawes Plan* (Chapel Hill, NC, 1976), p. 388. • 12 Henri Béraud, *Faut-il réduire l'Angleterre en esclavage?* (Paris, 1935), pp. 8, 19. • 13 Quoted in John C. Cairns, 'A Nation of Shopkeepers in Search of a Suitable France, 1919–1940', *American Historical Review*, vol. 79, no. 3 (1974), pp. 710–43. • 14 Simon Heffer (ed.), *Henry 'Chips' Channon: The Diaries, Vol. II: 1938–43* (London, 2021), 21 March 1939, p. 85. • 15 *The Times*, 22 March 1939; Ibid., 25 March 1939. • 16 FO 371/22923, Sargent Minute, 15 March 1939. • 17 See David Edgerton, *Britain's War Machine: Weapons, Resources, and Experts in the Second World War* (London, 2011). • 18 Noël Coward, *The Lyrics of Noël Coward* (London, 1965), p. 274. • 19 Roderick Macleod and Denis Kelly (eds), *The Ironside Diaries, 1937–1940* (London, 1962), 17 May 1940, p. 313. • 20 Quoted in Alistair Horne, *To Lose a Battle: France, 1940* (London, 1969), p. 84. • 21 Ben Pimlott (ed.), *The Political Diary of Hugh Dalton* (London, 1986), 11 September 1939, p. 299. • 22 Arthur Koestler, *Scum of the Earth* (London, 1941), p. 15. • 23 D. Barlone, *A French Officer's Diary: 23 August 1939–1 October 1940* (Cambridge, 1942), p. 4. • 24 André Beaufre, *Le Drame de 1940* (Paris, 1965), p. 190; Alexander Danchev and Daniel Todman (eds), *War Diaries, 1939–1945: Field Marshal Lord Alanbrooke* (London, 2001), 30 September 1939, p. 4, 5 November,

p. 13. • 25 Anthony Gibbs, *Gibbs and a Phoney War* (London, 1967), pp. 33–4, 49. • 26 Marc Bloch, *Strange Defeat* (London, 1949), pp. 69–70. • 27 Quoted in André Maurois, *Why France Fell* (London, 1941), p. 123. • 28 Quoted in Jean-Louis Crémieux-Brilhac, *Les Français de l'an 40, vol. I: la guerre, oui ou non?* (Paris, 1990), pp. 374, 381. • 29 CHAR 23/1/6, Spears to Churchill, 28 September 1939; Daladier quoted in Crémieux-Brilhac, *Les Français de l'an 40, vol. I*, p. 140. • 30 FO 371/24298, De La Warr to Halifax, 15 March 1940. • 31 Orville H. Bullitt (ed.), *For the President, Personal and Secret: Correspondence between Franklin D. Roosevelt and William C. Bullitt* (London, 1973), 6 February 1949, p. 310. • 32 Robert Self (ed.), *The Neville Chamberlain Diary Letters, Vol. IV: The Downing Street Years, 1934–1940* (Aldershot, 2005), NC to Ida, 30 March 1940, p. 512. • 33 CAB 99/3/1, Supreme War Council Minutes, 12 September 1939. • 34 David Dilks (ed.), *The Diaries of Sir Alexander Cadogan, OM, 1938–1945* (London, 1971), 22 September 1939, p. 218. • 35 Quoted in Talbot C. Imlay, *Facing the Second World War: Strategy, Politics, and Economics in Britain and France, 1938–1940* (Oxford, 2003), pp. 31, 51. • 36 Dilks (ed.), *Diaries of Sir Alexander Cadogan*, 22 September 1939, p. 218. • 37 Salisbury Papers, Box 63, Thomas to Cranborne, 25 September 1939. • 38 FO 800/317/30, Salisbury to Halifax, 22 September 1939; quoted in Joel Morley, 'The Memory of the Great War and Morale during Britain's Phoney War', *Historical Journal*, vol. 63, no. 2 (2020), p. 438. • 39 Self (ed.), *Neville Chamberlain Diary Letters, Vol. IV*, NC to Ida, 3 December 1939, p. 475. • 40 Jacques Mordal quoted in François Kersaudy, *Norway 1940* (London, 1990), p. 31.

II: *The Scandinavian Fiasco*

1 Quoted in Robert Edwards, *White Death: Russia's War on Finland, 1939–40* (London, 2006), p. 232. • 2 W. N. Medlicott, *The Economic Blockade, Vol. I* (London, 1952), p. xi • 3 FO 371/23659, Supplies of Swedish Iron Ore, 27 November 1939. • 4 Quoted in Medlicott, *Economic Blockade*, p. 46. • 5 In his rightly acclaimed account of the Norway campaign, *Norway, 1940* (London, 1990), François Kersaudy writes of 'Churchill's solitary crusade' to stop the iron ore traffic. • 6 Quoted in Talbot C. Imlay, *Facing the Second World War: Strategy, Politics, and Economics in Britain and France, 1938–1940* (Oxford, 2003), pp. 64, 59. • 7 CAB 99/3/1, Supreme War Council Minutes, 19 December 1939. • 8 Quoted in Imlay, *Facing the Second World War*, pp. 178–9. • 9 CAB 66/4, Churchill Memorandum, 'Norwegian Iron-Ore Traffic', 16 December 1939. • 10 Robert Rhodes James (ed.), *Winston S. Churchill: His Complete Speeches* (London, 1974), vol. 6, p. 6185. • 11 Chartwell Papers, CHAR 23/3, Halifax to Churchill, 26 January 1940. • 12 Quoted in Richard Wiggan, *Hunt the Altmark* (London, 1982), p. 126. • 13 Hickleton Papers, A7/8/3, Halifax Diary, 16 February 1940. • 14 Martin Gilbert (ed.), *The Churchill War Papers, Vol. I: At the Admiralty, September 1939–May 1940* (London, 1993), Churchill to Vian, 16 February 1940, p. 772; Alexander Papers, AVAR 5/4/1, 'Winston and the Altmark'. • 15 Malcolm Muggeridge (ed.), *Ciano's Diary, 1939–1943* (London, 1947), 19 February 1940, p. 210; *The Times*, 19 February 1940. • 16 Roderick Macleod and Denis Kelly (eds), *The Ironside Diaries, 1937–1940* (London, 1962), 1 February 1940, p. 214. • 17 Quoted in Imlay, *Facing the Second World War*, p. 67. • 18 Macleod and Kelly (eds), *Ironside Diaries*, 1 February 1940, p. 214. • 19 Air Chief Marshall Newall quoted in John Kennedy, *The Business of War: The War Narrative of Major-General Sir John Kennedy* (London, 1957), p. 48. • 20 *National Zeitung*, 13 March 1940. • 21 FO 371/24298, Minute by J. K. Roberts, 13 March 1940; FO 800/312/21, Campbell to Halifax, 23 March 1940. • 22 FO 371/24298, Cadogan Minute, 15 March 1940; FO 371/24298, Butler Minute, 20 March 1940. • 23 Jean Lacouture, *De Gaulle: The Rebel, 1890–1944* (London, 1990), p. 139. • 24 Macleod and Kelly (eds), *Ironside Diaries*, 26–27 March 1940, pp. 234–5. • 25 CAB 99/3/1, Supreme War Council Minutes, 28 March 1940. • 26 Ibid., Press Communiqué, 28 March 1940. • 27 FO 800/312/39, Campbell to Halifax, 7 April 1940 • 28 André Maurois, *Tragédie en France* (New York, 1940), p. 84. • 29 FO 800/312/30, Minute by Sir Alexander Cadogan, 31 March 1940. • 30 FO 800/312/28, Note by Neville Chamberlain of Conversation with Corbin, 31 March

1940. • 31 CAB 65/6/27, War Cabinet Minutes, 5 April 1940. • 32 John Harvey (ed.), *The Diplomatic Diaries of Oliver Harvey, 1937–1940* (London, 1970), 14 March 1940, p. 340. • 33 John Colville, *The Fringes of Power: Downing Street Diaries, 1939–1955* (London, 1985), 6 April 1940, p. 97. • 34 David Dilks (ed.), *The Diaries of Sir Alexander Cadogan, OM, 1938–1945* (London, 1971), 8 April 1940, p. 268. • 35 Macleod and Kelly (eds), *Ironside Diaries*, 9 April 1940, p. 249. • 36 Colville, *Fringes of Power*, 9 April 1940, p. 100. • 37 Ibid., 3 May 1940, p. 116. • 38 Adrian Carton de Wiart, *Happy Odyssey* (London, 1950), p. 169. • 39 Ibid., p. 170. • 40 FO 800/312/47, Campbell to Halifax, 29 April 1940. • 41 Quoted in Max Hastings, *All Hell Let Loose: The World at War, 1939–1945* (London, 2011), p. 50. • 42 Colville, *Fringes of Power*, 26 April 1940, p. 111. • 43 Quoted in Kersaudy, *Norway 1940*, p. 165. • 44 Quoted in Tim Bouverie, *Appeasing Hitler: Chamberlain, Churchill and the Road to War* (London, 2019), p. 395. • 45 Hansard, HC Deb, 7 May 1940, vol. 360, col. 1127. • 46 Hansard, HC Deb, 8 May 1940, vol. 360, col. 1283. • 47 Hansard, HC Deb, 7 May 1940, vol. 360, col. 1150. • 48 *The Private Diaries of Paul Baudouin* (London, 1948), 9 & 12 April 1949, pp. 9, 11.

III: The Fall

1 John Harvey (ed.), *Diplomatic Diaries of Oliver Harvey, 1937–1940* (London, 1970), 6 June 1940, p. 380. • 2 CAB 65/3/9, War Cabinet Minutes, Confidential Annex, 19 September 1939. • 3 *Documents diplomatiques français*, Series 1936–39, Vol. XIX (Paris, 1986), Gamelin to Daladier, 1 September 1939, pp. 357–8; quoted in Nicole Jordan, *The Popular Front and Central Europe: The Dilemmas of French Impotence, 1918–1940* (Cambridge, 1992), p. 297. • 4 Quoted in Alain Colignon, 'Belgium: Fragile Neutrality, Solid Neutralism', in Neville Wylie (ed.), *European Neutrals and Non-belligerents during the Second World War* (Cambridge, 2002), p. 106. • 5 Quoted in Rudolph Binion, 'Repeat Performance: A Psychohistorical Study of Leopold III and Belgian Neutrality', *History and Theory*, vol. 8., no. 2 (1969), p. 231. • 6 Quoted in Llewellyn Woodward, *British Foreign Policy in the Second World War, Vol. I* (London, 1970), p. 15. • 7 Davies Papers, Box 1, Folder 10, Joseph E. Davies Diary, April 1939. • 8 Quoted in Woodward, *British Foreign Policy in the Second World War, Vol. I*, p. 16. • 9 Brian Bond (ed.), *Chief of Staff: The Diaries of Lieutenant-General Sir Henry Pownall, Vol. I: 1933–1940* (London, 1972), 10 November 1939, p. 252. • 10 Roderick Macleod and Denis Kelly (eds), *The Ironside Diaries, 1937–1940* (London, 1962), 14 January 1940, p. 206; Paul Reynaud, *In the Thick of the Fight* (London, 1955), p. 251. • 11 Winston S. Churchill, *The Second World War, Vol. II: Their Finest Hour* (London, 1949), p. 38. • 12 *The Memoirs of General the Lord Ismay* (London, 1960), p. 126. • 13 *The Private Diaries of Paul Baudouin* (London, 1948), 16 May 1940, p. 32. • 14 Churchill, *Second World War, Vol. II*, p. 42. • 15 Reynaud, *In the Thick of the Fight*, p. 324. • 16 *Private Diaries of Paul Baudouin*, 16 May 1940, p. 32; *Memoirs of General the Lord Ismay*, p. 127. • 17 *Private Diaries of Paul Baudouin*, p. 33. • 18 CAB 79/4/33, Chiefs of Staff Committee Minutes, 15 May 1940; Alistair Horne, *To Lose a Battle: France 1940* (London, 1969), p. 323. • 19 Edward Spears, *Assignment to Catastrophe, Vol. I: Prelude to Dunkirk, July 1939–May 1940* (London, 1954), pp. 252–3. • 20 Quoted in Julian Jackson, *The Fall of France: The Nazi Invasion of 1940* (Oxford, 2003), pp. 93–4. • 21 Clare Boothe Luce, *European Spring* (London, 1941), p. 290. • 22 D. Barlone, *A French Officer's Diary* (Cambridge, 1942), p. 57. • 23 WO 106/1613, Gort to Ironside, 29 May 1940. • 24 Spears, *Assignment to Catastrophe, Vol. I*, p. 295. • 25 CAB 99/3/2, Supreme War Council Minutes, 31 May 1940. • 26 *Private Diaries of Paul Baudouin*, 24 May 1940, pp. 46, 47. • 27 FO 800/325/3, Halifax to Lothian, 21 November 1939. • 28 David Dilks (ed.), *The Diaries of Sir Alexander Cadogan, OM, 1938–1945* (London, 1971), p. 292. • 29 Ibid., 29 May 1940, p. 292. • 30 Malcolm Muggeridge (ed.), *Ciano's Diary, 1939–1943* (London, 1947), 27 May 1940, p. 255. • 31 Ibid., 9 June 1940, p. 263 & 7 June 1940, p. 262. • 32 Robert Self (ed.), *The Neville Chamberlain Diary Letters, Vol. IV: The Downing Street Years, 1934–1940* (Aldershot, 2005), NC to Hilda, 1 June 1940, pp. 534–5. • 33 FO 800/312/74, Campbell to Halifax, 30 May 1940. • 34 Spears, *Assignment to Catastrophe, Vol. I*, p. 319. • 35 Lord Moran, *Winston Churchill: The Struggle for Survival, 1940–1965* (London, 1966), p. 224. • 36 Lines

from Andrew Marvell's *An Horation Ode upon Cromwell's Return from Ireland*, which Churchill repeated during the Battle of France. • 37 Alexander Danchev and Daniel Todman (eds), *War Diaries, 1939–1945: Field Marshal Lord Alanbrooke* (London, 2001), pp. 74–5. • 38 Martin Gilbert (ed.), *The Churchill War Papers, Vol. II: Never Surrender, May 1940–December 1940* (London, 1994), Churchill to Ismay, 2 June 1940, p. 227. • 39 *Memoirs of General the Lord Ismay*, p. 142. • 40 Danchev and Todman (eds), *War Diaries*, 14 June 1940, p. 80. • 41 Ibid. • 42 Ibid., p. 81. • 43 Ben Pimlott (ed.), *The Second World War Diary of Hugh Dalton, 1940–45* (London, 1986), 3 June 1940, p. 34. • 44 Dilks (ed.), *Diaries of Sir Alexander Cadogan*, 2 June 1940, p. 293. • 45 CAB 65/13, War Cabinet Minutes, 4 June 1940. • 46 CAB 65/13, Campbell to Halifax, 5 June 1940. • 47 John Colville, *The Fringes of Power: Downing Street Diaries, 1939–1955* (London, 1985), 10 June 1940, p. 151. • 48 Edward Spears, *Assignment to Catastrophe, Vol. II: The Fall of France, June 1940* (London, 1954), p. 138. • 49 CAB 99/3/2, Supreme War Council Minutes, 11 June 1940. • 50 Spears, *Assignment to Catastrophe, Vol. II*, p. 143. • 51 Ibid., p. 149. • 52 *Memoirs of General the Lord Ismay*, p. 140. • 53 CAB 99/3/2, Supreme War Council Minutes, 11 June 1940. • 54 Spears, *Assignment to Catastrophe, Vol. II*, p. 150. • 55 Ibid., p. 158; *Memoirs of General the Lord Ismay*, p. 140. • 56 According to Spears, the Maréchal was anything but ashamed: 'Pétain looked in, paternal and accepting defeat joyfully almost. *"C'est la catastrophe, c'est la débandade"*, he said.' Spears Papers, SPRS 8/12, Diary, 12 June 1940.• 57 Spears, *Assignment to Catastrophe, Vol. II*, p. 170. • 58 Ibid., p. 205; CAB 99/3/2, Supreme War Council Minutes, 13 June 1940. • 59 Spears, *Assignment to Catastrophe, Vol. II*, p. 214. • 60 Ibid., p. 215. • 61 Churchill, *Second World War, Vol. II*, p. 162. • 62 Maxime Weygand, *Recalled to Service: The Memoirs of Maxime Weygand* (London, 1952), p. 153.

IV: Unfriendly Fire

1 Linlithgow Papers, MS EUR F 125/9, Amery to Linlithgow, 4 July 1940. • 2 'Vice Admiral Sir Cedric Swinton Holland, KCB', 18 October 2007, https://web.archive.org/web/20110724083959/http://www.admirals.org.uk/admirals/vadm/hollandcs.php • 3 Holland Papers, HND 3/4, Narrative of Events at Oran on 3 July 1940. • 4 Quoted in Warren Tute, *The Deadly Stroke* (London, 1973), p. 83. • 5 ADM 199/391, Somerville, Report of Proceedings 28 June–4 July 1940. • 6 Ibid., Appendix D. • 7 Quoted in Colin Smith, *England's Last War against France: Fighting Vichy, 1940–1942* (London, 2009), p. 65. • 8 Quoted in Albert Kammerer, *La Tragédie de Mers-el-Kébir: l'Angleterre et la flotte française* (Paris, 1945), p. 111. • 9 Holland Papers, HND 3/4, Narrative of Events at Oran on 3 July 1940. • 10 Quoted in David Brown, *The Road to Oran: Anglo-French Naval Relations, September 1939–July 1940* (London, 2004), p. 31. • 11 Edward Spears, *Assignment to Catastrophe, Vol. II: The Fall of France, June 1940* (London, 1954), p. 224. • 12 CAB 65/13, War Cabinet to Campbell, 16 June 1940. • 13 FO 371/24298, Sargent Minute, 28 February 1940. • 14 Ibid., Perth Memorandum, 14 March 1940. • 15 FO 371/24299, Sargent to Harvey, 11 April 1940. • 16 CAB 65/7, War Cabinet Minutes, 3 p.m. 16 June 1940. • 17 Spears, *Assignment to Catastrophe, Vol. II*, p. 291. • 18 Quoted in Julian Jackson, *The Fall of France: The Nazi Invasion of 1940* (Oxford, 2003), p. 138. • 19 Llewellyn Woodward, *British Foreign Policy in the Second World War, Vol. I* (London, 1970), p. 291. • 20 Ibid., pp. 293–4, Churchill to Pétain and Weygand, 17 June 1940. • 21 Lord Tyrell quoted in Patrick Beesly, *Very Special Admiral: The Life of Admiral J. H. Godfrey, CB* (London, 1980), p. 159; FO 371/24348, Campbell to FO, 22 June 1940. • 22 Quoted in Hervé Coutau-Bégarie and Claude Huan, *Darlan* (Paris, 1989), p. 268. • 23 Quoted in Woodward, *British Foreign Policy in the Second World War, Vol. I*, p. 307. • 24 Pleydell-Bouverie Papers, Diary, 22 June 1940; FO 371/24348, Campbell to FO, 22 June 1940. • 25 CAB 65/13, War Cabinet Minutes, 22 June 1940. • 26 Quoted in Brown, *Road to Oran*, p. 94. • 27 CAB 65/7, War Cabinet Minutes, 12 p.m., 24 June 1940. • 28 Holland Papers, HND 3/4, Narrative of Events at Oran on 3 July 1940. • 29 Jean Boutron, *De Mers el-Kébir à Londres* (Paris, 1980), p. 26. • 30 Ibid., p. 43. • 31 Holland Papers, HND 3/4, Narrative of Events at Oran on 3 July 1940, Captain Cedric Holland. • 32 Quoted in Arthur J. Marder, *From the Dardanelles to Oran: Studies of the Royal Navy in War and Peace, 1915–1940* (London, 1974), p. 245. • 33 Quoted in Coutau-Bégarie

and Huan, *Darlan*, p. 268. • 34 Holland Papers, HND 3/4, Narrative of Events at Oran on 3 July 1940. • 35 ADM 199/391, Somerville, Report of Proceedings 28 June–4 July 1940. • 36 Holland Papers, HND 3/4, Narrative of Events at Oran on 3 July 1940. • 37 Boutron, *De Mers el-Kébir à Londres*, p. 111. • 38 Michael Simpson (ed.), *The Somerville Papers: Selections from the Private and Official Correspondence of Admiral of the Fleet Sir James Somerville, GCB, GBE, DSO* (Aldershot, 1995), James Somerville to Mary Somerville, 4 July 1940, pp. 108–9. • 39 Holland Papers, HND 3/4, Holland to Somerville, 5 July 1940. • 40 Quoted in Jean Lacouture, *De Gaulle: The Rebel, 1890–1944* (London, 1990), p. 231; quoted in Marder, *From the Dardanelles to Oran*, p. 189. • 41 Édouard Herriot, *Épisodes, 1940–1944* (Paris, 1950), p. 75. • 42 ADM 186/797, Naval Staff History: Selected Bombardments (Mediterranean), 1940–1941, p. 8. • 43 Quoted in David Reynolds, *In Command of History: Churchill Fighting and Writing the Second World War* (London, 2004), p. 172. • 44 CAB, 80/14, Chiefs of Staff Paper, Implications of Action Contemplated in Respect of Certain French Ships, 30 June 1940. • 45 Alexander Papers, AVAR 5/4/38, Alexander to Churchill, 9 July 1940. • 46 *The Memoirs of Cordell Hull, Vol. I* (London, 1948), p. 799. • 47 PREM 3/457, Churchill to Halifax, 24 June 1940. • 48 Roosevelt Papers, PSF, Diplomatic Correspondence, Box 33, Great Britain Military Situation, Lothian to FDR, 4 July 1940.

V: Rebels with a Cause

1 Quoted in François Kersaudy, *Churchill and De Gaulle* (London, 1981), p. 80. • 2 FO 371/24321, Reports from Naval Attachés, 6–10 July 1940. • 3 FO 371/24241, American Survey Digest, 9 July 1940. • 4 ADM 199/822, Lothian to Halifax, 9 July 1940; James R. Leutze (ed.), *The London Observer: The Journal of General Raymond E. Lee, 1940–1941* (London, 1972), 4 July 1940, p. 11. • 5 Freya Stark, *Dust in the Lion's Paw: Autobiography, 1939–1946* (London, 1961), p. 58. • 6 Charles de Gaulle, *Mémoires de guerre, vol. I: l'appel, 1940–1942* (Paris, 1954), p. 1. • 7 *The Times*, 7 June 1940. • 8 Quoted in David Dilks (ed.), *The Diaries of Sir Alexander Cadogan, OM, 1938–1945* (London, 1971), p. 302. • 9 De Gaulle, *Mémoires de guerre, vol. I*, Documents, Appel du général de Gaulle aux Français, 18 June 1940, pp. 267–8. • 10 FO 371/24349, Strang Minute, 19 June 1940. • 11 Dilks (ed.), *Diaries of Sir Alexander Cadogan*, 19 & 20 June 1940, pp. 304–5. • 12 See 'General de Gaulle's Address (June 22, 1940)', https://franceintheus.org/IMG/pdf/General_de_Gaulles_Address_-_June_22_1940.pdf • 13 Quoted in Julian Jackson, *A Certain Idea of France: The Life of Charles de Gaulle* (London, 2018), p. 130. • 14 Ibid., p. 131. • 15 Chartwell Papers, CHAR 20/13/3, Churchill to Ismay, 24 June 1940. • 16 René Cassin, *Les Hommes partis de rien: le réveil de la France abattue, 1940–41* (Paris, 1975), p. 76. • 17 CAB 65/8, War Cabinet Conclusions, 28 June 1940. • 18 Cassin, *Les Hommes partis de rien*, p. 77. • 19 De Gaulle, *Mémoires de guerre, vol. I*, Documents, Termes de l'Accord du 7 août 1940, pp. 279–82. • 20 Sir Edward Spears, *Two Men Who Saved France: Pétain and De Gaulle* (London, 1966), p. 144–5. • 21 Ibid., p. 174. • 22 Ibid., p. 168. • 23 Spears Papers, MEC, Box 1, File 2, Spears to Admiral Sir Charles Little, 21 August 1940. • 24 Ibid., Spears to Dickens, 11 August 1940. • 25 Ibid., Dickens to Spears, 13 August 1940. • 26 Jean Lacouture, *De Gaulle, Vol. I: The Rebel, 1890–1944* (London, 1990), p. 250. • 27 De Gaulle, *Mémoires de guerre, vol. I*, pp. 86–7. • 28 PREM 3/276, Cusden to Foreign Office, 4 July 1940. • 29 Evelyn Waugh, *Men at Arms* (London, 1952), p. 144. • 30 Chartwell Papers, CHAR 20/13/3, WSC to Ismay, 5 June 1940. • 31 Quoted in Arthur Marder, *Operation 'Menace': The Dakar Expedition and the Dudley North Affair* (London, 1976), p. 12. • 32 Recollection by Rear-Admiral A. D. Nicholl, quoted ibid., pp. 16–17. • 33 Ibid., p. 17. • 34 De Gaulle, *Mémoires de guerre, vol. I*, p. 98. • 35 FO 371/24293, Lyon to Secretary of the Admiralty, 4 July 1940. • 36 Quoted in Marder, *Operation 'Menace'*, p. 46. • 37 Ibid., p. 47; Irwin Papers, 1/2, Summary of Report by the Inter-Service Security Board, Annex IV, The Dakar Operation. • 38 John A. Watson, *Échec à Dakar: septembre 1940* (Paris, 1968), p. 51. • 39 Sir Ronald Wingate, *Not in the Limelight* (London, 1959), p. 159. • 40 Quoted in Jackson, *Certain Idea of France*, p. 149. • 41 PREM 3/276, The Dakar Operation, October 1940. • 42 Spears Papers, SPRS 5/36, Dakar Diary, 16 September 1940; Irwin Papers, 1/1, The Dakar Operation, Official Report, Annex V, Signal 7. • 43 Major

John Watson, quoted in Marder, *Operation 'Menace'*, p. 106. • 44 Major John Watson, quoted in Marder, *Operation 'Menace'*, p. 106. • 45 Spears, *Two Men Who Saved France*, p. 196; quoted in Maurice Martin du Gard, *La Carte impériale: histoire de la France outre-mer, 1940–1945* (Paris, 1949), pp. 112–13. • 46 Spears Papers, SPRS 5/36, Dakar Diary, 23 September 1940. • 47 Emden Papers, 86/59/1, Journal, Dakar 23–25 September 1940. • 48 Spears, *Two Men Who Saved France*, p. 197. • 49 PREM 3/276, Churchill to Cunningham, 23 September 1940. 'Let 'em have it,' Churchill told Jock Colville when he reported that Dakar was resisting. 'Remember this: never maltreat your enemy by halves. Once the battle is joined, let 'em have it.' • 50 Irwin Papers, 1/2, Defeat before Dakar, p. 18. • 51 Ibid., p. 29. • 52 Ibid., Report on Menace, 7 October 1940, p. 20. • 53 Spears, *Two Men Who Saved France*, p. 185. • 54 PREM 3/276, Churchill to Cunningham and Irwin, 25 September 1940. • 55 Simon Heffer (ed.), *Henry 'Chips' Channon: The Diaries, Vol. II: 1938–43* (London, 2021), 25 September 1940, p. 412.

VI: The Battle for America

1 James R. Leutze (ed.), *The London Observer: The Journal of General Raymond E. Lee, 1940–1941* (London, 1972), p. 68. • 2 Quoted in Martin Gilbert, *Sir Horace Rumbold: Portrait of a Diplomat, 1869–1941* (London, 1973), p. 451. • 3 Admiral of the Fleet Viscount Cunningham of Hyndhope, KT, GCB, OM, DSO, *A Sailor's Odyssey: The Autobiography* (London, 1952), p. 238. • 4 Quoted in Christopher Thorne, *Allies of a Kind: The United States, Britain and the War against Japan* (London, 1978), p. 94; quoted in John Terraine, *The Right of the Line: the Royal Air Force in the European War, 1939–1945* (London, 1985), p. 170. • 5 Roberts Papers, Interview with Lord Colyton. Landing in London on 1 June, mid-way through the Dunkirk evacuation, the American writer Clare Boothe Luce found that everybody was still saying, 'England loses every battle but the last one.' • 6 Hickleton Papers, A7/8/4, Halifax Diary, 25 May 1940. • 7 Paul Addison and Jeremy A. Crang (eds), *Listening to Britain: Home Intelligence Reports on Britain's Finest Hour, May to September 1940* (London, 2010), p. 130. On 18 June 1940 – the day after the French request for an armistice – an analysis of Home Intelligence reports revealed that roughly 75 per cent of the population expected the war to continue. • 8 Mass Observation File Report 181, 'Capitulation Talk in Worktown', 19 June 1940, p. 5. • 9 Ibid. • 10 Martin Gilbert (ed.), *The Churchill War Papers, Vol. II: Never Surrender, May 1940–December 1940* (London, 1994), Randolph Churchill recollection, pp. 70–71. • 11 Robert Self (ed.), *Neville Chamberlain Diary Letters, Vol. IV: The Downing Street Years, 1934–1940* (Aldershot, 2005), NC to Ida, pp. 492–3. • 12 Quoted in David Reynolds, *The Creation of the Anglo-American Alliance, 1937–41: A Study in Competitive Co-operation* (London, 1981), p. 79. • 13 FO 371/24239, David Scott Minute, 28 February 1940. • 14 Royal Archives, Diaries of HM King George VI, 6 February 1940, Vol. I, p. 70. • 15 David Dilks (ed.), *The Diaries of Sir Alexander Cadogan, OM, 1938–1945* (London, 1971), 2 February 1940, p. 250; Sumner Welles, *The Time for Decision* (London, 1944), p. 61. • 16 Ickes Papers, Box 25, Diary Cuts, 6 April 1941. • 17 Self (ed.), *Neville Chamberlain Diary Letters, Vol. IV*, NC to Ida, 16 March 1940, p. 510. • 18 FO 371/24406, Vansittart minute, 18 March 1940. Vansittart was aware of the multiple 'assurances' the Foreign Office had received – including from the American Minister in London, Walton Butterworth – that 'internal [American] politics were almost entirely responsible for the tour'. • 19 Royal Archives, Diaries of HM King George VI, 13 March 1940, Vol. II, p. 97. • 20 Roosevelt Papers, Master Speech File, Fireside Chat No. 14, 3 September 1939. • 21 FO 371/24239, Lothian to Halifax, 29 April 1940. • 22 FO 115/3419585, Lothian to Halifax, 14 December 1939. • 23 Berle Papers, Box 211, Diary, 22 September 1939. • 24 Moffat Papers, MS Am 1407, vol. 42, 16 February 1939; quoted in Thorne, *Allies of a Kind*, p. 146. • 25 Robert Calder, *Beware the British Serpent: The Role of Writers in British Propaganda in the United States, 1939–1945* (Montreal, 2004), p. 43. • 26 Lord Casey, *Personal Experience, 1939–1946* (London, 1962), pp. 24–5. • 27 FO 371/24227, Hessell Tiltman, Report on General Position in the United States, 7 December 1939. • 28 Quoted in Robert E. Sherwood, *The White House Papers of*

Harry L. Hopkins, Vol. I: September 1939–January 1942 (London, 1948), p. 167. • 29 Berle Papers, Box 211, Diary, 26 May 1940. • 30 Beatrice Bishop Berle and Travis Beal Jacobs (eds), *Navigating the Rapids, 1918–1971: From the Papers of Adolf A. Berle* (San Diego, 1973). • 31 Chamberlain Papers, NC 2/24A, Diary, 19 May 1940. • 32 CAB 66/7/48, Chiefs of Staff Report, British Strategy in a Certain Eventuality, 25 May 1940. • 33 FO 371/25206, Halifax to Hankey, 15 July 1940. • 34 Quoted in David Reynolds, 'Lord Lothian and Anglo-American Relations, 1939–1940', *Transactions of the American Philosophical Society*, vol. 73, no. 2 (1983), p. 7. • 35 Roosevelt Papers, PSF, Safe File, Diplomatic Correspondence, Box 37, Kennedy to Roosevelt, 20 July 1939. • 36 Ickes Papers, Box 25, Diary Cuts, 6 April 1941; Berle Papers, Box 211, Diary, 5 May 1940. • 37 Ickes Papers, Diary, 12 May 1940, Vol. 31. • 38 Warren F. Kimball (ed.), *Churchill & Roosevelt: The Complete Correspondence* (Princeton, NJ, 1984), Churchill to Roosevelt, 15 May 1940, vol. 1, p. 37. • 39 John Colville, *The Fringes of Power: Downing Street Diaries, 1939–1955* (London, 1985), 19 May 1940, p. 136; Kimball (ed.), *Churchill & Roosevelt*, Churchill to Roosevelt, 20 May 1940, vol. 1, p. 40. • 40 Royal Archives, GVI/PRIV/DIARY/WAR/COPY/1940: 22 October, Conversation with Lothian. • 41 Orville H. Bullitt (ed.), *For the President, Personal and Secret: Correspondence between Franklin D. Roosevelt and William C. Bullitt* (London, 1973), pp. 427–8. • 42 Roosevelt Papers, PSF, Department Correspondence, Box 70, State Department, April–May 1940, Davies to Roosevelt, 23 May 1940. • 43 FO 371/24192, Lothian to Foreign Office, 18 May 1940. • 44 Ibid., Scott Minute, 20 May 1940. • 45 Hansard, HC Deb, 4 June 1940, vol. 361, col. 796; CHAR 20/14, Churchill to Lothian, 9 June 1940. • 46 Forrest C. Pogue, *George C. Marshall, Vol. II: Ordeal and Hope, 1939–1942* (New York, 1965), p. 50. • 47 Ibid., p. 53. • 48 FO 371/24230, Lothian to Foreign Office, 27 June 1940. • 49 FO 371/24241, Memorandum, US Press Prior to 14 July 1940. • 50 James A. Farley, *Jim Farley's Story: The Roosevelt Years* (New York, 1948), pp. 244–55. • 51 Quoted in Reynolds, *Creation of the Anglo-American Alliance*, pp. 119–20. • 52 Amanda Smith (ed.), *Hostage to Fortune: The Letters of Joseph P. Kennedy* (New York, 2001), p. 385. • 53 *Foreign Relations of the United States (FRUS) 1940, Vol. III: The British Commonwealth, The Soviet Union, The Near East and Africa* (Washington, DC, 1958), Doc. 25, Kennedy to Hull, 24 May 1940; Roosevelt Papers, PSF, Diplomatic Correspondence, Box 37, Kennedy to Roosevelt, 15 May 1940. 'Young man', the Ambassador told Lieutenant-Colonel Gerald Templer around 11 June 1940, 'England will be invaded in a few weeks' time and your country will have its neck wrung by Hitler like a chicken.' • 54 Quoted in George A. Lanyi, 'Review: The Problem of Appeasement', *World Politics*, vol. 15, no. 2 (1963), p. 324. • 55 John Wheeler-Bennett, *Special Relationships: America in Peace and War* (London, 1975), p. 72. • 56 FO 371/24245, Halifax to Beaverbrook, 16 December 1939. • 57 Johnson Papers, Folder 89, Herschel Johnson to Arabelle Johnson, 7 July 1940. • 58 Leutze (ed.), *London Observer*, 30 July 1940, p. 25. • 59 Henry Hardy (ed.), *Flourishing: Isaiah Berlin Letters, 1928–1946* (Cambridge, 2004), pp. 343, 346. • 60 Lothian Papers, GD40/17, Box 399, Lothian to Cazalet, 1 July 1940. • 61 Roosevelt Papers, Master Speech File, Box 52, File 1285, Address at the University of Virginia, 10 June 1940. • 62 Wheeler-Bennett, *Special Relationships*, p. 97. • 63 Rumbold Papers, Box 3, C, Anthony Rumbold to Etheldred Rumbold, 7 August 1940. • 64 Quoted in David Reynolds, *From World War to Cold War: Churchill, Roosevelt, and the International History of the 1940s* (Oxford, 2006), p. 95. • 65 Chartwell Papers, CHAR 2/396, Interview with Edgar Ansel Mowrer, 17 July 1940. • 66 Colville, *Fringes of Power*, 31 August 1940, p. 234. • 67 Congressional Record, Senate, 5 August 1940, vol. 86, part 9, p. 9826. • 68 FO 371/24241, Jock Balfour Minute, 7 August 1940. • 69 Elliott Roosevelt (ed.), *The Roosevelt Letters: Being the Personal Correspondence of Franklin Delano Roosevelt, Vol. III: 1928–1945* (London, 1952), Memorandum, 2 August 1940, p. 326. • 70 FO 371/24259, Lothian to Foreign Office, 22 August 1940. • 71 CAB 65/7, War Cabinet Minutes, 27 May 1940. • 72 FO 371/24255, Whitehead Minute, 14 July 1940. • 73 Balfour Papers, 'Diadems Askew', p. 176. • 74 Kimball (ed.), *Churchill & Roosevelt*, Churchill to Roosevelt, 31 July 1940, vol. 1, pp. 56–7. • 75 Balfour Papers, 'Diadems Askew', pp. 185–6. • 76 FO 371/24240, Halifax to WSC, 28 June 1940. • 77 *FRUS 1940, Vol. III*, Doc. 63, Kennedy to Hull, 29 August 1940. At one stage, Churchill, acutely aware of the vulnerability of his own domestic political position and fearing an unseemly wrangle over the scope and location of the bases, stated that he would rather 'do without the American destroyers' than submit to the perils and indignity of a formal contract. • 78 *Memoirs of Cordell Hull, Vol. I*, p. 837. • 79 *FRUS 1940, Vol. III*, Doc. 42, Lothian to Hull, 2 September 1940. • 80 Mark Chadwin, *The Hawks of World War II* (Chapel Hill, NC, 1968), p. 106; FO 371/24234, Lothian to Halifax, 9 September 1940. • 81 FO 371/24234, Lothian to Halifax, 9 September 1940; Franklin D. Roosevelt, Message to Congress on Exchanging Destroyers for British Naval and Air Bases, 3 September 1940, available at The American Presidency Project, https://www.presidency.ucsb.edu/documents/message-congress-exchanging-destroyers-for-british-naval-and-air-bases • 82 *New York Times*, 4 September 1940 • 83 Herbert Agar, *Britain Alone: June 1940–June 1941* (London, 1972), p. 148. • 84 Ivan Maisky, *Memoirs of a Soviet Ambassador: The War, 1939–1943* (London, 1967), p. 101; *FRUS 1940, Vol. III*, Doc. 60, Kennedy to Hull, 15 August 1940. • 85 CAB 65/8, War Cabinet Minutes, 14 August 1940. 'Every destroyer that you can spare is worth its weight in gold,' read a Foreign Office draft of Churchill's telegram to Roosevelt of 15 August 1940. When the Prime Minister asked what this meant, David Scott explained that £1,000,000 of gold was equivalent to 5 tons. Churchill thought this was 'a bit much' and so substituted 'rubies' for 'gold', 'the worth of a virtuous woman, you know'. • 86 Hansard, HC Deb, 20 August 1940, vol. 364, col. 1171.

VII: *The Reluctant Neutral*

1 Stanley G. Payne, *Franco and Hitler: Spain, Germany, and World War II* (New Haven, CT, 2008), p. 62. • 2 Quoted in Tim Bouverie, *Appeasing Hitler: Chamberlain, Churchill and the Road to War* (London, 2019), p. 75. • 3 Cato, *Guilty Men* (London, 1940) • 4 David Dilks (ed.), *The Diaries of Sir Alexander Cadogan, OM, 1938–1945* (London, 1971), 20 May 1940, p. 287. • 5 Quoted in D. R. Thorpe, *Eden: The Life and Times of Anthony Eden, First Earl of Avon, 1897–1977* (London, 2003), p. 153. • 6 B. H. Liddell Hart, *The Defence of Britain* (London, 1939), p. 68; Ivone Kirkpatrick, *The Inner Circle: Memoirs* (London, 1959), p. 195. • 7 FO 800/323/1, Hoare to Halifax, 3 June 1940; Hoare to Chamberlain, 6 June 1940, quoted in Sir Samuel Hoare, Viscount Templewood, *Ambassador on Special Mission* (London, 1946), p. 31. • 8 Ibid., p. 23. • 9 Ben Pimlott (ed.), *The Second World War Diary of Hugh Dalton, 1940–45* (London, 1986), 26 July 1940, p. 66. • 10 Ibid., 30 July 1940, p. 67. • 11 FO 800/323/1, Hoare to Halifax, 7 June 1940; Templewood Papers, Part XIII, File 8, Hoare to Beaverbrook, 6 June 1940. • 12 John Lomax, *The Diplomatic Smuggler* (London, 1965), p. 85. • 13 FO 800/323/1, Hoare to Halifax, 20 June 1940. • 14 FO 1093/233/1, Churchill to Eden and Wood, 25 September 1941. • 15 FO 954/27a/140, Hoare to Eden, 10 May 1941. • 16 Sherfield Papers, MS 518, Eccles to Makins, 1 November 1940. • 17 Ibid., Eccles to Makins, 5 November 1940. • 18 Sybil Eccles and David Eccles, *By Safe Hand: Letters, 1939–42* (London, 1983), David Eccles to Sybil Eccles, 20 July 1940, p. 141. • 19 FO 800/323, Dalton to Eccles, 27 August 1940. • 20 Sherfield Papers, MS 518, Eccles to Makins, 24 September 1940, Eccles to Makins, 5 November 1940. • 21 Ibid., Eccles to Makins, 24 September 1940. • 22 PREM 3/199, Churchill to Halifax, 21 June 1940. • 23 Warren F. Kimball (ed.), *Churchill & Roosevelt: The Complete Correspondence* (Princeton, NJ, 1984), Churchill to Roosevelt, 23 November 1940, vol. 1, p. 86. Although immovable on the subject of Gibraltar, Churchill was quite willing to see Spain expand in Morocco at the expense of France. 'I would far rather the Spaniards in Morocco than the Germans,' he minuted Halifax, 'and if the French have to pay for their abject attitude it is better that they should pay in Africa to Spain than in Europe to either of the guilty powers. Indeed, I think you should let them [the Spanish] know that we shall be no obstacle to their Moroccan ambitions, provided they preserve their neutrality in the war.' • 24 Berle Papers, Box 212, Diary, 2 December 1940. • 25 Eric C. Wendelin, Third Secretary at the US Embassy in Madrid, quoted ibid., Diary, 4 December 1940. • 26 *Foreign Relations of the United States (FRUS) 1941, Vol. II: Europe* (Washington, DC, 1959), Doc. 872, Weddell to Hull, 19 April 1941; *Documents on German Foreign Policy, 1918–1945, Series D, Vol. XII: The War Years, February 1–June 22, 1941* (London, 1962),

Von Stohrer to Foreign Ministry, 20 April 1941, p. 591. • 27 Thomas J. Hamilton, *Appeasement's Child: The Franco Regime in Spain* (London, 1943), p. 220. • 28 Lomax, *Diplomatic Smuggler*, pp. 87–9. • 29 Ibid., p. 86. • 30 PREM 4/21/2, Hillgarth to Churchill, 27 July 1940. • 31 Hamilton, *Appeasement's Child*, p. 207; Templewood Papers, Part XIII, File 16, Hoare to Churchill, 27 August 1940. • 32 Eccles and Eccles, *By Safe Hand*, p.101; ibid., David Eccles to Sybil Eccles, 30 August 1940, p. 148. • 33 Hoare, *Ambassador on Special Mission*, pp. 114–16; Quoted in J. A. Cross, *Sir Samuel Hoare: A Political Biography* (London, 1977), p. 338. • 34 Sherfield Papers, MS 518, Eccles to Makins, 12 November 1940. • 35 FO 371/24515, Churchill to Halifax, 24 July 1940. • 36 FO 371/49663, Interview with Charles Favrel, *Paris-Presse*, 26 October 1945. • 37 Malcolm Muggeridge (ed.), *Ciano's Diplomatic Papers* (London, 1948), p. 402. • 38 *FRUS 1940, Vol. II: General and Europe* (Washington, DC, 1957), Doc. 933, Weddell to Hull, 7 September 1940. • 39 *Arriba*, 5 September 1940. • 40 Quoted in David Wingeate Pike, *Franco and the Axis Stigma* (Basingstoke, 2008), p. 47. • 41 Sherfield Papers, MS 518, Eccles to Makins, 24 September 1940.

VIII: *Friend or Foe?*

1 Q. J. Reynolds, *Only the Stars Are Neutral* (New York, 1942). • 2 Sir Samuel Hoare, Viscount Templewood, *Ambassador on Special Mission* (London, 1946), p. 83. • 3 Templewood Papers, Part XIII, File 16, Hoare to Churchill, 27 June 1940. • 4 Harvey Papers, MS 56402, Peake to Harvey, 26 January 1940. • 5 *Foreign Relations of the United States (FRUS) 1940, Vol. III: The British Commonwealth, The Soviet Union, The Near East and Africa* (Washington, DC, 1958), Doc. 37, Weddell to Hull, 2 July 1940. • 6 Templewood Papers, Part XIII, File 2, Windsor Documents, Ribbentrop to Stohrer, 11 July 1940. • 7 FO 800/323/1, Halifax to Hoare, 8 July 1940. Although desirous of peace at almost any price, the Duke did not believe the time was right for him to play the role of peacemaker and was incredulous at the suggestion that he might one day reascend the throne. A fool and a defeatist no doubt but accusations of treachery appear wide of the mark. • 8 Sybil Eccles and David Eccles, *By Safe Hand: Letters, 1939–42* (London, 1983), David Eccles to Sybil Eccles, pp. 139, 132; quoted in Michael Bloch, *Operation Willi: The Plot to Kidnap the Duke of Windsor, July 1940* (London, 1984) p. 77. • 9 FO 371/24302, Policy towards Vichy Government, 27 September 1940. • 10 FO 371/24302, Policy towards Vichy Government, 27 September 1940. The Government's Chief Diplomatic Adviser, Sir Robert Vansittart, emphatically disagreed. 'It seems to me far too optimistic,' he minuted on Halifax's paper. 'The Dakar disaster is a great triumph for Laval, who is entirely pro-German and it is the Laval set who will be strengthened by this and, alas, no other element.' • 11 See Robert O. Paxton's seminal *Vichy France: Old Guard and New Order, 1940–1944* (New York, 1972), also Jean-Baptiste Duroselle, *L'Abîme, 1939–1945* (Paris, 1982) and Julian Jackson, *France: The Dark Years, 1940–1944* (Oxford, 2001). • 12 Quoted in Paxton, *Vichy France*, p. 61. • 13 Ibid. • 14 Quoted in Jackson, *France: The Dark Years*, p. 171. • 15 Quoted in Eberhard Jäckel, *La France dans l'Europe de Hitler* (Paris, 1968), p. 158. • 16 Malcolm Muggeridge (ed.), *Ciano's Diary, 1939–1943* (London, 1947), 4 October 1940, p. 296. • 17 *Documents on German Foreign Policy, 1918–1945 (DGFP), Series D, Vol. XI: The War Years, September 1, 1940–January 31, 1941* (London, 1961), Memorandum of a conversation between the Führer and Laval, 22 October 1940, p. 357. • 18 Quoted in Julian Jackson, *France on Trial: The Case of Marshal Pétain* (London, 2023), p. xxiii. • 19 FO 371/24334, Hoare to Halifax, 14 October 1940. • 20 Warren F. Kimball (ed.), *Churchill & Roosevelt: The Complete Correspondence* (Princeton, NJ, 1984), Churchill to Roosevelt, 25 October 1940, vol. 1, p. 77; ibid., Roosevelt to Churchill, 24 October 1941, vol. 1, p. 76. • 21 Louis Rougier, *Mission secrète à Londres: les accords Pétain–Churchill* (Paris, 1947), p. 72. • 22 Ibid., p. 79. • 23 FO 371/24302, Vansittart Minute, 27 September 1940. • 24 David Dilks (ed.), *The Diaries of Sir Alexander Cadogan, OM, 1938–1945* (London, 1971), 8 November 1940, pp. 334–5. • 25 CAB, 65/10, War Cabinet Minutes, 8 November 1940; CHAR 20/13/8, Churchill to Halifax, 8 November

1940. • 26 Eccles and Eccles, *By Safe Hand*, Letter from Roger Makins to David Eccles, 9 November 1940, p. 196. • 27 Quoted in Duroselle, *L'Abîme*, vol. 2, p. 276. • 28 John Colville, *The Fringes of Power: Downing Street Diaries, 1939–1955* (London, 1985), 28 October 1940, p. 277. • 29 Quoted in R. T. Thomas, *Britain and Vichy: The Dilemma of Anglo-French Relations, 1940–42* (London, 1979), p. 80. • 30 Spears Papers, SPRS 1/137/2d, *The Free French, Vichy and Ourselves*, undated memorandum. • 31 Final Text of the Articles of Agreement for a Treaty between Great Britain and Ireland as Signed, 6 December 1921, available at https://www.difp.ie/volume-1/1921/anglo-irish-treaty/214/#section-documentpage • 32 Winston S. Churchill, *The Second World War, Vol. I: The Gathering Storm* (London, 1948), p. 216. • 33 CAB 65/1/19, War Cabinet Minutes, 18 September 1940. • 34 CAB 65/1/50, War Cabinet Minutes, 17 October 1940. • 35 Avon Papers, AP 20/1/9/19, Eden Diary, 17 October 1939. • 36 CAB 66/2, The Need for Berehaven, 18 October 1939. • 37 Quoted in Robert Fisk, *In Time of War: Ireland, Ulster and the Price of Neutrality, 1939–1945* (Dublin, 1983), p. 98. • 38 Quoted in Earl of Longford and Thomas P. O'Neill, *Éamon de Valera* (Boston, 1971), p. xvi. • 39 CAB 66/2, Report by Sir John Maffey on His Interview with Mr de Valera on the 21 October 1939. Since 1937, when the Irish Government had abolished the post of Governor-General, there had been no British diplomatic representative in Dublin. De Valera wanted the British Government to send an ambassador but since this would be to recognise Ireland as a foreign country, outside the Commonwealth, the British refused. After many arguments, de Valera was persuaded to accept a 'representative', although he achieved the important semantic change of 'to Éire' rather than 'in Éire'. • 40 Chartwell Papers, CHAR 19/3/1, Churchill Minute to Pound, Philips and Godfrey, 24 September 1939. • 41 FO 371/23966, Irish Opinion and the War, 23 October 1939. • 42 DO 35/1109/6, Maffey to DO, 23 June 1941. • 43 PREM 3/131/2, Fifth Column In and Working from Éire, 8 June 1940. • 44 CAB 65/1/58, War Cabinet Minutes, 24 October 1939. • 45 CAB 66/1, Appendix II, Report by Sir John Maffey on His Visit to Dublin on 14 September 1939. • 46 Quoted in Fisk, *In Time of War*, p. 147 • 47 PREM 3/131/2, Craigavon to Chamberlain, 27 June 1940. • 48 Hansard, HC Deb, 5 November 1940, vol. 365, col. 1243. • 49 PREM 3/131/3, Maffey to Dominions Office, 20 January 1941. Churchill agreed. In February 1941, when fear of a German invasion of Ireland was running high, he told Major-General John Kennedy that he would not 'mind the Irish being mauled a bit before we go to the rescue. They have behaved so badly.' (Kennedy Papers, 4/2/3, Diary, 15 February 1941) • 50 DO 130/21, Maffey to Machtig, 4 March 1941. • 51 *FRUS 1941, Vol. III: The British Commonwealth; The Near East and Africa* (Washington, DC, 1959), Doc. 177, Gray to Hull, 1 May 1941. • 52 Quoted in Fisk, *In Time of War*, p. 305. • 53 Alsop Papers, Box 32, Folder 11, Undated Notes. • 54 DO/130/21, Maffey Memorandum, 6 January 1940. • 55 ADM 223/486, Irish Affairs, 28 March 1941. • 56 Robert Brennan, *Ireland Standing Firm: My Wartime Mission in Washington* and *Éamon de Valera: A Memoir* (Dublin, 2022), p. 47. • 57 *FRUS 1941, Vol. III*, Doc. 174, Gray to Hull, 25 April 1941. • 58 Quoted in Longford and O'Neill, *Éamon de Valera*, p. 393. • 59 *DGFP, Series D, Vol. VIII: The War Years, September 4, 1939–March 18, 1940* (London, 1954), Hempel to Ribbentrop, Doc. 216, 8 October 1939, p. 242. • 60 PREM 3/131/7A, Maffey Memorandum, 14 March 1941 • 61 *DGFP, Series D, Vol. IX: The War Years, March 18–June 22, 1940* (London, 1956), Hempel to Foreign Ministry, 17 June 1940, p. 601.

IX: Greek Tragedy

1 John Colville, *The Fringes of Power: Downing Street Diaries, 1939–1955* (London, 1985), 5 March 1941, p. 361. • 2 J. A. Gere and John Sparrow (eds), *Geoffrey Madan's Notebooks* (Oxford, 1981), p. 23. • 3 PREM 3/309/1, Churchill to Wavell, 17 December 1940. • 4 Malcolm Muggeridge (ed.), *Ciano's Diary, 1939–1943* (London, 1947), 12 October 1940, p. 297. • 5 Ibid. • 6 Ibid., 4 December 1940, p. 313. • 7 David Dilks (ed.), *The Diaries of Sir Alexander Cadogan, OM, 1938–1945* (London, 1971), 21 November 1940, p. 336. • 8 PREM 3/309/1, Eden

to Churchill, 1 November 1940. • 9 Quoted in Martin Gilbert, *Winston S. Churchill, Vol. VI: Finest Hour, 1939–1941* (London, 1983), p. 905. • 10 Chartwell Papers, CHAR 20/14, Churchill to Eden, 2 November 1940. • 11 Ibid., Churchill to Eden, 3 November 1940, • 12 Chartwell Papers, CHAR 20/36, Churchill to the Chiefs of Staff, 7 January 1941. • 13 CAB 69/2, Defence Committee Minutes, 8 January 1941. • 14 Ibid., Churchill to Wavell, 12 February 1941. • 15 Colville, *Fringes of Power*, 12 February 1941, p. 356. • 16 Kennedy Papers, 4/2/3, Diary, 11 February 1941. • 17 Ibid., 12 February 1941. • 18 Patrick J. Cosgrave, *R. A. Butler: An English Life* (London, 1981), p. 12. • 19 Dixon Papers, Journal of a Tour in the Levant, February–April 1941, 8 April 1941. • 20 Dilks (ed.), *Diaries of Sir Alexander Cadogan*, p. 345. • 21 Mallaby Papers, Tour with SoS for Foreign Affairs & CIGS, 12 February 1941. Previously unpublished, Mallaby's is one of three contemporary diaries kept by members of the mission, the others being Eden's and Pierson Dixon's. These latter two were drawn on, heavily, for their respective authors' memoirs but the unpublished manuscripts retain important details. • 22 Ibid., 13 February 1941. • 23 Quoted in Earl of Avon, *The Eden Memoirs, Vol. II: The Reckoning* (London, 1965), p. 197. • 24 Ibid., p. 198. • 25 Alex Danchev (ed.), *Establishing the Anglo-American Alliance: The Second World War Diaries of Brigadier Vivian Dykes* (London, 1990), February 1941, p. 51. • 26 James Marshall-Cornwall, *Wars and Rumours of Wars: A Memoir* (London, 1984), p. 185. • 27 Kennedy Papers, 4/2/2, Diary, 23 November 1940; CHAR 20/14, Churchill to Eden, 3 November 1940. • 28 Admiral of the Fleet Viscount Cunningham of Hyndhope, KT, GCB, OM, DSO, *A Sailor's Odyssey: The Autobiography* (London, 1952), p. 291. • 29 Quoted in Avon, *Reckoning*, p. 133; Marshall-Cornwall, *Wars and Rumours of Wars*, p. 183. • 30 Kennedy Papers, 4/2/2, Diary, 5 December 1940. • 31 John Kennedy, *The Business of War: The War Narrative of Major-General Sir John Kennedy* (London, 1957), p. 63; CAB 69/2, Defence Committee Minutes, 20 January 1941. • 32 Kennedy Papers, 4/2/2, Diary, 23 November 1940. • 33 Martin Gilbert (ed.), *The Churchill Documents, Vol. XVI: The Ever-Widening War, 1941* (Hillsdale, MI, 2011), Churchill to Eden, 20 February 1941, p. 245. • 34 Major General Sir Francis de Guingand, *Generals at War* (London, 1964), pp. 27, 29. • 35 Dilks (ed.), *Diaries of Sir Alexander Cadogan*, 24 February 1941, p. 358. • 36 Mallaby Papers, Tour with SoS for Foreign Affairs & CIGS, 25 February 1941. • 37 Sir Hughe Knatchbull-Hugessen, *Diplomat in Peace and War* (London, 1949), p. 161. • 38 Marshall-Cornwall, *Wars and Rumours of Wars*, p. 179. • 39 Ibid., p. 181. • 40 Dilks (ed.), *Diaries of Sir Alexander Cadogan*, 28 February 1941, p. 359. • 41 CHAR 20/49, Churchill to Eden, 1 March 1941. • 42 Quoted in Adrian Fort, *Wavell: The Life and Times of an Imperial Servant* (London, 2009), p. 197. • 43 CAB 65/22, Eden to Churchill, 6 March 1941. • 44 Avon, *Reckoning*, p. 216. • 45 John O. Iatrides (ed.), *Ambassador MacVeagh Reports: Greece, 1933–1947* (Princeton, NJ, 1980), 3 March 1941, pp. 305–6, 5 March 1941, pp. 308–9. • 46 Avon, *Reckoning*, p. 217. • 47 De Guingand, *Generals at War*, p. 37. • 48 C. L. Sulzberger, *A Long Row of Candles: Memoirs and Diaries, 1934–1954* (London, 1969), p. 110. • 49 Robert Rhodes James (ed.), *Winston S. Churchill: His Complete Speeches* (London, 1974), Conservative and Unionist Associations Central Council Meeting, 27 March 1941, vol. 6, p. 6366. • 50 Quoted in Desmond Flower and James Reeves (eds), *The War, 1939–1945* (London, 1960), p. 185. The British had a meagre eighty serviceable aircraft at the time of the invasion, facing a German strength of over 900. • 51 Kennedy Papers, 4/2/3, Diary, 12 April 1941. • 52 Iatrides (ed.), *Ambassador MacVeagh Reports*, 9 April 1941, p. 333. • 53 Butler Papers, RAB G/12, Halifax to RAB, 26 April 1941. • 54 Kennedy, *The Business of War*, pp. 138–9. • 55 Marshall-Cornwall, *Wars and Rumours of Wars*, p. 184. • 56 Kennedy Papers, 4/2/3, 12 April 1941; A. W. Martin and Patsy Hardy (eds), *Dark and Hurrying Days: Menzies' 1941 Diary* (Canberra, 1993), 14 April 1941, p. 112. • 57 Kennedy Papers, 4/2/3, 12 April 1941. • 58 Carl von Clausewitz, *On War* (Princeton, NJ, 1984), p. 607. • 59 Herbert Agar, *Britain Alone, June 1940–June 1941* (London, 1972), p. 190. • 60 Rhodes James (ed.), *Winston S. Churchill: His Complete Speeches,* Broadcast, col. 6, p. 6380. • 61 Quoted in Fort, *Wavell*, p. 206.

X: Desert War

1 Elke Fröhlich (ed.), *Die Tagebücher von Joseph Goebbels, Teil 1: Aufzeichnungen 1923–1941, Bd. IX, Dezember 1940–Juli 1941* (Munich, 1998), p. 252. • 2 Roald Dahl, *Going Solo* (London, 1986), p. 96. • 3 Ibid. p. 97. • 4 Freya Stark, *Dust in the Lion's Paw: Autobiography, 1939–1946* (London, 1961), 19 April 1941, p. 83. • 5 Llewellyn Woodward, *British Foreign Policy in the Second World War, Vol. I* (London, 1970), p. 577. • 6 Stark, *Dust in the Lion's Paw*, 20 April 1941, p. 81. • 7 *Documents on German Foreign Policy, Series D, Vol. XII: The War Years, February 1–June 22, 1941* (London, 1962), Chargé d'Affaires in Italy to German Foreign Ministry, 19 April 1941, p. 587. • 8 A. G. Dudgeon, *Hidden Victory: The Battle of Habbaniya, May 1941* (Stroud, 2000), p. 48. • 9 Ibid., p. 48. • 10 Trefor E. Evans (ed.), *The Killearn Diaries, 1934–1946* (London, 1972), 30 April 1941, p. 167. • 11 Quoted in Robert Lyman, *First Victory: Britain's Forgotten Struggle in the Middle East, 1941* (London, 2006), p. 74. • 12 Quoted in Robert Lyman, *Iraq, 1941: The Battles for Basra, Habbaniya, Fallujah and Baghdad* (Botley, Oxford, 2006), p. 42. • 13 Dudgeon, *Hidden Victory*, p. 55. • 14 Quoted in Lyman, *Iraq, 1941*, p. 43. • 15 David Dilks (ed.), *The Diaries of Sir Alexander Cadogan, OM, 1938–1945* (London, 1971), 3 May 1941, p. 375. • 16 Quoted in John Connell, *Wavell: Scholar and Soldier, to June 1941* (London, 1964), p. 435. • 17 Quoted in Harold E. Raugh Jr., *Wavell in the Middle East, 1939–1941: A Study in Generalship* (London, 1993), p. 213. • 18 John Verney, *Going to the Wars: A Journey in Various Directions* (London, 1955), pp. 69, 84–5. • 19 John Glubb, *The Story of the Arab Legion* (London, 1948), p. 257. • 20 *To War with Whittaker: The Wartime Diaries of the Countess of Ranfurly, 1939–1945* (London, 1994), 31 August 1942, p. 141. • 21 Somerset de Chair, *The Golden Carpet* (London, 1944), pp. 32–3. • 22 Ibid. p. 18. • 23 Glubb, *Story of the Arab Legion*, p. 269. • 24 Flanakin Papers, unpublished memoir, p. 22. • 25 De Chair, *Golden Carpet*, p. 37. • 26 Ibid., p. 28. • 27 Ibid., p. 71. • 28 Stark, *Dust in the Lion's Paw*, 22 May 1941, p. 107. • 29 Glubb, *Story of the Arab Legion*, p. 291. • 30 Quoted in Dudgeon, *Hidden Victory*, p. 139.

XI: Fighting France*

1 *Foreign Relations of the United States (FRUS) 1941, Vol. III : The British Commonwealth; The Near East and Africa* (Washington, DC, 1959), Doc. 778, Leahy to Hull, 12 June 1941. • 2 Chalk Papers, unpublished memoirs, pp. 20–21. • 3 *Documents on German Foreign Policy, 1918–1945, Series D, Vol. XII: The War Years, February 1–June 22, 1941* (London, 1962), Doc. No. 475, Record of Negotiations between Darlan and Abetz, 8 May 1941, p. 740. • 4 Quoted in A. B. Gaunson, *The Anglo-French Clash in Lebanon and Syria, 1940–45* (Basingstoke, 1987), p. 34. • 5 John Colville, *The Fringes of Power: Downing Street Diaries, 1939–1955* (London, 1985), 20 May 1941, p. 389. • 6 Sir Edward Spears, *Fulfilment of a Mission: The Spears Mission to Syria and Lebanon, 1941–1944* (London, 1977), p. 62. • 7 Ibid., p. 63. • 8 Quoted in Anthony Mockler, *Our Enemies the French: Being an Account of the War Fought between the French and the British, Syria, 1941* (London, 1976), p. 234. • 9 Georges Catroux, *Dans la bataille de Méditerranée, Égypte, Levant, Afrique du Nord, 1940–1944* (Paris, 1949), p. 125. • 10 Ibid., p. 127. • 11 Ibid., p. 128. • 12 PREM 3/422/6, Wavell to Chiefs of Staff, 21 May 1941 (author's italics). • 13 Ibid., Churchill to Wavell, 21 May 1941. • 14 Quoted in Jean-Luc Barré, *Devenir de Gaulle, 1939–1943* (Paris, 2003), p.196. • 15 Quoted in Gaunson, *Anglo-French Clash in Lebanon and Syria*, p. 5. • 16 Spears Papers, MEC, 1A, 10 April 1941. • 17 FO 371/24592, MacMichael to Foreign Office, 21 November 1940. • 18 Catroux, *Dans la bataille de Méditerranée, Égypte, Levant, Afrique du Nord*, p. 137. • 19 Quoted in Gavin Long, *Australia in the War of 1939–1945, Series 1: Army, Vol. II: Greece, Crete and Syria* (Canberra, 1953), p. 345. • 20 Quoted in James Barr, *A Line in the Sand: Britain, France and the Struggle That Shaped the Middle East* (London, 2011), p. 218. • 21 Boswood Papers, unpublished memoir. • 22 Quoted ibid., p. 218. • 23 Quoted in Alan Moorehead, *African Trilogy: The North African Campaign, 1940–43* (London, [1944] 1998), p. 171. • 24 Quoted in Trevor Royle, *Glubb Pasha: The Life and Times of Sir John Bagot Glubb,*

Commander of the Arab Legion (London, 1992), p. 277. • 25 John Masters, *The Road Past Mandalay: A Personal Narrative* (London, 1961), p. 56. • 26 *FRUS 1941, Vol. III*, Doc. 778, Leahy to Hull, 12 June 1941. • 27 Dahl, *Going Solo*, p. 190. • 28 Sherfield Papers, MS 518, David Eccles to Roger Makins, 26 May 1941. • 29 Hopkins Papers, Box 304, Hopkins to Roosevelt, February 1941. • 30 Sherfield Papers, MS 518, David Eccles to Roger Makins, 26 May 1941. • 31 Julian Jackson, *France: The Dark Years, 1940–1944* (Oxford, 2001), p. 183. • 32 Spears Papers, MEC, Box 2, File 5, Somerville Smith to Spears, 5 July 1941. • 33 Ibid., Box 1, File 5, Cairo Diary, 20 June 1941. • 34 Charles Mott-Radclyffe, *Foreign Body in the Eye: A Memoir of the Foreign Service Old and New* (London, 1975), p. 95. • 35 Charles de Gaulle, *Mémoires de guerre, vol. I: l'appel, 1940–1942* (Paris, 1954), p. 165. • 36 *The Memoirs of Lord Chandos* (London, 1962), p. 247. • 37 Spears Papers, MEC, Box 1, File 5, Cairo Diary, 21 July 1941. • 38 Ibid., Lampson to Eden, 21 July 1941. • 39 *Memoirs of Lord Chandos*, p. 248. • 40 Spears Papers, MEC, Box 1, File 5, Cairo Diary, 21 July 1941; Roberts Papers, Interview with Lord Colyton. • 41 Spears, *Fulfilment of a Mission*, p. 138. • 42 Quoted in Julian Jackson, *A Certain Idea of France: The Life of Charles de Gaulle* (London, 2018), p. 178. • 43 Quoted in Jean Lacouture, *De Gaulle, Vol. I: The Rebel, 1890–1944* (London, 1990), p. 304. • 44 Spears Papers, MEC, Box 2, File 5, Memorandum to Mission from Somerville Smith, 30 August 1941. • 45 PREM 3/120/5 Churchill to Eden, 27 August 1941. • 46 Spears Papers, MEC, Box 2, File 5, Memorandum to Mission from Somerville Smith, 30 August 1941. • 47 John Colville, *Footprints in Time* (London, 1976), p. 114. • 48 FO 954/8A/173, Meeting between Churchill and de Gaulle, 12 September 1941. • 49 Colville, *Footprints in Time*, p. 115.

XII: The Soviet Enigma

1 J. V. Stalin, *Works, Vol. VII: 1925* (Moscow, 1954), Speech to the Central Committee of the Communist Party, 19 January 1925, pp. 13–14. • 2 Robert Rhodes James (ed.), *Winston S. Churchill: His Complete Speeches* (London, 1974), 'The First Month of the War', 1 October 1939, vol. 6, p. 6161. • 3 Evelyn Waugh, *Men at Arms* (London, 1952), p. 4. • 4 Simon Heffer (ed.), *Henry 'Chips' Channon: The Diaries, Vol. II: 1938–43* (London, 2021), 22 August 1939, p. 188. • 5 FO 800/328/3, Maxwell-Scott to Halifax, 17 September 1939. • 6 Waugh, *Men at Arms*, pp. 5, 21. • 7 FO 371/23103, Butler Postscript, 21 September 1939. • 8 CAB 65/1, War Cabinet Conclusions, 18 September 1939. • 9 CAB 66/2, Notes on the General Situation, Churchill, 25 September 1939. • 10 Rhodes James (ed.), *Winston S. Churchill: His Complete Speeches*, 'The First Month of the War', 1 October 1939, vol. 6, p. 6161. • 11 Stuart Ball (ed.), *Parliament and Politics in the Age of Churchill and Attlee: The Headlam Diaries, 1935–1951* (Cambridge, 1999), 20 September 1939, p. 169. • 12 Ivo Banac (ed.), *The Diary of Georgi Dimitrov, 1933–1949* (New Haven, CT, 2003), 7 September 1939, p. 115. • 13 Strobe Talbott (ed.), *Khrushchev Remembers, Vol. I* (London, 1971), p. 128. • 15 Quoted in Timothy Snyder, *Bloodlands: Europe between Hitler and Stalin* (New York, 2010), p. 126. • 16 C. R. Attlee, A. Greenwood et al., *Labour's Aims in War and Peace* (London, 1940), pp. 73–4. • 17 Quoted in Talbot C. Imlay, *Facing the Second World War: Strategy, Politics, and Economics in Britain and France, 1938–1940* (Oxford, 2003), p. 178. • 18 Ball (ed.), *Parliament and Politics in the Age of Churchill and Attlee*, 11 October 1939, p. 172. • 19 Gabriel Gorodetsky (ed.), *The Complete Maisky Diaries* (New Haven, CT, 2017), 13 November 1939, vol. 2, p. 667. This parroting of Soviet propaganda would appear suspect were Churchill not to have expressed the same sentiments elsewhere. 'No doubt it appeared reasonable to the Soviet Union to take advantage of the present situation to regain some of the territory which Russia had lost as a result of the last war,' he told the War Cabinet on 16 November, three days after his meeting with Maisky. 'It was in our interests that the USSR should increase their strength in the Baltic, thereby limiting the risk of German domination in that area. For this reason it would be a mistake for us to stiffen the Finns against making concessions to the USSR.' • 20 FO 371/23697, Burgin to Halifax, 31 October 1939. • 21 Ibid., Fitzroy

Maclean Minute, 3 November 1939. • 22 Ibid., Halifax to Burgin, 8 November 1939. • 23
W. P. Crozier, *Off the Record: Political Interviews, 1933–1943* (London, 1973), Interview with Sir
Robert Vansittart, 10 November 1939, p. 105; FO 371/24845, Seeds to Foreign Office, 1 January 1940. • 24 Henderson Papers, Box 1, Steinhardt to Henderson, 2 March 1940. • 25 FO
371/24846, COS, Military Implications of Hostilities with Russia in 1940, 8 March 1940. • 26
A. P. Herbert, 'Baku or the Map Game'. • 27 FO 371/24846, Clark Kerr to Foreign Office,
4 March 1940. • 28 Ibid.; FO 371/24855, Le Rougetel to Foreign Office, 4 March 1940. • 29
FO 371/24846, Knatchbull-Hugessen to Foreign Office, 15 March 1940. • 30 FO 371/24846,
Vansittart Minute, 11 March 1940. • 31 John Colville, *The Churchillians* (London, 1981), p. 57.
• 32 Russell Papers, unpublished memoir. • 33 John Colville, *The Fringes of Power: Downing
Street Diaries, 1939–1955* (London, 1985), 12 December 1940, p. 309. • 34 Watchman, *What of
the Night?* (London, 1940), p. 159. • 35 Butler Papers, RAB E3/11, Clark Kerr to Butler, 20
March 1940; Russell Papers, unpublished memoir. • 36 George Bilainkin, *Diary of a Diplomatic Correspondent* (London, 1942), 4 July 1940, p. 145. • 37 FO 371/24844, Cripps to Foreign
Office, 2 July 1940. • 38 Ibid., Maclean Minute, 4 July 1940. • 39 Talbott (ed.), *Khrushchev
Remembers*, pp. 134, 166. • 40 Quoted in Stephen Kotkin, *Stalin, Vol. II: Waiting for Hitler,
1929–1941* (London, 2017), p. 774. • 41 Paul Schmidt, *Hitler's Interpreter* (London, 1951), p. 210.
• 42 *Documents on German Foreign Policy, 1918–1945 (DGFP)*, Series D, Vol. XI: *The War Years,
September 1, 1940–January 31, 1941* (London, 1961), Doc. No. 325, Record of the Conversation
between Ribbentrop and Molotov, 13 November 1940, p. 534. • 43 Schmidt, *Hitler's Interpreter*, p. 215; *DGFP*, Series D., Vol. XI, Doc. No. 326, Record of the Conversation between
Hitler and Molotov, 12 November 1940, p. 548. • 44 Quoted in Kotkin, *Stalin, Vol. II*, p. 809.
• 45 Quoted in Ian Kershaw, *Hitler, 1889–1936: Hubris* (London, 1998), p. 250. • 46 David Dilks
(ed.), *The Diaries of Sir Alexander Cadogan, OM, 1938–1945* (London, 1971), 17 August 1940, p.
321. • 47 FO/371/24844, Sargent Minute, 28 June 1940. • 48 FO 371/24852, Fitzroy Maclean
Minute, 1 August 1940. • 49 FO 371/26518, Cripps to Foreign Office, 24 March 1941. • 50
Winston S. Churchill, *The Second World War, Vol. III: The Grand Alliance* (London, 1950), pp.
322, 323. • 51 AVP RF, f. 06, op. 3, d. 75, p. 7, ll. 11–16, quoted in Gabriel Gorodetsky, *Grand
Delusion: Stalin and the German Invasion of Russia* (New Haven, CT, 1999), p. 174. • 52 John
Colville, *Footprints in Time* (London, 1976), pp. 111–12. • 53 Quoted in Roger Moorhouse,
The Devils' Alliance: Hitler's Pact with Stalin, 1939–1941 (London, 2014), p. 244. • 54 ' They
attacked us without declaring any grievances, without demanding any negotiations,' the
Vozhd was heard to say, bewildered, on the day of the German invasion. 'They attacked
us viciously, like gangsters.' (Ivo Banac (ed.), *The Diary of Georgi Dimitrov, 1933–1949* (New
Haven, CT, 2003), 22 June 1941, p. 166) • 55 Quoted in L. Dvoinykh and N. Tarkhova, 'What
Military Intelligence Reported: Historians Have a Chance to Analyse Soviet Dispatches on
the Eve of War', *Russian Studies in History: A Journal of Translations*, vol. 36, no. 3 (1997),
pp. 76–98. Author's italics.

XIII: Allied with Hell

1 Birkenhead Papers, Confidential Memorandum, Congressman Bradley of Michigan, 25
June 1941. • 2 Charles Burdick and Hans-Adolf Jacobsen (eds), *The Halder War Diary, 1939–
1942* (London, 1988), 3 July 1941, p. 446. • 3 Quoted in Max Domarus (ed.), *Hitler, Reden und
Proklamationen, 1932–1945, Band II: Untergang, Halbband II: 1941–1945* (Munich, 1965), p. 1664.
• 4 Royal Archives, GVI/PRIV/DIARY/WAR/COPY/1941: 23 June. • 5 Quoted in David
Carlton, *Churchill and the Soviet Union* (Manchester, 2000), p. 20. • 6 John Colville, *The
Fringes of Power: Downing Street Diaries, 1939–1955* (London, 1985), 21 June 1941, p. 404. • 7
Ibid., 22 June 1941, p. 405. • 8 Hopkins Papers, FDRPL, Box 307, Home Intelligence Report,
25 July 1941. • 9 W. P. Crozier, *Off the Record: Political Interviews, 1933–1943* (London, 1973),
Interview with Sir Robert Vansittart, 13 October 1941, p. 100. • 10 Birkenhead Papers, Confidential Memorandum, Congressman Bradley of Michigan, 25 June 1941. • 11 Berle Papers,

Box 213, Berle to Hopkins, 30 July 1941. • 12 Ibid., Box 213, Berle Memorandum, 31 July 1941. • 13 Roosevelt Papers, PSF, Diplomatic Correspondence, Roosevelt to Leahy, 26 June 1941. • 14 Davies Papers, Box 132, Diary, 29 September 1941. • 15 Yeaton Papers, Box 1, unpublished memoir, p. 37. • 16 Davies Papers, Box 1.10, Diary, 10 September 1941. • 17 Quoted in Robert E. Sherwood, *The White House Papers of Harry L. Hopkins, Vol. I: September 1939–January 1942* (London, 1948), p. 344. • 18 Roosevelt Papers, PSF, Safe File, Series 1, Russia 1939–1941, Hopkins to Roosevelt & Hull, 1 August 1941. • 19 Oumansky quoted in Robert Dallek, *Franklin D. Roosevelt and American Foreign Policy, 1932–1945* (New York, 1979), p. 280; Gabriel Gorodetsky (ed.), *The Complete Maisky Diaries* (New Haven, CT, 2017), 10 August 1941, vol. 3, p. 1141. • 20 David Reynolds and Vladimir Pechatnov (eds), *The Kremlin Letters: Stalin's Correspondence with Churchill and Roosevelt* (London, 2018), Churchill to Stalin, 20 July 1941, pp. 28–29. • 21 FO 371/29471, Exchanges between His Majesty's Government and the Soviet Government on the Subject of British Military Assistance to Russia, 19 November 1941; Reynolds and Pechatnov (eds), *Kremlin Letters*, Stalin to Maisky, 30 August 1941, p. 38. • 22 Winston S. Churchill, *The Second World War, Vol. III: The Grand Alliance* (London, 1950), pp. 406–7. • 23 CHAR 20/44, Churchill to Cripps, 28 October 1944. • 24 Lord Moran, *Winston Churchill: The Struggle for Survival, 1940–1965* (London, 1966), 22 September 1944, p. 185. • 25 Alexander Danchev and Daniel Todman (eds), *War Diaries, 1939–1945: Field Marshal Lord Alanbrooke* (London, 2001), p. 100. • 26 W. Averell Harriman and Elie Abel, *Special Envoy to Churchill and Stalin, 1941–1946* (New York, 1975), p. 3. • 27 Cecil H. King, *With Malice toward None: A War Diary* (London, 1970), 29 March 1941, p. 116; Harriman Papers, Box 158, Views from Mr Harriman's Conference, March 1941. • 28 Harold Balfour, *Wings over Westminster* (London, 1973), p. 175. • 29 *The Memoirs of General the Lord Ismay* (London, 1960), p. 230. • 30 Harriman and Abel, *Special Envoy to Churchill and Stalin*, p. 89. • 31 Ibid., p. 90. • 32 Beaverbrook Papers, BBK/D/100, Moscow Narrative. • 33 Russell Papers, unpublished memoir. • 34 Balfour, *Wings over Westminster*, p. 178. • 35 Beaverbrook Papers, BBK/D/100, Moscow Narrative, 1 October 1941. • 36 Quoted in Richard Langworth, 'Churchill and Bernard Shaw: a curious dichotomy, a fictitious exchange', The Churchill Project, Hillsdale College, 7 March 2020, https://winstonchurchill.hillsdale.edu/george-bernard-shaw/ • 37 Beaverbrook Papers, BBK/D/100, Notes by Minister of Moscow Conference. • 38 Harold Elvin, *A Cockney in Moscow* (London, 1958), 3 October 1941, p. 186. • 39 Beaverbrook Papers, BBK/D/102, Confidential Protocol, 1 October 1941. • 40 *Memoirs of General the Lord Ismay*, p. 228. • 41 Robert Rhodes James (ed.), *Winston S. Churchill: His Complete Speeches* (London, 1974), Broadcast, 20 January 1940, vol. 6, p. 6184. • 42 Reynolds and Pechatnov, *Kremlin Letters*, Stalin to Churchill, 11 November 1941, p. 67. • 43 John Kennedy, *The Business of War: The War Narrative of Major-General Sir John Kennedy* (London, 1957), p. 163. • 44 Amery Papers, AMEL 2/1/32, Amery to Eden, 29 August 1941. • 45 Colville, *Fringes of Power*, 29 August 1941, p. 432; John Harvey (ed.), *The War Diaries of Oliver Harvey, 1941–45* (London, 1978), 25 August 1941, p. 36. • 46 Hansard, HC Deb, 15 July 1941, vol. 373, col. 463. • 47 Pownall Papers, Pownall 2, Diary, 29 June 1941. • 48 Stuart Ball (ed.), *Parliament and Politics in the Age of Churchill and Attlee: The Headlam Diaries, 1935–1951* (Cambridge, 1999), 6 September 1941, p. 271. • 49 George Kennan, *Memoirs, 1925–1950* (London, 1968), pp. 133–4; Kennan quoted in David Mayers, 'Soviet War Aims and the Grant Alliance: George Kennan's Views, 1944–1946', *Journal of Contemporary History*, vol. 21, no. 1 (1986), p. 63; Steinhardt quoted in William Nester, *Franklin D. Roosevelt and the Art of Leadership: Battling the Great Depression and the Axis Powers* (Barnsley, 2024), p. 137. • 50 A. H. Birse, *Memoirs of an Interpreter* (New York, 1967), pp. 67–8. • 51 FO 371/29469, List of Secret and/or Technical Information Given or Promised to the Soviet Forces by the British Government since the Arrival of the British Military Mission in Moscow, 20 September 1941. • 52 Ibid., Cripps to Foreign Office, 20 September 1941. • 53 FO 181/963/7, Cripps to Foreign Office, 3 November 1941. • 54 Elvin, *Cockney in Moscow*, 22 June 1941, p. 56. • 55 Ibid., 21 July 1941, p. 98. • 56 The military historian David Stahel has argued convincingly that Barbarossa's failure was evident long before Army Group Centre began its final push for the Russian capital. See *Operation Typhoon: Hitler's March* on *Moscow, October 1941* (Cambridge, 2013); *The Battle for Moscow* (Cambridge, 2015); *Retreat from Moscow: A New History of Germany's Winter Campaign, 1941–1942* (New York, 2019).

XIV: 'In God's Good Time'

1 Harriman Papers, Box 159, Folder 5, Harriman to Bullitt, 21 May 1941. • 2 Michael E. Reilly, *Reilly of the White House* (New York, 1947), p. 66. • 3 Quoted in Kenneth S. Davis, *FDR: The War President, 1940–1943* (New York, 2000), p. 3. • 4 Roosevelt Papers, Master Speeches, FDR Speech File, Box 13, 4 March 1933. • 5 Hickleton Papers, A7/8/12, Halifax Diary, 3 February 1943. • 6 Ross T. McIntire, *Twelve Years with Roosevelt* (London, 1948), p. 5. • 7 Quoted in John Gunther, *Roosevelt in Retrospect* (London, 1950), p. 37–8. • 8 Eleanor Roosevelt, *This I Remember* (New York, 1950), p. 14. • 9 Morgenthau Papers, Presidential Diary, 15 May 1942. • 10 Frances Perkins, *The Roosevelt I Knew* (London, 1947), p. 9; Robert E. Sherwood, *The White House Papers of Harry L. Hopkins, Vol. I: September 1939–January 1942* (London, 1948), p. 10. • 11 Henry Hardy (ed.), *Flourishing: Isaiah Berlin Letters, 1928–1946* (Cambridge, 2004), Berlin to his parents, 16 August 1943, p. 456. • 12 Emma Soames (ed.), *Mary Churchill's War: The Wartime Diaries of Churchill's Youngest Daughter* (London, 2021), p. 56. • 13 George VI Papers, George VI Diary, 4 November 1940. A notable exception to this thinking was Walter Lippmann, who told members of the British Embassy that they would be better off with Willkie since FDR was such a poor administrator. • 14 Roosevelt Papers, Master Speech File, Box 55, 30 October 1940. • 15 Quoted in John Morton Blum (ed.), *From the Morgenthau Diaries, Vol. II: The Years of Urgency, 1938–1941* (Boston, 1965), p. 199. • 16 FO 371/24243, Scott Minute, 6 December 1940. • 17 Warren F. Kimball (ed.), *Churchill & Roosevelt: The Complete Correspondence* (Princeton, NJ, 1984), Churchill to Roosevelt, 7 December 1941, vol. 1, p. 109. • 18 Roosevelt Papers, Presidential Press Conferences, Press Conference 702, 17 December 1941. • 19 Hansard, HC Deb, 27 November 1941, vol. 376, col. 970. • 20 *Foreign Relations of the United States 1940, Vol. III: The British Commonwealth, The Soviet Union, The Near East and Africa* (Washington, DC, 1958), Doc. 30, 841.30/176, Memorandum by Hull of Conversation with Lothian, 11 June 1940. • 21 PREM 4/17/1, Beaverbrook to Churchill, 26 December 1940. • 22 Ibid., Draft Telegram Churchill to Roosevelt, December 1940. • 23 Sybil Eccles and David Eccles, *By Safe Hand: Letters, 1939–42* (London, 1983), Makins to Eccles, 28 March 1941, p. 250. • 24 Quoted in Max Hastings, *Finest Years: Churchill as Warlord, 1940–1945* (London, 2009), p. 175. • 25 PREM 4/17/2, Churchill to Sir Kingsley Wood, 20 March 1941; Donald Moggridge (ed.), *The Collected Writings of John Maynard Keynes, Vol. XXIII: Activities, 1940–1943: External War Finance* (Cambridge, 1978), p. 46. • 26 Blum (ed.), *From the Morgenthau Diaries, Vol. II*, p. 236. • 27 Morgenthau Papers, Morgenthau Presidential Diaries, Vol. 381, 10 March 1941. • 28 *The Secret Diary of Harold L. Ickes, Vol. III: The Lowering Clouds, 1939–1941* (London, 1955), 19 January 1941, p. 409; Berle Papers, Box 213, Memorandum 23 July 1941. • 29 Quoted in Wayne S. Cole, *Roosevelt and the Isolationists* (Lincoln, NE, 1983), p. 414. • 30 Fish quoted in Warren F. Kimball, *The Most Unsordid Act: Lend-Lease, 1939–1941* (Baltimore, MD, 1969), p. 154; Wheeler quoted in Lynne Olson, *Those Angry Days: Roosevelt, Lindbergh, and America's Fight over World War II, 1939–1941* (New York, 2013), pp. 274–5. Roosevelt called this 'the most untruthful . . . the most dastardly, unpatriotic thing . . . that has been said in public life in my generation'. • 31 Roosevelt Papers, Master Speech File, Fireside Chat, 29 December 1940. • 32 James R. Leutze (ed.), *The London Observer: The Journal of General Raymond E. Lee, 1940–1941* (London, 1972), 26 July 1941, p. 357. • 33 Quoted in Sherwood, *White House Papers of Harry L. Hopkins, Vol. I*, p. 237. • 34 Quoted in Robert E. Sherwood, *The White House Papers of Harry L. Hopkins, Vol. II: January 1942–July 1945* (London, 1949), p. 730. • 35 Ibid., p. 4. • 36 Ibid. • 37 *The Memoirs of General the Lord Ismay* (London, 1960), p. 213. • 38 *The Memoirs of Lord Chandos* (London, 1962), pp. 165–6. • 39 Lord Moran, *Winston Churchill: The Struggle for Survival, 1940–1965* (London, 1966), p. 6. • 40 Hopkins Papers, FDRL, Box 298, Hopkins to Roosevelt, 10 January 1941. Hopkins' friends were surprised

at the bond that had developed between the blue-blooded Prime Minister and this man 'who looks and acts like a farmer'. 'Hopkins' effectiveness was greater even than we had believed,' recorded the interventionist journalist Joseph Alsop in his notebook. 'The same curious genius Hop has for pleasing Roosevelt pleased Churchill . . . Hop has returned from England completely single-minded, judging every question solely in the light of winning the war.' (Alsop Papers, Box 32, Folder 12) • 41 Linlithgow Papers, MS EUR F 125/9, Amery to Linlithgow, 23 December 1940. • 42 Hickleton Papers, A4/410/4/8, Halifax to George VI, 28 January 1941. • 43 Quoted in Andrew Roberts, *The Holy Fox: A Biography of Lord Halifax* (London, 1991), p. 380. • 44 Peake Papers, Washington Diary, 30 January 1941; Hickleton Papers, A4/410/4/8, Halifax to King George VI, 16 May 1941. • 45 Hickleton Papers, A4/410/4/14, Halifax to Simon, 21 March 1941. • 46 Birkenhead Papers, Confidential Memorandum, Congressman Bradley of Michigan, 25 June 1941. • 47 Ibid., Interview with Air Vice-Marshal William MacNeece Foster. • 48 Ibid., Interview with Angus McDonnell. • 49 Ibid., Interview with John Wheeler Bennett; *Time*, 17 November 1941. • 50 Sherfield Papers, MS 518, Eccles to Makins, 4 June 1941. • 51 Fred L. Israel (ed.), *The War Diary of Breckinridge Long: Selections from the Years 1939–1944* (Lincoln, NE, 1966), 22 May 1941, p. 201; Turner quoted in Sherwood, *White House Papers of Harry L. Hopkins, Vol. I*, p. 275. • 52 Kennedy Papers 4/2/3, Diary, 27 April 1941. • 53 Cecil H. King, *With Malice toward None: A War Diary* (London, 1970), 19 February 1941, p. 108. • 54 Quoted in Llewellyn Woodward, *British Foreign Policy in the Second World War, Vol. II* (London, 1971), p. 14. • 55 Quoted in Nicholas Cull, *Selling War: The British Propaganda Campaign against American 'Neutrality' in World War II* (New York, 1995), p. 147. • 56 'How did public opinion about entering World War II change between 1939 and 1941?', United States Holocaust Memorial Museum website, https://exhibitions.ushmm.org/americans-and-the-holocaust/us-public-opinion-world-war-II-1939-1941, accessed 27 August 2024. • 57 Hopkins Papers, Box 302, *Fortune* survey, 10 July 1941. • 58 Harriman Papers, Box 159, Folder 3, Bullitt to Harriman, 29 April 1941. • 59 Stimson Papers, MS 465, Series XIV, Box 73, Folder 33, Diary, 22 April 1941. • 60 Roosevelt Papers, Master Speeches, File No. 1368-A, 27 May 1941. • 61 *Secret Diary of Harold L. Ickes, Vol. III*, 8 June 1941, pp. 536–8. • 62 Berle Papers, Box 212, Diary, 7 May 1941. • 63 PREM 3/469, Churchill to Eden, 2 May 1941.

XV: Atlantic Meeting – Pacific Infamy

1 Warren F. Kimball (ed.), *Churchill & Roosevelt: The Complete Correspondence* (Princeton, NJ, 1984), Roosevelt to Churchill, 20 January 1941, vol. 1, p. 134. • 2 John Colville, *The Fringes of Power: Downing Street Diaries, 1939–1955* (London, 1985), 1 August 1941, p. 423. • 3 David Dilks (ed.), *The Diaries of Sir Alexander Cadogan, OM, 1938–1945* (London, 1971), 5–6 August 1941, p. 396. • 4 H. V. Morton, *Atlantic Meeting* (London, 1943), p. 42. • 5 Jacob Papers, JACB 1/9, Diary, 6 August 1941. • 6 Quoted in Kimball, *Churchill and Roosevelt*, vol. 2, p. 355. • 7 Geoffrey C. Ward (ed.), *Closest Companion: The Unknown Story of the Intimate Friendship between Franklin Roosevelt and Margaret Suckley* (Boston, 1995), p. 141. • 8 Jacob Papers, JACB 1/9, Diary, 9 August 1941. • 9 Ibid., 11 August 1941. • 10 Colville, *Fringes of Power*, 10 August 1940, p. 215. • 11 Roosevelt Papers, Master Speech File, Box 58, Message to Congress, 6 January 1941; quoted in Llewellyn Woodward, *British Foreign Policy in the Second World War, Vol. II* (London, 1971), 'Joint Declaration by the President of the United States and Mr Winston Churchill, 14 August 1941', pp. 202–3. • 12 Woodward, *British Foreign Policy in the Second World War, Vol. II*, p. 200. • 13 Ibid., p. 202. • 14 Ibid. • 15 Hansard, HC Deb, 9 September 1941, vol. 374, col. 69. • 16 Amery Papers, AMEL 2/3/24, Amery to Linlithgow, 18 August 1941. • 17 Molotov Secretariat, Fund 6, Inventory 3 Auto, Case 281, File 21, Lozovsky to Molotov, 23 August 1941. • 18 Jacob Papers, JACB 1/9, Diary, 10 & 9 August 1941. • 19 Martin Papers, MART 1, Diary, 10 August 1941. • 20 Jacob Papers, JACB 1/9, Diary, 10 August 1941. • 21 W. H. Thompson, *I Was Churchill's Shadow* (London, 1951), p. 74. • 22 Chartwell Papers,

CHAR 20/48, Churchill to Attlee, 12 August 1941; ibid., Churchill to Attlee, 13 August 1941. • 23 CAB 65/19, War Cabinet Minutes, 19 August 1941. • 24 Royal Archives, GVI/PRIV/ DIARY/WAR/COPY/1941: 19 August. • 25 Martin Gilbert (ed.), *The Churchill Documents, Vol. XVI: The Ever-Widening War, 1941* (Hillsdale, MI, 2011), Churchill to Queen Elizabeth, 3 August 1941, p. 1032. • 26 Elliott Roosevelt, *As He Saw It* (New York, 1946), pp. 21–2. Author's italics. • 27 Morgenthau Papers, Diary, 14 May 1941, p. 253. • 28 Ibid., Presidential Diary, 17 May 1941, p. 254. • 29 *Sunday Times*, 31 August 1941. • 30 Hopkins Papers, Box 304, 'Anglo-Scot' to Hopkins, 9 January 1941. • 31 Buddell Papers, Doc. 26502, Diary, 21 June 1941. • 32 Gilbert (ed.), *Churchill Documents, Vol. XVI*, Churchill to Hopkins, 28 August 1941, p. 1125. • 33 Colville, *Fringes of Power*, 30 August 1941, p. 434. • 34 Quoted in Robert E. Sherwood, *The White House Papers of Harry L. Hopkins, Vol. I: September 1939–January 1942* (London, 1948), p. 368. • 35 Roosevelt Papers, Master Speeches, File 1381-B, Fireside Chat, 11 September 1941. • 36 Ibid., Master Speeches, File 1389-A, Navy Day Address, 27 October 1941. • 37 Quoted in Woodward, *British Foreign Policy in the Second World War, Vol. II*, p. 145. • 38 Stimson Papers, MS 465, Series XIV, Box 74, Diary, 7 December 1941. • 39 John G. Winant, *A Letter from Grosvenor Square: An Account of Stewardship* (London, 1948), pp. 198, 197. • 40 Richard M. Langworth. 'Dinner on the night that changed everything, 7 December 1941', The Churchill Project, Hillsdale College, 8 October 2021, https://winstonchurchill.hillsdale.edu/dinner-chequers-7dec41/

XVI: Forging the Alliance

1 Byron, *Childe Harold's Pilgrimage*, Canto III, Verse XXXV. 2 John G. Winant, *A Letter from Grosvenor Square: An Account of Stewardship* (London, 1948), p. 198. • 3 W. Averell Harriman and Elie Abel, *Special Envoy to Churchill and Stalin, 1941–1946* (New York, 1975), p. 112. • 4 Winant, *Letter from Grosvenor Square*, p. 199. • 5 Winston S. Churchill, *The Second World War, Vol. III: The Grand Alliance* (London, 1950), p. 538. • 6 Ibid., p. 540. • 7 An important corrective is provided by Brendan Simms and Charlie Laderman, *Hitler's American Gamble: Pearl Harbor and the German March to Global War* (London, 2021). • 8 Theodore H. White (ed.), *The Stilwell Papers* (London, 1949), 11 December 1941, p. 31. • 9 Arthur H. Vandenberg Jr (ed.), *The Private Papers of Senator Vandenberg* (London, 1953), p. 1. • 10 Quoted by M. Todd Bennett, *One World, Big Screen: Hollywood, the Allies, and World War II* (Chapel Hill, NC, 2012), p. 94. • 11 Stimson Papers, MS 465, Series XVI, Box 74, Diary, 7 December 1941. • 12 Martin Gilbert (ed.), *The Churchill Documents, Vol. XVI: The Ever-Widening War, 1941* (Hillsdale, MI, 2011), Churchill to George VI, 8 December 1941, p. 1585. • 13 Warren F. Kimball (ed.), *Churchill & Roosevelt: The Complete Correspondence* (Princeton, NJ, 1984), Roosevelt to Churchill, 10 December 1941, vol. 1, p. 286. • 14 Quoted in Ian Kershaw, *Hitler, 1936–1945: Nemesis* (London, 2000), p. 442. • 15 'Adolf Hitler: Speech Declaring War against the United States (December 11, 1941)', Jewish Virtual Library, https://www.jewishvirtuallibrary.org/hitler-s-speech-declaring-war-against-the-united-states, accessed 27 August 2024. • 16 Martin Papers, MART 1, Diary, 11 December 1941. • 17 Robert E. Sherwood, *The White House Papers of Harry L. Hopkins, Vol. I: September 1939–January 1942* (London, 1948), p. 446. • 18 Hickleton Papers, A7/8/10, Halifax Diary, 3 January 1942. • 19 Quoted in Sherwood, *White House Papers of Harry L. Hopkins, Vol. I*, p. 446. Churchill would later cast doubt on the anecdote yet it appears in several contemporary accounts (Jacob, Hollis and Kinna), while Churchill himself told Halifax that FDR was the only head of state he had 'received in the nude'. • 20 Ross T. McIntire, *Twelve Years with Roosevelt* (London, 1948), p. 132. • 21 Samuel I. Rosenman, *Working with Roosevelt* (New York, 1952), p. 295. • 22 Quoted in Doris Kearns Goodwin, *No Ordinary Time: Franklin and Eleanor Roosevelt – the Home Front in World War II* (New York, 1994), p. 312. • 23 Ibid., p. 311; also quoted in Michael S. Bell, 'The Declaration of the United States in the Aftermath of Pearl Harbor', National WWII Museum website, 3 January 2022, https://www.nationalww2museum.org/war/articles/

united-nations-declaration-1942 • 24 Quoted in Sherwood, *White House Papers of Harry L. Hopkins, Vol. I*, p. 449. • 25 Quoted in Victoria Schofield, *Wavell: Soldier and Statesman* (London, 2006), p. 231. • 26 Memorandum on the Conduct of the War, 16 December 1941, quoted in Martin Gilbert, *Churchill Documents, Vol. XVI*, pp. 1633–7. • 27 Stimson Papers, MS 465, Series XVI, Box 74, Diary, 19 December 1941. • 28 White (ed.), *Stilwell Papers*, Diary, 29 December 1941, p. 41. • 29 Ibid., Diary, 6 January 1942, pp. 46–7. • 30 Quoted in Forrest C. Pogue, *George C. Marshall, Vol. II: Ordeal and Hope, 1939–1942* (New York, 1965), p. 264. • 31 Jacob Papers, JACB 1/12, Diary, 23 December 1941 • 32 Alex Danchev (ed.), *Establishing the Anglo-American Alliance: The Second World War Diaries of Brigadier Vivian Dykes* (London, 1990), 27 December 1941, p. 79. • 33 Jacob Papers, JACB 1/12, Diary, 1 January 1942. • 34 Quoted in John Keegan (ed.), *Churchill's Generals* (London, 1991), p. 68. • 35 Robert Rhodes James (ed.), *Winston S. Churchill: His Complete Speeches* (London, 1974), Address before a Joint Session of Congress, 26 December 1941, vol. 6, pp. 6536–40. • 36 Ibid., Address to a Joint Session of the Canadian Parliament, vol. 6, p. 6544. • 37 Quoted in Llewellyn Woodward, *British Foreign Policy in the Second World War, Vol. II* (London, 1971), p. 214. • 38 Charles de Gaulle, *Mémoires de guerre, vol. I: l'appel, 1940–1942* (Paris, 1954), Documents, de Gaulle to Churchill, 10 December 1941, p. 490. • 39 H. G. Nicholas (ed.), *Washington Despatches, 1941–45: Weekly Political Reports from the British Embassy* (London, 1981), 1 August 1942, p. 62. • 40 Dean Acheson, *Present at the Creation: My Years in the State Department* (London, 1969), p. 12. • 41 Quoted in W. H. Chamberlain, *America's Second Crusade* (Chicago, 1950), p. 184.• 42 *Foreign Relations of the United States 1941, Vol. II: Europe* (Washington, DC, 1959), Doc. 486, Statement by the Secretary of State, 25 December 1941. Author's italics. • 43 Quoted in Michael S Neiberg, *When France Fell: The Vichy Crisis and the Fate of the Anglo-American Alliance* (Cambridge, MA, 2021), p. 139. • 44 Ibid. • 45 Quoted in François Kersaudy, *Churchill and De Gaulle* (London, 1981), pp. 173–4. • 46 FO 371/31872, Minute by Richard Law, 19 January 1942. • 47 Churchill, *Second World War, Vol. III*, p. 588. • 48 Quoted in Sherwood, *White House Papers of Harry L. Hopkins, Vol. I*, p. 491. • 49 Kimball (ed.), *Churchill & Roosevelt*, Roosevelt to Churchill, 30 January 1942, vol. 1, p. 337.

XVII: The Rising Sun

1 Quoted in Christopher Thorne, *Allies of a Kind: The United States, Britain, and the War against Japan, 1941–1945* (New York, 1978), p. 133 fn. • 2 Quoted in S. Woodburn Kirby, *The War against Japan, Vol. I: The Loss of Singapore* (London, 1957), Appendix 17, p. 525. • 3 Winston S. Churchill, *The Second World War, Vol. III: The Grand Alliance* (London, 1950), p. 551. • 4 Martin Gilbert (ed.), *The Churchill Documents, Vol. XVII: Testing Times, 1942* (Hillsdale, MI, 2014), Churchill to Wavell, 10 February 1942, p.236. • 5 John Kennedy, *The Business of War: The War Narrative of Major-General Sir John Kennedy* (London, 1957), p. 198. • 6 Robert Self (ed.), *The Neville Chamberlain Diary Letters, Vol. IV: The Downing Street Years, 1934–1940* (Aldershot, 2005), NC to Hilda, 28 July 1934, p. 82–3. • 7 FO/800/323/1, Halifax to Hoare, 8 July 1940. • 8 Kennedy, *Business of War*, p. 190. • 9 *The Memoirs of Cordell Hull, Vol. I* (London, 1948), p. 901; *Life*, 29 July 1940. • 10 Quoted in David Reynolds, *The Creation of the Anglo-American Alliance, 1937–41: A Study in Competitive Co-operation* (London, 1981), p. 134. • 11 John Colville, *The Fringes of Power: Downing Street Diaries, 1939–1955* (London, 1985), 26 January 1941, p. 346. • 12 Quoted in Andrew Roberts, *Churchill: Walking with Destiny* (London, 2018), p. 693. • 13 Quoted in Thorne, *Allies of a Kind*, p. 4. • 14 Little quoted in Stephen Roskill, *Naval Policy between the Wars, Vol. II: The Period of Reluctant Rearmament, 1930–1939* (London, 1976), p. 354; Thomas quoted in Christopher Bayly and Tim Harper, *Forgotten Armies: The Fall of British Asia, 1941–1945* (London, 2004), p. 116. • 15 Diana Cooper, *Trumpets from the Steep* (London, 1960), p. 103. • 16 Ian Morrison, *Malayan Postscript* (London, 1942), p. 37. • 17 Ibid., p. 38. • 18 CAB 66/20, British Administration in the Far East, 29 October 1941. • 19 Fred L. Israel (ed.), *The War Diary of Breckinridge Long: Selections from the Years 1939–1944*

(Lincoln, NE, 1966), 7 April 1942, p. 255. • 20 *The Times*, 14 March 1942. • 21 Quoted in Thorne, *Allies of a Kind*, p. 11. • 22 Nigel Nicolson (ed.), *Harold Nicolson: Diaries and Letters, Vol. II: 1939–1945* (London, 1967), 27 February 1942, p. 214. • 23 Winston S. Churchill, *The Second World War, Vol. IV: The Hinge of Fate* (London, 1951), p. 43. • 24 Quoted in Thorne, *Allies of a Kind*, p. 60. • 25 *Melbourne Herald*, 27 December 1941. • 26 Simon Heffer (ed.), *Henry 'Chips' Channon: The Diaries, Vol. II: 1938–43*, 13 February 1942, p. 728. • 27 Quoted in Bayly and Harper, *Forgotten Armies*, p. 146. • 28 Amery Papers, AMEL 2/1/32, Auchinleck to Amery, 10 November 1941. • 29 Quoted in Yasmin Khan, *The Raj at War: A People's History of India's Second World War* (London, 2015), p. 135. • 30 Ibid., p. 109. • 31 K. N. Panikkar (ed.), *Towards Freedom: Documents for the Movement of Independence in India, 1940, Part I* (New Delhi, 2009), p. 35. • 32 *The Collected Works of Mahatma Gandhi, Vol. LXXII: 16 April–11 September 1940* (New Delhi, 1978), 'To Every Briton', New Delhi, 2 July 1940; ibid., Gandhi to Kaur, 15 May 1940, p. 70; quoted in M. S. Venkataramani and B. K. Shrivastava, 'The United States and the "Quit India" Demand', *India Quarterly*, vol. 20, no. 2 (1964), p. 116. • 33 R. J. Moore, *Churchill, Cripps, and India, 1939–1945* (Oxford, 1979), p. 126. Another distinguished historian to have blamed a combination of Churchill and the Viceroy for the collapse of the Cripps mission is the Roosevelt scholar Warren F. Kimball. • 34 Bipan Chandra, Visalakshi Menon and Salil Misra (eds), *Towards Freedom: Documents on the Movement for Independence in India, 1942, Part 1* (New Delhi, 2016), 'Draft Declaration of the Proposals for Discussion with Indian Leaders', 30 March 1942, p. 96. • 35 Ibid., p. 97. • 36 Quoted in R. Coupland, *The Cripps Mission* (London, 1942), pp. 31–2. • 37 Coupland Papers, MSS. Brit. Emp. s. 15, Diary, 10 April 1942. • 38 Quoted in Peter Clarke, *The Cripps Version: The Life of Sir Stafford Cripps, 1889–1952* (London, 2002), p. 305. • 39 Quoted in Nicholas Owen, 'The Cripps Mission of 1942: A Reinterpretation', *Journal of Imperial and Commonwealth History*, vol. 30, no. 1 (2002), p. 81. • 40 Quoted in Clarke, *Cripps Version*, p. 305. • 41 Quoted in Owen, 'Cripps Mission of 1942', p. 82. • 42 Gilbert (ed.), *Churchill Documents, Vol. XVII*, Churchill to Cripps, 11 April 1942, p. 509. • 43 Hickleton Papers, A4/410/4/8, Halifax to George VI, 9 May 1942. • 44 Warren F. Kimball (ed.), *Churchill & Roosevelt: The Complete Correspondence* (Princeton, NJ, 1984), Roosevelt to Churchill, 11 April 1942, vol. 1, p. 446. • 45 Stimson Papers, MS 465, Series XVI, Box 75, Diary, 22 April 1942. • 46 Coupland Papers, MSS. Brit. Emp. s. 15, Diary, 31 March 1942.

XVIII: Fronts and Frontiers

1 Harold Elvin, *A Cockney in Moscow* (London, 1958), p. 169. • 2 FO 371/32874, Mr Eden's Visit to Moscow, Record of Interview between Eden and Stalin, 16 December 1941. • 3 David Reynolds and Vladimir Pechatnov (eds), *The Kremlin Letters: Stalin's Correspondence with Churchill and Roosevelt* (London, 2018), Stalin to Churchill, 11 November 1941, p. 67. • 4 PREM 3/399/7, Eden to Churchill, 5 January 1942. • 5 Quoted in Geoffrey Warner, 'From "Ally" to Enemy: Britain's Relations with the Soviet Union, 1941–1948', in Francesca Gori and Silvio Pons (eds), *The Soviet Union and Europe in the Cold War, 1943–1953* (Basingstoke, 1996), p. 295. • 6 AP 20/1/19/21, Diary, 14 November 1941; PREM 3/399/7, Churchill to Eden, 8 January 1942. • 7 CAB 66/21, Policy towards Russia, 28 January 1942. • 8 PREM 3/395/12, Halifax to Eden, 19 February 1942. • 9 Warren F. Kimball (ed.), *Churchill & Roosevelt: The Complete Correspondence* (Princeton, NJ, 1984), Roosevelt to Churchill, 18 March 1942, vol. 1, p. 421. • 10 Quoted in Reynolds and Pechatnov (eds), *Kremlin Letters*, p. 91. • 11 G. A. Arbatov, V. G. Komplektov and G. M. Korniyenko (eds), *Sovetsko-amerikanskie otnosheniia vo vremia Velikoi Otechestvennoi voiny, 1941–1945, Vol. I* (Moscow, 1984), Litvinov to Narkomindel, 12 March 1942, pp. 155–7. • 12 Berle Papers, Box 214, Diary, 2 May 1942. • 13 FO 371/32877, Eden minute, 15 March 1942. • 14 John Harvey (ed.), *The War Diaries of Oliver Harvey, 1941–45* (London, 1978), 15 March 1942, p. 109. • 15 FO 371/32877, Cadogan Minute, 10 March 1942. • 16 Berle Papers, Box 73, British–Soviet Negotiations, 3 April 1942. 'The treaty',

wrote Welles, 'is indefensible from every moral standpoint and equally indefensible from the standpoint of the future peace and stability of Europe.' • 17 Cazalet Papers, MS 917/1/4/11, Cazalet to Halifax, 15 April 1942. • 18 FO 954/25A/112, Cooper to Eden, 22 April 1942. • 19 Quoted in Tim Bouverie, *Appeasing Hitler: Chamberlain, Churchill and the Road to War* (London, 2019), p. 64; FO 954/25A/132, Harvie-Watt to Churchill, 24 April 1942. • 20 Winston S. Churchill, *The Second World War, Vol. I: The Gathering Storm* (London, 1948), p. 288; Q. J. Reynolds, *Only the Stars Are Neutral* (New York, 1942), p. 91. • 21 Quoted in Stephen Kotkin, *Stalin, Vol. I: Paradoxes of Power, 1878–1928* (London, 2014), p. 454; Stanisław Kot, *Conversations with the Kremlin and Dispatches from Russia* (London, 1963), p. xviii. • 22 David Dilks (ed.), *The Diaries of Sir Alexander Cadogan, OM, 1938–1945* (London, 1971), 20 June 1939, p. 189. • 23 Ibid., p. 454. • 24 Oleg A. Rzheshevsky (ed.), *War and Diplomacy: The Making of the Grand Alliance – Documents from Stalin's Archive* (Amsterdam, 1996), Molotov to Stalin, 23 May 1942, p. 121. • 25 Ibid., Stalin to Molotov, 24 May 1942, p. 122. • 26 Reynolds and Pechatnov (eds), *Kremlin Letters*, Roosevelt to Stalin, 11 April 1942, pp. 96–7. • 27 Morgenthau Papers, Series 2, Presidential Diaries, Book 5, 11 March 1942. • 28 CAB 69/4, Defence Committee Minutes, 14 April 1942. • 29 Kimball (ed.), *Churchill & Roosevelt*, Churchill to Roosevelt, 17 April 1942, vol. 1, p. 459. • 30 Kennedy Papers, 4/2/4, Diary, 10 March 1942. • 31 Alexander Danchev and Daniel Todman (eds), *War Diaries, 1939–1945: Field Marshal Lord Alanbrooke* (London, 2001), pp. 246, 249. • 32 Quoted in Robert E. Sherwood, *The White House Papers of Harry L. Hopkins, Vol. II: January 1942–July 1945* (London, 1949), p. 528. • 33 Albert C. Wedemeyer, *Wedemeyer Reports!* (New York, 1958), pp. 105–6. • 34 Kimball (ed.), *Churchill & Roosevelt*, Churchill to Roosevelt, 17 April 1942, vol. 1, p. 459. • 35 Winston S. Churchill, *The Second World War, Vol. IV: The Hinge of Fate* (London, 1951), pp. 289–90. • 36 Wedemeyer, *Wedemeyer Reports!*, p. 158. • 37 Ibid., p. 105. • 38 Albert Resis (ed.), *Molotov Remembers: Inside Kremlin Politics* (Chicago, 1993), p. 45. • 39 Ibid., p. 46. • 40 *Foreign Relations of the United States (FRUS) 1942, Vol. III: Europe* (Washington, DC, 1961), Doc. 471, Memorandum of Conference held at the White House by Samuel H. Cross, 30 May 1942. • 41 Ibid., Doc. 483, Press Release, 11 June 1942. • 42 Morgenthau Papers, Series 2, Vol. 5, Presidential Diaries, Book 5, 16 June 1942. The head of the European Affairs section of the State Department, Loy Henderson, tried to persuade the President against so definite a commitment but to no avail. • 43 Ibid., 11 March 1942. • 44 *Virginia Chronicle*, 7 May 1942. • 45 Quoted in P. M. H. Bell, *John Bull and the Bear: British Public Opinion, Foreign Policy, and the Soviet Union, 1941–1945* (London, 1990), p. 81; Kennedy Papers, 4/2/4, Diary, 1 March 1942. • 46 Lawford Papers, LWFD 02, Diary, 16 January 1942. • 47 A. P. Herbert, *Less Nonsense!* (London, 1944), p. 12. • 48 The statement appears in the Soviet record of the conversation over dinner on 29 May but not the American. Rzheshevsky (ed.), *War and Diplomacy*, Record of talks with Churchill, 9 June 1942, p. 269. • 49 Hickleton Papers, A7/8/12, Halifax Diary, 22 May 1943. • 50 Churchill, *Second World War, Vol. IV*, p. 344. • 51 Ibid., p. 428. • 52 W. Averell Harriman and Elie Abel, *Special Envoy to Churchill and Stalin, 1941–1946* (New York, 1975), p. 152. • 53 Martin Gilbert (ed.), *The Churchill Documents, Vol. XVII: Testing Times, 1942* (Hillsdale, MI, 2014), Clementine Churchill to Winston Churchill, 4 August 1942, p.1035; Lord Tedder, *With Prejudice: The War Memoirs of Marshal of the Royal Air Force Lord Tedder* (London, 1966), p. 328. • 54 FO 800/300, Clark Kerr Diary, 12 August 1942. • 55 Rowan Papers, unpublished memoir. • 56 Gerald Pawle, *The War and Colonel Warden: Based on the Recollections of C. R. Thompson, Personal Assistant to the Prime Minister, 1940–1945* (London, 1963), p. 194. • 57 V. M. Berezhkov, *Kak ia stal perevodchikom Stalina* (Moscow, 1993), p. 310. When Molotov reported that he had witnessed Churchill eating nothing but oatmeal and a barley-based coffee substitute at lunch that spring (surely a rare occurrence) the dictator reportedly replied, 'That was just a cheap show of democracy, Vyacheslav. He was just pulling your leg.' • 58 PREM 3/76a/12, Minutes of Meeting at the Kremlin, 12 August 1942. • 59 Ibid. • 60 *FRUS 1942, Vol. III*, Doc. 515, Harriman to Roosevelt, 13 August 1942; PREM 3/76a/12, Minutes of Meeting at the Kremlin, 12 August 1942. • 61 FO 800/300, Clark Kerr Diary, 12 August 1942. • 62 PREM 3/76a/12, Minutes of Meeting at the Kremlin, 12 August 1942; Lord Moran, *Winston Churchill: The Struggle for Survival, 1940–1965* (London, 1966),

12 August 1942, p. 55. • 63 Kimball (ed.), *Churchill & Roosevelt*, Churchill to Roosevelt, 13 August 1942, vol. 1, p. 561. • 64 Hickleton Papers, A4/410/4/16, Cadogan to Halifax, 29 August 1942; FO 800/300, Churchill to Attlee, 13 August 1942. • 65 PREM 3/76a/12, Meeting at the Kremlin, 13 August 1942. • 66 Tedder, *With Prejudice*, p. 332. • 67 Dilks (ed.), *Diaries of Sir Alexander Cadogan*, p. 471. • 68 Hickleton Papers, A4/410/4/16, Cadogan to Halifax, 29 August 1942. • 69 Gilbert (ed.), *Churchill Documents, Vol. XVII*, Churchill to War Cabinet, 14 August 1942, p.1077. • 70 FO 371/24844, Bruce Lockhart to Sargent, 8 June 1940. • 71 FO 800/300, Clark Kerr Diary, 14 August 1942. • 72 Ibid., 15 August 1942 • 73 Mark Clark, *Calculated Risk: His Personal Story of the War in North Africa and Italy* (London, 1951), p. 55; Rowan Papers, unpublished memoir. • 74 FO 800/300, Clark Kerr Diary, 15 August 1942. • 75 Ibid. • 76 Danchev and Todman (eds), *War Diaries*, p. 302; 13 August 1942, p. 300. • 77 Rowan Papers, unpublished memoir. • 78 Jacob Papers, JACB I, 1/16, Diary, 14 August 1942. • 79 FO 800/300, Clark Kerr Diary, 16 August 1942. • 80 Churchill, *Second World War, Vol. IV*, p. 446. • 81 Moran, *Struggle for Survival*, 15 August 1942, p. 63. • 82 FO 800/300, Clark Kerr Diary, 16 August 1942. • 83 Moran, *Struggle for Survival*, 15 August 1942, p. 64. • 84 Gilbert (ed.), *Churchill Documents, Vol. XVII*, Churchill to War Cabinet and Roosevelt, 16 August 1942, pp. 1087–8. • 85 Jacob Papers, JACB 1/16, Diary, 16 August 1942. • 86 General Sikorski Historical Institute (ed.), *Documents on Polish–Soviet Relations, 1939–1945: Vol. I, 1939–1943* (London, 1961), Minutes of Meeting held in the Kremlin between Sikorski and Stalin, 3 December 1941, p. 233. • 87 Jacob Papers, JACB 1/16, Diary, 15 August 1942.

XIX: The Flickering Torch

1 Quoted in Jean-Louis Crémieux-Brilhac, *La France libre: de l'appel du 18 juin à la Libération* (Paris, 1996), p. 442. • 2 Mark Clark, *Calculated Risk: His Personal Story of the War in North Africa and Italy* (London, 1951), p. 84. • 3 Clark Papers, War Diary, 22 October 1942. • 4 Ibid. • 5 Clark, *Calculated Risk*, pp. 86–7. • 6 Clark Papers, War Diary, 22 October 1942. • 7 Ibid. • 8 Stimson Papers, MS 465, Series XVI, Box 75, Folder 39, Diary, 23 & 27 July 1942. • 9 Ibid., Memorandum, 12 July 1942, Diary, 15 July 1942. • 10 Quoted in Ed Cray, *General of the Army: George C. Marshall, Soldier and Statesman* (New York, 1990), p. 328. • 11 Quoted in Robert E. Sherwood, *The White House Papers of Harry L. Hopkins, Vol. II: January 1942–July 1945* (London, 1949), p. 612. • 12 Quoted in Colin Smith, *England's Last War against France: Fighting Vichy, 1940–1942* (London, 2009), p. 338. • 13 Harold Macmillan, *War Diaries: Politics and War in the Mediterranean, January 1943–May 1945* (London, 1984), 23 March 1944, p. 393. • 14 Quoted in Douglas Porch, *Defeat and Division: France at War, 1939–1942* (Cambridge, 2022), p. 457. • 15 Clark Papers, War Diary, 7 November 1942. • 16 Alfred D. Chandler et al. (eds), *The Papers of Dwight D. Eisenhower: The War Years, Vol. II* (Baltimore, MD, 1970), Eisenhower to Chiefs of Staff, 8 November 1942, p. 672. • 17 Robert Murphy, *Diplomat among Warriors* (London, 1964), p. 164. • 18 Dwight D. Eisenhower, *Crusade in Europe* (London, 1948), p. 116. • 19 *Foreign Relations of the United States (FRUS) 1942, Vol. II: Europe* (Washington, DC, 1962), Doc. 374, Directive by President Roosevelt to Mr Robert Murphy, 22 September 1942. • 20 Murphy, *Diplomat among Warriors*, p. 165. • 21 Gerald Pawle, *The War and Colonel Warden: Based on the Recollections of C. R. Thompson, Personal Assistant to the Prime Minister, 1940–1945* (London, 1963), p. 208. • 22 George S. Patton, *War as I Knew It* (Boston, 1947), 8 November 1942, pp. 8–9. • 23 Quoted in Smith, *England's Last War against France*, p. 414. • 24 *FRUS 1942, Vol. II*, Doc. 428, The Chargé in France to the Secretary of State, 8 November 1942. • 25 André Beaufre, *La Revanche de 1945* (Paris, 1966), p. 132. • 26 Chandler et al. (eds), *Papers of Dwight D. Eisenhower*, Eisenhower to Combined Chiefs of Staff, 14 November 1942, p. 707. • 27 Quoted in James MacGregor Burns, *Roosevelt: The Soldier of Freedom, 1940–1945* (London, 1971), p. 294. • 28 Murphy, *Diplomat among Warriors*, p. 176. • 29 Clark Papers, War Diary, 10 November 1942. • 30 Quoted in A. L. Funk, *The Politics of TORCH: The Allied Landings and the Algiers Putsch, 1942* (Lawrence, KS, 1974), p. 233. • 31 Quoted in Porch, *Defeat and Division*, p. 531. • 32 Quoted

in William L. Langer, *Our Vichy Gamble* (Hamden, CT, [1947] 1965), p. 375. • 33 Quoted in Ian Ousby, *Occupation: The Ordeal of France, 1940–1944* (London, 1997), p. 268. • 34 Morgenthau Papers, Diary, Vol. 585, 17 November 1942. • 35 FO 371/32139, Jebb Memorandum, 16 November 1942. • 36 David Dilks (ed.), *The Diaries of Sir Alexander Cadogan, OM, 1938–1945* (London, 1971), 14 November 1942, p. 493. • 37 Quoted in Julian Jackson, *A Certain Idea of France: The Life of Charles de Gaulle* (London, 2018), p. 245. • 38 Charles de Gaulle, *Mémoires de guerre, vol. II: l'unité* (Paris, 1956), p. 51. • 39 Warren F. Kimball (ed.), *Churchill & Roosevelt: The Complete Correspondence* (Princeton, NJ, 1984), Churchill to Roosevelt, 17 November 1942, vol. 2, p. 7. • 40 Roosevelt Papers, Presidential Press Conferences, Press Conference No. 861, 4.05 p.m., 17 November 1942. • 41 Quoted in Crémieux-Brilhac, *France libre*, p. 442. • 42 De Gaulle, *Mémoires de guerre, vol. II*, Documents, de Gaulle to Tixier, 29 January 1942, p. 523. • 43 Cordell Hull, *Memoirs, Vol. II* (London, 1948), p. 1198. • 44 Kenneth Pendar, *Adventure in Diplomacy: The Emergence of General de Gaulle in North Africa* (London, 1966), p. 2. • 45 Avon Papers, AP 20/1/22, Diary, 24 December 1942. • 46 Kennedy Papers, 4/2/4, Diary, 11 & 17 November 1942. • 47 Robert Rhodes James (ed.), *Winston S. Churchill: His Complete Speeches* (London, 1974), Mansion House Speech, 10 November 1942, vol. 6, p. 6693.

XX: Casablanca

1 Dixon Papers, Diary, 22 January 1943. • 2 Hopkins Papers, Box 330, Book 7, Diary, 11 January 1943. • 3 Albert C. Wedemeyer, *Wedemeyer Reports!* (New York, 1958), pp. 191–2. • 4 Ibid., p. 169. • 5 JACB I 1/20, Diary, 3 January 1943. • 6 Quoted in Andrew Roberts, *Masters and Commanders: How Roosevelt, Churchill, Marshall and Alanbrooke Won the War in the West* (London, 2008), p. 337. • 7 Jacob Papers, JACB I 1/20, Diary, 13 January 1943. • 8 Wedemeyer, *Wedemeyer Reports!*, p. 192. • 9 Alex Danchev (ed.), *Establishing the Anglo-American Alliance: The Second World War Diaries of Brigadier Vivian Dykes* (London, 1990), 29 August 1942, p. 196; Roosevelt Papers, President's Secretary's File, Box 92, Anecdotes, Roosevelt to King, 12 August 1942. • 10 Admiral of the Fleet Viscount Cunningham of Hyndhope, KT, GCB, OM, DSO, *A Sailor's Odyssey: The Autobiography* (London, 1952), p. 466. • 11 Quoted in Lewis Lehrman, *Churchill, Roosevelt & Company: Studies in Character and Statecraft* (Guilford, CT, 2017), p. 151. • 12 Alexander Danchev and Daniel Todman (eds), *War Diaries, 1939–1945: Field Marshal Lord Alanbrooke* (London, 2001), p. 362, 18 January, p. 361. • 13 PREM 4/72/1, Churchill to Attlee, 19 January 1943. • 14 Danchev and Todman (eds), *War Diaries*, 20 January 1943, p. 364. • 15 Jacob Papers, JACB I 1/20, Diary, 19–23 January 1943. • 16 Quoted in Roberts, *Masters and Commanders*, p. 337. • 17 Quoted in Niall Barr, *Yanks and Limeys: Alliance Warfare in the Second World War* (London, 2015), p. 222. • 18 Ibid., p. 221. • 19 JACB I 1/21, Diary, 19–23 January 1943. • 20 Dixon Papers, Diary, 23 January 1943. • 21 Elliott Roosevelt, *As He Saw It* (New York, 1946), p. 66. • 22 Kenneth Pendar, *Adventure in Diplomacy: The Emergence of General de Gaulle in North Africa* (London, 1966), p. 146. • 23 Hopkins Papers, Box 330, Book 7, Diary, 22 January 1943. • 24 Harold Macmillan, *War Diaries: Politics and War in the Mediterranean, January 1943–May 1945* (London, 1984), 26 January 1943, p. 8. • 25 Lord Moran, *Winston Churchill: The Struggle for Survival, 1940–1965* (London, 1966), 24 January 1943, p. 82. • 26 Pendar, *Adventure in Diplomacy*, pp. 150–52. • 27 Macmillan, *War Diaries*, 26 January 1943, p. 10. • 28 Jacob Papers, JACB I, 1/20, Diary, 19–23 January 1943. • 29 Quoted in Douglas Porch, *Defeat and Division: France at War, 1939–1942* (Cambridge, 2022), p. 458. • 30 Robert Murphy, *Diplomat among Warriors* (London, 1964), p. 167. • 31 Ibid., p. 213. • 32 Mark Clark, *Calculated Risk: His Personal Story of the War in North Africa and Italy* (London, 1951), p. 147. • 33 FO 954/8B/359, Note of a Conversation between the Foreign Secretary and General de Gaulle, 17 January 1943. • 34 David Dilks (ed.), *The Diaries of Sir Alexander Cadogan, OM, 1938–1945* (London, 1971), 17 January 1943, p. 504. • 35 W. Averell Harriman and Elie Abel, *Special Envoy to Churchill and Stalin, 1941–1946* (New York, 1975), p. 191. • 36 Roosevelt, *As He Saw It*, p. 68. • 37 Fleet Admiral William D. Leahy, *I Was There* (London, 1950), pp. 173–4. Like the State Department, FDR believed the British owned de

Gaulle 'body, soul and britches'. • 38 Chartwell Papers, CHAR 20/127, Churchill to Eden, 18 January 1943, p. 155. • 39 John Harvey (ed.), *The War Diaries of Oliver Harvey, 1941–45* (London, 1978), 19 January 1943, p. 211. • 40 Quoted in François Kersaudy, *Churchill and De Gaulle* (London, 1981), p. 247. • 41 Charles de Gaulle, *Mémoires de guerre, vol. II: l'unité* (Paris, 1956), p. 77. • 42 Ibid., p. 78. • 44 Quoted in Kersaudy, *Churchill and De Gaulle*, p. 248. • 45 Moran, *Struggle for Survival*, 22 January 1943, p. 81. • 46 De Gaulle, *Mémoires de guerre, vol. II*, p. 80. • 47 Hopkins Papers, Box 330, Book 7, Diary, 22 January 1943. • 48 De Gaulle, *Mémoires de guerre, vol. II*, pp. 79–80. • 49 Quoted in A. L. Funk, *The Politics of TORCH: The Allied Landings and the Algiers Putsch, 1942* (Lawrence, KS, 1974), pp. 137–8. • 50 De Gaulle, *Mémoires de guerre, vol. II*, p. 81. • 51 Ibid., p. 85. • 52 Quoted in Harriman and Abel, *Special Envoy to Churchill and Stalin*, p. 187. • 53 Murphy, *Diplomat among Warriors*, p. 219. • 54 De Gaulle, *Mémoires de guerre, vol. II*, p. 86. • 55 Pendar, *Adventure in Diplomacy*, p. 148. • 56 Winston S. Churchill, *The Second World War, Vol. II: Their Finest Hour* (London, 1949), p. 162. • 57 Roosevelt Papers, Presidential Press Conferences, Conference No. 875, 24 January 1943. • 58 Quoted in Robert E. Sherwood, *The White House Papers of Harry L. Hopkins, Vol. II: January 1942–July 1945* (London, 1949), p. 693. • 59 *Foreign Relations of the United States, The Conferences at Washington, 1941–1942, and Casablanca, 1943* (Washington, DC, 1958), Doc. 335, Combined Chiefs of Staff Minutes, 18 January 1943. • 60 PREM 4/72/1, Churchill to Clement Attlee and War Cabinet, 19 January 1943. • 61 Harvey (ed.), *War Diaries of Oliver Harvey*, 14 November 1942, p. 183. • 62 David Reynolds and Vladimir Pechatnov (eds), *The Kremlin Letters: Stalin's Correspondence with Churchill and Roosevelt* (London, 2018), Stalin to Churchill, 27 November 1942, p. 182. • 63 Avon Papers, AP/20/9/403, Churchill to Eden, 5 November 1942. • 64 Gilbert and Arnn (eds), *Churchill Documents, Vol. XVIII*, Churchill to Attlee and Eden, 26 January 1943, p. 233. • 65 Gerald Pawle, *The War and Colonel Warden: Based on the Recollections of C. R. Thompson, Personal Assistant to the Prime Minister, 1940–1945* (London, 1963), p. 227. • 66 Jacob Papers, JACB I 1/20, Diary, 30 January 1943. • 67 Cadogan Papers, ACAD 7/2, unpublished memoirs. • 68 Jacob Papers, JACB 1/20, Diary, 30 January 1943. • 69 Moran, *Struggle for Survival*, 30 January 1943, p. 85. • 70 Cadogan Papers, ACAD 7/2, unpublished memoirs. • 71 Gilbert and Arnn (eds), *Churchill Documents, Vol. XVIII*, 'Morning Thoughts', 31 January 1943, p. 295; ibid., Minutes of Second Meeting, 30 January 1943, p. 278. • 72 Ibid., Churchill to Stalin, 2 February 1943, pp. 316–17. • 73 PREM 3/3/6, Eden to Churchill, 9 April 1943. • 74 John Colville, *The Fringes of Power: Downing Street Diaries, 1939–1955* (London, 1985), 4 March 1944, p. 476.

XXI: Special Relationship

1 Quoted in Robert E. Sherwood, *The White House Papers of Harry L. Hopkins, Vol. II: January 1942–July 1945* (London, 1949), p. 911. • 2 Martin Papers, MART 2, Letter to Rosalind Martin, 7 September 1943. • 3 Robert Rhodes James (ed.), *Winston S. Churchill: His Complete Speeches* (London, 1974), 6 September 1943, vol. 7, pp. 6823–7. • 4 Quoted in Stephen E. Ambrose, *Band of Brothers: E Company, 506th Regiment, 101st Airborne from Normandy to Hitler's Eagle's Nest* (New York, 1992), p. 48. • 5 Dixon Papers, Diary, 8 February 1944. • 6 Quoted in David Reynolds, *Rich Relations: The American Occupation of Britain, 1942–1945* (London, 1995), p. 169. The sample size was 3,711. • 7 FO 371/34116, An American Looks at American Troops in Britain, 11 March 1943. • 8 Harry Butcher, *My Three Years with Eisenhower* (New York, 1946), 17 January 1943, p. 239. • 9 Quoted in David Reynolds, *From World War to Cold War: Churchill, Roosevelt, and the International History of the 1940s* (Oxford, 2006), p. 227. • 10 CAB 106/708, The Allied Campaign in North Africa. • 11 *The Memoirs of General the Lord Ismay* (London, 1960), pp. 259, 263. Although the story is apocryphal it reflected Eisenhower's attitude and had the desired effect. • 12 See 'Frisch–Peierls Memorandum, March 1940', Atomic Archive, https://www.atomicarchive.com/resources/documents/beginnings/frisch-peierls.html, accessed 2 September 2024. • 13 Roosevelt Papers, President's Secretary's File, Safe File, Box 2, Bush to Roosevelt, 16 July 1941. • 14 Martin Gilbert and Larry

P. Arnn (eds), *The Churchill Documents, Vol. XVIII: One Continent Redeemed, January–August 1943* (Hillsdale, MI, 2015), Churchill to Hopkins, 27 February 1943, p. 518. • 15 Bush report, 16 December 1942, quoted in Richard G. Hewlett and Oscar E. Anderson Jr., *A History of the United States Atomic Energy Commission, Vol. I: The New World, 1939–1946* (Philadelphia, 1962) p. 267. • 16 Quoted in Sherwin, *World Destroyed*, pp. 74–6. • 17 PREM 3/139-8A, Anderson to Churchill, 11 January 1943. • 18 Gilbert and Arnn (eds), *Churchill Documents, Vol. XVIII*, Churchill to Hopkins, 27 February 1943, p. 519. • 19 *Foreign Relations of the United States (FRUS) 1943: Conferences at Washington and Quebec* (Washington, DC, 1970), Doc. 521, Agreement Relating to Atomic Energy, 19 August 1943. • 20 Ibid., Doc. 326, Memorandum by the Secretary of War's Special Assistant (Bundy), 22 July 1943. • 21 *FRUS: The Conferences at Malta and Yalta, 1945* (Washington, DC, 1955), Doc. 120, Roosevelt to Hull, 29 September 1944. • 22 Quoted in Sherwin, *World Destroyed*, p. 113. • 23 Fred L. Israel (ed.), *The War Diary of Breckinridge Long: Selections from the Years 1939–1944* (Lincoln, NE, 1966), 22 August 1941, p. 213; 29 January 1943, pp. 254–5. • 24 Albert C. Wedemeyer, *Wedemeyer Reports!* (New York, 1958), p. 188; H. G. Nicholas (ed.), *Washington Despatches, 1941–45: Weekly Political Reports from the British Embassy* (London, 1981), 9 October 1943, p. 257. • 25 FO 371/30655, King Minute, 11 May 1942. • 26 Alexander Danchev and Daniel Todman (eds), *War Diaries, 1939–1945: Field Marshal Lord Alanbrooke* (London, 2001), p. 365. • 27 Quoted in Alistair Horne, *Macmillan, the Official Biography: Vol. I: 1894–1956* (London, 1988), p. 160. • 28 FO 371/34121, Minuted by Alan Dudley, 8 November 1943; quoted in Benn Steil, 'Keynes: The Dunkirk Diplomat', *History Today*, vol. 63, no. 6, June 2013. • 29 FO 371/34117, Anglo-American Co-operation, 24 June 1943. • 30 FO 371/34119, Nevile Butler Minute, 11 August 1943. • 31 FO 371/30656, Postal and Telegraph Censorship Report on the United States of America, 11 September 1942; FO 371/30655, United States Criticism of British Action in the Far East, 21 February 1942. • 32 Quoted in Louise Holborn (ed.), *War and Peace Aims of the United Nations, September 1939–December 1942* (Boston, 1943), pp. 90–101. • 33 *Life*, 12 October 1942. • 34 FO 371/30715, Text of Willkie's War Statement. • 35 Wendell Willkie, *One World* (London, 1943), p. 167. • 36 Ibid., p. 14. • 37 Hickleton Papers, A4/410/4/8, 15 December 1942. • 38 Quoted in William Roger Louis, *Imperialism at Bay, 1941–45: The United States and the Decolonization of the British Empire* (Oxford, 1977), p. 14. • 39 Quoted in William Roger Louis, 'Churchill and the Liquidation of the British Empire', Kemper Lecture, 29 March 1998. • 40 PREM 4/42/9, Colonial Office Memorandum on Point III of the Atlantic Charter, August 1941. • 41 *Life*, 28 December 1942. • 42 FO 371/30656, Clark Kerr to Foreign Office, 28 September 1942. • 43 Taussig Papers, Box 47, Memorandum, 16 January 1945. • 44 Quoted in Andrew Roberts, *Churchill: Walking with Destiny* (London, 2018), p. 793. • 45 Hickleton Papers, A/4/410/4/8, Halifax to King George VI, 15 April 1943. • 46 See David Reynolds, 'The Churchill Government and the Black American Troops in Britain during World War II', *Transactions of the Royal Historical Society*, vol. 35 (1985), pp. 113–33. • 47 'As I Please', *Tribune*, 3 December 1943. • 48 Cecil H. King, *With Malice toward None: A War Diary* (London, 1970), 3 June 1944, p. 255. • 49 Quoted in Emily Charles, ' "They treated us royally"? Black Americans in Britain during WW2', Imperial War Museum website, https://www.iwm.org.uk/history/they-treated-us-royally-the-experiences-of-black-americans-in-britain-during-the-second-world-war, accessed 2 September 2024. • 50 'The American Century', *Life*, 17 February 1941. • 51 Quoted in Thorne, *Allies of a Kind*, p. 140. • 52 Quoted ibid., p. 139. • 53 PREM 4/42/9, Attlee to Churchill, 16 June 1942; Neil Smith, *American Empire: Roosevelt's Geographer and the Prelude to Globalization* (Berkeley, CA, 2003), p. 319. • 54 Warren F. Kimball (ed.), *Churchill & Roosevelt: The Complete Correspondence* (Princeton, NJ, 1984), Roosevelt to Churchill, 16 April 1942, vol. 1, p. 457. • 55 PREM 4/42/9, Campbell to Cadogan, 6 August 1942. • 56 Elliott Roosevelt, *As He Saw It* (New York, 1946), p. 115. Elliott's recollections are not always reliable but FDR expressed this view on so many other occasions – to Eden, to Churchill, to Hull, to Welles and before the Pacific War Council – that we may have faith in the sentiment of the quotation. • 57 Louis Adamic, *Dinner at the White House* (New York, 1946), p. 64. • 58 Quoted in Thorne, *Allies of a Kind*, p. 291. • 59 FO 371/34139, 'Anglo-American Relations in the Post War World', Yale Institute of

International Relations, May 1943. • 60 *Chicago Tribune*, 8 September 1943. • 61 *Boston Post*, 7 September 1943. • 62 *St Louis Post-Dispatch*, 7 September 1943. • 63 *New York Times*, 7 September 1943; *Buffalo Courier-Express*, 8 September 1943.

XXII: Stress and Strain

1 Orville H. Bullitt (ed.), *For the President, Personal and Secret: Correspondence between Franklin D. Roosevelt and William C. Bullitt* (London, 1973), Bullitt to Roosevelt, 29 January 1943, p. 579. • 2 Martin Gilbert and Larry P. Arnn (eds), *The Churchill Documents, Vol. XVIII: One Continent Redeemed, January–August 1943* (Hillsdale, MI, 2015), Churchill Press Conference Statement, 1 February 1943, pp. 307–8. • 3 David Reynolds and Vladimir Pechatnov (eds), *The Kremlin Letters: Stalin's Correspondence with Churchill and Roosevelt* (London, 2018), Stalin to Churchill, 16 February 1943, p. 212. • 4 Robert H. McNeal (ed.), *Sochineniia I. V. Stalina, Vol. II* (Stanford, CA, 1967), Speech to the Moscow Council of Workers' Deputies, 6 November 1942, pp. 72–3. • 5 Quoted in Reynolds and Pechatnov (eds), *Kremlin Letters*, p. 223. • 6 FO 800/298/1, Clark Kerr to Foreign Office, 26 May 1935. • 7 Inverchapel Papers, MS 12101/28, T. White, 'His Britannic Majesty's Ambassador', 23 March 1940. • 8 Quoted in *The Spectator*, 14 April 2017. • 9 FO 954/25A/128, Clark Kerr to Eden, 27 April 1942. • 10 FO 800/300, Clark Kerr to Warner, 3 October 1942. Molotov later presented Clark Kerr with a Tommy gun. • 11 Quoted in Donald Gillies, *Radical Diplomat: The Life of Archibald Clark Kerr, Lord Inverchapel, 1882–1951* (London, 1999), p. 152. • 12 FO 800/301, Clark Kerr to Foreign Office, 28 February 1943; ibid., Warner to Clark Kerr, 26 March 1943. • 13 Reynolds and Pechatnov (eds), *Kremlin Letters*, Stalin to Churchill, 21 April 1943, pp. 237–8. • 14 David Dilks (ed.), *The Diaries of Sir Alexander Cadogan, OM, 1938–1945* (London, 1971), 26 April 1943, p. 521. • 15 FO 688/29/19, O'Malley to Eden, 24 May 1943. • 16 Reynolds and Pechatnov (eds), *Kremlin Letters*, Stalin to Churchill, 4 May 1943, p. 246. • 17 McNeal (ed.), *Sochineniia I. V. Stalina, Vol. II*, May Day Address, p. 96; *Foreign Relations of the United States 1943, Vol. III: The British Commonwealth, Eastern Europe, the Far East* (Washington, DC, 1963), Doc. 390, Ambassador in the Soviet Union (Standley) to Secretary of State, 2 May 1943. • 18 Quoted in P. M. H. Bell, *John Bull and the Bear: British Public Opinion, Foreign Policy, and the Soviet Union, 1941–1945* (London, 1990), p. 70; Hickleton Papers, A7/8/12, Halifax Diary, 22 May 1943. • 19 FO 371/37019, Ministry of Information Special Supplement: 'Reflections on the Dissolution of the Comintern'. • 20 Ivo Banac (ed.), *The Diary of Georgi Dimitrov, 1933–1949* (New Haven, CT, 2003), 20 April 1941, pp. 155–6. • 21 Molotov Papers, Fund 6, Inventory 4, Business 26, Folder 2, Vyshinsky Diary, 11 June 1942. • 22 Quoted in Stephen Kotkin, *Stalin, Vol. II: Waiting for Hitler, 1929–1941* (London, 2017), p. 446. • 23 *Pravda*, 22 May 1943. • 24 Quoted in John Lewis Gaddis, *The United States and the Origins of the Cold War, 1941–1947* (New York, 1972), p. 41. • 25 Roosevelt Papers, President's Secretary's File, Box 92, Anecdotes, Roosevelt to Lamont, 12 November 1942. • 26 Quoted in Bell, *John Bull and the Bear*, pp. 69–70. • 27 H. G. Nicholas (ed.), *Washington Despatches, 1941–45: Weekly Political Reports from the British Embassy* (London, 1981), p. 157; Berle Papers, Box 213, Diary, 2 & 24 February 1943, Box 215, 5 August 1943. • 28 Bullitt (ed.), *For the President*, pp. 579–80. • 29 Roosevelt Papers, President's Secretary's File, Diplomatic Correspondence, Box 49, Roosevelt to Stalin, 5 May 1943. • 30 Davies Papers, Box 1.12, Diary, 14 March 1943. • 31 Ibid., Box 1.13, Diary, 12 April 1943. • 32 Warren F. Kimball (ed.), *Churchill & Roosevelt: The Complete Correspondence* (Princeton, NJ, 1984), Churchill to Roosevelt, 25 June 1943, vol. 2, p. 278. • 33 Roosevelt Papers, President's Secretary's File, Diplomatic Correspondence, Box 49, Roosevelt to Stalin, 5 May 1943. • 34 Reynolds and Pechatnov (eds), *Kremlin Letters*, Stalin to Churchill, 24 June 1943, pp. 269–70. • 35 Chartwell Papers, CHAR 20/113/63-64, Churchill to Clark Kerr, 16 June 1942. • 36 FO 800/301, Clark Kerr to Warner, 5 September 1943; Gabriel Gorodetsky (ed.), *The Complete Maisky Diaries* (New Haven, CT, 2017), vol. 3, p. 1483. • 37 W. Averell Harriman and Elie Abel, *Special Envoy to Churchill and Stalin, 1941–1946* (New York, 1975), pp. 225, 226. • 38 Avon Papers, AP 20/3/4, Diary, 26 August 1943. • 39 Reynolds and Pechatnov (eds), *Kremlin*

Letters, Stalin to Churchill and Roosevelt, 24 August 1943, p. 293. • 40 Sherfield Papers, MS 520, Makins to Strang, 19 February 1943. • 41 Nigel Nicolson (ed.), *Harold Nicolson: Diaries and Letters, Vol. II: 1939–1945* (London, 1967), 12 March 1943, p. 284. • 42 Quoted in François Kersaudy, *Churchill and De Gaulle* (London, 1981), p. 267. • 43 Sherfield Papers, MS 520, Makins to Strang, 7 April 1943. • 44 Hopkins Papers, Box 330, Monnet to Hopkins, 6 May 1943. • 45 FO 371/36047, Churchill to Attlee and Eden, 21 May 1943. • 46 CAB 65/38, War Cabinet Minutes, 23 May 1943. • 47 Coghill Papers, Doc. 7053, Diary, 29 November 1942. • 48 Charles de Gaulle, *Mémoires de guerre, vol. II: l'unité* (Paris, 1956), Documents, Telegram from the Délégation France combattante in Washington to the Comité national in London, 14 April 1943, pp. 462–3. • 49 Ibid., Moulin to de Gaulle, 15 May 1943, p. 475. • 50 Kenneth Pendar, *Adventure in Diplomacy: The Emergence of General de Gaulle in North Africa* (London, 1966), p. 167. • 51 CHAR 9/156B, Churchill Secret Session Speech, 10 December 1942. • 52 FO 954/8B/455, Churchill to Macmillan, 11 June 1943; CHAR 20/113/33, Macmillan to Churchill, 15 June 1943. • 53 Kimball (ed.), *Churchill & Roosevelt*, Roosevelt to Churchill, 22 July 1943, vol. 2, p. 340. • 54 Avon Papers, AP 20/3/4, Quebec Diary, 20 August 1943. • 55 Lawford Papers, LWFD 02, Diary, 20 August 1943. • 56 Avon Papers, AP 20/3/4, Quebec Diary, 20 August 1943. • 57 *The Memoirs of Cordell Hull, Vol. II* (London, 1948), p. 1241. • 58 Quoted in Jean Lacouture, *De Gaulle, Vol. I: The Rebel, 1890–1944* (London, 1990), p. 436. • 59 Charles Mott-Radclyffe, *Foreign Body in the Eye: A Memoir of the Foreign Service Old and New* (London, 1975), p. 101. • 60 Oxford Papers, MS R/02/1956, Diary, 15 November 1943. • 61 See Meir Zamir, *The Secret Anglo-French War in the Middle East: Intelligence and Decolonisation, 1940–1948* (Abingdon, 2015). • 62 Coghill Papers, Doc. 7053, Diary, 5 January 1942. • 63 Lord Casey, *Personal Experience, 1939–1946* (London, 1962), p. 126. • 64 Spears Papers, MEC, Box 1, File 1, Levant Diary, 23 August 1942. • 65 Sir Edward Spears, *Fulfilment of a Mission: The Spears Mission to Syria and Lebanon, 1941–1944* (London, 1977), p. 228. • 66 Coghill Papers, Doc. 7053, Diary, 28 November 1943. • 67 Georges Catroux, *Dans la bataille de Méditerranée, Égypte, Levant, Afrique du Nord, 1940–1944* (Paris, 1949), p. 421, • 68 Quoted in Julian Jackson, *A Certain Idea of France: The Life of Charles de Gaulle* (London, 2018), p. 287. • 69 Ibid., p. 286.

XXIII: The Big Three

1 James Leasor, *War at the Top: Based on the Experiences of General Sir Leslie Hollis* (London, 1959), p. 259. • 2 John Harvey (ed.), *The War Diaries of Oliver Harvey, 1941–45* (London, 1978), 29 September 1943, p. 302; Harriman Papers, Box 170, Folder 4, Part 1, Proposal of the USSR, 19 October 1943. • 3 FO 800/301, Moscow Conference Notes. • 4 Harriman Papers, Box 170, Folder 4, Part 1, Memorandum of Conversation between Hull and Molotov, 21 October 1943. • 5 Yee Wah Foo (ed.), *Chiang Kaishek's Last Ambassador to Moscow: The Wartime Diaries of Fu Bingchang* (Basingstoke, 2011), 30 October 1943, p. 113. • 6 Harvey (ed.), *War Diaries of Oliver Harvey*, 25 October 1943, p. 313. • 7 Avon Papers, AP 20/3/5, Diary, 22 October 1943; ibid., 21 October 1943. • 8 *The Memoirs of General the Lord Ismay* (London, 1960), p. 326. • 9 Harvey (ed.), *War Diaries of Oliver Harvey*, 30 October 1943, p. 316, 20 October 1943, p. 310. • 10 Harriman Papers, Box 170, Folder 7, Part 2, Harriman to Roosevelt and Hull, 30 October 1943. • 11 Ibid., Folder 8, Harriman to Churchill, 3 November 1943. • 12 Ibid., Folder 8, Harriman to Churchill, 3 November 1943. • 13 FO 371/36957, Eden to Churchill, 29 October 1943; Memorandum of Conversations with Monsieur A. J. Vyshinski, 4 December 1942. • 14 Quoted in Geoffrey Roberts, *Stalin's Wars: From World War to Cold War, 1939–1953* (New Haven, CT, 2006), p. 179. • 15 Hopkins Papers, Box 330, Folder 7, Harriman to State Department, 9 November 1943; J. V. Stalin, 'Speech at Celebration Meeting of the Moscow Soviet of Working People's Deputies and Moscow Party and Public Organizations', November 6, 1943, available at https://www.marxists.org/reference/archive/stalin/works/1943/11/06s.htm • 16 W. Averell Harriman and Elie Abel, *Special Envoy to Churchill and Stalin, 1941–1946* (New York, 1975), p. 236. • 17 Earl of Avon, *The Eden Memoirs, Vol. II: The Reckoning* (London,

1965), p. 416. • 18 Alexander Danchev and Daniel Todman (eds), *War Diaries, 1939–1945: Field Marshal Lord Alanbrooke* (London, 2001), 8 October 1943, p. 459. • 19 Warren F. Kimball (ed.), *Churchill & Roosevelt: The Complete Correspondence* (Princeton, NJ, 1984), Churchill to Roosevelt, 23 October 1943, vol. 2, pp. 555–6. • 20 *Foreign Relations of the United States (FRUS) 1943: The Conferences at Cairo and Tehran* (Washington, DC, 1961), Doc. 316, McCloy Memorandum for Harry Hopkins, 25 November 1943. • 21 Leasor, *War at the Top*, p. 245. • 22 Ibid., p. 258. • 23 *FRUS 1943: The Conferences at Cairo and Tehran*, Doc. 238, Minutes of the President's Meeting with the Joint Chiefs of Staff, 19 November 1943. • 24 Elliott Roosevelt, *As He Saw It* (New York, 1946), p. 151. • 25 Danchev and Todman (eds), *War Diaries*, p. 478. • 26 Sholto Douglas, *Years of Command* (London, 1966), p. 227. • 27 Theodore H. White (ed.), *The Stilwell Papers* (London, 1949), 23 November 1943, p. 230. • 28 Kennedy Papers, 4/2/5, Diary, 7 November 1943. • 29 Douglas, *Years of Command*, p. 229. • 30 Avon Papers, AP 20/3/5, Diary, 25 November 1943. • 31 PREM 4/27/1, Churchill to Eden, 5 November 1942. • 32 Quoted in Forrest C. Pogue, *George C. Marshall, Vol. III: Organizer of Victory, 1943–1945* (New York, 1973), p. 307. • 33 Lord Moran, *Winston Churchill: The Struggle for Survival, 1940–1965* (London, 1966), 25 November 1943, pp. 131–2. • 34 Quoted in John Lewis Gaddis, *The United States and the Origins of the Cold War, 1941–1947* (New York, 1972), p. 64. • 35 *FRUS 1943: The Conferences at Cairo and Tehran*, Doc. 358, Minutes of the Meeting between Roosevelt and Stalin, 28 November 1943; Harriman and Abel, *Special Envoy to Churchill and Stalin*, p. 266. • 36 Harriman and Abel, *Special Envoy to Churchill and Stalin*, p. 266. • 37 Ibid., p. 265. • 38 A. H. Birse, *Memoirs of an Interpreter* (New York, 1967), p. 155; *FRUS 1943: The Conferences at Cairo and Tehran*, Doc. 358, Minutes of the First Plenary Session, 28 November 1943. • 39 Quoted in Robert E. Sherwood, *The White House Papers of Harry L. Hopkins, Vol. II: January 1942–July 1945* (London, 1949), p. 775. • 40 CAB 80/77, 'Eureka' Minutes, First Plenary Session, 28 November 1943. • 41 *FRUS 1943: The Conferences at Cairo and Tehran*, Doc. 362, Minutes of the Dinner Hosted by Roosevelt, 28 November 1943. • 42 Ibid., Doc. 363, Charles E. Bohlen, Memorandum of Marshal Stalin's Views as Expressed on Evening of 28 November 1943. • 43 Ibid. Stalin's presence in Leipzig is by no means certain. Although there is no record of it beyond this reference, it is possible that he visited the city on his way to, or on his way back from, the Fifth Congress of the Russian Social Democratic Labour Party in London. Alternatively, he may have been appropriating Lenin's alleged joke that if German revolutionaries ever stormed a railway station, they would stop first to buy tickets. • 44 Avon Papers, AP 20/3/5, Diary, 28 November 1943. • 45 Danchev and Todman (eds), *War Diaries*, 29 November 1943, p. 485. • 46 *FRUS 1943: The Conferences at Cairo and Tehran*, Doc. 364, Combined Chiefs of Staff Minutes, 28 November 1943. • 47 Sergo Beria, *Beria, My Father: Inside Stalin's Kremlin* (London, 2001), p. 93. • 48 John R. Deane, *The Strange Alliance: The Story of American Efforts at Wartime Co-operation with Russia* (London, 1947), p. 42. • 49 CAB 80/77, 'Eureka' Minutes, Second Plenary Session, 29 November 1943. • 50 Deane, *Strange Alliance*, p. 44. • 51 *Memoirs of General the Lord Ismay*, p. 338. • 52 Stimson Papers, MS 465, Series XIV, Box 76, Folder 45, Diary, 5 December 1943. • 53 *FRUS 1943: The Conferences at Cairo and Tehran*, Doc. 368, Minutes of the Dinner at the Soviet Legation, 29 November 1943. • 54 Winston S. Churchill, *The Second World War, Vol. V: Closing the Ring* (London, 1952), p. 330. • 55 Hickleton Papers, A7/8/12, Halifax Diary, 16 March 1943. • 56 *FRUS 1943, Vol. III: The British Commonwealth, Eastern Europe, The Far East* (Washington, DC, 1963), Doc. 17, Hopkins to Roosevelt, 17 March 1943. • 57 Morgenthau Papers, Diaries, 18 August 1944. • 58 Boettiger Papers, Box 13, Folder 1, John Boettiger to Anna Boettiger, 30 November 1943. • 59 Moran, *Struggle for Survival*, 29 November 1943, pp. 139–40. • 60 Frances Perkins, *The Roosevelt I Knew* (London, 1947), pp. 70–71. • 61 Danchev and Todman (eds), *War Diaries*, 30 November 1943, p. 486. • 62 *FRUS 1943: The Conferences at Cairo and Tehran*, Doc. 375, Minutes of the Dinner Held at the British Legation, 30 November 1943. • 63 Moran, *Struggle for Survival*, 30 November 1943, p. 143. • 64 Kimball (ed.), *Churchill & Roosevelt*, Churchill to Roosevelt, 1 December 1943, vol. 2, p. 615. • 65 *FRUS 1943: The Conferences at Cairo and Tehran*, Doc. 375, Minutes of the Dinner Held at the British Legation, 30 November 1943. • 66 Quoted in Frank Freidel, *Franklin D. Roosevelt: A Rendezvous with*

Destiny (Boston, 1990), p. 493. • 67 Roosevelt Papers, Press Conferences, Press Conference No. 927, 17 December 1943; ibid., Master Speech File, Box 76, Fireside Chat, 24 December 1943. • 68 Morgenthau Diaries, quoted in Christopher Thorne, *Allies of a Kind: The United States, Britain, and the War against Japan, 1941–1945* (New York, 1978), p. 276.

XXIV: The Fourth Policeman

1 Elliott Roosevelt (ed.), *The Roosevelt Letters: Being the Personal Correspondence of Franklin Delano Roosevelt, Vol. III: 1928–1945* (London, 1952), p. 483. • 2 *Time*, 1 November 1937. • 3 Graham Peck, *Two Kinds of Time* (Boston, 1950), p. 378. • 4 Quoted in Jay Taylor, *The Generalissimo: Chiang Kai-shek and the Struggle for Modern China* (Cambridge, MA, 2009), p. 155. • 5 Peck, *Two Kinds of Time*, p. 379; Fujiko Isono (ed.), *Owen Lattimore: China Memoirs – Chiang Kai-shek and the War against Japan* (Tokyo, 1990), p. 164. • 6 Quoted in Taylor, *Generalissimo*, pp. 49–50. • 7 Quoted in Rana Mitter, *China's War with Japan, 1937–1945: The Struggle for Survival* (London, 2013), p. 243. • 8 Ibid., p. 313. • 9 Roosevelt Papers, PSF, Subject File, Box 132, Lauchlin Currie, Soong May-ling to Currie, 18 May 1942. • 10 Ibid., Safe File, Box 2, Chiang Kai-shek to T. V. Soong for transmission to Roosevelt, 25 February 1942. • 11 FO 800/300, Clark Kerr to Eden, 13 February 1942. • 12 Quoted in Mitter, *China's War with Japan*, p. 244. • 13 Peck, *Two Kinds of Time*, p. 35. • 14 *Foreign Relations of the United States (FRUS) 1942: China* (Washington, DC, 1956), Doc. 17, Magruder to War Department, 10 February 1942. • 15 Quoted in Barbara W. Tuchman, *Stilwell and the American Experience in China, 1911–1945* (New York, 1970), p. 126. • 16 Quoted in J. D. M. Pringle, *China Struggles for Unity* (London, 1939), p. 71. • 17 John Gunther, *Procession: Dominant Personalities of Four Decades as Seen by the Author of the 'Inside' Books* (New York, 1965), p. 157; John Gunther, 'Inside Asia', *The Argus* (Melbourne), 17 June 1939. • 18 Joseph Alsop, *I've Seen the Best of It: Memoirs* (New York, 1992), p. 203. • 19 John Morton Blum (ed.), *From the Morgenthau Diaries, Vol. III: The Years of War, 1941–1945* (Boston, 1965), p. 94. The British provided £50 million to be spent on war purchases within the sterling area. • 20 Theodore H. White (ed.), *The Stilwell Papers* (London, 1949), Joseph Stilwell to Winifred Stilwell, 1 March 1942, p. 68. • 21 Quoted in Alan K. Lathrop, 'The Employment of Chinese Nationalist Troops in the First Burma Campaign', *Journal of Southeast Asian Studies*, vol. 12, no. 2 (1981), p. 419. • 22 White (ed.), *Stilwell Papers*, 25 May 1942, p. 116. • 23 Quoted in Hans Van de Ven, *China at War: Triumph and Tragedy in the Emergence of the New China* (London, 2017), pp. 165–6. • 24 White (ed.), *Stilwell Papers*, 10 July 1942, p. 132, 1 April 1942, p. 95, 12 September 1942, p. 149, 1 August 1942, p. 136, 19 June 1942, p. 123. • 25 Quoted in Charles F. Romanus and Riley Sunderland, *Stilwell's Mission to China* (Washington, DC, 1953), p. 172. • 26 *FRUS 1942: China*, Doc., 91, Hornbeck Memorandum, 27 June 1942. • 27 Tuchman, *Stilwell and the American Experience in China*, p. 333. • 28 White (ed.), *Stilwell Papers*, 5 October 1942, p. 158. • 29 Wendell Willkie, *One World* (London, 1943), p. 110. • 30 Gardner Cowles, *Mike Looks Back: The Memoirs of Gardner Cowles, Founder of 'Look' Magazine* (New York, 1985), p. 89. • 31 FO 371/35775, Hayter to Clarke, 2 March 1943. • 32 'Soong Mei-Ling, "Addresses to the House of Representatives and to the Senate", February 18, 1943', USC US–China Institute, https://china.usc.edu/soong-mei-ling-"addresses-house-respresentatives-and-senate"-february-18-1943, accessed 3 September 2024. • 33 *Life*, 19 April 1943. • 34 *FRUS 1943: The Conferences at Cairo and Tehran* (Washington, DC, 1961), Doc. 365, Minutes of the Meeting between Roosevelt and Stalin, 29 November 1943. • 35 *FRUS 1943, Vol. III: The British Commonwealth, Eastern Europe, the Far East* (Washington, DC, 1963), Doc. 23, Hopkins Memorandum of Meeting between Roosevelt, Hull and Eden, 27 March 1943. • 36 Martin Gilbert (ed.), *The Churchill Documents, Vol. XVII: Testing Times, 1942* (Hillsdale, MI, 2014), Churchill to Eden, 21 October 1942, p. 1296. • 37 Moran, *Struggle for Survival*, 24 June 1954, p. 559. • 38 FO 371/35780, David Nelson Rowe, 'China's Military Potential and the Enforcement of Peace', September 1943. • 39 *Zhongyang ribao* editorial, 13 January 1943, quoted in Dong Wang, *China's Unequal Treaties: Narrating National History* (Lanham, MD, 2005), p. 93. • 40 Quoted in Herbert Feis, *The China Tangle:*

The American Effort in China from Pearl Harbor to the Marshall Mission (Princeton, NJ, 1953), p. 62. • 41 Winston S. Churchill, *The Second World War, Vol. V: Closing the Ring* (London, 1952), pp. 289–90. • 42 Lord Halifax, *Fullness of Days* (London, 1957), p. 250. • 43 Quoted in Mitter, *China's War with Japan*, p. 313. • 44 Ismay Papers, 4/14/5, Grimsdale to Ismay, 15 August 1942. • 45 Roosevelt Papers, Map Room Papers, Box 10, Chiang Kai-shek to Roosevelt, 9 December 1943. • 46 Roosevelt Papers, Secretary's File, Diplomatic Correspondence, Box 27, China, July–December 1944, Summary of a Memorandum by John Service, 1 July 1944. • 47 Quoted in Christopher Thorne, *Allies of a Kind: The United States, Britain, and the War against Japan, 1941–1945* (New York, 1978), pp. 42, 68; quoted in Tuchman, *Stilwell and the American Experience in China*, p. 158; Hopkins Papers, Box 334, Book 9, Davies to Hopkins, 23 January 1944. • 48 Edgar Snow, *Red Star over China* (New York, 1937), p. 94. • 49 Quoted in Van de Ven, *China at War*, p. 146. • 50 Zhisui Li, *The Private Life of Chairman Mao* (London, 1994), p. 568. • 51 Hopkins Papers, Box 334, Book 9, Davies to Hopkins, 23 January 1944. • 52 *FRUS 1944, Vol. VI: China* (Washington, DC, 1967), Doc. 416, John Service Memorandum, 28 July 1944. • 53 Quoted in Mitter, *China's War with Japan*, p. 330. • 54 Quoted in Tuchman, *Stilwell and the American Experience in China*, p. 473. • 55 Roosevelt Papers, Map Room Papers, Box 10, Chiang Kai-shek to Roosevelt, 8 July 1944. • 56 White (ed.), *Stilwell Papers*, 16 September 1944, p. 303. • 57 Ibid., 15 September, p. 303; quoted in Charles F. Romanus and Riley Sunderland, *Stilwell's Command Problems* (Washington, DC, 1956), p. 435. • 58 White (ed.), *Stilwell Papers*, 19 September 1944, p. 305. • 59 Roosevelt Papers, Map Room Papers, Box 10, Roosevelt to Chiang Kai-shek, 16 September 1944. • 60 Quoted in John Paton Davies Jr, *China Hand: An Autobiography* (Philadelphia, 2012), p. 203. • 61 White (ed.), *Stilwell Papers*, 19 September 1944, p. 305. • 62 Ibid., Joseph Stilwell to Winifred Stilwell, 21 September 1944, p. 305. • 63 Quoted in Taylor, *Generalissimo*, p. 289. • 64 *New York Times*, 31 October 1944. • 65 Ibid.

XXV: Turncoats and Partisans

1 Fitzroy Maclean, *Eastern Approaches* (London, 1949), p. 281. • 2 Warren F. Kimball (ed.), *Churchill & Roosevelt: The Complete Correspondence* (Princeton, NJ, 1984), Churchill to Roosevelt, 26 July 1943, vol. 2, p. 348. • 3 Caccia Papers, MS 671/05/04, Harold Caccia to Nancy Caccia, 4 October 1943. • 4 Kimball (ed.), *Churchill & Roosevelt*, Churchill to Roosevelt, 31 July 1943, vol. 2, p. 369. • 5 Winston S. Churchill, *The Second World War, Vol. I: The Gathering Storm* (London, 1948), p. 9. • 6 Kimball (ed.), *Churchill & Roosevelt*, Churchill to Roosevelt, 31 July 1943, vol. 2, p. 369. • 7 PREM 3/243/5, Sforza to Berle, 23 September 1943. • 8 Ibid., Reuter Message from New York, 1 October 1943. • 9 Nigel Nicolson (ed.), *Harold Nicolson: Diaries and Letters, Vol. II: 1939–1945* (London, 1967), Harold Nicolson to Benedict and Nigel Nicolson, 8 December 1944, p. 417; PREM 3/243/5, Personalities Report on Count Carlo Sforza, 1 October 1943. • 10 David Dilks (ed.), *The Diaries of Sir Alexander Cadogan, OM, 1938–1945* (London, 1971), 11 October 1943, p. 566. • 11 Quoted in Elisabeth Barker, *Churchill and Eden at War* (London, 1978), p. 167. • 12 Harold Macmillan, *War Diaries: Politics and War in the Mediterranean, January 1943–May 1945* (London, 1984), 26 October 1943, p. 266. • 13 Ivo Banac (ed.), *The Diary of Georgi Dimitrov, 1933–1949* (New Haven, CT, 2003), 20 June 1944, pp. 322–3. • 14 PREM 3/243/12, Churchill to Eden, 10 June 1944. • 15 Quoted in Llewellyn Woodward, *British Foreign Policy in the Second World War, Vol. II* (London, 1971), p. 543. • 16 Quoted in Barker, *Churchill and Eden at War*, p. 177. • 17 Kimball (ed.), *Churchill & Roosevelt*, Churchill to Roosevelt, 6 December 1944, vol. 3, pp. 438–9. • 18 Sherfield Papers, MS 521, Further Reflections on the Sforza Incident, December 1944. • 19 *Daily Telegraph*, 5 December 1941. • 20 Chartwell Papers, CHAR 20/36/11, Churchill to Ismay, 28 November 1941. • 21 Banac (ed.), *Diary of Georgi Dimitrov*, Dimitrov to Tito, 10 August 1942, p. 234. • 22 FO 371/33469. • 23 Quoted in Walter E. Roberts, *Tito, Mihailović and the Allies, 1941–1945* (Durham, NC, [1973] 1987), p. 27. • 24 Ibid., p. 70. • 25 F. W. D. Deakin, *The Embattled Mountain* (London, 1971), p. 14. • 26 Quoted in Michael Lees,

The Rape of Serbia: The British Role in Tito's Grab for Power, 1943–1944 (New York, 1990), p. 217. • 27 Maclean, *Eastern Approaches*, pp. 26, 24. • 28 Harold Eeman, *Clouds over the Sun: Memories of a Diplomat, 1942–1958* (London, 1981), pp. 33–4. • 29 Maclean, *Eastern Approaches*, p. 281. • 30 Ibid., pp. 305–6. • 31 Quoted in Halik Kochanski, *Resistance: The Underground War in Europe, 1939–45* (London, 2022), p. 480. • 32 Maclean, *Eastern Approaches*, p. 326. • 33 Deakin, *Embattled Mountain*, p. 80. • 34 FO 371/37615, Report by Brigadier F. H. R. Maclean, Commanding Allied Military Mission to the Partisan Forces in Yugoslavia, 6 November 1943. • 35 Quoted in Roberts, *Tito, Mihailović and the Allies*, p. 102. • 36 Ibid., p. 260. • 37 Maclean, *Eastern Approaches*, pp. 402–3. • 38 Dixon Papers, Diary, 13 August 1944. • 39 Ibid. • 40 FO 371/44263, Churchill to Eden, 31 August 1944; ibid., Eden's handwritten comments. • 41 Chartwell Papers, CHAR 20/173/32-33, Churchill to Hopkins, 12 October 1944. • 42 Quoted in Heather Williams, *Parachutes, Patriots and Partisans: The Special Operations Executive and Yugoslavia, 1941–1945* (London, 2003), p. 161. • 43 Quoted in Kochanski, *Resistance*, p. 732. • 44 Ibid., p. 750. • 45 Clarke Papers, *Sunday Telegraph*, 29 July 1990.

XXVI: Brave New World

1 FO 371/38516, Lieutenant Miles Report, 'The President at Home', November 1943. 2 Quoted in Max Hastings, *All Hell Let Loose: The World at War, 1939–1945* (London, 2011), p. 535. • 3 *Foreign Relations of the United States (FRUS) 1943: The Conferences at Cairo and Tehran* (Washington, DC, 1961), Doc. 362, Tripartite Dinner, Bohlen Minutes, 28 November 1943; ibid., Doc. 379, Tripartite Political Meeting, Bohlen Minutes, 1 December 1943. • 4 CAB 66/45, Minutes of Plenary Tripartite Meeting, 1 December 1943; quoted in Geoffrey Roberts, *Stalin's Wars: From World War to Cold War, 1939–1953* (New Haven, CT, 2006), p. 186. • 5 *FRUS 1943: The Conferences at Cairo and Tehran*, Doc. 362, Tripartite Dinner, Bohlen Minutes, 28 November 1943. • 6 Quoted in Michael R. Beschloss, *The Conquerors: Roosevelt, Truman and the Destruction of Hitler's Germany, 1941–1945* (New York, 2002), pp. 75–6. • 7 Morgenthau Papers, Diaries, Series 1, Vol. 768, Diaries, 4 September 1944. • 8 Ibid. • 9 Quoted in Henry L. Feingold, *The Politics of Rescue: The Roosevelt Administration and the Holocaust, 1938–1945* (New Brunswick, NJ, 1970), p. 206. • 10 Ibid., p. 257. • 11 Morgenthau Papers, Presidential Diary, 19 August 1944. • 12 Stimson Papers, MS 465, Series XIV, Box 76, Folder 48, Memorandum on Post-war Treatment of Germany, 5 September 1944. • 13 Quoted in John M. Blum (ed.), *From the Morgenthau Diaries, Vol. III: The Years of War, 1941–1945* (Boston, 1965), p. 369. • 14 Lord Moran, *Winston Churchill: The Struggle for Survival, 1940–1965* (London, 1966), 13 September 1944, p. 177. • 15 Morgenthau Papers, Presidential Diary, 15 September 1944. • 16 Morgenthau Papers, Diary, Record of a Conversation between Morgenthau and White, 18 October 1944. • 17 Moran, *Struggle for Survival*, 13 September 1944, p. 178. • 18 Henry L. Stimson and McGeorge Bundy, *On Active Service in Peace and War* (New York, 1948), p. 581; *Völkischer Beobachter*, quoted in Beschloss, *Conquerors*, p. 144. • 19 Morgenthau Papers, Diary, 28 September 1944. • 20 Agreed Recommendations of the Dumbarton Oaks Conference, 28 September 1944, quoted in Llewellyn Woodward, *British Foreign Policy in the Second World War, Vol. V* (London, 1976), p. 152. • 21 Quoted in Stephen Wertheim, *Tomorrow, the World: The Birth of US Global Supremacy* (Cambridge, MA, 2020), p. 142. • 22 Bowman Papers, MS 58, Memorandum of a Conversation with Churchill at Chequers, 15 April 1944. • 23 Chartwell Papers, CHAR 20/67/8, Churchill Minute to Eden, 18 October 1942. • 24 Ibid., Churchill Minute to Eden, 21 October 1942. • 25 *FRUS 1943: The Conferences at Cairo and Tehran*, Doc. 519, Charles E. Bohlen Memorandum, 15 December 1943. • 26 Quoted in Robert Dallek, *Franklin D. Roosevelt and American Foreign Policy, 1932–1945* (New York, 1979), p. 459. • 27 Roosevelt Papers, PSF, Department Correspondence, Box 74, Roosevelt to Cordell Hull, 24 January 1944. • 28 Quoted in Walter La Feber, 'Roosevelt, Churchill and Indochina, 1942–1945', *American Historical Review*, vol. 80, no. 5 (1975), p. 1291. • 29 Quoted in Christopher Thorne, *Allies of a Kind: The United States, Britain, and the War against Japan, 1941–1945* (New York, 1978), p. 466. • 30 Quoted in La Feber, 'Roosevelt,

Churchill and Indochina', p. 1285. • 31 Robert Rhodes James (ed.), *Winston S. Churchill: His Complete Speeches* (London, 1974), Lord Mayor's Luncheon, 10 November 1942, vol. 6, p. 6695. • 32 Roosevelt Papers, PSF, Subject File, Box 166, Taussig Report, 17 December 1942. • 33 Quoted in David Dilks (ed.), *The Diaries of Sir Alexander Cadogan, OM, 1938–1945* (London, 1971), p. 578. • 34 The Foreign Office noted that the word 'independence' appeared 'no less than six times in the same sentence'. FO 371/35311, Gladwyn Jebb, Preliminary Analysis of Mr. Hull's Draft, 2 April 1943. • 35 FO 371/35311, Law to Stanley, 22 November 1943; *FRUS 1943, Vol. I: General* (Washington, DC, 1963), Doc. 608, Minutes of the Eleventh Session of the Tripartite Conference, 29 October 1943. • 36 Thomas M. Campbell and George C. Herring (eds), *The Diaries of Edward R. Stettinius, Jr., 1943–1946* (New York, 1975), 17 March 1944, p. 39. • 37 Bowman Papers, MS 58/015/001, Churchill, Report by Isaiah Bowman on Chequers Conversation, 15 April 1944. • 38 Theodore H. White (ed.), *The Stilwell Papers* (London, 1949), 10 November 1943, p. 283; quoted in John H. Sbrega, 'Anglo-American Relations and the Selection of Mountbatten as Supreme Allied Commander, South East Asia', *Military Affairs*, vol. 46, no. 3 (1982), pp. 139–45. • 39 *FRUS 1943: China* (Washington, DC, 1957), Doc. 796, Cover Note re Memorandum by John Paton Davies, 26 October 1943. • 40 Quoted in Thorne, *Allies of a Kind*, p. 293. Author's italics. • 41 Quoted ibid., pp. 292–3, 160. • 42 Campbell and Herring (eds), *Diaries of Edward R. Stettinius, Jr.*, p. 45. • 43 *FRUS 1943, Vol. III: The British Commonwealth, Eastern Europe, the Far East* (Washington, DC, 1963), Doc. 59, 'United States' Policy on Limitations on British Gold and Dollar Balances', Dean Acheson, 2 November 1943. • 44 Ibid., Doc. 61, Record of a Meeting Held in the Treasury, 16 December 1943. • 45 Morgenthau Papers, Presidential Diaries, 19 August 1944. • 46 Clement Attlee, Hansard, HC Deb, 24 February 1942, vol. 378, col. 25. • 47 Quoted in Roy Harrod, *The Life of John Maynard Keynes* (London, 1951), p. 512. • 48 Campbell and Herring (eds), *Diaries of Edward R. Stettinius, Jr.*, 21 November 1944, p. 175. • 49 Donald Moggridge (ed.), *The Collected Writings of John Maynard Keynes, Vol. XXIV: Activities, 1944–1946: The Transition to Peace* (London, 1979), p. 410. • 50 Quoted in Thorne, *Allies of a Kind*, p. 280. • 51 Quoted in Chan Kit-cheng, 'The United States and the Question of Hong Kong, 1941–45', *Journal of the Hong Kong Branch of the Royal Asiatic Society*, vol. 19 (1979), p. 11. • 52 John Colville, *The Fringes of Power: Downing Street Diaries, 1939–1955* (London, 1985), 25 November 1944, p. 528. • 53 Quoted in Benn Steil, *The Battle of Bretton Woods: John Maynard Keynes, Harry Dexter White, and the Making of a New World Order* (Princeton, NJ, 2013), p. 176. • 54 Donald Moggridge (ed.), *The Collected Writings of John Maynard Keynes, Vol. XXV: Activities, 1940–44: Shaping the Post-war World – The Clearing Union* (London, 1980), Keynes to Eady, p. 363. • 55 Harrod, *Life of John Maynard Keynes*, p. 558.

XXVII: The Polish Agony

1 *Documents on Polish–Soviet Relations (DPSR), Vol. I: 1939–1943* (London, 1961), Minutes of a Meeting Held in the Kremlin between Kot and Stalin, 14 November 1941, p. 210. • 2 Joseph Retinger, *Memoirs of an Eminence Grise* (Brighton, 1972), p. 144; quoted in Vojtech Mastny, 'The Beneš–Stalin–Molotov Conversations in December 1943: New Documents', *Jahrbücher für Geschichte Osteuropas*, vol. 20, no. 3 (1972), p. 377. • 3 Quoted in Halik Kochanski, *The Eagle Unbowed: Poland and the Poles in the Second World War* (London, 2012), p. 331; John Harvey (ed.), *The War Diaries of Oliver Harvey, 1941–45* (London, 1978), 9 February 1944, p. 330. • 4 *DPSR: Vol. II, 1943–1945* (London, 1968), Record of a Conversation between Mikołajczyk and Eden, 11 January 1944, p. 135 • 5 Quoted in Llewellyn Woodward, *British Foreign Policy in the Second World War, Vol. II* (London, 1971), p. 202. • 6 Stanisław Mikołajczyk, *The Pattern of Soviet Domination* (London, 1948), p. 57. • 7 FO 954/20A, Conversation between Mikołajczyk and Churchill, 6 February 1944. • 8 Lawford Papers, LWFD 02/07, 14 January 1944. • 9 Dixon Papers, Diary, 7 February 1944; FO 954/20A/66, O'Malley to Eden, 13 February 1944. • 10 FO 371/954/20A/14, O'Malley to Eden, 22 January 1944. • 11 Edward Raczynski, *In Allied London* (London, 1962), Illustration no. 20. • 12 Quoted

in Agnieszka Morriss, 'The BBC Polish Service during World War II', unpublished PhD thesis, City, University of London (2016), p. 200; FO 954/20B, Beaverbrook to Eden, 26 August 1944. FO 954/20B, Beaverbrook to Eden, 26 August 1944. • 13 Dixon Papers, Diary, 14 February 1944. • 14 David Reynolds and Vladimir Pechatnov (eds), *The Kremlin Letters: Stalin's Correspondence with Churchill and Roosevelt* (London, 2018), Stalin to Churchill, 4 February 1944, p. 372. • 15 Quoted in Mastny, 'Beneš–Stalin–Molotov Conversations in December 1943', p. 377. • 16 Harvey (ed.), *War Diaries of Oliver Harvey*, 8 February 1944, p. 329. • 17 Reynolds and Pechatnov (eds), *Kremlin Letters*, Churchill to Stalin, 20 February 1944, p. 378. • 18 FO 954/20A/119, Clark Kerr to Foreign Office, 28 February 1944. • 19 Reynolds and Pechatnov (eds), *Kremlin Letters*, Stalin to Churchill, 23 March 1944, p. 401. • 20 Sherfield Papers, MS 521, Makins to Harvey, 27 January 1944. • 21 Roosevelt Papers, PSF, Diplomatic Correspondence, Box 49, Russia 1945, Notes of an Interview with Maxim Litvinov, 28 December 1944. • 22 FO 371/43304, Eden Minute, 3 April 1944. • 23 FO 954/20A, Churchill to Eden, 8 May 1944. • 24 Quoted in Kochanski, *Eagle Unbowed*, p. 391. • 25 G. A. Arbatov, V. G. Komplektov and G. M. Kornienko (eds), *Sovetsko-amerikanskie otnosheniia vo vremia Belikoi Otechestvennoi voiny, 1941–1945, Vol. 1* (Moscow, 1984), Litvinov to Narkomindel, 12 March 1942, pp. 155–7. Two months later, FDR later repeated these sentiments to Molotov. Oleg A. Rzheshevsky (ed.), *War and Diplomacy: The Making of the Grand Alliance – Documents from Stalin's Archives* (Amsterdam, 1996), Record of Talks with Roosevelt, 29 May 1942, pp. 173–5; Mary E. Glantz, *FDR and the Soviet Union: The President's Battles over Foreign Policy* (Lawrence, KS, 2005), p. 102. • 26 Quoted in Robert Rhodes James, *Victor Cazalet: A Portrait* (London, 1976), p. 282. • 27 Quoted in Vojtech Mastny, *Russia's Road to the Cold War: Diplomacy, Warfare, and the Politics of Communism, 1941–1945* (New York, 1979), p. 131. • 28 *Foreign Relations of the United States (FRUS) 1943: The Conferences at Cairo and Tehran* (Washington, DC, 1961), Doc. 378, Bohlen Minutes of a Meeting between Roosevelt and Stalin, 1 December 1943. • 29 George F. Kennan, 'Comment', *Survey*, vol. 21, no. 1–2 (1975), pp. 29–36; Walter Lippmann Oral History, Columbia University, Butler Library, 217. • 30 Quoted in Robert I. Gannon, *The Cardinal Spellman Story* (London, 1963), pp. 222–4. • 31 Mikołajczyk, *Pattern of Soviet Domination*, p. 65. • 32 *FRUS 1944, Vol. III: The British Commonwealth and Europe* (Washington, DC, 1965), Doc. 1182, Stettinius Record of a Conversation between Roosevelt and Mikołajczyk, 12 June 1944. • 33 Mikołajczyk, *Pattern of Soviet Domination*, p. 65. • 34 Harvey (ed.), *War Diaries of Oliver Harvey*, 30 July 1944, p. 348. • 35 Quoted in Kochanski, *Eagle Unbowed*, p. 406. • 36 Lieutenant John Ward, Warsaw Uprising 1944 website, https://web.archive.org/web/20190719070935/http://www.warsawuprising.com/doc/dispatches2.htm, accessed 5 September 2024. Churchill objected to this muzzling of the press, urging Bracken, on 23 August, to allow the facts to speak for themselves. • 37 *DPSR, Vol. II: 1943–1945* (London, 1968), Note on a Conversation between Mikołajczyk and Stalin, 3 August 1944, p. 313. • 38 FO 954/20B/239, Stalin to Churchill, 5 August 1944. • 39 *FRUS 1944, Vol. III*, Doc. 1261, Harriman to Roosevelt and Hull, 15 August 1944. • 40 Reynolds and Pechatnov (eds), *Kremlin Letters*, Stalin to Roosevelt and Churchill, 20 August 1944, p. 462. • 41 Warren F. Kimball (ed.), *Churchill & Roosevelt: The Complete Correspondence* (Princeton, NJ, 1984), Churchill to Roosevelt, 25 August 1944, vol. 3, p. 295. • 42 Ibid., Roosevelt to Churchill, 26 August 1944, vol. 3, p. 296. • 43 Avon Papers, AP 20/1, Diary, 3 September 1944. • 44 Kimball (ed.), *Churchill & Roosevelt*, Churchill to Roosevelt, 4 September 1944, vol. 3, p. 309. • 45 Ibid., War Cabinet to Soviet Government, 4 September 1944, vol. 3, p. 310. • 46 Quoted in P. M. H. Bell, *John Bull and the Bear: British Public Opinion, Foreign Policy, and the Soviet Union, 1941–1945* (London, 1990), p. 139. • 47 Quoted ibid., p. 152. • 48 Berle Papers, Box 216, Diary, 23 September 1944. • 49 *DPSR, Vol. II*, Proceedings of the Moscow Conference on Polish Affairs, 13 October 1944, p. 409. • 50 Mikołajczyk, *Pattern of Soviet Domination*, p. 107. • 51 Ibid., p. 108. • 52 Earl of Avon, *The Eden Memoirs, Vol. II: The Reckoning* (London, 1965), p. 486; Winston S. Churchill, *The Second World War, Vol. VI: Triumph and Tragedy* (London, 1954), p. 205. • 53 *DPSR, Vol. II*, Note of a Conversation between Mikołajczyk and Churchill, 14 October 1944, p. 418. • 54 Lunghi Papers, LUNG 1/4, Tribute to Sir Winston Churchill. • 55 Quoted in Jan Karski, *The Great Powers & Poland,*

1919–1945: From Versailles to Yalta (Lanham, MD, 1985), p. 561. • 56 *DPSR, Vol. II*, Roosevelt to Mikołajczyk, 17 November 1944, p. 468. • 57 Walter Millis (ed.), *The Forrestal Diaries* (London, 1952), Forrestall to Palmer Hoyt, 2 September 1944, p. 32. • 58 Arthur Bliss Lane, *I Saw Poland Betrayed: An American Ambassador Reports to the American People* (Indianapolis, 1948), pp. 66–7. • 59 Reynolds and Pechatnov (eds), *Kremlin Letters*, Churchill to Stalin, 3 December 1944, p. 506. • 60 Ibid., Stalin to Churchill, 8 December 1944, p. 512. • 61 Ibid., Stalin to Roosevelt, 27 December 1944, p. 525.

XXVIII: Spheres of Influence

1 Berle Papers, Box 216, Diary, 26 August 1944. • 2 Oleg A. Rzheshevsky (ed.), *War and Diplomacy: The Making of the Grand Alliance – Documents from Stalin's Archives* (Amsterdam, 1996), Stalin to Molotov, 1 June 1942, p. 204. • 3 Robert H. McNeal (ed.), *Sochineniia I. V. Stalina, Vol. III* (Stanford, CA, 1967), Stalin Address to the Moscow Council of Worker's Deputies, 6 November 1944, pp. 165–70. • 4 Milovan Djilas, *Conversations with Stalin* (London, 1962), p. 70. 'One could see', wrote Đilas, that Churchill had left a 'deep impression on the communist leaders as a far-sighted and dangerous "bourgeois statesman".' (p. 106) • 5 Ibid., p. 71; quoted in Dmitri Volkogonov, *Stalin: Triumph and Tragedy* (London, 1991), p. 491. • 6 Quoted in Vojtech Mastny, 'The Beneš–Stalin–Molotov Conversations in December 1943: New Documents', *Jahrbücher für Geschichte Osteuropas*, vol. 20, no. 3 (1972), p. 377. • 7 Alexander Danchev and Daniel Todman (eds), *War Diaries, 1939–1945: Field Marshal Lord Alanbrooke* (London, 2001), 27 July 1944, p. 575. • 8 FO 371/43306, Sargent to Eden, 18 August 1944. • 9 Kenneth Young (ed.), *The Diaries of Sir Robert Bruce Lockhart, Vol. II: 1939–1965* (London, 1980), 4 April 1942, p. 157. • 10 FO 371/40696, Cooper to Eden, 30 May 1944. • 11 Ibid., Harvey Minute, 25 June 1944. • 12 Ibid., Jebb Minute, 18 June 1944. • 13 Ibid., Sargent Minute, 30 June 1944, Eden Minute, 2 July 1944. • 14 Quoted in M. J. Sherwin, *A World Destroyed: The Atomic Bomb and the Grand Alliance* (New York, 1975), p. 62. • 15 Quoted in W. Averell Harriman and Elie Abel, *Special Envoy to Churchill and Stalin, 1941–1946* (New York, 1975), p. 346. • 16 *Foreign Relations of the United States (FRUS) 1944, Vol. IV: Europe* (Washington, DC, 1966), Doc. 826, Kennan to State Department, September 1944. • 17 Chartwell Papers, CHAR 20/187, Minutes of the First Plenary Meeting at the Citadel, Quebec, 13 September 1944. • 18 Wheeler-Bennett Papers, F 2/2, Notes on Lunch with Churchill, 12 August 1954. • 19 Warren F. Kimball (ed.), *Churchill & Roosevelt: The Complete Correspondence* (Princeton, NJ, 1984), Churchill to Roosevelt, 1 July 1944, vol. 3, p. 227. Author's italics. • 20 Danchev and Todman (eds), *War Diaries*, 23 June 1944, pp. 561–2. • 21 PREM 3/66/7, Minute Churchill to Eden, 4 May 1944. • 22 David Dilks (ed.), *The Diaries of Sir Alexander Cadogan, OM, 1938–1945* (London, 1971), 13 November 1943, p. 575. • 23 Kimball (ed.), *Churchill & Roosevelt*, Churchill to Roosevelt, 11 June 1944, vol. 3, p. 179. • 24 Quoted in Elisabeth Barker, *Churchill and Eden at War* (London, 1978), p. 281. • 25 Quoted in Martin Gilbert and Larry P. Arnn (eds), *The Churchill Documents, Vol. XX: Normandy and Beyond, May–December 1944* (Hillsdale, MI, 2018) Chiefs of Staff Committee Minutes, 8 September 1944, p. 1301. • 26 Kimball (ed.), *Churchill & Roosevelt*, Churchill to Roosevelt, 29 September 1944, vol. 3, p. 341. • 27 David Reynolds and Vladimir Pechatnov (eds), *The Kremlin Letters: Stalin's Correspondence with Churchill and Roosevelt* (London, 2018), Roosevelt to Stalin, 4 October 1944, p. 480. • 28 FO 800/302, Minutes of a Meeting between Churchill, Stalin, Eden and Molotov, 9 October 1944. • 29 Kimball (ed.), *Churchill & Roosevelt*, Churchill to Roosevelt, 5 October 1944, vol. 3, p. 345. • 30 FO 800/302, Minutes of a Meeting between Churchill, Stalin, Eden and Molotov, 9 October 1944; Winston S. Churchill, *The Second World War, Vol. VI: Triumph and Tragedy* (London, 1954), p. 198. • 31 Churchill, *Second World War, Vol. VI*, p. 202. • 32 Charles E. Bohlen, *The Transformation of American Foreign Policy* (New York, 1969), p. 33. • 33 *FRUS 1944, Vol. IV*, Doc. 915, Harriman to Roosevelt, 10 October 1944. • 34 Kimball (ed.), *Churchill & Roosevelt*, Churchill to Roosevelt, 18 October 1944, vol. 3, p. 359. • 35 Ibid., Churchill to Roosevelt, 11 October 1944, vol. 3, p. 353. • 36 Gilbert and Arnn (eds), *Churchill Documents,*

Vol. XX, Winston Churchill to Clementine Churchill, 13 October 1944, p. 1648. • 37 Elliott Roosevelt, *As He Saw It* (New York, 1946), p. 150; John Colville, *The Fringes of Power: Downing Street Diaries, 1939–1955* (London, 1985), 9 January 1945, p. 550. • 38 Sir Reginald Leeper, *When Greek Meets Greek* (London, 1950), p. 3. • 39 CAB 66/50, Eden Memorandum for War Cabinet, 3 June 1944. • 40 Harold Macmillan, *War Diaries: Politics and War in the Mediterranean, January 1943–May 1945* (London, 1984), 19 January 1945, p. 654. • 41 Ibid., 18 October 1944, p. 557. • 42 Ibid., 27 October 1944, p. 565. • 43 Ibid., 29 October 1944, p. 567. • 44 Gilbert and Arnn (eds), *Churchill Documents, Vol. XX*, Churchill to Leeper, 5 December 1944, p. 2110. • 45 Ibid., Churchill to Scobie, 5 December 1944, pp. 2100–2101. • 46 Macmillan, *War Diaries*, 8 December 1944, p. 599. • 47 Quoted in Halik Kochanski, *Resistance: The Underground War in Europe, 1939–45* (London, 2022), p. 183. • 48 Hansard, HC Deb, 8 December 1944, vol. 404, col. 928. • 49 Leeper, *When Greek Meets Greek*, p. 107. • 50 J. E. R. W. Egremont, *Wyndham and Children First* (London, 1968), pp. 125–6. • 51 Leeper, *When Greek Meets Greek*, p. 114. • 52 George VI Papers, Diary, 9 December 1944. • 53 Harold Macmillan, *The Blast of War, 1939–1945* (London, 1967), p. 625. • 54 Colville, *Fringes of Power*, Colville to Martin, 26 December 1944, p. 541. • 55 Caccia Papers, MS 671/05/04/01/01/06, Harold Caccia to Nancy Caccia, 27 December 1944. • 56 Quoted in Gilbert and Arnn (eds), *Churchill Documents, Vol. XX*, Ministry of Foreign Affairs Conference Minutes, 26 December 1944, pp. 2360, 2362. • 57 Dixon Papers, Diary, 26 December 1944. • 58 Colville, *Fringes of Power*, 18 January 1945, p. 553. • 59 Hansard, HC Deb, 18 January 1945, vol. 407, cols 400–406. • 60 Scobie Papers, Diary, 6 December 1944. • 61 Chartwell Papers, CHAR 20/209, Churchill to Eden, 19 January 1945.

XXIX: Yalta

1 Quoted in David Reynolds, *In Command of History: Churchill Fighting and Writing the Second World War* (London, 2004), p. 464. • 2 Quoted in Diana Preston, *Eight Days at Yalta: How Churchill, Roosevelt and Stalin Shaped the Post-war World* (London, 2019), p. 86, • 3 Quoted in Reynolds, *In Command of History*, p. 473; Lord Moran, *Winston Churchill: The Struggle for Survival, 1940–1965* (London, 1966), 7 February 1945, p. 226. • 4 Halsted Papers, Box 84, Folder 11, Yalta Notes, Diary, 2 February 1945. • 5 Quoted in Preston, *Eight Days at Yalta*, p. 86; quoted in Martin Gilbert, *Winston S. Churchill, Vol. VII: Road to Victory, 1941–1945* (London, 1986), p. 1172. • 6 Michael E. Reilly, *Reilly of the White House* (New York, 1947), p. 212. • 7 Quoted in Gilbert, *Winston S. Churchill, Vol. VII*, p. 1172; *Foreign Relations of the United States (FRUS): The Conferences at Malta and Yalta, 1945* (Washington, DC, 1955), Doc. 328, Bohlen Minutes of Meeting between Roosevelt and Stalin, 4 February 1945. • 8 Ismay Papers, 4/4, Ismay to Burrows, 19 March 1945; Dixon Papers, Pierson Dixon to Alexandra 'Ismene' Dixon, 13 February 1945. • 9 Lawford Papers, LWFD 02/08, Diary, 9 February 1945. • 10 David Dilks (ed.), *The Diaries of Sir Alexander Cadogan, OM, 1938–1945* (London, 1971), Alexander Cadogan to Theodosia Cadogan, 4 February 1945, p. 703. • 11 James Leasor, *War at the Top: Based on the Experiences of General Sir Leslie Hollis* (London, 1959), p. 281. • 12 *FRUS: Conferences at Malta and Yalta*, Doc. 66, Hopkins to Roosevelt, 24 January 1945. • 13 Halsted Papers, Box 85, Radio Address by Senator Robert A. Taft, 29 January 1951. • 14 Quoted in William Bullitt, 'How we won the war and lost the peace', *Life*, 30 August 1948; Chester Wilmot, *The Struggle for Europe* (London, 1952), p. 628. • 15 *FRUS: Conferences at Malta and Yalta*, Doc. 267, JCS to Roosevelt, 23 January 1945. • 16 Warren F. Kimball (ed.), *Churchill & Roosevelt: The Complete Correspondence* (Princeton, NJ, 1984), Churchill to Roosevelt, 10 January 1945, vol. 3, pp. 505–6. • 17 Earl of Avon, *The Eden Memoirs, Vol. II: The Reckoning* (London, 1965), p. 504. • 18 Dixon Papers, Diary, 1 February 1945. • 19 Avon Papers, AP 20/3/11, Diary, 1 February 1945. • 20 Charles E. Bohlen, *Witness to History, 1929–1969* (London, 1973), p. 172. • 21 Avon Papers, AP 20/3/11, Diary, 2 February 1945. • 22 Interview with Sergo Beria, George Washington University, Oral History, https://nsarchive2.gwu.edu/coldwar/beria.html, accessed 6 September 2024. • 23 Eleanor Roosevelt, *This I Remember* (New York, 1950), p. 265. • 24 Bohlen, *Witness to History*, p. 180. • 25 *FRUS: Conferences at*

Malta and Yalta, Doc. 328, Bohlen Minutes of Meeting between Roosevelt and Stalin, 4 February 1945. • 26 C. L. Sulzberger, *The Last of the Giants* (New York, 1970), p. 12. • 27 Quoted in Julian Jackson, *A Certain Idea of France: The Life of Charles de Gaulle* (London, 2018), p. 353. • 28 W. Averell Harriman and Elie Abel, *Special Envoy to Churchill and Stalin, 1941–1946* (New York, 1975), p. 377. • 29 *FRUS: Conferences at Malta and Yalta*, Doc. 328, Bohlen Minutes of Meeting between Roosevelt and Stalin, 4 February 1945. • 30 FO 954/9B/458, Churchill to Eden, 19 January 1945. • 31 Bohlen, *Witness to History*, p. 185. • 32 Quoted in S. M. Plokhy, *Yalta: The Price of Peace* (New York, 2010), p. 94. • 33 Bohlen, *Witness to History*, p. 183. • 34 PREM 3/51/4, 'Argonaut' Minutes, First Plenary Meeting, 5 February 1945. • 35 Avon Papers, AP 20/3/11, Diary, 6 February 1945. • 36 Quoted in Lydia V. Pozdeeva, 'Soviet Union: Territorial Diplomacy', in David Reynolds, Warren F. Kimball and A. O. Chubarian (eds), *Allies at War: The Soviet, American, and British Experience, 1939–1945* (New York, 1994), p. 373. • 37 Robert H. McNeal (ed.), *Sochineniia I. V. Stalina, Vol. III* (Stanford, CA, 1967), Stalin Radio Address, 9 May 1945, p. 198. • 38 *FRUS: Conferences at Malta and Yalta*, Doc. 336, Bohlen Minutes, Second Plenary Session, 5 February 1945. • 39 PREM 3/51/4, 'Argonaut' Minutes, First Plenary Meeting, 5 February 1945. • 40 Quoted in Gilbert, *Winston S. Churchill, Vol. VII*, p. 1207. • 41 Lawford Papers, LWFD 02/08, Diary, 10 February 1945. • 42 *FRUS: Conferences at Malta and Yalta*, Doc. 457, Bohlen Minutes, Dinner at the Vorontsov Palace, 10 February 1945. • 43 Ibid., Doc. 352, Bohlen Minutes, Third Plenary Session, 6 February 1945. • 44 Ibid., Doc. 331, Bohlen Minutes, Dinner at the Livadia Palace, 4 February 1945. • 45 Quoted in Stephen Wertheim, *Tomorrow, the World: The Birth of US Global Supremacy* (Cambridge, MA, 2020), p. 142. • 46 John R. Deane, *The Strange Alliance: The Story of American Efforts at Wartime Co-operation with Russia* (London, 1947), p. 228. • 47 *FRUS: Conferences at Malta and Yalta*, Doc. 255, Harriman to Roosevelt, 15 October 1944. • 48 Ibid., Doc. 260, Harriman to Roosevelt, 15 December 1944. • 49 *FRUS 1943: The Conferences at Cairo and Tehran* (Washington, DC, 1961), Doc. 371, Bohlen Minutes, Roosevelt–Churchill–Stalin Lunch, 30 November 1943. • 50 Quoted in Forrest C. Pogue, *George C. Marshall, Vol. III: Organizer of Victory, 1943–1945* (New York, 1973), p. 526. • 51 Avon Papers, AP 20/13/36A, Russia and the Far East, 27 January 1945. • 52 FO 371/54073, Churchill to Eden and Ismay, 23 October 1944. • 53 CAB 120/714, Churchill to Eden, 28 January 1945. • 54 *FRUS: Conferences at Malta and Yalta*, Doc. 393, Bohlen Minutes, Roosevelt–Stalin Meeting, 8 February 1945. • 55 Ibid. • 56 Robert E. Sherwood, *The White House Papers of Harry L. Hopkins, Vol. II: January 1942–July 1945* (London, 1949), p. 855. • 57 FO 371/40444, Grigg to Eden, 24 August 1944. • 58 Avon Papers, AP 20/13, Eden to Churchill, Prisoners of War, 9 February 1945. • 59 *FRUS: Conferences at Malta and Yalta*, Doc. 504, Agreement between United States and Soviet Union Concerning Liberated Prisoners of War and Civilians, 11 February 1945. • 60 Quoted in Nikolai Tolstoy, *Victims of Yalta* (London, 1977), p. 138. • 61 Ibid., pp. 139–40. • 62 Roosevelt Papers, PSF, Diplomatic Correspondence, Box 48, Arciszewski to Roosevelt, 3 February 1945. • 63 Harriman & Abel, *Special Envoy*, p. 369 • 64 PREM 3/51/4, 'Argonaut' Minutes, Third Plenary Meeting, 6 February 1945. • 65 Quoted in Plokhy, *Yalta*, p. 166. • 66 *FRUS: Conferences at Malta and Yalta*, Doc. 354, Matthews Minutes, Third Plenary Session, 6 February 1945; PREM 3/51/4, 'Argonaut' Minutes, Third Plenary Meeting, 6 February 1945. • 67 PREM 3/51/4, 'Argonaut' Minutes, Third Plenary Meeting, 6 February 1945. • 68 Quoted in Plokhy, *Yalta*, p. 176. • 69 *FRUS: Conferences at Malta and Yalta*, Doc. 377, Roosevelt to Stalin, 6 February 1945. • 70 PREM 3/51/4, 'Argonaut' Minutes, Fourth Plenary Session, 7 February 1945. • 71 *FRUS: Conferences at Malta and Yalta*, Doc. 399, Hiss Collection, US Proposal on Poland, 8 February 1945. • 72 PREM 3/51/4, 'Argonaut' Minutes, Fifth Plenary Meeting, 8 February 1945. • 73 *FRUS: Conferences at Malta and Yalta*, Doc. 394, Bohlen Minutes, Fifth Plenary Session, 8 February 1945. • 74 Ibid., Doc. 405, Page Minutes, Foreign Ministers Meeting, 9 February 1945. • 75 Martin Gilbert and Larry P. Arnn (eds), *The Churchill Documents, Vol. XXI: The Shadows of Victory, January–July 1945* (Hillsdale, MI, 2018), 'Argonaut' Minutes, Sixth Plenary Meeting, 9 February 1945, pp. 416–17, 421. • 76 *FRUS: Conferences at Malta and Yalta*, Doc. 424, Matthews Minutes, Sixth Plenary Session, 9 February 1945. • 77 Gilbert and Arnn (eds), *Churchill Documents, Vol. XXI*, Eden to Churchill, 10 February 1945,

Churchill to Eden, 10 February 1945, p. 434. • 78 FRUS: *Conferences at Malta and Yalta*, Doc. 501, Protocol of the Proceedings of the Crimea Conference, 11 February 1945. • 79 Fleet Admiral William D. Leahy, *I Was There* (London, 1950), p. 370. • 80 PREM 4/309/9, Protocol of the Proceedings of the Crimea Conference, 'Declaration on Liberated Europe'. • 81 Albert Resis (ed.), *Molotov Remembers: Inside Kremlin Politics* (Chicago, 1993), p. 51. • 82 John Colville, *The Fringes of Power: Downing Street Diaries, 1939–1955* (London, 1985), 9 January 1945, p. 550; Moran, *Struggle for Survival*, 6 February 1945, p. 225. • 83 Gilbert and Arnn (eds), *Churchill Documents, Vol. XXI*, Sarah Oliver to Clementine Churchill, 8 February 1945, p. 391. • 84 Colville, *Fringes of Power*, 23 February 1945, p. 563. • 85 Avon, *Reckoning*, p. 513. • 86 George VI Papers, Diary, 23 January 1945. • 87 Davies Papers, 1/6, Diaries, 10 January 1945. • 88 Dilks (ed.), *Diaries of Sir Alexander Cadogan*, Alexander Cadogan to Theodosia Cadogan, 11 February 1945, pp. 708–9. • 89 Dixon Papers, Pierson Dixon to Alexandra 'Ismene' Dixon, 13 February 1945. • 90 Gilbert and Arnn (eds), *Churchill Documents, Vol. XXI*, Sarah Oliver to Clementine Churchill, 9 February 1945, p. 412. • 91 Ibid., 'Argonaut' Conference, Birse Notes, Dinner Toasts, 8 February 1945, p. 405; *FRUS: Conferences at Malta and Yalta*, Doc. 403, Bohlen Minutes, Dinner, 8 February 1945. • 92 Gilbert and Arnn (eds), *Churchill Documents, Vol. XXI*, 'Argonaut' Conference, Birse Notes, Dinner Toasts, 8 February 1945, p. 406. • 93 Sherwood, *White House Papers of Harry L. Hopkins, Vol II*, p. 859. • 94 Bohlen, *Witness to History*, p. 200. • 95 Moran, *Struggle for Survival*, 6 February 1945, p. 225. • 96 Quoted in Reynolds, *In Command of History*, p. 468. • 97 Gilbert and Arnn (eds), *Churchill Documents, Vol. XXI*, 'Argonaut' Conference, Birse Notes, Dinner Toasts, 8 February 1945, p. 405. • 98 Ben Pimlott (ed.), *The Second World War Diary of Hugh Dalton, 1940–45* (London, 1986), 23 February 1945, p. 836.

XXX: *Triumph and Tragedy*

1 Roosevelt Papers, Master Speech File, Box 86. • 2 *Time*, 19 February 1945. • 3 *The Times*, 13 February 1945. • 4 I. Laufer and G. P. Kynin (eds), *SSSR i Germanskii vopros* (Moscow, 1996), Doc. 144, pp. 606–8. • 5 Ivan Mikhailovich Maiskii, *Izbrannaia perepiska s rossiiskimi korrespondentami* (Moscow, 2005), vol. 2, Doc. 550, p. 161. • 6 CAB 65/51, War Cabinet Minutes, Confidential Annex, 19 February 1945. • 7 Ibid., War Cabinet Minutes, Confidential Annex, 21 February 1945 • 8 John Colville, *The Fringes of Power: Downing Street Diaries, 1939–1955* (London, 1985), 27 February 1945, p. 565. • 9 Hansard, HC Deb, 27 February 1945, vol. 408, cols 1280, 1284. • 10 Roosevelt Papers, Master Speeches File, Box 86, Address to Congress, 1 March 1945. • 11 Samuel I. Rosenman, *Working with Roosevelt* (New York, 1952), p. 479. • 12 David Reynolds and Vladimir Pechatnov (eds), *The Kremlin Letters: Stalin's Correspondence with Churchill and Roosevelt* (London, 2018), Roosevelt to Stalin, 17 March 1944, p. 553. • 13 Warren F. Kimball (ed.), *Churchill & Roosevelt: The Complete Correspondence* (Princeton, NJ, 1984), Churchill to Roosevelt, 8 March 1945, vol. 3, p. 547. • 14 Ibid., Roosevelt to Churchill, 11 March 1945, vol. 3, p. 562. • 15 Avon Papers, AP 20/13/111, Eden to Churchill, 7 April 1945. • 16 Kimball (ed.), *Churchill & Roosevelt*, Churchill to Roosevelt, 8 March 1945, vol. 3, p. 549. • 17 Ibid., Churchill to Roosevelt, 13 March 1945, vol. 3, pp. 564–5. • 18 Quoted in Sean McMeekin, *Stalin's War: A New History of the Second World War* (London, 2021), p. 611. • 19 Harriman Papers, Kathleen Harriman to Mary Harriman, 8 March 1945. • 20 Quoted in Reynolds and Pechatnov (eds), *Kremlin Letters*, p. 556. • 21 Kimball (ed.), *Churchill & Roosevelt*, Churchill to Roosevelt, 1 April 1945, vol. 3, p. 605. • 22 Reynolds and Pechatnov (eds), *Kremlin Letters*, Roosevelt to Stalin, 4 April, p. 573. • 23 Kimball (ed.), *Churchill & Roosevelt*, Roosevelt to Churchill, 6 April 1945, vol. 3, p. 617. • 24 Ibid., Roosevelt to Churchill, 11 April 1945, vol. 3, p. 630. • 25 *The Memoirs of Marshal Zhukov* (London, 1971), p. 589. • 26 *Foreign Relations of the United States (FRUS) 1945, Vol. V: Europe* (Washington, DC, 1969), Doc. 628, Harriman to Stettinius, 13 April 1945. • 27 Thomas M. Campbell and George C. Herring (eds), *The Diaries of Edward R. Stettinius, Jr., 1943–1946* (New York, 1975), 13 April 1945, p. 318. • 28 Harry S Truman, *Memoirs, Vol. I: Year of Decisions* (London, 1955), p. 85.

• 29 Ibid., p. 73; IWM, Harriman Oral History. • 30 W. Averell Harriman and Elie Abel, *Special Envoy to Churchill and Stalin, 1941–1946* (New York, 1975), p. 454. • 31 FO 954/20D, Churchill to Eden, 4 May 1945. • 32 Colville, *Fringes of Power*, 28 February 1945, p. 566. • 33 CAB 120/691, Operation Unthinkable, 22 May 1945. • 34 Truman, *Memoirs, Vol. I*, p. 346. • 35 *FRUS 1945: The Conference at Berlin (The Potsdam Conference), Vol. II* (Washington, DC, 1960), Doc. 1382. • 36 Alexander Danchev and Daniel Todman (eds), *War Diaries, 1939–1945: Field Marshal Lord Alanbrooke* (London, 2001), 23 July 1945, p. 709. • 37 Quoted in D. F. Fleming, *The Cold War and Its Origins, 1917–1960* (Garden City, NY, 1961), vol. 1, p. 329. • 38 *FRUS 1945, Vol. V*, Doc. 650, Harriman to Byrnes, 11 July 1945; Hansard, HC Deb, 16 August 1945, vol. 413, col. 84.

Epilogue

1 Quoted in David Reynolds, *In Command of History: Churchill Fighting and Writing the Second World War* (London, 2004), p. 464. • 2 Frederick L. Schuman, *American Policy toward Russia since 1917* (New York, 1928), pp. 153–4. • 3 PREM 3/399/7, Eden to Churchill, 5 January 1942. • 4 Ibid. • 5 *The Memoirs of Marshal Zhukov* (London, 1971), p. 583. • 6 V. M. Berezhkov, *Kak ia stal perevodchikom Stalina* (Moscow, 1993), p. 253. • 7 Roosevelt Papers, PSF, Diplomatic Correspondence, Box 49, Russia 1945, Notes of an Interview with Maxim Litvinov, 28 December 1944. • 8 Vojtech Mastny, *Russia's Road to the Cold War: Diplomacy, Warfare, and the Politics of Communism, 1941–1945* (New York, 1979), p. 309. • 9 George Kennan, *Memoirs, 1925–1950* (London, 1968), pp. 133–4. • 10 Berle Papers, Box 213, Berle Memorandum, 31 July 1941. • 11 Charles E. Bohlen, *Witness to History, 1929–1969* (London, 1973), pp. 175–6. • 12 Edgar Snow, *Journey to the Beginning* (London, 1959), p. 357. • 13 Quoted in Forrest C. Pogue, *George C. Marshall, Vol. III: Organizer of Victory, 1943–1945* (New York, 1973), p. 530. • 14 Arthur H. Vandenberg Jr (ed.), *The Private Papers of Senator Vandenberg* (Boston, 1952), 21 April 1943, p. 46, 1 May 1943, p. 48. • 15 Robert Rhodes James (ed.), *Winston S. Churchill: His Complete Speeches* (London, 1974), vol. 6, p. 6429. • 16 Mastny, *Russia's Road to the Cold War*, p. 310. • 17 Hickleton Papers, A7/8/4, Halifax Diary, 25 May 1940. • 18 Sir Owen O'Malley, *The Phantom Caravan* (London, 1954), p. 233. • 19 Quoted in Richard Overy, *Blood and Ruins: The Great Imperial War, 1931–1945* (London, 2021), p. 564. • 20 Quoted in Robert Service, *Stalin: A Biography* (London, 2004), p. 486.

Index

About the Author

Tim Bouverie is the author of *Sunday Times* bestseller *Appeasing Hitler: Chamberlain, Churchill and the Road to War*, which was short-listed for the Orwell Prize. He studied history at Christ Church, Oxford, and was the 2020–21 Alistair Horne Fellow at St Antony's College, Oxford.